Antiquarian Catalogues of Musical Interest

Antiquarian Catalogues of Musical Interest

Compiled by

James Coover

Mansell Publishing Limited
London and New York

First published 1988 by
Mansell Publishing Limited, *A Cassell Imprint*
Artillery House, Artillery Row, London SW1P 1RT
125 East 23rd Street, Suite 300, New York 10010, U.S.A.

British Library Cataloguing in Publication Data
Coover, James
    Antiquarian catalogues of musical interest
    1. Music. Indexes. Bibliographies
    I. Title
    016.01678
\ISBN 0–7201–1979–0

Library of Congress Cataloging-in-Publication Data
Coover, James, 1925–
    Antiquarian catalogues of musical interest / compiled by James
Coover.
        p.   cm.
    Includes indexes.
    ISBN 0–7201–1979–0 : $72.00 (U.S.)
    1. Music—Bibliography—Catalogs—Bibliography.   2. Antiquarian
booksellers—Catalogs—Bibliography.   I. Title.
ML152.C65   1988
016.78—dc 19   88–8396
                                                                                 CIP
                                                                                 MN

This book has been printed and bound in Great Britain.
Printed by Redwood Burn Ltd. on Redwood Book
Wove paper, and bound by WBC Bookbinders.

Contents

Preface

The initial version of this checklist, when it appeared in 1981,[1] included approximately 3,000 catalogues, bulletins, and lists (this edition contains 5,531) from some 570 antiquarians (in this one they number 640). It was issued, first, as a device to solicit addenda and corrigenda from persons in position to help expand its coverage. Secondly, it was hoped that it would heighten the awareness of those who saw it to the ephemeral nature of the documents it listed and the need to preserve them. That first edition lacked indexes; this has two — one by place and dealer, another by subject. That edition offered no historical information about the antiquarian trade; happily, this one includes Albi Rosenthal's entertaining and informative essay on that topic.[2]

The items listed here are antiquarian catalogues in which fixed prices, usually printed, are set against each lot or item. Omitted are auction catalogues and also what are called 'vendors' catalogues — listings prepared by firms who collect from various publishers current and in-print materials ordered by customers which they then funnel back to those buyers.

When book-collecting, -selling, or the book trade are discussed or scrutinized, the antiquarian segment has always been considered peripheral. Much has been written about historic auctions, colourful auctioneers, important consignors and consignments, remarkable collectors and their phenomenal buys. Antiquarian sales attract relatively little of that kind of attention. Auctions seem more glamourous; they involve real people in immediate, social interactions who are often distinguished — or at least famous or well-to-do. Most of the interactions arising from antiquarian sales, on the other hand, consist mainly of letters travelling between mail boxes. In general, too, the materials put up at auctions tend to be more precious than many of those offered by small antiquarian firms. And the surviving records of them are more complete; thousands of 'marked' auction catalogues showing who bought each lot and how much was paid for it remain publicly available. For each of these there are often many copies, for after the sales, most auctioneers have filled orders for 'marked' copies prepared by their staff. Others exist, of course, that were marked by persons present at the actual auctions. Who bought what items from an antiquarian's sale catalogue, however, remains a mystery, buried in the antiquarian's records, and there is little likelihood that the business records of their sales will become available.

Both auction catalogues and antiquarian catalogues are equally ephemeral, and ephemera disappear — those having to do with music at a seemingly more rapid rate than some other types. In the introduction to the earlier *Checklist*, I labelled them endangered species and pointed to the incompleteness of sets credited to a number of dealers in that publication:

> Even modest, incomplete sets of catalogues issued by famous and important dealers such as List & Francke, Herman Baron, Karl Max Poppe, Leo Liepmannssohn, Hans Schneider, Maggs, The First Edition Bookshop, Salloch, and dozens of others in this century — some since World War II — are already difficult to locate.

As Rosenthal says, 'No printed or other matter gravitates more automatically, more powerfully towards the wastebasket!' Gwyn Walters of the National Library of Wales, is more graphic; in an article about the scarcity of such catalogues, he notes that they disappear after sales as rapidly as betting slips after a race.[3] Even sixty years ago Edward Newton was comparing their rarity with that of incunables or Shakespeare folios.[4] The most telling evidence, however, emerges from the following pages: 1) the higgledy-piggledy scattering among great libraries of incomplete sets of dealers' lists;[5] and 2) the revelation that many dealers (for example Herman Baron, Walter Ricke, William Reeves, and others) do not themselves possess complete sets of their own catalogues.

Even truer for ephemera than for other printed materials, the earlier they were issued, the fewer the examples of them that have survived. Only 2 per cent of the catalogues in this list were issued before 1850, only 7 per cent (or 440) between 1850 and 1900, and a meagre 21 per cent (1,208) between 1900 and 1950. Fully 70 per cent postdate 1950 reflecting a surge of interest in used, out-of-print, and rare materials after World War II, so too the number of dealers eager to supply it, and so too the number of catalogues they issued and distributed. They went to a growing and increasingly widespread group of potential customers,[6] for the world had shrunk. And because they have been issued in greater numbers than those of a hundred years ago, more have survived in libraries' collections. (To date, but for how long?)

Preservation alone, however, is not enough. Unfortunately, in many libraries where such ephemera have been collected (or at least not discarded), if catalogued at all, the access thus provided is sub-standard. (As Walters remarks, 'The ubiquitous Anglo-American cataloging code offers little practical advice' about what to do with such problem materials.) Usually they are not catalogued at all; in a few places, a scholar may be fortunate and find a manuscript handlist or card file in some reference librarian's desk — but it is not likely. Only a handful of libraries' card or printed catalogues include bibliographically acceptable citations for sale catalogues.[7] A knowledgeable, smartly-planned, systematic search for specific catalogues from particular dealers, or for particular kinds of material, or on a special topic usually has about as much chance of success as a search based on sheer serendipity — except in a few institutions like the Grolier Club in New York City and the Vereeniging ter Bervordering van de Belangen des Boekhandels in Amsterdam where collecting, preserving, and making such ephemera accessible have been urgent goals for many years.

If most libraries neglect the proper cataloguing of dealers' lists that they may still have on hand, they have also, unfortunately, done little to enrich or to complete the collections they have. Few libraries' development policies, in fact, take notice of either auction or antiquarian catalogues, much less offer guidelines for their acquisition or their disposal.

They live in limbo. Query most librarians about the catalogues that may be in their collections and a conversation like this is apt to follow: 'Did you look in the card catalogue? None there? I didn't *think* we had any. There may be some recent ones in Mr. X's office, but no old ones; if any of those were saved, they would be downstairs in the 'Y' Department. They might have saved them for some reason. Oh, you've checked there and they are not? Well, I guess we don't have any. Why did you need them?' which usually stands as a euphemism for 'Of what earthly use can they be!' Colleagues who asked the same question in a number of large libraries in Germany a few years ago received remarkably similar answers — and found no catalogues. All such searches, correspondence with libraries and collectors, a study of the literature about the antiquarian trade, and the evidence in this list — amply support Rosenthal's, Walter's and others contentions and legitimate their alarm.

But do their uses warrant the concern expressed here? In his essay, Rosenthal talks about the quality of catalogues issued by various musicsellers' catalogues but touches only briefly on their historical importance or utility. No one catalogue — or even a complete set of dealer's catalogues — is of overwhelming significance, but these sets, if carefully studied, can be made to yield surprisingly useful information, some of which is nowhere else available. Rosenthal notes that the ninety-year series of antiquarian and auction catalogues from Leo Liepmannssohn and his successor, Otto Haas (about 250 in all), form a 'veritable encyclopedia of musical literature'. In them — as in many other dealers' catalogues — the citations manifest the highest bibliographical standards, while the annotations invariably include erudite remarks on the identification and relationship of authors and texts, on various editions, states, and versions, sometimes on the provenance of the copy cited[8] — and often on the music itself. Their prices disclose a financial value and degree of rarity for that particular moment, and those, over a period of time, serve as a record of public taste.[9] The item which in one decade elicits no interest in the trade may be re-evaluated in time and then — having grown scarce — will be found to be surprisingly 'old and rare', and often even 'important'. The kinds of material various dealers handled or made their specialty reflects not only changing economic conditions and general historical events — the tides of European wars and shifting sources of supplies — but also, again, taste.[10] And taste is always an interesting subject, in whatever way information about it may be revealed.

The catalogues of those dealers who have specialized in one or several areas of musical literature, along with catalogues in which thorough indexes to the contents have been provided, can be extraordinarily useful to those engaged in subject bibliography. Index I to this checklist, by Subject and Type of Material, provides a starting place for such work.

And finally, sale catalogues tell us about the trade — when dealers were active, with whom they associated, where they were located (Reeves & Turner, one of the predecessors of William Reeves in this list, occupied premises at six addresses in the course of only 27 years), which libraries they bought and sold, and sometimes their personal opinions on topics of trade concern.

Part of the history of music is the history of the music trade, which has been little explored to date. When it receives the thorough-going attention it deserves, catalogues from antiquarians, along with those issued by publishers and auctioneers, will be primary source materials. Whatever use will be made of them, before they can be studied we must know what exists and where. I hope this checklist, like the provisional one that preceded it, will answer part of that need as well as awaken interest in this special resource.

Notes

[1] It was entitled a *Provisional Checklist of Priced Antiquarians' Catalogues Containing Musical Materials* and was issued in a limited number of photocopies by the University Libraries of the State University of New York at Buffalo, N.Y.

[2] Reprinted from *Fontes artis musicae* 5 (1958): 80–89, by permission of the Editor, Mr Andre Jurres and the International Association of Music Libraries. The importance of this essay was earlier recognized, and it was reprinted by my colleague, Dr Carol June Bradley, in her *Reader in Music Librarianship* (81–89), published by Microcard Editions Books in 1973.

[3] Gwyn Walters, 'Early Sale Catalogues: Problems and Perspectives', pp. 106–25 in *Sale and Distribution of Books from 1700*, ed. by Robin Myers and Michael Harris (Oxford: Oxford Polytechnic Press, 1982).

[4] Edward Newton, *The Sale Catalogue of Dr. Johnson's Library*. (New York: E.B. Hackett, 1925).

[5] Note how the catalogues issued by Ifan Kyrle Fletcher, nos. 1007–72, are scattered among the private and institutional collections inventoried for this checklist.

[6] Widely dispersed like the dealers themselves. In this list German dealers number 181 (39 in Berlin); U.S., 138 (44 in New York City); the U.K., 113 (66 in London); Holland, 60 (24 in Amsterdam); Italy, 43 (13 in Rome); France 45, (40 in Paris); Austria, 26 (22 in Vienna); Switzerland, 17; Belgium, 16; Denmark, 13; and five or fewer in Spain, Portugal, Hungary, Norway, Czechoslovakia, Brazil, and Canada.

[7] Perhaps the most notable example of a printed music catalogue that includes them is that of the famous Paul Hirsch collection now in the British Library. The first major national library to print a catalogue solely of its antiquarian sale catalogues was the Royal Library of Belgium with Jean Blogie's *Répertoire des catalogues de ventes de livres imprimés* (Brussels: Fl. Tulkens, 1982).

[8] The Antiquarian Richard Macnutt, like others, provides information about provenance in his annotations to items in his catalogues number 103 and 104, but he may be the first music antiquarian in history to include, as well, an index to those owners.

[9] It would be risky to depend too much on prices as a measure of public taste today

since prices being asked for some books presently coming off the presses are collectors' prices, long before the manufacturing stage is past.

[10] Through a study of the catalogues of a little-known, seventeenth-century, London bookseller, D.W. Krummel has shown, in a brilliant essay, that the firm's imports were highly influential in acquainting English musicians with the works of Italian composers of the seventeenth century. 'Venetian Baroque Music in a London Bookshop: the Robert Martin Catalogues, 1633–60', pp. 1–27 in *Music and Bibliography: Essays in Honor of Alex Hyatt King*, ed. by Oliver Neighbour (New York: Clive Bingley, 1980).

Acknowledgements

Copies of the preliminary edition of this list were sent to colleagues and various libraries hoping to elicit from them addenda and corrigenda. Some of them responded in magnificent fashion by inventorying their own or their library's collection of antiquarian catalogues and adding materially to this edition. I thank especially D.W. Krummel who undertook to inventory his entire collection which is, doubtless, one of the largest in private hands in the United States. Mr Evan Bonds, then Music Librarian at the University of Virginia, sent me citations for all of the music antiquarian catalogues in that University's libraries that were not in the original list. Dr Harold Samuel, Music Librarian at Yale University, donated large quantities of antiquarian catalogues to the collections at the State University of New York at Buffalo, many of which are recorded in these pages. Mr Stephen Fry, Head of the Music Library at the University of California at Los Angeles, not only donated a similar number to the collections in Buffalo but allowed me access to his library's stacks in order to inventory what was there.

So, too, did many other libraries and librarians, and a number of music antiquarians. To all I am very grateful. Charles Lindahl and Neil Bunker searched a sizeable uncatalogued backlog at the Eastman School of Music in Rochester, N.Y. to isolate and organize materials in which they thought I might be interested. Jean Bowen, Head of the Reference Division of the Music Division of the New York Public Library made some rather complicated arrangements that facilitated my going through that library's large uncatalogued collection. As has been the case for a decade, Robert Nikirk, Librarian of the Grolier Club in New York City allowed me almost unlimited access to that library's extraordinary collections of auction and antiquarian catalogues, a convenient place to work on them — and more importantly, encouragement and advice. Oliver Neighbour and his staff in the Music Room at the British Library made it possible for me to examine with significant economies of time the sale catalogues collected actively by Paul Hirsch. In Holland, I received generous assistance from both the Vereeniging ter Bervordering van de Belangen des Boekhandels in Amsterdam and the Gemeentemuseum in Den Haag. The latter houses a rich collection of sale catalogues formed by another famous collector, Daniel Francois Scheurleer. Each library answered graciously many queries sent them by mail.

Several antiquarians — Herman Baron, William Reeves, Nigel Simeone, and Theodore Front — permitted me to search through their collections of antiquarian's catalogues, and those explorations produced additional citations for this list. Perhaps as useful were discussions with them about the antiquarian music trade. A number of other dealers generously agreed to review and edit the listing of their own catalogues which I sent to them in draft form, and their contributions have markedly improved the accuracy and coverage of this checklist. Those who helped include Hans Schneider, Herman Baron, William Salloch, Walter Ricke, Robert Hearn (Bel Canto Books), Annemarie Schnase, J.B. Muns, V.-A. Heck, Ulrich Druner, J. & J. Lubrano, J. & M. Morton-Smith, Musica Antiqua, Portico Librerias, Kurt Stein, Peter Wood, G.N. Landre, and Martin Silver. Several others checked not only the list of their *own* publications but those of their predecessors, as well: Richard Macnutt (his own and Leonard Hyman's), Dan Fog (his and Knud Larsen's), Theodore Front (his and E.E. Gottlieb's), William Reeves (his and his many predecessors'), and Kenneth Mummery (his and Harold Reeves'). (These dealers are the only locations for a sizeable number of catalogues in the checklist. When that is the case, the firm name is placed in brackets at the right margin.)

On a visit to West Germany, Mrs Diane Parr Walker and her husband, at my request, asked a number of libraries for information about their holdings of antiquarian catalogues. What they learned forms the basis of some of the gloomy comments in the Preface, but their assistance was timely and appreciated.

Several persons were influential in transforming the data for the basic list (pp. 1–346) from floppy discs into camera-ready copy — Mr Roger Campbell, Assistant Manager of Academic Computing in the University Computing Services at SUNY at Buffalo; the Vice-President for University Services at that institution, Mr Robert Wagner, who directed the attention of the computing services under his authority to this project; and Mr Robert Kettle, candidate for a PhD. in Music History at the same school, who was responsible for some rather heroic, last-minute programming and tidying-up to achieve the text that appears here.

To all I am deeply grateful.

ALBI ROSENTHAL (LONDON)

The "Music Antiquarian" *

Since Roman times, when "antiquarius" was used first to describe a writing master, later an official in charge of copying codices, the term "antiquarian" has appeared in a variety of shapes and meanings. In Italian, "antiquario" was synonymous with art collector, more rarely also with art dealer, until most recent times, similar to "antiquaire" in France. Murray's New English Dictionary defines the word "antiquarian" thus: *"adjective and noun; a) of, or connected with the study of antiquities b) applied to a large size of drawing paper"*. The term is only rarely used as a noun. In German, French, and Italian the word is now generally understood to mean someone dealing commercially in old objects or books.

The fact that the definition itself is elusive, not to say dubious, has its historical causes, which may become apparent when we try to look into the origin of the species and its evolution a little closer. A Music Antiquarian is, for our present purpose, one who deals commercially in music books, music editions, or music manuscripts which are out of print, or otherwise unobtainable, and, by implication, objects originating in earlier periods.

In attempting to outline the Music Antiquarian in his social function and historical significance we shall try to investigate to what extent he mirrors, follows, or influences certain trends in musical taste, musical scholarship, and collecting standards. For long periods his contours merge with those of the general bookseller, publisher, auctioneer, or even art dealer: it is for this reason, perhaps, that no one has ventured to enquire into his remoter ancestry up to now.

There have been many retrospective periods in history which sought inspiration and spiritual nourishment from the artistic creations of earlier ages. It is in these periods that antiquarians flourish, and may first have established themselves. One of the earliest, if not the earliest reference to such dealers is contained in the following edict of the year 832 A.D.— a period, we may observe, which is characterised by its revival of interest in classical art forms. This 9th-century edict[1] warns bishops and abbots to *"watch their ecclesiastical treasures very carefully, lest some of the jewels, vases, or other valuable objects may disappear through the perfidy or negligence of their custodians, because it has come to our ears that dealers, both Jewish and non-Jewish, boast that they can buy from them anything that takes their fancy."*

In the 14th century, Richard de Bury (1281—1345) made some wise and amusing observations about booksellers in his famous *Philobiblon*.

The Renaissance and Humanism produced booksellers like Vespasiano da Bisticci in Florence, and others who are the first fully recognisable ancestors of their modern counterparts.

Music could play only an incidental rôle in the revival of classical studies, and in the activities of such booksellers: apart from learned speculations about Greek and Roman music, the only tangible classical monuments that could exercise the humanist's curiosity were the theoretical works of Ptolemy and a few others, and some later ones such as Augustine and Boethius.

---

* Paper read to the International Music Libraries Association, United Kingdom Branch, at Chaucer House, London W.C. 1., on 19 February, 1958
[1] Monumenta Germaniae Historica, Legum Tomus III, p. 364 § 23.

The first music item ever to figure on a printed catalogue may be found on that remarkable broadside printed in Nuremberg in 1474, in which Regiomontanus, an outstanding humanist, lists his completed and forthcoming publications. Among the latter is *Musica Ptolemei cum Expositione Porphyrii*[2].

Organised bookselling on an important scale really began with the bi-annual Book Fairs at Frankfurt am Main and Leipzig in the middle of the 16th century. New publications from all over Europe were exhibited, and the catalogues published in connection with these Fairs from 1564 onwards are a bibliographical source of the first order. They contain, on the whole, only newly published works. As early as 1572, however, Georg Willer's catalogue of the new publications at the Frankfurt Fair mentions on the title the inclusion of some older editions.

A retrospective catalogue covering the publications of the past twenty-eight years was issued by Georg Willer in 1592. There are no fewer than twenty pages of *LIBRI MUSICI VARIAEQUE CANTIONES LATINAE POTISSIMUM TAM SACRAE QUAM PROFANAE ... alphabetico ordine nominibus autorum.* Part II of this great catalogue comprises a further nine-page section of *Teutsche Music Bücher*, Part III a similar section of Italian, Spanish and French music books which had been exhibited at the Fair from 1568 to 1592[3].

A facsimile of the music sections of two similar catalogues, compiled by Georg Draudius in 1611 and 1625 respectively, was recently published by Konrad Ameln[4]. Both these catalogues contain, the title says, "*Music Books printed almost as many years ago as we may remember, and many of which are still to be found in Bookshops.*"

An English counterpart to these catalogues — but one not connected with a Trade Fair — is the "*Seconde Parte of the Catalogue of English Printed Books: Eyther written in our own tongue, or translated out of any other language: which concerneth the Sciences Mathematicall as Arthmetick, Geometrie, Astronomie, Astrologie, Musick, the Arte of Warre and Navigation ... by ANDREW MAUNSELL Booke-seller. London, James Roberts for Andrew Maunsell, 1595.*" (STC 17669.)

This is the first printed English Catalogue containing books on music and music editions. While not in the strict sense a bookseller's catalogue, it is — like the catalogues of Willer and Draudius mentioned above[5]—a catalogue by a bookseller, and, to some extent, for booksellers. In the preface addressed to the "*Master, Wardens and Assistants of the Companie of Stationers and ... Bookesellers in generall*", Maunsell says: "*... seeing also many singuler Bookes, not only of Divinitie, but of other excellent Arts, after the First Impression, so spent and gone, that they lie even as it were buried in some few studies: that men desirous of such kind of Bookes, cannot aske for that they never heard of, and the Booke-seller cannot shew that he hath not: I have thought good in my poor estate to undertake this most tire-some businesse ... thinking it is as necessarie for the Bookseller (considering the number and nature of them) to have a catalogue of our English Bookes: as the Apothecarie his Dispensatorium, or the Schoolemaster his Dictionarie.*"

---

[2] Regiomontanus died before work on the book was put in hand, and Ptolemy's treatise on music was not published for almost another hundred years.

[3] A bibliography of the music books listed in the Frankfurt Fair Catalogues was published by Albert Göhler in 1902 (*Die Messkataloge im Dienst der musikalischen Geschichtsforschung.* in Sammelbände d. IMG, & *Verzeichnis der in den Frankfurter und Leipziger Meßkatalogen 1564—1759 angezeigten Musikalien,* Leipzig, 1902).

[4] Bärenreiter-Verlag.

[5] See also their Italian prototype, Antonio Francesco Doni's *La Libraria* (first edition 1550).

The section "Of Musicke" begins with "A Brief Instruction to Musicke, collected by P. Delamote Frenchman, Prin. by Tho. Vautrollier. 1574. 8". William Bathe's Introduction to ... Musicke, Oxford, 1584, the Service book printed by John Day (in 1560), the Psalmes of 1563 and 1579, and those of John Wolfe and Thomas Este (East) of 1585 and 1594 respectively are also listed. There are three items under: "Lute" (Adrian Le Roy, translated by F. Ke. Gentleman. A briefe and plaine Instruction to set all Musicke ... in Tableture for the Lute ... James Rowbothum. 1574); "Gitterne". A brief ... instruction ... to learne ... the Gitterne. Pri. for James Rowbothum in 4. (n.d.) and "Citterne". A new booke of Citterne lessons ... Pri. for William Barley. 1593. 4.

The catalogues quoted so far are an indication of the better organisation and the expansion of the general book trade in the countries of Western Europe. Even when they list publications considerably earlier than their date, they nevertheless are designed to give as complete a picture as possible of the new output, including what we would term "second-hand" or out-of-print publications. No really "antiquarian", retrospective trend can be read into these catalogues: for the reader of 1595 a lute manual of 1574 was as contemporary as a theoretical treatise of 1569, or a song book of 1571 [6].

It is not until the 17th century that we come across evidence of music collecting, and of a definite antiquarian interest in old music and music books. We may assume that scholars like Christopher Simpson or Thomas Mace in England, Athanasius Kircher or, earlier still, Vincenzo Galilei, Mersenne, and others, gathered round themselves music and music treatises of the past which they used for, and quoted in, their works.

One of the greatest music libraries that ever existed was the marvellous collection assembled by King João IV of Portugal (1604—1656), at Lisbon. One copy only of the catalogue, printed in 1649, survives (Bibliothèque Nat., Paris). Its 525 pages are eloquent proof of the unbelievable wealth of that music library, without any doubt the richest in the world at the time. The first volume of the catalogue—two more were planned but never printed—is, alas, all that survives [7]: the whole collection was swallowed up by the earth in the great Lisbon earthquake of 1755. Two months before his death, on September 4th, 1656, the King concluded the acquisition of an entire music collection for which his librarian had negotiated with the Amsterdam bookseller Blaeu. The King himself had studied and annotated the lists submitted by the bookseller, and agreed to the very large purchase price. (In his Will, the King left detailed instructions concerning the future preservation of the music library.)

According to O. E. Deutsch (his article on Music Collections in Grove, 5th edition), the earliest English music collection is that of Samuel PEPYS (died in 1703), preserved in Magdalene College, Cambridge. Both Pepys and Evelyn wrote of their frequent visits to London bookshops, among them Playford's Music Shop. It would not be surprising if evidence of even earlier music collections in Britain could be found.

However, for information on the availability of early music books and editions we have to look mainly to Auction Sale catalogues: the system of book auctions seems to have

---

[6] It may be worth recording that the earliest known register of books exported to the New World, listing a consignment of books shipped by the Seville bookseller Diego de Montoya to Pedro de Ochoa de Ontegui in Mexico in the year 1586, contains one copy of Musica de Cabeçon, in pergamino, price 14 Reis. (Printed in 1578). Two further copies were contained in another case in the same shipment. The first book-sale in the Americas was held in Mexico in 1576. On this occasion several copies of Martin de Tapia's Bergel de Musica (1570), and Alonso de Castillo's Arte de Canto Llano were sold. These are the earliest music books to become known across the Atlantic.

[7] The catalogue was reprinted in 1874, and a biographical volume added by Joaquim de Vasconcellos in 1900. This volume includes numerous documents relating to the growth of the music library.

originated in Holland—one of the earliest was held by Ludwig Elzevir at Amsterdam in 1604—and soon spread to England, where the first book auction was held by William Cooper, bookseller, in 1676. Sale catalogues were only rarely collected systematically, even by libraries, but the British Museum and Bodleian Library have a large number of them, going back to the late 17th century. A most useful list of the English Auction Catalogues containing Music, compiled by Mr. Wakeling, is available in the Music Room of the British Museum.

Apparently the earliest English Music Auction took place at Dewing's Coffee-House in Popes Head Alley, near the Royal Exchange, on December 17th, 1691. A copy of the 16-page 8vo catalogue is preserved in the British Museum (*A Catalogue of Ancient and Modern Musick Books, both Vocal & Instrumental, with divers Treatises about the same, and several Musical Instruments, as also of a Collection of Books in History Divinity and Physick.*) There is no indication of the original owner of that collection nor of the auctioneer, but a prominent advertisement in the catalogue for the *"newly printed the 2d Book of Apollo's Banquet . . . sold by Henry Playford . . ."* makes it probable that the collection was assembled by the elder Playford, who had died a few years earlier (there are also several lots of 20 sets each of music books printed by him in the 1660's and 1670's). The collection here offered for sale is extraordinarily rich, both in English and foreign 16th and 17th century music. Among the latter the works of most of the great Italian madrigalists, Peri's *Euridice*, Monteverdi's *Lamento d'Arianna*, and similar treasures are listed. Among French works we find French songs for four voices by Ronsard, editions of Claude Lejeune, etcetera, and there is also *"an old Spanish Book that Treats about and is full of Musick, di Antonio de Cubicon"* (Cabezon).

Even more important for our purpose is a 4-page 4to catalogue, printed in 1690, of which only one copy appears to survive, according to Wing's Short Title Catalogue (P 2428): that preserved in the Bodleian Library, Oxford: it is, I believe, the earliest antiquarian music catalogue printed in England. While Playford's catalogue of 1691 discussed above was an auction catalogue, the present one has all the elements of a bookseller's catalogue [8]. Though fairly long, it will be worth quoting the title of this 1690 catalogue in full *"A Curious Collection of Musicke-Books both Vocal and Instrumental (and several rare copies in Three and Four Parts, fairly prick'd) by the Best Masters, Formerly designed to have been sold by way of Auction: But the reason of its beeing put off, was, that several Gentlemen, Lovers of Musick, living remote from London, having a desire for some of this Collection, and could not be there, they are here set down in order, with the rates, being lower than could be afforded otherwise. The collection is to be sold by Henry Playford, at his house at the lower end of Arundel Street in the Strand; where the Collection may be viewed four Days after the Publication in the Gazette. All Gentlemen and Ladies that desire any of these Collections, sending in time the number and the price, may have them delivered, they being designed to be sold off in a Fortnight . . . Catalogues may be had gratis of Mr. Knight Bookseller . . . Mr. Carr at his Shop . . . (etc.) . . . at Mr. Henry Playford's . . . and of Mr. Dolliff, Bookbinder in Oxford."*

The copy in the Bodleian Library has a ms. note on the title: *Donum Fr. Dolliff, XI Jun. 1690.*

Originally designed to be auctioned, the 121 lots are now offered, as the title informs us, at their affixed prices, to the Gentlemen and Ladies that may buy them. (The custom of

---

[8] See also Wm. C. Smith's article *Playford. Some hitherto unnoticed catalogues of early music*, in Musical Times, July/Aug. 1926.

fixing a time limit within which orders should be sent is a feature encountered in book-sellers' catalogues throughout the 18th century: the period varies with the size of the catalogue). Thus, the modern antiquarian music catalogue was, one is tempted to speculate, born through the inability of gentlemen residing in the country to attend the auctions held in town: we certainly have the title of Henry Playford's catalogue to suggest the point. Nor is it a surprising one: it is in this period and the following century that art and book collections were formed, and flourished in the country houses of the aristocracy.

The catalogue lists a collection of mostly English printed and manuscript music of the 17th century, and a few music books, including a few 16th century items. The earliest is item 93 "GLARINIA, a large Treatise on Musick in Latin, 4 shillings" which is, no doubt, a copy of Glareanus, *Dodekachordon*, Basle, 1547. The bulk is made up of vocal and instrumental part books by Morley, Tomkins, Campion, Lawes, Wilbye, Locke, Ferabosco, and many others. Such a catalogue, and the auction catalogues mentioned before, prove that music collecting and dealing in music was by then an established custom. Henry Playford's antiquarian music catalogue did not, however, start a fashion: in spite of his pioneering example we are forced to consult auction and general booksellers' catalogues in our search for old music throughout the 18th century. It is also certain that since the 16th century music publishers carried stocks of old music editions, and that much of the antiquarian music trade was a by-product of their activities.

Towards the middle of the 18th century several firms of antiquarian booksellers are established in London. Their main ambition appears to have been to amass enormous numbers of books from private libraries, and to offer them in catalogues often containing 20, 30, or 40,000 items.

The well-known firm of T. OSBORNE, of Gray's Inn, issued "*A Catalogue of the Libraries of the late Dr. Cromwell Mortimer Secretary to the Royal Society, Edm. Pargiter, Esq., and many others too tedious to mention; all purchased this last summer ... the whole together being a much larger collection than any ever yet sold by any bookseller in England which will begin to be sold ... on 26 November 1753 and for the conveniency of the Nobility and Gentlemen who live at a distance will continue selling every day till November 1754.*" The catalogue contains under the sections "*Antiquities, Inscriptions, Medals, Mathematicks and other Arts and Sciences*" a number of old music books, valued at a few shillings.

Osborne & Shipton's *Catalogue of near two hundred thousand volumes* issued five years later, 1758, contains a copy of Caroso, Il Ballarino, Venice, 1581, for 5 shillings, and others on music.

Later in the century Thomas Payne & Son issued similar catalogues, among whose lots are listed some music items, with prices; the highest figure, in 1790, is affixed to "Burney's Present State of Music in Germany and Italy, 3 volumes, neat and gilt, 1775 — 12 shillings." "*The Dancing Master, 2 volumes, 1686*", on the other hand was to be had for 5 shillings, and William Bathe's *Brief Introduction to the Skill of Song*, 1597, for two shillings — indeed for a song!

It is not surprising that these booksellers failed to price items according to their rarity: on looking through some of these enormous catalogues one is struck by the uniformity of the prices, and their uniformly low level. This was, indeed, a kind of whole-sale bookselling which must, on the other hand, have attracted discriminating buyers.

The manner of distribution of these catalogues is described in a note in Osborne & Shipton's two-volume catalogue of 1754: "*Notwithstanding these two large volumes of the catalogue are attended with a great Expence, they are, as usual, sent to the most eminent Coffee-*

Houses in and near Town, for Gentlemen's perusal, who are earnestly desired not to take them away; and if taken away, a fine laid upon the landlord or landlady of the House; for, as this Sale will continue for two years, they will always be an amusement to Gentlemen."

Although several notable music collections were formed in England at this time, there was, as it seems, no bookseller who made a special point of offering more music material than his rivals. It may be significant to remember that this was the era of the encyclopaedists: an epoch still far removed from the trends toward specialisation, which was to alter the picture so decisively in the ensuing century.

It is the period in which Dr. Burney and others, such as Dr. Pepusch, William Boyce, and Hawkins built up their music collections. The autograph MS of Dr. Burney's Journal, mostly portions not included in the published version, contains some revealing passages concerning his collecting methods and relations with booksellers: *"Went out book hunting at stalls, old shops, &c.",* he writes soon after his arrival in Paris in the summer of 1770. *"I went into La rue St. Jacques (a long street filled with booksellers) not so much to purchase books as to collect catalogues to examine at my leisure. However, I purchased so many books of Canto Fermo, such as Offices, Graduals, Missals, Rituals, Antiphoners, &c., in order to get a thorough knowledge of the Romish Church Music, that at my return to England I shall perhaps be taken up at Dover for a Jesuit come over to propagate the papal doctrines."* ... *"At last, after several vain attempts, I met with Lacombe, Garrick's bookseller; performed my commissions to him from my friend and made some purchases for myself. I found him an intelligent conversible man ... I gave him a list of books and pamphlets relative to Music to procure for me which Nourn's correspondent had sought in vain. Lacombe promised me to find more during my absence in Italy. Some of them on musical controversy he furnished me with, bound up together for his own use."* ... *"Met with the Abbé Roussier at La Chevardière's Music Shop and we were soon made acquainted and had a great deal of musical talk ... This Abbé has a great collection of books on Musick. I shewed him my catalogue which seemed to make his mouth water. "Ah, Monsieur", (he said) "vous êtes bien riche!"*

In Milan Dr. Burney writes: *"Tuesday, 17th. Spent in hunting after source books...".* In Venice: *"There are no music shops nor is any music engraved stampt or printed with types ... But the number of booksellers in the fine street called La Merceria is very considerable. I found in no one place so many old Treatises and authors on the subject of music as here ... The principal booksellers in Venice at present are Pasquali, Raimondini, Bettinelli, Occhi, & Antonio di Castro."*

In Florence: *"Mr Joseph Molini from whom I have received much assistance ... at Florence, has been so kind as to undertake to send the books which I collected here and at Bologna to England, directed to his brother. They began a second time to be too much for my trunk and would have been a horrible embarrassment at the entrance into the Pope's territories ... where they say all books are examined by the Inquisition."*

Burney's notes are both amusing and illuminating. He is surely the first music scholar who admits that he visits bookshops not so much to purchase books, as to collect catalogues! On the other hand, he was a substantial and discriminating customer, and his beloved Library, which was auctioned in London in 1814, proves it: the sale catalogue, partly with prices reached at the auction, is preserved in the British Museum. The sale of music took seven weekdays. The books on music which were to be auctioned a few weeks later were withdrawn and sold en bloc to the British Museum in the following year (1815).

It may be useful to sum up at this point what the evidence so far adduced means in terms of the story of the Music Antiquarian. The personalities we have so far encountered behind the counter were either auctioneers, general booksellers, or music publishers. Music editions of the past are often met with, even listed in seperate sections in bookseller's catalogues, but they rarely assume more than incidental importance. Their largely haphasard and uneven prices prove that no definite trends in antiquarian music dealing and collecting had crystallised up to the end of the 18th century.

The great music historians of the century, however, paved the way for a new appreciation of old music. While the works of Dr. Burney, Hawkins, and comparable continental scholars made facts and perspectives of music history accessible and intelligible to a wide public, the musical monuments of the past assumed living shape in their own right only with the romantic revival towards the turn of the century and after. The musical revivalist movements—we need only mention the name of Palestrina as an example—led to what we might call musical historicism—a development which had a profound effect on musical outlook and scholarship. It brought in its train an unprecedented interest in the music of earlier ages, and all the resources of ever more exact and exacting methods of research were brought to bear on the interpretation of its surviving monuments. The provision of source books, the extension of bibliographical exploration to the field of music books and editions, the search for hitherto neglected music of earlier centuries became more and more vital to scholars, libraries, and the newly founded Faculties of Music History.

On the Continent, above all in Germany, this trend is reflected in the appearance of booksellers' catalogues devoted entirely to old music. The Berlin booksellers R. Friedländer & Sohn, established in 1828, compiled a catalogue of the music collection of A. Westrow, which was auctioned in 1853. The firm of L. E. Lanz in Weilburg issued a music catalogue in 1854 entitled *Verzeichnis einer Sammlung antiquarischer Musikwerke* (Catal. II). Similar ones followed in 1860 and 1861. In 1859 L. F. Maske's Antiquariat, Breslau, issued their catalogue 44, containing the fine collection of Johann Theodor Mosewius. J. D. Class of Heilbronn issued a whole series of music catalogues between 1860 and 1865. Richard Zeune compiled three remarkable music catalogues for the Berlin antiquarian bookseller E. Mecklenburg in 1860 and 1861. (Nos. 10, 12, and 13). Several antiquarian music catalogues were issued by Kirchhoff & Wigand in Leipzig between 1860 and 1865. Others were issued by Asher & Co. of Berlin (specially catals. 68 and 74 of 1862 and 1863) and, notably, by the house of List & Franke of Leipzig.

The catalogues of that firm are well suited to illustrate some aspects of the antiquarian music trade of that period. Within a few years of its Catalogue One of 1862, this firm offered for sale a number of distinguished private music libraries: those of H. Schellenberg of Leipzig, Landsberg of Rome, Strauch of Ernstthal, Kieber of Oederan, and others. The mere fact that such private collections could now be purchased and offered for sale by music antiquarians, is undoubtedly a measure of their growing importance: the sale of similar collections was previously entrusted without exception to auction houses.

The catalogues of List & Francke contain other features worthy of note: the descriptive notes, for instance, are mostly in French, although the catalogues were issued in Germany. The practice of issuing catalogues in foreign languages became widespread in the German-speaking countries. Ludwig Rosenthal writes in the Foreword to his music catalogue in 1880: "*A cause de l'intérêt universel des matériaux nous sommes forcés à donner ce catalogue en français, quoique notre connaissance de cette langue internationale ait bien des lacunes. Nous sommes prêts à donner des explications éventuelles sur ce qui pourra paraitre obscur.*" The use of an international language is an indication both of the growing international connections of the antiquarian bookseller and, of course, of the fact that buyers were increasingly to be found in France and the Anglo-Saxon countries[9].

In England, too, greater prominence is given to music in booksellers' catalogues even in the first half of the 19th century. Thomas Thorpe's catalogue of 1834, for instance, refers on the cover to "an extraordinary assemblage of MSS ... of the late William Radcliffe, including collections of Elizabethan Madrigals with Music". (The descriptions also are becoming more elaborate, lists of Incipits are given in full, and short biographical notes on the composers are added.) Thomas Kerslake, bookseller at Bristol, underlines music prominently on the cover of one of his catalogues about the same time. The firm of Bernard Quaritch, established in 1847, soon begins to include music in its catalogues. While catal. 24, issued in 1851, contains under the heading Games, Sports & Music only four items, three on music and one on shooting, catalogue 50, October 1852, comprises 120 music items under the heading "MUSIC, SONGS. *The most curious collection of Old English Songs and Ballads ever offered for sale*." In England, especially, the antiquarian music market continued to be further stimulated by auction sales of important music collections.

Perhaps the very existence of a parody of a music catalogue may be taken as a sign that such catalogues were well established and widely known. As early as 1862 such a parody was printed by R. Lonsdale, aimed at Dr. Rimbault and his library, under the title *Catalogue of the Extensive Library of Dr. Rainbeau FRS, FSA, ASS, which Messrs Topsy Turvy & Co. will put up for public competition on Saturday, October 1862.* Here are a few samples chosen partly for their relevance to music dealers and their catalogues:

Lot 1   Doctor Rainbeau's handkerchief, spectacles, and case (much soiled).

Lot 13 "HOW CAN I LIVE?" or, The poor Musick Professor's outcrie against his rich brethren for taking the allowance on Musick from him and dealing at the cheap shoppes by which he and his family are like to be ruined. 8vo. 1862.

Lot 50 DUFFIN's ART OF PUFFING, or the Music Seller's Day Book.

Lot 92 Beethoven's Works, Moscheles edition, the most correct.

Lot 93 Beethoven's Works, Bennett's edition, the most correct.

Lot 94 Beethoven's Works, Benedict's edition, the most correct.

Lot 95 Beethoven's Works, Liszt's edition, the most correct.

Lot 96 Beethoven's Works, Hummel's edition, the most correct.

and so on and so forth.

The antiquarian Music Catalogues now reflect the most conspicuous feature of 19th-century scholarship: that of specialisation. The generation of Fétis, Coussemaker, Bellermann, Jacobsthal, and others, had opened new perspectives to musical research, and had established musicology as a discipline in its own right. Within a short time its literature and range became so vast that the bookseller had to specialise in this field, if he was to serve the expanding circle of customers adequately.

The process was a gradual one, and music buying lagged behind the achievements of musical scholarship. This may be deduced from the following words written by Johannes Wolf: "*Is it not extraordinary that at a time when Heinrich Bellermann and Philip Spitta were occupying Chairs in Music History, when Robert Eitner was active with bibliographical*

[9] Some of the voluminous English 18th-century catalogues had Prefaces and Selling Conditions in French and English.

research, when Chrysander was doing his brilliant work, that Leo Liepmannssohn was offering one of the earliest German organ tablatures, the MS of Ileborgh von Stendal of 1448, for 40 marks without finding a buyer in Germany—so that the precious MS was sold abroad?" Wolf also points out that even the extraordinarily low prices were no inducement to librarians at a time when music was studiously overlooked even in the cataloguing of libraries, with the sole exception, as far as Germany was concerned, of the Berlin Staats-bibliothek.

The name of Leo Liepmannssohn just quoted provides an opportunity for referring briefly to this remarkable personality, who did so much to create the very conception of the Music Antiquarian in the current sense of the word. "Small and round in stature", wrote Prager in his little booklet Silhouettes of Antiquarian Booksellers, "suffering from asthma in his later years, but nevertheless smoking incessantly—clever, vivacious eyes set in a pink face with short beard, the high dome of his head framed by short white hair. An amusing talker, fond of telling stories, he could sometimes be prevailed upon to display his mastery of the piano. I have heard him play Chopin with perfect technique while at the same time keeping his beloved cigar going. An extremely learned and friendly man, in spite of his pronounced sarcasm."

Leo Liepmannssohn first established himself in Paris in 1866, in the rue des Saints-Pères. One of his early catalogues, No: 33 of 1870 contains 1141 items, many of them of outstanding rarity. The hallmark of the specialist bookseller is clearly discernible even in his first catalogues. Titles are fully given, collations are added to the more important items. There is a far greater diversity of prices—a much wider and at the same time more solid scale of values, based on intimate knowledge of the music reference works, music history, and current collecting tastes. He notes not only references to existing literature, but indicates results of his own research. In his description of Froberger's Diverse ingegnosissime ... Partite, Toccate, Canzone, &c., he points out that this work was not printed in 1714, as Fétis had it, but in 1693. He also says that, as the edition speaks of Froberger as "nunc piae memoriae", he must have died in or before that year, not in 1695, as Fétis had stated.

Liepmannssohn, especially after reopening in Berlin in 1873, became the leading specialist in antiquarian music, and the firm retained its pre-eminence after it had been taken over in 1903 by Otto Haas, on whom this Association bestowed an Honorary Membership in 1953. The long series of almost 250 catalogues issued by that firm is, perhaps, quite apart from being a veritable encyclopaedia of musical literature, the most continuous and reliable record of the trends in music buying, and the availability of material over a period of almost ninety years. Great private collections were being formed in that period—the names of Matthew, Ecorcheville, Wolffheim, Cortot, Hirsch, may alone suffice to illustrate the point. Collections are now built and organised primarily on the lines demanded by musicology. In an article on Musik-Bibliophilie. Aus den Erfahrungen eines Musik-Sammlers, 1927, Paul Hirsch gives the six guiding points which governed his acquisitions. Number one is: "Wissenschaftliche Bedeutung." Preservation, rarity, typographical merit, binding, and illustrations come after this consideration.

Public and University Libraries continued in increasing measure to buy systematically to satisfy the rapidly and universally growing need for source material and specialised literature. It is this need which provided the stimulus for music antiquarians in several countries to keep abreast with research in the descriptions and composition of their catalogues. In England, the house of Reeves issued its first music catalogue in 1875, and thus inaugurated a long series of astonishingly rich catalogues. R. Legouix became a well-known music specialist in Paris. Several of the leading general antiquarian booksellers issued important and well-edited music catalogues: Ludwig Rosenthal's catalogue 26 *Bibliotheca Musica* issued in 1880 in Munich comprises well over 2,000 music items, Jacques Rosenthal's catalogue I, 1895, is entirely devoted to music. Many of its numbers were acquired by the British Museum. Martin Breslauer issued his scholarly and finely produced catalogue „Das deutsche Lied" in 1908, L. S. Olschki in Florence, Quaritch in London, and others, published similar special music catalogues of value. Between the two world wars, and later, new and important firms established themselves both in England, on the Continent, and in America, whose names will be familiar to you—I hope for unimpeachable reasons.

The antiquarian bookseller knows very well that no printed or other matter gravitates more automatically, more powerfully towards the wastepaper basket than his catalogues. Only by giving them bibliographical and typographical thrust in the opposite direction can he achieve the ideal result: namely that not only the goods offered therein should be sold, but that the catalogues themselves should become the faithful satellites of the music-bibliographer, -librarian, and -historian.

"*Booksellers' catalogues*", as Mr. C. B. Oldman wrote in *Collecting Musical First Editions*, 1938, "*contain some of the fullest and most reliable information on the subject of musical first editions that (the collector) is likely to find anywhere. In particular some of the catalogues recently issued . . . are models of careful research and invaluable as works of reference.*"

The usefulness of music dealers' catalogues as sources of bibliographical information was recognised by Petzhold, who gave a list of those he thought noteworthy in his 'Bibliotheca Bibliographica', 1866. Eitner's Quellenlexikon contains innumerable references to copies of music books in booksellers' catalogues. One wishes sometimes that certain bibliographies should not be quite so adamant in excluding copies held or listed by dealers when enumerating known copies: their editors may rightly point to difficulties arising from quoting from such transient sources, but they have only themselves to blame if the music antiquarian then writes "only one copy in X's bibliography", although it is a book of which several copies may have been prominently described in dealers' catalogues within most recent memory.

Music antiquarians' catalogues were perhaps for the first time collected systematically by Paul Hirsch, and will figure under the names of the firms in the forthcoming part of the Hirsch Library Accessions Catalogue of the British Museum. In some public libraries antiquarian booksellers' catalogues are still, by tradition, consigned not, perhaps, to the "Enfer", but certainly to the Purgatory of the stacks. Their rescue from this anonymous and uncatalogued twilight is a labour of love which is not without reward to music historians and -bibliographers alike.

An enquiry into the nature of music antiquarians' catalogues in the last 100 years might well yield interesting information. If I have been able to draw the attention of music librarians to this somewhat neglected branch of musical literature—and by neglect I do not mean that they have neglected to order from these catalogues—this sketchy and tentative survey may have served a useful purpose.

Sources and Related Readings

BibdMS[1]   *Bibliographie des Musikschrifttums.* Frankfurt a.M.: F. Hofmeister, 1936–.

Block, Andrew. *Book Collector's Vade Mecum.* London: D. Archer, 1932.

––––––. *A Short History of the Principal London Antiquarian Booksellers and Book Auctioneers.* London: D. Archer, 1933.

Blogie, Jeanne. *Répertoire des catalogues de ventes de livres imprimés.* vol. 1: *Catalogue belges appartenant à la Bibliothèque royale Albert Ier.* Brussels: Fl. Tulken, 1982. (Centre national de l'archéologie et de l'histoire du livre, Publications no. 4)

Bohatta, Hanns. 'Die Bedeutung der Antiquariats- und Auktionskataloge für den Bibliographen', *Archiv für Bibliographie, Buch- und Bibliothekswesen,* 2. Jg., Heft 2 (1928): 72–79.

Bohatta, Hanns and Franz Hodes. *Internationale Bibliographie der Bibliographien.* Frankfurt a.M.: Klostermann, 1939–50.

Book Selling and Book Buying: Aspects of the Nineteenth-century British and North American Book Trade. Ed. Richard G. Landon. Chicago: American Library Association, [1978].

Brown, Richard and Stanley Brett. *The London Bookshop: Part One of a Pictorial Record of the Antiquarian Book Trade. Portraits and Premises.* London: Private Library Association, 1971.

Coral, Lenore. 'Music Dealers and Antiquarians'. In *The New Grove Dictionary of Music and Musicians.* Ed. Stanley Sadie. Vol. 12: 828–30. London: Macmillan, 1980.

Curwen, Henry. *A History of Booksellers, the Old and the New.* London: Chatto & Windus [1873].

---

[1] Sigla in this column are employed in the checklist to indicate secondary sources of citations for catalogues not seen by the compiler.

DBT   *Danske bogmarked.* 1, 1854–   . Kobenhavn: Danske forlaeggerforen-
           ing, 1854.
               Title varies. Aug. 1915–Dec. 1947 as *Dansk boghandler-tidende.*

           Eitner, Robert. *Buch- und Musikalienhändler, Büch- und Musikalien-
           drucker nebst Notenstecher.* Leipzig: Breitkopf & Härtcl, 1904.

           Field, Eugene. 'The Malady Called Catalogitis', in Targ, William.
           Bouillabaisse for Bibliophiles, pp. 329–35. Cleveland and New York:
           World Publishing Co., 1955.

           Fischer, Jürgen. 'Die Kataloge des Musikantiquariats Hans Schneider',
           in *Festschrift Hans Schneider, hrsg. von Rudolf Elvers und Ernst Vogel,*
           pp. 75–86. München: Verlag Ernst Vogel, 1981.

           Fog, Dan. 'Eine dänischer Sortimentskatalog vom Jahre 1787: Analyse
           und Kommentar'. In *Ibid.* pp. 89–110.

Ganley   Ganley, Eric H. *Catalogues.* Forest Hills, N.Y.: 1950–.

           Gough, Richard. 'The Progress of Selling Books by Catalogue', *Gentle-
           man's Magazine,* 1788. Reprint in Nichols, John, *Literary Anecdotes of
           the Eighteenth Century,* vol. 3, pp. 608–93. London: Nichols, Son and
           Bentley, 1812.

Heck   Heck, V.A., firm. *Kataloge und Liste.* Vienna, 1923–.

           Holzbauer, Hermann. *Musikantiquariat und Verleger dazu. Für Hans
           Schneider.* Tutzing: Verlegt bei Hans Schneider, 1986. (Schriften der
           Universitätsbibliothek Eichstätt, 9)

           Hortschansky, Klaus. 'The Musician as Music Dealer in the Second Half
           of the 18th century', in *The Social Status of the Professional Musician
           from the Middle Ages to the 19th Century,* ed. by Walter Salmen, pp.
           109–218. New York: Pendragon, 1983.

ZiMG   Internationale Musik-Gesellschaft. *Zeitschrift.* 1.–15. Jg., 1899–1914.
           Leipzig: Breitkopf & Härtel, 1899–1914.

JbP   *Jahrbuch der Musikbibliothek Peters.* 1.–47. Jahrg., 1894–1940. Leip-
           zig: C.F. Peters, 1894–1940; Reprint, Vaduz: Kraus, 1965.

           'Katalogeingänge'. In issues of the *Börsenblatt für den deutschen Buch-
           handel, Frankfurter Ausgabe.* Jg. 1–. 6. Okt. 1945–. Frankfurt a.M.,
           etc., 1945–.

           King, Alexander Hyatt. *Some British Collectors of Music.* Cambridge:
           Cambridge University Press, 1963.

           Knight, Charles. *Shadows of the Old Booksellers.* London: George Rout-
           ledge [s.d.].

Lambertini, Michel'angelo. *Bibliophilie musicale. Edition abrégée.* Viseu: Andrade & Ca., 1924.

IBAK Loh, Gerhard. *Internationale Bibliographie der Antiquariats-, Auktions- und Kunst-Kataloge, 'IBAK',* bearb. von Gerhard Loh. Leipzig: Universitäts-bibliothek, 1960–.

Lugt, Frits. *Répertoire des catalogues de ventes publiques intérresant l'art ou la curiosité.* La Haye: Martinus Nijhoff, 1938.

MfM *Monatshefte für Musikgeschichte.* 1.–37. Jahrg., 1869–1905. Berlin: Trautwein; Leipzig: Breitkopf & Härtel, 1869–1905.

Petzholdt Petzholdt, Julius. *Bibliotheca bibliographica. Kritische Verzeichnis.* Leipzig: Engelmann, 1866.

Po[llard], A[lfred] W. 'Book-collecting', *Encyclopedia Britannica*, 11th ed., 1910.

Pollard, Graham and Albert Ehrman. *The Distribution of Books by Catalogue . . . to 1800.* Cambridge: Roxburghe Club, 1965.

Roberts, William. The Book-hunter in London. Chicago: McClurg, 1895.

––––––. *The Earlier History of English Bookselling.* London: Sampson Low, Marston, Searle & Rivington, 1889.

Rosenthal, Albi. 'Die Lagerkatalog des Musikantiquariats Leo Liepmannssohn (1866–1935)'. In *Festschrift Hans Schneider zum 60. Geburtstag,* hrsg. *von Rudolf Elvers und Ernst Vögel.* pp. 193–216. München: Verlag Ernst Vögel, 1981.

Schaal, Richard. 'Die Bedeutung der Mikropie für den Antiquar', *Börsenblatt für den deutsche Buchhandel, Frankfurter Ausg.,* Nr. 21/22 (1 April 1949): A153.

––––––. 'Der Bildungsgang des Musikantiquars', *Ibid.,* Nr. 47 (28 June 1949): 329–30.

––––––. 'Musikverlag und Musikalienhandel', in *Die Musik in Geschichte und Gegenwart.* Hrsg. von Friedrich Blume. Kassel [etc.]: Bärenreiter, 1949–87.

Schneider Schneider, Hans, firm. *Kataloge. . . .* 1–. 1949–. Tutzing über München, 1949–.

Shaylor, Joseph. *The Fascination of Books, with Other Papers on Books and Bookselling.* New York: Putnam's Sons, 1912.

Slater, John Herbert. *Round and About the Book-stalls: A Guide for the Book-hunter.* London: L. Upcott Gill, 1891.

Taylor, Archer. *Book Catalogues: Their Variety and Uses*. Chicago: Newberry Library, 1957.

Vereeniging ter bervordering van de belangen des boekhandels, Amsterdam. *Catalogus der Bibliotheek*, 1–. Amsterdam: P. N. Van Kampen & Zoon, 1885–.
> See especially the voluminous listings of auction and antiquarian catalogues in Deel 4, 1934 and Deel VIII, *Supplement-catalogus, 1932–1973*, published 1979.

Walters, Gwyn. 'Early Sale Catalogues: Problems and Perspectives', in *Sale and Distribution of Books from 1700*. Ed. Robin Myers and Michael Harris, pp. 106–125. [Oxford]: Oxford Polytechnic Press [1982].

Wendt, Bernhard. 'Zur Geschichte des deutschen Antiquariatsbuchhandels', *Zeitschrift für Bücherfreund*, Jg. 38, 3. Folge, Heft 5 (1934): 103–08.

––––––. *Der Versteigerungs- und Antiquariats-Katalog im Wandel dreier Jahrhunderte*. Leipzig: Liebisch, 1937.

Wolf, Johannes. 'Antiquariat und Musikwissenschaft', *Aus Wissenschaft und Antiquariat: Festschrift ... Gustav Fock*, pp. 167–700. Leipzig: [Fock] 1929.

List of Abbreviations

ALS	Autograph Letter, Signed
Angeb.	Angebot
Antiq.	Antiquarian
Ausg.	Ausgabe(n)
Ausz.	Auszug, Auszüge
Autogr.	Autograph(s)
Bibliogr.	Bibliography(ies)
Biogr.	Biography(ies)
Bks.	Books
Cat.	Catalogue(s)
chmbr.	chamber
Coll.	Collection(s)
d.	die, der, das
do.	ditto
Dr.	Drucke
Ed.	Edition(s)
Facs., Faks.	Facsimile(s)
Hist., hist.	History, historical
Hymnol.	Hymnology
Hpschd.	Harpsichord
i.a.	inter alia
Illus.	Illustration(s)
incl.	Including
Instr.	Instrument(s)
Jhs.	Jahrhunderts
Lit.	Literatur(e)
M.	Music, -ik, -ique
mcal.	musical
min.	miniature
misc.	miscellaneous
Ms., Mss.	manuscript(s)
Nwsltr.	Newsletter
prakt.	praktisch
prtd.	printed
Slg.	Sammlung

Th.	Theater, Theatre
u.	und
wissen.	wissenschaft
Wks.	Works

List of Libraries and Collections Cited

Siglum

1   Compiler/State University of New York at Buffalo
2   The British Library (London)
3   Gemeentemuseum (Den Haag)
4   The Grolier Club (New York City)
5   Paul Hirsch Collection, British Library (London)
6   D.W. Krummel (Urbana, Illinois)
7   The Library of Congress (Washington, D.C.)
8   The Library and Museum of the Performing Arts (New York)
9   William Reeves (London)
10 Sibley Library, Eastman School of Music (Rochester, N.Y.)
11 Nigel Simeone (Tunbridge Wells, Kent)
12 Vereeniging ter Bevordering van de Belangen des Boekhandels (Amsterdam)
13 University of Virginia (Charlottesville, Virginia)
14 University of California at Los Angeles
15 Generally available

Sigla for Sources of Citations

Numbers from the table above are used at the right margin in the checklist to indicate where copies of the catalogues, lists, and bulletins were examined. Sigla indicating the sources of citations for works that were not examined at first hand are also printed at the right margin. They appear in square brackets [ ] and include: (1) the name of an antiquarian who owns a copy of a catalogue that was not found elsewhere (e.g., [Macnutt]); (2) codes for items noted in the secondary literature but not found in the collections surveyed (e.g., [Petzholdt], whose *Bibliotheca bibliographica* is included in the 'Sources and Related Readings,'; and (3) RISM sigla for libraries known to own copies of listed catalogues (e.g. [F–Pn]).

Elements of the Citations

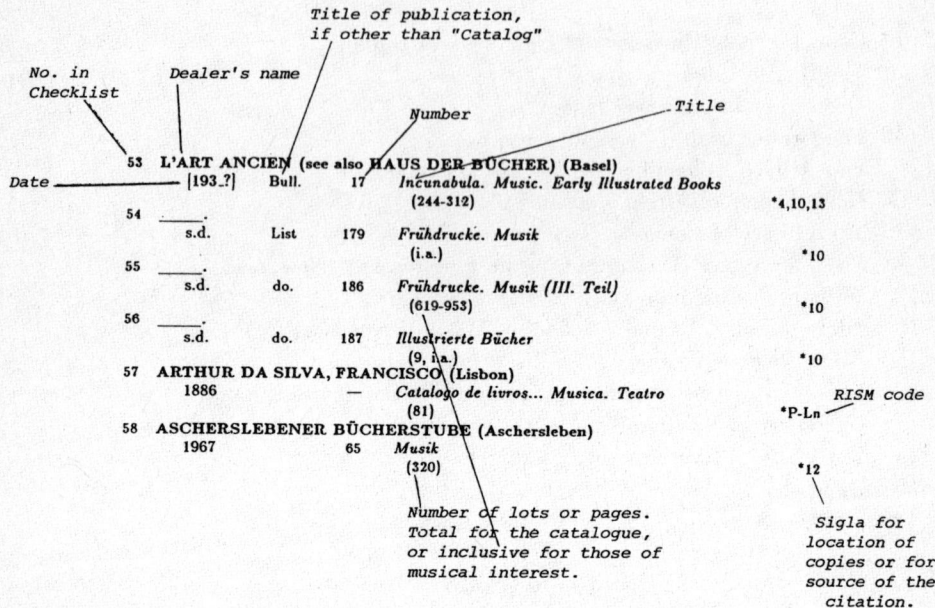

Title of publication,
if other than "Catalog"

No. in
Checklist

Dealer's name

Number

Title

53 **L'ART ANCIEN** (see also **HAUS DER BÜCHER**) (Basel)

Date ——— [193.?]   Bull.   17   *Incunabula. Music. Early Illustrated Books*
                                  (244-312)   *4,10,13

54 ___.
     s.d.   List   179   *Frühdrucke. Musik*
                          (i.a.)   *10

55 ___.
     s.d.   do.   186   *Frühdrucke. Musik (III. Teil)*
                          (619-953)   *10

56 ___.
     s.d.   do.   187   *Illustrierte Bücher*
                          (9, i.a.)   *10

57 **ARTHUR DA SILVA, FRANCISCO** (Lisbon)
     1886   —   *Catalogo de livros... Musica. Teatro*
                          (81)   RISM code
                                                                 *P-Ln

58 **ASCHERSLEBENER BÜCHERSTUBE** (Aschersleben)
     1967   65   *Musik*
                          (320)   *12

Number of lots or pages.
Total for the catalogue,
or inclusive for those of
musical interest.

Sigla for
location of
copies or for
source of the
citation.

The Checklist

1 **ACKERMANN, THEODORE (Munich)**
    1870   14   *Theoretisch und praktische Musik*
                                       [MFM]

2 _____.
    1871   18   *Kirchenmusik*
                                         [MFM]

3 _____.
    1876   45   *Ältere und neuere Musik*
                      (546)   [MFM]

4 _____.
    1877   ?   *Coll: Tucher v. Simmelsdorf*
                      (883)   [MFM]

5 _____.
    1878   60   *Ältere und neuere Musik. Kirchenmusik*
                                          *3,12

6 _____.
    1881   74   *Coll: [unnamed]. Musiksammlung ...*
                      (1235)   [MFM]

7 _____.
    1884   120   *Bücher und Musik*
                                          [MFM]

8 _____.
    1886   156   *Musikliteratur*
                                          *8

9 _____.
    1886   160   *Bücher und Porträts*
                                          [MFM]

10 _____.
    1887   211   *Bücher und Porträts*
                                          [MFM]

11 _____.
    1888   213   *Mythologie ... Volkslieder*
                      (333)   *3

12 _____.
    1893   347   *Geschichte d. Musik. Theoret. Werke, etc.*
                                        *8

13 _____.
    1900   467   *[Musikgeschichte, -theorie. Komische Oper]*
                      (841)   [MFM]

14 _____.
    [1934]   581   *Musik u. Musikgeschichte. Lied. Oper*
                      (2588)   *1,3,5,12

15 **ALBERT, EBERHARD (Freiburg i. Br.)**
    [1959]   83   *Kunst. Kunstgeschichte. Musik. Theater*
                      (2078)   *12

16 **ALDER, ROBERT (Bern)**
    [1960]   65   *Coll: Meyer, G. Musik und Literatur*
                      (475)   *12

1 Compiler/State University of New York (Buffalo)   **2** The British Library (London)   **3** Gemeentemuseum (Den Haag)   **4** The Grolier Club (N.Y.C.)   **5** Hirsch Collection, British Library (London)   **6** D.W. Krummel (Urbana)   **7** Library of Congress (Washington, D.C.)   **8** Library and Museum of the Performing Arts (N.Y.C.)   **9** William Reeves (London)   **10** Sibley Library, Eastman School of Music (Rochester)   **11** Nigel Simeone (Tunbridge Wells, Kent)   **12** Vereeniging ter Bervordering van de Belangen des Boekhandels (Amsterdam)   **13** University of Virginia (Charlottesville)   **14** University of California at Los Angeles   **15** Generally available

17 **ALICKE, PAUL (Dresden)**
    s.d.   189   *Coll: Schurig, A., 2.Tl. Musik u. Theater*
                               (1-551)   *3

18 **ALLEN, WALTER C. (Highland Park, N.J.)**
    1973/74   1/13   *Allen's Poop Sheet*
                            (pp.1-12)   *1

19 _____.
    1974/75   1/14   *Allen's Poop Sheet*
                            (pp.1-11)   *1

20 **ALLIED BOOK SHOP (N.Y.C.?)**
    1967   501   *Russian antiquarian music*
                                                          *8

21 **ALTREE BOOKSHOP (N.Y.C.)**
    1934   9   *American music ... Art*
                              (668)   *1

22 **ALMACEN DE LA CARRERA DE S. GERONIMO (Madrid)**
    1824   ?   *Musica vocal e instrumental*
                              (17p.)   *8

23 **AMERICAN ART ASSOCIATION (N.Y.C.)**
    1923   —   *Coll: Bieber, A. Songbooks*
                              708   *12

24 **L'AMI DU BIBLIOPHILE (Montpellier)**
    1958   —   *Beaux livres ... Musique*
                                                 [Ganley #311]

25 **LES AMIS DE LA MUSIQUE (Brussels)**
    194_-   1-   *Musique, revue mensuelle*
                                          *1,44- *8,14-

26 **ANTIQUA (Amsterdam)**
    1966   List   7   *Books on Music*
                                                          *8

27 _____.
    [1967]   do.   14   *Musical Literature*
                              (739)   *1,6,8,13

28 _____.
    [1968]   do.   17   *Books on Musicology*
                                (197)   *1,6,8,13

29 _____.
    [1969]   do.   19   *Musicology*
                                (229)   *1,6,8,12,13

30 _____.
    [1970?]   do.   21   *Books on Musicology*
                                (1000)   *1,6,8,13

31 _____.
    [1971]   do.   26   *Musicology*
                                (317)   *1,12

32 _____.
    [1978]   do.   31   *Books on Musicology and Ethnomusicology*
                                (799)   *8,12

---

1 Compiler/State University of New York (Buffalo) **2** The British Library (London) **3** Gemeentemuseum (Den Haag) **4** The Grolier Club (N.Y.C.) **5** Hirsch Collection, British Library (London) **6** D.W. Krummel (Urbana) **7** Library of Congress (Washington, D.C.) **8** Library and Museum of the Performing Arts (N.Y.C.) **9** William Reeves (London) **10** Sibley Library, Eastman School of Music (Rochester) **11** Nigel Simeone (Tunbridge Wells, Kent) **12** Vereeniging ter Bervordering van de Belangen des Boekhandels (Amsterdam) **13** University of Virginia (Charlottesville) **14** University of California at Los Angeles **15** Generally available

33 **ANTIQUA (Amsterdam) (continued)**
    [1962-   Nwslt   1-   *[Newsletters]*
                                                                        *1,6,10,12

34 _____ .
    [1971]   Bklst   10   *Musicology*
                                (227)   *1,12,13

35 _____ .
    [1972]   Bklst   14   *Musicology. Theater*
                                (249)   *1,6,12,13

36 **ANTIQUARIAT AM LÜTZOWPLATZ (Berlin)**
    1924   14   *Theater. Geschichte. Tanz. Musik*
                                                                  *5

37 **ANTIQUARIAT D'EENDT**
    1954   101   *50 numeros sur la musique*
                                  (50)   *8

38 **ANTIQUARIATO [LIBRARIE ITALIANE RIUNITE] (Bologna)**
    1931   21   *Teatro e musica*
                                                             *1,12

39 **ANTIQUARIUM (Bethany, Connecticut)**
    1983   —   *Music. Musicology. History. Composers*
                                  (132)   *13

40 **ARGUS (Baarn)**
    [1968]   6   *Dutch and Flemish Songbooks*
                                  (265)   *1,6,12

41 **ARIOSO (Paris)**
    1979   —   *40 Rare Full Scores of Operas*
                                  (40)   *1,8

42 _____ .
    1980   —   *Full Scores*
                                  (691)   *1,8

43 _____ .
    1982   —   *Full Scores*
                                  (407)   *1

44 **ARNOLD, F. W. (Elberfeld)**
    1860?   —   *Catalog d. Musikalien-Leih-Anstalt*
                                                              *8

45 **ARNOUL, GARNIER, LIBRAIRIE (Paris)**
    1969   21   *Les arts du spectacle*
                                                               *8

46 _____ .
    1971   22   *Les arts du spectacle*
                                                               *8

47 _____ .
    1973   23-24   *Molière ... Théâtre. Musique*
                                  (1510-1937)   *10

48 _____ .
    1976   25-26   *Spectacle, 16-18s. Théâtre. Danse. Musique*
                                  (1605-2221)   *1,10,13

---

49 **ARNOUL, GARNIER, LIBRAIRIE (Paris) (continued)**
    1978   27-28   *Spectacles ...*
                            (1058-1652)   *10,13

50 ____.
    1980   29-30   *Comédie française. Danse. Musique. Chansons*
                            (1643-2160)   *1,10

51 **ARS MUSICAE (Jean Leguy. Paris)**
    1979   —   *Principaux livres sur l'orgue*
                            (8p.)   *1

52 ____.
    1981   —   *Livres sur l'orgue*
                            (8p.)   *1

53 **L'ART ANCIEN (see also HAUS DER BÜCHER) (Basel)**
    [193_?] Bull.   17   *Incunabula. Music. Early Illustrated Books*
                            (244-312)   *4,10,13

54 ____.
    s.d.   List   179   *Frühdrucke. Musik*
                            (i.a.)   *10

55 ____.
    s.d.   do.   186   *Frühdrucke. Musik (III. Teil)*
                            (619-953)   *10

56 ____.
    s.d.   do.   187   *Illustrierte Bücher*
                            (9, i.a.)   *10

57 **ARTHUR DA SILVA, FRANCISCO (Lisbon)**
    1886   —   *Catalogo de livros... Musica. Teatro*
                            (81)   *P-Ln

58 **ASCHERSLEBENER BÜCHERSTUBE (Aschersleben)**
    1967   65   *Musik*
                            (320)   *12

59 ____.
    [1970]   91   *Musik. Theater*
                            (222)   *12

60 **ASHBROOK, H. F. (London)**
    7/1949   2   *Music Literature (and a few Scores)*
                            (237)   *2,8

61 ____.
    11/1949   3   *Music Literature*
                            (234)   *2

62 ____.
    8/1950   4   *Music Literature*
                            (309)   *2,8

63 ____.
    12/1950   5   *Music Literature*
                            (313)   *2,8

64 ____.
    7/1951   6   *Music Literature*
                            (367)   *2,8

---

1 Compiler/State University of New York (Buffalo)   **2** The British Library (London)   **3** Gemeentemuseum (Den Haag)   **4** The Grolier Club (N.Y.C.)   **5** Hirsch Collection, British Library (London)   **6** D.W. Krummel (Urbana)   **7** Library of Congress (Washington, D.C.)   **8** Library and Museum of the Performing Arts (N.Y.C.)   **9** William Reeves (London)   **10** Sibley Library, Eastman School of Music (Rochester)   **11** Nigel Simeone (Tunbridge Wells, Kent)   **12** Vereeniging ter Bervordering van de Belangen des Boekhandels (Amsterdam)   **13** University of Virginia (Charlottesville)   **14** University of California at Los Angeles   **15** Generally available

65 **ASHBROOK, H. F. (London) (continued)**
      |1953| 7   *Collected Eds. Musicology and some Scores*
                               (910)   *2,9,11

66 **ASHER, A., & CO. (Berlin)**
      186_   68   *"Extrait"*
                               (1720-2022)   *5

67 _____.
      1863   74   *Coll: Anon. Musique ancienne*
                               (267)   *8

68 _____.
      1873   103   *Livres à figure. Beaux-arts. Musique*
                               (453)   *8

69 **ATLANTIS LIVROS LTDA (Sao Paulo)**
      1975   —   *Musicos e gravacoes*
                               (pp.1-4)   *1

70 **BAER, E. (London)**
      1946   NS.11   *Books. Prints. Drawings [and Music]*
                               (4454-5215)   *10

71 **BAER, JOSEPH (Frankfurt a.M.)**
      1884   140   *Musik. Theater. Tanz*
                                                                            *3

72 _____.
      1884   148   *Musik. Theater. Tanz*
                               (490)   *3,7

73 _____.
      1887   208   *Musik und Theater*
                               (903)   *3

74 _____.
      1889   248   *Musik. Theater. Volkslieder*
                               (1273)   *3

75 _____.
      1892   295   *Coll: Hauff, J. C. Theater und Musik*
                               (1399)   *3,12

76 _____.
      1900   433   *Autographen [including musicians']*
                                                                            *US-Bp

77 _____.
      1901   446   *Musik. Musiker-autographen*
                               (687)   *5,12

78 _____.
      190-   449   *Musikwissenschaft*
                               (8078-8452)   *3

79 _____.
      [1908]   555   *Musikgeschichte*
                               (2425)   *12

80 _____.
      [1909]   566   *Musik und Theater. Autographen*
                                                                            *12

1 Compiler/State University of New York (Buffalo) 2 The British Library (London) 3 Gemeentemuseum
(Den Haag) 4 The Grolier Club (N.Y.C.) 5 Hirsch Collection, British Library (London) 6 D.W.
Krummel (Urbana) 7 Library of Congress (Washington, D.C.) 8 Library and Museum of the Performing
Arts (N.Y.C.) 9 William Reeves (London) 10 Sibley Library, Eastman School of Music (Rochester)
11 Nigel Simeone (Tunbridge Wells, Kent) 12 Vereeniging ter Bervordering van de Belangen des
Boekhandels (Amsterdam) 13 University of Virginia (Charlottesville) 14 University of California at Los
Angeles 15 Generally available

81 **BAER, JOSEPH (Frankfurt a.M.) (continued)**
    [19__]   573   *Musik. Theater und Oper*
                                     (1431)   *5,7,12
82 _____.
    [19_]   691   *Musik. Lied. Tanz. Autographen*
                                     (2422)   *3,8,12,13
83 _____.
    [19__]   750   *(Pt. 3) One thousand Books*
                                     (651-1000)   *5,7,8,10
84 _____.
    1930   769   *Musik. Oper. Lied. Liturgik. Tanz*
                                     (1431)   *1,5,8,12,13
85 _____.
    [19__]   774   *Firsts in Literature, Science, Fine Arts*
                                     (407-15)   *13
86 _____.
    [19__]   792   *Theologie und Musica Sacra*
                                     (1760)   *7
87 **BAER, LEO (Paris)**
    193_   9   *Fine Arts. Music. History. Sports. Pastimes*
                                     (4298-4319)   *13
88 **BÄRENREITER-ANTIQUARIAT (Kassel)**
    [1940]   34   *Musikwissenschaft*
                                     (256)   *6
89 _____.
    [1950]   46   *Musikliteratur*
                                     (1344)   *1
90 _____.
    1952   50   *Musikliteratur*
                                     (2736)   *1
91 _____.
    1953   51   *Gesamtausg. Denkmäler. Faks. Volkslied*
                                     (506)   *1
92 _____.
    1954   52   *Musikbücher. Theorie. Geschichte*
                                     (3485)   *1,6,13
93 _____.
    1955   53   *Musik und Theater*
                                     (1529)   *1,6,11
94 _____.
    1958   54   *Musikliteratur*
                                     (1168)   *1,6
95 _____.
    1961   [55?]   *Musik und Musik Bücher*
                                     (112p.)   *6
96 _____.
    1963   56   *Musica antiqua*
                                     (186)   *1,6,12,13

1 Compiler/State University of New York (Buffalo)   **2** The British Library (London)   **3** Gemeentemuseum (Den Haag)   **4** The Grolier Club (N.Y.C.)   **5** Hirsch Collection, British Library (London)   **6** D.W. Krummel (Urbana)   **7** Library of Congress (Washington, D.C.)   **8** Library and Museum of the Performing Arts (N.Y.C.)   **9** William Reeves (London)   **10** Sibley Library, Eastman School of Music (Rochester) **11** Nigel Simeone (Tunbridge Wells, Kent)   **12** Vereeniging ter Bevordering van de Belangen des Boekhandels (Amsterdam)   **13** University of Virginia (Charlottesville)   **14** University of California at Los Angeles   **15** Generally available

97   **BÄRENREITER-ANTIQUARIAT (Kassel) (continued)**

97	1963		—	*Musik und Musik Bücher* (115p.)	*6
98	_____. 1966		57	*Miscellanea Musicologica* (650)	*1,6,12
99	_____. 1969		58	*Musica una scripta mille* (1000)	*1,6,12,13
100	_____. 1975		59	*Varia musica et musicologica* (1000)	*1,6,13
101	_____. 1980		60	*Miscellanea musica et musicologica* (1135)	*1,6,13
102	_____. 1982		61	*Pratum musica* (1345)	*14
103	_____. 1984		62	*Musica Jubilans* (465)	*14
104	_____ 1957	Liste	A1	*Orgel- und Klaviermusik. Schulen* (280)	*1
105	_____ 1957	do.	A2	*Klavierauszüge* (328)	*1
106	_____. 1957	do.	A3	*Instrumental Kammermusik* (271)	*1

107   **BARNETT, WILLIAM**

107	1951	M-4	*Musicology* (356)	*8
108	_____. 1951	M-5	*Music* (272)	*8
109	_____. 1951?	M-5	*Idem.* (89)	*8
110	_____. 1952	M-9	*Music Books* (?)	*8
111	_____. 1952	M-10	*idem.* (?)	*8
112	_____. 195_	M-11	*1000 Books about Music* (1000)	*8

113 **BARNETT, WILLIAM (continued)**
    195_   M-12   *Musicology*
                              (218)   *8

114 _____.
    195_   M-13   *Books about Music*
                              (450)   *8

115 _____.
    195_?   M-58   *Musicology*
                              (597)   *8

116 _____.
    195_?   M-64   *[Music books]*
                              (64)   *8

117 **BARON, H. (London)**
    1950   1   *Scores and Instrumental Music*
                              (238)   *1

118 _____.
    1951   2   *Full, Vocal Scores. Chmbr.music. Music Lit.*
                              (526)   *1

119 _____.
    1951   3   *Music of 6 Centuries*
                              (343)   *1

120 _____.
    1951   4   *Orchestral Materials*
                              (var.)   *1

121 _____.
    1951   5a   *Full Scores*
                              (205)   *1

122 _____.
    1951   5b   *Orchestral Materials. Pianoforte Music*
                              (114)   *1

123 _____.
    1951   5c   *Vocal Music*
                              (233)   *1

124 _____.
    1951   5d   *Musical Literature*
                              (87)   *1,8

125 _____.
    1951   6   *Orchestral Material*
                              (171)   *1

126 _____.
    1952   7   *Music*
                              (382)   *1,8

127 _____.
    1052   8   *Orchestral Material*
                              (167)   *1

128 _____.
    1952   9a   *Musical Literature*
                              (247)   *1,8

1 Compiler/State University of New York (Buffalo)   **2** The British Library (London)   **3** Gemeentemuseum (Den Haag)   **4** The Grolier Club (N.Y.C.)   **5** Hirsch Collection, British Library (London)   **6** D.W. Krummel (Urbana)   **7** Library of Congress (Washington, D.C.)   **8** Library and Museum of the Performing Arts (N.Y.C.)   **9** William Reeves (London)   **10** Sibley Library, Eastman School of Music (Rochester)   **11** Nigel Simeone (Tunbridge Wells, Kent)   **12** Vereeniging ter Bervordering van de Belangen des Boekhandels (Amsterdam)   **13** University of Virginia (Charlottesville)   **14** University of California at Los Angeles   **15** Generally available

129 **BARON, H. (London) (continued)**

	1952		9b	*Music* (599)	*1
130	_____.				
	1952-53	Lists	1-10	*[Music and Musical Literature]*	*1
131	_____.				
	1953?	do.	10A	*Scores, Engr., Lithographed and Manuscript* (200)	[Baron]
132	_____.				
	1954	Cat.	10B	*Instrumental Music, pre-1850* (297)	*1
133	_____.				
	1954		10C	*Musical Literature, 1700-1850. Libretti* (82)	*1,8
134	_____.				
	1954		11	*Rare Books, Mainly O.-P. Facsimiles* (342)	[Baron]
135	_____.				
	1954		12	*Music (Modern Editions)* (492)	*1
136	_____.				
	1954		13	*Musical Literature* (213)	[Baron]
137	_____.				
	1954		14	*[Not found]*	*?
138	_____.				
	1954		15	*Music Published before 1850* (519)	[Baron]
139	_____.				
	1954		16	*Music Lit. History. Biography. Bibliography* (189)	[Baron]
140	_____.				
	1954		17	*Vocal and Instrumental Music* (514)	*1
141	_____.				
	1955?		18	*Musical Literature. Scholarly Editions* (387)	*1,6
142	_____.				
	1955		19	*Music, Old and New* (260)	*1,6,9
143	_____.				
	1955		20	*Musical Literature* (233)	*1,6,9
144	_____.				
	1955		21	*Music of 5 Centuries* (275)	*1,6

1 Compiler/State University of New York (Buffalo)   **2** The British Library (London)   **3** Gemeentemuseum (Den Haag)   **4** The Grolier Club (N.Y.C.)   **5** Hirsch Collection, British Library (London)   **6** D.W. Krummel (Urbana)   **7** Library of Congress (Washington, D.C.)   **8** Library and Museum of the Performing Arts (N.Y.C.)   **9** William Reeves (London)   **10** Sibley Library, Eastman School of Music (Rochester)   **11** Nigel Simeone (Tunbridge Wells, Kent)   **12** Vereeniging ter Bervordering van de Belangen des Boekhandels (Amsterdam)   **13** University of Virginia (Charlottesville)   **14** University of California at Los Angeles   **15** Generally available

145	**BARON, H. (London) (continued)**				
	1955	22	*Musical Literature*		
			(173)		*1,6
146	_____.				
	1955	23	*Choral Music*		
			(303)		*6
147	_____.				
	1955?	24	*Vocal and Instrumental Music*		
			(535)		*1
148	_____.				
	1955?	25	*Musicology*		
			(444)		*1,6,9
149	_____.				
	1956?	26	*Music and Musical Literature*		
			(308)		*6
150	_____.				
	1956	27	*Vocal and Instrumental Music, 1652-1860*		
			(221)		*6,9
151	_____.				
	1956	28	*Musical Literatur, 19th and 20th Century*		
			(317)		*6
152	_____.				
	1956	29	*Music, New and Out of Print*		
			(398)		*6
153	_____.				
	1956	30	*Spanish Music and Music Lit. Modern Eds.*		
			(188)		[Baron]
154	_____.				
	1956	31	*Music Literature, 19th and 20th Centuries*		
			(264)		[Baron]
155	_____.				
	1956	32	*Music in 19th and 20th Century Editions*		
			(383)		[Baron]
156	_____.				
	1957	33	*Music Literature published since 1850*		
			(244)		[Baron]
157	_____.				
	1957	35	*Music Literature of the 17th-19th Centuries*		
			(140)		[Baron]
158	_____.				
	1957	36	*Musical Literature*		
			(354)		*8,9
159	_____.				
	1957	37	*Operas and Operetta*		
			(308)		*9
160	_____.				
	1957	38	*Music Literature, 1588-1957*		
			(315)		*8,9

1 Compiler/State University of New York (Buffalo)   **2** The British Library (London)   **3** Gemeentemuseum (Den Haag)   **4** The Grolier Club (N.Y.C.)   **5** Hirsch Collection, British Library (London)   **6** D.W. Krummel (Urbana)   **7** Library of Congress (Washington, D.C.)   **8** Library and Museum of the Performing Arts (N.Y.C.)   **9** William Reeves (London)   **10** Sibley Library, Eastman School of Music (Rochester)   **11** Nigel Simeone (Tunbridge Wells, Kent)   **12** Vereeniging ter Bevordering van de Belangen des Boekhandels (Amsterdam)   **13** University of Virginia (Charlottesville)   **14** University of California at Los Angeles   **15** Generally available

161   **BARON, H. (London) (continued)**

	1957	39	*Orchestra Materials. Vocal and Instr. Music* (159)	[Baron]
162	____. 1958	40	*Coll: Dent, E. J. Books. Music Lit.* (430)	*9
163	____. 1958	41	*Coll: Dent, E. J. Scores, Vocal & Instr.* (400)	*8
164	____. 1958	42	*Chamber Music, Parts and a few Scores* (256)	*9
165	____. 1958	43	*Music Literature. Part I. Part II* (735)	*9
166	____. 1958	44	*Rare Music, 1583-1799* (68)	*9
167	____. 1958	45	*Secular Vocal Music, 18th-19th Centuries* (229)	*9
168	____. 1958	46	*Musical Literature* (305)	*9
169	____. 1959	47	*Vocal & Orchestral Music - Modern Editions* (675)	*9
170	____. 1959	48&49	*Musical Bibliogr., History, Biogr., Theory* (1343)	*6,8,9
171	____. 1960	50	*Religious Music, Lit. Notation. Hymnology* (367)	*8,14
172	____. 1961	51	*Musical Literature, 1525-1960* (800)	*8,14
173	____. 1961	52	*Vocal & Orchestral Music, 19-20th Centuries* (500)	*14
174	____. 1961	53	*Coll: Oldman. Musical Lit. Mozartiana* (332)	*1,6,10
175	____. 1962	54	*ALS. Manuscripts* (200)	*1,6,10,13,14
176	____. 1962	55a	*Keyboard Music. Chamber Music. A-L* (330)	*1,6,10,13,14

177 **BARON, H. (London) (continued)**

	1962	55b	*Keyboard Music. Chamber Music, M-Z* (331-631)	*1,6,10,13,14
178	_____.			
	1962	56	*Musical Literature* (351)	*1,6,10,13,14
179	_____.			
	1962	57	*Folk Song. Books on Instruments* (336)	*1,6,10,13,14
180	_____.			
	1962	58	*Musical Literature, 1630-* (337)	*1,6,10,13
181	_____.			
	1962	59	*Chamber Music* (229)	*1,6,10,13
182	_____.			
	1962	60a	*Musical Biography* (480)	*1,6,10,13
183	_____.			
	1962	60b	*Musical Biography* (481-1106)	*1,6,10,13
184	_____.			
	1962	61	*Musical Bibliography + Supplement* (223+315)	*1,6,10,13,14
185	_____.			
	1962	62	*Music of the British Isles before 1840* (116)	*1,6,10,13
186	_____.			
	1962	63	*Musical Literature* (380)	*1,6,10,13
187	_____.			
	1962	64	*Opera, 1582-, Part I* (336)	*1,6,10,13,14
188	_____.			
	1963	65	*Church Music. Musical Literature* (355)	*1,6,10,13,14
189	_____.			
	1963	66	*Organ Music. Musical Literature* (119)	*1,6,10,13,14
190	_____.			
	1964	67	*Methods and Treatises* (333)	*1,6,10,12,14
191	_____.			
	1964	68	*100 Musical Rarities* (100)	*1,6,10,13,14
192	_____.			
	1964	69	*75 Rare Books on Music* (139)	*1,6,10,13,14

193	**BARON, H. (London) (continued)**			
	1964	70	*Folksong and Popular Music*	
			(161)	*1,6,10,13,14
194	_____.			
	1965	71	*ALS. Holographs*	
			(220)	*1,6,10,13,14
195	_____.			
	1965	72	*Books on Music*	
			(750)	*1,6,13,14
196	_____.			
	1965	73	*Keyboard Music*	
			(479)	*1,6,10,13,14
197	_____.			
	1965	74	*Methods and Early Books on Music*	
			(121)	*1,10,13,14
198	_____.			
	1966	75	*Songs. Chansons. Cantatas*	
			(166)	*1,6,10,13,14
199	_____.			
	1966	76	*Autograph Letters of Musicians*	
			(125)	*6,10,13,14
200	_____.			
	1966	77	*Musical Literature*	
			(733)	*1,6,10,13
201	_____.			
	1967	78	*Church Music. Oratorio*	
			(378)	*1,6,10,13
202	_____.			
	1967	79	*Facs. Eds. Musical Iconography. Portraits*	
			(211)	*6,10,13,14
203	_____.			
	1967	80	*Methods and Treatises*	
			(165)	*1,6,10,13,14
204	_____.			
	1967	81	*Lieder. Arias. Cantatas. Choral Music*	
			(240)	*1,6,10,13,14
205	_____.			
	1967	82	*Musical Literature*	
			(748)	*1,6,10,13,14
206	_____.			
	1968	83	*Orchestral Scores*	
			(328)	*1,6,10,13,14
207	_____.			
	1968	84	*Vocal Scores*	
			(467)	*1,6,10,13,14
208	_____.			
	1968	85	*Full Scores*	
			(210)	*1,13,14

1 Compiler/State University of New York (Buffalo)   **2** The British Library (London)   **3** Gemeentemuseum (Den Haag)   **4** The Grolier Club (N.Y.C.)   **5** Hirsch Collection, British Library (London)   **6** D.W. Krummel (Urbana)   **7** Library of Congress (Washington, D.C.)   **8** Library and Museum of the Performing Arts (N.Y.C.)   **9** William Reeves (London)   **10** Sibley Library, Eastman School of Music (Rochester)   **11** Nigel Simeone (Tunbridge Wells, Kent)   **12** Vereeniging ter Bervordering van de Belangen des Boekhandels (Amsterdam)   **13** University of Virginia (Charlottesville)   **14** University of California at Los Angeles   **15** Generally available

209	**BARON, H. (London) (continued)**			
	1968	86	*Musical Literature* (648)	*1,6,10,13,14
210	_____.			
	1968	87	*ALS. Photos, etc.* (245)	*1,6,10,13,14
211	_____.			
	1968	unn.	*Summer List: Instrumental and Chamber Music* (321)	*1,6,10,13,14
212	_____.			
	1969	88	*Vocal Scores. Songs. Full Scores* (670)	*1,6,10,13,14
213	_____.			
	1969	89	*Musical Lit. Periodicals, 19th Century* (548)	*1,6,13,14
214	_____.			
	1969	90	*Musical Lit. Periodicals, 19th Century* (606)	*1,6,10,13,14
215	_____.			
	1970	91	*Music Publishing in France, 1700-1800* (292)	*1,6,10,13,14
216	_____.			
	1970	92	*Books on Music* (577)	*1,6,10,13,14
217	_____.			
	1970	93	*Full and Vocal Scores. Songs* (339)	*1,6,10,13,14
218	_____.			
	1971	94	*Keyboard Music* (1271)	*1,6,10,13,14
219	_____.			
	1971	95	*Musical Literature. Books on the Violin* (491)	*1,6,10,13,14
220	_____.			
	1971	96	*Methods and Treatises* (215)	*1,6,10,13,14
221	_____.			
	1971	97	*Opera Vocal Scores* (561)	*1,6,10,13,14
222	_____.			
	1972	98	*Musical Literature. Facsimile Editions* (683)	*1,6,10,13,14
223	_____.			
	1972	99	*Keyboard Music* (597)	*1,6,10,13,14
224	_____.			
	1972	100	*Music Written or Printed before 1600: I* (22)	*1,6,13,14

1 Compiler/State University of New York (Buffalo)   **2** The British Library (London)   **3** Gemeentemuseum (Den Haag)   **4** The Grolier Club (N.Y.C.)   **5** Hirsch Collection, British Library (London)   **6** D.W. Krummel (Urbana)   **7** Library of Congress (Washington, D.C.)   **8** Library and Museum of the Performing Arts (N.Y.C.)   **9** William Reeves (London)   **10** Sibley Library, Eastman School of Music (Rochester)   **11** Nigel Simeone (Tunbridge Wells, Kent)   **12** Vereeniging ter Bervordering van de Belangen des Boekhandels (Amsterdam)   **13** University of Virginia (Charlottesville)   **14** University of California at Los Angeles   **15** Generally available

225 **BARON, H. (London) (continued)**

	1972	101	*Secular Vocal Music* (450)	*1,6,13,14
226	_____.			
	1972	102	*Musical Literature* (429)	*1,6,13,14
227	_____.			
	1973	103	*Folk Songs* (243)	*1,6,13,14
228	_____.			
	1973	104	*Musical Literature* (338)	*1,6,13,14
229	_____.			
	1974	105	*Musical Literature* (1032)	*1,6,13,14
230	_____.			
	1975	106	*Religious Music. Oratorio. Addenda* (587)	*1,6,13,14
231	_____.			
	1975	107	*Opera* (632)	*1,6,13,14
232	_____.			
	1975	108	*Musical Literature* (861)	*1,6,13,14
233	_____.			
	1977	109	*Music for Pianoforte. Addenda* (1300)	*1,13,14
234	_____.			
	1977	110	*Around the Pianoforte* (335)	*1,13,14
235	_____.			
	1977	111	*Coll: Verchaly. Musical Literature* (989)	*1,13
236	_____.			
	1977	112	*Secular Vocal Music in Autograph and Mss.* (778)	*13,14
237	_____.			
	1978	113	*Opera. Printed and Manuscript Scores* (503)	*1,13
238	_____.			
	1978	114	*Coll: Linden, A. van der. Musical Lit.* (1076)	*1,13
239	_____.			
	1979	115	*Colls: Dannreuther and Berri. Music Lit.* (939)	*1,6,13
240	_____.			
	1980	116	*Full Scores. Addenda* (807,808-95)	*15

1 Compiler/State University of New York (Buffalo)   **2** The British Library (London)   **3** Gemeentemuseum (Den Haag)   **4** The Grolier Club (N.Y.C.)   **5** Hirsch Collection, British Library (London)   **6** D.W. Krummel (Urbana)   **7** Library of Congress (Washington, D.C.)   **8** Library and Museum of the Performing Arts (N.Y.C.)   **9** William Reeves (London)   **10** Sibley Library, Eastman School of Music (Rochester) **11** Nigel Simeone (Tunbridge Wells, Kent)   **12** Vereeniging ter Bervordering van de Belangen des Boekhandels (Amsterdam)   **13** University of Virginia (Charlottesville)   **14** University of California at Los Angeles   **15** Generally available

241   **BARON, H. (London) (continued)**
      1981   117   *Musical Literature*
                                  (727)   *15
242   _____.
      1981   unn. *A Collection of Vocal Scores*
                                  (165)   *15
243   _____.
      1981   118   *A German Miscellany*
                                  (217)   *15
244   _____.
      1982   119   *Keyboard Music, A-L*
                                  (795)   *15
245   _____.
      1982   120   *Musical Lit. since 1800. Methods. Treatises*
                                  (1050)   *15
246   _____.
      1982   121   *Vocal Scores - Operas, Operettas. Portraits*
                                  (872)   *15
247   _____.
      1982   122   *Music Published since 1896*
                                  (813)   *15
248   _____
      1983   123   *Musical Rarities. Programmes and Handbills*
                                  (114)   *15
249   _____.
      1983   124   *French Opera Prior to 1760*
                                  (107)   *15
250   _____.
      1983   125   *Keyboard Music*
                                  (680,381)   *15
251   _____.
      1983   126   *Engl. & Amer. Bks. on Music. Jls. Programs*
                                  (896)   *15
252   _____.
      1984   127   *Full Scores*
                                  (332)   *15
253   _____.
      1984   128   *Music on Military and Patriotic Themes*
                                  (343)   *15
254   _____
      [1952]   Misc.   unn. *Collected Editions*
                                  (8p.)   *6
255   _____.
      n.d.   Misc.   unn. *Collected Editions and Anthologies*
                                  (10p.)   *6
256   _____.
      n.d.   Misc.   unn. *Musical Periodicals*
                                  (8p.)   *6

1 Compiler/State University of New York (Buffalo)   2 The British Library (London)   3 Gemeentemuseum (Den Haag)   4 The Grolier Club (N.Y.C.)   5 Hirsch Collection, British Library (London)   6 D.W. Krummel (Urbana)   7 Library of Congress (Washington, D.C.)   8 Library and Museum of the Performing Arts (N.Y.C.)   9 William Reeves (London)   10 Sibley Library, Eastman School of Music (Rochester)   11 Nigel Simeone (Tunbridge Wells, Kent)   12 Vereeniging ter Bervordering van de Belangen des Boekhandels (Amsterdam)   13 University of Virginia (Charlottesville)   14 University of California at Los Angeles   15 Generally available

257 **BARON, H. (London) (continued)**
    n.d.   Misc.   unn.   *Musical Periodicals*
                          (8p.)   *6

258 -----
    6/1955   Misc.   unn.   *Musical Periodicals*
                          (152)   *6

259 -----
    6/1959   Misc.   unn.   *Collected Editions*
                          (125)   *6

260 _____.
    1/1972   Misc.   unn.   *Collections of Music. Collected Editions*
                          (161)   *1,6

261 _____.
    1/1972   Misc.   unn.   *Musical Periodicals and Yearbooks*
                          unn.   *1,6

262 _____.
    4/1972   Misc.   unn.   *Full Scores*
                          (169)   *1,6

263 _____.
    4/1973   Misc.   unn.   *Full Scores. Chamber Music*
                          (387)   *1,6

264 _____.
    1974   Misc.   unn.   *Books on Music*
                          (549)   *1,6

265 _____.
    7/1980   Misc.   unn.   *Musical Literature*
                          (292)   *1,6

266 _____.
    198-?   Misc.   A   *Musical Biography*
                          (258)   *6

267 _____.
    198-?   Misc.   B   *Musical Reference Works*
                          (27)   *6

268 _____.
    198-?   Misc.   C   *Musical History*
                          (154)   *6

269 _____.
    198-?   Misc.   D   *Folk Song. Folk Dance. Literature and Music*
                          (77)   *6

270 **BARTOLOTTI, (Milan?)**
    1881   —   *Coll: Muoni, D. Libretti*
                          (53)   US-MdBJ

271 **BATTISTELLI, (Milan)**
    1907   —   *Coll: Muoni, D. Autographs. Manuscripts*
                                                      US-IaU

272 **BAUER, ARTHUR (Berlin)**
    1964   —   *Musik*
                          (127)   [IBAK]

---

1 Compiler/State University of New York (Buffalo)   **2** The British Library (London)   **3** Gemeentemuseum (Den Haag)   **4** The Grolier Club (N.Y.C.)   **5** Hirsch Collection, British Library (London)   **6** D.W. Krummel (Urbana)   **7** Library of Congress (Washington, D.C.)   **8** Library and Museum of the Performing Arts (N.Y.C.)   **9** William Reeves (London)   **10** Sibley Library, Eastman School of Music (Rochester)   **11** Nigel Simeone (Tunbridge Wells, Kent)   **12** Vereeniging ter Bervordering van de Belangen des Boekhandels (Amsterdam)   **13** University of Virginia (Charlottesville)   **14** University of California at Los Angeles   **15** Generally available

273 **BAUR, J. ("Successeur de L. Liepmannssohn," Paris)**
    1873   4   *Livres anciens et modernes*
                              (881)   *5
274 **BAYRHOFFER NACHFOLGER J. JAEGER (Düsseldorf)**
    1850-57   —   *Musikalien-Leihanstalt /Catalogs & suppls./*
                              (19252)   *8
275 **BAYREUTHER MUSIKANTIQUARIAT (Bayreuth)**
    1954   —   *Katalog 1954*
                              (2034)   *1,6
276 _____.
    1955   —   *Festspiel-Katalog*
                              (802+pls)   *1,9,11
277 _____.
    1956   —   *Musica theorica*
                              (1702)   *1,9,12
278 _____.
    1957   —   *Musikdrucke. Musikliteratur. Varia*
                              (1275)   *1,6,9
279 _____.
    1958   —   *Autographen. Musikdrucke. Musikliteratur*
                              (1170)   *1,6,9
280 **BEBB, RICHARD (London)**
    6/1980   —   *Books on Singers and Instrumentalists*
                              (8pp.)   *9
281 **BECK, C. H. (Nördlingen)**
    1892   208   *Musik. Liturgik. Hymnologie*
                              (1414)   *8,12
282 _____.
    1894   219   *Coll: Schletterer, H. M. /Musik. Teil/*
                              (169pp.)   [Bob]
283 **BEIJERS, J. L. (Utrecht)**
    1872   21   *Musique. Theatre. Danse*
                              (742)   *12
284 _____.
    1877   49   *Boeken over Muziekgeschiedenis*
                              (481)   *12
285 _____.
    1884   92   *Tooneel. Muziek. Liedboekjes*
                              (1600)   *12
286 _____.
    188_   92   *Musique. Theatre*
                              (1013)   *12
287 _____.
    188_   165   *Musique. Theatre*
                              (1259)   *8,12
288 _____.
    188_   173   *Musique. Theatre*
                              (1249)   *12

1 Compiler/State University of New York (Buffalo)   2 The British Library (London)   3 Gemeentemuseum (Den Haag)   4 The Grolier Club (N.Y.C.)   5 Hirsch Collection, British Library (London)   6 D.W. Krummel (Urbana)   7 Library of Congress (Washington, D.C.)   8 Library and Museum of the Performing Arts (N.Y.C.)   9 William Reeves (London)   10 Sibley Library, Eastman School of Music (Rochester)   11 Nigel Simeone (Tunbridge Wells, Kent)   12 Vereeniging ter Bervordering van de Belangen des Boekhandels (Amsterdam)   13 University of Virginia (Charlottesville)   14 University of California at Los Angeles   15 Generally available

289 **BEIJERS, J. L. (Utrecht) (continued)**
189_?   184   *Theoretisch und praktische Musik*
(857)   *8

290 _____.
1903?   209   *Musikliteratur. Partituren*
(902)   *12

291 **BEIMA, JAN (Arnhem)**
1960?   88   *Bladmuziek en enkele Boeken*
(494)   *12

292 **BEL CANTO BOOK SHOP [later BEL CANTO BOOKS] (Union, N.J.)**
1957   2   *Books on Music*
(206)   *8

293 _____.
195_   3   *Special List*
(692)   *8

294 _____.
1959   7   *Books on Music*
(399)   *6,8

295 _____.
1959   8   *Books on Music*
(813)   *6

296 _____.
1960   9   *Books on Music*
(1000)   *6,13

297 _____.
1962   11   *Books on Music*
(713)   *13

298 _____.
1962   12   *Books on Music*
(874)   *6

299 _____.
1964   13   *Books on Music*
(1086)   *1,6

300 _____.
1964   14   *Books on Music*
(1000)   *1,6,8

301 _____.
1966   15   *Books on Music*
(790)   *1,6,8

302 _____.
1979   16   *Books about Music and Musicians*
(1240)   *1,13

303 _____.
1980   17   *Books about Music and Musicians*
(791)   *1,13

304 _____.
1982   18   *Books about Music and Musicians*
(744)   *1,13

1 Compiler/State University of New York (Buffalo)   **2** The British Library (London)   **3** Gemeentemuseum (Den Haag)   **4** The Grolier Club (N.Y.C.)   **5** Hirsch Collection, British Library (London)   **6** D.W. Krummel (Urbana)   **7** Library of Congress (Washington, D.C.)   **8** Library and Museum of the Performing Arts (N.Y.C.)   **9** William Reeves (London)   **10** Sibley Library, Eastman School of Music (Rochester)   **11** Nigel Simeone (Tunbridge Wells, Kent)   **12** Vereeniging ter Bervordering van de Belangen des Boekhandels (Amsterdam)   **13** University of Virginia (Charlottesville)   **14** University of California at Los Angeles   **15** Generally available

305 **BEL CANTO BOOK SHOP** (Union, N.J.) (continued)
    1982   19   *Books about Music and Musicians*
                           (733)   *1,13
306 ____
    1983   20   *Books about Music and Musicians*
                           (560)   *1
307 ____.
    1984   21   *Books about Music and Musicians*
                           (561)   *1
308 ____.
    1985   22   *Books about Music and Musicians*
                           (608)   *1
309 ____.
    1963   Spec.   2   *[Books about Music]*
                           (349)   *6
310 **BELMORE, H. W.** (Rome)
    19_   15   *Old and Rare Books*
                           (336-56)   *13
311 **BERÈS, PIERRE** (N.Y.C.)
    1939   3   *Books. Autographs*
                           (83-93,i.a.)   *10
312 ____.
    1941   5   *ALS. Mss., including Composers, Singers*
                           (229-69)   *10
313 ____.
    1952   22   *Music*
                           (365)   *8
314 ____.
    1953   24   *Coll: Black, Frank. Music*
                           (168)   *8
315 ____.
    1947   List   37   *Music and Musical Literature*
                           (257)   *8,13
316 ____.
    1948?   do.   46   *Music and Musical Literature*
                           (258)   *1
317 ____.
    1949   do.   53   *Coll: Photiades. Music. Musical Literature*
                           (324)   *1
318 ____.
    195_   do.   59   *ALS. Mss. [including Music]*
                           (241)   *1
319 ____.
    195_   do.   62   *Coll: Vines, R. Music and Musical Lit.*
                           (516)   *1
320 **BERGMANS, W.** (Tilburg)
    1950   —   *Gids voor Kerkmuziek*
                           (144)   *12

321 **BERMANN & ALTMANN (Vienna)**
     18—   74   *Musik u. Dramaturgie. Aesthetik. Geschichte*
                         (pp.1-48)   *8
322 _____.
     1897   127   *Musik und Theater*
                         (?)   *8
323 **BERTLING, RICHARD (Dresden)**
     1887   —   *Theorie u. Geschichte. Praktische Musik*
                         (1376)   *5
324 _____.
     1888?   7   *Musikalische Literatur. Musikalien*
                         (?)   *3
325 _____.
     1889   9   *Musikalische Literatur. Musikalien*
                         (235)   *3
326 _____.
     1889   11   *Autographen von Musikern*
                         (109)   *3
327 _____.
     1889   12   *Musikalische Literatur und Musikalien*
                         (345)   *3
328 _____.
     1889   15   *Musikalische Literatur und Musikalien*
                         (?)   *4
329 _____.
     1891   16   *Musikalische Literatur und Musikalien*
                         (326)   *3
330 _____.
     1891   17   *Autographen [including musicians]*
                         (684)   *3
331 _____.
     1892   20   *Hymnologie und Kirchenmusik*
                         (676)   *3,8
332 _____.
     1892   21   *Musikalische Literatur*
                         (1146)   *3,8
333 _____.
     1894   25   *Autographen [including musicians]*
                         (1146)   *3
334 _____.
     1894   27   *Musikwissenschaft und Musikalien*
                         (1326)   *3
335 _____.
     1894   28   *Musikwissenschaft und Musikalien*
                         (1138)   *3,8
336 _____.
     1895   29   *Autographen [including musicians]*
                         (541)   *3

1 Compiler/State University of New York (Buffalo)   2 The British Library (London)   3 Gemeentemuseum (Den Haag)   4 The Grolier Club (N.Y.C.)   5 Hirsch Collection, British Library (London)   6 D.W. Krummel (Urbana)   7 Library of Congress (Washington, D.C.)   8 Library and Museum of the Performing Arts (N.Y.C.)   9 William Reeves (London)   10 Sibley Library, Eastman School of Music (Rochester)   11 Nigel Simeone (Tunbridge Wells, Kent)   12 Vereeniging ter Bervordering van de Belangen des Boekhandels (Amsterdam)   13 University of Virginia (Charlottesville)   14 University of California at Los Angeles   15 Generally available

337 **BERTLING, RICHARD (Dresden) (continued)**
    1899   32   *Musikwissenschaft und Musikalien*
                           (2456)   *5

338 _____.
    1900   36   *Autographen /including musicians/*
                           (4820)   [MFM]

339 _____.
    1903   48   *Hymnologie. Liturgik*
                           (600)   *5

340 _____.
    1905   52   *Musikwissenschaft und Musikalien*
                                                                         *4,5

341 _____.
    1905   53   *Porträts von Musikern*
                           (1014)   *5

342 _____
    1905   54   *Musikliteratur des Alterthums*
                           (780)   *3,5

343 _____.
    1905   55   *Musikliteratur. Wagner-Sammlung*
                           (1191)   *3,5

344 _____.
    1909   67   *Musiker-Autographen*
                           (539)   *12

345 _____.
    1910   68   *Musikgeschichte*
                           (1176)   *5,12

346 _____.
    1910   69   *Musiklehre und Instrumentenkunde*
                           (1230)   *7,12

347 _____.
    s.d.   70   *Porträts. Theater. Musik*
                           (2415)   *4,5,7,12

348 _____.
    1911   72   *Autographen /including musicians/*
                           (?)   *4,7

349 **BERTOLA, Dr. CELSO (Torino)**
    1969   —   *Musica, Libri e Documenti*
                           (183)   *8

350 _____.
    9/1976   —   *Letteratura musicale. Canto e piano. Varia*
                           (206)   *1

351 _____.
    11/1976   —   *Letteratura musicale. Canto e piano. Varia*
                           (610)   *1

352 _____.
    1977   —   *Spartiti manoscritti*
                           (68)   *1

---

1 Compiler/State University of New York (Buffalo)   **2** The British Library (London)   **3** Gemeentemuseum (Den Haag)   **4** The Grolier Club (N.Y.C.)   **5** Hirsch Collection, British Library (London)   **6** D.W. Krummel (Urbana)   **7** Library of Congress (Washington, D.C.)   **8** Library and Museum of the Performing Arts (N.Y.C.)   **9** William Reeves (London)   **10** Sibley Library, Eastman School of Music (Rochester)   **11** Nigel Simeone (Tunbridge Wells, Kent)   **12** Vereeniging ter Bervordering van de Belangen des Boekhandels (Amsterdam)   **13** University of Virginia (Charlottesville)   **14** University of California at Los Angeles   **15** Generally available

353 **BERTOLA, Dr. CELSO (Torino) (continued)**
    2/1977   —   *Musica strumentale. Partiture*
                               (649)   *1,8

354   ——.
    4/1977   4   *Letteratura musicale. Canto e piano. Varia*
                               (541)   *1,8

355   ——.
    11/l977   —   *Letteratura musicale. Canto e piano. Varia*
                               (658)   *1,8

356   ——.
    [1978]   —   *La Canzonette in Italia*
                               (229)   *8

357   ——.
    3/1978   —   *Musica*
                               (413)   *8

358   ——.
    11/1978   —   *Musica*
                               (300)   *8

359 **BERTRAM, GUSTAV (Sondershausen)**
    1861   45-47   *Verzeichnis... I.-III.Abth.*
                               (?)   [Petzholdt]

360 **BEYER. P. H. & SOHN (Leipzig)**
    1937   87   *Musik. Theater. Tanz*
                               (300)   [BibDMS'37]

361 **BIBLO & TANNEN (N.Y.C.)**
    1952   71   *World of Entertainment*
                               (?)   *8

362 **BIELEFELD, A. (Karlsruhe and Offenburg)**
    1869   6   *Architecture. Musikwissenschaft. Theorie*
                               (630-732)   *8

363   ——.
    1873   24   *Theater*
                               (?)   *12

364   ——.
    1880?   53   *Musikliteratur und Hymnologie*
                               (626)   *5,8

365   ——.
    1885   112   *Bibliotheca musica I*
                               (1159)   *5,8

366   ——.
    1885   118   *Bibliotheca musica II*
                               (1531)   *5,8

367   ——.
    s.d.   158   *Literatur. Curiosa. Musik*
                               (?)   *12

368   ——.
    1900   —   *Geschichte der Musik*
                               (1151)   *5

---

1 Compiler/State University of New York (Buffalo)   **2** The British Library (London)   **3** Gemeentemuseum (Den Haag)   **4** The Grolier Club (N.Y.C.)   **5** Hirsch Collection, British Library (London)   **6** D.W. Krummel (Urbana)   **7** Library of Congress (Washington, D.C.)   **8** Library and Museum of the Performing Arts (N.Y.C.)   **9** William Reeves (London)   **10** Sibley Library, Eastman School of Music (Rochester)   **11** Nigel Simeone (Tunbridge Wells, Kent)   **12** Vereeniging ter Bervordering van de Belangen des Boekhandels (Amsterdam)   **13** University of Virginia (Charlottesville)   **14** University of California at Los Angeles   **15** Generally available

369 **BINGHAM, TONY (London)**
    1972   5   *A Selection of Books, Tutors and Prints*
                       (48)   *8

370 **BIRETT'SCHE ANTIQUARIATS-BUCHHANDLUNG F. BUTSCH see BUTSCH, F.**

371 **BITTNER, HERBERT (N.Y. and Rome)**
    [1939]   [1]   *Music. Autographs. 1st Editions. Portraits*
                   (108)   *5,10

372 _____.
    1940   4   *Music. Autographs. Orch. & Vocal Scores*
                   (149)   *5

373 _____.
    s.d.   8   *Music. 1st & Early Eds. Autographs. Books*
                   (149)   *5

374 _____.
    s.d.   12   *Musique et théâtre*
                   (301)   *1,5

375 -----
    1931?   17   *Arts and Sciences*
                   (596-700)   *13

376 _____.
    1931   18   *Beaux arts. Musique. Théâtre*
                   (153)   *1,3,7,13

377 **BJÖRCK & BÖRJESSEN (Stockholm)**
    1934   289   *Musik. Theater*
                   (1725)   *7,12

378 **BLACKWELL'S MUSIC SHOP (Oxford)**
    1926   206   *Liturgical Books. Hymnology*
                   (654)   *12

379 _____.
    [1958]   642   *Instrumental Music*
                   (40pp.)   *6,8

380 _____.
    1958?   656   *Vocal Music*
                   (1532)   *6,8

381 _____.
    1958   673   *Books on Music*
                   (1041)   *8

382 _____.
    1958   693   *Antiquarian Music and Books on Music*
                   (1477)   *1,8,11,12

383 _____.
    1961   714   *Instrumental Music*
                   (1860)   *8

384 _____.
    1961   737   *Books on Music*
                   (1684)   *8,13

1 Compiler/State University of New York (Buffalo)   **2** The British Library (London)   **3** Gemeentemuseum (Den Haag)   **4** The Grolier Club (N.Y.C.)   **5** Hirsch Collection, British Library (London)   **6** D.W. Krummel (Urbana)   **7** Library of Congress (Washington, D.C.)   **8** Library and Museum of the Performing Arts (N.Y.C.)   **9** William Reeves (London)   **10** Sibley Library, Eastman School of Music (Rochester)   **11** Nigel Simeone (Tunbridge Wells, Kent)   **12** Vereeniging ter Bervordering van de Belangen des Boekhandels (Amsterdam)   **13** University of Virginia (Charlottesville)   **14** University of California at Los Angeles   **15** Generally available

385   **BLACKWELL'S MUSIC SHOP (Oxford) (continued)**

	1962	756	*Instrumental Music*	
			(4095)	*6,13
386	____.			
	1963	762	*Books on Music*	
			(1670)	*12
387	____.			
	1963	763	*Books on Music*	
			(2486)	*6,13
388	____.			
	1964	782	*Vocal Music*	
			(2135)	*6,12
389	____.			
	1964	788	*Secondhand Books on Music*	
			(1588)	*6,8,13
390	____.			
	1965	794	*Secondhand Books on Music*	
			(1444)	*12,13
391	____.			
	1966	796	*Instrumental Music*	
			(2700)	*13
392	____.			
	1967	808	*Instrumental and Chamber Music*	
			(3858)	*6
393	____.			
	1966	809	*Books on Music*	
			(1933)	*6,12,13
394	____.			
	1966	822	*Music*	
			(1451)	*6,8,12,13
395	____.			
	1967	833	*Vocal Music*	
			(2471)	*6,12
396	____.			
	1969	872	*Music for Pianoforte*	
			(1910)	*12
397	____.			
	1970	913	*Music*	
			(2988)	*6,8,12
398	____.			
	1971	943	*Instrumental Music: Woodwind and Brass*	
			(3259)	*12
399	____.			
	1972	945	*Music and Books*	
			(1258)	*6,8,12,13
400	____.			
	1974	994	*Books on Music*	
			(3572)	*6,11

1 Compiler/State University of New York (Buffalo)   2 The British Library (London)   3 Gemeentemuseum (Den Haag)   4 The Grolier Club (N.Y.C.)   5 Hirsch Collection, British Library (London)   6 D.W. Krummel (Urbana)   7 Library of Congress (Washington, D.C.)   8 Library and Museum of the Performing Arts (N.Y.C.)   9 William Reeves (London)   10 Sibley Library, Eastman School of Music (Rochester) 11 Nigel Simeone (Tunbridge Wells, Kent)   12 Vereeniging ter Bervordering van de Belangen des Boekhandels (Amsterdam)   13 University of Virginia (Charlottesville)   14 University of California at Los Angeles   15 Generally available

401 **BLACKWELL'S MUSIC SHOP (Oxford) (continued)**

	1974	1002	*Antiquarian Music and Books* (1027)	*6,8,13
402	____. 1975	1025	*Antiquarian Music and Books* (967)	*6,8,13
403	____. 1976	A1063	*Antiquarian Music and Books* (1122)	*6,11,13
404	____. 1977	M1091	*Antiquarian Music and Books* (830)	*13
405	____. 1978	M1107	*Antiquarian Music and Books* (940)	*13
406	____. 1979	M1132	*Antiquarian Music and Books* (810)	*6,13
407	____. 1980	M1150	*Antiq. Music and Secondhand Books on Music* (879)	*1
408	____. 1982	M1161	*Second-hand Books on Music. Periodicals* (1042)	*1
409	____. 1983	M1167	*Music. Books. Periodicals* (866)	*1
410	____. 1984	M1180	*Music. Books. Periodicals* (866)	*1

411	____. 1955	List	112	*Music* (1322)	*6,8
412	____. 1959	do.	150	*Books on Music* (8pp.)	*12
413	____. 1962	do.	170	*Secondhand Music* (1364)	*6,12
414	____. 1959-	Bull.	1-	*Bulletins, no. 1-*	*15

415 **BLOCH, EDUARD (Berlin)**

	[189_?]	*Theater Musik* (40pp.)	*8

416 **BOEHLAU ANTIQUARIAT (Vienna)**

	1978	155	*Katalog* (1838-1951)	*13

---

1 Compiler/State University of New York (Buffalo)   **2** The British Library (London)   **3** Gemeentemuseum (Den Haag)   **4** The Grolier Club (N.Y.C.)   **5** Hirsch Collection, British Library (London)   **6** D.W. Krummel (Urbana)   **7** Library of Congress (Washington, D.C.)   **8** Library and Museum of the Performing Arts (N.Y.C.)   **9** William Reeves (London)   **10** Sibley Library, Eastman School of Music (Rochester)   **11** Nigel Simeone (Tunbridge Wells, Kent)   **12** Vereeniging ter Bervordering van de Belangen des Boekhandels (Amsterdam)   **13** University of Virginia (Charlottesville)   **14** University of California at Los Angeles   **15** Generally available

417 **BOERNER, C. G. (Leipzig)**

	1906	4	*Theater und Musik. Dramen*	
			(?)	*1,4,5,12

418 _____.

	1910	16	*Musik. Autographen. Mss. Bücher*	
			(456)	*4,7,8

419 _____.

	191_	22	*Autographen*	
			(1073-1311)	*4

420 _____.

	1910	27	*Coll: Wagener. Aus der Sammlung ...*	
			(269)	*1,8,12

421 **BOLLETINO BIBLIOGRAFICO MUSICALE (Milan)**

	5/1929	2	*Letteratura musicale*	
			(1194)	*1

422 _____.

	11/1929	3	*Letteratura musicale*	
			(3361)	*8,10

423 _____.

	1930	4	*Letteratura musicale. Biografi*	
			(364)	*1,8

424 _____.

	10/1930	5	*Letteratura musicale*	
			(1549)	*1,10

425 _____.

	1931	6	*Letteratura musicale*	
			(628)	*1,8

426 _____.

	1931	7	*Letteratura musicale*	
			(557)	*8

427 _____.

	11/1931	8	*Letteratura musicale. Danza. Teatro*	
			(539)	*8,10,13

428 _____.

	1/1932	9	*Letteratura musicale. Danza. Teatro*	
			(384)	*8,10

429 _____.

	2/1932	10	*Letteratura musicale. Danza. Teatro*	
			(412)	*8,13

430 _____

	1933?	16	*Letteratura musicale. Biog. Bibliog. Danza*	
			(540)	*1,10

431 _____.

	193_	18	*Letteratura musicale. Biog. Bibliog. Danza*	
			(762)	*1,10

432 _____.

	1939?	19	*Letteratura musicale. Biog. Bibliog. Danza*	
			(506)	*1,10

1 Compiler/State University of New York (Buffalo)   **2** The British Library (London)   **3** Gemeentemuseum (Den Haag)   **4** The Grolier Club (N.Y.C.)   **5** Hirsch Collection, British Library (London)   **6** D.W. Krummel (Urbana)   **7** Library of Congress (Washington, D.C.)   **8** Library and Museum of the Performing Arts (N.Y.C.)   **9** William Reeves (London)   **10** Sibley Library, Eastman School of Music (Rochester)   **11** Nigel Simeone (Tunbridge Wells, Kent)   **12** Vereeniging ter Bevordering van de Belangen des Boekhandels (Amsterdam)   **13** University of Virginia (Charlottesville)   **14** University of California at Los Angeles   **15** Generally available

433 **BOOK AND RECORD SHOP (N.Y.C.)**
    1944   1   *No. 1-9. Miscellany*
                        (221)   *8

434 _____.
    1945   2   *No. 1-6. Miscellany*
                        (160)   *8

435 _____.
    1946   3   *No. 1-3. Miscellany*
                        (554)   *8

436 _____.
    1947   4   *No. 1-3. Miscellany*
                        (?)   *8

437 _____.
    1948   5   *No.1-3. Miscellany*
                        (919)   *8

438 _____.
    1949   6   *No. 1-3. Miscellany*
                        (541)   *8

439 **BOOK AND TACKLE SHOP (Chestnut Hill, Mass.)**
    1977   7   *Music Books*
                        (345)   *1

440 **BOOK FARM (Hattiesburg, Miss.)**
    1940   —   *Books and Music of the Conferderacy*
                        (809-921)   *13

441 **BOOK SEARCH SERVICE ((Avondale Estates, Georgia)**
    1973   20   *Music and Hymnology Books*
                        (228)   *8

442 _____.
    1974   21   *Music and Hymnology Books*
                        (113)   *8

443 _____.
    197_   28   *Music and Hymnology Books*
                        (371)   *10

444 _____.
    198_?   29   *Music and Hymnology Books*
                        (340)   *10

445 _____.
    1980   30   *Music and Hymnology Books*
                        (411)   *10

446 **BOOKS UNLIMITED (N.Y.C.?)**
    1949   5   *Selected musical Bibliography*
                        (53)   *8

447 **BORROMEO, C. (Paris)**
    197_?   [1]   *Some rare musical Scores*
                        (22)   *10

448 _____.
    197_?   [2]   *Some Rare Musical Scores*
                        (18)   *10

---

1 Compiler/State University of New York (Buffalo)   **2** The British Library (London)   **3** Gemeentemuseum (Den Haag)   **4** The Grolier Club (N.Y.C.)   **5** Hirsch Collection, British Library (London)   **6** D.W. Krummel (Urbana)   **7** Library of Congress (Washington, D.C.)   **8** Library and Museum of the Performing Arts (N.Y.C.)   **9** William Reeves (London)   **10** Sibley Library, Eastman School of Music (Rochester)   **11** Nigel Simeone (Tunbridge Wells, Kent)   **12** Vereeniging ter Bervordering van de Belangen des Boekhandels (Amsterdam)   **13** University of Virginia (Charlottesville)   **14** University of California at Los Angeles   **15** Generally available

449   **BOTTEGA D'ERASMO (Torino)**
      1953   75   *Musica*
                              (208)   *8

450   _____.
      1956   244   *Musica*
                              (241)   *8

451   _____.
      1960   —   *Musica*
                              (?)   [IBAK]

452   **BOUTEFOY, R. (Paris)**
      1935   170   *Bibliothèque musicale*
                              (740)   *8

453   **BOUVIER, H., and CO.. (Bonn)**
      1961   59   *Musik*
                              (296)   *12

454   **BOWES & BOWES (Cambridge)**
      [1924]   419   *Theological and Liturgical Works*
                              (2288)   *2,12

455   _____.
      1934   470   *Theological and Liturgical Works*
                              (1587)   *12

456   **BRAUS-RIGGENBACH [formerly HENNING OPPERMAN, q.v.] (Basel)**
      148   470   *Musikliteratur und Autographen*
                              (945)   *4,10

457   **BRECHER, L. & A. (Brno)**
      1934?   34   *Coll: Almeria, Countess of Esterhazy*
                              (477)   *4,5,8,10,12

458   **BREITKOPF & HÄRTEL (Leipzig)**
      1836   —   *Musikalien [including holographs]*
                              (12166)   *5

459   _____.
      1899   —   *Antiq. Musikalien I. Instrumentalmusik II.*
                              (2v.)   *7

460   **BRESLAUER, MARTIN (Berlin)**
      1908   3   *Das deutsche Lied*
                              (?)   *10,11,12

461   _____.
      1908   —   *Musik*
                              (?)   *12

462   _____.
      19__   69   *Recent Acquisitions... Music & Opera*
                              (i.a.)   *1

463   **BRIDEL, MAURICE (Lausanne)**
      1950   1   *Coll: Zborowsky. Danse. Théâtre. Musique*
                              (519)   *4

464   _____.
      1952   2   *Théâtre. Chansons-musique*
                              (471-537+)   *4

1 Compiler/State University of New York (Buffalo)   **2** The British Library (London)   **3** Gemeentemuseum (Den Haag)   **4** The Grolier Club (N.Y.C.)   **5** Hirsch Collection, British Library (London)   **6** D.W. Krummel (Urbana)   **7** Library of Congress (Washington, D.C.)   **8** Library and Museum of the Performing Arts (N.Y.C.)   **9** William Reeves (London)   **10** Sibley Library, Eastman School of Music (Rochester)   **11** Nigel Simeone (Tunbridge Wells, Kent)   **12** Vereeniging ter Bervordering van de Belangen des Boekhandels (Amsterdam)   **13** University of Virginia (Charlottesville)   **14** University of California at Los Angeles   **15** Generally available

465 **BRIDEL, MAURICE (Lausanne) (continued)**
    1966   6   *Danse ancienne et moderne*
                    (275)   *₊*

466 **BRILL, E. J. (Leiden)**
    1877   —   *Liedboeken*
                    (?)   **12*

467 **BRINSER, MARLIN (Irvington, N.J.)**
    1970-71   —   *Books on Music*
                   (14pp.)   **8*

468 **_____.**
    1977   —   *Books on Music - over 1500 Titles*
                    (?)   **8*

469 **_____.**
    1982   —   *Books on Music*
                   (4pp.)   **1*

470 **BROCKHAUS, F. A. (Leipzig)**
    1902   —   *Handbücher [including Music Literature]*
                    (?)   **7*

471 **BROCKHAUSEN & BRÄUER (Vienna)**
    s.d.   9   *Coll: Barb, H. A.I: Musikwissenschaft*
                    (477)   **8*

472 **BRONS ORCHESTRAL SERVICE (London)**
    1949   —   *Orchestrations. Instrumental Solos, etc.*
                   (36pp.)   **8*

473 **BROWSER'S BOOKS (Falmouth, Cornwall)**
    s.d.   List   —   *Collector's Corner [Sheet Music]*
                    (225)   **1*

474 **_____.**
    s.d.   do.   101   *Victorian and Edwardian Illustrators*
                    (?)   [not located]

475 **_____.**
    s.d.   do.   102   *Pre-1850 Songs*
                    (?)   [not located]

476 **_____.**
    s.d.   do.   103   *Victorian Keybd. Music (Polkas, Galops...)*
                    (?)   [not located]

477 **_____.**
    s.d.   do.   104   *1910-1920 Songs and Music*
                    (83)   **1*

478 **_____.**
    s.d.   do.   105   *1920s Music*
                    (120)   **1*

479 **_____.**
    s.d.   do.   106   *1930s Music*
                    (119)   **1*

480 **_____.**
    s.d.   do.   107   *2d World War Numbers [Sheet Music]*
                    (?)   [not located]

---

1 Compiler/State University of New York (Buffalo)   **2** The British Library (London)   **3** Gemeentemuseum (Den Haag)   **4** The Grolier Club (N.Y.C.)   **5** Hirsch Collection, British Library (London)   **6** D.W. Krummel (Urbana)   **7** Library of Congress (Washington, D.C.)   **8** Library and Museum of the Performing Arts (N.Y.C.)   **9** William Reeves (London)   **10** Sibley Library, Eastman School of Music (Rochester)   **11** Nigel Simeone (Tunbridge Wells, Kent)   **12** Vereeniging ter Bervordering van de Belangen des Boekhandels (Amsterdam)   **13** University of Virginia (Charlottesville)   **14** University of California at Los Angeles   **15** Generally available

481 **BROWSER'S BOOKS (Falmouth, Cornwall) (continued)**
  s.d. do. 108 *1950s and 1960s [Sheet Music]*
            (?)   [not located]

482 _____.
  s.d. do. 109 *Cornish Songs and Ballads*
            (?)   [not located]

483 _____.
  s.d. do. 110 *Reprints [Sheet Music]*
            (?)   [not located]

484 **BRUDVIG, R. L. (Minneapolis, Minnesota)**
  197_   1 *Books about Music*
            (256)   *1

485 _____.
  197_   2 *Books about Music*
            (62)   *1

486 _____.
  197_   3 *Books about Literature*
            (?)   *1

487 _____.
  197_   4 *Books about Theater*
            (241)   *1

488 _____.
  197_   5 *Books about Music and Dance*
            (469)   *1,8

489 _____.
  1977   9 *Books about Music/Dance*
            (226)   *1

490 _____.
  1977   10 *Books about Music*
            (233)   *1

491 _____.
  1977   12 *Books about Music*
            (251)   *1

492 _____.
  1977   14 *Books about Opera*
            (99)   *1

493 _____.
  s.d.   ? *Books about Music and Dance*
            (986)   *1,8

494 _____.
  s.d.   19 *Music and Dance*
            (766)   *1

495 _____.
  1983   83-07 *Books on Music*
            (683)   *1

496 **BRUINE, P. J. de see BOM, D. G.**

---

1 Compiler/State University of New York (Buffalo) 2 The British Library (London) 3 Gemeentemuseum (Den Haag) 4 The Grolier Club (N.Y.C.) 5 Hirsch Collection, British Library (London) 6 D.W. Krummel (Urbana) 7 Library of Congress (Washington, D.C.) 8 Library and Museum of the Performing Arts (N.Y.C.) 9 William Reeves (London) 10 Sibley Library, Eastman School of Music (Rochester) 11 Nigel Simeone (Tunbridge Wells, Kent) 12 Vereeniging ter Bevordering van de Belangen des Boekhandels (Amsterdam) 13 University of Virginia (Charlottesville) 14 University of California at Los Angeles 15 Generally available

497　"DER BÜCHERWURM" see LÜBKE, G. and HANNMANN, HANS

498　"DER BÜCHERWURM" [later incarnation] (Heidelberg)
　　　　1980　　　　　　　　23　　*Kunst. Musik. Musiker. Theater*
　　　　　　　　　　　　　　　　　(?)

499　BURNETT & SIMEONE (London and Tunbridge Wells, Kent)
　　　　1982　　　　　　　　4　　*Music of the Eighteenth Century*
　　　　　　　　　　　　　　　　　(119)　　　　　　　　　　　　　　　　　　　*15

500　_____.
　　　　1982　　　　　　　　5　　*500 Years of Music [and Books]*
　　　　　　　　　　　　　　　　　(50)　　　　　　　　　　　　　　　　　　　　*15

501　_____.
　　　　1983　　　　　　　　7　　*Antiquarian Music. Music Lit. Full Scores*
　　　　　　　　　　　　　　　　　(287)　　　　　　　　　　　　　　　　　　　*15

502　_____.
　　　　1983　　　　　　　　8　　*Johannes Brahms, 1833-1897*
　　　　　　　　　　　　　　　　　(205)　　　　　　　　　　　　　　　　　　　*15

503　_____.
　　　　1983　　　　　　　　9　　*Antiq. Music. 1st Editions. Women Composers*
　　　　　　　　　　　　　　　　　(369)　　　　　　　　　　　　　　　　　　　*15

504　_____.
　　　　6/1984　　　　　　　10　　*Music since Wagner. Libretti. Postcards*
　　　　　　　　　　　　　　　　　(650)　　　　　　　　　　　　　　　　　　　*15

505　_____.
　　　　9/1984　　　　　　　11　　*Antiquarian Music [and Music Literature]*
　　　　　　　　　　　　　　　　　(555)　　　　　　　　　　　　　　　　　　　*15

506　BURSTEIN, HAROLD M. (Waltham, Mass.)
　　　　1971　　　　List　　781　　*Music and Songsters*
　　　　　　　　　　　　　　　　　(59)　　　　　　　　　　　　　　　　　　　　*1

507　_____.
　　　　1982　　　　do.　　182!　*Music*
　　　　　　　　　　　　　　　　　(27)　　　　　　　　　　　　　　　　　　　*1,13

508　BUTSCH, FIDELIS (BIRETT'SCHES ANTIQUARIAT) (Augsburg)
　　　　1846　　　　　　　—　　*Seltene Notendrucke*
　　　　　　　　　　　　　　　　　(42pp.)　　　　　　　　　　　　　　　　　　*7

509　CADENZA BOOKSELLER (Smithtown, N.Y.)
　　　　1980　　　　　　　1　　*[Books on Music]*
　　　　　　　　　　　　　　　　　(215)　　　　　　　　　　　　　　　　　　*1,8

510　_____.
　　　　s.d.　　　　　　　2　　*[Books on music]*
　　　　　　　　　　　　　　　　　(?)　　　　　　　　　　　　　　　　　　　*1,8

511　_____.
　　　　1981　　　　　　　3　　*[Musical Literature]*
　　　　　　　　　　　　　　　　　[30pp.]　　　　　　　　　　　　　　　　　　*1

512　_____.
　　　　1982　　　　　　　4　　*Books about Music and Musicians*
　　　　　　　　　　　　　　　　　(581)　　　　　　　　　　　　　　　　　　　*1

1 Compiler/State University of New York (Buffalo)　　**2** The British Library (London)　　**3** Gemeentemuseum (Den Haag)　　**4** The Grolier Club (N.Y.C.)　　**5** Hirsch Collection, British Library (London)　　**6** D.W. Krummel (Urbana)　　**7** Library of Congress (Washington, D.C.)　　**8** Library and Museum of the Performing Arts (N.Y.C.)　　**9** William Reeves (London)　　**10** Sibley Library, Eastman School of Music (Rochester)　　**11** Nigel Simeone (Tunbridge Wells, Kent)　　**12** Vereeniging ter Bevordering van de Belangen des Boekhandels (Amsterdam)　　**13** University of Virginia (Charlottesville)　　**14** University of California at Los Angeles　　**15** Generally available

513	**CADENZA BOOKSELLER** (Smithtown, N.Y.) (continued)			
	1982	4a	*Books about Music and Musicians* (222)	*15
514	____.			
	1983	5	*Books about Music and Musicians* (305)	*15
515	____.			
	1984	6	*Music Literature. Jazz and Jazz Musicians* (567)	*15
516	**CALKIN & BUDD** (London)			
	1844	—	*Misc. Coll. of Music. Treatises. History* (3447)	*1
517	____.			
	1849	—	*First Supplement* (3448-4248)	*1
518	**CALVARY, S. & CO.** (Berlin)			
	1866	48	*Musik* (20pp.)	*8
519	____.			
	s.d.	194	*Kulturgeschichte und Musik* (2499)	*8
520	**CANTABRIGIA** (Cambridge, Mass.)			
	195_?	7	*Folklore. Folkmusic. Folkdance* (289)	*6,8
521	____.			
	195_?	10	*Ethos. (Folklore. Folkmusic)* (706)	*6,8
522	____.			
	195_?	11	*Of America's Past* (544)	*6,8
523	____.			
	195_?	18	*Folklore. Folkmusic. Folkdance* (577)	*8
524	____.			
	195_?	19	*Folklore. Folkmusic. Folkdance* (865)	*8
525	____.			
	196_?	20	*Of America's Past* (621)	*8
526	____.			
	196_?	21	*Folklore. Folkmusic. Folkdance* (589)	*8
527	____.			
	196_?	23	*Folklore. Folkmusic. Folkdance* (857)	*8
528	____.			
	196_?	24	*Folklore. Folkmusic. Folkdance* (623)	*8

1 Compiler/State University of New York (Buffalo)   **2** The British Library (London)   **3** Gemeentemuseum (Den Haag)   **4** The Grolier Club (N.Y.C.)   **5** Hirsch Collection, British Library (London)   **6** D.W. Krummel (Urbana)   **7** Library of Congress (Washington, D.C.)   **8** Library and Museum of the Performing Arts (N.Y.C.)   **9** William Reeves (London)   **10** Sibley Library, Eastman School of Music (Rochester) **11** Nigel Simeone (Tunbridge Wells, Kent)   **12** Vereeniging ter Bervordering van de Belangen des Boekhandels (Amsterdam)   **13** University of Virginia (Charlottesville)   **14** University of California at Los Angeles   **15** Generally available

529   **CANTABRIGIA (Cambridge, Mass.) (continued)**
      196_?   25   *Folklore. Folkmusic. Folkdance*
                                   (832)   *8
530   **CAPPELEN, J. W. (Oslo)**
      1966   203   *Musikk-teater*
                                   (968)   [IBAK]
531   _____.
      1967   211   *[Kunst. Musik]*
                                   (656)   [IBAK]
532   **CARLEBACH, ERNST (Heidelberg)**
      1896   211   *Theater und Musik*
                                   (1065)   *8,12
533   _____.
      1896   216   *Theater und Musik*
                                                                             *8,12
534   _____.
      1899   235   *Deutsche Literatur. Theater. Musik*
                                   (2031)   *8,12
535   **CARLSOHN, ERICH (Leipzig)**
      1929   18   *Lieder von Goethe*
                                   (269)   *13
536   _____.
      1930   22   *Deutsche Lied. Instrumental Musik*
                                                                              *7
537   **CARTHAUS, J. F. (Bonn)**
      1905   —   *Coll: Koester, K.*
                                   (36pp.)   [BiBB]
538   **CASA LIQUIDORA (Lisbon)**
      1916   —   *Coll: [unnamed]. Musical Instruments*
                                                                        [Lambertini]
539   **EL CASCERO (N.Y.C.)**
      1967-68   15   *Music. Books. Scores*
                                   (52pp.)   *8
540   **CASIMIRI-CAPRA (Rome)**
      1963   178   *Organo armonia*
                                   (224pp.)   *8
·541 _____.
      1963   179   *Domenico Bartilucci*
                                   (26pp.)   *8
542   _____.
      1967   208   *Musica. Dischi*
                                   (208pp.)   *8
543   **CHAMONAL, FRANCOIS (Paris)**
      1969   —   *Regionalisme. Musique. Varia*
                                   (228-59)   *6,13
544   _____.
      1980?   —   *[Rare] Musique. Théâtre. Danse*
                                   (141)   *1,9

---

1 Compiler/State University of New York (Buffalo)   **2** The British Library (London)   **3** Gemeentemuseum (Den Haag)   **4** The Grolier Club (N.Y.C.)   **5** Hirsch Collection, British Library (London)   **6** D.W. Krummel (Urbana)   **7** Library of Congress (Washington, D.C.)   **8** Library and Museum of the Performing Arts (N.Y.C.)   **9** William Reeves (London)   **10** Sibley Library, Eastman School of Music (Rochester)   **11** Nigel Simeone (Tunbridge Wells, Kent)   **12** Vereeniging ter Bervordering van de Belangen des Boekhandels (Amsterdam)   **13** University of Virginia (Charlottesville)   **14** University of California at Los Angeles   **15** Generally available

545 **CHAPOTTE, H. (Lima, Peru)**
    1951   —   *Peruvian Music*
                         (33pp.)   *8

546 **CHENE, GENE DE (Los Angeles)**
    1971   —   *Music Books*
                         (1600)   *8

547 **CHEROKEE BOOK SHOP (Hollywood)**
    197_   88   *Music Literature*
                         (684)   *1,8

548 _____.
    1976   105   *Music. Cinema*
                         (1-691)   *14

549 **CHIAPPINI, LIBRERIA (Rome)**
    1968   11   *Musica. Musicologia. Roma*
                         (577)   *8

550 _____.
    1969   16-17   *Arte. Archeologia. Musicologia. Storia*
                         (881)   *8

551 **CHISWICK PRESS (London)**
    1905?   —   *Coll: [unnamed]. Autographs and Manuscripts*
                                                        *2

552 **CLUNES, ALEC (London)**
    1956   5   *Music and Musical Literature*
                         (422)   *8,9,11,13

553 _____.
    1957   8   *Music and Musical Literature*
                         (432)   *,6,9,11

554 _____.
    1957   9   *Theatre*
                         (501-656)   *13

555 _____.
    1957   10   *Music. Musical Literature*
                         (522)   *8,11

556 _____.
    1958   12   *Music and Musical Literature*
                         (468)   *11

557 _____.
    1959   14   *Music and Musical Literature*
                         (522)   *8,11

558 **COEBERGH, H. (Haarlem)**
    1955   61   *Antiq. Kunst og Muziek*
                         (8201-8558)   *12

559 **COHEN, FRIEDRICH (Bonn)**
    1900   98   *Coll: Posonyi. Autogr.-Sammlung II: Musiker*
                         (1611)   *3,4

560 **COHN, ALBERT (Berlin)**
    1876   112   *Alte Musik*
                         (85)   *12

---

1 Compiler/State University of New York (Buffalo)   **2** The British Library (London)   **3** Gemeentemuseum (Den Haag)   **4** The Grolier Club (N.Y.C.)   **5** Hirsch Collection, British Library (London)   **6** D.W. Krummel (Urbana)   **7** Library of Congress (Washington, D.C.)   **8** Library and Museum of the Performing Arts (N.Y.C.)   **9** William Reeves (London)   **10** Sibley Library, Eastman School of Music (Rochester) **11** Nigel Simeone (Tunbridge Wells, Kent)   **12** Vereeniging ter Bervordering van de Belangen des Boekhandels (Amsterdam)   **13** University of Virginia (Charlottesville)   **14** University of California at Los Angeles   **15** Generally available

561 **COHN, ALBERT (Berlin) (continued)**
  1878   119 *Musique ancienne*
           (156)   *5,12
562 ———.
  1878   123 *Theoret., hymnol. und praktische Musik*
           (232)   *5,12
563 ———.
  1880   132 *Coll: Cohn, A. Livres rares, anciennes*
           (256-309)   *8
564 ———.
  1881   140 *Theoretisch und praktische Musik*
           (331)   *5,12
565 ———.
  1882   141 *Theoretisch und praktische Musik. Tanzkunst*
           (703)   *3,5,8,12
566 ———.
  1882   145 *[Supplement to Katalog 141?]*
                       *4,5,12
567 ———.
  1884   163 *Autographen und historische Dokumente*
                       *5
568 ———.
  1885   164 *Deutsche Bücher. Hymnologie*
           (235-321)   *3
569 ———.
  1885   169 *Theoretisch und prakt. Musik. Autographen*
           (501)   *8,12
570 ———.
  1886   173 *Autographen und historische Dokumente*
           (pp.99-104)   *5
571 ———.
  1887   182 *Coll: Grell, E.*
           (773)   *3,5
572 ———.
  1891   200 *Bücher aus allen Gebieten*
           (1123-82)   *3
573 ———.
  1900   218 *Autographen. Briefe. Musikmanuskripte*
                       [ZiMG]
574 **COLLEGE BOOK SERVICE (Port Washington, N. Y.)**
  s.d.   Bull.   29 *Music History. Biography*
           (608)   *1
575 **COLLETT'S HOLDINGS LTD. (Wellingsborough, U. K.)**
  1976   Info.   1 *Music List*
           (6pp.)   *14
576 **COLLEY-CIBBER MUSIC (Twickenham/Guildford, U.K.)**
  10/1983   1 *Music Literature*
           (370)   *15

---

1 Compiler/State University of New York (Buffalo) **2** The British Library (London) **3** Gemeentemuseum (Den Haag) **4** The Grolier Club (N.Y.C.) **5** Hirsch Collection, British Library (London) **6** D.W. Krummel (Urbana) **7** Library of Congress (Washington, D.C.) **8** Library and Museum of the Performing Arts (N.Y.C.) **9** William Reeves (London) **10** Sibley Library, Eastman School of Music (Rochester) **11** Nigel Simeone (Tunbridge Wells, Kent) **12** Vereeniging ter Bervordering van de Belangen des Boekhandels (Amsterdam) **13** University of Virginia (Charlottesville) **14** University of California at Los Angeles **15** Generally available

577   **COLLEY-CIBBER MUSIC (Twickenham/Guildford, U.K.) (continued)**
        2/1984   2   *Music Literature with American Supplement*
                                      (513,174)   *15

578   _____.
        5/1984   3   *Music Lit. Publ. Letters. Americana Suppl.*
                                        (327,158)   *15

579   _____.
        10/1984   4   *Scores. Suppl.: Piano, Chamber, Vocal Music*
                                      (247)   *15

580   **CONSTAPEL (The Hague)**
        1759   —   *Coll: [unnamed]*
                                      (?)   *3,12

581   _____.
        1760   —   *Coll: [unnamed]*
                                      (?)   *3

582   _____.
        1771   —   *Coll: Pooten*
                                      (16 lvs.)   *3

583   _____.
        1772   —   *Coll: [unnamed]*
                                      (4 lvs.)   *3

584   _____.
        1774   —   *Coll: [unnamed]*
                                      (4 lvs.)   *3

585   **CONWAY, NOEL & CO. (London)**
        [189_]   —   *Rare, Interesting ALS, Mss. Mendelssohniana*
                                    (pp.37-56)   *8,9

586   **CORBELLINI, MARIO (Rome)**
        4/1953   —   *[Including] Musica e Musicologia*
                                    (1-74)   *6

587   _____.
        11/1953   —   *[Including] Musica, Canto e Danza*
                                    (1-185)   *6

588   _____.
        11/1954   —   *[Including] Musica, Canto e Danza*
                                    (1-199)   *6

589   _____.
        12/1955   —   *[Including] Musica, Canto e Danza*
                                    (1-279)   *6

590   _____.
        1958   —   *"Spectacula"*
                                      (1-248)   *6

591   _____.
        1960   —   *Musica ... Aeronautica*
                                      (402)   [IBAK]

592   _____.
        1966   —   *Cinema. Musica. Teatro. Folklore*
                                      (826)   *8

---

1 Compiler/State University of New York (Buffalo)   **2** The British Library (London)   **3** Gemeentemuseum (Den Haag)   **4** The Grolier Club (N.Y.C.)   **5** Hirsch Collection, British Library (London)   **6** D.W. Krummel (Urbana)   **7** Library of Congress (Washington, D.C.)   **8** Library and Museum of the Performing Arts (N.Y.C.)   **9** William Reeves (London)   **10** Sibley Library, Eastman School of Music (Rochester)   **11** Nigel Simeone (Tunbridge Wells, Kent)   **12** Vereeniging ter Bervordering van de Belangen des Boekhandels (Amsterdam)   **13** University of Virginia (Charlottesville)   **14** University of California at Los Angeles   **15** Generally available

593 **CORBELLINI, MARIO (Rome) (continued)**
    1967   —   *Spettacolo*
                      (865)   *8

594   ____.
    12/1967   —   *"Spectacula." Musica. Teatro. Cinema*
                    (1-399)   *8

595   ____.
    1969   —   *Musica. Teatro. Cinema*
                    (584)   *6,8,12

596   ____.
    1970   —   *Musica. Teatro*
                    (612)   *8

597   ____.
    1971   —   *Musica. Teatro. Cinema*
                    (748)   *8

598   ____.
    1972   —   *"Spectacula"*
                    (1-300)   *1,8

599   ____.
    1974   —   *Spettacolo e Folklore*
                    (1-250)   *1,8

600 **CORNER BOOK SHOP (N.Y.C.)**
    1967?   M67   *Music. Radio. TV*
                    (613)   *1,6

601 **COSTA-BORGNA, F. (Paris)**
    1/1910   —   *Musique ancienne et moderne*
                    (?)   *5

602   ____.
    1911?   —   *Musique ancienne et moderne*
                    (?)   *5

603   ____.
    1911?   —   *Musique ancienne et moderne*
                    (?)   *5

604   ____.
    1912?   —   *Musique ancienne et moderne*
                    (?)   *5

605   ____.
    1913   —   *Musique ancienne et moderne*
                    (275)   *5,8

606   ____.
    1914   —   *Musique ancienne et moderne*
                    (303)   *5,8

607   ____.
    1918   —   *Musique ancienne et moderne*
                    (270)   *8

608   ____.
    7/1919   —   *Musique ancienne et moderne*
                    (268)   *8

609 **COSTA-BORGNA, F. (Paris) (contiued)**
      11/1919   —   *Musique ancienne et moderne*
                                (303)   *8

610 _____.
      5/1920   —   *Musique ancienne et moderne*
                                  (261)   *8

611 _____.
      11/1920   —   *Musique ancienne et moderne*
                                  (252)   *8

612 _____.
      5/1921   —   *Musique ancienne et moderne*
                                  (256)   *8

613 _____.
      11/1921   —   *Musique ancienne et moderne*
                                  (285)   *8

614 _____.
      5/1922   —   *Musique ancienne et moderne*
                                  (282)   *8

615 _____.
      11/1922   —   *Musique ancienne et moderne*
                                  (259)   *8

616 _____.
      3/1923   —   *Musique ancienne et moderne*
                                  (307)   *8

617 _____.
      7/1923   —   *Musique ancienne et moderne*
                                  (286)   *8

618 _____.
      7/1923   —   *Musique ancienne et moderne*
                                  (286)   *8

619 _____.
      3/1924   —   *Musique ancienne et moderne*
                                  (280)   *8

620 _____.
      6/1924   —   *Musique ancienne et moderne*
                                  (288)   *8

621 _____.
      7/1925   —   *Musique ancienne et moderne*
                                  (287)   *8

622 **LIBRARIE C. COULET & A. FAURÉ (Paris)**
      1972   —   *Spectacles: Théâtre. Cinema. Musique. Mss.*
                                  (961-1657)   *8

623 **COX, LISA (Chulmleigh, U. K.)**
      1983?   1   *Books. Libretti. Photos. ALS. Scores. Mss.*
                                  (155)   *15

624 _____.
      1984?   2   *Books. Libretti. Photos. ALS. Scores. Mss.*
                                  (168)   *15

---

1 Compiler/State University of New York (Buffalo)   **2** The British Library (London)   **3** Gemeentemuseum (Den Haag)   **4** The Grolier Club (N.Y.C.)   **5** Hirsch Collection, British Library (London)   **6** D.W. Krummel (Urbana)   **7** Library of Congress (Washington, D.C.)   **8** Library and Museum of the Performing Arts (N.Y.C.)   **9** William Reeves (London)   **10** Sibley Library, Eastman School of Music (Rochester)   **11** Nigel Simeone (Tunbridge Wells, Kent)   **12** Vereeniging ter Bervordering van de Belangen des Boekhandels (Amsterdam)   **13** University of Virginia (Charlottesville)   **14** University of California at Los Angeles   **15** Generally available

625 **COX, LISA (Chulmleigh, U. K.) (continued)**
  1984/85   3   *[Music and Music Literature. ALS. Mss.]*
                              (236)   *15
626 **CREYGHTON (Bilthoven)**
  [1955]   18   *Diss. Music Lit. in First and Early Editions*
                              (100)   *8
627 _____.
  [195_]   22   *Vokalmusik*
                              (385)   *6,8,9,12
628 _____.
  [195_]   23   *General [Music] Literature*
                              (177)   *6,8
629 _____.
  [195_]   24   *Musik-Literatur*
                              (150)   *6
630 _____.
  [195_]   25   *Musikliteratur und Zeitschriften*
                              (101)   *6,8
631 _____.
  [1957]   26   *[Music and Musical Literatur]*
                              (139)   *9
632 _____.
  [195_]   27   *Musikliteratur*
                              (549)   *6,8,9,12
633 _____.
  1960   28   *Miscellaneous [Music, i.a.]*
                              (167)   *6,8,9
634 _____.
  1961   29   *Miscellaneous [Music, i.a.]*
                              (167)   *6,8,9,11,12
635 _____.
  1962   30   *Miscellaneous [Music, i.a.]*
                              (217)   *8,9
636 _____.
  [1963]   31   *... Music*
                              (231)   *8,9,11
637 _____.
  [1963]   32   *Miscellaneous [Music i.a.]*
                              (184)   *6,8,10,13
638 _____.
  [1963]   33   *Opera and Ballet*
                              (559)   *6,10,11,13
639 _____.
  [1963?]   34   *Miscellaneous [Music i.a.]*
                              (331)   *6,10
640 _____.
  [1964]   35   *Miscellaneous [and Music]*
                              (294)   *6,10

641 **CREYGHTON (Bilthoven) (continued)**

641	[1964?]		36	*Miscellaneous [and Music]* (145)	*10
642	____. [1965]		37	*Miscellaneous [and Music]* (262)	*6,8,10
643	____. [1968]		38	*Musical Literature. Facsimiles. Theater* (294)	*1,6,8,10
644	____. [1969]		39	*Literature on Musicology and Theater* (453)	*1,6,8,10,13
645	____. [1969]		40	*Printed Music. Literature on Musicology* (311)	*1,8,10,13
646	____., [1970?]		41	*Lit. on Musicology. Printed Music. Theater* (310)	*1,8,10,13
647	____. 1971		42	*Musical Literature. Instrumental Music* (350)	*1,8,10,13
648	____. [1971]		—	*Coll: "A Private Collection"* (96pp.)	*1
649	____. 1972		43	*Autographs. Musical Literature. Vocal Music* (308)	*1,8,10,13
650	____. 1979		50	*Musical Literature. Printed Music* (270)	*1,8,13
651	____. [1959]	Lijst	6	*Muziekliteratur* (309)	*8,12
652	____. 1958	do.	7	*Complete Works and Denkmaeler* (113)	*8
653	____. 1958	do.	8	*Instr. Music in First and Early Editions* (211)	*8,12
654	____. 1958	do.	9	*Musical Dissertations* (17)	*8
655	____. 1959	do.	10	*Catalogues* (63)	*8
656	____. 1959	do.	11	*Yearbooks and Memorial Works* (21)	*8

1 Compiler/State University of New York (Buffalo)   2 The British Library (London)   3 Gemeentemuseum (Den Haag)   4 The Grolier Club (N.Y.C.)   5 Hirsch Collection, British Library (London)   6 D.W. Krummel (Urbana)   7 Library of Congress (Washington, D.C.)   8 Library and Museum of the Performing Arts (N.Y.C.)   9 William Reeves (London)   10 Sibley Library, Eastman School of Music (Rochester)   11 Nigel Simeone (Tunbridge Wells, Kent)   12 Vereeniging ter Bervordering van de Belangen des Boekhandels (Amsterdam)   13 University of Virginia (Charlottesville)   14 University of California at Los Angeles   15 Generally available

657 **CREYGHTON (Bilthoven) (continued)**
    1959   do.   12   *Mozartiana*
                               (182)   *8

658 _____ .
    1959   do.   13   *Complete Sets or Separate Volumes*
                               (64)   *8

659 _____ .
    1959   do.   14   *Music Literature*
                               (138)   *8,12

660 _____ .
    1959   do.   15   *Complete Sets or Separate Volumes*
                               (144)   *8

661 _____ .
    1959   do.   16   *Vocal Scores with Text*
                               (250)   *8

662 _____ .
    1959   do.   17   *Vocal Scores with Text*
                               (70)   *8

663 _____ .
    1959   do.   18   *Full Scores*
                               (16)   *8

664 _____ .
    1959   do.   20   *Catalogues and Dictionaries*
                               (66)   *8

665 _____ .
    1959   do.   21   *Lit. about Instruments. Works of G. Kastner*
                               (24)   *8

666 _____ .
    1959   do.   22   *General Musical Literature*
                               (73)   *8

667 _____ .
    1959   do.   23   *Psalms, Hymns, Masses*
                               (84)   *8

668 _____ .
    1959   do.   24   *Instrumental Music in First and Early Eds.*
                               (243)   *8

669 _____ .
    1959   do.   25   *Instrumental Music in First and Early Eds.*
                               (168)   *6,8

670 _____ .
    1960   do.   29   *Instrumental Music in First and Early Eds.*
                               (150)   *6,12

671 _____ .
    1960   do.   33   *Miscellaneous [Music i.a.]*
                               (124)   *8

672 _____ .
    1960   do.   36   *Miscellaneous [Music, i.a.]*
                               (90)   [IBAK]

---

1 Compiler/State University of New York (Buffalo)   **2** The British Library (London)   **3** Gemeentemuseum (Den Haag)   **4** The Grolier Club (N.Y.C.)   **5** Hirsch Collection, British Library (London)   **6** D.W. Krummel (Urbana)   **7** Library of Congress (Washington, D.C.)   **8** Library and Museum of the Performing Arts (N.Y.C.)   **9** William Reeves (London)   **10** Sibley Library, Eastman School of Music (Rochester)   **11** Nigel Simeone (Tunbridge Wells, Kent)   **12** Vereeniging ter Bervordering van de Belangen des Boekhandels (Amsterdam)   **13** University of Virginia (Charlottesville)   **14** University of California at Los Angeles   **15** Generally available

673 **CREYGHTON (Bilthoven) (continued)**

| | 1960 | do. | 37 | *Alphons Diepenbrock* | |
| | | | | (40) | [IBAK] |

674 ——

| | 1960 | do. | 38 | *Schulmusik-Literatur* | |
| | | | | (165) | [IBAK] |

675 ——.

| | 1960 | do. | 39 | *Vocal Scores* | |
| | | | | (128) | [IBAK] |

676 ——.

| | 1960 | do. | 40 | *Musical Literature* | |
| | | | | (75) | [IBAK] |

677 ——.

| | 1960 | do. | 41 | *Vocal Scores Published by Lauweryns* | |
| | | | | (28) | [IBAK] |

678 ——.

| | 1960 | do. | 42 | *Miscellaneous [Music i.a.]* | |
| | | | | (135) | [IBAK] |

679 ——.

| | 1960 | do. | 44 | *Miscellaneous [Music, i.a.]* | |
| | | | | (101) | [IBAK] |

680 ——.

| | 1961 | do. | 46 | *Miscellaneous [Music, i.a.]* | |
| | | | | (115) | [IBAK] |

681 ——.

| | 1961 | do. | 48 | *Miscellaneous [Music, i.a.]* | |
| | | | | (148) | [IBAK] |

682 ——.

| | 1961 | do. | 49 | *Miscellaneous [Music, i.a.]* | |
| | | | | (152) | *11 |

683 ——.

| | 1961 | do. | 51 | *Miscellaneous [Music, i.a.]* | |
| | | | | (120) | *11 |

684 ——.

| | 1961 | do. | 53 | *Full Scores* | |
| | | | | (259) | *11 |

685 ——.

| | 1961 | do. | 55 | *Miscellaneous [Music i.a.]* | |
| | | | | (166) | *6,11 |

686 ——.

| | 1961 | do. | 57 | *Miscellaneous [Music, i.a.]* | |
| | | | | (148) | *6,11 |

687 ——.

| | 1962 | do. | 59 | *Musical Literature* | |
| | | | | (195) | *6,11 |

688 ——.

| | 1962 | do. | 60 | *Miscellaneous [Music i.a.]* | |
| | | | | (140) | *6,11 |

1 Compiler/State University of New York (Buffalo)   **2** The British Library (London)   **3** Gemeentemuseum (Den Haag)   **4** The Grolier Club (N.Y.C.)   **5** Hirsch Collection, British Library (London)   **6** D.W. Krummel (Urbana)   **7** Library of Congress (Washington, D.C.)   **8** Library and Museum of the Performing Arts (N.Y.C.)   **9** William Reeves (London)   **10** Sibley Library, Eastman School of Music (Rochester)   **11** Nigel Simeone (Tunbridge Wells, Kent)   **12** Vereeniging ter Bervordering van de Belangen des Boekhandels (Amsterdam)   **13** University of Virginia (Charlottesville)   **14** University of California at Los Angeles   **15** Generally available

689 **CREYGHTON (Bilthoven) (continued)**

	1962	do.	61	*Miscellaneous [Music, i.a.]* (160)	*6,11
690	_____.				
	1962	do.	63	*Miscellaneous [Music, i.a.]* (171)	*6,11
691	_____.				
	1962	do.	65	*Miscellaneous [Music, i.a.]* (125)	*6,11
692	_____.				
	1962	do.	66	*Vocal Scores* (190)	*6
693	_____.				
	1962	do.	67	*Musicology* (18)	[IBAK]
694	_____.				
	1962	do.	69	*Miscellaneous [Music i.a.]* (133)	*6
695	_____.				
	1962	do.	70	*Miscellaneous [Music, i.a.]* (155)	
696	_____.				
	1962	do.	72	*Miscellaneous [Music, i.a.]* (140)	*6
697	_____.				
	1963	do.	74	*Miscellaneous [Music, i.a.]* (117)	*6
698	_____.				
	1963	do.	76	*East-European Musicology* (150)	*6
699	_____.				
	1963	do.	77	*Miscellaneous [Music i.a.]* (170)	*6
700	_____.				
	1963	do.	78	*Miscellaneous [Music, i.a.]* (175)	*6
701	_____.				
	1963	do.	79	*Miscellaneous [Music, i.a.]* (125)	*6
702	_____.				
	1964	do.	83	*Musik* (152)	*6
703	_____.				
	1964	do.	84	*Musik* (135)	*6
704	____.				
	1964	do.	86	*Musicology and Theatre* (140)	*6

705 **CREYGHTON (Bilthoven) (continued)**
    1965   do.   89   *Dissertations on Musicology and Theatre*
                           (80)   *6

706 _____.
    1965   do.   90   *Miscellaneous [Music i.a.]*
                           (90)   [IBAK]

707 _____.
    1965   do.   91   *Miscellaneous [Music, i.a.]*
                           (152)   [IBAK]

708 _____.
    1965   do.   93   *Full Scores*
                           (140)   *6,8

709 _____.
    1966   do.   95   *Musicology and Theatre*
                           (125)   *6,8

710 _____.
    1966   do.   97   *Miscellaneous. Musicology and Theatre*
                           (150)   *6

711 _____.
    1966   do.   98   *Opera. Full Scores*
                           (200)   *6,8

712 _____.
    1966   do.   100   *Musicology and Theatre*
                           (150)   *6

713 _____.
    1966   do.   102   *Vocal Scores*
                           (170)   *6,8

714 _____.
    1966   do.   103   *Vocal Scores*
                           (175)   *6,8

715 _____.
    1966   do.   104   *Franz Liszt*
                           (305)   [IBAK]

716 _____.
    1967   do.   106   *Musicology and Theatre*
                           (97)   *6

717 _____.
    1967   do.   107   *Musicology and Theatre*
                           (123)   *6

718 _____.
    1967   do.   109   *Musicology and Theatre*
                           (151)   [IBAK]

719 _____.
    1967   do.   111   *Musicology and Theatre*
                           (120)   *8

720 _____.
    1967   do.   112   *Musicology and Theatre*
                           (72)   [IBAK]

1 Compiler/State University of New York (Buffalo)   **2** The British Library (London)   **3** Gemeentemuseum (Den Haag)   **4** The Grolier Club (N.Y.C.)   **5** Hirsch Collection, British Library (London)   **6** D.W. Krummel (Urbana)   **7** Library of Congress (Washington, D.C.)   **8** Library and Museum of the Performing Arts (N.Y.C.)   **9** William Reeves (London)   **10** Sibley Library, Eastman School of Music (Rochester)   **11** Nigel Simeone (Tunbridge Wells, Kent)   **12** Vereeniging ter Bervordering van de Belangen des Boekhandels (Amsterdam)   **13** University of Virginia (Charlottesville)   **14** University of California at Los Angeles   **15** Generally available

721 **CREYGHTON (Bilthoven) (continued)**

1967	do.	113	*Musicology and Theatre* (166)	*6,8

722 _____.
1968	do.	115	*Musicology and Theatre* (114)	*6,8

723 _____.
1968	do.	118	*Musicology and Theatre* (183)	*6

724 _____.
1969	do.	119	*Musicology and Theatre* (102)	*6

725 _____.
3/1970	do.	125	*Musicology and Theatre* (177)	*8

726 _____.
2/1971	do.	132	*Musicology and Theatre* (150)	*8

727 _____.
4/1972	do.	137	*Antiquarian Vocal Music* (107)	*8

728 _____.
5/1972	do.	138	*Coll: "Musicologist," the Library of a* (129)	*8

729 _____.
6/1972	do.	139	*Antiquarian Instrumental Music* (130)	*8

730 _____.
10/1972	do.	141	*Antiquarian Music List* (129)	*8,13

731 _____.
11/1972	do.	143	*Antiquarian Literature on Music and Theatre* (175)	*8

732 _____.
11/1972	do.	144	*Antiquarian Music Periodicals* (143)	*8

733 _____.
12/1972	do.	145	*Interesting Antiquarian Items on Musicology* (76)	*8

734 _____.
12/1972	do.	146	*Antiquarian Books on Musicology and Theatre* (205)	*8

735 _____.
8/1973	do.	148	*Antiq. Instr. Music in First and Early Eds.* (123)	*8

736 _____.
12/1973	do.	152	*Antiquarian Music Literature* (120)	*8,13

1 Compiler/State University of New York (Buffalo)   **2** The British Library (London)   **3** Gemeentemuseum (Den Haag)   **4** The Grolier Club (N.Y.C.)   **5** Hirsch Collection, British Library (London)   **6** D.W. Krummel (Urbana)   **7** Library of Congress (Washington, D.C.)   **8** Library and Museum of the Performing Arts (N.Y.C.)   **9** William Reeves (London)   **10** Sibley Library, Eastman School of Music (Rochester)   **11** Nigel Simeone (Tunbridge Wells, Kent)   **12** Vereeniging ter Bevordering van de Belangen des Boekhandels (Amsterdam)   **13** University of Virginia (Charlottesville)   **14** University of California at Los Angeles   **15** Generally available

737 **CREYGHTON (Bilthoven) (continued)**

| | 1/1974 | do. | 153 | *Antiquarian Literature. Theatre*
 (22) | *8 |

738 _____.

| | 4/1974 | do. | 156 | *Antiquarian Instrumental Music*
 (108) | *8,13 |

739 _____.

| | 6/1974 | do. | 158 | *First and Early Editions*
 (52) | *8,13 |

740 _____.

| | 1974 | do. | 159 | *Antiquarian Books on Musicology and Theatre*
 (97) | *13 |

741 _____.

| | 9/1974 | do. | 160 | *Antiquarian Literature on Music and Theatre*
 (225) | *8 |

742 _____.

| | 10/1974 | do. | 162 | *Antiquarian Books on Musicology and Theatre*
 (151) | *8 |

743 _____.

| | 11/1974 | do. | 163 | *Antiquarian Literature on Music and Theatre*
 (172) | *8 |

744 _____.

| | 1975 | do. | 170 | *Antiquarian Music and Musical Literature*
 (106) | *8,12 |

745 _____.

| | 11/1975 | do. | 176 | *Antiquarian Music and Musical Literature*
 (38) | *8 |

746 _____.

| | 1976 | do. | 177 | *Antiquarian Lit. on Musicology and Theatre*
 (178) | *8,12 |

747 _____.

| | 1976 | do. | 178 | *Antiquarian Music and Musical Literature*
 (135) | *8,12,13 |

748 _____.

| | 11/1980 | do. | 180 | *Musical Literature*
 (219) | *1,8 |

749 **CULTURA (Ft. Worth Texas)**

| | 1967 | | 108 | *Music and Books about Music*
 (731) | *1 |

750 _____.

| | 1967 | | 109 | *Music and Books about Music*
 (498) | *1 |

751 _____.

| | 1968 | | 110 | *Musica Rara Publications* | *1 |

752 _____.

| | 1968 | | 111 | *Music and Music Literature*
 (1586) | *1,10,11,13 |

1 Compiler/State University of New York (Buffalo)   **2** The British Library (London)   **3** Gemeentemuseum (Den Haag)   **4** The Grolier Club (N.Y.C.)   **5** Hirsch Collection, British Library (London)   **6** D.W. Krummel (Urbana)   **7** Library of Congress (Washington, D.C.)   **8** Library and Museum of the Performing Arts (N.Y.C.)   **9** William Reeves (London)   **10** Sibley Library, Eastman School of Music (Rochester)   **11** Nigel Simeone (Tunbridge Wells, Kent)   **12** Vereeniging ter Bervordering van de Belangen des Boekhandels (Amsterdam)   **13** University of Virginia (Charlottesville)   **14** University of California at Los Angeles   **15** Generally available

753	**CULTURA (Ft. Worth Texas) (continued)**			
	1970	112	*Music and Music Literature* (1490)	*1,10,13
754	____.			
	1970	113a	*Music and Music Literature, A-L* (1218)	*1,10,13
755	____.			
	1971	113b	*Music and Music Literature, L-Z+* (4059)	*1,10,13
756	____.			
	1972	114a	*Music and Music Literature* (1031)	*1,11,13
757	____.			
	1973	114b	*Pianoforte and Vocal Scores* (1902)	*1,10,13
758	____.			
	1973	115	*Music and Music Literature, A-I* (1025)	*1,10,13
759	____.			
	1974	115a	*Music and Music Literature, I-Z* (2137)	*1,10,13
760	____.			
	1975	116	*Music and Music Literature* (847)	*1,10,13
761	____.			
	1975	117	*Orchestral Materials. Full Scores, etc.* (1070)	*1,10
762	____.			
	1976	119	*Rare, o-o-p and Antiquarian Items* (931)	*1,10
763	____.			
	1977	120	*Books on Music, H-M* (1583)	*1,10
764	____.			
	1977	121	*Books on Music, M-S* (2379)	*1,10,12
765	____.			
	1978	122	*Books on Music, S-Z* (2957)	*1,10,13
766	____.			
	1978	123	*Rare, o-o-p and Antiquarian Vocal Music* (998)	*1,10
767	____.			
	1979	124	*Music Lit. Vocal Scores. Spanish Music* (925)	*1
768	____.			
	1980	125	*Piano-Vocal and Full Scores of Operas* (1469)	*1

1 Compiler/State University of New York (Buffalo)   2 The British Library (London)   3 Gemeentemuseum (Den Haag)   4 The Grolier Club (N.Y.C.)   5 Hirsch Collection, British Library (London)   6 D.W. Krummel (Urbana)   7 Library of Congress (Washington, D.C.)   8 Library and Museum of the Performing Arts (N.Y.C.)   9 William Reeves (London)   10 Sibley Library, Eastman School of Music (Rochester)   11 Nigel Simeone (Tunbridge Wells, Kent)   12 Vereeniging ter Bervordering van de Belangen des Boekhandels (Amsterdam)   13 University of Virginia (Charlottesville)   14 University of California at Los Angeles   15 Generally available

769 **CULTURA (Ft. Worth Texas) (continued)**
     1982   126   *Vocal and Full Scores of Opera, etc.*
                              (1001)   *1

770 **DABNEY, Q. M. (Washington, D. C.)**
     1975   75/1   *Old, Used, Rare and o.p. Books on Music*
                              (208)   *1,12,13

771 _____.
     1975   75/4   *Old, Used, Rare and o.p. Books on Music*
                              (154)   *12

772 _____.
     1976   156   *Old, Used, Rare and o.p. Books on Music*
                              (386)   *1,8

773 _____.
     1977   169   *Old, Used, Rare and o.p. Books on Music*
                              (449)   *1,8,13

774 **DAMKÖHLER, R.**
     1840?   4   *[Music]*
                                                                              *5

775 **DANCE MART (Brookln, N. Y.)**
     1981-82   —   *Rare Bks. Jls. Autogrs. relating to Dance*
                              (17pp.)   *1

776 **DANNAPEL, E. (Dresen)**
     s.d.   Liste 164   *Musik.2. Folge, Mi-Z*
                              (165)   *5

777 **DAUBER & PINE BOOKSHOP (N.Y.C.)**
     [1933]   139   *Books on Violins. Music BOOKS*
                              (?)   *7

778 **DAVIDTS (Paris?)**
     1763   —   *Coll: Boissiere, P. de la*
                                                                [Pincherle:438]

779 **DAWSON RARE BOOKS (London)**
     1980   279   *Rare Books on Music, Theatre and Dance*
                              (297)   *8,11,12

780 **DEIBLER, J. (Vienna)**
     1919?   8   *Coll: unnamed. Musikalien. Erstausgaben*
                              (1231)   *4

781 **DEKKER & NORDEMANN (Amsterdam)**
     1974   List   11   *Coll: Fokker, A. D. Music Theory & History*
                              (35)   *1,8

782 _____.
     1976   do.   25   *Fine Arts - Music*
                              (35)   *1,8

783 _____.
     1976   do.   31   *Fine Arts. Illustrated Books. Music*
                              (117-45)   *1,13

784 _____.
     1977   do.   36   *Music*
                              (23)   *1,8,13

1 Compiler/State University of New York (Buffalo) **2** The British Library (London) **3** Gemeentemuseum (Den Haag) **4** The Grolier Club (N.Y.C.) **5** Hirsch Collection, British Library (London) **6** D.W. Krummel (Urbana) **7** Library of Congress (Washington, D.C.) **8** Library and Museum of the Performing Arts (N.Y.C.) **9** William Reeves (London) **10** Sibley Library, Eastman School of Music (Rochester) **11** Nigel Simeone (Tunbridge Wells, Kent) **12** Vereeniging ter Bervordering van de Belangen des Boekhandels (Amsterdam) **13** University of Virginia (Charlottesville) **14** University of California at Los Angeles **15** Generally available

785 DEKKER & NORDEMANN (Amsterdam) (continued)
    1978   do.   50   *Old and Rare Books ... Musical Literature*
                             (325-43)   *1
786 DE KORNE, HENRI see KORNE, HENRI DE

787 DETKEN & ROCHOLL
    1928   11   *Musica e musicisti*
                           (56pp.)   [Ganley:31]
788 DETLOFF, C. (Basel)
    1875   17   *Belletristik. Kunst. Musik*
                                                  *12
789 _____.
    18   79   *31 Ausserd. Belletristik. Kunst. Musik*
                                                  *12
790 DEUTSCHER BUCH- EXPORT UND -IMPORT, GMBH (Leipzig)
    1968   2   *Musik- Theater*
                           (48pp.)   *8
791 DICHTER, HARRY, MUSICAL AMERICANA (Atlantic City, N.J.)
    1973   10   *Songs and Music*
                           (380)   *6
792 DOBLINGER, L., MUSIKANTIQUARIAT (Vienna)
    196-   [1]   *First & Earliest Printings of Haydn, Mozart*
                           (34pp.)   *1,6,8
793 _____.
    1968   34   *Klaviermusik, vier, sechs und acht Händen*
                         (34pp.)   *8
794 _____.
    1968   35   *Antiquarische-Musikbücher [und Musik]*
                         (2113)   *8
795 _____.
    1974   41   *Klavierauszüge*
                         (16pp.)   *8
796 _____.
    9/1974   —   *Einmaliges Angebot*
                         (6pp.)   *8
797 _____.
    1980   42   *Musik. Faksimiles*
                         (328+21)   *12
798 DÖRFFEL, FELIX (Darmstadt)
    1960   21   *Autographen. Musik und Theater*
                         (189)   [IBAK]
799 _____.
    1962   27   *Autographen. Musik und Theater*
                       (124)   [IBAK]
800 _____.
    1963   33   *Coll: Feith. 2.Abth., Musik und Theater*
                       (?)   [IBAK]

---

1 Compiler/State University of New York (Buffalo)   2 The British Library (London)   3 Gemeentemuseum (Den Haag)   4 The Grolier Club (N.Y.C.)   5 Hirsch Collection, British Library (London)   6 D.W. Krummel (Urbana)   7 Library of Congress (Washington, D.C.)   8 Library and Museum of the Performing Arts (N.Y.C.)   9 William Reeves (London)   10 Sibley Library, Eastman School of Music (Rochester)   11 Nigel Simeone (Tunbridge Wells, Kent)   12 Vereeniging ter Bervordering van de Belangen des Boekhandels (Amsterdam)   13 University of Virginia (Charlottesville)   14 University of California at Los Angeles   15 Generally available

801	**DÖRFFEL, FELIX (Darmstadt) (continued)**			
	1963	36	*Autogr aphen. Dichter ... Musiker*	
			(47)	[IBAK]
802	_____.			
	1964	39	*Autographen. Dichter ... Musiker*	
			(40)	[IBAK]
803	_____.			
	1964	40	*Coll: Scholz, K. W. Autographen*	
			(40)	[IBAK]
804	_____.			
	1964	41	*Coll: Haeberlin*	
			(52)	[IBAK]
805	_____.			
	1965	[43]	*Autographen. Musik und Theater*	
			(32)	[IBAK]
806	_____.			
	1965	45	*Coll: Tischer & Jagenberg*	
			(23)	[IBAK]

807 **DOERLING, F. (Hamburg)**
1931?   108   *Musikgeschichte. Theorie. Praktische Musik*
                                                        *5,8,10,13

808 **DONALD, W. (West Kirby, U. K.)**
[193-?]   *Engraved Music, mostly of the 18th Century*
                   (2pp.)   *13

809 **DORBON, LUCIEN (Paris)**
s.d.   639   *Coll: Prod'homme. Théâtre. Musique. Danse*
                   (1625)   *1,13

810	**DRESDNER ANTIQUARIAT**			
	[1960]	220	*Bildende Kunst. Musik. Tanz. Theater*	
			(524)	[IBAK]
811	_____.			
	1962	247	*Bilden de Kunst. Musik. Tanz. Theater*	
			(667)	[IBAK]
812	_____.			
	1962	301	*Kunst/Musik/Tanz/Theater*	
			(609)	[IBAK]
813	_____.			
	1963	308	*Kunst-, Musik- und Theaterwissenschaft*	
			(597)	[IBAK]
814	_____.			
	1963	318	*Kunst - Musik - Theater*	
			(609)	[IBAK]
815	_____.			
	[1964]	323	*Kunst - Musik - Theater*	
			(452)	[IBAK]
816	_____.			
	[1964]	330	*Kunst - Musik - Theater*	
			(551)	[IBAK]

1 Compiler/State University of New York (Buffalo)   **2** The British Library (London)   **3** Gemeentemuseum (Den Haag)   **4** The Grolier Club (N.Y.C.)   **5** Hirsch Collection, British Library (London)   **6** D.W. Krummel (Urbana)   **7** Library of Congress (Washington, D.C.)   **8** Library and Museum of the Performing Arts (N.Y.C.)   **9** William Reeves (London)   **10** Sibley Library, Eastman School of Music (Rochester)   **11** Nigel Simeone (Tunbridge Wells, Kent)   **12** Vereeniging ter Bervordering van de Belangen des Boekhandels (Amsterdam)   **13** University of Virginia (Charlottesville)   **14** University of California at Los Angeles   **15** Generally available

817 **DRESDNER ANTIQUARIAT** (continued)
    [1965]   339   *Kunst - Musik - Theater*
                                (640)   [IBAK]

818   _____.
    [1966]   352   *Kunst - Musik - Theater*
                                (649)   [IBAK]

819 **DRÜNER, ULRICH**(Stuttgart)
    4/1983   List   1   *Alte Musikdrucke des 18. Jahrhunderts*
                                (105)   *15

820   _____.
    5/1983   do.   2   *Musikdrucke des l0. Jahrhunderts*
                                (228)   *15

821   _____.
    2/1984   do.   3   *Musique ancienne. Mss. Autographs. Bücher*
                                (228)   *15

822   _____.
    3/1984   do.   4   *Musik d. l9. Jhdts. (Klavier. Orgel. Opern)*
                                (458)   *15

823   _____.
    6/1984   do.   5   *M.drucke u. M.bücher d. l8. u. l9. Jhdts.*
                                (259)   *15

824   _____.
    12/1984   do.   6   *Musique ancienne: Mss. Autogr. Bücher...*
                                (250)   *15

825   _____.
    12/1984   do.   7   *Musik des l9. Jahrhunderts*
                                (278)   *15

826 **DUNK, J. H. (Rotterdam)**
    1872   —   *Coll: Broedelet, H. W., et al*
                                (pp.128-34)   *12

827   _____.
    1904   —   *Coll: de Ridder, H. H., Jr.*
                                (pp.181-206)   *12

828 **DUNNEBEIL, HANS (Brlin)**
    s.d.   —.   *Coll: Fleischer, Oskar. [Music & Music Lit.]*
                                (ca.800)   *8

829 **DUWAER & NAESSENS (Amsterdam)**
    s.d.   —   *Fransche Muziek*
                                (?)   *12

830 **EASTMA N, HARLAN H. (Springvale, Maine)**
    1/1983   —   *Pre-Ci vil War Sheet Music*
                                (165)   *1

831 **EATON, PETER (Weedon, Aylesbury)**
    19__   —   *Music and Art*
                                (1-526)   *10

832 **ECKE, GEORG (Berlin)**
    s.d.   238   *Biographie. Prakt. u. theoret. Musik. Autogr.*
                                (681)   *1,8

---

1 Compiler/State University of New York (Buffalo)   **2** The British Library (London)   **3** Gemeentemuseum (Den Haag)   **4** The Grolier Club (N.Y.C.)   **5** Hirsch Collection, British Library (London)   **6** D.W. Krummel (Urbana)   **7** Library of Congress (Washington, D.C.)   **8** Library and Museum of the Performing Arts (N.Y.C.)   **9** William Reeves (London)   **10** Sibley Library, Eastman School of Music (Rochester)   **11** Nigel Simeone (Tunbridge Wells, Kent)   **12** Vereeniging ter Bervordering van de Belangen des Boekhandels (Amsterdam)   **13** University of Virginia (Charlottesville)   **14** University of California at Los Angeles   **15** Generally available

833 **EDELMANN, MORITZ (Nuremburg)**
     s.d.   2   *Kultur - und Sittengeschichte*
                                                                     *1

834 _____.
     1901?   4   *Coll: Auberlen, Ad. Minnesang u. Meistersang*
                          (2122)   *4,8,12

835 _____.
     s.d.   *Alte und neue Musik. Lied*
                          (1107)   *10,12

836 **EDWARDS, F. (London)**
     1921   417   *Painting. Music. Drama*
                                                               *1

837 **EDWARDS, H. E. (Camarillo, CA.)**
     197-   V-K.   *Books on Music*
                          (1339)   *1

838 _____.
     1978?   U-L   *Books on Music*
                          (195)   *1

839 **EGGERT, WILHELM (Berlin)**
     s.d.   1   *Musik. Bücher und Zeitschriflen*
                          (678)   *9

840 _____.
     s.d.   17   *Musik*
                          (277)   *12

841 **ELLIS, MESSRS. (London)**
     s.d.   ?   *Music Ser. 4: Rare old String Music*
                          (133)   *1,12

842 _____.
     s.d.   ?   *Music Ser. 7: Old Song Books*
                          (140)   *3,12

843 _____.
     s.d.   197   *Music Ser. 22:Rare Books and Mss.*
                          (307)   *4,12

844 _____.
     s.d.   207   *Music Ser.23: Rare Bks. English Songs Books*
                          (387)   *1,4,8,12

845 _____.
     s.d.   217   *Music Ser. 24:Rare Books and Manuscripts*
                          (349)   *1,4,12

846 _____.
     1925   233   *Music Ser.25: Books ... including Rarities*
                          (307)   *1,3,4,12,13

847 _____.
     1928   258   *Music Ser. 26:Rare Books and Manuscripts*
                          (314)   * *1,4,12,13

848 _____.
     1929?   269   *Italian Art. Manuscripts [including Music]*
                          (100-141)   *4,13

---

1 Compiler/State University of New York (Buffalo)   **2** The British Library (London)   **3** Gemeentemuseum (Den Haag)   **4** The Grolier Club (N.Y.C.)   **5** Hirsch Collection, British Library (London)   **6** D.W. Krummel (Urbana)   **7** Library of Congress (Washington, D.C.)   **8** Library and Museum of the Performing Arts (N.Y.C.)   **9** William Reeves (London)   **10** Sibley Library, Eastman School of Music (Rochester)   **11** Nigel Simeone (Tunbridge Wells, Kent)   **12** Vereeniging ter Bervordering van de Belangen des Boekhandels (Amsterdam)   **13** University of Virginia (Charlottesville)   **14** University of California at Los Angeles   **15** Generally available

849   **ELLIS, MESSRS. (London) (continued)**

	1930	277	*Rare old Music ... charming English Pieces* (222)	*1,4,8,10
850	1930	—	*Music 30* (138)	*4,10
851	1931	281	*Old & Rare Books & Mss. relating to Music* (279)	*1,4,8,10
852	1932	287	*Old & Rare Books & Mss. relating to Music* (262)	*1,4,8,10,12
853	1932	293	*_____. Supplement of Engraved Portraits* (238)	*1,4,8,10,12
854	1933	297	*Rare old Music and a few ALS* (242)	*1,8,10,12,13
855	1933	301	*Rare old Music.* (223)	*1,4,8,10,13
856	1934	304	*Liturgical and Devotional Books* (197)	*12
857	1934	307	*... sundry choice, but inexpensive Pieces* (253)	*1,8,9,10,12
858	1934	311	*Catalogue of Music* (445)	*10,13
859	1935	319	*Choice and Rare Music* (138)	*1,9,10,12
860	1935	324	*Coll: Willmott, Miss. Rare old Music* (124)	*1,7,13
861	1936	330	*Old and Rare Music* (186)	*1,9,10,13
862	1936	331	*Manuscript Material* (171-99)	*13
863	]1936	336	*Music* (362)	*7,10,12,13
864	1936	339	*Old English Songs and Songbooks. Rare Books* (635)	*13

1 Compiler/State University of New York (Buffalo)   **2** The British Library (London)   **3** Gemeentemuseum (Den Haag)   **4** The Grolier Club (N.Y.C.)   **5** Hirsch Collection, British Library (London)   **6** D.W. Krummel (Urbana)   **7** Library of Congress (Washington, D.C.)   **8** Library and Museum of the Performing Arts (N.Y.C.)   **9** William Reeves (London)   **10** Sibley Library, Eastman School of Music (Rochester)   **11** Nigel Simeone (Tunbridge Wells, Kent)   **12** Vereeniging ter Bervordering van de Belangen des Boekhandels (Amsterdam)   **13** University of Virginia (Charlottesville)   **14** University of California at Los Angeles   **15** Generally available

865 **ELLIS, MESSRS. (London) (continued)**

	1937	342	... *Books and Mss. of musical Interest* (624)	*1,7,10,13
866	_____.			
	1937	344	*Mss., Books, Portraits of Musical Interest* (449)	*10
867	_____.			
	1937	346	*Rare Books, some of Musical Interest* (121-64)	*7,10,12
868	_____.			
	1938	351	*Rare Books, some of Musical Interest* (102-24)	*13
869	_____.			
	1940	347c	*Rare Musical Works. Collections of Songs* (79)	*10,13
870	_____.			
	194_?	352	*Catalogue of Rare Books and Music.* (64-97)	*10

871 **ELLIS & ELVEY and ELLIS & WHITE (London)**

	s.d.	37	*Books. Manuscripts. Madrigals. Rare Music* (429-54)	*4
872	_____.			
	1883?	52	... *including Mozart Autographs* (397-98)	*4
873	_____.			
	[1897]	85	*Rare Books on Music* (381-618)	*4
874	_____.			
	1897	87	*Choice Books. Rare Books on Music* (1195)	*9,12
875	_____.			
	1900	IV	*Art and Science of Music* (589)	*8,12
876	_____.			
	1902	VI	*Books Relating to Music.Portraits. ALS* (553)	*4,8,9,12
877	_____.			
	1903	100	... *including Books on Music* (383-544)	*4,12
878	_____.			
	1905	VII	*Pt.I: A-Pow (Portion of J. Marshall Coll.)* (868)	*4,9
879	_____.			
	1906	VIII	*Pt.II: Pont-Zarl. ALS. Mss. Portraits* (872-1992)	*4,8,9
880	_____.			
	1907	IX	*Pt.III: Engravings & Prints. Books & Music* (1993-2630)	*4,9

1 Compiler/State University of New York (Buffalo) **2** The British Library (London) **3** Gemeentemuseum (Den Haag) **4** The Grolier Club (N.Y.C.) **5** Hirsch Collection, British Library (London) **6** D.W. Krummel (Urbana) **7** Library of Congress (Washington, D.C.) **8** Library and Museum of the Performing Arts (N.Y.C.) **9** William Reeves (London) **10** Sibley Library, Eastman School of Music (Rochester) **11** Nigel Simeone (Tunbridge Wells, Kent) **12** Vereeniging ter Bervordering van de Belangen des Boekhandels (Amsterdam) **13** University of Virginia (Charlottesville) **14** University of California at Los Angeles **15** Generally available

881 **ELLIS & ELVEY and ELLIS & WHITE (London) (continued)**
    1908   X   *Rare Books relating to Music*
                           (490)   *4,9

882 _____.
    1909   XI   *Rare Books relating to Music*
                           (414)   *4,9

883 _____.
    1910   XII   *Rare Books relating to Music*
                           (469)   *4,9

884 _____.
    1911   XIII   *Rare Books on Music. Compositions. Psalms*
                           (512)   *4

885 _____.
    1911   138   *Mss. Illustrated Books. Musical Mss.*
                           (86-199 and i.a   .)*4

886 _____.
    1912   XIV   *Rare Books relating to Music*
                           (470)   *4

887 _____.
    1913   XV   *Rare Books relating to Music*
                           (452)   *4,9

888 _____.
    1913   XVI   *Musical Books and Mss.*
                           (454)   *4,9,13

889 _____.
    1914   XVII   *Rare Books on Music. Music. Wagner*
                           (472)   *4,13

890 _____.
    1915   XVIII   *Rare Books on Music. Music*
                           (453)   *4

891 _____.
    1916   XIX   *Rare Books.. Music. Printings of Handel*
                           (459)   *4,13

892 _____.
    1917   XX   *Rare Books on Music, Printed and Mss. Music*
                           (420)   *4,13

893 _____.
    1918   XXI   *Coll: Cummings, W.H. Rare Bks. & Mss. Music*
                           (619)   *4

894 _____.
    1921?   225   *Rare Books and Mss. [including Music]*
                           (167-89)   *4

895 **ELSBERG, DOROTHY (West Stockbridge, Massachusetts)**
    1977   List   1   *Music Literature*
                           (104)   *1,14

896 _____.
    1977   do.   2   *idem.*
                           (103,   *8

---

1 Compiler/State University of New York (Buffalo)   2 The British Library (London)   3 Gemeentemuseum (Den Haag)   4 The Grolier Club (N.Y.C.)   5 Hirsch Collection, British Library (London)   6 D.W. Krummel (Urbana)   7 Library of Congress (Washington, D.C.)   8 Library and Museum of the Performing Arts (N.Y.C.)   9 William Reeves (London)   10 Sibley Library, Eastman School of Music (Rochester)   11 Nigel Simeone (Tunbridge Wells, Kent)   12 Vereeniging ter Bervordering van de Belangen des Boekhandels (Amsterdam)   13 University of Virginia (Charlottesville)   14 University of California at Los Angeles   15 Generally available

897   **ELSBERG, DOROTHY (West Stockbridge, Massachusetts) (continued)**

	1978	do.	3	*idem.*	
				(119)	*1,14
898	_____.				
	1979	do.	4	*idem.*	
				(156)	*1
899	_____.				
	1979	do.	5	*idem.*	
				(160)	*1
900	_____.				
	1980	do.	6	*idem.*	
				(212)	*1
901	_____.				
	1980	do.	7	*idem.*	
				(168)	*1
902	_____.				
	1980	do.	9	*idem.*	
				(133)	*1
903	_____.				
	1980	do.	10	*idem.*	
				(137)	*1
904	_____.				
	1981	do.	11	*idem.*	
				(176)	*1,8
905	_____.				
	1981	do.	12	*idem.*	
				(115)	*1
906	_____.				
	1981	do.	13	*idem.*	
				(173)	*1
907	_____.				
	1982	do.	14	*idem.*	
				(165)	*15
908	_____.				
	1982	do.	15	*idem.*	
				(152)	*15
909	_____.				
	2/1983	do.	16	*idem.*	
				(287)	*15
910	_____.				
	9/1983	do.	17	*idem.*	
				(293)	*15
911	_____.				
	2/1984	do.	18	*idem.*	
				(171)	*15
912	_____.				
	6/1984	do.	19	*idem.*	
				(180)	*15

1 Compiler/State University of New York (Buffalo)   **2** The British Library (London)   **3** Gemeentemuseum (Den Haag)   **4** The Grolier Club (N.Y.C.)   **5** Hirsch Collection, British Library (London)   **6** D.W. Krummel (Urbana)   **7** Library of Congress (Washington, D.C.)   **8** Library and Museum of the Performing Arts (N.Y.C.)   **9** William Reeves (London)   **10** Sibley Library, Eastman School of Music (Rochester) **11** Nigel Simeone (Tunbridge Wells, Kent)   **12** Vereeniging ter Bervordering van de Belangen des Boekhandels (Amsterdam)   **13** University of Virginia (Charlottesville)   **14** University of California at Los Angeles   **15** Generally available

913 **ELTE, MEYER (La Haye)**
  10/1930   19   *Beaux-arts*
          (784-838)   *10

914 **ENAULT, LIBRAIRIE GABRIEL (Paris)**
  12/1950   —   *Musique*
          (30pp.)   *8

915 **ENGEL, GABRIEL (N.Y.C.)**
  1957   29   *First Editions including Music*
          (?)   *6

916 **EON (Exp., Nice)**
  1898   —   *Coll: Helminger, E.*
          (pp.1-51)   *3

917 **EPWORTH (London)**
  [1966]   —   *Music*
          (51)   [IBAK]

918 **ERASMUS ANTIQUARIAT (Amsterdam)**
  [1972]   288   *Books on Musicology*
          (647)   *12

919 **ERASMUSHAUS. HAUS DER BÜCHER AG see HAUS DER BÜCHER**

920 **EVANGELISCHE BUCHHANDLUNG see MÜLLER, MAX**

921 **FAUSTUS (London)**
  1974   60   *Periodicals. Theater.. Music & Literature*
          (67, i.a.)   *8

922 **FELDMAN, THEODORE (N.Y.C.)**
  1948   70   *Music and Music Biography. Opera*
          (369)   *8

923 _____.
  1949   74   *Theatrical Books. Ballet. Bayreuth*
          (1077)   *1

924 _____.
  1954   92   *Music and Musical Literature*
          (323)   *8

925 **FENNING, J. O'D. (Dun Laoghaire, Eire)**
  1980   1   *Old Music, 1740-1830*
          (482)   *1,8,13

926 **FERROW, DAVID (Great Yarmouth, Norfolk)**
  1984   —   *Coll: Maine, Rev. Basil. Books on Music*
          (421)   *11

927 **FINZI (Milan)**
  1931   18   *Teatro e musica*
                   *7

928 **FIRST EDITION BOOKSHOP (London)**
  1934   12/1   *First Editions of Music by Great Composers*
          (135)   *6,10

1 Compiler/State University of New York (Buffalo) **2** The British Library (London) **3** Gemeentemuseum (Den Haag) **4** The Grolier Club (N.Y.C.) **5** Hirsch Collection, British Library (London) **6** D.W. Krummel (Urbana) **7** Library of Congress (Washington, D.C.) **8** Library and Museum of the Performing Arts (N.Y.C.) **9** William Reeves (London) **10** Sibley Library, Eastman School of Music (Rochester) **11** Nigel Simeone (Tunbridge Wells, Kent) **12** Vereeniging ter Bervordering van de Belangen des Boekhandels (Amsterdam) **13** University of Virginia (Charlottesville) **14** University of California at Los Angeles **15** Generally available

929 **FIRST EDITION BOOKSHOP** (London) (continued)

	11/1934	15/2	*First and Early Eds. ... by great Composers* (142)
930 ____.			
	2/1953	16/3	*French Music [Introd. by Calvocoressi]* (127)
931 ____.			
	3/1936	/4	*First Editions of Music. Russian Composers* (188)
932 ____.			
	1/1937	/5	*Brahms, Chopin, Wagner [etc.] - First Eds.* (252)
933 ____.			
	5/1937	25/6	*Handel. First and Early Editions* (155)
934 ____.			
	5/1937	25/6	*Suppl. to Catalogue 25 (the 6th of Music)* (24)
935 ____.			
	5/1937	/7	*Rare Music published in England* (175)
936 ____.			
	11/1937	/8	*Orchestral & Chamber Music. Scores & Parts* (445)
937 ____.			
	1939	34/10	*Music of the Last 100 Years* (248)
938 ____.			
	194-?	35/11	*Orchestral Scores and Parts* (824)
939 ____.			
	194-	36/12	*Orchestral Scores and Parts* (238)
940 ____.			
	194-	37/13	*Opera* (777)
941 ____.			
	5/1949	38/14	*Pianoforte Music* (759)
942 ____.			
	1950	39/15	*150 Years of Instrumental Music* (917)
943 ____.			
	1951	40/16	*Books on Music. Collected Editions* (511)
944 ____.			
	1951	41/17	*Instrumental Music, 18th Century. Haydn* (1008)

929: *10,13
930: *10,12
931: *10
932: *10
933: *10
934: *8
935: *10,11
936: *10
937: *10,11
938: *6,8,11
939: *8,11,13
940: *11
941: *10,11,13
942: *1,11
943: *1,11,12
944: *1,11

1 Compiler/State University of New York (Buffalo)   2 The British Library (London)   3 Gemeentemuseum (Den Haag)   4 The Grolier Club (N.Y.C.)   5 Hirsch Collection, British Library (London)   6 D.W. Krummel (Urbana)   7 Library of Congress (Washington, D.C.)   8 Library and Museum of the Performing Arts (N.Y.C.)   9 William Reeves (London)   10 Sibley Library, Eastman School of Music (Rochester)   11 Nigel Simeone (Tunbridge Wells, Kent)   12 Vereeniging ter Bervordering van de Belangen des Boekhandels (Amsterdam)   13 University of Virginia (Charlottesville)   14 University of California at Los Angeles   15 Generally available

945 **FIRST EDITION BOOKSHOP** (London) (continued)

	1952	42/18	*Vocal Music. The Wesleys* (913)	*1,11
946	_____.			
	1953	43/19	*Music Published by John Walsh* (313)	*1,8,11
947	_____.			
	1953	44/20	*Music for the Stage. Gilbert & Sullivan* (1034)	*1,8,11,13
948	_____.			
	1953	45/21	*Books on Music. Portraits. Collected Eds.* (526)	*1,8,13
949	_____.			
	1954	46/22	*Orchestral Music. Full Scores and Parts* (691)	*1,8,11,13
950	_____.			
	1954	47/23	*Musical Mss. Autograph Letters* (344)	*1,6,8,11,13
951	_____.			
	1954	48/24	*Books. Portraits. Song Books & Collections* (575)	*1,6,8,11,13
952	_____.			
	1955	49/25	*Pianoforte Music. Ballet. Dance* (635)	*1,6,8,11,13
953	_____.			
	1955	50/26	*18th Century Vocal Music. Sheet Music* (672)	*1,6,8,11,13
954	_____.			
	1955	51/27	*18th Century Instrumental Music* (610)	*1,6,8,11,13
955	_____.			
	1956	52/28	*Operas and Ballets, 1800-1950. Libretti* (549)	*1,6,8,11,13
956	_____.			
	1956	53/29	*Mozart* (150)	*1,11,13
957	_____.			
	1956	54/30	*Books on Music. Portraits & Collected Eds.* (594)	*1,6,8,11,13
958	_____.			
	1956	55/31	*Orchestral & Chamber Music, 1800-1950* (666)	*1,6,8,11,13
959	_____.			
	1957	56/32	*Three Centuries of Vocal Music, 1650-1950* (782)	*1,6,8,11,13
960	_____.			
	1957	57/33	*Instr.Music, 1680-1820. Ballet. Dance Music* (640)	*1,6,8,11,13

1 Compiler/State University of New York (Buffalo) **2** The British Library (London) **3** Gemeentemuseum (Den Haag) **4** The Grolier Club (N.Y.C.) **5** Hirsch Collection, British Library (London) **6** D.W. Krummel (Urbana) **7** Library of Congress (Washington, D.C.) **8** Library and Museum of the Performing Arts (N.Y.C.) **9** William Reeves (London) **10** Sibley Library, Eastman School of Music (Rochester) **11** Nigel Simeone (Tunbridge Wells, Kent) **12** Vereeniging ter Bervordering van de Belangen des Boekhandels (Amsterdam) **13** University of Virginia (Charlottesville) **14** University of California at Los Angeles **15** Generally available

961	**FIRST EDITION BOOKSHOP** (London) (continued)			
	1958	58/34	*Books on Music. Collected Editions* (708)	*1,6,8,11,13
962	_____.			
	1958	59/35	*Opera: Scores. Vocal Scores. Libretti* (699)	*1,6,8,11
963	_____.			
	1958	60/36	*Handel. Haydn* (32)	*1,6,8,11
964	_____.			
	1958	61/37	*Orchestral Scores & Parts, 1800-1950* (372)	*1,6,8,10,11
965	_____.			
	1958	62/38	*Rare Music, Morley to Stravinsky, 1595-1912* (386)	*1,6,8,11
966	_____.			
	1960	63/39	*Rare Books & Music, 1558-1917* (434)	*1,6,8,11,12
967	_____.			
	1961	64/40	*Four Centuries of Vocal Music* (568)	*1,6,8,10,11
968	_____.			
	1962	65/41	*Opera and Ballet* (900)	*1,6,8,10,12
969	_____.			
	1962	66/42	*Opera and Ballet [Suppl. to Catalogue 41]* (201)	*1,8,10,11
970	_____.			
	1962	67/43	*Rare Music, 17th-19th Centuries* (447)	*1,6,8,10,11
971	_____.			
	1963	68/44	*17th, 18th, 19th Century Books on Music* (367)	*1,6,8,10,11
972	_____.			
	1963	69/45	*Inexpensive Books on Music and the Cinema* (509)	*1,6,8,10,12
973	_____.			
	1963	70/46	*Orchestral Scores & Parts, 1800-1950* (381)	*1,6,8,10,11
974	_____.			
	1963	71/47	*100 Musical Rarities, 17th-19th Centuries* (100)	*1,6,8,10,12
975	_____.			
	1964	72/48	*Coll: Calvocoressi, M.D. Vocal Music* (544)	*1,6,8,10,12
976	_____.			
	1964	73/49	*Coll: Calvocoressi, M.D. Instrum. Music* (101)	*6,8,10,11,12

1 Compiler/State University of New York (Buffalo)   **2** The British Library (London)   **3** Gemeentemuseum (Den Haag)   **4** The Grolier Club (N.Y.C.)   **5** Hirsch Collection, British Library (London)   **6** D.W. Krummel (Urbana)   **7** Library of Congress (Washington, D.C.)   **8** Library and Museum of the Performing Arts (N.Y.C.)   **9** William Reeves (London)   **10** Sibley Library, Eastman School of Music (Rochester) **11** Nigel Simeone (Tunbridge Wells, Kent)   **12** Vereeniging ter Bervordering van de Belangen des Boekhandels (Amsterdam)   **13** University of Virginia (Charlottesville)   **14** University of California at Los Angeles   **15** Generally available

977 **FIRST EDITION BOOKSHOP (London) (continued)**

	1965	75/51	*Music for the Stage* (905)	*1,6,10,11,12
978	_____. 1965	76/52	*Recent Acquisitions [Books and Music]* (180)	*1,6,10,11,12
979	_____. 1965	77/53	*Pianoforte Music* (613)	*1,6,10,11,12
980	_____. 1966	78/54	*16th-19th Century Rare Books and Music* (292)	*1,6,10,11,12
981	_____. 1967	79/55	*Instr. Music of the 18th & 19th Centuries* (251)	*1,6,8,10,12
982	_____. 1967	80/56	*Opera & Ballet* (564)	*1,6,8,10,12
983	_____. 1967	81/57	*100 Rare & Interesting Items. Theory* (666)	*1,8,10,11,12
984	_____. 1968	82/58	*A Catalogue of Catalogues* (666)	*1,8,10,11,12
985	_____. 1968	83/59	*Music & Rare Books on Music* (257)	*1,6,8,10,12
986	_____. 1969	84/60	*Opera & Ballet* (467)	*1,6,8,10,12
987	_____. 1969	85/61	*Books (mostly Reference) on Music* (197)	*1,6,11,12
988	_____. 1969	86/62	*Instrumental Music* (506)	*1,6,8,10,12
989	_____. 1970	87/63	*Music Mss. ALS. Treatises* (312)	*1,6,8,10,12
990	_____. 1970	88/64	*Music for the Pianoforte* (528)	*1,6,8,10,12
991	_____. 1970	89/65	*18th Century Vocal & Instrumental Music* (70)	*1,6,8,10,12
992	_____. 1971	90/66	*Vocal Music, Sacred and Secular. Song Books* (364)	*1,10,12

1 Compiler/State University of New York (Buffalo)   **2** The British Library (London)   **3** Gemeentemuseum (Den Haag)   **4** The Grolier Club (N.Y.C.)   **5** Hirsch Collection, British Library (London)   **6** D.W. Krummel (Urbana)   **7** Library of Congress (Washington, D.C.)   **8** Library and Museum of the Performing Arts (N.Y.C.)   **9** William Reeves (London)   **10** Sibley Library, Eastman School of Music (Rochester) **11** Nigel Simeone (Tunbridge Wells, Kent)   **12** Vereeniging ter Bervordering van de Belangen des Boekhandels (Amsterdam)   **13** University of Virginia (Charlottesville)   **14** University of California at Los Angeles   **15** Generally available

993 **FIRST EDITION BOOKSHOP (London) (continued)**
        1971   91/67   *Opera*
                                     (341)   *1,8,10,11,12

994 _____.
        1972   92/68   *Recent Acquisitions*
                                     (300)   *1,11,12

995 _____.
        s.d.   List   [1]   *Operas*
                                     (110)   *11

996 _____.
        s.d.   do.   2   *Reference Books. Music*
                                     (116)   *11

997 _____.
        1/1960   do.   3   *Opera and Ballet*
                                     (199)   *11

998 _____.
        5/1960   do.   4   *Recent Acquisitions*
                                     (245)   *6,11

999 **FISCHBACHER, LIBRAIRIE (Paris)**
        1902   5   *Musique et théâtre*
                                     (16pp.)   *8,11

1000 _____.
        1909   —   *Guide de l'amateur: Musique. Musiciens*
                                     (60pp.)   *8

1001 _____.
        1914   —   *Ouvrages de littérature et critique musicale*
                                     (34pp.)   *8

1002 _____.
        1919   —   *Ouvrages de littérature et critique musicale*
                                     (?)   *8

1003 _____.
        1927   —   *Ouvrages sur la musique*
                                     (?)   *8

1004 _____.
        1928   —   `*Ouvrages sur la musique*
                                     (?)   *8

1005 _____.
        1931   —   *Ouvrages sur la musique*
                                     (?)   *8

1006 **FLETCHER, C. & I. K. (London)**
        8/1953   List   76   *Music List /mimeo/*
                                     (96)   *8

1007 **FLETCHER, IVAN KYRLE (London)**
        1936?   3   *Dance. Rare Books. ALS. Music. Programmes*
                                     (170)   *4

1008 _____.
        1939   10   *Coll: Birch-Reynardson, H. Old Music*
                                     (703)   *4,10

---

1 Compiler/State University of New York (Buffalo)   **2** The British Library (London)   **3** Gemeentemuseum (Den Haag)   **4** The Grolier Club (N.Y.C.)   **5** Hirsch Collection, British Library (London)   **6** D.W. Krummel (Urbana)   **7** Library of Congress (Washington, D.C.)   **8** Library and Museum of the Performing Arts (N.Y.C.)   **9** William Reeves (London)   **10** Sibley Library, Eastman School of Music (Rochester) **11** Nigel Simeone (Tunbridge Wells, Kent)   **12** Vereeniging ter Bervordering van de Belangen des Boekhandels (Amsterdam)   **13** University of Virginia (Charlottesville)   **14** University of California at Los Angeles   **15** Generally available

1009	**FLETCHER, IVAN KYRLE (London) (continued)**			
	1942!	38	*Music Books. Ballet. ALS. Engraved Music* (336)	*5,10
1010	_____.			
	1936	56	*History of Music. Opera. Ballet* (431)	*1,12,13
1011	_____.			
	1937	62	*Theatre. Books. Mss. Opera, Opera Prints* (1442-1822)	*4
1012	_____.			
	194-	71	*Old Music* ?	*5,6,8,10
1013	_____.			
	1946	100	*Rare Books. Mss. Maps. Music* (lot 12)	*4
1014	_____.			
	1946	117	*Dance*	*1
1015	_____.			
	1948?	124	*Music & Books relating to Music*	*5,9,10
1016	_____.			
	1950?	144	*Music & Dance* (603)	*1,5,9,10
1017	_____.			
	1950	150	*Rare Books. Mss. Maps. Music* (i.a.)	*4,10
1018	_____.			
	1952	153	*Dance. Rare Books* (351)	*1,8
1019	_____.			
	1952	154	*Music & Dance* (340)	*1,5,12
1020	_____.			
	1953	162	*History of Entertainment* (779)	*8,10,12
1021	_____.			
	1954	167	*Music. Ballet. Opera. Mozart* (450)	*1,5,8,9,12
1022	_____.			
	1955	171	*Theatre. Ballet. Opera* (370-474)	*10
1023	_____.			
	1957	180	*History of Entertainment* (385-541)	*10,12
1024	_____.			
	1958?	187	*History of Entertainment. Ballet. Opera* (354-541)	*1

1 Compiler/State University of New York (Buffalo)   **2** The British Library (London)   **3** Gemeentemuseum (Den Haag)   **4** The Grolier Club (N.Y.C.)   **5** Hirsch Collection, British Library (London)   **6** D.W. Krummel (Urbana)   **7** Library of Congress (Washington, D.C.)   **8** Library and Museum of the Performing Arts (N.Y.C.)   **9** William Reeves (London)   **10** Sibley Library, Eastman School of Music (Rochester) **11** Nigel Simeone (Tunbridge Wells, Kent)   **12** Vereeniging ter Bervordering van de Belangen des Boekhandels (Amsterdam)   **13** University of Virginia (Charlottesville)   **14** University of California at Los Angeles   **15** Generally available

1025   **FLETCHER, IVAN KYRLE (London) (continued)**

	1959	190	*Coll: Clarence, et al. Entertainment* (503)	*3,12
1026	_____. 1960	194	*History of Entertainment* (583)	*12
1027	_____. 1962	200	*History of Entertainment* (881)	*10,12,13
1028	_____. 1962	203	*A Theatrical Miscellany* (178-281)	*13
1029	_____. 1963	208	*Autographs. Rare Books. Music* (423)	*10,12
1030	_____. 1963	209	*History of Entertainment* (647)	*6,10,12
1031	_____. 1964	210	*Autographs. Books. Music. Prints* (311-86)	*8,12,13
1032	_____. 1964	213	*Autographs. Books. Music. Prints* (555)	*10,12,13
1033	_____. 1964	214	*History of Entertainment* (982)	*8,10,12,13
1034	_____. 1965	215	*Autographs. Rare Books. Music. Prints* (434)	*10,12,13
1035	_____. 1965	216	*Opera* (683)	*6,8,10,12,13
1036	_____. 1965	217	*Rare Books. Autographs. Music. Prints* (499)	*6,10,12
1037	_____. 1965	218	*Popular Entertainment* (757)	*6,10,12,13
1038	_____. 1966	219	*Autographs. Books. Music. Prints* (502)	*6,10,12,13
1039	_____. 1966	220	*Entertainments. Theatre. Opera. Dance* (506A-733)	*8
1040	_____. 1966	221	*Entertainments. Theatre. Opera. Dance* (629-760)	*8

1 Compiler/State University of New York (Buffalo)   **2** The British Library (London)   **3** Gemeentemuseum (Den Haag)   **4** The Grolier Club (N.Y.C.)   **5** Hirsch Collection, British Library (London)   **6** D.W. Krummel (Urbana)   **7** Library of Congress (Washington, D.C.)   **8** Library and Museum of the Performing Arts (N.Y.C.)   **9** William Reeves (London)   **10** Sibley Library, Eastman School of Music (Rochester)   **11** Nigel Simeone (Tunbridge Wells, Kent)   **12** Vereeniging ter Bevordering van de Belangen des Boekhandels (Amsterdam)   **13** University of Virginia (Charlottesville)   **14** University of California at Los Angeles   **15** Generally available

1041   **FLETCHER, IVAN KYRLE (London) (continued)**

	1967		224	*Entertainments. Theatre. Opera. Dance*
				(365-418) *8,13
1042 _____.				
	1967		225	*New Spirit in the Theatre, 1899-1930*
				(744-976) *13
1043 _____.				
	1967		227	*Books. Autographs. Music*
				(481)976) *12
1044 _____.				
	1968		228	*Entertainment*
				(387-548) *13
1045 _____.				
	1969		232	*Theatre of the 19th Century*
				(272-314,368-57 5) *13
1046 _____.				
	1971		233	*ALS. Mss. Drawings. Photos*
				(306) *13
1047 _____.				
	1972		234	*Entertainment*
				(319) *13
1048 _____.				
	1953	List	64	*Books on the Opera*
				(85) *8
1049 _____.				
	6/1953	do.	70	*Books about Music*
				(115) *8
1050 _____.				
	8/1953	do.	76	*Music-List [i.e. ALS!]*
				(93) *8
1051 _____.				
	3/1955	do.	98	*Theatre and other Forms of Entertainment*
				(208) *8
1052 _____.				
	1959	do.	184	*History of Entertainment*
				(212) *12
1053 _____.				
	1960	do.	187	*History of Entertainment*
				(246) *12
1054 _____.				
	1960	do.	188	*History of Entertainment*
				(269) *12
1055 _____.				
	1961	do.	193	*Theatre & Ballet*
				(137) *12
1056 ____.				
	1961	do.	194	*Theatre & Dance*
				(269) *12

1 Compiler/State University of New York (Buffalo)   **2** The British Library (London)   **3** Gemeentemuseum (Den Haag)   **4** The Grolier Club (N.Y.C.)   **5** Hirsch Collection, British Library (London)   **6** D.W. Krummel (Urbana)   **7** Library of Congress (Washington, D.C.)   **8** Library and Museum of the Performing Arts (N.Y.C.)   **9** William Reeves (London)   **10** Sibley Library, Eastman School of Music (Rochester)   **11** Nigel Simeone (Tunbridge Wells, Kent)   **12** Vereeniging ter Bervordering van de Belangen des Boekhandels (Amsterdam)   **13** University of Virginia (Charlottesville)   **14** University of California at Los Angeles   **15** Generally available

1057 **FLETCHER, IVAN KYRLE (London) (continued)**
      1962   do.   212   *History of Entertainment*
                                    (347)   *12

1058 ____.
      1962   do.   213   *History of Entertainment*
                                    (432)   *12

1059 ____.
      1962   do.   215   *History of Entertainment* (176) *12

1060 ____.
      1963   do.   217   *Opera Libretti* (235) *13

1061 ____.
      1963   do.   219   *Theatre & Dance* (163) *12

1062 ____.
      1964   do.   228   *History of Entertainment* (239) *12

1063 ____.
      1964   do.   230   *Ballet* (260) *12

1064 ____.
      1964   do.   231   *Ballet* (83) *12

1065 ____.
      2964   do.   233   *History of Entertainment* (328) *12

1066 ____.
      1965   do.   235   *History of Entertainment* (?) *12

1067 ____.
      1965   do.   237   *History of Entertainment* (?) *12

1068 ____.
      1965   do.   238   *History of Entertainment* (?) *12

1069 ____.
      1966   do.   244   *History of Entertainment* (374) *12

1070 ____.
      1967   do.   250   *History of Entertainment* (334) *6

1071 ____.
      1967   do.   253   *History of Entertainment* (336) *12

1072 ____.
      1969   do.   270   *History of Entertainment* (503) *12

1073	**FLINT, J. H. (Amsterdam)**					
	[1966]		170	*Fine Arts & Music*		
				(503)		*12
1074	**FOCK, GUSTAV (Leipzig)**					
	192_		546	*Bücher und Musikalien*		
				(1309)		*3,12
1075	_____.					
	192_		578	*Bücher und Musikalien*		
				(1058)		*12
1076	_____.					
	192_		578	*Bücher und Musikalien*		
				(1058)		*12
1077	_____.					
	1930?		589	*Musikwissenschaft*		
				(954)		*8
1078	_____.					
	1930		624	*Coll: Seidl, A. Musik. Theater*		
				(2493)		*1,5,8,10,13
1079	**FOG, DAN (Copenhagen)**					
	3/1959	Kat.	63	*Music Literature*		
				(392)		*6
1080	_____.					
	4/1959		64	*Folk Music*		
				(385)		*1
1081	_____.					
	9/1959		65	*Orchestral Scores and Sets*		
				(426)		*1
1082	_____.					
	10/1959		66	*Klaviermusik. Piano Music*		
				(924)		*1
1083	_____.					
	11/1959		67	*Musical Literature. Early Music Editions*		
				(211)		*8
1084	_____.					
	2/1960		68	*Oper und Operette*		
				(603)		*1,6
1085	_____.					
	2/1960		69	*Forlagskatalog*		
						*Fog
1086	_____.					
	2/1960		70	*Verlagskatalog. Danish Music*		
				(455)		*Fog
1087	_____.					
	3/1960	Essay	71	*Peter Heise ... Fortegnelse*		
						*Fog
1088	_____.					
	3/1960	Kat.	72	*Choral Music*		
				(755)		*1,6

1 Compiler/State University of New York (Buffalo)   **2** The British Library (London)   **3** Gemeentemuseum (Den Haag)   **4** The Grolier Club (N.Y.C.)   **5** Hirsch Collection, British Library (London)   **6** D.W. Krummel (Urbana)   **7** Library of Congress (Washington, D.C.)   **8** Library and Museum of the Performing Arts (N.Y.C.)   **9** William Reeves (London)   **10** Sibley Library, Eastman School of Music (Rochester) **11** Nigel Simeone (Tunbridge Wells, Kent)   **12** Vereeniging ter Bervordering van de Belangen des Boekhandels (Amsterdam)   **13** University of Virginia (Charlottesville)   **14** University of California at Los Angeles   **15** Generally available

1089 **FOG, DAN (Copenhagen) (continued)**

	5/1960		73	*Musikkatalog for biblioteker* (1404)	*Fog
1090	____.				
	2/1961		124	*Vocal Scores* (331)	*6
1091	____.				
	3/1961	Spec.	125	*Orchestral Scores and Materials* (?)	*Fog
1092	____.				
	4/1961	Cat.	126	*Ballet Music and Literature. Bournonville* (666)	*1,6
1093	____.				
	9/1961	Kat.	127	*Orgelmusik* (837)	*Fog
1094	____.				
	10/1961		128	*Vokal Kirkemusik. Vocal Church Music* (340)	*Fog
1095	____.				
	5?/1962	Spec.	131	*Instrumentalmusik. Vokalmusik. Periodica* (93)	*6
1096	____.				
	6/1962	Kat.	132	*Swedish Music and Music Literature* (172)	*Fog
1097	____.				
	9/1962		133	*Musik Lit. und Musik in Erst- u. Frühausg.* (229)	*1,6,10
1098	____.				
	10/1962		134	*Klavierpartituren, Erst- und Frühausgaben* (221)	*1,6,10
1099	____.				
	11/1962		135	*Kammermusik, Erst- und Frühausgaben* (389)	*1,6,8,10
1100	____.				
	1/1963		136	*Orchestra Materials. Full Scores. Varia* (478)	*1,6,10
1101	____.				
	2/1963		137	*Vocal Scores. Ballets in Piano Score* (612)	*Fog
1102	____.				
	9/1963		138	*Kirkemusik. Organ and Sacred Music* (591)	*1,6,8,10
1103	____.				
	10/1963		139	*Seltene Musikliteratur und Musikdrucke* (150)	*1,8,10
1104	____.				
	12/1963		140	*Musiklitteratur* (779)	*1,6,10

1 Compiler/State University of New York (Buffalo)   **2** The British Library (London)   **3** Gemeentemuseum (Den Haag)   **4** The Grolier Club (N.Y.C.)   **5** Hirsch Collection, British Library (London)   **6** D.W. Krummel (Urbana)   **7** Library of Congress (Washington, D.C.)   **8** Library and Museum of the Performing Arts (N.Y.C.)   **9** William Reeves (London)   **10** Sibley Library, Eastman School of Music (Rochester)   **11** Nigel Simeone (Tunbridge Wells, Kent)   **12** Vereeniging ter Bervordering van de Belangen des Boekhandels (Amsterdam)   **13** University of Virginia (Charlottesville)   **14** University of California at Los Angeles   **15** Generally available

1105 **FOG, DAN (Copenhagen) (continued)**
       2/1964   141   *Vocal and Pocket Scores*
                                 (490)   *1,6,10

1106 _____.
       3/1964   142   *Orchestral Materials. Full Scores*
                                 (450)   *1,6,10

1107 _____.
       5/1964   143   *Musikkatalog for Biblioteker*
                                 (2410)   *Fog

1108 _____.
       6/1964   144   *Books on Music. Full Scores*
                                 (188)   *1,6,10

1109 _____.
       9/1964   145   *Danish Music. Books. Scores*
                                 (395)   *1,6,10

1110 _____.
      10/1964   146   *Chamber Music, New and Old*
                                 (433)   *1,6,10

1111 _____.
      11/1964   147   *Svensk Musikhistorie, I*
                                 (284)   *1,6,10

1112 _____.
      11/1964   Spec.   148   *Music and Books on Music*
                                 (152)   *6

1113 _____.
      12/1964   Liste   149   *Operetten, Klavierauszüge*
                                 (186)   *Fog

1114 _____.
      12/1964   Kat.   150   *Svensk Musikhistorie, II. Vokalmusik*
                                 (303)   *1,6,10

1115 _____.
       1/1965   151   *Orchestral Materials. Full Scores*
                                 (210)   *1,6,10

1116 _____.
       2/1965   152   *Books on Music*
                                 (808)   *1,6,8,10

1117 _____.
       3/1965   153   *Dansk Kirke-, Skole- og Folkesang*
                                 (374)   *1,8,10

1118 _____.
       4/1965   154   *Sange med Klaver*
                                 (738)   *1,6,10

1119 _____.
       5/1965   155   *Carl Nielsen, 1865-1965*
                                 (260)   *Fog

1120 _____.
      11/1965   156   *Jean Sibelius, 186551965*
                                 (196)   *1,10

1 Compiler/State University of New York (Buffalo)   **2** The British Library (London)   **3** Gemeentemuseum (Den Haag)   **4** The Grolier Club (N.Y.C.)   **5** Hirsch Collection, British Library (London)   **6** D.W. Krummel (Urbana)   **7** Library of Congress (Washington, D.C.)   **8** Library and Museum of the Performing Arts (N.Y.C.)   **9** William Reeves (London)   **10** Sibley Library, Eastman School of Music (Rochester)   **11** Nigel Simeone (Tunbridge Wells, Kent)   **12** Vereeniging ter Bervordering van de Belangen des Boekhandels (Amsterdam)   **13** University of Virginia (Charlottesville)   **14** University of California at Los Angeles   **15** Generally available

1121   **FOG, DAN (Copenhagen) (continued)**
      6/1965   157   *Kammermusik*
                                  (365)   *1,6,10

1122   _____.
      8/1965   Liste   158   *Operetten. Klavierausz.*
                                    (183)   *6

1123   _____.
      8/1965   do.   159   *Operetten. Aufführungsmaterialen*
                                    (51)   *Fog

1124   _____.
      10/1965   do.   160   *Richard Wagner*
                                    (261)   *6

1125   _____.
      11/1965   do.   161   *Saertilbud til Biblioteker*
                                    (167)   *Fog

1126   _____.
      12/1965   Kat.   162   *Piano Solo*
                                    (207)   *6,10

1127   _____.
      1/1966   163   *Svensk Musikhistorie, III*
                                    (448)   *6,8

1128   _____.
      2/1966   Liste   164   *Musiklitteratur. Periodica*
                                    (169)   *6

1129   _____.
      3/1966   do.   165   *Musiklitteratur*
                                    (493)   *6

1130   _____.
      5/1965   Spec.   166   *Sonder-Offerte*
                                    (?)   *Fog

1131   _____.
      5/1966   do.   167   *Special Offer*
                                    (25)   *6

1132   _____.
                      Kat.   168   *[Not issued]*

1133   _____.
      5/1966   169   *Orchestral Materials. Full Scores*
                                    (284)   *Fog

1134   _____.
      9/1966   170   *Nordisk Musiklitteratur*
                                    (480)   *Fog

1135   _____.
      10/1966   171   *Nordisk Musik*
                                    (345)   *Fog

1136   _____.
      11/1966   Liste   172   *Bücher und Noten*
                                    (241)   *Fog

1 Compiler/State University of New York (Buffalo)   **2** The British Library (London)   **3** Gemeentemuseum (Den Haag)   **4** The Grolier Club (N.Y.C.)   **5** Hirsch Collection, British Library (London)   **6** D.W. Krummel (Urbana)   **7** Library of Congress (Washington, D.C.)   **8** Library and Museum of the Performing Arts (N.Y.C.)   **9** William Reeves (London)   **10** Sibley Library, Eastman School of Music (Rochester)   **11** Nigel Simeone (Tunbridge Wells, Kent)   **12** Vereeniging ter Bervordering van de Belangen des Boekhandels (Amsterdam)   **13** University of Virginia (Charlottesville)   **14** University of California at Los Angeles   **15** Generally available

1137	FOG, DAN (Copenhagen) (continued)				
	11/1966	do.	173	*Kammer-musik* (417)	*8
1138	____.				
	12/1966	do.	174	*Klavierpartituren* (378)	*8,13
1139	____.				
	1/1967	do.	175	*Chamber Music ... in unused First Editions* (102)	*13
1140	____.				
	1/1967	do.	176	*Orchestral Works - in unused First Editions* (431)	*13
1141	____.				
	2/1967	Spec.	177	*Niels Gade Compositions. Books* (76)	*Fog
1142	____.				
			178	*[Not issued]*	
1143	____.				
	3/1967	Liste	179	*Niels W. Gade* (234)	*6
1144	____.				
	4/1967	Kat.	180	*Musikliteratur. Denkmäler. Gesamtausgaben* (247)	*8,10
1145	____.				
	6/1967		181	*Musikliteratur* (632)	*1,6,10
1146	____.				
	9/1967		182	*Nordisk Musiklitteratur* (707)	*1,10
1147	____.				
	10/1967		183	*Orkestermusik* (596)	*1,6,10
1148	____.				
			184	*[Not issued]*	
1149	____.				
	2/1968		185	*Musikliteratur. Volks-Musik. Faksimileausg.* (491)	*1,8,10
1150	____.				
	2/1968	Liste	186	*Antiquaria. Für Kenner und Liebhaber* (54)	*1,6,8
1151	____.				
	4/1968	Kat.	187	*Nordisk Vokalmusik* (525)	*1,6,8,10
1152	____.				
	5/1968	Liste	188	*Musiklitteratur* (197)	* 1,6,8

1 Compiler/State University of New York (Buffalo)   2 The British Library (London)   3 Gemeentemuseum (Den Haag)   4 The Grolier Club (N.Y.C.)   5 Hirsch Collection, British Library (London)   6 D.W. Krummel (Urbana)   7 Library of Congress (Washington, D.C.)   8 Library and Museum of the Performing Arts (N.Y.C.)   9 William Reeves (London)   10 Sibley Library, Eastman School of Music (Rochester)   11 Nigel Simeone (Tunbridge Wells, Kent)   12 Vereeniging ter Bervordering van de Belangen des Boekhandels (Amsterdam)   13 University of Virginia (Charlottesville)   14 University of California at Los Angeles   15 Generally available

1153   **FOG, DAN (Copenhagen) (continued)**

1153	6/1968	Spec.	189	*Orchestermaterialien* (250)	*6,8

1153	6/1968	Spec.	189	*Orchestermaterialien* (250)	*6,8
1154 _____.	8/1968	Kat.	190	*Musical Literature. Bibliography. Berggreen* (352)	*6,8,10
1155 _____.	9/1968	Liste	191	*Classics of Russian Music* (412)	*6
1156 _____.	10/1968	do.	192	*Folkemusik* (220)	*6,8
1157 _____.	11/1968	do.	193	*Vocal Scores. Books on Music* (191)	*1,6
1158 _____.	11/1968	do.	194	*Nordisk Musik* (348)	*Fog
1159 _____.	12/1968	do.	195	*Vocal Scores. Opera* (215)	*1,6,8
1160 _____.	1/1969	do.	196	*Gesamtausgaben. Musikliteratur. Kataloge* (260)	*1,6,8
1161 _____.	3/1969	Kat.	197	*Musik i Skandinavien, Early and Rare* (1151)	*1,6,8,10
1162 _____.	5/1969	Liste	198	*Full and Vocal Scores* (444)	*1,6,10
1163 _____.	6/1969	do.	199	*Musikliteratur* (245)	*1,6,8
1164 _____.	6/1969	do.	200	*Full Scores and Orchestral Materials* (292)	*1
1165 _____.	6/1969	Spec.	201	*Musical Literature, Rare and o.p.* (105)	*1
1166 _____.	9/1969	Liste	202	*Musikliteratur* (989)	*1,6,8
1167 _____.	11/1969	do.	203	*First & Early Editions. Musical Literature* (137)	*6,8
1168 _____.	11/1969	Kat.	204	*Kammermusik* (419)	*1,6,8,10

1 Compiler/State University of New York (Buffalo)   **2** The British Library (London)   **3** Gemeentemuseum (Den Haag)   **4** The Grolier Club (N.Y.C.)   **5** Hirsch Collection, British Library (London)   **6** D.W. Krummel (Urbana)   **7** Library of Congress (Washington, D.C.)   **8** Library and Museum of the Performing Arts (N.Y.C.)   **9** William Reeves (London)   **10** Sibley Library, Eastman School of Music (Rochester) **11** Nigel Simeone (Tunbridge Wells, Kent)   **12** Vereeniging ter Bervordering van de Belangen des Boekhandels (Amsterdam)   **13** University of Virginia (Charlottesville)   **14** University of California at Los Angeles   **15** Generally available

1169 **FOG, DAN (Copenhagen) (continued)**

	12/1969	Liste	205	*Seltene Kammermusik* (56)	*Fog
1170 _____.					
	1/1970	do.	206	*100 musikalische Seltenheiten* (100)	*6
1171 _____.					
	2/1970	do.	207	*Ballet Rarities* (54)	*1,6,8
1172 _____.					
	3/1970	do.	208	*Vocal Scores in First and Early Editions* (322)	*1,6
1173 _____.					
	4/1970	do.	209	*Musikliteratur* (291)	*Fog
1174 _____.					
	5/1970	do.	210	*Musikliteratur* (495)	*1,6
1175 _____.					
	6/1970	do.	211	*Kammermusik, besonders 1900-1950* (297)	*1,13
1176 _____.					
	9/1970	do.	212	*Musikliteratur* (186)	*1
1177 _____.					
	11/1970	do.	213	*idem.* (1633)	*1,8,13
1178 _____.					
	12/1970	do.	214	*Vocal Scores* (420)	*1,8
1179 _____.					
	1/1971	do.	215	*Auserlesene Musikdrucke und Musikliteratur* (250)	*1,13
1180 _____.					
	2/1971	do.	216	*Full Scores* (578)	*1,8,13
1181 _____.					
	3/1971	do.	217	*Music for 2 Pianos, 4 Hands* (382)	*1,8,13
1182 _____.					
	4/1971	do.	218	*Orchestral Sets* (150)	*1,8
1183 _____.					
	5/1971	do.	219	*Classical Russian and Polish Music* (715)	*1,8,13
1184 _____.					
	6/1971	do.	220	*Church Music. Folk Music. Books* (324)	*1

1 Compiler/State University of New York (Buffalo)   2 The British Library (London)   3 Gemeentemuseum (Den Haag)   4 The Grolier Club (N.Y.C.)   5 Hirsch Collection, British Library (London)   6 D.W. Krummel (Urbana)   7 Library of Congress (Washington, D.C.)   8 Library and Museum of the Performing Arts (N.Y.C.)   9 William Reeves (London)   10 Sibley Library, Eastman School of Music (Rochester)   11 Nigel Simeone (Tunbridge Wells, Kent)   12 Vereeniging ter Bevordering van de Belangen des Boekhandels (Amsterdam)   13 University of Virginia (Charlottesville)   14 University of California at Los Angeles   15 Generally available

1185 **FOG, DAN (Copenhagen) (continued)**

	7/1971	do.	221	*Periodica. Bibliographie. Rara. Literatur* (422)	*1,13
1186 _____.					
	9/1971	do.	222	*Music for Cembalo - Clavier - Fortepiano* (258)	*8,13
1187 _____.					
	10/1971	Kat.	223	*Methods. Books on Music. Rara* (316)	*1,13
1188 _____.					
	10/1971	Liste	224	*Russian Music* (106)	*1,13
1189 _____.					
	11/1971	do.	225	*Orgel- og Kirkemusik* (104)	*Fog
1190 _____.					
	11/1971	do.	226	*Full Scores. Orchestral Sets* (125)	*1,8,13
1191 _____.					
	12/1971	do.	227	*Vocal Scores. Ballet. Early Editions. Books* (129)	*1,13
1192 _____.					
	1/1972	do.	228	*Violin-Music* (156)	*1,8,13
1193 _____.					
	2/1972	do.	229	*Kammermusik, alt und neu* (419)	*1,13
1194 _____.					
	2/1972	do.	230	*Vokalmusik [1800-1850]* (239)	*1,8,13
1195 _____.					
	3/1972	do.	231	*Le concert au salon. First & Early Editions* (266)	*1,8,13
1196 _____.					
	4/1972	do.	232	*Musiklitteratur* (148)	*Fog
1197 _____.					
	5/1972	do.	233	*Le pianiste au l9ème siècle* (574)	*1,8,13
1198 _____.					
	5/1972	do.	234	*Klavierpartitur - Vocal Scores* (311)	*8
1199 _____.					
	5/1972	do.	235	*Musicalia. Denkmäler. Gesamtausgaben* (235)	*8
1200 _____.					
	6/1972	do.	236	*Vocal Scores. Songs. Hymnals. Folk Songs* (196)	*Fog

1 Compiler/State University of New York (Buffalo) **2** The British Library (London) **3** Gemeentemuseum (Den Haag) **4** The Grolier Club (N.Y.C.) **5** Hirsch Collection, British Library (London) **6** D.W. Krummel (Urbana) **7** Library of Congress (Washington, D.C.) **8** Library and Museum of the Performing Arts (N.Y.C.) **9** William Reeves (London) **10** Sibley Library, Eastman School of Music (Rochester) **11** Nigel Simeone (Tunbridge Wells, Kent) **12** Vereeniging ter Bevordering van de Belangen des Boekhandels (Amsterdam) **13** University of Virginia (Charlottesville) **14** University of California at Los Angeles **15** Generally available

1201	FOG, DAN (Copenhagen) (continued)				
	7/1972	Kat.	237	Skandinavisk Musik. Rare Editions (546)	*1,13
1202	___.				
	?/1972	Cat.	—	Publications and Remainders (164)	*1
1203	___.				
	7/1972	Liste	238A	Russian Music (132)	*1,8,13
1204	___.				
	9?/1972	do.	238	Music for Viola (157)	*8
1205	___.				
	9?/1972	do.	239	[Not issued?]	
1206	___.				
	10/1972	Spec.	—	Special Offer (22)	*1,8,13
1207	___.				
	11/1972	Liste	240	Mixtum Compositum. First & Early Editions (175)	*1,8,13
1208	___.				
	12/1972	do.	241	Musiklitteratur (632)	*1,8,13
1209	___.				
	12/1972	do.	242	Franz Liszt. Piano Music in Early Editions (311)	*1,8,13
1210	___.				
	1/1973	do.	243	Vocal Scores in First and Early Editions (525)	*1,8,13
1211	___.				
	2/1973	do.	244	Elf Nordiske Komponister (710)	*1,8,13
1212	___.				
	3/1973	do.	245	Musicalia: a Strange Mixture (139)	*1,8,13
1213	___.				
	4/1973	do.	246	Volksmusik. Choralbücher. Liturgie (240)	*1,8,13
1214	___.				
	5/1973	Spec.	0573	Musikliteratur. Musikalier (130)	*1
1215	___.				
	5/1973	Liste	248	Musica Selecta (139)	*1,8,13
1216	___.				
	6/1973	Spec.	0673	Bach - Gade - Haydn - Mozart - etc. (49)	*1,8

1 Compiler/State University of New York (Buffalo)   2 The British Library (London)   3 Gemeentemuseum (Den Haag)   4 The Grolier Club (N.Y.C.)   5 Hirsch Collection, British Library (London)   6 D.W. Krummel (Urbana)   7 Library of Congress (Washington, D.C.)   8 Library and Museum of the Performing Arts (N.Y.C.)   9 William Reeves (London)   10 Sibley Library, Eastman School of Music (Rochester)   11 Nigel Simeone (Tunbridge Wells, Kent)   12 Vereeniging ter Bervordering van de Belangen des Boekhandels (Amsterdam)   13 University of Virginia (Charlottesville)   14 University of California at Los Angeles   15 Generally available

1217	**FOG, DAN (Copenhagen) (continued)**				
	6/1973	Liste	249	*Ballet. Opera. Theater. Books. Periodicals* (285)	*1,8,13
1218	____.				
	6/1973	do.	250	*Full Scores. Orchestral Sets* (285)	*1,8,13
1219	____.				
	8/1973	do.	251	*Study Scores* (427)	*1,8,13
1220	____.				
	9/1973	do.	252	*Music of the Nations. Folk Songs, etc.* (281)	*1,8,13
1221	____.				
	10/1973	do.	253	*Kammermusik* (306)	*1,8,13
1222	____.				
	11/1973	do.	254	*Chor-Musik* (517)	*1,8,13
1223	____.				
	11/1973	do.	255	*Violin & Piano* (298)	*1,8,13
1224	____.				
	1/1974	do.	256	*Organ Music. Books on Church Music* (466)	*1,8
1225	____.				
	2/1974	do.	257	*Vocal Scores* (339)	*1,8,13
1226	____.				
	3/1974	do.	258	*Musikliteratur. Anhang: Volksmusik. Instrs.* (1214)	*1,8,13
1227	____.				
	5/1974	do.	259	*Periodica. Bibliography* (348)	*1,13
1228	____.				
	5/1974	do.	260	*Libretti* (219)	*1,8,13
1229	____.				
	8/1974	do.	261	*Piano a 4 mains* (345)	*13
1230	____.				
	8/1974	do.	262	*Sange med klaver. Skandinaviske Komponister* (659)	*1,8,13
1231	____.				
	9/1974	do.	263	*Musikliteratur* (234)	*1,8,13
1232	____.				
	9/1974	do.	264	*Lieder und Gesänge* (400)	*1,8

1 Compiler/State University of New York (Buffalo)   2 The British Library (London)   3 Gemeentemuseum (Den Haag)   4 The Grolier Club (N.Y.C.)   5 Hirsch Collection, British Library (London)   6 D.W. Krummel (Urbana)   7 Library of Congress (Washington, D.C.)   8 Library and Museum of the Performing Arts (N.Y.C.)   9 William Reeves (London)   10 Sibley Library, Eastman School of Music (Rochester)   11 Nigel Simeone (Tunbridge Wells, Kent)   12 Vereeniging ter Bervordering van de Belangen des Boekhandels (Amsterdam)   13 University of Virginia (Charlottesville)   14 University of California at Los Angeles   15 Generally available

1233 **FOG, DAN (Copenhagen) (continued)**

	10/1974	do.	265	*Vocal Scores* (383)	*1,8,13
1234 _____.	12/1974	do.	266	*Musicalia. First and Early Editions* (179)	*1,8,13
1235 _____.	1/1975	do.	267	*Antiquaria* (252)	*1,8,13
1236 _____.	3/1975	do.	268	*Music Lit. Liturgy. Organ. Folk Music* (302)	*13
1237 _____.	6/1975	do.	269	*Musica Selecta. Early Eds. Vocal Scores* (164)	*1,8,13
1238 _____.	6/1975	do.	270	*Klaviermusik des l9ten Jahrhunderts* (462)	*1,8,13
1239 _____.	8/1975	do.	271	*Musiklit. Liturgie. Orgel. Zeitschriften* (1762)	*1,8,13
1240 _____.	9/1975	do.	272	*Musik til klassiske danske Digtere* (215)	*Fog
1241 _____.	9/1975	do.	273	*Kammermusik* (431)	*1,13
1242 _____.	10/1975	do.	274	*Musicalia. Instrumental Music* (272)	*1,8,13
1243 _____.	11/1975	do.	275	*Musikliteratur. Musik* (226)	*1,8,13
1244 _____.	12/1975	do.	276	*Chamber Music, Early Eds.Violin & Piano* (300)	*13
1245 _____.	1/1976	do.	277	*Study Scores* (738)	*1,8,13
1246 _____.	1/1976	do.	278	*Klavierauszüge* (426)	*8,13
1247 _____.	2/1976	Spec.	0276	*Foliopartiten* (157)	*8,13
1248 _____.	2/1976	do.	279	*Swedish Music (l9th Century)* (771)	*13

1 Compiler/State University of New York (Buffalo)   **2** The British Library (London)   **3** Gemeentemuseum (Den Haag)   **4** The Grolier Club (N.Y.C.)   **5** Hirsch Collection, British Library (London)   **6** D.W. Krummel (Urbana)   **7** Library of Congress (Washington, D.C.)   **8** Library and Museum of the Performing Arts (N.Y.C.)   **9** William Reeves (London)   **10** Sibley Library, Eastman School of Music (Rochester)   **11** Nigel Simeone (Tunbridge Wells, Kent)   **12** Vereeniging ter Bervordering van de Belangen des Boekhandels (Amsterdam)   **13** University of Virginia (Charlottesville)   **14** University of California at Los Angeles   **15** Generally available

1249 **FOG, DAN (Copenhagen) (continued)**

	3/1976	do.	280	*Klavierauszüge. Early Editions* (275) *8,13
1250 ____.	3/1976	do.	281	*Antiquaria. Early Music. Liturgy. Folkmusic* (184) *13
1251 ____.	3/1976	do..	0376	*Violin and Piano* (?) *Fog
1252 ____.	3/1976	Liste	280	*Klavierauszüge. Early Editions* (275) *8,13
1253 ____.	4/1976	do.	282	*Musikliteratur* (676) *Fog
1254 ____.	4/1976	Spec.	0476	*Kammermusik* (?) *Fog
1255 ____.	?/1976	Liste	283	*Full and Vocal Scores. Early Editions* (225) *1,13
1256 ____.	7/1976	do.	284	*Hymnals and Liturgy. Vocal Choral Music* (416) *1,8,13
1257 ____.	9/1976	do.	285	*Music Lit. Chmbr.Music, First & Early Eds.* (757) *1,8,13
1258 ____.	8/1976	Spec.	0876	*Violoncello and Piano* (267) *1,8,13
1259 ____.	9/1976	do.	286	*Musikliteratur* (167) *1,8,13
1260 ____.	10/1976	Liste	287	*Full Scores. Performing Materials* (851) *1,8,13
1261 ____.	11/1976	do.	288	*Chamber Music. Violin and Piano* (470) *1
1262 ____.	12/1976	do.	289	*Vocal Scores. Early Editions. Musiklit.* (271) *1,8,13
1263 ____.	12/1976	do.	290	*Vocal Scores* (351) *1,8
1264 ____.	2/1977	do.	291	*Musikliteratur. Early Eds. Vocal Scores* (404) *1,8,13

1 Compiler/State University of New York (Buffalo)   2 The British Library (London)   3 Gemeentemuseum (Den Haag)   4 The Grolier Club (N.Y.C.)   5 Hirsch Collection, British Library (London)   6 D.W. Krummel (Urbana)   7 Library of Congress (Washington, D.C.)   8 Library and Museum of the Performing Arts (N.Y.C.)   9 William Reeves (London)   10 Sibley Library, Eastman School of Music (Rochester) 11 Nigel Simeone (Tunbridge Wells, Kent)   12 Vereeniging ter Bervordering van de Belangen des Boekhandels (Amsterdam)   13 University of Virginia (Charlottesville)   14 University of California at Los Angeles   15 Generally available

1265 FOG, DAN (Copenhagen) (continued)
      3/1977   do.   292   *Sange med Klaver*
                            (747)   *1,8

1266 _____.
      4/1977   do.   293   *Coll: Unnamed. Musical Literature*
                            (497)   *1,8

1267 _____.
      4/1977   do.   294   *Selected Vocal Scores. Ballet Piano Scores*
                            (236)   *1

1268 _____.
      5/1977   do.   295   *Kammermusik*
                            (409)   *1,8,13

1269 _____.
      5/1977   do.   296   *Music for 2 Pianos, 4 Hands*
                            (447)   *1,8

1270 _____.
      7/1977   do.   297   *Kammermusik. Partituren.*
                            (342)   *1,8

1271 _____.
      9/1977   do.   298   *Musikliteratur. Liturgy. Organ. Instruments*
                            (2125)   *1

1272 _____.
      11/1977   do.   299   *Klaviermusik*
                            (600)   *1

1273 _____.
      11/1977   do.   300   *Russian Music*
                            (179)   *1,8

1274 _____.
      12/1977   do.   301   *Early Eds. Vocal Scores. Musikliteratur*
                            (224)   *1,8

1275 _____.
      1/1978   Kat.   302   *Musicus Danicus*
                            (811)   *1,10

1276 _____.
      2/1978   Liste   303   *Piano Duet. Organ Music*
                            (664)   *1

1277 _____.
      4/1978   do.   304   *Musikliteratur. Early Eds. Harp Music*
                            (1069)   *1,13

1278 _____.
      5/1978   do.   305   *Flute Music*
                            (345)   *1

1279 _____.
      6/1978   do.   306   *Violinmusik*
                            (?)   *Fog

1280 _____.
      6/1978   do.   307   *Full Scores. Vocal Scores*
                            (673)   *Fog

1 Compiler/State University of New York (Buffalo)   2 The British Library (London)   3 Gemeentemuseum (Den Haag)   4 The Grolier Club (N.Y.C.)   5 Hirsch Collection, British Library (London)   6 D.W. Krummel (Urbana)   7 Library of Congress (Washington, D.C.)   8 Library and Museum of the Performing Arts (N.Y.C.)   9 William Reeves (London)   10 Sibley Library, Eastman School of Music (Rochester)   11 Nigel Simeone (Tunbridge Wells, Kent)   12 Vereeniging ter Bervordering van de Belangen des Boekhandels (Amsterdam)   13 University of Virginia (Charlottesville)   14 University of California at Los Angeles   15 Generally available

1281	**FOG, DAN (Copenhagen) (continued)**				
	8/1978	do.	308	*First & Early Editions (mainly Flute Music)* (123)	*1
1282	_____.				
	10/1978	Kat.	309	*Vokalmusik* (509)	*1,10,13
1283	_____.				
	11/1978		310	*Musikliteratur. First and Early Editions* (610)	*1,10,13
1284	_____.				
	12/1978	Liste	311	*Kammermusik* (417)	*8
1285	_____.				
	12/1978	do.	312	*Music for Viola - Violoncello - Violin* (606)	*8
1286	_____.				
	12/1978	do.	313	*Norsk Musik* (900)	*1,8
1287	_____.				
	1/1979	do.	314	*Orgelmusik. Koralbøger. Litteratur.* (453)	*Fog
1288	_____.				
	1/1979	do.	315	*Musik. Musikliteratur* (660)	*1
1289	_____.				
	5/1979	do.	316	*Piano Music* (920)	*1,13
1290	_____.				
	6/1979	do.	317	*Musik. Musikliteratur* (1155)	*1
1291	_____.				
	6/1979	do.	318	*Vocal Scores. Early Editions* (909)	*1
1292	_____.				
			319	*[Not issued]*	
1293	_____.				
	9/1979	do.	320	*Kammermusik. Musik. Musikliteratur* (388)	*1
1294	_____.				
	10/1979	do.	321	*Full Scores. Performing Materials* (656)	*1
1295	_____.				
	11/1979	do.	322	*Musica Selecta, Fine & Rare. Early Eds.* (388)	*1,10,13
1296	_____.				
	11/1979	do.	323	*August Bournonville. Music and Libretti* (250)	*1

1 Compiler/State University of New York (Buffalo)   **2** The British Library (London)   **3** Gemeentemuseum (Den Haag)   **4** The Grolier Club (N.Y.C.)   **5** Hirsch Collection, British Library (London)   **6** D.W. Krummel (Urbana)   **7** Library of Congress (Washington, D.C.)   **8** Library and Museum of the Performing Arts (N.Y.C.)   **9** William Reeves (London)   **10** Sibley Library, Eastman School of Music (Rochester) **11** Nigel Simeone (Tunbridge Wells, Kent)   **12** Vereeniging ter Bervordering van de Belangen des Boekhandels (Amsterdam)   **13** University of Virginia (Charlottesville)   **14** University of California at Los Angeles   **15** Generally available

1297 **FOG, DAN (Copenhagen) (continued)**
    12/1979   do.   324   *British Music*
                           (340)   *1

1298 _____.
    1/1980   do.   325   *Musikliteratur*
                           (1988)   *1

1299 _____.
    3/1980   do.   326   *Autografe. Musiker Breve*
                           (471)   *1,13

1300 _____.
    4/1980   Spec.   —   *Orgelmusik*
                           (313)   *Fog

1301 _____.
    4/1980   Liste   327   *Piano Music, l9th Century*
                           (543)   *1

1302 _____.
    5/1980   do.   328   *Vocal Scores. Musikliteratur*
                           (468)   *1,13

1303 _____.
    5/1980   Spec.   —   *Dansk Romancer og Sange. Libretti*
                           (506)   *Fog

1304 _____.
    6/1980   Liste   329   *Music for 2 Pianos, 4 Hands*
                           (404)   *1

1305 _____.
    6/1980   do.   330   *Musikliteratur. Chamber Music*
                           (279)   *1

1306 _____.
    9/1980   do.   331   *Musik. Musikliteratur*
                           (590)   *1

1307 _____.
    9/1980   do.   332   *Klaviermusik*
                           (896)   *1

1308 _____.
    10/1980   Spec.   1080   *Deutsche topographische Musik*
                           (182)   *Fog

1309 _____.
    11/1980   Liste   333   *Music of Scandinavia*
                           (679)   *1

1310 _____.
    12/1980   do.   334   *Musik. Musikliteratur*
                           (498)   *1,13

1311 _____.
    12/1980   do.   335   *Study Scores*
                           (406)   *1

1312 _____.
    1/1981   Spec.   0181   *American Sheet Music from the 19th Century*
                           (177)   *1

1 Compiler/State University of New York (Buffalo)   **2** The British Library (London)   **3** Gemeentemuseum (Den Haag)   **4** The Grolier Club (N.Y.C.)   **5** Hirsch Collection, British Library (London)   **6** D.W. Krummel (Urbana)   **7** Library of Congress (Washington, D.C.)   **8** Library and Museum of the Performing Arts (N.Y.C.)   **9** William Reeves (London)   **10** Sibley Library, Eastman School of Music (Rochester)   **11** Nigel Simeone (Tunbridge Wells, Kent)   **12** Vereeniging ter Bervordering van de Belangen des Boekhandels (Amsterdam)   **13** University of Virginia (Charlottesville)   **14** University of California at Los Angeles   **15** Generally available

1313 **FOG, DAN (Copenhagen) (continued)**
     2/1981   do.   0281   *Johannes Brahms. Early Editions*
                                   (261)   *1

1314 _____.
     2/1981   Liste   336   *Vokalmusik*
                                   (1000)   *1

1315 _____.
     3/1981   do.   337   *Musikliteratur. Klavierauszüge. Musikalien*
                                   (618)   *1

1316 _____.
     5/1981   Spec.   0581   *Musik für Gitarre*
                                   (193)   *1

1317 _____.
     5/1981   Liste   338   *Klavierausz. Foliopartituren. Kammermusik*
                                   (1050)   *1

1318 _____.
     5/1981   do.   339   *Piano à 4 mains*
                                   (715)   *1

1319 _____.
     6/1981   do.   340   *Musik. Musikliteratur*
                                   (609)   *1

1320 _____.
     9/1981   do.   341   *Music Literature*
                                   (443)   *1

1321 _____.
     9/1981   do.   342   *Faks.-Drucke. Musiklit. Erst- u. Frühdrucke*
                                   (381)   *1

1322 _____.
     10/1981   do.   343   *Carl Nielsen*
                                   (282)   *1

1323 _____.
     10/1981   do.   344   *Klavierauszüge. Dirigierpartituren*
                                   (398)   *1

1324 _____.
     10/1981   do.   345   *Studienpartituren*
                                   (612)   *1

1325 _____.
     12/1981   do.   346   *Musikliteratur*
                                   (1719)   *1

1326 _____.
     12/1981   do.   347   *Musikalien*
                                   (313)   *1

1327 _____.
     2/1982   do.   348   *Orgelmusik- und Literatur*
                                   (610)   *15

1328 _____.
     2/1982   do.   349   *Klaviermusik aus Scandinavien, 1825-1950*
                                   (610)   *15

1 Compiler/State University of New York (Buffalo)　2 The British Library (London)　3 Gemeentemuseum (Den Haag)　4 The Grolier Club (N.Y.C.)　5 Hirsch Collection, British Library (London)　6 D.W. Krummel (Urbana)　7 Library of Congress (Washington, D.C.)　8 Library and Museum of the Performing Arts (N.Y.C.)　9 William Reeves (London)　10 Sibley Library, Eastman School of Music (Rochester)　11 Nigel Simeone (Tunbridge Wells, Kent)　12 Vereeniging ter Bervordering van de Belangen des Boekhandels (Amsterdam)　13 University of Virginia (Charlottesville)　14 University of California at Los Angeles　15 Generally available

1329 **FOG, DAN (Copenhagen) (continued)**

	3/1982	do.	350	*Musikalien. Musikliteratur* (616)	*15
1330 ____.	5/1982	Spec.	8205	*Den Danske Revy, 1875-1900* (633)	*Fog
1331 ____.	5/1982	Liste	351	*Klavierauszüge. Libretti. Theaterliteratur* (966)	*15
1332 ____.	6/1982	do.	352	*Musikalien. Musikliteratur* (754)	*15
1333 ____.	9/1982	do.	353	*idem.* (151)	*15
1334 ____.	9/1982	do.	354	*Dirigierpartituren* (467)	*15
1335 ____.	9/1982	do.	355	*Kammermusik. Harmonium mit Instrumenten* (391)	*15
1336 ____.	10/1982	do.	356	*Musikalien in praktischen Ausgaben* (1213)	*15
1337 ____.	10/1982	Spec.	1082	*Antiquaria: Flöte* (160)	*15
1338 ____.	10/1982	Liste	357	*Musikliteratur. Musikalien* (783)	*15
1339 ____.	11/1982	do.	358	*Musikerbriefe. Musikalien. Musikliteratur* (766)	*15
1340 ____.	1/1983	do.	359	*Musiker Völker. Volkslieder. Volkstänze* (386)	*15
1341 ____.	1/1983	do.	360	*Musikliteratur ü. Musikinstrumente* (239)	*15
1342 ____.	2/1983	Spec.	8302	*Musiklitteratur paa Dansk* (336)	*15
1343 ____.	3/1983	Liste	361	*Musik. Musiklit. Kataloge. Bibliographie* (892)	*15
1344 ____.	3/1983	Spec.	8303	*Study Scores. Pop. Beat. Rock. Jazz* (874)	*15

1345 **FOG, DAN (Copenhagen) (continued)**

	4/1983	Liste	362	*Klaviermusik*
				(517)	*15

1346 _____.

| | 4/1983 | do. | 363 | *Klaviermusik /4- and 8-hand/* |
| | | | | (540) | *15 |

1347 _____.

| | 5/1983 | do. | 364 | *Musikliteratur. Musikalien* |
| | | | | (879) | *15 |

1348 _____.

| | 5/1983 | do. | 365 | *Scandinavia Yesterday: Music. Bibliographie* |
| | | | | (311) | *15 |

1349 _____.

| | 6/1983 | Spec. | 8306 | *Violine, Viola, Violoncello Kammermusik* |
| | | | | (522) | *15 |

1350 _____.

| | 6/1983 | Liste | 367 | *Orchestermaterialen. Full Scores* |
| | | | | (299) | *15 |

1351 _____.

| | 7/1983 | do. | 368 | *Musikalien. Musikerbriefe. Musikliteratur* |
| | | | | (365) | *15 |

1352 _____.

| | 9/1983 | Spec. | 8309 | *Voice and Piano. Piano Music* |
| | | | | (199) | *15 |

1353 _____.

| | 10/1983 | do. | 8310 | *Violin Music* |
| | | | | (200) | *15 |

1354 _____.

| | 11/1983 | Liste | 370 | *Music for Flute and Violin. Chamber Music* |
| | | | | (293) | *15 |

1355 _____.

| | 11/1983 | do. | 371 | *Orgelmusik. Choralbücher. Chormusik* |
| | | | | (625) | *15 |

1356 _____.

| | 12/1983 | do. | 372 | *Musikalien. Musikliteratur* |
| | | | | (621) | *15 |

1357 _____.

| | 2/1984 | do. | 373 | *Musikliteratur* |
| | | | | (1455) | *15 |

1358 _____.

| | 2/1984 | Spec. | 8402 | *Klaviermusik. Sang & Klaver* |
| | | | | (199) | *15 |

1359 _____.

| | 3/1984 | do. | 374 | *Musikalien. Musikliteratur* |
| | | | | (724) | *15 |

1360 _____.

| | 4/1984 | do. | 8404 | *Skandinavisk Musikliteratur* |
| | | | | (745) | *15 |

1 Compiler/State University of New York (Buffalo)   **2** The British Library (London)   **3** Gemeentemuseum (Den Haag)   **4** The Grolier Club (N.Y.C.)   **5** Hirsch Collection, British Library (London)   **6** D.W. Krummel (Urbana)   **7** Library of Congress (Washington, D.C.)   **8** Library and Museum of the Performing Arts (N.Y.C.)   **9** William Reeves (London)   **10** Sibley Library, Eastman School of Music (Rochester) **11** Nigel Simeone (Tunbridge Wells, Kent)   **12** Vereeniging ter Bervordering van de Belangen des Boekhandels (Amsterdam)   **13** University of Virginia (Charlottesville)   **14** University of California at Los Angeles   **15** Generally available

1361 **FOG, DAN (Copenhagen) (continued)**

	5/1984	Liste	375	*Kammermusik. Klavierauszüge. Partituren* (1477)	*15
1362 ____.	5/1984	do.	376	*Musikverlagskataloge. Musikalien. Musiklit.* (801)	*15
1363 ____.	6/1984	Spec.	8406	*Klaviermusik. Musiklitteratur. Tillaeg* (256)	*15
1364 ____.	6/1984	do.	8407	*Specialofferte* (10)	*15
1365 ____.	7?/1984	Liste	377	*Klavierauszüge. Musikalien. Musikliteratur* (671)	*15
1366 ____.	8/1984	Spec.	8408	*Piano Scores. Operetta. Folksongs* (323)	*15
1367 ____.	9/1984	do.	8409	*Songbooks. Folksong. Folkdance* (227)	*15
1368 ____.	11/1984	do.	8411	*Musik om (saersforsorgen)* (764)	*15
1369 ____.	11/1984	Liste	378	*Musikliteratur. Musikalien* (792)	*15
1370 ____.	11/1984	do.	379	*Dokumentar-Materialen. Musik. Musiklit.* (890)	*15
1371 ____.	12/1984	do.	380	*Klaviermusik. Musikliteratur* (969)	*15

1372 **"FOLIA" (Amersfoort, Neth.)**

	197_?		51	*Antiquarian Music* (633)	*1,13
1373 ____.	s.d.	Lijst	106	*Antiquarian Music* (277)	*10

1374 **FOLKLORE ASSOCIATES (Hatboro, PA.)**

	1959		1	*Old & New Books: Folklore, Folksong, Ballad* (420)	*8
1375 ____.	1959		2	*Old & New Books: Folklore, Folksong, Ballad* (310)	*8
1376 ____.	1961		4	*Old & New Books: Folklore, Folksong, Ballad* (413)	*8

---

1 Compiler/State University of New York (Buffalo)   **2** The British Library (London)   **3** Gemeentemuseum (Den Haag)   **4** The Grolier Club (N.Y.C.)   **5** Hirsch Collection, British Library (London)   **6** D.W. Krummel (Urbana)   **7** Library of Congress (Washington, D.C.)   **8** Library and Museum of the Performing Arts (N.Y.C.)   **9** William Reeves (London)   **10** Sibley Library, Eastman School of Music (Rochester) **11** Nigel Simeone (Tunbridge Wells, Kent)   **12** Vereeniging ter Bervordering van de Belangen des Boekhandels (Amsterdam)   **13** University of Virginia (Charlottesville)   **14** University of California at Los Angeles   **15** Generally available

1377 **FOLKLORE ASSOCIATES** (Hatboro, PA.) (continued)
      1967   11   *Old & New Books: Folklore, Folksong, Ballad*
                               (402)   *8

1378 **THE FOOTNOTE** (N.Y.C.)
      1973   2   *Dance and Music Books*
                               (18pp.)   *8

1379 _____.
      1974   3   *Dance and Music Books*
                               (22pp.)   *8

1380 _____.
      1975   4   *Dance and Music Books*
                               (14pp.)   *8

1381 _____.
      1977   6   *Dance and Music Books*
                               (22pp.)   *8

1382 _____.
      1977   List   D   *[Dance and Music Books]*
                               (2pp.)   *8

1383 _____.
      1978   do.   F   *Dance and Music Books*
                               (4pp.)   *8

1384 **FOREIGN AND INTERNATIONAL BOOK CO.** (N.Y.C.)
      1947   A   *Latin-American Music - Folklore*
                               (236)   *8

1385 **FORNI, ARNALDO, LIBRERIA** (Bologna)
      1961   48   *Musica*
                               (286)   *12

1386 _____.
      1969   13   *Dance and Musical Instruments*
                                                         *1

1387 _____.
      1970   Spec.   16   *Musica*
                                                      *12

1388 **FORREST, JIM, GUITAR MUSIC** (Garden Grove, CA.)
      1/1982   1   *[Stock List]*
                             (3 lvs.)   *1

1389 **FOSTER, MARK** (Champaign, Illinois)
      1977   —   *Books for the Choral Conductor*
                             (447)   *1

1390 **FOYLE, W. & G., LTD.** (London)
      1921   15   *Music and Books on the Drama*
                               (14pp.)   *5

1391 _____.
      1924   15[!]   *Music and Books on the Drama*
                               (51pp.)   *5,7

1392 _____.
      2/1924   15[!]   *Catalogue Dept. Music*
                               (13pp.)   *5

---

1 Compiler/State University of New York (Buffalo)   **2** The British Library (London)   **3** Gemeentemuseum (Den Haag)   **4** The Grolier Club (N.Y.C.)   **5** Hirsch Collection, British Library (London)   **6** D.W. Krummel (Urbana)   **7** Library of Congress (Washington, D.C.)   **8** Library and Museum of the Performing Arts (N.Y.C.)   **9** William Reeves (London)   **10** Sibley Library, Eastman School of Music (Rochester)   **11** Nigel Simeone (Tunbridge Wells, Kent)   **12** Vereeniging ter Bervordering van de Belangen des Boekhandels (Amsterdam)   **13** University of Virginia (Charlottesville)   **14** University of California at Los Angeles   **15** Generally available

1393 **FOYLE, W. & G., LTD. (London) (continued)**
        6/1928   *Music and Drama*
                        (24pp.)   *5

1394   _____.
        8/1929   *Music and Drama*
                        (32pp.)   *5,10

1395   _____.
      11/1930   *Music and Drama*
                        (39pp.)   *5,7

1396   _____.
      11/1931   *Music and Drama*
                        (87pp.)   *5,7,10

1397   _____.
        2/1932   *[Suppl.to Cat.15]: Rare Books. Music. Dance*
                        ?   *5

1398   _____.
      12/1932   *Music and Drama*
                        (88pp.)   *10,13

1399   _____.
        4/1934   *Music and Drama*
                        (108pp.)   *10

1400   _____.
        6/1935   *Music and Drama*
                        (112pp.)   *8,10

1401   _____.
        4/1936   *Music and Drama*
                        (136pp.)   *10,13

1402   _____.
        8/1937   *Rare and Interesting Music and Music Books*
                        (336)   *1,11

1403   _____.
        7/1940   *Books on Music and Drama*
                        (156pp.)   *10

1404   _____.
        4/1950   *Books on Music and Drama*
                        (106pp.)   *8

1405 **FRANK, J., ANTIQUARIAT (LUDWIG LAZARUS) (Würzburg)**
        s.d.   Anzgr   157   *Medezin [etc.] Music*
                        (789-900)   *10

1406   _____.
        n.d.   do.   175   *Geschichte. Kultur. Musik*
                        (628-54)   *13

1407 **FRANZ, L., & CO. (Leipzig)**
        1929   Heft   8   *Antiq. Zeitschriften-Markt*
                        (181-205)   *10

1408   _____.
        1930   do.   9   *[idem.]: Musik und Theater*
                        (458)   *1,5,8,10,12

---

1 Compiler/State University of New York (Buffalo)   **2** The British Library (London)   **3** Gemeentemuseum (Den Haag)   **4** The Grolier Club (N.Y.C.)   **5** Hirsch Collection, British Library (London)   **6** D.W. Krummel (Urbana)   **7** Library of Congress (Washington, D.C.)   **8** Library and Museum of the Performing Arts (N.Y.C.)   **9** William Reeves (London)   **10** Sibley Library, Eastman School of Music (Rochester)   **11** Nigel Simeone (Tunbridge Wells, Kent)   **12** Vereeniging ter Bervordering van de Belangen des Boekhandels (Amsterdam)   **13** University of Virginia (Charlottesville)   **14** University of California at Los Angeles   **15** Generally available

1409	**FRENSDORFF, ERNST (Berlin)**			
	19_?	9	*Theatergeschichte u. Schauspielkunst. Musik*	
			(878-1063)	*1
1410	**FRIEDRICH, GEORG (Breslau)**			
	1871	21	*/Includes Music/*	
			(1299-1424)	*12
1411	**FRIESE MUZIEKHANDEL (Leeuwarden)**			
	1959	379	*Vooraadlijst*	
			(539)	*12
1412	_____.			
	1959	380	*Vooraadlijst*	
			(659)	*12
1413	_____.			
	1959	388	*Vooraadlijst*	
			(782)	*12
1414	**FROMANNSCHE BUCHHANDLUNG (Jena)**			
	1921?	9	*Kunst. Musik. Theater*	
			(1345)	*12
1415	**FRONT, THEODORE (Los Angeles, CA.)**			
	1962	1	*Books on Music. Music Editions. ALS*	
			(2325)	*1,6,8,12,13
1416	_____.			
	1963	2	*Music Editions. Books on Music*	
			(1833)	*1,6,8,12,13
1417	_____.			
	1965	3	*Antiquarian Books. New Publications*	
			(1761)	*1,6,8,11,12
1418	_____.			
	1966	4	*Music Editions, Old and New*	
			(1723)	*6,8,11,12,13
1419	_____.			
	1967	5	*Books on Music (Antiquarian and New)*	
			(1865)	*6,11,13
1420	_____.			
	1967	6	*Musical Editions (Old and New)*	
			(678)	*1,6,8,11,13
1421	_____.			
	1968	7	*Books on Music (Antiquarian and New)*	
			(2538)	*1,6,8,11,13
1422	**FRONT, THEODORE (Beverly Hills, CA.)**			
	1969	8	*Musical Eds. (Antiquarian/New). Autographs*	
			(1154)	*1,6,8,11,13
1423	_____.			
	1969	9	*Books on Music*	
			(2193)	*1,6,8,11,13
1424	_____.			
	1970	10	*Musical Eds. (Antiquarian/New). Autographs*	
			(1601)	*1,6,8,11,13

1 Compiler/State University of New York (Buffalo)   **2** The British Library (London)   **3** Gemeentemuseum (Den Haag)   **4** The Grolier Club (N.Y.C.)   **5** Hirsch Collection, British Library (London)   **6** D.W. Krummel (Urbana)   **7** Library of Congress (Washington, D.C.)   **8** Library and Museum of the Performing Arts (N.Y.C.)   **9** William Reeves (London)   **10** Sibley Library, Eastman School of Music (Rochester)   **11** Nigel Simeone (Tunbridge Wells, Kent)   **12** Vereeniging ter Bervordering van de Belangen des Boekhandels (Amsterdam)   **13** University of Virginia (Charlottesville)   **14** University of California at Los Angeles   **15** Generally available

1425   **FRONT, THEODORE (Beverly Hills, CA.) (continued)**

	1970	11	*Books on Music, A-MOS* (2002)	*1,6,8,11,13
1426	____. 1970	12	*Books on Music, Mozart-Z* (3488)	*1,6,8,11,13
1427	____. 1971	13	*Musical Eds. (Antiquarian & New). Mss.* (2507)	*1,6,8,11,13
1428	____. 1972	14	*Antiquarian Books on Music* (1331)	*1,6,8,11,13
1429	____. 1972	15	*Antiquarian Music* (679)	*1,6,8,11,13
1430	____. 1973-	16-18	*New Books on Music*	*15
1431	____. 1973-	19-21	*New Music*	*15
1432	____. 1974	22	*Antiquarian Music* (593)	*1,6,8,11,13
1433	____. 1974	23	*Antiquarian Books on Music* (2326)	*1,6,8,11,13
1434	____. 1975-	24-26	*New Books on Music*	*15
1435	____. 1975	27	*Antiquarian Music and Books on Music* (90)	*1,6,8,11,13
1436	____. 1975	28	*Keyboard Music* (980)	*15
1437	____. 1977	28-30	*[New Instrumental Music]*	*15
1438	____. 1977	31	*Antiquarian Books on Music* (1056)	*15
1439	____. 1978	32	*Antiquarian Music* (549)	*15
1440	____. 1978	33	*Antiquarian Vocal Scores. Musical Comedies* (619)	*15

1 Compiler/State University of New York (Buffalo)   **2** The British Library (London)   **3** Gemeentemuseum (Den Haag)   **4** The Grolier Club (N.Y.C.)   **5** Hirsch Collection, British Library (London)   **6** D.W. Krummel (Urbana)   **7** Library of Congress (Washington, D.C.)   **8** Library and Museum of the Performing Arts (N.Y.C.)   **9** William Reeves (London)   **10** Sibley Library, Eastman School of Music (Rochester)   **11** Nigel Simeone (Tunbridge Wells, Kent)   **12** Vereeniging ter Bervordering van de Belangen des Boekhandels (Amsterdam)   **13** University of Virginia (Charlottesville)   **14** University of California at Los Angeles   **15** Generally available

1441   **FRONT, THEODORE (Beverly Hills, CA.) (continued)**
       1979   34   *Ethnomusicology. Books. Records*
                                 (176)   *15

1442   _____.
       1979   35   *Antiquarian Books and Music*
                                 (380)   *15

1443   _____.
       1979   36   *Biography. History. Opera. Singing*
                                 (325)   *15

1444   _____.
       1980   37   *Music for the Oboe*
                                 (128)   *15

1445   _____.
       1981   38   *Antiquarian Books on Music*
                                 (838)   *15

1446   _____.
       1981   39   *Antiquarian Music*
                                 (1109)   *15

1447   _____.
       1982   40   *Preview Edition of Catalogue 40*
                                 (441-669)   *15

1448   **FRONT, THEODORE (Van Nuys, CA.)**
       1983   41   *Series*
                                 (536)   *15

1449   _____.
       1983   42   *Antiquarian Books. Music. Mss.*
                                 (327)   *15

1450   _____.
       1984   43   *Music of Eastern Europe*
                                 (1028)   *15

1451   **GACH, JOHN (Baltimore, Maryland)**
       1974?   —   *Offers in Music and Dance*
                                 (312)   *1

1452   _____.
       1976   18   *Music*
                                 (201)   *1

1453   _____.
       1977   22   *Music and Dance*
                                 (414)   *1

1454   _____.
       1978   unn.   *Music and Dance*
                                 (524)   *1

1455   **GAD, G. E. C. (Copenhagen)**
       1929   —   *Musik. Teater. Digtekunst. Literatur*
                                 (20pp.)   [DBT'29]

1456   **GANLEY, ERIC H. (Forest Hills, N. Y.)**
       1949   1   *Music and Books on Music*
                                 (245)   *5,10

---

1 Compiler/State University of New York (Buffalo)   **2** The British Library (London)   **3** Gemeentemuseum (Den Haag)   **4** The Grolier Club (N.Y.C.)   **5** Hirsch Collection, British Library (London)   **6** D.W. Krummel (Urbana)   **7** Library of Congress (Washington, D.C.)   **8** Library and Museum of the Performing Arts (N.Y.C.)   **9** William Reeves (London)   **10** Sibley Library, Eastman School of Music (Rochester)   **11** Nigel Simeone (Tunbridge Wells, Kent)   **12** Vereeniging ter Bervordering van de Belangen des Boekhandels (Amsterdam)   **13** University of Virginia (Charlottesville)   **14** University of California at Los Angeles   **15** Generally available

1457 **GANLEY, ERIC H. (Forest Hills, N. Y.) (continued)**
      1950   2   *Music and Books on Music (New, Old, Rare)*
                                   (348)   *1,10

1458 _____.
      1950   3   *Music and Books on Music*
                                   (268)   *1,10

1459 _____.
      1950   4   *Music and Books on Music*
                                   (441)   *1,10

1460 _____.
      1951   5   *Music and Books on Music*
                                   (453)   *1,10

1461 _____.
      1951   6   *Music and Books on Music*
                                   (560)   *1,8,10

1462 _____.
      1951   7   *Music and Books on music*
                                   (573)   *1,8,10

1463 _____.
      1952   8   *Music and Books on Music*
                                   (638)   *1,6,8,10

1464 _____.
      1952   9   *Music and Books on Music*
                                   (555)   *1,6,8,10

1465 _____.
      1952   10   *Music and Books on Music*
                                   (539)   *1,6,8,10

1466 _____.
      1952   *Special List. Music and Books on Music*
                                   (327)   *1,8

1467 _____.
      1952   11   *Music and Books on Music (New, Old, Rare)*
                                   (484)   *1,6,8,10

1468 _____.
      1953   12   *Music and Books on Music*
                                   (600)   *1,6,10

1469 _____.
      1953   13   *Music and Books on Music*
                                   (554)   *1,8,10

1470 _____.
      1953   14   *Music and Books on Music*
                                   (605)   *1,8,10

1471 _____.
      1954   15   *Music and Books on Music*
                                   (300)   *1,10,13

1472 _____.
      1954   16   *Music and Books on Music*
                                   (825)   *1,6,10

1 Compiler/State University of New York (Buffalo) **2** The British Library (London) **3** Gemeentemuseum
(Den Haag) **4** The Grolier Club (N.Y.C.) **5** Hirsch Collection, British Library (London) **6** D.W.
Krummel (Urbana) **7** Library of Congress (Washington, D.C.) **8** Library and Museum of the Performing
Arts (N.Y.C.) **9** William Reeves (London) **10** Sibley Library, Eastman School of Music (Rochester)
11 Nigel Simeone (Tunbridge Wells, Kent) **12** Vereeniging ter Bervordering van de Belangen des
Boekhandels (Amsterdam) **13** University of Virginia (Charlottesville) **14** University of California at Los
Angeles **15** Generally available

1473 **GANLEY, ERIC H. (Forest Hills, N. Y.) (continued)**

	1954	17	*Music and Books on Music* (661)	*6
1474	____.			
	1955	18	*Music and Books on Music* (809)	*1,8,10,13
1475	____.			
	1955	19	*Music and Books on Music* (809)	*1,8,10,13
1476	____.			
	1955	20	*Music and Books on Music* (558)	*1,6,8,10,13
1477	____.			
	1956	21	*Music and Books on Music* (815)	*1,6,13
1478	____.			
	1956	22	*Music and Books on Music* (835)	*1,6,13
1479	____.			
	1957	23	*Music and Books on Music* (848)	*1,6,13
1480	____.			
	1957	24	*Music and Books on Music* (850)	*1,6,13
1481	____.			
	1957	25	*Music and Books on Music* (880)	*1,6,13
1482	____.			
	1958	26	*Music and Books on Music* (809)	*1,6,13
1483	____.			
	1958	27	*Music and Books on Music* (844)	*1,13
1484	____.			
	1958	28	*Music and Books on Music* (828)	*1,6,8,13
1485	____.			
	1959	29	*Music and Books on Music* (835)	*1,6,8,13
1486	____.			
	1959	30	*Music and Books on Music* (848)	*1,6,8,13
1487	____.			
	1959	31	*Music and Books on Music* (786)	*1,6,8,13
1488	____.			
	1960	32	*Music and Books on Music* (754)	*1,6,8,13

1 Compiler/State University of New York (Buffalo)   2 The British Library (London)   3 Gemeentemuseum (Den Haag)   4 The Grolier Club (N.Y.C.)   5 Hirsch Collection, British Library (London)   6 D.W. Krummel (Urbana)   7 Library of Congress (Washington, D.C.)   8 Library and Museum of the Performing Arts (N.Y.C.)   9 William Reeves (London)   10 Sibley Library, Eastman School of Music (Rochester)   11 Nigel Simeone (Tunbridge Wells, Kent)   12 Vereeniging ter Bevordering van de Belangen des Boekhandels (Amsterdam)   13 University of Virginia (Charlottesville)   14 University of California at Los Angeles   15 Generally available

1489	**GANLEY, ERIC H. (Forest Hills, N. Y.) (continued)**			
	1960	33	*Music and Books on Music* (797)	*1,6,8,13
1490	_____.			
	1960	34	*Music and Books on Music* (832)	*8,11,13
1491	_____.			
	1961	35	*Music and Books on Music* (831)	*8,11,13
1492	_____.			
	1961	36	*Music and Books on Music* (844)	*11,13
1493	_____.			
	1961	37	*Music and Books on Music* (840)	*11,13
1494	_____.			
	1962	38	*Music and Books on Music* (1768)	*11,13
1495	_____.			
	1962	39	*Clearance Sale. Music and Books on Music* (1778)	*11,13
1496	**GANZ, CHARLES (Paris)**			
	s.d.	List 26	*Musicologie. Chamber Music. Parts* (399)	*8,11
1497	_____.			
	s.d.	do. 27	*Musicologie. Chamber Music. Parts* (252)	*8,11
1498	_____.			
	s.d.	do. 28	*Livres sur la musique* (468)	*11
1499	_____.			
	s.d.	do. 29	*Musique instrumentale et vocale* (263)	*11
1500	_____.			
	s.d.	do. 30	*Livres sur la musique. Musicologie* (549)	*8,11
1501	**GANZ, MINNIE CH. (Paris)**			
	1955	31	*Musique et livres sur la musique* (641)	*9
1502	_____.			
	1956	32	*Musique et livres sur la musique* (100)	*9
1503	_____.			
	1956/57	33	*Musique et livres sur la musique* (421)	*9
1504	_____.			
	1957	34	*Musique vocale et instrumentale* (365)	*9,11

1505   **GANZ, MINNIE CH. (Paris) (continued)**
      1957   35   *Livres sur la musique*
                                    (546)   *1,9

1506   ____.
      1958   36   *Musique d'orchestre*
                                    (522)   *1,9

1507   ____.
      5/1959   37   *Cent ans de musique du chambre*
                                    (532)   *9,11

1508   ____.
      1959-60   38   *Livres sur la musique*
                                    (506)   *9,11

1509   ____.
      1960   39   *Musique et livres sur la musique.*
                                    (675)   *8

1510   ____.
      1960   40   *Livres sur la musique*
                                    (830)   *1,8

1511   ____.
      1952   41   *Le musique jusqu'au début au l9e siècle*
                                    (276)   *8

1512   ____.
      1962   42   *Le musique jusqu'au début au l9e siècle*
                                    (276)   *1

1513   **GARD BOOK (York)**
      1/1978   7   *Music and Musical Books*
                                    (394)   *11

1514   ____.
      1/1979   14   *Music and Musical Books*
                                    (802)   *11

1515   **GATSBY'S MUSIC (East Rochester, N. Y.)**
      10/1979   —   *Sheet Music Sale*
                                    (380)   *8

1516   **GAVEAU, MAISON (Paris)**
      1909   —   *Catalogue de musicologie. Anthologies ...*
                                    (41pp.)   *1

1517   **GEERING, A. & R. (Basel)**
      1922   250   *Neuester Erwerbungen*
                                    (64pp.)   *7

1518   ____.
      s.d.   265   *Handel. Musik*
                                                                             *12

1519   ____.
      [1923]   400   *Livres anciens. Autographe. Musique*
                                                                             *4,12

1520   ____.
      s.d.   402   *Autographe*
                                    (1031-1326)   *4,10

---

1 Compiler/State University of New York (Buffalo)   **2** The British Library (London)   **3** Gemeentemuseum (Den Haag)   **4** The Grolier Club (N.Y.C.)   **5** Hirsch Collection, British Library (London)   **6** D.W. Krummel (Urbana)   **7** Library of Congress (Washington, D.C.)   **8** Library and Museum of the Performing Arts (N.Y.C.)   **9** William Reeves (London)   **10** Sibley Library, Eastman School of Music (Rochester)   **11** Nigel Simeone (Tunbridge Wells, Kent)   **12** Vereeniging ter Bervordering van de Belangen des Boekhandels (Amsterdam)   **13** University of Virginia (Charlottesville)   **14** University of California at Los Angeles   **15** Generally available

1521 **GEERING, A. & R. (Basel) (continued)**
      [1925]   403   *Musikgeschichte und Theorie. Lied. Mss.*
                            (104pp.)   *1,4,7,9,10

1522 **GEIGER & JEDELE (Stuttgart)**
      1895   228   *Theoretisch u. praktische Werke. Operntexte*
                            (990)   [MfM]

1523 **GEORGE'S, WM., & SONS, LTD. (Bristol)**
      1933   411   *Music and the Drama*
                            (1-336)   *8

1524 _____.
      1962   547   *Coll: Atchley. Theology. Liturgy. Church M.*
                            (876-1172)   *4

1525 _____.
      1984   672   *Antiq. ... Books. Mozart Collection*
                            (1-341)   *15

1526 **GERRA, FERDINANDO (Rome)**
      s.d.   2   *Autografi. Libri [including Music]*
                            (282)   *5

1527 _____.
      s.d.   6   *Autografi. Libri [including Music]*
                            (27pp.)   *8

1528 _____.
      s.d.   7   *Autografi. Libri [including Music]*
                            (20pp.)   *8

1529 **GERSCHEL, O. (Stuttgart)**
      1924   111   *Theater - Musik*
                            (1883)   *1,3,5,12

1530 **GEYER, H. (Vienna)**
      1969   —   *Musik in Geschichte und Praxis*
                            (404)   *1,6,10

1531 **GILHOFER & RANSCHBURG (Lucerne and Vienna)**
      [1886]   —   *Coll: Unnamed*
                            (4pp.)   *US-CA

1532 _____.
      1901   64   *Coll: Hajdecki*
                            (59pp.)   *5,7,8,12

1533 _____.
      1902   67   *Coll: Preyer, G. von*
                            (1069)   *5

1534 _____.
      [1906]   83   *Coll: Volkmann, R.*
                            (3174)   *5,7,12

1535 _____.
      191_   153   *Coll: Unnamed*
                            ?   *4

1536 _____.
      195_   155   *Musik Seltenheiten. Kirchenmusik*
                            (1770)   *4,5,12

---

1 Compiler/State University of New York (Buffalo)   **2** The British Library (London)   **3** Gemeentemuseum (Den Haag)   **4** The Grolier Club (N.Y.C.)   **5** Hirsch Collection, British Library (London)   **6** D.W. Krummel (Urbana)   **7** Library of Congress (Washington, D.C.)   **8** Library and Museum of the Performing Arts (N.Y.C.)   **9** William Reeves (London)   **10** Sibley Library, Eastman School of Music (Rochester) **11** Nigel Simeone (Tunbridge Wells, Kent)   **12** Vereeniging ter Bervordering van de Belangen des Boekhandels (Amsterdam)   **13** University of Virginia (Charlottesville)   **14** University of California at Los Angeles   **15** Generally available

1537 **GILHOFER & RANSCHBURG (Lucerne and Vienna) (continued)**
    195_   157   *Coll: Unnamed*
                             ?   *4

1538 _____.
    19__   209   *Alte Drucke [including Music]*
                             (313-26)   *3

1539 _____.
    1927   213   *Musik*
                             (1414)   *1,7,8,10,13

1540 _____.
    1936   259   *Musik. Mss. Autographen*
                             (293)   *4,8,12,13

1541 _____.
    19__   272   *Autographen ... deutsche Musiker*
                             (238, i.a.)   *8,13

1542 _____.
    s.d.   Anzgr   103   *Anzeiger: Musik*
                             ?   *7

1543 _____.
    1907   1   *Bibl. d. Bücherfreundes. Musiklit. u. Musik*
                             (152pp.)   Heck Liste 279

1544 **GLASER, EDWIN V. (Sausalito, CA.)**
    1982   37   *Music and Musicians*
                             (48)   *13

1545 **GLOGAU, M., JR. (Hamburg)**
    1933   81   *Kunst. Musik. Theater. Zeitschriften*
                             (674-765)   *10

1546 **GODAI, HELMUT (Vienna)**
    1966   33   *... Varia. Musik*
                             (670)   [IBAK]

1547 _____.
    1968   38   *Musik. Varia*
                             (611)   *12

1548 **GÖTTINGER ANTIQUARIAT (Göttingen)**
    4/1983   M83   *Musik. Periodica. Literatur. Noten. Theater*
                             (2038)   *1

1549 **GOLDSCHEIDER, GABY (Windsor, Berkshire)**
    s.d.   17   *Entertainment [including Music and Dance]*
                             (601)   *9

1550 **GOLDSCHMIDT, LUCIEN (N.Y.C.)**
    1954   N.S.4   *Special List 81: ALS & Mss., Books & Scores*
                             (161)   *8

1551 _____.
    1954   N.S.5   *Special List #82. Music Theory and History*
                             (339)   *1,8,10

1552 **GOTHIER, FERNAND (Liège)**
    1962   172   *Livres anciens. Musique. Chansons*
                             (676)   [IBAK]

---

1 Compiler/State University of New York (Buffalo) **2** The British Library (London) **3** Gemeentemuseum (Den Haag) **4** The Grolier Club (N.Y.C.) **5** Hirsch Collection, British Library (London) **6** D.W. Krummel (Urbana) **7** Library of Congress (Washington, D.C.) **8** Library and Museum of the Performing Arts (N.Y.C.) **9** William Reeves (London) **10** Sibley Library, Eastman School of Music (Rochester) **11** Nigel Simeone (Tunbridge Wells, Kent) **12** Vereeniging ter Bervordering van de Belangen des Boekhandels (Amsterdam) **13** University of Virginia (Charlottesville) **14** University of California at Los Angeles **15** Generally available

1553 **GOTHIER, FERNAND (Liège) (continued)**
      196_   361   *Belgique ... Musique*
                           (756) |IBAK|

1554 **GOTHIER, LIBRAIRIE PAUL (Liège)**
      1981   454   *L'amateur ... Musique, Théâtre*
                          (254-61,521-683)   ) *8

1555 **GOTTLIEB, ERNEST (Los Angeles, CA.) [Succeeded by T. FRONT]**
      194_   1   *Hist. Science & Theory of Music. First Eds.*
                        (169)   *1

1556 _____ .
      194_   2   *History of Music, excluding Monographs*
                        (171)   *10

1557 _____ .
      194_   3   *Richard Wagner*
                        (46)   *8

1558 _____ .
      194_   4   *Strauss & Mahler. Mss. and Autographs*
                        (257)   *1,8,10

1559 _____ .
      194_   5   *Art Song. Church Song. Musical Folklore*
                        (317)   *8,10

1560 _____ .
      194_   6   *J. S. Bach*
                        (156)   *8,10

1561 _____ .
      1950   7   *Theory of Music, Part I*
                        (410)   *1,8,10

1562 _____ .
      195_   8   *Theory of Music, Part II*
                        (438)   *1,8,10

1563 _____ .
      195_   9   *Haydn, Mozart and their Period*
                        (263)   *1,8,10

1564 _____ .
      195_   11   *Musicology, Part I: Beethoven*
                        (500)   *1,8,10

1565 _____ .
      195_   14   *Musicology and Music Editions*
                        (30)   *8

1566 _____ .
      195-   15   *Musicology, Part II: Instruments*
                        (377)   *1,8,10

1567 _____ .
      195_   16   *Musical Folklore*
                        (390)   *1,8,10

1568 _____ .
      195_   17   *Musicology. Musical Instruments*
                        (390)   *1,8,10

---

1 Compiler/State University of New York (Buffalo) **2** The British Library (London) **3** Gemeentemuseum (Den Haag) **4** The Grolier Club (N.Y.C.) **5** Hirsch Collection, British Library (London) **6** D.W. Krummel (Urbana) **7** Library of Congress (Washington, D.C.) **8** Library and Museum of the Performing Arts (N.Y.C.) **9** William Reeves (London) **10** Sibley Library, Eastman School of Music (Rochester) **11** Nigel Simeone (Tunbridge Wells, Kent) **12** Vereeniging ter Bevordering van de Belangen des Boekhandels (Amsterdam) **13** University of Virginia (Charlottesville) **14** University of California at Los Angeles **15** Generally available

1569	**GOTTLIEB, ERNEST** (Los Angeles, CA.) (continued)			
	195_	18	*Musicology. Sacred Music* (396)	*1,8
1570	_____.			
	1952	19	*Musicology. Aesthetics. Philosophy ...* (411)	*1,8,10
1571	_____.			
	1952	22	*Musical Literature before 1850* (282)	*1,8,10
1572	_____.			
	1953	23	*Musical Literature (A-He). Mss. Autographs* (614)	*1,8,10
1573	_____.			
	1953	24	*Small Selection of important Musicologica* (152)	*8
1574	_____.			
	1953	25	*Musical Literature (Hi-P)* (613)	*1,10
1575	_____.			
	1953?	26	*Musical Literature (Q-Sche)* (293)	*10
1576	_____.			
	1954?	27	*[Musical Literature]* (76)	*8
1577	_____.			
	1954?	28	*Musical Lit. (Schi-Ty). Books. Mss. Autogrs.* (243)	*8,10
1578	_____.			
	195_	29	*Musical Lit. (U-Z). Books. Mss. Autographs* (243)	*8,10
1579	_____.			
	195_	30	*Theater - Dance - Opera - Film* (715)	*1,8,10
1580	_____.			
	195_	31	*Musical Lit. (A-C). Mss. Autographs* (256)	*10
1581	**GOTTSCHALK, PAUL** (Berlin)			
	1917	5?	*Autographen* (?)	*3,12
1582	_____.			
	1918	6	*Mss. Bücher* ?	*4,12
1583	_____.			
	191_	?	*ALS [including Musicians']* (78)	*4
1584	_____.			
	1930	10	*Orig. Mss. of the World's Greatest Composers* (20pp.)	*4,5,7,8

1 Compiler/State University of New York (Buffalo)   **2** The British Library (London)   **3** Gemeentemuseum (Den Haag)   **4** The Grolier Club (N.Y.C.)   **5** Hirsch Collection, British Library (London)   **6** D.W. Krummel (Urbana)   **7** Library of Congress (Washington, D.C.)   **8** Library and Museum of the Performing Arts (N.Y.C.)   **9** William Reeves (London)   **10** Sibley Library, Eastman School of Music (Rochester) **11** Nigel Simeone (Tunbridge Wells, Kent)   **12** Vereeniging ter Bervordering van de Belangen des Boekhandels (Amsterdam)   **13** University of Virginia (Charlottesville)   **14** University of California at Los Angeles   **15** Generally available

1585 **GRÄFE UND UNZER** (Königsberg)
      1938   83   *Musikliteratur*
                           (221)   [JbP'38]

1586 **GRANT, JOHN** (Edinburgh)
      12/1921   —   ... *Music Lit. Instr. Music. Pianoforte*
                        (pp.3-23)   *5

1587 _____.
      1927   —   *Music and Literature*
                        (1721)   *12

1588 _____.
      1932   —   *Music and Literature*
                        (1-1195)   *3,13

1589 _____.
      1933   —   *Fine Arts & Music*
                        (1219)   *12

1590 _____.
      5/1935   —   *Fine Arts & Music*
                        (1501-1983)   *10

1591 _____.
      11/1936   —   *Music, Instrumental and Vocal. Holographs*
                        (1-432)   *4,10

1592 _____.
      10/1938   —   ... *Music and Musical Literature*
                        (391-948)   *10

1593 _____.
      3/1940   —   ... *Music Books. Music and Songs*
                        (498-995)   *5,10

1594 _____.
      9/1950   —   *Books on Art, Music and Literature*
                        (842-1405)   *4,10

1595 _____.
      1/1954   —   ... *Music and Books on Music*
                        (pp.27-42)   *5,13

1596 **GRAUPE, P.** (Berlin)
      19_ _   57   *Politische Lied*
                          (?)   *12

1597 **GREEN BOOK SHOP** (N.Y.C.)
      [1965]   101   *The Lively Arts*
                        (376-533)   *6

1598 **LE GRENIER DU COLLECTIONNEUR** (Brussels)
      1970   13   *Spectacles. Pt.III. Chansons. Music. Danse*
                        (248-319&i.a.)   *8

1599 **GREVELL, H.** (London)
      1993   3   *Valuable Coll. of Books. Liturgy. Early Music*
                        (325-59)   *4

1600 **GROBE, CHARLES** (Wilmington, Delaware)
      s.d.   1   *Vocal and Instrumental Music. Works on Music*
                        (423)   *8

---

1 Compiler/State University of New York (Buffalo)   **2** The British Library (London)   **3** Gemeentemuseum (Den Haag)   **4** The Grolier Club (N.Y.C.)   **5** Hirsch Collection, British Library (London)   **6** D.W. Krummel (Urbana)   **7** Library of Congress (Washington, D.C.)   **8** Library and Museum of the Performing Arts (N.Y.C.)   **9** William Reeves (London)   **10** Sibley Library, Eastman School of Music (Rochester) **11** Nigel Simeone (Tunbridge Wells, Kent)   **12** Vereeniging ter Bervordering van de Belangen des Boekhandels (Amsterdam)   **13** University of Virginia (Charlottesville)   **14** University of California at Los Angeles   **15** Generally available

1601   **GROEN, N. V. (Amsterdam)**
     [1965]   146   *Arts and Music*
                        (584)   *12

1602   **GRØNHOLT PEDERSENS BOGHUS (Copenhagen)**
     [1961]   87   *Musik. Filologi. Ordbøger*
                        (1549)   *12

1603   **GRÜNDEL, EMIL (Leipzig)**
     1886   —   *Antiquarische Musikalien*
                        (?)   [MfM]

1604   **GRUENER, B. R. (Amsterdam)**
     1969   16   *Music*
                        (59)   *1,8,12,13

1605   ____.
     [1969]   29   *Music*
                        (54)   *8,12

1606   ____.
     1970   39   *Music*
                        (107)   *1,8,12

1607   ____.
     1971   50   *Music*
                        (125)   *1,8,12

1608   **GRUYTER, WALTER D. (Berlin)**
     1929   18   *Musik und Theater*
                        (21pp.)   *7

1609   **GSELLIUS (Berlin)**
     [1963]   249   *Kunst. Musik. Theater*
                        (1755)   *12

1610   ____.
     [1967]   254   *Kunst. Musik. Theater*
                        (2044)   *12

1611   ____.
     [1967]   9   *Angebot: Kunst. Musik. Theater*
                        (706)   *12

1612   **GÜNTHER, MAX (Berlin)**
     1965   208   *Kunst - Theater - Musik*
                        (638)   [IBAK]

1613   ____.
     1966   216   *Film - Theater - Musik*
                        (763)   [IBAK]

1614   ____.
     1967   224   *Film - Theater - Musik*
                        (645)   [IBAK]

1615   **GUZMAN, ANTONIO DE (Madrid)**
     [1965]   59   *... Musica*
                        (433-75)   *6

1616   **GYSBERS EN VAN LOON (Arnhem)**
     1960   402   *Kunst. Muziek. Geschiedenis*
                        (421)   [IBAK]

---

1 Compiler/State University of New York (Buffalo)   **2** The British Library (London)   **3** Gemeentemuseum (Den Haag)   **4** The Grolier Club (N.Y.C.)   **5** Hirsch Collection, British Library (London)   **6** D.W. Krummel (Urbana)   **7** Library of Congress (Washington, D.C.)   **8** Library and Museum of the Performing Arts (N.Y.C.)   **9** William Reeves (London)   **10** Sibley Library, Eastman School of Music (Rochester)   **11** Nigel Simeone (Tunbridge Wells, Kent)   **12** Vereeniging ter Bervordering van de Belangen des Boekhandels (Amsterdam)   **13** University of Virginia (Charlottesville)   **14** University of California at Los Angeles   **15** Generally available

1617	____.				
	1960	415	*Boekkunst. Muziek. Militaria*		
			(303)		[IBAK]
1618	____.				
	1961	445	*Kunst. Musikgeschichte. Kulturgeschichte*		
			(297)		[IBAK]
1619	____.				
	1961	457	*Musikgeschichte. Exakte Wissenschaft*		
			(284)		[IBAK]
1620	____.				
	[1961]	462	*Fine Arts. Music. Dutch Topography*		
			(270)		[IBAK]
1621	____.				
	1961	467	*Muziekgeschiedenis*		
			(296)		[IBAK]
1622	____.				
	[1962]	533	*... Muziek ...*		
			(203-71)		*6
1623	____.				
	1964	615	*Volkslieder. Niederlande*		
			(276)		[IBAK]
1624	____.				
	1964	629	*Kunst. Musik. Porzellende*		
			(241)		[IBAK]
1625	____.				
	1964	631	*Kunst. Musik. Niederlande*		
			(276)		[IBAK]
1626	____.				
	1965	650	*Muziekgeschiedenis*		
			(1-45)		*1
1627	____.				
	1965	702	*Muziek. Muziekinstrumenten. Lieder. Orgel*		
			(243)		[IBAK]
1628	____.				
	1967	775	*Sitten und Gebräuche. Musik. Theater*		
			(219)		[IBAK]
1629	____.				
	1980	1428	*... Orgels. Beiaarden. Muziek*		
			(82-150)		*1
1630	____.				
	1980	1441	*Muziek. Orgels. Bieaarden*		
			(110-85)		*1
1631	____.				
	1980	1462	*Muziek*		
			(102-35)		*1
1632	____.				
	1981	1510	*Folklore. Muziek. Volkslied*		
			(111-40)		*1

1 Compiler/State University of New York (Buffalo)   **2** The British Library (London)   **3** Gemeentemuseum (Den Haag)   **4** The Grolier Club (N.Y.C.)   **5** Hirsch Collection, British Library (London)   **6** D.W. Krummel (Urbana)   **7** Library of Congress (Washington, D.C.)   **8** Library and Museum of the Performing Arts (N.Y.C.)   **9** William Reeves (London)   **10** Sibley Library, Eastman School of Music (Rochester)   **11** Nigel Simeone (Tunbridge Wells, Kent)   **12** Vereeniging ter Bervordering van de Belangen des Boekhandels (Amsterdam)   **13** University of Virginia (Charlottesville)   **14** University of California at Los Angeles   **15** Generally available

1633   GYSBERS EN VAN LOON (Arnhem) (continued)
        1981   1522   ... Muziek. Tooneel
                                (147-76)   *1
1634   _____.
        1982   1541   ...Muziek. Instrumenten. Dans
                                (156-203)   *1
1635   _____.
        1982   1543   Boek ... Volkskunst
                                (85-230)   *1
1636   _____.
        1982   1550   ... Muziek. Film
                                (163-201)   *1
1637   _____.
        1982   1567   Muziek. Tooneel. Theater. Muziekinstrumenten
                                (153-208)   *1
1638   _____.
        1983   1400!   Muziek. Tooneel. Beiaarden
                                (223-54)   *1
1639   _____.
        1983   1609   Muziek. Tooneel. Dans en Theater
                                (160-99)   *1
1640   _____.
        1984   1630e   Muziek. Tooneel. Dans en Theater. Beiaarden
                                (163-210)   *1
1641   _____.
        1984   1646   Muziek. Tooneel. Orgen en Beiaarden
                                (146-69)   *1
1642   HAAS, OTTO (London) [Successor to LEO LIEPMANNSSOHN, q.v.]
        [1936]   1   Musical Literature
                                (219)   *1,8,9,13
1643   _____.
        [1936]   2   Music. Tablatures
                                (689)   *8,9,13
1644   _____.
        [1936]   3   Music. Literature
                                (830)   *1,8,9,12,13
1645   _____.
        [1937]   4   Music. Literature
                                (547)   *1,9,12,13
1646   _____.
        [1938]   5   Music Scores. Vocal and Instrumental Music
                                (924)   *1,8,9,12,13
1647   _____.
        [1938]   6   Music and Music Literature
                                (657)   *1,8,9,12
1648   _____.
        [1938]   7   Autograph Letters and Manuscripts
                                (1-232)   *1,8,9,12

1 Compiler/State University of New York (Buffalo)   2 The British Library (London)   3 Gemeentemuseum
(Den Haag)   4 The Grolier Club (N.Y.C.)   5 Hirsch Collection, British Library (London)   6 D.W.
Krummel (Urbana)   7 Library of Congress (Washington, D.C.)   8 Library and Museum of the Performing
Arts (N.Y.C.)   9 William Reeves (London)   10 Sibley Library, Eastman School of Music (Rochester)
11 Nigel Simeone (Tunbridge Wells, Kent)   12 Vereeniging ter Bervordering van de Belangen des
Boekhandels (Amsterdam)   13 University of Virginia (Charlottesville)   14 University of California at Los
Angeles   15 Generally available

1649 **HAAS, OTTO (London)** [Successor to **LEO LIEPMANNSSOHN, q.v.**] (continued)
    [1938]   8   *Music Bibliography. Biography. Coll. Works*
                          (445)   *1,8,9,12,13

1650 _____.
    [1938]   9   *Full Opera Scores*
                          (?)   US-Bp

1651 _____.
    [1938]   10   *Autograph Letters and Manuscripts*
                          (1-123)   *1,8,9,12

1652 _____.
    [1938]   11   *History of Music. Collected Works. Biography*
                          (406)   *1,8,9,12,13

1653 _____.
    [1939]   12   *Vocal Music*
                          (612)   *1,8,9,12,13

1654 _____.
    [1940]   13   *Theory and Science of Music*
                          (746)   *1,9,12,13

1655 _____.
    194_   14   *Instrumental Music*
                          (486)   *1,9,13

1656 _____.
    [1941]   15   *Musical Literature*
                          (444)   *1,8,9,13

1657 _____.
    [1941]   16   *Musical Biography*
                          (619)   *1,9,13

1658 _____.
    [1942]   17   *Series. Scores. Instrumental and Vocal Music*
                          (686)   *1,6,8,9,13

1659 _____.
    [1942]   18   *Musical Literature*
                          (444)   *1,9,13

1660 _____.
    [1943]   19   *Opera. Dramatic Music. Theatre. Dance*
                          (1303)   *1,9,13

1661 _____.
    [1944]   20   *Coll: Moffat, A. Chamber & Harpsichord Music*
                          (700)   *1

1662 _____.
    [1945]   21   *Musical Literature*
                          (830)   *11

1663 _____.
    [194_]   22   *Instrumental Music*
                          (809)   *1,10,13

1664 _____.
    [194_]   23   *Musical Literature*
                          (871)   *1,12,13

---

1 Compiler/State University of New York (Buffalo)   **2** The British Library (London)   **3** Gemeentemuseum (Den Haag)   **4** The Grolier Club (N.Y.C.)   **5** Hirsch Collection, British Library (London)   **6** D.W. Krummel (Urbana)   **7** Library of Congress (Washington, D.C.)   **8** Library and Museum of the Performing Arts (N.Y.C.)   **9** William Reeves (London)   **10** Sibley Library, Eastman School of Music (Rochester)   **11** Nigel Simeone (Tunbridge Wells, Kent)   **12** Vereeniging ter Bervordering van de Belangen des Boekhandels (Amsterdam)   **13** University of Virginia (Charlottesville)   **14** University of California at Los Angeles   **15** Generally available

1665   **HAAS, OTTO (London) [Successor to LEO LIEPMANNSSOHN, q.v.] (continued)**
     [194_]   24   *Autograph Letters and Mss.*
                            (?)   *1,12

1666   _____.
     [1947]   25   *Music and Musical Literature. Rare Works*
                   (150)   *1,10,12,13

1667   _____.
     [1947?]   26   *Vocal and Instrumental Music*
                   (500)   *6,10,13

1668   _____.
     [1948?]   27   *Musical Literature. Bibliography*
                   (1000)   *1,6,10,12,13

1669   _____.
     [1950]   28   *Rare Music and Musical Literature. ALS*
                   (300)   *1,6,10,12,13

1670   _____.
     [195_]   29   *Musical Literature. Biography. Bibliography*
                   (1100)   *1,8,10,12,13

1671   _____.
     [195_]   30   *Rare Music and Musical Literature. ALS*
                   (200)   *1,8,10,11,12

1672   _____.
     [195_]   31   *Musical Literature*
                   (883)   *1,6,8,13

1673   _____.
     [195_]   32   *Orchestral and Vocal Scores. Songs*
                   (777)   *1,8,10,11,13

1674   _____.
     [195_]   33   *Autograph Letters and Manuscripts*
                   (1-136)   *1,6,8,10

1675   _____.
     [195_]   34   *Music Bibliography. History. Opera*
                   (861)   *1,6,10,12,13

1676   _____.
     [195_]   35   *Rare Music Books and Editions. Bibliography*
                   (224)   *1,6,8,10,11,13

1677   _____.
     [195_]   36   *Music and Musicology*
                   (725)   *6,8,10,11,13

1678   _____.
     1959   37   *Rare Music, Boethius to Webern*
                   (183)   *1,6,8,10,12,13

1679   _____.
     1955?   Misc.   —   *Musicology. Recent Purchases*
                   (140)   *1

1680   _____.
     1958   List   1   *Recent Purchases*
                   (219)   *8

1681 **HAAS, OTTO** (London) [Successor to **LEO LIEPMANNSSOHN**, q.v.] (continued)
     s.d.   do.   —   *Old Chamber Music*
                                    (312)   *13
1682 _____.
     [1972?]   do.   —   *Rare Music Exhibited at Antiquarian Book Fair*
                                    (12pp.)   *8,11
1683 **HAASE, P., & SÖNS** (Copenhagen)
     195_?   2   *Musik Litteratur*
                                    (1117)   *9
1684 _____.
     195_?   —   *Musik Litteratur*
                                    (705)   *9
1685 **HACHETTE, DEPT. ÉTRANGER** (Paris)
     1957   —   *Musique et musiciens*
                                    (108pp.)   *1
1686 **HACKE, ERNST MAX** (Schloss Kaibitz b. Kemnath-Stadt)
     1962   5   *Königl. Hofoper bis zu Carows Lachbühne*
                                    (574)   [IBAK]
1687 _____.
     1962   6   *Bühnenwerke, Tl. 1*
                                    (1243)   [IBAK]
1688 _____.
     1962   6[?]   *Bühnenwerke, T. 2. Oper. Operette*
                                    (334)   [IBAK]
1689 _____.
     1963?   9   *Weber. Wagner. Wahnfried*
                                    (597)   *12
1690 _____.
     1963   12   *Königl. Hofoper bis zum Kabarett*
                                    (348)   [IBAK]
1691 _____.
     1964   15   *Richard Strauss ... ll. Juni 1964*
                                    (223)   [IBAK]
1692 _____.
     1964   17   *Wagner. Tannhaeuser. Bayreuth*
                                    (346)   *12
1693 _____.
     1965   20   *Theater. Film. Musik. Litteratur*
                                    (329)   *12
1694 _____.
     1965   24   *Richard Wagner.Werk und Interpreten*
                                    (277)   *12
1695 _____.
     1966   34   *90 Jahre Bayreuther Festspiele*
                                    (440)   [IBAK]
1696 _____.
     1967   40   *Richard Wagner*
                                    (228)   *12

---

1 Compiler/State University of New York (Buffalo)   **2** The British Library (London)   **3** Gemeentemuseum (Den Haag)   **4** The Grolier Club (N.Y.C.)   **5** Hirsch Collection, British Library (London)   **6** D.W. Krummel (Urbana)   **7** Library of Congress (Washington, D.C.)   **8** Library and Museum of the Performing Arts (N.Y.C.)   **9** William Reeves (London)   **10** Sibley Library, Eastman School of Music (Rochester)   **11** Nigel Simeone (Tunbridge Wells, Kent)   **12** Vereeniging ter Bervordering van de Belangen des Boekhandels (Amsterdam)   **13** University of Virginia (Charlottesville)   **14** University of California at Los Angeles   **15** Generally available

1697 **HACKE, ERNST MAX (Schloss Kaibitz b. Kemnath-Stadt) (continued)**

	1967		43	*Richard Wagner (2 vols.)*
				(636)	*12

1698 _____.

	1968		51	*Richard Wagner*
				(96)	*12

1699 _____.

	[1959]	Liste	1	*Theater. Film. Musik*
				(312)	*12

1700 _____.

	1960	do.	5	*Lustspiele. Operette ... Schallplatten*
				(157)	[IBAK]

1701 _____.

	1960	do.	6	*... Musikgeschichte*
				(158-345)	*6

1702 _____.

	1961	do.	13	*Kabarett. Komödie. Operette. Tanz*
				(233)	*12

1703 _____.

	1961	do.	19	*Richard Wagner*
				(100)	*12

1704 _____.

	1963	do.	33	*Musik. Oper. Operette. Lied. Konzert. Chor*
				(169)	*12

1705 _____.

	1963	do.	34	*Theater und Musik*
				(164)	[IBAK]

1706 _____.

	1964	do.	43	*Moderne Literatur. Theater. Musik*
				(147)	*12

1707 _____.

	1965	do.	48	*Theater. Musik. Tanz*
				(194)	*12

1708 _____.

	1965	do.	52	*Weltliteratur. Theater. Film. Musik*
				(185,155)	*12

1709 _____.

	196_	do.	66	*Theater. Literatur. Musik. Kunst*
				(84)	*12

1710 _____.

	s.d.	do.	72	*Theater. Film. Operette*
				(93)	*12

1711 _____.

	s.d.	do.	90	*Theater. Film. Musik*
				(159)	*12

1712 **HAGARTY & McBURNIE (Toronto)**

	1981		1	*Music. Books*
				(399)	*1,8

1 Compiler/State University of New York (Buffalo) 2 The British Library (London) 3 Gemeentemuseum (Den Haag) 4 The Grolier Club (N.Y.C.) 5 Hirsch Collection, British Library (London) 6 D.W. Krummel (Urbana) 7 Library of Congress (Washington, D.C.) 8 Library and Museum of the Performing Arts (N.Y.C.) 9 William Reeves (London) 10 Sibley Library, Eastman School of Music (Rochester) 11 Nigel Simeone (Tunbridge Wells, Kent) 12 Vereeniging ter Bervordering van de Belangen des Boekhandels (Amsterdam) 13 University of Virginia (Charlottesville) 14 University of California at Los Angeles 15 Generally available

1713 **HAGARTY & McBURNIE** (Toronto) (continued)
      1982   2   *Music. Books*
                    (434)   *1,8

1714 _____.
      1983   3   *Music. Books*
                    (463)   *1,8

1715 _____.
      1984   List   1   *Music and Music Literature*
                    (82)   *1

1716 **HALLE, J.** (Munich)
      1930?   37   *Musica sacra et profana. Mss. Autographs*
                    (600)   *1,4,5,12,13

1717 _____.
      1931?   66   *Musica sacra et profana*
                    (600)   *5

1718 _____.
      1932?   72   *Alte Musik. Bücher. Porträts*
                    (563)   *4,5,8,10,13

1719 **HALLER, FRITZ** (Munich)
      1962   55   *Neuerwerbungen Musik Literatur. Noten*
                    (319)   *12

1720 _____.
      1962   193   *Germanistik. Dissertationen. Noten*
                    (200)   *12

1721 **HALLESCHES ANTIQUARIAT** (Halle/Saale)
      [1960]   16   *Musik*
                    (449)   [IBAK]

1722 ─────
      1962   35   *Musik. Theater*
                    (620)   *12

1723 _____.
      1965   48   *Musik. Theater. Tanz*
                    (655)   *12

1724 _____.
      1966   55   *Musik. Theater. Tanz. Film*
                    (606)   *12

1725 _____.
      1970   73   *Musik. Theater. Tanz. Film*
                    (1-562,700-51)   *8

1726 _____.
      1972   79   *Musik. Theater. Tanz. Film*
                    (563)   *12

1727 _____.
      1974   85   *Theologie. Gesangbücher*
                    (683-817,842-74)   ) *8

1728 **HALLIDAY, BERNARD** (Leicester)
      1935   194   *ALS of Literary Men, Artists and Musicians*
                    (794,i.a.)   *4

1729 **HALLIDAY, BERNARD (Leicester) (continued)**
      1937   213   *ALS of Literary Men, Artists and Musicians*
                                 (1927,i.a.)   *4

1730 **HAMMER MOUNTAIN BOOK HALLS (Schenectady, N.Y.)**
      1980   21   *Performing Arts*
                                 (1-115)   *10

1731 **HANKE, FRANZ, (Zürich)**
      1865?   97   *Musikalien und Musikwissenschaft*
                                 (6000)   US-Cn

1732 **HANNMANN, HEINZ ("DER BÜCHERWURM") (Berlin)**
      1950?   225   *Musik. Lied. Tanz*
                                 (2151)   *6

1733 **HANRAHAN. J. & J. (Portsmouth, N.H.)**
      1975   List   15   */Music/*
                                 (123-207)   *8

1734 **HARDOU (Paris)**
      1874   —   *Liquidation de la Maison Legouix*
                                 (3367)   *8

1735 **HAROLD, W., & CO. (London)**
      1899   [1]   *Second-hand Music and Musical Literature*
                                 (20pp.)   *9,13

1736 _____.
      1900   2   *Music and Musical Lit., Ancient and Modern*
                                 (36pp.)   *9

1737 _____.
      1900   3   *Music and Musical Lit., Ancient and Modern*
                                 (pp.37-60)   *9

1738 **HAROLD & CO. (London) [the W. is dropped]**
      1900   4   *Music and Musical Lit., Ancient and Modern*
                                 (pp.61-82)   *9

1739 _____.
      1901   5   *Music and Musical Lit., Ancient and Modern*
                                 (pp.83-104)   *9

1740 _____.
      1901   6   *Music and Musical Lit., Ancient and Modern*
                                 (pp.106-28)   *9

1741 _____.
      1901   7   *Music and Musical Lit., Ancient and Modern*
                                 (pp.130-52)   *9

1742 _____
      1902   8   *Music and Musical Lit., Ancient and Modern*
                                 (pp.154-76)   *9

1743 _____.
      1902   9   *Music and Musical Lit., Ancient and Modern*
                                 (pp.178-200)   *9

1744 _____.
      1902   10   *Music and Musical Lit., Ancient and Modern*
                                 (pp.202-224)   *9

1 Compiler/State University of New York (Buffalo)   2 The British Library (London)   3 Gemeentemuseum
(Den Haag)   4 The Grolier Club (N.Y.C.)   5 Hirsch Collection, British Library (London)   6 D.W.
Krummel (Urbana)   7 Library of Congress (Washington, D.C.)   8 Library and Museum of the Performing
Arts (N.Y.C.)   9 William Reeves (London)   10 Sibley Library, Eastman School of Music (Rochester)
11 Nigel Simeone (Tunbridge Wells, Kent)   12 Vereeniging ter Bervordering van de Belangen des
Boekhandels (Amsterdam)   13 University of Virginia (Charlottesville)   14 University of California at Los
Angeles   15 Generally available

1745 **HAROLD & CO. (London) (continued)**

	1903	11	*Music and Musical Lit., Ancient and Modern* (pp.226048)	*9
1746	_____.			
	1903	12	*Music and Musical Lit., Ancient and Modern* (pp.250-72)	*7,9
1747	_____.			
	1903	13	*Music and Musical Lit., Ancient and Modern* (pp.274-96)	*9
1748	_____.			
	1903	14	*Music and Musical Lit., Ancient and Modern* (pp.198-320)	*9
1749	_____.			
	1904	15	*Music and Musical Lit., Ancient and Modern* (pp.322-44)	*9
1750	_____.			
	1904	16	*Music and Musical Lit., Ancient and Modern* (pp.346-86)	*9
1751	_____.			
	1904	17	*Music and Musical Lit., Ancient and Modern* (pp.388-410)	*9
1752	_____.			
	1904	18	*Music and Musical Lit., Ancient and Modern* (pp.412-34)	*9
1753	_____.			
	1904	19	*Music and Musical Lit., Ancient and Modern* (pp.436-58)	*9
1754	_____.			
	1904	20	*Music and Musical Lit., Ancient and Modern* (pp.460-82)	*9
1755	_____.			
	1905	21	*Music and Musical Lit., Ancient and Modern* (pp.484-510)	*9
1756	_____.			
	1905	22	*Music and Musical Lit., Ancient and Modern* (pp.512-40)	*9
1757	_____.			
	1905	23	*Music and Musical Liy., Ancient and Modern* (PP.542-68)	*9
1758	_____.			
	1905	24	*Music and Musical Lit., Ancient and Modern* (pp.570-94)	*9
1759	_____.			
	1906	25	*Music and Musical Lit., Ancient and Modern* (PP.596-626)	*9
1760	_____.			
	1906	26	*Music and Musical Lit., Ancient and Modern* (pp.628-54)	*9

1 Compiler/State University of New York (Buffalo) **2** The British Library (London) **3** Gemeentemuseum (Den Haag) **4** The Grolier Club (N.Y.C.) **5** Hirsch Collection, British Library (London) **6** D.W. Krummel (Urbana) **7** Library of Congress (Washington, D.C.) **8** Library and Museum of the Performing Arts (N.Y.C.) **9** William Reeves (London) **10** Sibley Library, Eastman School of Music (Rochester) **11** Nigel Simeone (Tunbridge Wells, Kent) **12** Vereeniging ter Bervordering van de Belangen des Boekhandels (Amsterdam) **13** University of Virginia (Charlottesville) **14** University of California at Los Angeles **15** Generally available

1761	**HAROLD & CO. (London) (continued)**			
	1906		27	*Music and Musical Lit., Ancient and Modern*
				(pp.656-82) *9
1762	**HARPAGON ASSOCIATES (San Francisco)**			
	1968	List	2	*Music and Dance*
				(98,97) *1
1763	_____.			
	1971	Cat.	12	*Music and Dance*
				(476,176) *1
1764	**HARPER, LATHROP (N.Y.C.)**			
	1972		209	*Fine Books and Manuscripts. Rare Music*
				(176-234) *6,8,12,13
1765	_____.			
	1978		232	*Incunabula*
				(i.a.) *1,8
1766	**HARRASSOWITZ, O. (Leipzig and Wiesbaden)**			
	1881		78	*Kunstliteratur. Musik*
				? *12
1767	_____.			
	1888		140	*Geschichte und Theorie der Musik*
				? [MfM]
1768	_____.			
	1896		212	*Kunst. Musik. Theater*
				(885-1082) *12
1769	_____.			
	1900		254	*Kunst. Musik. Theater*
				(1509-1758) *12
1770	_____.			
	1908		310	*Kunst. Musik. Theater*
				(1659-1933) *12
1771	_____.			
	1913		358	*Kunst. Archeologie. Musik. Theater*
				(1864-2145) *4,12
1772	_____.			
	1932		438	*Volkskunde. Kulturgeschichte. Musik. Theater*
				(2880) *3
1773	_____.			
	198_?	Spec.	6	*Coll: Mayer-Reinach, A. Books and Scores*
				(36pp.) *1
1774	**HARRWITZ, MAX (Berlin)**			
	1914?		108	*Musik*
				(1045) *3,4,5,6,12
1775	**HARTUNG, HERMANN (Leipzig)**			
	1866		104	*Musik. Theater. Kunst*
				(14pp.) *1,12
1776	_____.			
	1867		108	*Musik. Theater. Kunst*
				(411) *1

1777 **HARTUNG, HERMANN (Leipzig) (continued)**

	1870	134	*Aesthetik. Musik. Theater. Kunst* (644)	*1,12

1778 _____.

	1870	136	*Musik. Theorie und Literatur der Musik* (2628)	*1,8,12

1779 _____.

	1872	151	*Musikalien. Theorie und Literatur der Musik* (1491)	*1

1780 _____.

	1875	164	*Musikalien* (1260)	*1

1781 **HARVEY, GLYNN (Southern Pines, No. Carolina)**

	1951	Op. 1	*Song Albums* (34+)	*8

1782 _____.

	195_?	Op. 2	*Opera. Musical Scores* ([26])	*8

1783 **HARVEY, LION (N.Y.C. and Wappingers Falls, N. Y.)**

	1969	—	*Spring. Books pertaining to Music* (798)	*12

1784 _____.

	1970	—	*Jan.-June. Books pertaining to Music* (1475)	*8,11,12

1785 _____.

	1971	—	*Autumn. Books pertaining to Music* (1256)	*11,12,13

1786 _____.

	1971	—	*Winter. Books on Music* (1108)	*1,6

1787 _____.

	1972	10	*Books on Music* (1187,112)	*1,8,12,13

1788 _____.

	1972	11	*Books on Music* (1154)	*1

1789 _____.

	1973	12	*Books on Music* (91)	*1,6

1790 _____.

	1973	13	*Books on Music* (1130)	*1,12

1791 _____.

	1974	14	*Books on Music* (921)	*13

1792 _____.

	1977	16	*Books on Music* (1559)	*1

---

1 Compiler/State University of New York (Buffalo)   **2** The British Library (London)   **3** Gemeentemuseum (Den Haag)   **4** The Grolier Club (N.Y.C.)   **5** Hirsch Collection, British Library (London)   **6** D.W. Krummel (Urbana)   **7** Library of Congress (Washington, D.C.)   **8** Library and Museum of the Performing Arts (N.Y.C.)   **9** William Reeves (London)   **10** Sibley Library, Eastman School of Music (Rochester)   **11** Nigel Simeone (Tunbridge Wells, Kent)   **12** Vereeniging ter Bervordering van de Belangen des Boekhandels (Amsterdam)   **13** University of Virginia (Charlottesville)   **14** University of California at Los Angeles   **15** Generally available

1793 **HARVEY, LION (N.Y.C. and Wappingers Falls, N. Y.) (continued)**
    1977   17   *Books on Music*
                        (572)   *1,12

1794 **HASBACH. A. L. (Vienna)**
    1967   81   *Musik. Theater. Film*
                        (472)   *12

1795 _____.
    1969   89   *Theater. Musik. Film*
                        (523)   *12

1796 **HATCHWELL, RICHARD (Little Sommerfield, Wilts.)**
    c.1963   Misc.   5   *Coll: David, F. Engr., Ms. Music, 18-19th c.*
                        (167)   *9

1797 _____.
    [1965]   do.   10   *Engraved and Ms. Music, 18-19th Centuries*
                        (187)   *6,13

1798 **HAUS DER BÜCHER (Basel)**
    s.d.   644   *Autographen. Musikgeschichte und Theorie*
                        (?)   *4,9

1799 _____.
    [1963]   706-7   *Deutsche Literatur d. Barockzeit. (2 vols.)*
                        (i.a.)   *4,12

1800 _____.
    1969   736   *Musikerautographen*
                        (158)   *6,8,12

1801 _____.
    1/1978   788   *M.autographen. Prakt. Musik. Zeitschriften*
                        (1127)   *13

1802 **HAZLETT, DICK (West Palm Beach, Florida)**
    [1980]   5   *20th Century Literature. Pop Music*
                        (1693)   *1,8

1803 _____.
    1982   6   *Jazz and Pop*
                        (500)   *1

1804 **HECK, V. A. (Vienna)**
    1923   9   *Musik. Volks- und Kirchenlied*
                        (395-519)   *4,12

1805 _____.
    192_   10   *Autographen ...*
                        (1-365)   *10

1806 _____.
    192_   24   *Coll: Hanslick, E. Musik und Theater*
                        (1046)   *4,5,12,13

1807 _____.
    1927?   25?   *Mss.*
                        (68)   *7

1808 _____.
    1927?   26   *Musik-Manuskripte. Musiker-Briefe. Autogr.*
                        (180)   *4,8,10,12

---

1 Compiler/State University of New York (Buffalo)   **2** The British Library (London)   **3** Gemeentemuseum (Den Haag)   **4** The Grolier Club (N.Y.C.)   **5** Hirsch Collection, British Library (London)   **6** D.W. Krummel (Urbana)   **7** Library of Congress (Washington, D.C.)   **8** Library and Museum of the Performing Arts (N.Y.C.)   **9** William Reeves (London)   **10** Sibley Library, Eastman School of Music (Rochester)   **11** Nigel Simeone (Tunbridge Wells, Kent)   **12** Vereeniging ter Bervordering van de Belangen des Boekhandels (Amsterdam)   **13** University of Virginia (Charlottesville)   **14** University of California at Los Angeles   **15** Generally available

1809   **HECK, V. A. (Vienna) (continued)**

	192_	28	*Autographen*	
			(252)	*4,10
1810	_____.			
	192_	33	*Wertvolle Autographen [including Wagner]*	
			(223)	*8
1811	_____.			
	1927	38	*L. v. Beethoven: Mss. Briefe. Erstdrucke*	
			(?)	[Heck]
1812	_____.			
	192_	39	*Musik-Manuskripte, Bach bis Strauss*	
			(24)	*4,5,7,10,11,13
1813	_____.			
	1928?	42	*Musiker-Autographen*	
			(223)	*4,7,9
1814	_____.			
	1928	44	*Franz Schubert*	
			(237)	*1
1815	_____.			
	192_	46	*Coll: Brahms, J. Nachlass. Briefe. Mss.*	
			(?)	*5,7,13
1816	_____.			
	192_	47	*Interessante Musiker-Autographen*	
			(259)	*13
1817	_____.			
	192_	50	*Interessante alte Bücher*	
			(786-851)	*13
1818	_____.			
	s.d.	51	*Interessante alte Bücher*	
			(249-67)	*13
1819	_____.			
	s.d.	52	*Bibliothek eines Germanisten*	
			(459-704)	*13
1820	_____.			
	1923	54	*Autographen [including Musiker]*	
			(i.a.)	*7,8,10,13
1821	_____.			
	1931 .	57	*Musikliteratur. Anhang: Beethoven-Literatur*	
			(87,52)	*5,7,13
1822	_____.			
	1934	58	*Interessante Autographen*	
			(105)	*5
1823	_____.			
	1935	61	*Querschnitt durch unser Autographenlager*	
			(380)	*7
1824	_____.			
	193_	69	*Autographen*	
			(367)	*4,5,7,9,10,13

1 Compiler/State University of New York (Buffalo)   **2** The British Library (London)   **3** Gemeentemuseum (Den Haag)   **4** The Grolier Club (N.Y.C.)   **5** Hirsch Collection, British Library (London)   **6** D.W. Krummel (Urbana)   **7** Library of Congress (Washington, D.C.)   **8** Library and Museum of the Performing Arts (N.Y.C.)   **9** William Reeves (London)   **10** Sibley Library, Eastman School of Music (Rochester)   **11** Nigel Simeone (Tunbridge Wells, Kent)   **12** Vereeniging ter Bervordering van de Belangen des Boekhandels (Amsterdam)   **13** University of Virginia (Charlottesville)   **14** University of California at Los Angeles   **15** Generally available

1825   **HECK, V. A. (Vienna) (continued)**

	1938	70	*Autographen*
			(522)
			*4,7
1826	_____.		
	1947	125	*Musik*
			(212)
			[Heck]
1827	_____.		
	1947	128	*Musik*
			(149)
			[Heck]
1828	_____.		
	1949	135	*Musik*
			(208)
			*8
1829	_____.		
	s.d.	162	*Tanzmusik des 19. Jahrhunderts*
			(287)
			*1,8
1830	_____.		
	1951	163	*Autographen berühmter Musiker*
			(126)
			*1
1831	_____.		
	1951	167	*Musik-Literatur*
			(329)
			*1
1832	_____.		
	1951	168	*Alte Noten*
			(221)
			*11
1833	_____.		
	1952	176	*Musik und Theater*
			(325)
			*1
1834	_____.		
	1952	180	*Alte Noten*
			(313)
			*1
1835	_____.		
	1952	196	*Musik Literatur*
			(470)
			*9
1836	_____.		
	1954	205	*Autographen berühmter Musiker*
			(486)
			*9
1837	_____.		
	1957	213	*Musikalische Seltenheiten, I-II*
			(806)
			*9
1838	_____.		
	1961	235	*Kammermusik in modernen Ausgaben*
			(414)
			[IBAK]
1839	_____.		
	1962	237	*Coll: Schlosser, J. von*
			(2.Tl., 763)
			*5,6
1840	_____.		
	1963	242	*Noten in alten Ausgaben*
			(584)
			*6

1 Compiler/State University of New York (Buffalo)   2 The British Library (London)   3 Gemeentemuseum (Den Haag)   4 The Grolier Club (N.Y.C.)   5 Hirsch Collection, British Library (London)   6 D.W. Krummel (Urbana)   7 Library of Congress (Washington, D.C.)   8 Library and Museum of the Performing Arts (N.Y.C.)   9 William Reeves (London)   10 Sibley Library, Eastman School of Music (Rochester) 11 Nigel Simeone (Tunbridge Wells, Kent)   12 Vereeniging ter Bervordering van de Belangen des Boekhandels (Amsterdam)   13 University of Virginia (Charlottesville)   14 University of California at Los Angeles   15 Generally available

1841 HECK, V. A. (Vienna) (continued)

	1964	245	*Lieder und Tanzmusik*	
			(1440)	*6
1842	_____.			
	1964	247	*Musik und Theater*	
			(1026)	*5,6,13
1843	_____.			
	1966	257	*Noten*	
			(967)	*1,6,12,13
1844	_____.			
	1967	265	*Musik und Theater*	
			(1352)	*1,6,8,12,13
1845	_____.			
	1968	269	*Noten*	
			(841)	*1,6,8,12,13
1846	_____.			
	1969	274	*Autographe*	
			(741)	*8
1847	_____.			
	1970	279	*Musik und Theater*	
			(1475)	*6,13
1848	_____.			
	1972	288	*Musik und Theater*	
			(1501)	*6,13
1849	_____.			
	1974	302	*Lieder*	
			(536))	*6,8,13
1850	_____.			
	1974	304	*Musik und Theater*	
			(1297)	*8,13
1851	_____.			
	1975	306	*Tanz*	
			(1117)	*1,6,8
1852	_____.			
	1977	318	*Musik*	
			(1673)	*13
1853	_____.			
	1982	341	*Coll: Müller von Asow. Tl. I, Musiklit.*	
			(1312)	*11,13
1854	_____.			
	1983	346	*Die Musik*	
			(1390)	*13

1855 HEERDEGEN, F. (Nuremburg)

	1868?	278	*Musik-Katalog*	
			(91pp.)	[Schneider 82]
1856	_____.			
	1969?	279	*Musik-Katalog*	
			(91pp.)	[Schneider 82]

1 Compiler/State University of New York (Buffalo)   **2** The British Library (London)   **3** Gemeentemuseum (Den Haag)   **4** The Grolier Club (N.Y.C.)   **5** Hirsch Collection, British Library (London)   **6** D.W. Krummel (Urbana)   **7** Library of Congress (Washington, D.C.)   **8** Library and Museum of the Performing Arts (N.Y.C.)   **9** William Reeves (London)   **10** Sibley Library, Eastman School of Music (Rochester) **11** Nigel Simeone (Tunbridge Wells, Kent)   **12** Vereeniging ter Bervordering van de Belangen des Boekhandels (Amsterdam)   **13** University of Virginia (Charlottesville)   **14** University of California at Los Angeles   **15** Generally available

1857 **HEERDEGEN, F. (Nuremburg) (continued)** ·
    [1870]   315   *Musik-Katalog*
    ·   (91pp.)   [Schneider 82]

1858 **HEFFER, W., & SONS (Cambridge)**
    1935   462   *Secondhand Books on Music. Rare Early Music*
                      (417)   *10, US-Pv

1859 _____.
    193_   479   *Secondhand Books on Music. Rare Early Music*
                      (155)   *10

1860 _____.
    1936   494   *Music and Musical Literature*
                      (239)   *10,US-Pv

1861 _____.
    193-   508   *Music and Musical Literature*
                      (742)   *9,10

1862 _____.
    1938   525   *Music and Musical Literature*
                      (636)   *1,4,10,US-Pv

1863 _____.
    1939   553   *Music and Musical Literature*
                      (1123)   *1,4,8,9,10,11

1864 _____.
    1939   559   *Music and Musical Literature*
                      (810)   *3,4,8,10,US-Pv

1865 _____.
    1940   572   *Music and Musical Literature*
                      (865)   *4,9,10,US-Pv

1866 _____.
    1941   591   *Music and Musical Literature*
                      (1002)   *1,4,9,10,11

1867 _____.
    1942   597   *Music and Musical Literature*
                      (685)   *1,9,10,US-Pv

1868 _____.
    1943   605   *Music and Musical Literature*
                      (1142)   *9,10,11,US-Pv

1869 _____.
    1947   615   *Music and Musical Literature*
                      (2021)   *4,9,11,US-Pv

1870 _____.
    s.d.   845   *Performing Arts ... Music*
                      (815-1375)   *6,8

1871 **HENNING, THEODORE (Berlin)**
    1962   274   *Musik. Theater. Tanz*
                      (670+)   [IBAK]

1872 **HENRICI, KARL ERNST (Berlin)**
    s.d.   7   *Autographen*
                      (1-169)   *3

---

1 Compiler/State University of New York (Buffalo)   **2** The British Library (London)   **3** Gemeentemuseum (Den Haag)   **4** The Grolier Club (N.Y.C.)   **5** Hirsch Collection, British Library (London)   **6** D.W. Krummel (Urbana)   **7** Library of Congress (Washington, D.C.)   **8** Library and Museum of the Performing Arts (N.Y.C.)   **9** William Reeves (London)   **10** Sibley Library, Eastman School of Music (Rochester)   **11** Nigel Simeone (Tunbridge Wells, Kent)   **12** Vereeniging ter Bervordering van de Belangen des Boekhandels (Amsterdam)   **13** University of Virginia (Charlottesville)   **14** University of California at Los Angeles   **15** Generally available

1873 **HERITAGE BOOKSHOP (Los Angeles, CA.)**
    1979   —   *Scarce o.p. Books on Music*
                              (209)   *1,8,13

1874 **HERTZ, ALEX. (Jackson Heights, N. Y.)**
    1950   List   1   *Music*
                              (61)   *8

1875 **HESSE, J. (Ellwangen)**
    1887   —   *[Seltenheiten von Musikdrucken]*
                              ?   [MfM19:77]

1876 **HIERSEMANN, KARL (Leipzig)**
    1906   330   *Musik und Theater*
                              ?   *3
1877 _____.
    1908   352   *Musik und Theater. Mss.*
                            (270)   *4,5,9,12
1878 _____
    1911   392   *Coll: Olmeda. Musik und Liturgie*
                            (335)   *1,4,5,9,12
1879 _____.
    1925   551   *Musik und Liturgie*
                            (929)   *1,4,5,9,10,12
1880 _____.
    s.d.   623   *Kostume. Uniformen ... Musik. Theater*
                          (593-912)   *10,13
1881 _____.
    1938   651   *Uniformen ... Musik. Theater. Tanz*
                          (736-1036)   *10

1882 **HIGHAM, CHARLES (London)**
    1890   —   *Coll: Vaughan, et al. Bibliotheca hymnologica*
                          (1792)   *4

1883 **HINTERBERGER, HEINRICH (Vienna)**
    1935?   2   *[including Musik]*
                            ?   *7
1884 _____.
    1935   4   *Musiker-Autographen*
                            (90)   *1,5,12
1885 _____.
    1935   7   *Autogr. und histor. Dokumente. Mozart Mss.*
                          (82-93)   *5,12,13
1886 _____.
    1936   9   *Coll: Zweig,S. M.alische Meisterhandschriften*
                          (232-304)   *4
1887 _____.
    1936   11   *Autogr. II: Musiker und Componisten*
                          (i.a.)   *10
1888 _____.
    1936?   12   *Coll: Schenker. Musik und Theater*
                          (394)   *5,12,13

---

1 Compiler/State University of New York (Buffalo)   **2** The British Library (London)   **3** Gemeentemuseum (Den Haag)   **4** The Grolier Club (N.Y.C.)   **5** Hirsch Collection, British Library (London)   **6** D.W. Krummel (Urbana)   **7** Library of Congress (Washington, D.C.)   **8** Library and Museum of the Performing Arts (N.Y.C.)   **9** William Reeves (London)   **10** Sibley Library, Eastman School of Music (Rochester)   **11** Nigel Simeone (Tunbridge Wells, Kent)   **12** Vereeniging ter Bervordering van de Belangen des Boekhandels (Amsterdam)   **13** University of Virginia (Charlottesville)   **14** University of California at Los Angeles   **15** Generally available

1889 **HINTERBERGER, HEINRICH (Vienna) (continued)**
    1937   18   *Coll: Zweig,S. Autogr. u. Dokumente. Mozart*
                             ?   ?

1890 _____.
    1937   20   *Coll: Zweig, S.*
                       ?   *4,9,12

1891 **The HIPPOGRIFF (Sweet Briar, Virginia)**
    1983   3   *Music*
                  (42)   *13

1892 **HODGSON, MESSRS. (London)**
    1961/62   —   *Coll: Holmes, Edward. Books and Music*
                  (585)   *10

1893 **HÖNISCH, RUDOLPH (Leipzig)**
    1921   15   *Colls.: Müller-Reuter und H. Riemann*
                  (2028)   *1,5,7,10,12

1894 _____.
    s.d.   16   *Colls: Müller-Reuter und H. Riemann*
                  (2584)   *8,13

1895 _____.
    s.d.   29   *Musikalien und Musikliteratur*
                  (2227)   *3,5,7,8,10,13

1896 _____.
    [1926]   62   *Musik- und Theater-geschichte*
                  (324)   *12

1897 _____.
    1928   70   *Colls: Kipke and Segnitz. Musik und Theater*
                  (2124)   *1,3,10,12

1898 **HOEPLI, U. (Milan)**
    1899   125   *Teatro. Musica*
                  (?)   *12

1899 _____.
    1951   —   *Teatro e musica*
                  (380)   *8

1900 **HOLLEYMAN & TREACHER, LTD. (Brighton, U.K.)**
    1956   51   *Music and Musical Literature*
                  (1117)   *8

1901 _____.
    1972   115   *Music and Musical Literature*
                  (1012)   *8

1902 **HOLLYWOOD BOOK SERVICE (Hollywood, CA.)**
    1957   —   *Performing Arts*
                  (1454)   *6

1903 **HOLLYWOOD BOOK SHOP (Los Angeles, CA.)**
    1978   22   *Folkmusic*
                  (115)   *8

1904 **HOLMES, T,. & CO. (Hove, Sussex)**
    s.d.   1   *Books in all Departments [including Music]*
                  (32pp.)   *9

---

1 Compiler/State University of New York (Buffalo)   **2** The British Library (London)   **3** Gemeentemuseum (Den Haag)   **4** The Grolier Club (N.Y.C.)   **5** Hirsch Collection, British Library (London)   **6** D.W. Krummel (Urbana)   **7** Library of Congress (Washington, D.C.)   **8** Library and Museum of the Performing Arts (N.Y.C.)   **9** William Reeves (London)   **10** Sibley Library, Eastman School of Music (Rochester)   **11** Nigel Simeone (Tunbridge Wells, Kent)   **12** Vereeniging ter Bervordering van de Belangen des Boekhandels (Amsterdam)   **13** University of Virginia (Charlottesville)   **14** University of California at Los Angeles   **15** Generally available

1905	**HOLMES, T. & CO. (Hove, Sussex) (continued)**			
	1913	2	*Old Music and Musical Literature* (32pp.)	*1,9
1906	_____.			
	1913	3	*Books in all Departments [including Music]* (6pp.)	*9
1907	_____.			
	1913	4	*Books in all Departments [including Music]* (pp.17-32)	*9
1908	_____.			
	1914	5	*Old Music and Musical Literature* (48pp.)	*1,9
1909	_____.			
	[1914]	5[!]	*idem. [including "items from no. 2"]* (28pp.)	*1,9
1910	_____.			
	1914	6	*Old Music and Musical Literature* (32pp.)	*1,9
1911	_____.			
	1914	7	*Old Music and Musical Literature* (40pp.)	*1,8,9
1912	_____.			
	1914?	8	*Old Music and Musical Literature* (40pp.)	*8,9
1913	**HOLMES, T. & CO. (by A. N. MAY, in continuation, Exmouth)**			
	1914?	9	*Old Music and Musical Literature* (40pp.)	*1,9
1914	_____.			
	19_?	10	*Old Music and Musical Literature* (32pp.)	*1,8,9
1915	_____.			
	19_?	11	*Old Music and Musical Literature* (24pp.)	*1,9
1916	_____.			
	1926?	12	*Old Music and Musical Literature* (40pp.)	*1,8,9
1917	_____.			
	1927?	13	*Old Music and Musical Literature* (40pp.)	*7,9
1918	_____.			
	192_	14	*Old Music and Musical Literature* (36pp.)	*1,9,13
1919	**HOOSIER BOOKSHOP (Indianapolis, Indiana)**			
	s.d.	List	35	*Catalogue of Books ... American Sheet Music* (222-46)	*10
1920	**HORTUS MUSICUS: IL CENTRO ITALIANE ... (Rome)**			
	1978	8	*Scelta di opere ... interesse musicali* (539)	*10,14

1 Compiler/State University of New York (Buffalo) 2 The British Library (London) 3 Gemeentemuseum (Den Haag) 4 The Grolier Club (N.Y.C.) 5 Hirsch Collection, British Library (London) 6 D.W. Krummel (Urbana) 7 Library of Congress (Washington, D.C.) 8 Library and Museum of the Performing Arts (N.Y.C.) 9 William Reeves (London) 10 Sibley Library, Eastman School of Music (Rochester) 11 Nigel Simeone (Tunbridge Wells, Kent) 12 Vereeniging ter Bervordering van de Belangen des Boekhandels (Amsterdam) 13 University of Virginia (Charlottesville) 14 University of California at Los Angeles 15 Generally available

1921 **HORTUS MUSICUS: IL CENTRO ITALIANE ... (Rome) (continued)**
    1980   11   *Libri di musica*
                         (1645)   *1,8,13,14

1922   _____.
    1981   14   *Libri di musica*
                         (794)   *10

1923 **HOTTLE, KEN (Allentown, Penn.)**
    1967   —   *Hymnology*
                         (3 lvs.)   *14

1924 **HOVINGH, C. (Haarlem)**
    1959   9   *Kunst. Muziek. Tooneel*
                         (362)   *12

1925   _____.
    1961   18   *Muziek*
                         (422-794)   *12

1926   _____.
    1962   35   *Kunst. Muziek*
                         (2409-2911)   *12

1927   _____.
    1962   39   *Muziek*
                         (4309-4774)   *12

1928   _____.
    1963   41   *Bibliographie. Kunst. Muziek*
                         (558)   *12

1929   _____.
    1966   70   *Bladmuziek*
                         (2231-2881)   *12

1930 **HOWES BOOKSHOP LTD. (Hastings, Sussex)**
    1963   153   */including/ Music and Dancing*
                         (2412-2857)   *5

1931   _____.
    1964   156   *Literature. The Arts. Folklore. Music*
                         (2284-2502)   *4,5

1932   _____.
    1965   159   *Literature. The Arts. Folklore. Music*
                         (2877-3054)   *4,5

1933 **HUBER, ALOIS HILMER (Salzburg)**
    1910?   42   *Musik und Theater*
                         (1-652)   *4,5

1934 **HUG & CO. (Zurich)**
    s.d.   1   *Coll: d'Albert, E.*
                         (254)   *5

1935   _____.
    s.d.   —   *Musik aus vier Jarhunderten, 1400-1800*
                         (60pp.)   *8

1936 **HUGENDUBEL, H. (Munich)**
    s.d.   13   *Deutsch Sprache. Musik. Theater*
                         ?   *12

1937 **HYMAN, LEONARD (Reading) [Succeeded by R. MACNUTT, q.v.]**

	1941	[1]	*Opera Libretti. Books. Autographs*	
			(unn.)	*Macnutt
1938	____.			
	1943	[2]	*Books and Periodicals*	
			(unn.)	*Macnutt
1939	____.			
	1943	[3]	*Books*	
			(unn.)	*Macnutt
1940	____.			
	1943	[4]	*Books*	
			(unn.)	*Macnutt
1941	____.			
	1943	5	*Music Literature*	
			(unn.)	*Macnutt
1942	____.			
	1943	6	*Music Literature*	
			(unn.)	*Macnutt
1943	____.			
	1943	7	*Music Literature*	
			(unn.)	*Macnutt
1944	____.			
	1943	8	*Music and Music Literature*	
			(unn.)	*Macnutt
1945	____.			
	1944	[9]	*Music Literature*	
			(unn.)	*Macnutt
1946	____.			
	1944	10	*Music Literature. Autographs. Sheet Music*	
			(unn.)	*Macnutt
1947	____.			
	1944	11	*Music Literature*	
			(unn.)	*Macnutt
1948	____.			
	1944	12	*Modern Music Literature*	
			(unn.)	*Macnutt
1949	____.			
	1944	13	*Music and Music Literature*	
			(unn.)	*Macnutt
1950	____.			
	1944	14	*Music and Music Literature*	
			(unn.)	*Macnutt
1951	____.			
	1944	15	*Music and Music Literature*	
			(unn.)	*Macnutt
1952	____.			
	1944	16	*Music*	
			(unn.)	*Macnutt

1 Compiler/State University of New York (Buffalo)   **2** The British Library (London)   **3** Gemeentemuseum (Den Haag)   **4** The Grolier Club (N.Y.C.)   **5** Hirsch Collection, British Library (London)   **6** D.W. Krummel (Urbana)   **7** Library of Congress (Washington, D.C.)   **8** Library and Museum of the Performing Arts (N.Y.C.)   **9** William Reeves (London)   **10** Sibley Library, Eastman School of Music (Rochester)   **11** Nigel Simeone (Tunbridge Wells, Kent)   **12** Vereeniging ter Bervordering van de Belangen des Boekhandels (Amsterdam)   **13** University of Virginia (Charlottesville)   **14** University of California at Los Angeles   **15** Generally available

1953 **HYMAN, LEONARD (Reading) (continued)**

	1944	17	*Books on Music* (unn.)	*Macnutt
1954	_____.			
	1944	18	*Music and Music Literature* (98)	*Macnutt
1955	_____.			
	1944	19	*Music and Music Literature* (69)	*Macnutt
1956	_____.			
	n.d.	20	*Music and Music Literature* (71)	*Macnutt
1957	_____.			
	1945	21	*Music and Music Literature* (62)	*Macnutt
1958	_____.			
	1945	22	*Music and Music Literature* (72)	*Macnutt
1959	_____.			
	1945	23	*Instruments & Instrumentalists. Min. Scores* (74)	*Macnutt
1960	_____.			
	1945	24	*Music Literature* (76)	*Macnutt
1961	_____.			
	1945	25	*Music and Music Literature* (137)	*Macnutt
1962	_____.			
	1945	26	*Old Music and Music Literature* (46)	*Macnutt
1963	_____.			
	1945	27	*Music Literature, Old and Modern* (103)	*Macnutt
1964	_____.			
	1945?	28?	*?* (?)	[not located]
1965	_____.			
	1945	29	*Music and Music Literature* (77)	*Macnutt
1966	_____.			
	1946	30	*Orchestral and Chamber Music* (114)	*Macnutt
1967	_____.			
	1946	31	*Music Literature* (89)	*Macnutt
1968	_____.			
	1946	32	*Music Literature (including Autograph Letters)* (148)	*Macnutt

1 Compiler/State University of New York (Buffalo)   **2** The British Library (London)   **3** Gemeentemuseum (Den Haag)   **4** The Grolier Club (N.Y.C.)   **5** Hirsch Collection, British Library (London)   **6** D.W. Krummel (Urbana)   **7** Library of Congress (Washington, D.C.)   **8** Library and Museum of the Performing Arts (N.Y.C.)   **9** William Reeves (London)   **10** Sibley Library, Eastman School of Music (Rochester) **11** Nigel Simeone (Tunbridge Wells, Kent)   **12** Vereeniging ter Bervordering van de Belangen des Boekhandels (Amsterdam)   **13** University of Virginia (Charlottesville)   **14** University of California at Los Angeles   **15** Generally available

1969	HYMAN, LEONARD (Reading) (continued)			
	1946	33	*Music Literature*	
			(77)	*Macnutt
1970	_____.			
	1946	34	*Books on Music and Musicians*	
			(98)	*Macnutt
1971	_____.			
	1947	35	*Music Literature. Dance*	
			(603)	*10,11
1972	_____.			
	1947	36	*Music Literature*	
			(82)	*Macnutt
1973	_____.			
	1947	37	*Orchestral and Chamber Music*	
			(349)	*1,10,13
1974	_____.			
	1947	—	*Books on Theatre, Opera, Ballet and Dancing*	
			(81)	*11
1975	_____.			
	1947	—	*Music Biography and Criticism*	
			(67)	*11
1976	_____.			
	1947	—	*Music Biography and Criticism*	
			(74)	*Macnutt
1977	_____. [business moved to London]			
	1947	38	*Music Literature and Music*	
			(404)	*Macnutt,13
1978	_____.			
	1948	—	*Vocal Scores*	
			(103)	*Macnutt
1979	_____.			
	1948	—	*Modern Music Literature*	
			(82)	*Macnutt
1980	_____.			
	1948	—	*Chamber Music*	
			(77)	*Macnutt,10
1981	_____.			
	1948	39	*Music Literature and Music*	
			(406)	*10,12
1982	_____.			
	1948	40	*Music Biography and Music*	
			(418)	*8,10,13
1983	_____.			
	1948	41	*Books mostly Printed before 1800*	
			(374)	*Macnutt
1984	_____.			
	1949	42	*Books and Pamphlets on ... Musical Instruments*	
			(314)	*10

1 Compiler/State University of New York (Buffalo)   **2** The British Library (London)   **3** Gemeentemuseum (Den Haag)   **4** The Grolier Club (N.Y.C.)   **5** Hirsch Collection, British Library (London)   **6** D.W. Krummel (Urbana)   **7** Library of Congress (Washington, D.C.)   **8** Library and Museum of the Performing Arts (N.Y.C.)   **9** William Reeves (London)   **10** Sibley Library, Eastman School of Music (Rochester)   **11** Nigel Simeone (Tunbridge Wells, Kent)   **12** Vereeniging ter Bervordering van de Belangen des Boekhandels (Amsterdam)   **13** University of Virginia (Charlottesville)   **14** University of California at Los Angeles   **15** Generally available

1985 **HYMAN, LEONARD (London) (continued)**

1985	1949	43	*Music* (303)	*9,13
1986	1949	44	*Music* (303)	*8,13
1987	1949-50	45	*Coll: Landau. Music and Music Literature* (232)	*1,9,13
1988	1950	46	*Rare Music and some Music Literature* (326)	*9,10,13
1989	1950	47	*Books on Musical Instruments* (264)	*10,13
1990	1950	48	*Vocal Music* (578)	*9,10
1991	1950	49	*Orchestral Scores and Parts* (350)	*1
1992	1950	50	*Rare old Music & Music Literature. Autographs* (606)	*1,10
1993	1951	51	*British Music and Music Lit. Bach. Handel* (434)	*1,8,10
1994	1951	52	*Music Literature and Music* (331)	*1,8,10
1995	1951	53	*Music Literature and Music* (363)	*1,10
1996	1951	54	*Books & Pamphlets on Music & Music Literature* (350)	*1,10
1997	1952	55	*Biography. Hist. Dictionaries. Bibliographies* (553)	*1,8,10
1998	1952	56	*Rare Music* (668)	*1,8,10,13
1999	1952	57	*Music and Music Literature* (408)	*1,13
2000	1952	58	*Music and Music Literature. Portraits* (364)	*1,13

1 Compiler/State University of New York (Buffalo) 2 The British Library (London) 3 Gemeentemuseum (Den Haag) 4 The Grolier Club (N.Y.C.) 5 Hirsch Collection, British Library (London) 6 D.W. Krummel (Urbana) 7 Library of Congress (Washington, D.C.) 8 Library and Museum of the Performing Arts (N.Y.C.) 9 William Reeves (London) 10 Sibley Library, Eastman School of Music (Rochester) 11 Nigel Simeone (Tunbridge Wells, Kent) 12 Vereeniging ter Bervordering van de Belangen des Boekhandels (Amsterdam) 13 University of Virginia (Charlottesville) 14 University of California at Los Angeles 15 Generally available

2001	**HYMAN, LEONARD (London) (continued)**			
	1953	59	*Rare Music and Music Literature*	
			(410)	*1,10,13
2002	_____.			
	1953	60	*Music. Music Literature*	
			(374)	*8,10,13
2003	_____.			
	1953	61	*Music Literature. Music by British Composers*	
			(725)	*1.13
2004	_____.			
	1953	62	*17th and 18th Century Music*	
			(711)	*1,8,10,13
2005	_____.			
	1954	63	*Books and Booklets on Musical Instruments*	
			(323)	*1,10,13
2006	_____.			
	1954	—	*21 Musical Rarities (printed or autograph)*	
			(21)	*Macnutt
2007	_____.			
	1954	64	*Music and Music Literature*	
			(438)	*1,8,10
2008	_____.			
	1954	65	*Scores. Biography. Books on Violin*	
			(533)	*1,8,10
2009	_____.			
	1955	66	*Music and Music Lit. Biographies (I-W)*	
			(368)	*1,8,10,13
2010	_____.			
	1955	67	*Music and Music Literature*	
			(329)	*10,13
2011	_____.			
	1955	68	*Music for Voice. Books on Singing*	
			(546)	*1,8,10
2012	_____.			
	1955	69	*Scores and Parts*	
			(344)	*1,8,10
2013	_____.			
	1955	—	*Mozart, 1756-1956*	
			(421)	*8,13
2014	_____.			
	1956	70	*Music Literatur and Music*	
			(376)	*1,8,10
2015	_____.			
	1956	71	*Music from 1600 to 1860*	
			(227)	*1,8,10
2016	_____.			
	1956	72	*Music and Music Literature before 1840*	
			(428)	*1,8,10,13

1 Compiler/State University of New York (Buffalo) **2** The British Library (London) **3** Gemeentemuseum (Den Haag) **4** The Grolier Club (N.Y.C.) **5** Hirsch Collection, British Library (London) **6** D.W. Krummel (Urbana) **7** Library of Congress (Washington, D.C.) **8** Library and Museum of the Performing Arts (N.Y.C.) **9** William Reeves (London) **10** Sibley Library, Eastman School of Music (Rochester) **11** Nigel Simeone (Tunbridge Wells, Kent) **12** Vereeniging ter Bervordering van de Belangen des Boekhandels (Amsterdam) **13** University of Virginia (Charlottesville) **14** University of California at Los Angeles **15** Generally available

2017	**HYMAN, LEONARD (London) (continued)**			
	1957	73	*Music Literature* (424)	*1,8,10
2018	____.			
	1957	74	*Vocal Music* (342)	*1,8,10
2019	____.			
	1957	75	*Engraved Portraits. Music and Music Literature* (312)	*1,8,10
2020	____.			
	1957	76	*Antiq. Music & Music Lit. Scores. Portraits* (240)	*10,13
2021	____.			
	1957	—	*Mozart Manuscript. Beethoven First Editions* (16)	*10
2022	____.			
	1958	77	*Antiq. Music Books. Periodicals* (331)	*1,10,13
2023	____.			
	1958	78	*Music Biographies. Min. Scores. Antiq. Music* (356)	*1,10
2024	____.			
	1958	79	*Vocal Music* (242)	*10
2025	____.			
	1958	80	*History. Dictionaries. Instruments* (295)	*1,8
2026	____.			
	1959	81	*Scarce Music and Music Literature* (287)	*8,10
2027	____.			
	1959	82	*Music and Music Literature. Autograph Letters* (212)	*10
2028	____.			
	1959	83	*Antiquarian Music. Scores. Books* (312)	*9,10
2029	____.			
	1960	85	*Shakespeareana. Music and Music Literature* (400)	*1
2030	**HYMAN, LEONARD (MUSIC) LTD. (London)**			
	1960-61	86	*Rare Music and Music Literature* (328)	*Macnutt
2031	____. [prop., **RICHARD MACNUTT**]			
	1961	87	*Rare Music and Music Literature* (450)	*1,4
2032	____.			
	1961	88	*Music and Music Literature* (456)	*1,4,8,10

1 Compiler/State University of New York (Buffalo)   2 The British Library (London)   3 Gemeentemuseum (Den Haag)   4 The Grolier Club (N.Y.C.)   5 Hirsch Collection, British Library (London)   6 D.W. Krummel (Urbana)   7 Library of Congress (Washington, D.C.)   8 Library and Museum of the Performing Arts (N.Y.C.)   9 William Reeves (London)   10 Sibley Library, Eastman School of Music (Rochester)   11 Nigel Simeone (Tunbridge Wells, Kent)   12 Vereeniging ter Bervordering van de Belangen des Boekhandels (Amsterdam)   13 University of Virginia (Charlottesville)   14 University of California at Los Angeles   15 Generally available

2033 **HYMAN, LEONARD (MUSIC) LTD. (Lonodn) (continued)**
    1961   89   *Music and Music Literature*
                               (467)   *1,4,8

2034   _____.
    1962   90   *Music and Music Literature*
                               (419)   *1,4,6,8

2035   _____.
    1961   91   *Music and Music Literature*
                               (808)   *1,4,6,8,10

2036   _____.
    1963   92   *Music and Music Literature*
                               (585)   *1,4,6,8

2037   _____.
    1963   93   *Music and Music Literature*
                               (504)   *1,4,6,8

2038   _____.
    1963   —   *Music and Books by Berlioz*
                               (268)   *14

2039   _____.
    1961   List   1   *Autographs: Composers, Conductors, etc.*
                               (100)   *8

2040   _____.
    1961   do.   2   *Biography and Criticism*
                               (158)   *8

2041   _____.
    1962   do.   3   *Autographs. Composers, Conductors, etc.*
                               (243)   *8

2042   _____.
    1962   do.   4   *Portraits of Musicians (excluding Singers)*
                               (554)   *8

2043 **HYRE, KENNETH M. (Los Angeles, CA.)**
    1981?   7   *Opera. Ballet. Dance*
                               (640)   *1

2044 **ICHTHYSVERLAG (Stuttgart)**
    1972   —   *Modernes Antiquariat*
                               (pp.27-29)   *13

2045 **INTERNATIONAL AUTOGRAPHS (N.Y.C.)**
    s.d.   14   *ALS. Mss. and Documents*
                               (1-86)   *8 (incomplete)

2046   _____.
    1975   25   *ALS. Mss. and Documents*
                               (1-86)   *1,8

2047 **IREDALE, A. (Torquay)**
    1884   16   *[Musical Works... Catalogue on application]*
                               (?)   [not located]

2048 **ISLER, PETER G. (Basel)**
    1983   M1   *Bücher. Partituren. Klavierausz., 1768-1978*
                               (303)   *15

---

1 Compiler/State University of New York (Buffalo)   **2** The British Library (London)   **3** Gemeentemuseum (Den Haag)   **4** The Grolier Club (N.Y.C.)   **5** Hirsch Collection, British Library (London)   **6** D.W. Krummel (Urbana)   **7** Library of Congress (Washington, D.C.)   **8** Library and Museum of the Performing Arts (N.Y.C.)   **9** William Reeves (London)   **10** Sibley Library, Eastman School of Music (Rochester)   **11** Nigel Simeone (Tunbridge Wells, Kent)   **12** Vereeniging ter Bervordering van de Belangen des Boekhandels (Amsterdam)   **13** University of Virginia (Charlottesville)   **14** University of California at Los Angeles   **15** Generally available

2049 **ISRAEL, B. M. (Amsterdam)**
      1936   27   *Muziek*
                                 (368)   *12

2050 **JAMMES, P. (Paris)**
      1934?   55   *[untitled]*
                                 (3757-4126)   *3,5

2051 _____.
      1934?   56   *[untitled]*
                                 (4658-872)   *3,5

2052 _____.
      193_   57   *[untitled]*
                                 (5491-673)   *3

2053 _____.
      1934?   59   *[untitled]*
                                 (609-90)   *3

2054 **JEFFERY, BRIAN (London)**
      1983   1   *Music (18th Century). Guitar Music. Americana*
                                 (175)   *1

2055 **JOACHIMSTHAL, MUZIEKANTIQUARIAT (Utrecht)**
      [1964]   1   *Literature. Music. Autographs*
                                 (352)   *6,10,12,13

2056 _____.
      [1965]   2   *Prints. Mss. Musicology*
                                 (380)   *8,11,12

2057 _____.
      [1966]   3   *[Musical Literature]*
                                 (440)   *8,11,13,14

2058 _____.
      [?]   4   *[Musical Literature]*
                                 (285)   *6,8,14

2059 _____.
      1966   5   *[Musical Literature]. Miscellaneous*
                                 (345)   *10,12,13,14

2060 _____.
      [1968]   6   *Musical Literature*
                                 (219)   *1,8,10,12,13

2061 _____.
      [1969]   7   *Miscellaneous. Songbooks*
                                 (538)   *1,8,10,11,13

2062 _____.
      [1970]   8   *[Musical Literature]*
                                 (491)   *8,12,13,14

2063 _____.
      [1972]   9   *[Musical Literature]*
                                 (171)   *12,13

2064 _____.
      [1978]   10   *[Musical Literature]*
                                 (419)   *11,13,14

1 Compiler/State University of New York (Buffalo)   2 The British Library (London)   3 Gemeentemuseum
(Den Haag)   4 The Grolier Club (N.Y.C.)   5 Hirsch Collection, British Library (London)   6 D.W.
Krummel (Urbana)   7 Library of Congress (Washington, D.C.)   8 Library and Museum of the Performing
Arts (N.Y.C.)   9 William Reeves (London)   10 Sibley Library, Eastman School of Music (Rochester)
11 Nigel Simeone (Tunbridge Wells, Kent)   12 Vereeniging ter Bervordering van de Belangen des
Boekhandels (Amsterdam)   13 University of Virginia (Charlottesville)   14 University of California at Los
Angeles   15 Generally available

2065 **JOACHIMSTHAL, MUZIEKANTIQUARIAT (Utrecht) (continued)**
 1979   25   *[Music Literature]*
                                  (696)   *1,13
2066 _____.
       [1969]   List   ?   *Coll: Collegium "Audi et Tace"*
                                  (49)   *1,3,13
2067 _____.
       [1967?]   2   *Stocklist [Music Literature]*
                                  (558)   *8
2068 _____.
       [1967?]   3   *Stocklist [idem.]*
                                  (328)   *1,8,10
2069 _____.
       [1968?]   4   *Music Stocklist*
                                  (328)   *1,8,10,11
2070 _____.
       12/1969   5   *Stocklist [Music]*
                                  (351)   *11
2071 _____.
       1/1970   6   *Miscellaneous (Stocklist)*
                                  (343)   *11
2072 _____.
       2/1970   7   *Stocklist [Music]*
                                  (450)   *11
2073 _____.
       197_   8   *Stocklist [Music]*
                                  (347)   *11
2074 _____.
       197_   9   *Catalogues. Congresses. Programs. Yearbooks*
                                  (237)   *11
2075 _____.
       19__   —   *Vocal Scores [Stocklist?]*
                                  (410)   *6
2076 _____.
       s.d.   Misc.   —   *Books on the Organ*
                                  (8pp.)   *1,10
2077 _____.
       1967?   do.   —   *Biographies, old and new*
                                  (792)   *1,13
2078 _____.
       1968   do.   —   *Documentation 1968: Vol. I:1*
                                  (16pp.)   *13
2079 **JOB & ENKE (N.Y.C.)**
       1874   —   *Imported and domestic Music. Instruments*
                                  (?)   *7
2080 **JONG, E. D. DE (Doetinchem)**
       s.d.   2   *[German, French, English Books on Music]*
                                  (?)   *12

---

1 Compiler/State University of New York (Buffalo)   **2** The British Library (London)   **3** Gemeentemuseum (Den Haag)   **4** The Grolier Club (N.Y.C.)   **5** Hirsch Collection, British Library (London)   **6** D.W. Krummel (Urbana)   **7** Library of Congress (Washington, D.C.)   **8** Library and Museum of the Performing Arts (N.Y.C.)   **9** William Reeves (London)   **10** Sibley Library, Eastman School of Music (Rochester)   **11** Nigel Simeone (Tunbridge Wells, Kent)   **12** Vereeniging ter Bervordering van de Belangen des Boekhandels (Amsterdam)   **13** University of Virginia (Charlottesville)   **14** University of California at Los Angeles   **15** Generally available

2081   "JOURNALFRANZ" ARNULF LIEBING see LIEBING, ARNULF

2082   JUX, DR. H. (Berlin)
      1960   44   *Allgemeine Musikgeschichte. Theater. Film*
                         (1971)   [IBAK]

2083   _____.
      1962   59   *Musik. Theater*
                         (2048)   [IBAK]

2084   KAMPFFMEYER, TH. (Berlin)
      1899   388   *Werke a. d. Gebiete d. Musik u. d. Theaters*
                         (56pp., incompl   ete)*8

2085   KANTOROWICZ, E. (Berlin)
      1900   30   */Moderne Werke ü. Musik/*
                         (?)   [ZiMG]

2086   KARAFIAT, FR. [later WILLIAM] (Brno)
      1914   47   */not examined/*
                         (?)   *4

2087   KARMIOLE, KENNETH (Los Angeles, CA.)
      1978   —   *Performing Arts*
                         (233)   *13

2088   KARNO, HOWARD (Santa Monica, CA.)
      1979?   14   *Performing Arts of Latin America*
                         (147)   *14

2089   _____.
      1979?   30   *Performing Arts of Latin America*
                         (361)   *8,14

2090   _____.
      1979?   55   *Performing Arts*
                         (423)   *14

2091   _____.
      1983   138   *Literature. Theatre. Dance and Music*
                         (1792)   *8

2092   KATZBICHLER, EMIL (Munich/Giebings)
      [1963]   1   *Musikliteratur*
                         (554)   *6,8

2093   _____.
      [1963?]   2   *Musikliteratur. Musikdrucke*
                         (700)   *6

2094   _____.
      [1963?]   3   *Musikliteratur. Studienpartituren*
                         (590)   *6

2095   _____.
      [1954]   4   *Musikliteratur*
                         (518)   *6

2096   _____.
      [1964?]   5   ?
                         (?)   [not located]

---

1 Compiler/State University of New York (Buffalo)   **2** The British Library (London)   **3** Gemeentemuseum (Den Haag)   **4** The Grolier Club (N.Y.C.)   **5** Hirsch Collection, British Library (London)   **6** D.W. Krummel (Urbana)   **7** Library of Congress (Washington, D.C.)   **8** Library and Museum of the Performing Arts (N.Y.C.)   **9** William Reeves (London)   **10** Sibley Library, Eastman School of Music (Rochester)   **11** Nigel Simeone (Tunbridge Wells, Kent)   **12** Vereeniging ter Bervordering van de Belangen des Boekhandels (Amsterdam)   **13** University of Virginia (Charlottesville)   **14** University of California at Los Angeles   **15** Generally available

2097   **KATZBICHLER, EMIL**   (Munich/Giebings) (continued)

	[1964?]	6	*Musikliteratur* (420)	*6,8
2098	_____. [1965]	7	*Musikliteratur. Klavierauszüge* (583)	*6,12
2099	_____. [1965]	8	*Miscellanea* (759)	*6,8,10,12,14
2100	_____. [1965]	9	*Musikliteratur. Klavierauszüge* (236)	*6,12
2101	_____. [1965]	10	*Musikliteratur. Klavierauszüge* (320)	*6,10,12
2102	_____. [1966]	11	*Musikdrucke* (211)	*1,6,8,12
2103	_____. [1966]	12	*Musikliteratur* (677)	*1,6,12
2104	_____. [1967]	13	*Musikdrucke* (285)	*1,6,12
2105	_____. [1967]	14	*Musikliteratur* (830)	*1,6,8,12,14
2106	_____. [1967]	15	*Musikliteratur* (1000)	*1,6,8,14
2107	_____. [1967]	16	*Musikliteratur* (707)	*1,6,8,14
2108	_____. [1968]	17	*Musikliteratur. Partituren* (1519)	*1,6,10,12,14
2109	_____. [1968]	18	*Musikliteratur. Musikdrucke* (877)	*1,6,8,10,12,14
2110	_____. [1968]	19	*Musikliteratur. Musikdrucke* (1042)	*1,6,8,10,12,14
2111	_____. [1969]	20	*Musikliteratur. Musica Sacra* (1274)	*1,6,8,10,13,14
2112	_____. [1970]	21	*Musikliteratur. 100 Klavierauszüge* (1000)	*1,6,8,12,14

1 Compiler/State University of New York (Buffalo)   **2** The British Library (London)   **3** Gemeentemuseum (Den Haag)   **4** The Grolier Club (N.Y.C.)   **5** Hirsch Collection, British Library (London)   **6** D.W. Krummel (Urbana)   **7** Library of Congress (Washington, D.C.)   **8** Library and Museum of the Performing Arts (N.Y.C.)   **9** William Reeves (London)   **10** Sibley Library, Eastman School of Music (Rochester)   **11** Nigel Simeone (Tunbridge Wells, Kent)   **12** Vereeniging ter Bervordering van de Belangen des Boekhandels (Amsterdam)   **13** University of Virginia (Charlottesville)   **14** University of California at Los Angeles   **15** Generally available

2113 **KATZBICHLER, EMIL (Munich/Giebings) (continued)**

	1970	22	*Musikliteratur* (622)	*1,6,10,12
2114	____. [1971]	23	*Musikliteratur. Vokalmusik* (975)	*1,6,8,10,13,14
2115	____. [1972]	24	*Musikliteratur. Klavierauszüge* (1391)	*1,8,10,13,14
2116	____. [1972]	25	*Musikliteratur* (1245)	*1,6,8,10,12,14
2117	____. 1975	26	*Musikliteratur, A - P* (1219)	*1,8,10,14
2118	____. 197_	27	*Musikdrucke. Musikliteratur, R - Z* (744)	*1,8,10,13,14
2119	____. 1978	28	*Musikliteratur. Klavier- und Kammermusik* (971)	*1,8,10,13,14
2120	____. 1979	19	*Musikliteratur. Musica Rara* (957)	*1,8,10,13,14
2121	____. 1980	30	*Musikliteratur. Alte und seltene Notendrucke* (852)	*1,6,8,14
2122	____. 1982	31	*Musiklit. Musikdrucke. Erst- und Frühdrucke* (786)	*15
2123	____. 1983	32	*Musikliteratur und Musik* (1174)	*15

2124 **KAUFFMANN, J. (Frankfurt a. M.)**

	188_	12	*Musikalische Literatur* (?)	[not located]
2125	____. 1896?	23	*Musikalische Synagogen-Verzeichnis* (?)	*8
2126	____. 1900?	33	*Musikalische Synagogen-Verzeichnis* (?)	*8
2127	____. 1906	55	*Musikalien* (?)	[not located]
2128	____. 1912?	67	*Musikalien* (?)	[not located]

1 Compiler/State University of New York (Buffalo)   **2** The British Library (London)   **3** Gemeentemuseum (Den Haag)   **4** The Grolier Club (N.Y.C.)   **5** Hirsch Collection, British Library (London)   **6** D.W. Krummel (Urbana)   **7** Library of Congress (Washington, D.C.)   **8** Library and Museum of the Performing Arts (N.Y.C.)   **9** William Reeves (London)   **10** Sibley Library, Eastman School of Music (Rochester)   **11** Nigel Simeone (Tunbridge Wells, Kent)   **12** Vereeniging ter Bervordering van de Belangen des Boekhandels (Amsterdam)   **13** University of Virginia (Charlottesville)   **14** University of California at Los Angeles   **15** Generally available

2129 KAUFFMANN, J. (Frankfurt a. M.) (continued)
      1925   —   Synagogen-componisten und ihre Werke
                              (?)   [not located]
2130 KAUFFMANN, RICHARD (Stuttgart)
      1902   94   /Musik und Musikliteratur/
                              (?)   *7
2131 KERLER, HEINRICH (Ulm)
      1900   278 Coll: Engel, F. Theater. Oper. Partituren
                              (?)   [ZiMG]
2132 _____.
      [1908]   375 Coll: Köstlin, H. und A. Zumsteeg
                              (1785)   *5,7
2133 _____.
      s.d.   417 Geschichte der Musik
                              (?)   *5,7
2134 KERSHNER, M. (N.Y.C.)
      19_   155 Nature of Literature. Music. Art
                              (1398-1495)   *13
2135 KERST, ROLF (Göttingen)
      1960   349z Musik. Theater. Tanz
                              (1149)   [IBAK]
2136 _____.
      1960   379s Musik. Theater. Tanz
                              (573)   [IBAK]
2137 _____.
      1961   408k Musik. Theater. Tanz
                              (1038)   [IBAK]
2138 _____.
      [1962]   451c Musik. Tanz. Theater. Film
                              (955)   [IBAK]
2139 _____.
      [1963]   481b Musik. Theater. Film. Tanz
                              (999)   *6
2140 _____.
      [1964]   516g Musik. Tanz. Theater. Film
                              (1004)   *6
2141 _____.
      [1965]   554 Musik. Tanz. Theater. Film
                              (998)   *6
2142 _____.
      [1968]   607k Kunst- und Musik-wissenschaft
                              (1243k-1378k)   *1
2143 _____.
      [1968]   614z Musik. Theater. Tanz
                              (1274)   *1,12
2144 _____.
      [1970]   645b Musik. Theater. Tanz
                              (939)   *1,12

2145 **KERST, ROLF (Göttingen) (continued)**
  [1971]   676 *Musik. Theater. Tanz*
         (1432)   *1,12

2146   _____.
  [1980]   M80 *Musik. Tanz. Theater. Film*
         (1455)   *1

2147 **KEW BOOKS (Richmond, Surrey and N.Y.C.)**
  1976   — *Wagner*
         (751)   *1,14

2148   _____.
  1983   — *Wagner Centenary Catalogue*
         (775)   *1

2149   _____.
  1984?   — *Wagner Centenary Supplement*
         (64)   *1

2150 **KIENREICH, JOS. A. (Graz)**
  [1967]   216 *Bildende Kunst. Musik. Tanz*
         (339)   [IBAK]

2151 **KIRCHOFF & WIGAND (Leipzig)**
  1861   57 *Musikalien und Werke ü. Musik*
         (?)   [Petzholdt]

2152   _____.
  1862   61 *Musikalien und Werke ü. Musik*
         (?)   [Petzholdt]

2153   _____.
  1862   68 *Musikalien und Werke ü. Musik*
         (628)   *12

2154   _____.
  1863   74 *Musikalien und Werke ü. Musik*
         (?)   [Petzholdt]

2155   _____.
  1863   85 *Musikalien und Werke ü. Musik*
         (?)   [Petzholdt]

2156   _____.
  1/1864   94 *Musikalien und Werke ü. Musik*
         (835)   *8

2157   _____.
  1864   109 *Musikalien und Werke ü. Musik*
         (?)   [Petzholdt]

2158   _____.
  1865   122 *Musikalien und Werke ü. Musik*
         (778)   [Petzholdt]

2159   _____.
  6/1866   158 *Philologie. Musikwissenschaft*
         (445-682)   *8

2160   _____.
  1869   247 *Musikwissenschaft und Musikalien*
         (552)   *12

---

1 Compiler/State University of New York (Buffalo) **2** The British Library (London) **3** Gemeentemuseum (Den Haag) **4** The Grolier Club (N.Y.C.) **5** Hirsch Collection, British Library (London) **6** D.W. Krummel (Urbana) **7** Library of Congress (Washington, D.C.) **8** Library and Museum of the Performing Arts (N.Y.C.) **9** William Reeves (London) **10** Sibley Library, Eastman School of Music (Rochester) **11** Nigel Simeone (Tunbridge Wells, Kent) **12** Vereeniging ter Bervordering van de Belangen des Boekhandels (Amsterdam) **13** University of Virginia (Charlottesville) **14** University of California at Los Angeles **15** Generally available

2161 **KIRCHOFF & WIGAND (Leipzig) (continued)**
      9/1869   252   *Geschichte der Musik. Ältere Musik. Opern*
                                 (2785)   *8,12

2162 _____.
      1870   265   *Musikalien. Hymnologie*
                                 (?)   [MfM]

2163 _____.
      1870   285   *Musikalien und Schriften ü. Musik*
                                 (?)   [MfM]

2164 _____.
      1870   286   *Musikwissenschaft und Musikalien*
                                 (2388)   *8,12

2165 _____.
      1871   305   *Musikwissenschaft. Praktische Musik*
                                 (1560)   *12

2166 _____.
      1871   319   *Musikwissenschaft. Praktische Musik*
                                 (?)   *12

2167 _____.
      1873   366   *Musikwissenschaft. Praktische Musik*
                                 (2235)   *12

2168 _____.
      1873   386   *Musikwissenschaft. Praktische Musik*
                                 (2531)   *5

2169 _____.
      1874   415   *Musikwissenschaft. Praktische Musik*
                                 (2531)   *12

2170 _____.
      1874   420   *Musikwissenschaft und Musikalien*
                                 (2425)   *12

2171 _____.
      1874   444   *Musikwissenschaft und Musikalien*
                                 (2164)   *12

2172 _____.
      1876   474   *Musikwissenschaft und Musikalien*
                                 (?)   *12

2173 _____.
      1877   505   *Musikwissenschaft und Musikalien*
                                 (1808)   *12

2174 _____.
      1878   534   *Musikwissenschaft und Musikalien*
                                 (1723)   *12

2175 _____.
      1879   562   *Musikwissenschaft und Musikalien*
                                 (1554)   *12

2176 _____.
      1880   574   *Musikwissenschaft und Musikalien*
                                 ?   *12

2177   **KIRCHOFF & WIGAND (Leipzig) (continued)**
     1880   591   *Musikwissenschaft und Musikalien*
                                  (1541)   *12

2178   _____.
     1881   617   *Musikwissenschaft und Musikalien*
                                    (1494)   *12

2179   _____.
     1882   645   *Bücher und Musikalien*
                                    (1483)   *12

2180   _____.
     1883   678   *Musikwissenschaft und Musikalien*
                                    (1536)   *5,12

2181   _____.
     1884   709   *Musikwissenschaft und Musikalien*
                                    (1649)   *5,12

2182   _____.
     1887   791   *Musikwissenschaft und Musikalien*
                                    (1661)   *5

2183   _____.
     1888   814   *?*
                                    (1238)   [MfM]

2184   _____.
     1889   834   *Coll: Nohl*
                                    (?)   *4

2185   _____.
     1891   881   *Musikwissenschaft*
                                    (1190)   *12

2186   _____.
     1893   915   *Musikwissenschaft und Musikalien*
                                    (1313)   *12

2187   _____.
     1894   936   *Musikwissenschaft und Musikalien*
                                    (1249)   *12

2188   _____.
     1895   952   *Musikwissenschaft. Praktische Musik*
                                    (1531)   *12

2189   _____.
     1898   1016   *Musikwissenschaft. Praktische Musik*
                                    (1178)   *12

2190   _____.
     1899   1033   *Musikwissenschaft. Praktische Musik*
                                    (?)   [ZiMG]

2191   _____.
     1900   —   */Werke des 18. und 19. Jahrhunderts/*
                                    (?)   [not located]

2192   **KLEIN, ELLIOT, LTD. (N.Y.C.)**
     1979   3   *Folksong, Folk Medicine and Gypsies*
                                    (533)   *8

---

1 Compiler/State University of New York (Buffalo)   **2** The British Library (London)   **3** Gemeentemuseum (Den Haag)   **4** The Grolier Club (N.Y.C.)   **5** Hirsch Collection, British Library (London)   **6** D.W. Krummel (Urbana)   **7** Library of Congress (Washington, D.C.)   **8** Library and Museum of the Performing Arts (N.Y.C.)   **9** William Reeves (London)   **10** Sibley Library, Eastman School of Music (Rochester)   **11** Nigel Simeone (Tunbridge Wells, Kent)   **12** Vereeniging ter Bervordering van de Belangen des Boekhandels (Amsterdam)   **13** University of Virginia (Charlottesville)   **14** University of California at Los Angeles   **15** Generally available

2193 **KLEMMING, H. (Stockholm)**
    1871   2   *Musikalier och Musiklitteratur*
                    (808)   *12

2194 **KNUF, FRITS (Amsterdam)**
    1959   42   *Muziekwetenschap. Muziek voor Pianoforte*
                    (476)   *8,14

2195 _____.
    [1961]   54   *Oude Uitg. Kinderboeken. Liedboekjes*
                    (605)   *12

2196 _____.
    [1971]   99   *Rederijkes. Lied- en Volsboeken*
                    (317)   *12

2197 _____.
    [197-]   —   *Colls: Cronheim, Mengelberg and Vreedenburg*
                    (872)   *1,10,13

2198 _____.
    [1976]   121   *Colls: Cronheim, Mengelberg, Vreedenberg (2)*
                    (373)   *1

2199 _____.
    [197-]   —   *Books on Music*
                    (296)   *1,8,13,14

2200 _____.
    [1979]   132   *Music [and Musical Literature]*
                    (166)   *8,10,13,14

2201 _____.
    1981   —   *Rare Music Collection*
                    (13pp.)   *13

2202 _____.
    1975   Bull.   1   *Bibliography ... Rare old Books*
                    (173)   *8

2203 **KOEHLER, K. F. (Leipzig)**
    1885   410   *Kunst. Musik*
                    (?)   *4

2204 _____.
    1905   5__   *Bücher und Musikalien*
                    (?)   *12

2205 _____.
    1911   5__   *Bücher und Musikalien*
                    (?)   *12

2206 _____.
    1914   N.F.3   *Deutsche Literatur. Theater. Musik*
                    (?)   *12

2207 _____.
    1922   55   *Musik. Theater*
                    (?)   *12

2208 _____.
    1923   177   *Musikgeschichte*
                    (?)   *12

---

1 Compiler/State University of New York (Buffalo)   **2** The British Library (London)   **3** Gemeentemuseum (Den Haag)   **4** The Grolier Club (N.Y.C.)   **5** Hirsch Collection, British Library (London)   **6** D.W. Krummel (Urbana)   **7** Library of Congress (Washington, D.C.)   **8** Library and Museum of the Performing Arts (N.Y.C.)   **9** William Reeves (London)   **10** Sibley Library, Eastman School of Music (Rochester)   **11** Nigel Simeone (Tunbridge Wells, Kent)   **12** Vereeniging ter Bervordering van de Belangen des Boekhandels (Amsterdam)   **13** University of Virginia (Charlottesville)   **14** University of California at Los Angeles   **15** Generally available

2209　**KOEHLER, K. F. (Leipzig) (continued)**
　　　　1926　　　　　5　　*Büchertisch: [Musik und Theater]*
　　　　　　　　　　　　　　(1344-597,662-7)　　　　　　　　　　　67) *5

2210　　____.
　　　　1930　　　　　18　　*Büchertisch: [Musik und Theater]*
　　　　　　　　　　　　　　(1751-2098)　　　　　　　　　　　　　　　*13

2211　**KOEHLER, PAUL (Leipzig)**
　　　　1924　　Anz.　　22　　*Literatur. Musik. Theater. Kunst*
　　　　　　　　　　　　　　(1750)　　　　　　　　　　　　　　　　　*12

2212　**KOEHLER & VOLCKMAR & CO. (Leipzig/Stuttgart)**
　　　　1926　　　　　—　　*Barsortiments Lagerkatalog*
　　　　　　　　　　　　　　(?)　　　　　　　　　　　　　　　　　　*12

2213　　____.
　　　　1928　　　　　—　　*Lagerkatalog*
　　　　　　　　　　　　　　(?)　　　　　　　　　　　　　　　　　　*12

2214　**KOENIG'S, BENJAMIN, COUNTRY BOOKSHOP (Plainfield, Vt.)**
　　　　1977　　　　　—　　*Bell Books: the second List*
　　　　　　　　　　　　　　(4pp.)　　　　　　　　　　　　　　　　　*8

2215　**KOERPER, J. (Vienna)**
　　　　1906　　　　　19　　*Kunst und Musik*
　　　　　　　　　　　　　　(?)　　　　　　　　　　　　　　　　　　*12

2216　**KOK, BOEKENTOKO A. (Amsterdam)**
　　　　1958　　　　　54　　*Muziekgeschiedenis*
　　　　　　　　　　　　　　(8pp.)　　　　　　　　　　　　　　　　　*12

2217　　____.
　　　　1959　　　　　62　　*Tooneel. Film. Ballet. Muziek*
　　　　　　　　　　　　　　(6pp.)　　　　　　　　　　　　　　　　　*12

2218　　____.
　　　　[1960]　　　　78　　*Kunst. Muziek*
　　　　　　　　　　　　　　(300-545)　　　　　　　　　　　　　　[IBAK]

2219　　____.
　　　　1960　　　　　91　　*Muziek. Muziekgeschiedenis. Dans*
　　　　　　　　　　　　　　(6pp.)　　　　　　　　　　　　　　　　　*12

2220　　____.
　　　　1960　　　　　105　　*Muziekgeschiedenis. Ballet*
　　　　　　　　　　　　　　(6pp.)　　　　　　　　　　　　　　　　[IBAK]

2221　　____.
　　　　1961　　　　　123　　*Muziek*
　　　　　　　　　　　　　　(6pp.)　　　　　　　　　　　　　　　　　*12

2222　　____.
　　　　1963　　　　　182　　*Varia. Ballet. Muziek*
　　　　　　　　　　　　　　(10pp.)　　　　　　　　　　　　　　　[IBAK]

2223　　____.
　　　　1963　　　　　186　　*Muziek-literatur en Biografieen*
　　　　　　　　　　　　　　(312)　　　　　　　　　　　　　　　　[IBAK]

2224　　____.
　　　　1963　　　　　188　　*Muziek. Folklore*
　　　　　　　　　　　　　　(313-694)　　　　　　　　　　　　　　　*12

---

1 Compiler/State University of New York (Buffalo)　　**2** The British Library (London)　　**3** Gemeentemuseum (Den Haag)　　**4** The Grolier Club (N.Y.C.)　　**5** Hirsch Collection, British Library (London)　　**6** D.W. Krummel (Urbana)　　**7** Library of Congress (Washington, D.C.)　　**8** Library and Museum of the Performing Arts (N.Y.C.)　　**9** William Reeves (London)　　**10** Sibley Library, Eastman School of Music (Rochester)　　**11** Nigel Simeone (Tunbridge Wells, Kent)　　**12** Vereeniging ter Bervordering van de Belangen des Boekhandels (Amsterdam)　　**13** University of Virginia (Charlottesville)　　**14** University of California at Los Angeles　　**15** Generally available

2225 **KOK, BOEKENTOKO A. (Amsterdam) (continued)**
    1964   212   *Muziek*
                              (350)   *12

2226   _____.
    1965   238   *Kunst. Muziek. Tooneel*
                              (100-696)   *12

2227   _____.
    1965   247   *Muziek. Ballet*
                              (600-1149)   *12

2228 **KOLVOORD, R. (Windsor, Vt.)**
    1942   List   —   *Music and Musical Literature*
                              (217)   *8

2229 **KOOIMAN, E. (Wageningen)**
    1941   1   *Bevattende Muziekliteratur. Dans en Tooneel*
                              (285)   *3

2230   _____.
    1941   2   *Muziek en Muziekliteratur*
                              (1048, with #3)   *12

2231   _____.
    1942   3   *Muziek en Muziekliteratur*
                              (1048, with #2)   *12

2232   _____.
    s.d.   35   *Muziek en Muziekliteratur*
                              (500)   *12

2233   _____.
    1959   90   *Muziekliteratur*
                              (380)   *12

2234   _____.
    1959-61   91-94   *Muziekliteratur en Muziek*
                              (?)   *12

2235 **KORNE, HENRI DE (Utrecht)**
    1958   17   *Muziek*
                              (390)   *12

2236   _____.
    1958   18   *Muziek*
                              (299)   *12

2237   _____.
    1960   23   *Muziekliteratur*
                              (102)   [IBAK]

2238   _____.
    1960   24   *[Klavierauszüge]. Muziekliteratur*
                              (247)   *10

2239   _____.
    1961   25   *Books on Music*
                              (204)   *13

2240   _____.
    1961   26   *Books on Music*
                              (208)   *6

1 Compiler/State University of New York (Buffalo)   **2** The British Library (London)   **3** Gemeentemuseum (Den Haag)   **4** The Grolier Club (N.Y.C.)   **5** Hirsch Collection, British Library (London)   **6** D.W. Krummel (Urbana)   **7** Library of Congress (Washington, D.C.)   **8** Library and Museum of the Performing Arts (N.Y.C.)   **9** William Reeves (London)   **10** Sibley Library, Eastman School of Music (Rochester)   **11** Nigel Simeone (Tunbridge Wells, Kent)   **12** Vereeniging ter Bervordering van de Belangen des Boekhandels (Amsterdam)   **13** University of Virginia (Charlottesville)   **14** University of California at Los Angeles   **15** Generally available

2241	**KORNE, HENRI DE (Utrecht) (continued)**			
	1961	27	*Books on Music* (196)	*6
2242	_____.			
	1962	28	*Books on Music. Orchestral Scores* (218+)	*6,13
2243	_____.			
	1962	29	*Books on Music* (137)	*6,8,10,13
2244	_____.			
	[1963]	30	*Autograph Orchestral Scores. Vocal Scores* (216)	*6,8,10,13
2245	_____.			
	[1963]	31	*Musical Literature. Orchestral & Vocal Scores* (239)	*6,8,10,13
2246	_____.			
	[1963]	32	*Music. Orchestral Scores. Musical Literature* (201)	*6,8,10
2247	_____.			
	[1964]	33	*Musical Literature* (207)	*6,8,10,13
2248	_____.			
	[1964]	34	*Vocal Scores* (229)	*6,8,10
2249	_____.			
	[1964]	35	*Musical Literature* (126)	*6,8,10,13
2250	_____.			
	[1965]	36	*Musical Literature. Vocal Scores* (111)	*6,8,10,13
2251	_____.			
	[1965]	37	*Muziekliteratur* (157)	*12
2252	_____.			
	[1964]	List 1	*Music - Musicology* (55)	[IBAK]
2253	**KOSKY, J. (London)**			
	1975	—	*Music* (205)	*1,8
2254	_____.			
	1975	3	*Miniature and Study Scores* (361)	*1,8
2255	_____.			
	1975	5	*Books and Music* (79-147)	*1,8
2256	_____.			
	1975	6	*Music* (111)	*8

1 Compiler/State University of New York (Buffalo)   **2** The British Library (London)   **3** Gemeentemuseum (Den Haag)   **4** The Grolier Club (N.Y.C.)   **5** Hirsch Collection, British Library (London)   **6** D.W. Krummel (Urbana)   **7** Library of Congress (Washington, D.C.)   **8** Library and Museum of the Performing Arts (N.Y.C.)   **9** William Reeves (London)   **10** Sibley Library, Eastman School of Music (Rochester)   **11** Nigel Simeone (Tunbridge Wells, Kent)   **12** Vereeniging ter Bervordering van de Belangen des Boekhandels (Amsterdam)   **13** University of Virginia (Charlottesville)   **14** University of California at Los Angeles   **15** Generally available

2257   **KOSKY, J. (London) (continued)**
      1975   7   *Opera Scores*
                               (225)   *8

2258   **KRAFT, LEOPOLD (Vienna)**
      1888?   —   *Musik-katalog*
                               (16pp.)   [VdDM]

2259   _____.
      1892?   —   *idem.*
                               (17pp.)   [VdDM]

2260   **KRAUS, HANS P. (Vienna)**
      1934   2   *Coll: Proksch, J.*
                               (1717)   *1,5,6,8,10,12

2261   _____.
      s.d.   Angeb   22   *Old, Rare and Interesting Books and Music*
                               (91)   *5

2262   **KRAUS, HANS P. (N.Y.C.)**
      1942   List   7   *Music. Old and New Books. Some 1st Editions*
                               (66)   *8

2263   _____.
      1944   do.   34   *Russian Music. European Music. Musical Lit.*
                               (411)   *1,10

2264   _____.
      [1948]   do.   111   *Russian Music*
                               (212)   *13

2265   _____.
      s.d.   do.   125   *180 Rare Books and Mss.*
                               (61-70)   *13

2266   _____.
      [1950]   do.   140   *Early Music. Items from the Landau Collection*
                               (24)   *13

2267   _____.
      1952   do.   152   *Books & Periods. on Folklore, Music, Dance*
                               (569)   *8

2268   _____.
      s.d.   do.   194   *The Arts III:4-Music, Theatre, Ballet, Opera*
                               (46-72)   ,10

2269   _____.
      s.d.   do.   202   *Old Music. Rare Books and Mss.*
                               (52)   *8,10

2270   _____.
      1955   Bull.   9   *Books on Music. Scores. Periodicals*
                               (155)   *8

2271   _____.
      19577   do.   34   *Music*
                               (128)   *12

2272   **"DE KRING" (Fred. W. van der Wal) (Amsterdam)**
      [1962]   104   *Music. Theatre*
                               (299)   [IBAK]

---

1 Compiler/State University of New York (Buffalo)   **2** The British Library (London)   **3** Gemeentemuseum (Den Haag)   **4** The Grolier Club (N.Y.C.)   **5** Hirsch Collection, British Library (London)   **6** D.W. Krummel (Urbana)   **7** Library of Congress (Washington, D.C.)   **8** Library and Museum of the Performing Arts (N.Y.C.)   **9** William Reeves (London)   **10** Sibley Library, Eastman School of Music (Rochester)   **11** Nigel Simeone (Tunbridge Wells, Kent)   **12** Vereeniging ter Bervordering van de Belangen des Boekhandels (Amsterdam)   **13** University of Virginia (Charlottesville)   **14** University of California at Los Angeles   **15** Generally available

2273 **KRISCHE, THEODOR (Erlangen)**
    s.d.   —   *Musik. Tanz. Theater*
                              (192)   *13

2274 **KUBASTA & VOIGT (Vienna)**
    1875   37   *Musik und Theaterwissenschaft*
                       ?   *12

2275 **KUBON & SAGNER (Munich)**
    19_   2394   *Kunst. Arch. Film. Theater. Musik*
                              (124)   *1

2276 _____.
    1964   3056   *Bulgarien. Kunst. Musik. Theater*
                              (29)   [IBAK]

2277 _____.
    1965   3092   *Sowjetunion. Kunst. Musik. Theater*
                              (98)   [IBAK]

2278 _____.
    1965   3104   *Polen. Ethnogr. Film. Kunst. Musik*
                              (135)   [IBAK]

2279 _____.
    1965   3110   *Jugoslawien. Theater. Musik. Kunst*
                              (74)   [IBAK]

2280 _____.
    1965   3154   *Kunst. Musik. Theater. Film*
                              (88)   [IBAK]

2281 _____.
    1965   3161   *Böhmen, Mähren. Kunst. Musik. Theater*
                              (19)   [IBAK]

2282 _____.
    1966   3195   *Jugoslawien. Musik. Theater. Kunst*
                              (4pp.)   [IBAK]

2283 _____.
    1966   3226   *Polen. Kunst. Musik. Theater*
                              (3pp.)   [IBAK]

2284 _____.
    1966   3293   *Bulgarien. Kunst. Musik. Theater*
                              (5pp.)   [IBAK]

2285 _____.
    1966   3325   *Jugoslawien. Kunst. Musik. Film. Theater*
                              (4pp.)   [IBAK]

2286 **KUIJPER, A. (Haarlem)**
    1908-09   —   *Muziek-catalogus voor 1908-09*
                              (71pp.)   *12

2287 **KULTURA (Budapest)**
    1963   164   *Music*
                              (98)   *12

2288 **LA CERRA, PATRICK (Chicgao, Ill.)**
    1978   2   *Music Literature*
                              (304)   *1,8

2289 **LACKINGTON, J. (London)**
     1793   —   *Catalogue for 1793*
                         (6604-836)   *4

2290 **LÄMLIN, H. (Schaffhausen)**
     1861   —   *Sammlung von Musikalien*
                         (422)   [Petzholdt]

2291 **LAFFITTE, L. (Marseilles)**
     1924   28   *Sciences. Théâtre. Musique*
                         (?)   *12

2292 _____.
     1936   74   *Musique. Théâtre. Chasse*
                         (?)   *12

2293 **LANDRÉ, G. N. (Harlingen)**
     s.d.   10   *[Musical Literature. Dance. Theatre]*
                         (206)   *10

2294 _____.
     s.d.   11   *[Musical Literature. Dance. Theatre]*
                         (222)   *10

2295 _____.
     s.d.   20   *Books on Music, Music-hall, Theatre*
                         (1008)   *10

2296 _____.
     197_?   23   *[Musical Literature]*
                         (387)   *10

2297 _____.
     197_?   24   *[Musical Literature]*
                         (271)   *8,10

2298 _____.
     /1977   25   *General Music Literature*
                         (784)   *1,8,10,11

2299 _____.
     9/1977   26   *General Music Literature*
                         (367)   *1,8,10,11

2300 _____.
     11/1977   27   *General Music Literature*
                         (385)   *8,10,11

2301 _____.
     /1977   28   *Theatre. Dance. Music Hall. Chansons*
                         (246)   *1

2302 _____.
     12/1977   29   *Basic Catalogue*
                         (1134)   *1,10,11

2303 _____.
     /1977?   30   *General Music Literature*
                         (249)   *1,8,10,11

2304 _____.
     2/1978   31   *Books on Music. Theatre. Dance. Chansons*
                         (209)   *1,10,11

2305   **LANDRÉ, G. N. (Harlingen) (continued)**
     /1978   32   *Books on Music. Theatre. Dance. Chansons*
                          (210)   *1,8,10

2306   _____.
     4/1978   33   *Books on Music*
                          (196)   *1,8,10,11

2307   _____.
     5/1978   34   *Books on Music. Nederlandse Koormuziek*
                          (1-111,720-897)   *1,8,10,11

2308   _____.
     6?/1978   35   *Books on Music. Liederen*
                          (1034)   *1,10

2309   _____.
     7/1978   36   *Books on Music*
                          (445)   *1,8,10

2310   _____.
     /1978   37   *Bargain List of Books on Music*
                          (1-249,1035-461)   )*1,8,10,11

2311   _____.
     /1978   38   *Books. Church Music. Theatre. Dance. Chansons*
                          (2148)   *1,10,11

2312   _____.
     /1978   39   *Books on Music*
                          (406)   *1,8,10,11

2313   _____.
     1/1979   40   *Books on Music*
                          (416)   *1,10,11

2314   _____.
     /1979   41   *Books on Music*
                          (382)   *1,8

2315   _____.
     /1979   42   *Books on Music*
                          (302)   *1,8,10

2316   _____.
     /1979   43   *Books on Music. Kinderlied. Theatre. Dance*
                          (344)   *1,8,10

2317   _____.
     /1979   44   *Books on Music. Sheetmusic. Pop*
                          (312)   *1,8,10

2318   _____.
     /1979   45   *Books. Dutch Songbooks. Theatre. Dance*
                          (3089)   *1,8,10

2319   _____.
     /1979   46   *Bladmuziek*
                          (?)   *1,8,10

2320   _____.
     /1980   47   *Books on Music. Film. Miniature Scores*
                          (653)   *1,8,10

1 Compiler/State University of New York (Buffalo)   **2** The British Library (London)   **3** Gemeentemuseum (Den Haag)   **4** The Grolier Club (N.Y.C.)   **5** Hirsch Collection, British Library (London)   **6** D.W. Krummel (Urbana)   **7** Library of Congress (Washington, D.C.)   **8** Library and Museum of the Performing Arts (N.Y.C.)   **9** William Reeves (London)   **10** Sibley Library, Eastman School of Music (Rochester) **11** Nigel Simeone (Tunbridge Wells, Kent)   **12** Vereeniging ter Bervordering van de Belangen des Boekhandels (Amsterdam)   **13** University of Virginia (Charlottesville)   **14** University of California at Los Angeles   **15** Generally available

2321 **LANDRÉ, G. N. (Harlingen) (continued)**

	/1980	48	*Books on Music. Bladmuziek. Kinderlieder*	
			(369)	*1,8,10
2322	_____.			
	/1980	49	*Books on Music. Bladmuziek. Dutch Songbooks*	
			(450)	*1,8,10
2323	_____.			
	/1980	50	*Books on Music. Neue Musik*	
			(418)	*1,8,10
2324	_____.			
	/1980	51	*Books on Music*	
			(329)	*8,10
2325	_____.			
	/1980	52	*Books on Music. Volksmuziek. Miniature Scores*	
			(481)	*8
2326	_____.			
	/1980	53	*Books on Music. Rare Books. Theatre. Dance*	
			(336)	*1,8,10
2327	_____.			
	/1980	54	*Books on Music. Theatre. Dance. Film*	
			(922)	*1,10
2328	_____.			
	/1980	55	*Books on Music. Festschriften*	
			(403)	*1,10*1,10
2329	_____.			
	/1980	56	*Bladmuziek. New Books on Music*	
			(422)	*1,8,10
2330	_____.			
	/1980	57/2	*Books on Music*	
			(2629)	*1,8,10
2331	_____.			
	/1980	58	*Books on Music*	
			(368)	*1,10
2332	_____.			
	/1980	59	*Books on Music. Chansons. Theatre. Film*	
			(360)	*1,8,10
2333	_____.			
	/1980	60	*Books on Music*	
			(380)	*1,10
2334	_____.			
	/1981	61	*Books on Music. Volksmuziek*	
			(327)	*1,10
2335	_____.			
	/1981	62	*Books on Music. A-Z*	
			(427)	*1,10
2336	_____.			
	/1981	63	*Composers. General. Varia*	
			(505)	*1,8,10

1 Compiler/State University of New York (Buffalo)   **2** The British Library (London)   **3** Gemeentemuseum (Den Haag)   **4** The Grolier Club (N.Y.C.)   **5** Hirsch Collection, British Library (London)   **6** D.W. Krummel (Urbana)   **7** Library of Congress (Washington, D.C.)   **8** Library and Museum of the Performing Arts (N.Y.C.)   **9** William Reeves (London)   **10** Sibley Library, Eastman School of Music (Rochester) **11** Nigel Simeone (Tunbridge Wells, Kent)   **12** Vereeniging ter Bevordering van de Belangen des Boekhandels (Amsterdam)   **13** University of Virginia (Charlottesville)   **14** University of California at Los Angeles   **15** Generally available

2337	**LANDRÉ, G. N. (Harlingen) (continued)**			
	/1981	64	*General. Composers. Church Music. Theory* (453)	*1,10
2338	_____.			
	/1981	65	*Books on Music. Old, Rare Books* (430)	*1,8,10
2339	_____.			
	/1982	66	*Books on Music. Miniscores* (436)	*1,8,10
2340	_____.			
	/1982	67	*Books on Music. Kerkmuziek* (394)	*1,8,10
2341	_____.			
	/1982	68	*Books on Music. Old and Rare Books* (226)	*1,8,10
2342	_____.			
	/1982	69	*Music and Music Literature* (392)	*1,8
2343	_____.			
	1983?	70	*Music and Music Literature* (389)	*1,8
2344	_____.			
	1983	71	*Music and Music Literature* (486)	*1,8
2345	_____.			
	1983	72	*Music and Music Literature* (465)	*1,8
2346	_____.			
	1983	73	*Music and Music Literature* (350)	*1,8
2347	_____.			
	1983	74	*Music and Music Literature* (405)	*1,8
2348	_____.			
	1983	75	*Music and Music Literature* (426)	*1,8
2349	_____.			
	1983/4	76	*33rpm Records. Music and Music Literature* (458)	*1,8
2350	_____.			
	1984?	77	*Music and Music Literature* (436)	*1,8
2351	_____.			
	1984	78	*Music and Music Literature* (700)	*1,8
2352	_____.			
	1984	79	*Music and Music Literature* (496)	*1,8

1 Compiler/State University of New York (Buffalo)   **2** The British Library (London)   **3** Gemeentemuseum (Den Haag)   **4** The Grolier Club (N.Y.C.)   **5** Hirsch Collection, British Library (London)   **6** D.W. Krummel (Urbana)   **7** Library of Congress (Washington, D.C.)   **8** Library and Museum of the Performing Arts (N.Y.C.)   **9** William Reeves (London)   **10** Sibley Library, Eastman School of Music (Rochester) **11** Nigel Simeone (Tunbridge Wells, Kent)   **12** Vereeniging ter Bervordering van de Belangen des Boekhandels (Amsterdam)   **13** University of Virginia (Charlottesville)   **14** University of California at Los Angeles   **15** Generally available

2353 **LANDRÉ, G. N. (Harlingen) (continued)**
      1984   80   *Catalogues. Music and Music Literature*
                            (482)   *1,8

2354 _____.
      1984   81   *Music. Music Literature. Periodica*
                            (583)   *1,8

2355 _____.
      1984   82   *Music Literature. Sheetmusic. Recordings*
                            (534)   *1,8

2356 _____.
      1980?   List   10   *[Music Literature]*
                            (206)   *1,8,14

2357 _____.
      1980?   do.   11   *[Music Literature]*
                            (222)   *8,14

2358 _____.
      1982   do.   13   *Music Literature and Periodicals*
                            (265)   *1,8

2359 _____.
      1982   do.   14   *Music Lit. & Periodicals. Antiquarian Books*
                            (163)   *1,8

2360 _____.
      1983   do.   15A   *Books on String Instruments*
                            (94)   *1,8

2361 _____.
      1984   do.   16B   *Books on Keyboard Instruments*
                            (103)   *1,8

2362 _____.
      1984   do.   17   *?*
                            (?)   [not located]

2363 _____.
      1984   do.   18   *Music Literature*
                            (178)   *1,8

2364 **LANDRÉ & MEESTERS (Amstelveen)**
      s.d.   Kat.   14   *Books on Music, Music-hall. Dance. Theatre*
                            (1045)   *10

2365 _____.
      1976   Lflet   6   *Books on Music. Theatre. Dance. Music-hall*
                            (198)   *8

2366 _____.
      1976?   do.   9   *Books on Music*
                            (177)   *8

2367 _____.
      1976?   do.   12   *Books on Music*
                            (187)   *8

2368 _____.
      1976?   do.   16   *Books on Music*
                            (140)   *8

---

1 Compiler/State University of New York (Buffalo)   **2** The British Library (London)   **3** Gemeentemuseum (Den Haag)   **4** The Grolier Club (N.Y.C.)   **5** Hirsch Collection, British Library (London)   **6** D.W. Krummel (Urbana)   **7** Library of Congress (Washington, D.C.)   **8** Library and Museum of the Performing Arts (N.Y.C.)   **9** William Reeves (London)   **10** Sibley Library, Eastman School of Music (Rochester)   **11** Nigel Simeone (Tunbridge Wells, Kent)   **12** Vereeniging ter Bervordering van de Belangen des Boekhandels (Amsterdam)   **13** University of Virginia (Charlottesville)   **14** University of California at Los Angeles   **15** Generally available

2369 **LANDRÉ & MEESTERS (Amstelveen) (continued)**
     1976?   do.   18   *Books on Music*
                               (262)   *8

2370 **LANG, C. (Rome and Zürich)**
     1910?   20   *Geschichte des Theaters. Mss.*
                              ?   *12

2371 _____.
     1914   23   *Musique*
                            (182)   *3

2372 _____.
     191_   26   *Geschichte des Theaters. Libretti*
                            (1405)   *5

2373 **LANGENHUYSEN, C. L. VAN (Amsterdam)**
     s.d.   Bull.   5   *Nederl. Tooneel. Livres rares*
                               (736)   *12

2374 _____.
     s.d.   do.   9   *Musicalia et litterature musicale*
                             (305)   *12

2375 **LANZ, L. G. (Weilburg)**
     1854   —   *Antiquarische Musikwerke*
                           (32pp.)   [Petzholdt]

2376 **LAPICCIRELLA, LEONARDO (Florence)**
     1957   2   *Autografi di musicisti*
                           (260)   *1

2377 _____.
     1961?   —   *Autografi musicisti, concertisti /ecc./*
                          (253)   *1,6

2378 **LARSEN, KNUD (Copenhagen) [Succeeded by FOG, DAN, q.v.]**
     8/1953   9   *Flöjte og obo*
                           (290)   *8

2379 _____.
     [1953]   10   *Klaverudtg. Lommepartitur. Boeger*
                           (766)   *8

2380 _____.
     [1954]   11   *Violin Music*
                           (637)   *8

2381 _____.
     [195_]   13   *Vokalmusik*
                           (1000)   *1

2382 _____.
     1954?   14   *Klavermusik, 4-6-8 haender*
                           (?)   *8

2383 _____.
     [1954]   15   *Vocal Scores. Books on Music. Orchestral Music*
                           (464)   *1,8

2384 _____.
     [1954]   17   *Flöjtenmusik. Kammermusik*
                           (356)   *1,8

---

1 Compiler/State University of New York (Buffalo)   **2** The British Library (London)   **3** Gemeentemuseum
(Den Haag)   **4** The Grolier Club (N.Y.C.)   **5** Hirsch Collection, British Library (London)   **6** D.W.
Krummel (Urbana)   **7** Library of Congress (Washington, D.C.)   **8** Library and Museum of the Performing
Arts (N.Y.C.)   **9** William Reeves (London)   **10** Sibley Library, Eastman School of Music (Rochester)
11 Nigel Simeone (Tunbridge Wells, Kent)   **12** Vereeniging ter Bervordering van de Belangen des
Boekhandels (Amsterdam)   **13** University of Virginia (Charlottesville)   **14** University of California at Los
Angeles   **15** Generally available

2385 **LARSEN, KNUD [Succeeded by FOG, DAN, q.v.] (continued)**

     [1954]   21   *Books about Music*
                                (579)   *1,6,8

2386   _____.

     [195_]   22   *Pocket Scores. Chamber Music*
                                (589)   *1,6,8

2387   _____.

     [195_]   12   *Music for Two*
                                (700)   *6

2388   _____.

     [195_]   24   *Books on Music. Vocal Scores. Ballets*
                                (520)   *1,6

2389   _____.

     [195_]   25   *Chamber Music*
                                (297)   *1,6,8

2390   _____.

     [195_]   26   *Books on music*
                                (500)   *1,6,8

2391   _____.

     [195_]   27   *Antiquaria*
                                (359)   *6

2392   _____.

     [195_]   28   *Full Scores. Orchestral Materials. Vocal Music*
                                (783)8   *1,6,8

2393   _____.

     [195_]   30   *Organ Music. Hymns. Vocal Music. Literature*
                                (669)   *1,6

2394   _____.

     [1956?]   33   *Scores. Music Literature*
                                (424)   *1,6

2395   _____.

     1956?   34   *Kammermusik*
                                (438)   *1,6

2396   _____.

     1956?   36   *Musikliteratur*
                                (351)   *1,6,8

2397   _____.

     1956?   37   *Full Scores. Orchestral Sets. Choral Works*
                                (930)   *1,6

2398   _____.

     1956?   38   *Chamber Music. Study Scores*
                                (318)   *6,8

2399   _____.

     1956   39   *Musikliteratur. Volksmusik. Kataloge*
                                (301)   *1,6

2400   _____.

     1956   40   *Carl Nielsen*
                                (267+)   *1,6

2401   **LARSEN, KNUD (Copenhagen) (continued)**
        1956   41   *Vocal Scores*
                              (181)   *1,6

2402   _____.
        1956   42   *Full Scores. Orchestral Sets*
                              (305)   *1,6

2403   _____.
        1956   43   *Chamber Music*
                              (311)   *1,6

2404   _____.
        1956   44   *Musikliteratur. Klavierpartituren*
                              (299)   *1,6

2405   _____.
        1957   46   *Danish Music and Music Literature*
                              (425)   *1,6

2406   _____.
        1957   47   *Vocal Music*
                              (591)   *1,6

2407 -_____.
        1957   48   *Piano Music*
                              (547)   *1,6

2408   _____.
        1957   50   *Violin Music*
                              (471)   *1,6

2409   _____.
        1957   51   *Musikliteratur. Varia*
                              (194)   *1,6

2410   _____.
        1957   52   *Kammermusik*
                              (436)   *1,6

2411   _____.
        1957   53   *Cellomusik*
                              (335)   *1,6

2412   _____.
        1957   54   *Flute Music*
                              (268)   *1,6,8,12

2413   _____.
        1957   55   *Old Music. Music Literature*
                              (212)   *1,6

2414   _____.
        1958   57   *Danish Music Literature. Hymns. Folk Music*
                              (385)   *1,6

2415   _____.
        1958   59   *Musikliteratur. Periodica*
                              (391)   *1,6,12

2416   _____.
        1958   60   *Opera. Choral Works. Ballets*
                              (642)   *1,6,12

1 Compiler/State University of New York (Buffalo)   **2** The British Library (London)   **3** Gemeentemuseum (Den Haag)   **4** The Grolier Club (N.Y.C.)   **5** Hirsch Collection, British Library (London)   **6** D.W. Krummel (Urbana)   **7** Library of Congress (Washington, D.C.)   **8** Library and Museum of the Performing Arts (N.Y.C.)   **9** William Reeves (London)   **10** Sibley Library, Eastman School of Music (Rochester)   **11** Nigel Simeone (Tunbridge Wells, Kent)   **12** Vereeniging ter Bevordering van de Belangen des Boekhandels (Amsterdam)   **13** University of Virginia (Charlottesville)   **14** University of California at Los Angeles   **15** Generally available

2417 **LARSEN, KNUD (Copenhagen) (continued)**
      1958   61   *Operas*
                              (580)   *1
2418 _____.
      1959   62   *D. Frederik / R. Kuhlau /catalogues/*
                              (127)   *1,6,10
2419 **LAURIA, ARTHUR (Paris)**
      19__   —   *Danse - Fêtes - Musique - Théâtre. 2.pt.*
                              (152+pls.)   *1
2420 **LEAMINGTON BOOK SHOP (Washington, D. C.)**
      195_   5   *Incunabula. Heraldry. Bibliography*
                              (226, i.a.)   *8
2421 _____.
      1952   6   *Incunabula. 18th Century Music. Violin-making*
                              (219 i.a.)   *8
2422 _____.
      s.d.   7   *Bibles. Incunabula. Americana. Music*
                              (269)   *8
2423 _____.
      s.d.   8   *Rare old Books /a few Music/*
                              (207)   *8
2424 _____.
      [195_]   9   *Musick*
                              (243)   *1,6,8,9,10
2425 _____.
      [195_]   10   *Incunabula. Americana. Miscellanea. Musicana*
                              (248 i.a.)   *6,8
2426 _____.
      [195_]   11   *Incunabula. Illus. Books ... Liturgies. Music*
                              (288)   *6,8
2427 _____.
      [195_]   12   *Bibliographies ...*
                              (227 i.a.)   *6,8
2428 _____.
      [195_]   13   *Rare Books /a few Music/*
                              (184 i.a.)   *6,8
2429 _____.
      [195_]   14   *Incunabula and Americana /a few Music/*
                              (206 i.a.)   *6,8
2430 _____.
      [1957]   15   *Music*
                              (310)   *1,6,8,14
2431 _____.
      [195_]   16   *Rare Books /including Music/*
                              (245 i.a.)   *1,6,8
2432 _____.
      [195_]   19   *Music*
                              (260)   *1,6,8,10,13

2433 **LEAMINGTON BOOK SHOP (Washington, D. C.) (continued)**
    [195.]   20   *Rare Books. Bibles. Incunables. Music*
                                   (i.a.)   *6,8,14

2434   _____.
    [196.]   22   *Rare. Unusual. Unique [including Music]*
                                   (195 i.a.)   *1,8,14

2435   _____.
    1962   24   *Rare Books ... Bibles. Liturgies. Music*
                                   (i.a.)   *8,14

2436   _____.
    1963   25   *Music and Americana*
                                   (260)   *8,14

2437   _____.
    1963   26   *Rare Books ...*
                                   (278 i.a.)   *6,8

2438   _____.
    1964   27   *Americana [including Music]*
                                   (i.a.)   *8,13,14

2439   _____.
    [1965]   28   *Music*
                                   (210)   *1,6,8,10,12,14

2440   _____.
    1965   29   *Rare Unusual. Unique*
                                   (220)   *6,8

2441   _____.
    1966   30   *Ephemera. Pams. Broadsides. Mss.*
                                   (i.a.)   *14

2442   _____. **(moved to Fredericksburg, Virginia)**
    s.d.   31   *Rare Books [including Music and Liturgy]*
                                   (240)   *1,8,14

2443   _____.
    1968   32   *Musick*
                                   (250)   *1,8,10,12,14

2444   _____.
    1969   34   *Rare old Books [including Music]*
                                   (200)   *1,8

2445   _____.
    1969   35   *Musick. Treatises. Histories. Scores*
                                   (200)   *1,6,8,9,12

2446   _____.
    4/1970   37   *Bibles. Americana. Music Scores and Histories*
                                   (200 i.a.)   *1,8

2447   _____.
    1971   38   *Rare Books. Incunabula... Liturgies. Music*
                                   (211 i.a.)   *1,8

2448   _____.
    1971   39   *Rare Scores. Treatises*
                                   (200)   *1,8

---

1 Compiler/State University of New York (Buffalo)   **2** The British Library (London)   **3** Gemeentemuseum (Den Haag)   **4** The Grolier Club (N.Y.C.)   **5** Hirsch Collection, British Library (London)   **6** D.W. Krummel (Urbana)   **7** Library of Congress (Washington, D.C.)   **8** Library and Museum of the Performing Arts (N.Y.C.)   **9** William Reeves (London)   **10** Sibley Library, Eastman School of Music (Rochester)   **11** Nigel Simeone (Tunbridge Wells, Kent)   **12** Vereeniging ter Bervordering van de Belangen des Boekhandels (Amsterdam)   **13** University of Virginia (Charlottesville)   **14** University of California at Los Angeles   **15** Generally available

2449 **LEAMINGTON BOOK SHOP (Fredericksburg, Va.) (continued)**
      1972   40   *Rare Books. Bibles. Liturgies. Music*
                              (200 i.a.)   *1,8,11,13

2450 _____.
      197_   41   *Libri rarissimi*
                              (200 i.a.)   *8,11

2451 **LEAKLEY BOOK SEARCH (Winthrop Harbor, Ill.)**
      1975   10   *Resource Materials List: Music*
                              (141)   *8

2452 **van LEEUWEN, J. W. (Leiden)**
      1905   152   *Musique*
                              (170-464)   *3

2453 **LEFEBVRE, CHARLES (Bordeaux)**
      1879   —   *Pétite collection de livres sur la musique*
                              (19pp.)   *8

2454 **LEGACY BOOKS (Hatboro, Pa.) [Formerly FOLKLORE ASSOCIATES, q.v.]**
      1970   101   *Ballads. Folksongs. Ethnomusicology. Carols*
                              (421)   *8

2455 _____.
      1971/72   102   *Folksong. Ballads. Carols. Ethnomusicology*
                              (1-403)   *8,10

2456 _____.
      1972   103   *Folksong. Ballads. Folk Dance*
                              (1-180)   *10

2457 _____.
      197_   104   *Myth. Custom. Folk Dance. Folksong. Blues*
                              (1-269)   *8

2458 _____.
      1975   105   *Folk Song. Ballads. Blues, etc.*
                              (1-327)   *8

2459 _____.
      1977   —   *Folksong. Instrs. Ethnic Music. Blues. Ballads*
                              (254)   *8

2460 _____.
      1977   —   *MLA Convention Exhibit Catalogue. Folklore*
                              (26pp.)   *8,14

2461 _____.
      1978   —   *MLA Convention Exhibit Catalogue. Folklore*
                              (24pp.)   *8

2462 **LEGOUIX, GUSTAVE (Paris)**
      [19_]   1   *Musique instrumentale*
                              (?)   *5

2463 _____.
      [1909?]   2   *Partitions, piano et chant*
                              (?)   *5,8

2464 _____.
      [1909?]   3   *Partitions d'orchestra. Opéras*
                              (?)   *5,8

---

1 Compiler/State University of New York (Buffalo)   2 The British Library (London)   3 Gemeentemuseum (Den Haag)   4 The Grolier Club (N.Y.C.)   5 Hirsch Collection, British Library (London)   6 D.W. Krummel (Urbana)   7 Library of Congress (Washington, D.C.)   8 Library and Museum of the Performing Arts (N.Y.C.)   9 William Reeves (London)   10 Sibley Library, Eastman School of Music (Rochester)   11 Nigel Simeone (Tunbridge Wells, Kent)   12 Vereeniging ter Bervordering van de Belangen des Boekhandels (Amsterdam)   13 University of Virginia (Charlottesville)   14 University of California at Los Angeles   15 Generally available

2465 **LEGOUIX, GUSTAVE (Paris) (continued)**
      [1909?]   4   *Musique vocale ancienne*
                                  (?)   *5

2466 _____ .
      [1909?]   5   *Musique et le théâtre*
                                  (?)   *5,8

2467 _____ .
      [19__]   6   *Chant ancien. Livres sur la musique*
                                  (1260)   *3,5,8,13

2468 _____ .
      [19__]   7   *Chant ancienne*
                                  (?)   *5

2469 _____ .
      [19__]   8   *Livres sur la musique. Théâtre*
                                  (1068-2120)   *3,5,8

2470 _____ .
      [19__]   9   *Livres sur la musique. Théâtre*
                                  (2122-693)   *3,5,8

2471 _____ .
      [19__]   10   *Partitions*
                                  (?)   *5,8

2472 _____ .
      [19__]   11   *Coll: Picquot & Cartier. Musique instrumentale*
                                  (426)   *3,5,8

2473 _____ .
      [19__]   12   *Oeuvres instrumentales*
                                  (?)   *5,10,13

2474 _____ .
      [1924?]   13   *Livres sur la musique. Bibliographies.*
                                  (995)   *3,5,8,10

2475 _____ .
      [192_]   14   *Musique instrumentale, 17-19 siècles*
                                  (448)   *3,5,8,10,13

2476 _____ .
      1931   15   *Coll: B ... Oeuvres vocales*
                                  (364)   *5,8,10

2477 _____ .
      [193_]   16   *Musique vocale*
                                  (996-1613)   *3,5,8,10,13

2478 _____ .
      [193_]   17   *Éditions ancienne et originales*
                                  (608)   *5,8,13

2479 _____ .
      [193_]   18   *Coll: Tiersot. Litérature. Musique*
                                  (664)   *5,8

2480 _____ .
      1953?   List   5   *Musique instrumentale. Anciennes éditions*
                                  (188)   *8

1 Compiler/State University of New York (Buffalo)   **2** The British Library (London)   **3** Gemeentemuseum (Den Haag)   **4** The Grolier Club (N.Y.C.)   **5** Hirsch Collection, British Library (London)   **6** D.W. Krummel (Urbana)   **7** Library of Congress (Washington, D.C.)   **8** Library and Museum of the Performing Arts (N.Y.C.)   **9** William Reeves (London)   **10** Sibley Library, Eastman School of Music (Rochester)   **11** Nigel Simeone (Tunbridge Wells, Kent)   **12** Vereeniging ter Bervordering van de Belangen des Boekhandels (Amsterdam)   **13** University of Virginia (Charlottesville)   **14** University of California at Los Angeles   **15** Generally available

2481 **LEHMANN, PAUL (Berlin)**
       1898   92   *Deutsch Lit. und Sprache. Musikwissenschaft*
                                (3463-720)   *8

2482 **LEIBER, LIBRAIRIE (Paris)**
       [1866?]   —   *Ouvrages anciens sur la musique*
                               (?)   *3

2483 **LELANT, PIERRE (Antwerp)**
       [1963]   4   *Literature. Musicographie. Guerres*
                               (?)   *12

2484 _____ .
       [196_]   5   *Literature. Musicographie. Guerres*
                               (?)   *12

2485 _____ .
       [1964]   7   *Literature. Musicographie. Guerres*
                               (?)   *12

2486 _____ .
       [196_]   8   *Literature. Muscographie*
                               (?)   *12

2487 _____ .
       [1965]   9   *Literature. Musicographie*
                               (?)   *12

2488 _____ .
       [1966]   —   *Literature. Musicographie. Collections*
                               (605)   *12

2489 _____ .
       [1968]   15   *Literature. Guerres. Musicographie*
                               (588)   *12

2490 **LELIEVELD, MUZIEKANTIQUARIAT (Den Haag))**
       2/1968   6   *Zangmuziek. Klavieruitreksels*
                               (748)   *8

2491 _____ .
       6/1968   10   *Muziekliteratuur*
                               (572)   *8

2492 _____ .
       1969   14   *Muziekliteratur*
                               (293)   *12

2493 _____ .
       [196_]   32   *Muziekliteratur*
                               (511)   *10

2494 _____ .
       [1970?]   —   *Muziekliteratur*
                               (336)   *12

2495 _____ .
       [197_]   45   *Oude Drukken. Tijdschriften*
                               (529)   *8,10,11

2496 _____ .
       [197_]   49   *Muziekliteratur*
                               (501)   *11

---

1 Compiler/State University of New York (Buffalo) **2** The British Library (London) **3** Gemeentemuseum (Den Haag) **4** The Grolier Club (N.Y.C.) **5** Hirsch Collection, British Library (London) **6** D.W. Krummel (Urbana) **7** Library of Congress (Washington, D.C.) **8** Library and Museum of the Performing Arts (N.Y.C.) **9** William Reeves (London) **10** Sibley Library, Eastman School of Music (Rochester) **11** Nigel Simeone (Tunbridge Wells, Kent) **12** Vereeniging ter Bervordering van de Belangen des Boekhandels (Amsterdam) **13** University of Virginia (Charlottesville) **14** University of California at Los Angeles **15** Generally available

2497   **LELIEVELD, MUZIEKANTIQUARIAT (Den Haag)) (continued)**

	[197_]	51	*Pianomuziek*	
			(2260)	*11
2498	[197_]	52	*Muziekliteratur*	
			(920)	*1
2499	[197_]	58	*Oude Drukken*	
			(1288)	*8,11
2500	[197_]	59	*Muziekliteratur*	
			(671)	*11
2501	[197_]	60	*[Pianoforte Music]*	
			(2840)	*11
2502	4/1974	—	*[untitled. Music and Music Literature]*	
			(1435)	*8,11
2503	[197_]	62	*Muziekliteratur*	
			(927)	*11
2504	[197_]	63	*Orgelliteratur. Orgelmuziek*	
			(710)	[Front]
2505	[197_]	64	*Zangliteratur. Opera. Zangsmuziek*	
			(2704)	*8
2506	[197_]	68	*Muziekliteratur*	
			(924)	*8
2507	[197_]	69	*Pianoliteratur en Pianomuziek*	
			(520)	*1,8
2508	[197_]	73	*Muziekliteratur*	
			(750)	*8
2509	5/1975	74	*Oude Drukken*	
			(387)	*8,11
2510	[1975]	78	*Musical Literatur*	
			(783)	*1
2511	[1975]	79	*Chansons. Chor. Lied. Opera. Zangers*	
			(774)	*1,14
2512	[1976]	80	*Opera en Operetten*	
			(873)	*14

2513 **LELIEVELD, MUZIEKANTIQUARIAT (Den Haag)) (continued)**

	[1976]	82	*Muziek Tijdschrift* (438)	*14
2514	____. [1976]	85	*[Musical Literature]* (674)	*1
2515	____. [1976]	88	*Pianoliteratur/Pianomuziek* (2958)	*1,11
2516	____. [1977]	89	*Literature. Chansons. Opera. Lied* (962)	*1
2517	____. [1977]	91	*First and rare Editions* (568)	*1
2518	____. [1977]	92	*Music Literature* (977)	*1
2519	____. [1977]	94	*[Music and Music Literature]* (230)	*1,10
2520	____. [1977]	95	*Muziekliteratur* (783)	*1
2521	____. [1977]	98	*Zangliteratur. Chor. Opera* (957)	*1,10
2522	____. [1977]	99	*Musical Literature* (1061)	*1
2523	____. [1977]	100	*Old Prints* (535)	*1
2524	____. [1977]	104	*[Music and Musical Literature]* (230)	*1
2525	____. [197_]	107	*[Zangliteratur]* (734)	*1
2526	____. [197_]	108	*[Music and Musical Literature]* (316)	*1
2527	____. [1978]	110	*Original Editions* (434)	*1
2528	____. [1978]	111	*Muziek Literatur* (787)	*1,14

1 Compiler/State University of New York (Buffalo)   **2** The British Library (London)   **3** Gemeentemuseum (Den Haag)   **4** The Grolier Club (N.Y.C.)   **5** Hirsch Collection, British Library (London)   **6** D.W. Krummel (Urbana)   **7** Library of Congress (Washington, D.C.)   **8** Library and Museum of the Performing Arts (N.Y.C.)   **9** William Reeves (London)   **10** Sibley Library, Eastman School of Music (Rochester)   **11** Nigel Simeone (Tunbridge Wells, Kent)   **12** Vereeniging ter Bervordering van de Belangen des Boekhandels (Amsterdam)   **13** University of Virginia (Charlottesville)   **14** University of California at Los Angeles   **15** Generally available

2529 **LELIEVELD, MUZIEKANTIQUARIAT (Den Haag)) (continued)**

	[197_]	112	*Oude en zeldzame Drukken* (895)	*1,13
2530	_____. 1980	114	*Zang Literatur* (831)	*1,14
2531	_____. 1980	116	*New Music [antiquarian]* (1111)	*1,10,13
2532	_____. 1980	117	*Franz Liszt* (308)	*1
2533	_____. 1981	119	*First and Rare Editions* (497)	*1
2534	_____. 1981	122	*Muziekliteratur* (1232)	*1
2535	_____. [198_]	125	*Oude en zeldzame Drukken* (687)	*1,8,13
2536	_____. 1982	126	*Muziekliteratur* (593)	*1,13
2537	_____. 1982	127	*Orkestpartiten en material* (375)	*1,13
2538	_____. 1982	128	*First and Rare Editions* (461)	*1
2539	_____. 1983	130	*Muziek van 1850-1960* (1042)	*1
2540	_____. 1983	131	*First Editions* (451)	*1
2541	_____. 1983	132	*Reference Works* (843)	*1
2542	_____. 1983	133	*Muziek van 1880 tot en met 1950* (1427)	*1
2543	_____. 1983	134	*First Editions* (602)	*1
2544	_____. 1983?	136	*Books on Music* (957)	*1

1 Compiler/State University of New York (Buffalo)   2 The British Library (London)   3 Gemeentemuseum (Den Haag)   4 The Grolier Club (N.Y.C.)   5 Hirsch Collection, British Library (London)   6 D.W. Krummel (Urbana)   7 Library of Congress (Washington, D.C.)   8 Library and Museum of the Performing Arts (N.Y.C.)   9 William Reeves (London)   10 Sibley Library, Eastman School of Music (Rochester) 11 Nigel Simeone (Tunbridge Wells, Kent)   12 Vereeniging ter Bervordering van de Belangen des Boekhandels (Amsterdam)   13 University of Virginia (Charlottesville)   14 University of California at Los Angeles   15 Generally available

2545 **LELIEVELD, MUZIEKANTIQUARIAT (Den Haag)) (continued)**
    1984   137   *Music and Music Literature, 1870-1960*
                            (1333)   *15

2546 _____.
    1984   138   *Music and Music Literature*
                            (1002)   *15

2547 _____.
    1984   139   *Music Literature*
                            (1043)   *15

2548 **LEMPERTZ, MATHIAS (Bonn)**
    s.d.   300   *Memoiren. Biographie. Tagebücher [und Musik]*
                            (i.a.)   *13

2549 **LENGFELD, M. (Cologne)**
    1928   34   *Coll: Kyllmann*
                           (500)   *5,12

2550 _____.
    [1929]   36   *M.geschichte. Theorie. Praktische Musik. Lied*
                           (1851)   *5,6,12,13

2551 _____.
    1930   37   *[Coll: Friedländer]. Schubert... Romantik*
                           (1363)   *1,6,8,9,10,13

2552 _____.
    [193_]   38   *Musikliteratur*
                           (148)   *3,5,8,10,13

2553 _____.
    [193_]   39   *Musik. Bücher. Praktische Musik*
                           (1381)   *3,5,10,13

2554 _____.
    [193_]   40   *Alte und neu Opern*
                           (333)   *5,8,13

2555 _____.
    1932   42   *Autographen [ed. by Kinsky]*
                           (571,xv pls.)   *5,10,13

2556 _____.
    [193_]   44   *Musikalische Seltenheiten. Musikbücher*
                           (320)   *1,3,8,9,10,13

2557 _____.
    1933   46   *Praktische Musik - Musikbücher*
                           (362)   *1,5,8,10

2558 _____.
    1934?   47   *Musikalische Seltenheiten. Praktische Musik*
                           (414)   *1,5,8,9,10,13

2559 _____.
    1935   50   *Praktische Musik. Bücher. Portraits*
                           (1587)   *3,5,8,9,10,13

2560 _____.
    1936?   53   *Musikliteratur*
                           (188)   *5

2561 **LENGFELD, M. (Cologne) (continued)**
    1937   55   *Musikautographen und Musikhandschriften*
                          (127)   *1,8,9,10

2562 _____.
    1937   56   *Musikalische Seltenheiten*
                          (20pp.)   *5,8

2563 _____.
    1938   59   *Musikbibliographie*
                          (770)   *5,8,10,13

2564 **LESSER, H. (Breslau)**
    1873   3   *Coll: Koehler. Theoretisch & praktische Musik*
                          (370)   *5

2565 _____.
    s.d.   253   *Theater. Musik. Lieder. Volkslieder*
                          (560)   *8

2566 **LEVI, R. (Stuttgart)**
    1904   152   *Neueste Erwerbung. Musik und Theater*
                          (1550-707)   *5

2567 _____.
    1911   189   *Coll: Obrist. Bücher. Musik. Autographen*
                          (106)   *5

2568 _____.
    1912   198   *Coll: Proelss. Lit. Theater. Musik. Kunst*
                          (1543)   *5

2569 **LEVIN, RICHARD (Copenhagen)**
    1970   169   *Musik*
                          (374)   *1

2570 **LEVIN & MUNKSGAARD (Copenhagen)**
    [1929?]   7   *Breve og manuskripter ... Komponisten*
                          (67-91)   *13

2571 **LIBRAIRIE D'ARGENCES (Paris)**
    [1960]   41   *Beaux arts. Musicologie*
                          (1867)   *12

2572 **LIBRAIRIE DES ACADEMIES (Brussels)**
    s.d.   Bull. 4   *Musique. Livres anciens et modernes*
                          (1-514)   *1

2573 **LIBRAIRIE BONAPARTE (Paris)**
    1981   —   *Spectacles. Musique. Opéra. Danse. Music-hall*
                          (713)   *8

2574 _____.
    1983   —   *Spectacles. Musique. Opéra. Danse. Music-hall*
                          (904)   *8

2575 **LIBRAIRIE ENCYCLOPÉDIQUE (Brussels)**
    1942   4   *Histoire de l'art. Philologie. Musique*
                          (407)   *12

2576 _____.
    1947   7   *Histoire de l'art. Philologie. Musique*
                          (709)   *12

2577   **LIBRAIRIE ENCYCLOPÉDIQUE (Brussels) (continued)**
[1973]   List   508   *Musique. Théâtre. Ballet*
                         (1-119,279)   *13
2578   **LIBRAIRIE MUSICALE (Brussels)**
1948   23   *Musique*
                       (243)   *13
2579   _____.
1948   24   *Musique*
                       (260)   *13
2580   _____.
1948   25   *Musique*
                       (233)   *13
2581   _____.
1949   28   *Musique*
                       (253)   *13
2582   _____.
1949   35   *Musique*
                       (284)   *13
2583   _____.
1949   36   *Musique*
                       (298)   *13
2584   _____.
1950   38   *Musique*
                                                                        *13
2585   _____.
1950   40   *Musique*
                       (347)   *13
2586   _____.
1950   43   *Musique*
                       (258)   *13
2587   **LIBRERIA CORBELLINI see CORBELLINI**

2588   **LIBRERIA DANTE (DITTA ORESTE COZZINI) (Florence)**
1979   29   *Libri antichi e moderni [including Musica]*
                       (892)   *1
2589   **LIBRERIA ITALIANE RIUNITE see ANTIQUARIATO**

2590   **LIBRERIA MIRTO (Madrid)**
2/1966   —   *Spanish Music and Musical Literature*
                      (97)   *8[typed]
2591   **LIBRERIA MUSICALE (Milan)**
[19_]   1   *Catalogo letteratura musicale*
                     (499)   *5,10,13
2592   _____.
1932   2   *Catalogo letterature musicale*
                      (363)   *10,13

1 Compiler/State University of New York (Buffalo)   **2** The British Library (London)   **3** Gemeentemuseum (Den Haag)   **4** The Grolier Club (N.Y.C.)   **5** Hirsch Collection, British Library (London)   **6** D.W. Krummel (Urbana)   **7** Library of Congress (Washington, D.C.)   **8** Library and Museum of the Performing Arts (N.Y.C.)   **9** William Reeves (London)   **10** Sibley Library, Eastman School of Music (Rochester)   **11** Nigel Simeone (Tunbridge Wells, Kent)   **12** Vereeniging ter Bervordering van de Belangen des Boekhandels (Amsterdam)   **13** University of Virginia (Charlottesville)   **14** University of California at Los Angeles   **15** Generally available

2593 **LIBRERIA MUSICALE (Milan) (continued)**
    1932   3   *Catalogo letterature musicale*
                       (362)   *10

2594 ____ .
    [193_]   4   *Catalogo letteratura musicale*
                       (424)   *5

2595 ____ .
    1933   5   *Catalogo letteratura musicale*
                       (390)   *5,10

2596 ____ .
    1934   6   *Catalogo letteratura musicale*
                       (933)   *10

2597 **LIBRERIA NUOVA (Lucca)**
    1900   —   *Partiture manoscritte e stampate*
                       ?   [ZiMG]

2598 **LIBRERIA ROMANA (Rome)**
    1903   —   *Coll: Rosati. Biblioteca musicale*
                       (481)   *4

2599 **LICOSA SANSONI (Florence)**
    1974   5   *Letteratura musicale e teatrale. Strumenti*
                       (1108)   *1,6,8,10,13

2600 **LIEBING, ARNULF (Würzburg)**
    1960   69   *Musik und Theater*
                       (851)   *12

2601 ____ .
    1967   86   *Musik. Literatur. Kunst*
                       (803)   *6,8,12

2602 **LIEBISCH, BERNHARD (Leipzig)**
    1910   180   *Coll: Langhans. Musik. Lied*
                       ?   *5,6,8,12

2603 ____ .
    1921   242   *Kunst. Musik. Theater*
                       (2792)   *5,12

2604 ____ .
    1929   284   *Liturgik und Hymnologie*
                       (3646)   *10,12

2605 ____ .
    1934   304   *... Musik. Theater*
                       (2276)   *10

2606 **LIEPMANNSSOHN & DUFOUR (Paris)**
    1867?   4   *Beaux-arts. Musique. Danse*
                       (907-1202)   *A. Rosenthal

2607 ____ .
    [18_]   9   *Musique - Chansons - Danse*
                       (2767-3126)   *A. Rosenthal

2608 ____ .
    [18_]   12   *Musique*
                       (4052-443)   *A. Rosenthal

1 Compiler/State University of New York (Buffalo) 2 The British Library (London) 3 Gemeentemuseum (Den Haag) 4 The Grolier Club (N.Y.C.) 5 Hirsch Collection, British Library (London) 6 D.W. Krummel (Urbana) 7 Library of Congress (Washington, D.C.) 8 Library and Museum of the Performing Arts (N.Y.C.) 9 William Reeves (London) 10 Sibley Library, Eastman School of Music (Rochester) 11 Nigel Simeone (Tunbridge Wells, Kent) 12 Vereeniging ter Bervordering van de Belangen des Boekhandels (Amsterdam) 13 University of Virginia (Charlottesville) 14 University of California at Los Angeles 15 Generally available

2609 **LIEPMANNSSOHN & DUFOUR (Paris) (continued)**
        [18_]   17   *Musiques. Chansons. Danse*
                                 (1315-944)   *A. Rosenthal

2610 _____.
        [18_]   19   *Figures - Beaux arts - Musique*
                                 (2557-3059)   *A Rosenthal

2611 _____.
        [18_]   21   *Musique - Chansons - Danse*
                                 (3341-886)   *A. Rosenthal

2612 _____.
        1869   25   *Musique - Danse*
                                 (1146)   *3,8

2613 _____.
        1869   29   *Coll: Choron. Musique. Danse*
                                 (1360)   *8

2614 _____.
        1870   33   *Coll: [Cartier]. Collection musicale*
                                 (1141)   *3

2615 _____.
        5/1872   35   *Musique. Théâtre*
                                 (1228)   *3

2616 _____.
        6/1872   37   *Musique. Autographes*
                                 (821)   *3

2617 **LIEPMANNSSOHN, LEO (Berlin) [Succeeded by OTTO HAAS, q.v.]**
        1874   1   *Linguistik - Miscellanean*
                                 (497)   *A. Rosenthal

2618 _____.
        1874   2   *Livres rares et curieux ... Musique*
                                 (378-414)   *A. Rosenthal

2619 _____.
        1874   3   *Ouvrages ... relatifs à la musique*
                                 (345)   *A. Rosenthal

2620 _____.
        1876   8   *Musik (theoretisch und praktisch). Tanz*
                                 (466)   *12

2621 _____.
        1876   9   *Musik (theoretisch und praktisch). Tanz*
                                 (460,461-737)   *7,8,12

2622 -_____.
        1879   15   *Coll: Lindner, E. O.*
                                 (98pp.)   *5,7,8

2623 _____.
        1881   21   *Theoretisch und praktische Musik. Libretti*
                                 (1245)   *12

2624 _____.
        1882   22   *Coll: Müller, J. [M.Literatur]. Hymnologie*
                                 (3345)   *7,8,US-Bp

2625 **LIEPMANNSSOHN, LEO** (Berlin) (continued)

2625	1883	24	*Theoretisch und praktische Musik. Tanz* (730)	*7,12
2626	____. 1883	27	*Theoretisch und praktische Musik. Tanz* (327)	*7,12
2627	____. 6/1884	32	*Autographen (Bach, Händel, Mozart, et al)* (578)	*7
2628	-____. 1884	34	*Coll: Teschner, G. W. Gesangsliteratur* (1208)	*7,12
2629	____. 1885	36,37	*Musik - Tanz - Portraits (2v.)* (955,956-1610)	*12
2630	____. 1885	39	*Musiktexte (Opern. Oratorien. Ballet)* (1393)	*7,12
2631	____. 1885	40	*Autographen /including Musiker/* (588, i.a.)	*7
2632	____. 1885	42	*Theologie. Hymnologie* (1292)	*7
2633	____. 9/1885	43	*Opern. Oratorien. Gesangskompositionen* (550)	*7
2634	____. 1885	45	*Geschichte und Theorie der Musik. Tanz* (673)	*7,12
2635	____. 7/1886	47	*Geschichte und Theorie der Musik. Tanz* (492)	*7
2636	____. 10/1886	50	*Instrumental-musik* (618)	*7,12
2637	____. 12/1886	51	*Opern und Vokalmusik* (812)	*7,12
2638	____. 12/1886	52	*Geschichte u. Theorie d. Musik. Tanz* (1142)	*7
2639	____. 1887	54	*Autographen. Musiker. Sänger, et al* (545)	*7
2640	____. 1887	56	*Coll: Grell, E. Instrumental- und Vokal-Musik* (894)	*A. Rosenthal

1 Compiler/State University of New York (Buffalo)   **2** The British Library (London)   **3** Gemeentemuseum (Den Haag)   **4** The Grolier Club (N.Y.C.)   **5** Hirsch Collection, British Library (London)   **6** D.W. Krummel (Urbana)   **7** Library of Congress (Washington, D.C.)   **8** Library and Museum of the Performing Arts (N.Y.C.)   **9** William Reeves (London)   **10** Sibley Library, Eastman School of Music (Rochester) **11** Nigel Simeone (Tunbridge Wells, Kent)   **12** Vereeniging ter Bervordering van de Belangen des Boekhandels (Amsterdam)   **13** University of Virginia (Charlottesville)   **14** University of California at Los Angeles   **15** Generally available

2641 **LIEPMANNSSOHN, LEO (Berlin) (continued)**

	1887	57	*Geschichte u. Theorie d. Musik. Tanz* (259)	*7,12
2642	_____.			
	1887	58	*Colls: Grell, E. & Wilhelm von Redern* (557)	*7,12
2643	_____.			
	1887	59	*Coll: von Redern, W. Schauspieler-Autogr.* (824)	*7
2644	_____.			
	1887	60	*Autographen. Sängern et al [Anhang zu 59]* (136)	*7
2645	_____.			
	1888	62	*Musikliteratur. Letzte Erwerbungen* (562)	*7,12
2646	_____.			
	1888	63	*Autographen [including Musiker]* (606)	*7
2647	_____.			
	1888	65	*Coll: Commer, F. Musik und Hymnologie* (680)	*7,12
2648	_____.			
	1888	66	*Coll: Commer, F. Musiklit. u. Musikalien* (555)	*7
2649	_____.			
	1888	68	*Autographen von Musikern und Buhnenkünstler* (728)	*7
2650	_____.			
	9/1888	69	*Portraits von Musikern und Buhnenkünstlern* (441)	*7
2651	_____.			
	1888	71	*Geschichte und Theorie d. Musik. Musikdrucke* (2170)	*A. Rosenthal
2652	_____.			
	1889	73	*Dramatische Musik* (390)	*7,12
2653	_____.			
	1889	75,76	*Colls: Grell, Commer, von Redern. Musik-Mss.* (694,634)	*7,8,12
2654	_____.			
	1889	78	*Instrumental-Musik* (646)	*12
2655	_____.			
	1889	79	*Musikliteratur. Letzte Erwerbungen* (229)	*7,12
2656	_____.			
	1889	80	*Autographen aller Art [incl. Musiker], A-K* (633, i.a.)	*A. Rosenthal

---

1 Compiler/State University of New York (Buffalo)   **2** The British Library (London)   **3** Gemeentemuseum (Den Haag)   **4** The Grolier Club (N.Y.C.)   **5** Hirsch Collection, British Library (London)   **6** D.W. Krummel (Urbana)   **7** Library of Congress (Washington, D.C.)   **8** Library and Museum of the Performing Arts (N.Y.C.)   **9** William Reeves (London)   **10** Sibley Library, Eastman School of Music (Rochester) **11** Nigel Simeone (Tunbridge Wells, Kent)   **12** Vereeniging ter Bervordering van de Belangen des Boekhandels (Amsterdam)   **13** University of Virginia (Charlottesville)   **14** University of California at Los Angeles   **15** Generally available

2657 **LIEPMANNSSOHN, LEO (Berlin) (continued)**

	1889	81	*Autographen aller Art [incl. Musiker]. L-Z* (634-1129, i.a.	) *7
2658	_____.			
	1890	82	*Vokalmusik (weltlich und geistlich). Oper* (812)	*7
2659	_____.			
	1890	83	*Vokalmusik (Schluss 82 und Anhang zu 73)* (1473)	*12
2660	_____.			
	1890	85	*Musikliteratur. Letzte Erwerbungen* (477)	*7
2661	_____.			
	1890	86	*Autographen [including Musiker]* (725, i.a.)	*7
2662	_____.			
	1891	87	*Musik - Tanz - Theater - Musikalien* (416)	*8,12
2663	_____.			
	1891	88	*Musikliteratur* (292)	*7
2664	_____.			
	1891	89	*Coll: Lasserre, V. Musique instrumentale* (550)	*7,12
2665	_____.			
	1891	90	*Musikliteratur. Vokal- u. Instrumental-Musik* (986)	*7,12
2666	_____.			
	1892	91	*Musikliteratur. Letzte Erwerbungen* (154)	*7,12
2667	_____.			
	1892	94	*Musikliteratur* (686)	*7,12
2668	_____.			
	1892	95	*Autographen aller Art [including Musiker]* (732, i.a.)	*7
2669	_____.			
	̄ ̄ ̄ ̇92	98	*Musikliteratur* (185)	*7
2670	_____.			
	1893	100	*Geschichte und Theorie d. Musik. Musikdrucke* (1877)	*7,12
2671	_____.			
	1893	101	*Musikliteratur. Vokal- und Instrumental-Musik* (449)	*7
2672	_____.			
	1893	102	*Musiker-Autographen* (757)	*7

2673 **LIEPMANNSSOHN, LEO** (Berlin) (continued)

	1893	103	*Musikliteratur. Vokal- und Instrumental-Musik* (291)	*7
2674	____. 1894	105	*Dramatische Musik und grössere Gesangswerke* (658)	*7,12
2675	____. 4/1894	107	*Musikliteratur* (242)	*7,12
2676	____. 5/1894	108	*Instrumentalmusik* (999)	*7,12
2677	____. 6/1894	110	*Musikliteratur. Vokal- und Instrumental-Musik* (343)	*7,12
2678	____. 11/1894	111	*Musikliteratur. Vokal- und Instrumental-Musik* (309)	*7
2679	____. 1/1895	112	*Autographen [including Musiker]* (i.a.)	*7
2680	____. 3/1895	114	*Musikliteratur. Vokal- und Instrumental-Musik* (235)	*7,12
2681	____. 9/1895	116	*Musikliteratur nebst älteren Musikalien* (215)	*7
2682	____. 11/1895	117	*Ältere Instrumentalmusik (f. Streichinstr.)* (415)	*7
2683	____. 1/1896	118	*Musikliteratur* (114)	*7
2684	____. 2/1896	119	*Älterer Instrumentalmusik* (332)	*7,12
2685	____. 4/1896	120	*Musikliteratur (vorw. seltene Broschüren)* (348)	*7,12
2686	____. 9/1896	122	*Dramatische Musik. Partituren. Klavier-ausz.* (457)	*7,12
2687	____. 10/1896	123	*Musiker-Autographen* (819)	*7,12
2688	____. 11/1896	124	*Musikliteratur. Vokal- und Instrumental-Musik* (339)	*7,12

2689   **LIEPMANNSSOHN, LEO** (Berlin) (continued)

2689	4/1897	126	*Musiklit. Alte M.drucke. Wagner. Musikalien* (550)	*7
2690	_____. 7/1897	127	*Autographen [including Musiker]* (1211)	*7,12
2691	_____. 12/1897	129	*Musikliteratur* (255)	*7,12
2692	_____. 3/1898	130	*Musiker-Portraits* (382)	*7,12
2693	_____. 1898	131	*Musikliteratur* (465)	*7,12
2694	_____. 1898	132	*Autographen [including Musiker]* (1316,i.a.)	*12
2695	_____. 1898	133	*Wagner - Berlioz - Liszt* (483)	*7
2696	_____. 1898	134	*Musikliteratur. Musikalien. Handschriften* (305)	*7
2697	_____. 1898	135	*Vokalmusik* (665)	*7,12
2698	_____. 1898	136	*Instrumentalmusik* (684)	*7,12
2699	_____. 1899	137	*Musikliteratur. Musik. Seltene Musikdrucke* (277)	*7,12
2700	_____. 1899	138	*Musikliteratur. Geschichte. Bibliographien* (690)	*7,12
2701	_____. 1899	139	*Opern. Oratorien. Gesangwerke* (548)	*7,12
2702	_____. 1899	140	*Musik-Literatur* (682)	*7,12
2703	_____. 1899	141	*Autographen [including Musiker]* (421-882)	*1,12
2704	_____. 1899	142	*Musikliteratur* (653)	*7,12

1 Compiler/State University of New York (Buffalo)   **2** The British Library (London)   **3** Gemeentemuseum (Den Haag)   **4** The Grolier Club (N.Y.C.)   **5** Hirsch Collection, British Library (London)   **6** D.W. Krummel (Urbana)   **7** Library of Congress (Washington, D.C.)   **8** Library and Museum of the Performing Arts (N.Y.C.)   **9** William Reeves (London)   **10** Sibley Library, Eastman School of Music (Rochester)   **11** Nigel Simeone (Tunbridge Wells, Kent)   **12** Vereeniging ter Bervordering van de Belangen des Boekhandels (Amsterdam)   **13** University of Virginia (Charlottesville)   **14** University of California at Los Angeles   **15** Generally available

2705 **LIEPMANNSSOHN, LEO (Berlin) (continued)**
       1900   144   *Coll: Vasconcellos. Span. u. Port. Musik*
                                  (291)   *7
2706 _____.
       1900   145   *Musikliteratur. Ältere Instrumentalmusik*
                                  (564)   *7
2707 _____.
       1901   147   *Musik-Literatur. Musiker-Portraits*
                                  (466)   *7,12
2708 _____.
       1901   149   *Musikliteratur. Musikalien*
                                  (230)   *7,12
2709 _____.
       1901   150   *... Musikalien zur Geschichte Berlins*
                                  (494)   *7,12
2710 _____.
       1901   151   *Porträts von Musikern, et al*
                                  (611)   *7,12
2711 _____.
       1902   152   *Musikliteratur. Ältere Musikalien*
                                  (235)   *7,12
2712 _____. [**Prop.: Otto Haas. See HAAS catalogues, 1936-]**
       1903   153   *Musikliteratur*
                                  (1222)   *7,12
2713 -_____.
       1904   154   *Colls: Picquot, L. & J. B. Cartier. A-E*
                                  (970)   *7,12
2714 _____.
       1904   155   *Autographen /including Musiker/*
                                  (688)   *7,12
2715 _____.
       3/1906   156   *Colls: Rust, F. W. & R. Eitner. Theorie*
                                  (633)   *7,12
2716 _____.
       [1906]   157   *Instr.-Musik. 2.Abth. F-N (Fortsetzg. v. 54)*
                                  (1260)   *7,12
2717 _____.
       9/1906   158   *Colls: Bovet, A. & F. Förster. Autographen*
                                  (2141)   *7,12
2718 _____.
       [1906]   160   *Musikalien u. Bücher. Musikalischen Notation*
                                  (164)   *7,12
2719 _____.
       [1906]   161   *Deutsche Lit.,A-H. Musikalische Kompositionen*
                                  (i.a.)   *7,12
2720 _____.
       [1906]   162   *Colls: Eitner, R. and H. Riemann*
                                  (757)   *7,12

2721 **LIEPMANNSSOHN, LEO (Berlin) (continued)**

	2/1907	163	*Autographen ... II. Musiker* (631-950)	*7,12
2722	____. [1907]	164	*Deutsche Lit. 2.Teil,I-P (Fortsetzung v. 161)* (1742-2820)	*7,12
2723	____. 5/1907	165	*Colls: Rust, F. W. & R. Eitner, et al* (1715)	*7,12
2724	____. [1907]	166	*Deutsche Lit. 3.Teil,Q-Z (Fortsetzung v. 164)* (2821-4319)	*7,12
2725	____. [1908]	167	*Colls: Picquot, Cartier, Rust, Matthew* (1455)	*7,12
2726	____. [1908]	168	*Deutsche Lit. [Nachtrag zu 161, 164, 166]* (795)	*7,12
2727	____. 5/1908	169	*Colls: Picquot, Cartier, Rust, Matthew* (739)	*7,12
2728	____. [1908]	170	*Coll: Matthew, J. E. Musiklit. Liturgie. Tanz* (1204)	*7,8,12
2729	____. 12/1908	171	*Coll: Matthew, J.E. Musiklit. Zeitschriften* (1092)	*7,8,12
2730	____. 11/1909	172	*Coll: Matthew, J.E. Bibliographie. Kataloge* (1800)	*7,8,12
2731	____. 1909	—	*Musique d'occasion* (2211)	*A. Rosenthal
2732	____. [1910]	173	*Coll: Matthew, J.E.. Biographien. Briefe ...* (2012)	*7,12
2733	____. 10/1910	174	*Musiker-Autographen. Manuskripte* (2337)	*5,9,12
2734	____. 10/1910	175	*Musikliteratur. Tabulaturen* (224)	*7,9,13
2735	____. [1910]	176	*Instrumente: Bau, Geschichte, Lehre* (1470)	*7
2736	____. [1911]	178	*Akustik. Notenschrift* (563)	*7

1 Compiler/State University of New York (Buffalo)   **2** The British Library (London)   **3** Gemeentemuseum (Den Haag)   **4** The Grolier Club (N.Y.C.)   **5** Hirsch Collection, British Library (London)   **6** D.W. Krummel (Urbana)   **7** Library of Congress (Washington, D.C.)   **8** Library and Museum of the Performing Arts (N.Y.C.)   **9** William Reeves (London)   **10** Sibley Library, Eastman School of Music (Rochester)   **11** Nigel Simeone (Tunbridge Wells, Kent)   **12** Vereeniging ter Bervordering van de Belangen des Boekhandels (Amsterdam)   **13** University of Virginia (Charlottesville)   **14** University of California at Los Angeles   **15** Generally available

2737 **LIEPMANNSSOHN, LEO (Berlin) (continued)**

[1911] 179 *Primitive, antike, orientalische Musik*
                (703)   *7

2738 _____.
       9/1912 181 *Colls: Liliencron, Fuchs, Grüters*
                     (2093)   *7

2739 _____.
       5/1913 182 *Musiker-Biographien*
                     (2242)   *7

2740 _____.
       [1913?] — *Partitions*
                    (1169)   *A. Rosenthal

2741 _____.
       [1913?] — *Partitions*
                    (2315)   *A. Rosenthal

2742 _____.
       [1913?] — *Musique religieuse, vocale*
                    (902)   *A. Rosenthal

2743 _____.
       [1913] 183 *Musikalisches Seltenheiten. Tabulaturen*
                     (260)   *6,7

2744 _____.
       [1913] 184 *Autographen [including Musiker]*
                     (516-760)   *7

2745 _____.
       [1914] 185 *Opern. Oratorien. Gesangwerke*
                     (1352)   *7

2746 _____.
       4/1914 186 *Musik-Kataloge, Bibliographie. Geschichte*
                     (1934)   *7

2747 _____.
       9/1915 189 *Vokalmusik. Klavierauszuege, 1. Teil, A-F*
                     (1238)   *12,13

2748 _____.
       2/1916 190 *Musiker-Autographen. Manuskripte*
                     (2023)   *7

2749 _____.
       6/1916 192 *Vokalm.. Klav.-ausz., 2.Tl., G-M [Suppls.189]*
                     (1847)   *12

2750 _____.
       10/1916 193 *Vokalm., Klav.-ausz., (Forsetzg. von 192)*
                      (1958)   *12

2751 _____.
       11/1916 194 *Opern. Oratorien. Gesangswerke [Suppls. 185]*
                      (219)   *12

2752 _____.
       6/1917 196 *Colls: Stockhausen, J. & L. Lüstner. Orch. M.*
                     (765)   *6,12

---

1 Compiler/State University of New York (Buffalo) **2** The British Library (London) **3** Gemeentemuseum (Den Haag) **4** The Grolier Club (N.Y.C.) **5** Hirsch Collection, British Library (London) **6** D.W. Krummel (Urbana) **7** Library of Congress (Washington, D.C.) **8** Library and Museum of the Performing Arts (N.Y.C.) **9** William Reeves (London) **10** Sibley Library, Eastman School of Music (Rochester) **11** Nigel Simeone (Tunbridge Wells, Kent) **12** Vereeniging ter Bervordering van de Belangen des Boekhandels (Amsterdam) **13** University of Virginia (Charlottesville) **14** University of California at Los Angeles **15** Generally available

2753 LIEPMANNSSOHN, LEO (Berlin) (continued)

	6/1917	197	*Theorie. Aesthetik. Kunstgesang* (264)	*12,13
2754	_____. 9/1917	198	*Autographen [including Musiker] [Suppls. 190]* (686-998)	*7
2755	_____. 12/1917	199	*Musikgeschichte u. Musik-Biographien* (1295)	*7,13
2756	_____. 1/1918	200	*Musikliteratur. Musikwerke* (264)	*12,13
2757	_____. 10/1918	202	*Instrumental-Musik. Kammermusik, 1.Teil, A-F* (632)	*12,13
2758	_____. 12/1918	203	*Seltene Musikliteratur. Tanz. Liturgie* (105)	*12,13
2759	_____. 3/1924	208	*Musik-Autographen. Manuskripte* (745)	*12
2760	_____. 6/1924	209	*Musikliteratur* (493)	*12,13 *12,13
2761	_____. 11/1924	210	*Musikgeschichte, -bibliographie. Kataloge* (1423)	*1,9,11,13
2762	_____. [1925]	213	*Colls: Kretzschmar, H. & E. Vogel. M.-biogr.* (2084)	*7,11,13
2763	_____. [1925]	214	*Colls: Kretzschmar, H. & E. Vogel. M.-gesch.* (334,30)	*7,11,13,US-Pv
2764	_____. 12/1925	215	*Autographen. I: Musiker. III: M.porträts* (1091)	*7
2765	_____. 5/1926	216	*Opern. Oratorien. Gesangswerke... Stimmen* (1232)	*1,7,8,11,13
2766	_____. [1926]	217	*Instrumental-Musik in Orchesterpartituren* (688)	*1,7,8,11
2767	_____. 9/1927	218	*Musikgeschichte. Oper. Bibliographie* (1848)	*1,6,7,11,13
2768	_____. [1930]	221	*Musikliteratur. Tabulaturen* (931)	*1,6,9,11,13

1 Compiler/State University of New York (Buffalo)   **2** The British Library (London)   **3** Gemeentemuseum (Den Haag)   **4** The Grolier Club (N.Y.C.)   **5** Hirsch Collection, British Library (London)   **6** D.W. Krummel (Urbana)   **7** Library of Congress (Washington, D.C.)   **8** Library and Museum of the Performing Arts (N.Y.C.)   **9** William Reeves (London)   **10** Sibley Library, Eastman School of Music (Rochester)   **11** Nigel Simeone (Tunbridge Wells, Kent)   **12** Vereeniging ter Bervordering van de Belangen des Boekhandels (Amsterdam)   **13** University of Virginia (Charlottesville)   **14** University of California at Los Angeles   **15** Generally available

2769   **LIEPMANNSSOHN, LEO (Berlin) (continued)**

	12/1930	222	*Musiker-Biographien* (2167)	*1,6,7,8,11,13
2770	____. 10/1931	223	*Musikbibliographie und Notation. Kataloge* (600)	*1,6,8,11,13
2771	____. [1931]	224	*Musikgeschichte. Exotische Musik. Gesamtausg.* (1653)	*1,6,8,11,13
2772	____. 2/1932	226	*... II.Goethe in der Musik* (430)	*1,8,13,US-Pv
2773	____. 4/1932	227	*Instrumental-Musik. Choralbücher* (316)	*1,11,13,US-Pv
2774	____. 6/1932	228	*Musiker-autographen. Mss. Porträts* (487)	*7,8,9,13,US-Pv
2775	____. 12/1932	229	*Vokalmusik. Klavier-ausz., 1.Teil, A-K* (1614)	*1,13,US-Pv
2776	____. 4/1933	230	*Opern. Oratorien. Gesangswerke* (900)	*1,11,US-Pv
2777	____. 4/1933	231	*Instrumental-Musik. Stimmen-Material* (606)	*1,8,13,US-Pv
2778	____. 4/1933	232	*Johannes Brahms [incl. Autogr., Portraits]* (291)	*8,12
2779	____. 10/1933	233	*Vokalmusik. Klavier-ausz. 2.Tl., L-Z* (2104)	*8,12,13,US-Pv
2780	____. 10/1933	234	*Musikliteratur. Gesamtausg. ... Zeitschriften* (493)	*1,13,US-Pv
2781	____. [1934]	236	*Musiker-Autographen. Porträts* (613)	*9,12,13
2782	____. 12/1934	237	*Colls: Friedländer, M. & W. Wolffheim* (1107)	*1,6,13,US-Pv
2783	____. 5/1935	238	*Colls: Friedländer, M. & W. Wolffheim* (2200)	*1,6,13,US-Pv
2784	**LIPSIUS & TISCHER (Kiel)** [1938]	153	*Colls: Lutgendorff & Leiburg, Tl. 2* (1145)	*4,12

2785   **LISSA, GEORG (Berlin)**
       1900   27   *[includes neuere Musikwerke ...]*
                                    (?)   [MfM]

2786   **LIST & FRANCKE (Leipzig)**
       1859   —   *Coll: Landsberg, L.*
                                    (28pp.)   *3,5,7

2787   _____.
       1862   —   *Theoretische und praktische Musik*
                                    (?)   [Petzholdt]

2788   _____.
       1863   8   *Coll: Schellenberg, H.*
                                    (39pp.)   *12

2789   _____.
       1865   21   *Theoretische Werke ü. Musik. Musikalien.*
                                    (2030)   [Petzholdt]

2790   _____.
       1865   24   *Theoretische Werke ü. Musik. Musikalien*
                                    (881)   *12

2791   _____.
       1869?   51   *Werthvollen Sammlung theoret. u. prakt. Musik*
                                    (?)   [MfM]

2792   _____.
       1870   —   *Coll: Bach, A.W. Theoret. u. praktische Musik*
                                    (60pp.)   *8

2793   _____.
       1871   72   *Theoretisch und praktische Musik*
                                    (1224)   [MfM]

2794   _____.
       1873   83   *Coll: Baumgart, E. F. Theoretische Werke*
                                    (1313)   *12

2795   _____.
       187_   92   *Werthvollen Slg. Musik u. theoretische Werke*
                                    (1392)   *5

2796   _____.
       1874   96   *Theoretische Werke ü. Musik. Musikalien*
                                    (1430)   [MfM]

2797   _____.
       1876   107   *Coll: Merkel, C. L.*
                                    (2156)   *3,4,12

2798   _____.
       1878?   124   *Theoretische Werke ü. Musik. Musikalien*
                                    (1850)   *12

2799   _____.
       1881   144   *Coll: Hahn, A. Musik und Musikalien*
                                    (2044)   *12

2800   _____.
       1881   150   *Colls: Wenzel, E. F. & Naumannn*
                                    (2070)   *5,12

2801	**LIST & FRANCKE (Leipzig) (continued)**			
	1884	164	*Colls: Hummel, J. N. & Zopf*	
			(2271)	*5,7,12
2802	____.			
	1886	182	*Colls: Ritter, A. G. & Grabau*	
			(3194)	*3,12
2803	____.			
	1887	185	*Werthvollen Sammlung theoretische Werke*	
			(969)	*3,5,12
2804	____.			
	1889	200	*Wissenschaften*	
			(?)	*12
2805	____.			
	1889	208	*Theoretische Werke ü. Musik. Theater*	
			(2654)	*12
2806	____.			
	1890	214	*Gesangs-Musik*	
			(?)	*3
2807	____.			
	1890	217	*Stolberg-Slg. Kirchenmusik und Hymnologie*	
			(884)	*3,12
2808	____.			
	1892	230	*Coll: Trautermann, G. Musikwissenschaft*	
			(3142)	*3,4,12
2809	____.			
	1894	248	*Theoretische Werke ü. Musik. Theater*	
			(932)	*3
2810	____.			
	1896	272	*Coll: Kossmaly, C. Theoret. u. prakt. Musik*	
			(2655)	*1,3,12
2811	____.			
	1898	292	*Colls: Fischer, Dr. & Hartensteinn*	
			(1902)	*12
2812	____.			
	1899	300	*Coll: Paul, O. M.autographen. Prakt.Musik*	
			(1787)	*12
2813	____.			
	1899	311	*Coll: Böhme, F. M. Musik. Theater. Autogr.*	
			(2320)	*8,12
2814	____.			
	1901	324	*Coll: Boers, J. C.*	
			(2519)	*7,8,12
2815	____.			
	1902	335	*Coll: Apunn, A. Geschichte u Theorie. Musik*	
			(2533)	*7,12
2816	____.			
	1903	353	*Musikliteratur. Praktische Musik. Theater*	
			(2817)	*5,12

1 Compiler/State University of New York (Buffalo)   **2** The British Library (London)   **3** Gemeentemuseum (Den Haag)   **4** The Grolier Club (N.Y.C.)   **5** Hirsch Collection, British Library (London)   **6** D.W. Krummel (Urbana)   **7** Library of Congress (Washington, D.C.)   **8** Library and Museum of the Performing Arts (N.Y.C.)   **9** William Reeves (London)   **10** Sibley Library, Eastman School of Music (Rochester)   **11** Nigel Simeone (Tunbridge Wells, Kent)   **12** Vereeniging ter Bervordering van de Belangen des Boekhandels (Amsterdam)   **13** University of Virginia (Charlottesville)   **14** University of California at Los Angeles   **15** Generally available

2817 **LIST & FRANCKE** (Leipzig) (continued)
    1904   360   *Coll: Rosati, V. M.literatur. Musik. Theater*
                                (1051)   *7,12

2818 _____.
    1905   37_   *Coll: Galluzzi, G. Bücher und Autographen*
                                (3479)]   *7

2819 _____.
    1905   372   *Coll: Musiol, R. P. J.*
                                (3292)   *5,7,12

2820 _____.
    1907   384   *Musikliteratur. Musikalien*
                                (2651)   *3,5,12

2821 _____.
    1909   404   *Musikliteratur. Musikalien*
                                (2714)   *12

2822 _____.
    1912   430   *Musikliteratur. Musikalien*
                                (2588)   *5,12,13

2823 _____.
    1914   443   *Musikliteratur. Musikalien. Theater*
                                (2250)   *3,5

2824 _____.
    1915   455   *Musikliteratur. Musikalien. Theater*
                                (2776)   *4,5,12

2825 _____.
    1918   466   *Coll: Tottmann, A. M.literatur. Musikalien*
                                (2742)   *4,12

2826 _____.
    1920?   470   *Coll: Becker, H.*
                                (29pp.)   [ZfMW]

2827 _____.
    1922   474   *Musikliteratur. Musikalien. Theater*
                                (2282)   *12

2828 _____.
    1924   475   *Alte Hausmusik (-1830)*
                                (1169)   *1

2829 **LOCKNER, CHARLES H.** (N.Y.C.)
    1952   301   *Music*
                                (750)   *6

2830 **LOESCHER, ERMANNO** (Rome)
    s.d.   53   *Musica*
                                (?)   *7

2831 **LOLIÉE, MARC** (Paris)
    1957?   90   *Lettres autographes et mss de musiciens*
                                (188)   *9

2832 **LONSDALE, C.** (London) [late **BIRCHALL & CO.**]
    1860?   —   *Printed and Ms. Music, Pt. II*
                                (?)   [Fetis 5214]

2833 **LONSDALE, C. (London) (continued)**

	1860	—	*1st Suppl. Unique, rare ... Music. Treatises* (475-956)	*8

2834 ____.

	1861	—	*4th Suppl. Unique, rare ... Music. Treatises* (1082-344)	*8

2835 ____.

	1862	—	*5th Suppl. Books. Autographs. Mss.* (1345-752)	*8

2836 **LORENTZ, ALFRED (Leipzig)**

	1935?	29	*Schönen Kunst. Kunstgewerbe. Theoret. Musik* (1716,i.a.)	*8

2837 ____.

	s.d.	32	*Kunstliteratur. Theater. Musik* (pp.101-11)	*12

2838 ____.

	1961	Angeb	476	*Musikwissenschaft* (76) [IBAK]

2839 ____.

	1962	do.	510	*Musik und Theater* (33) [IBAK]

2840 **LOUNZ, GREGORY (N.Y.C.)**

	11/1948	List	71	*Foreign Books on music. Foreign Music* (330) *8

2841 ____.

	9/1949	do.	86	*Books on Music* (517) *8

2842 ____.

	1/1951	do.	92	*Foreign Books on Music. Organs & Organ Music* (426) *8

2843 **LUBRANO, J. & J. (South Lee, Mass.)**

	1979	1	*Old and rare Books. Autographs* (917)	*1,6,8,10

2844 ____.

	1980	2	*Old and rare books. Autographs* (447)	*1,6,10

2845 ____.

	1980	3	*Music and Dance* (150)	*1,6,8,10

2846 ____.

	1980	4	*Music and Dance* (573)	*1,6,8,10

2847 ____.

	1981	5	*Old and rare Books. Music and Dance* (1000)	*1,8

2848 ____.

	1981	6	*Old & rare Books. Prints. Autographs. Scores* (2178)	*1,8

---

1 Compiler/State University of New York (Buffalo) **2** The British Library (London) **3** Gemeentemuseum (Den Haag) **4** The Grolier Club (N.Y.C.) **5** Hirsch Collection, British Library (London) **6** D.W. Krummel (Urbana) **7** Library of Congress (Washington, D.C.) **8** Library and Museum of the Performing Arts (N.Y.C.) **9** William Reeves (London) **10** Sibley Library, Eastman School of Music (Rochester) **11** Nigel Simeone (Tunbridge Wells, Kent) **12** Vereeniging ter Bervordering van de Belangen des Boekhandels (Amsterdam) **13** University of Virginia (Charlottesville) **14** University of California at Los Angeles **15** Generally available

2849 **LUBRANO, J. & J. (South Lee, Mass.) (continued)**
  1981   7   *Old and rare Books. Prints. Autographs*
            (554)   *1,8

2850 ____.
  1982   8   *Music and Dance*
            (917)   *1,8,10

2851 ____.
  1982   9   *Music. Dance. Theatre. Film*
            (1803)   *1,8

2852 ____.
  1983   10   *Music. Dance. Theatre*
            (297)   *8

2853 ____.
  1983   11   *Dance Prints*
            (20,93pp.)   *1

2854 ____.
  1983   12   *Coll: A Scholar's Music Library*
            (977)   *1

2855 ____.
  1984   13   *Music and Music Literatur*
            (255)   *15

2856 ____.
  1984   14   *Printed Music and Music Prints*
            (601)   *15

2857 **LUBRANO, LUIGI (Naples)**
  [1930]   47   *Teatro e musica*
            (16pp.)   [Schneider 82]

2858 **LÜBKE, G.(Berlin) ["DER BÜCHERWURM"]**
  1937   174   *Musik. Theater*
            (1017)   [BibDMS'37]

2859 ____
  s.d.   191   *Theater/Musik*
            (2164)   *5

2860 ____.
  1952   218   *Theater und Drama. Film. Opera. Tanz*
            (2630)   *8

2861 ____.
  1954   225   *Musik. Lied. Tanz*
            (2143)   *13

2862 **LUNDQUIST, ABR. (Stockholm)**
  1904   —   *Musik-katalog*
            (?)   *7

2863 **LYNGE OG SØHN, HERM. H. J. (Copenhagen)**
  1941   117   *Musik. Teater*
            (2108)   *12

2864 ____.
  1949   169   *Musik. Teater. Boghistorie*
            (1670)   *12

---

1 Compiler/State University of New York (Buffalo)   **2** The British Library (London)   **3** Gemeentemuseum (Den Haag)   **4** The Grolier Club (N.Y.C.)   **5** Hirsch Collection, British Library (London)   **6** D.W. Krummel (Urbana)   **7** Library of Congress (Washington, D.C.)   **8** Library and Museum of the Performing Arts (N.Y.C.)   **9** William Reeves (London)   **10** Sibley Library, Eastman School of Music (Rochester) **11** Nigel Simeone (Tunbridge Wells, Kent)   **12** Vereeniging ter Bervordering van de Belangen des Boekhandels (Amsterdam)   **13** University of Virginia (Charlottesville)   **14** University of California at Los Angeles   **15** Generally available

2865 **LYNGE OG SØHN, HERM. H. J.** (Copenhagen) (continued)
    [1965]   263   *Musik. Teater. Sange. Ballet*
                                 (2165)   *8,12

2866 _____.
    1950   List   16   *Musik. Tijdskrifter. Bøger om Musik*
                                 (1-404)   *8

2867 **MC CALL, DAN** (N.Y.C.)
    1974   E   *Sheet Music List*
                                 (24pp.)   *8

2868 _____.
    1974   G   *Sheet Music List*
                                 (23pp.)   *8

2869 **MACNUTT, RICHARD** (London) [Successor to **LEONARD HYMAN**, q.v.]
    [1965]   94   *Music. Music Literature ... Mss. ALS*
                                 (812)   *4,6,8,10,11,14

2870 _____.
    [1965]   95   *Music*
                                 (100)   *6,8,10,11,12,14

2871 _____.
    [1965]   96   *Music Books. ALS*
                                 (924)   *6,10,14

2872 _____.
    [1965]   97   *Music Books. ALS*
                                 (75)   *6,10,11,14

2873 _____. **(Tunbridge Wells, Kent)**
    [1966?]   98   *Mss. Association Copies. ALS*
                                 (119)   *1,4,6,10,11,14

2874 _____.
    [1967]   99   *Music and its Literature. Autographs. Mss.*
                                 (599)   *1,6,8,10,11,13

2875 _____.
    1968   100   *First and Rare Editions. Mss.*
                                 (100)   *1,8,10,13,14

2876 _____.
    1970   101   *Early Music and Books. Mss. Ballet*
                                 (200)   *1,6,8,10,11

2877 _____.
    1970   102   *Autographs. Musical Mss. ALS*
                                   (200)   *1,6,14

2878 _____.
    1971   103   *Opera, 1751-1800*
                                 (300)   *1,6,8

2879 _____.
    [1972]   104   *Books. Printed and Ms. Music. Autographs. ALS*
                                 (142)   *1,6,14

2880 _____.
    1973   105   *Books. Printed and Ms. Music. Autographs. ALS*
                                 (122)   *1,6,8,13,14

---

1 Compiler/State University of New York (Buffalo)   **2** The British Library (London)   **3** Gemeentemuseum (Den Haag)   **4** The Grolier Club (N.Y.C.)   **5** Hirsch Collection, British Library (London)   **6** D.W. Krummel (Urbana)   **7** Library of Congress (Washington, D.C.)   **8** Library and Museum of the Performing Arts (N.Y.C.)   **9** William Reeves (London)   **10** Sibley Library, Eastman School of Music (Rochester)   **11** Nigel Simeone (Tunbridge Wells, Kent)   **12** Vereeniging ter Bervordering van de Belangen des Boekhandels (Amsterdam)   **13** University of Virginia (Charlottesville)   **14** University of California at Los Angeles   **15** Generally available

2881   **MACNUTT, RICHARD (London) (continued)**
     1975   106   *Books. Printed and Ms. Music. Autographs. ALS*
                      (152)   *1,6,8,11,14

2882   _____.
     1975   107   *Books. Printed and Ms. Music. Autographs. Als*
                      (135)   *1,8,11,14

2883   _____.
     1977   108   *Antiquarian Music and Music Lit. ALS. Mss.*
                      (504)   *1,6,8,11,13

2884   _____.
     1979   109   *Music. Theatre. Ballet*
                      (317)   *1,6,11

2885   _____.
     [1980]   110   *Antiq. Music & Music Lit. ALS. Mss. Libretti*
                      (239)   *1,8,11

2886   _____.
     [1980?]   111   *Printed and manuscript Music. ALS. Mss. Ballet*
                      (259)   *1,8,11

2887   _____.
     1983   112   *Music. Music Lit. Letters. Iconography*
                      (241)   *15

2888   _____.
     [1975]   List   —   *FRIMAIRE: Antiq. Music & Music Lit. ALS. Mss.*
                      (29)   *15

2889   _____.
     [1975]   do.   —   *SAGGITARIUS: Antiq. Music & Music Lit. ALS.*
                      (26)   *15

2890   _____.
     [1976]   do.   —   *PLUVIOSE: Antiq. Music & Music Lit. ALS. Mss.*
                      (45)   *15

2891   _____.
     [1976]   do.   —   *GERMINAL: Antiq. Music & Music Lit. ALS. Mss.*
                      (44)   *15

2892   _____.
     [1976]   do.   —   *FLOREAL: Antiq. Music & Music Lit. ALS. Mss.*
                      (41)   *15

2893   _____.
     1971   4to.   2   *Opera vocal scores*
                      (383)   *1,8,13

2894   _____.
     [1971]   do.   3   *Rare printed music*
                      (48)   *1,6,8,11,13

2895   _____.
     [1971]   do.   4   *Rare Books on music. Ballet. Theatre*
                      (46)   *1,6,8,11,13

2896   _____.
     [1971]   do.   5   *ALS and Mss.*
                      (69)   *1,6,8,11,13

1 Compiler/State University of New York (Buffalo)   **2** The British Library (London)   **3** Gemeentemuseum (Den Haag)   **4** The Grolier Club (N.Y.C.)   **5** Hirsch Collection, British Library (London)   **6** D.W. Krummel (Urbana)   **7** Library of Congress (Washington, D.C.)   **8** Library and Museum of the Performing Arts (N.Y.C.)   **9** William Reeves (London)   **10** Sibley Library, Eastman School of Music (Rochester)   **11** Nigel Simeone (Tunbridge Wells, Kent)   **12** Vereeniging ter Bervordering van de Belangen des Boekhandels (Amsterdam)   **13** University of Virginia (Charlottesville)   **14** University of California at Los Angeles   **15** Generally available

2897 **MACNUTT, RICHARD (London) (continued)**
      [1972]   do.   6   *ALS and Mss.*
                                 (?)   *8,11
2898 _____.
      [1972]   do.   7   *Music Published before 1801*
                                 (70)   *1,6,8,11
2899 _____.
      [1972]   do.   8   *ALS and Mss.*
                                 (141)   *1,8,11
2900 _____.
      1973   do.   9   *ALS and Mss.*
                                 (173)   *6,8,11,13,14
2901 _____.
      1973   do.   10   *Music. Ballet. Theatre*
                                 (140)   *1,8,11,13,14
2902 _____.
      1974   do.   11   *ALS and Mss.*
                                 (250)   *8,11
2903 _____.
      1975   do.   12   *Opera to 1800. Music Books. Autographs*
                                 (106)   *1,6,8,11,13
2904 _____.
      1977   do.   —   *N.Y. Book Fair*
                                 (453)   *1,8,13
2905 _____.
      [1979]   do.   13   *Music. Ballet. Theatre*
                                 (201)   *8,11
2906 _____.
      1980   do.   14   *A Miscellany*
                                 (108)   *1,6,8,11,14
2907 _____.
      1980   do.   15   *Another Miscellany*
                                 (188)   *1,11,13
2908 _____.
      1982   do.   16   *Dance. Theatre*
                                 (739)   *1
2909 _____.
      1982   do.   17   *Vocal Scores. Autogrs. Keybd.Music. Libretti*
                                 (437)   *15
2910 **MAGDEBURGER ANTIQUARIAT (Magdeburg)**
      1968   55   *Kunst. Musik*
                                 (649)   *12
2911 **MAGGS BROS. (London)**
      1918   363   *Drama and Music*
                                 (650)   *12
2912 _____.
      1919   377   *Drama and Music*
                                 (955)   *12

---

1 Compiler/State University of New York (Buffalo)   **2** The British Library (London)   **3** Gemeentemuseum (Den Haag)   **4** The Grolier Club (N.Y.C.)   **5** Hirsch Collection, British Library (London)   **6** D.W. Krummel (Urbana)   **7** Library of Congress (Washington, D.C.)   **8** Library and Museum of the Performing Arts (N.Y.C.)   **9** William Reeves (London)   **10** Sibley Library, Eastman School of Music (Rochester)   **11** Nigel Simeone (Tunbridge Wells, Kent)   **12** Vereeniging ter Bervordering van de Belangen des Boekhandels (Amsterdam)   **13** University of Virginia (Charlottesville)   **14** University of California at Los Angeles   **15** Generally available

2913	**MAGGS BROS. (London) (continued)**				
	1926		476	*Books. Mss. Autographs. Engravings* (264)	*1,6,10,13
2914	_____.				
	1928		512	*Music. Early Books. Mss. Autographs* (537)	*1,6,8,10,12,13
2915	_____.				
	1931		557	*Music. Early Books. Mss. Autographs* (409)	*1,6,12,13
2916	_____.				
	1936		621	*The Noel* (684)	*12
2917	_____.				
	1958		849	*Florence and Tuscany: Music* (593)	*1,8,10,12
2918	_____.				
	1968		913	*Music, Pt. I* (250)	*1,6,8,10,12
2919	_____.				
	1970		925	*Music, Pt. II: 18th and 19th Centuries* (607)	*1,8,12
2920	_____.				
	1974		950	*Music, Pt. III: 20th Century* (757)	*1,6,8
2921	_____.				
	1978		983	*Music prior to 1840* (234)	*1,8
2922	_____.				
	1980		1003	*Music prior to 1840* (173)	*1,13
2923	_____.				
	1981		1012	*English Composers of the 20th Century ... Mss.* (754)	*8
2924	_____.				
	1983		1033	*Music prior to 1840* (166)	*8
2925	_____.				
	4/1975	Misc.	1	*... including 100 Items on Bells* (189)	*8,9
2926	_____.				
	12/1975	do.	2	*Songs and their Singers* (325)	*8,11
2927	_____.				
	11/1976	do.	3	*200 Items on the Dance* (200)	*1,8
2928	_____.				
	1925	Spec.	–	*Rare Spanish & Portuguese Books on Music* (19)	*3[typed]

1 Compiler/State University of New York (Buffalo)   2 The British Library (London)   3 Gemeentemuseum (Den Haag)   4 The Grolier Club (N.Y.C.)   5 Hirsch Collection, British Library (London)   6 D.W. Krummel (Urbana)   7 Library of Congress (Washington, D.C.)   8 Library and Museum of the Performing Arts (N.Y.C.)   9 William Reeves (London)   10 Sibley Library, Eastman School of Music (Rochester)   11 Nigel Simeone (Tunbridge Wells, Kent)   12 Vereeniging ter Bervordering van de Belangen des Boekhandels (Amsterdam)   13 University of Virginia (Charlottesville)   14 University of California at Los Angeles   15 Generally available

2929 **MAIERS, WILLIAM C. (So. Lyndeborough, N.H.)**
[1954]   Flyer   16   *Old Sheet Music. One Hundred Years Ago*
(15pp.)   *8

2930 **MAKAREWICH, JOHN (Van Nuys, CA.)**
1970   186   *Performing Arts*
(842,66,1207-67)   1)*14

2931 **MALOTA, FRANZ (Vienna)**
s.d.   60   *Autographen-Katalog [25 Beethoven!]*
(300)   *7

2932 **MARINI, EDOARDO (Trieste)**
1961   39   *Musicologia*
(323)   [IBAK]

2933 **MARINI & CO., T. DE (Florence)**
1909   10   *Manuscrits ...*
?   *12

2934 **MARKERT, KARL (Leipzig)**
[1961]   107   *Musik*
(679)   [IBAK]

2935 _____.
[1964]   140   *Musik*
(557)   [IBAK]

2936 _____.
1965   163   *Theater und Musik. Tanz. Film*
(557)   *12

2937 _____.
1968   197   *Theater und Musik. Tanz. Film*
(559)   *12

2938 **MARLBOROUGH RARE BOOKS LTD. (London)**
s.d.   8   *Coll: Reeves, H. ALS & Documents [Musicians]*
(174+)   *8

2939 _____.
s.d.   13   *Coll: Reeves. H. Music. Theatre*
(629)   *4,9

2940 _____.
s.d.   38   *Illustrated Books ... and important Music Mss.*
(625-29)   *4

2941 **MARTIN, JEAN-MARIE (Hollogne-aux-Pierres, Belgium)**
[1962]   List   5   *Musique vocale*
(605)   *6

2942 _____.
6/1964   do.   —   *Books on Music*
(38)   *6

2943 _____.
9/1964   do.   —   *Musique vocale*
(308)   *6

2944 _____.
1/1965   do.   —   *Partitions ... Publications Sovietiques. Varia*
(705)   *6

---

1 Compiler/State University of New York (Buffalo)   **2** The British Library (London)   **3** Gemeentemuseum (Den Haag)   **4** The Grolier Club (N.Y.C.)   **5** Hirsch Collection, British Library (London)   **6** D.W. Krummel (Urbana)   **7** Library of Congress (Washington, D.C.)   **8** Library and Museum of the Performing Arts (N.Y.C.)   **9** William Reeves (London)   **10** Sibley Library, Eastman School of Music (Rochester)   **11** Nigel Simeone (Tunbridge Wells, Kent)   **12** Vereeniging ter Bervordering van de Belangen des Boekhandels (Amsterdam)   **13** University of Virginia (Charlottesville)   **14** University of California at Los Angeles   **15** Generally available

2945 **MARTIN, JEAN-MARIE** (Hollogne-aux-Pierres, Belgium) **(continued)**

	3/1965	do.	— *Full Scores*	
			(50)	*6
2946	____.			
	9/1965	do.	— *Partitions*	
			(295)	*6
2947	____.			
	9/1965	do.	— *Partitions*	
			(340)	*6
2948	____.			
	11/1965	do.	— *Livres sur la musique*	
			(295)	*6
2949	____.			
	9/1966	do.	— *Opera in Full orchestral Scores*	
			(340)	*6
2950	____.			
	1/19067	do.	— *... Vocal Works in Full Score. Complete Works*	
			(408)	*10
2951	____.			
	2/1967	do.	— *Full Scores*	
			(401)	*10
2952	____.			
	3/1967	so.	— *Vocal Scores*	
			(915)	*1,6,8
2953	____.			
	9/1967	do.	— *Opera & Oratorios Full Scores. Vocal Scores*	
			(270)	*1,6,8
2954	____.			
	1/1968	do.	— *Books on Music. Russian Music*	
			(244)	*1,8
2955	____.			
	3/1968	do.	— *Full Scores. Study Scores. Complete Editions*	
			(628)	*8
2956	____.			
	3/1968	do.	— *Vocal Scores*	
			(1288)	*1,6,8
2957	____.			
	5/1968	do.	— *Opera Full Scores. Scores of Rarity*	
			(209)	*1,6
2958	____.			
	9/1968	do.	— *Opera and Vocal Works. Full Scores. Coll.Eds.*	
			(682)	*1,8,14
2959	____.			
	1/1969	do.	— *Vocal Music. First and Early Editions*	
			(1076)	*1,6,8,14
2960	____.			
	2/1969	do.	— *Books on Music*	
			(298)	*1,8,14

1 Compiler/State University of New York (Buffalo)   **2** The British Library (London)   **3** Gemeentemuseum (Den Haag)   **4** The Grolier Club (N.Y.C.)   **5** Hirsch Collection, British Library (London)   **6** D.W. Krummel (Urbana)   **7** Library of Congress (Washington, D.C.)   **8** Library and Museum of the Performing Arts (N.Y.C.)   **9** William Reeves (London)   **10** Sibley Library, Eastman School of Music (Rochester)   **11** Nigel Simeone (Tunbridge Wells, Kent)   **12** Vereeniging ter Bervordering van de Belangen des Boekhandels (Amsterdam)   **13** University of Virginia (Charlottesville)   **14** University of California at Los Angeles   **15** Generally available

2961 **MARTIN, JEAN-MARIE** (Hollogne-aux-Pierres, Belgium) (continued)
    3/1969   do.   —   *Full and Study Scores. Complete Editions*
                                  (682)   *1,8,14

2962 _____.
    9/1969   do.   —   *Vocal Scores*
                                    (1210)   *1,6,8,10,14

2963 _____.
    2/1970   do.   —   *Books on Music. Autographs*
                                    (617)   *1,6,8,10,14

2964 _____.
    3/1970   do.   -   *Opera and Vocal Works in Full Scores*
                                    (342)   *1,6,8,10,14

2965 _____.
    9/1970   do.   —   *Vocal Scores*
                                    (1236)   *1,6,8,10,14

2966 _____.
    3/1971   do.   —   *Full and Study Scores. Complete Editions*
                                    (1010)   *1,10,11,14

2967 _____.
    4/1971   do.   —   *Books on Music. Facsimiles. Signed Scores*
                                    (602)   *1,8,10,12,14

2968 _____.
    9/1971   do.   —   *Vocal Scores*
                                    (1711)   *1,6,8,10,12,14

2969 _____.
    3/1973   do.   —   *Full and Study Scores. Complete Editions*
                                    (1217)   *1,6,8,11,14

2970 _____.
    3/1974   do.   —   *Vocal Scores*
                                    (2377)   *1,6,8,10,12,14

2971 _____.
    9/1976   do.   —   *Full and Study Scores. Complete Editions*
                                    (1618)   *1,8,11,13,14

2972 _____.
    [1977?]   do.   —   *Opera in Full Scores*
                                    (52)   *6

2973 _____.
    12/1978   do.   —   *New Acquisitions [Music and Music Literature]*
                                    (316)   *8

2974 **MARTIN, PHILIP** (York, U.K.)
    1976   2   *General Catalogue: Music Books*
                                    (260)   *10,14

2975 _____.
    1978   7   *General Catalogue: Music Books*
                                    (251)   *10

2976 _____.
    1979   8   *General Catalogue: Music Books*
                                    (368)   *8,10,13,14

---

1 Compiler/State University of New York (Buffalo) 2 The British Library (London) 3 Gemeentemuseum (Den Haag) 4 The Grolier Club (N.Y.C.) 5 Hirsch Collection, British Library (London) 6 D.W. Krummel (Urbana) 7 Library of Congress (Washington, D.C.) 8 Library and Museum of the Performing Arts (N.Y.C.) 9 William Reeves (London) 10 Sibley Library, Eastman School of Music (Rochester) 11 Nigel Simeone (Tunbridge Wells, Kent) 12 Vereeniging ter Bevordering van de Belangen des Boekhandels (Amsterdam) 13 University of Virginia (Charlottesville) 14 University of California at Los Angeles 15 Generally available

2977	**MARTIN, PHILIP (York, U.K.) (continued)**			
	1979	9	*Piano*	
			(755)	*8
2978	_____.			
	1980	10	*[Music Literature]*	
			(630)	*8
2979	_____.			
	1980	11	*Solo Songs and Song Albums*	
			(1237)	*8
2980	_____.			
	1980	12	*Organ Music*	
			(506)	*8˙
2981	_____.			
	1980	13	*Piano Music*	
			(678)	*8,10
2982	_____.			
	1981	14	*Organ Music*	
			(444)	*8,10
2983	_____.			
	1981	15	*General Catalogue [Music and Music Literature]*	
			(606)	*8,10
2984	_____.			
	1982	16	*General Catalogue [Music and Music Literature]*	
			(705)	*8,10
2985	_____.			
	1982	17	*Opera and Oratorio Scores*	
			(606)	*8
2986	_____.			
	1982	18	*Church Music. Books. Organ and Choral Scores*	
			(749)	*8
2987	_____.			
	1983	21	*Piano, Strings, Chamber, Voice, Winds, etc.*	
			(882)	*8
2988	_____.			
	1983	22	*General Catalogue [Music and Music Literature]*	
			(600)	*8
2989	_____.			
	1983	23	*?*	
			(?)	[not located]
2990	_____.			
	1983	24	*General Catalogue [including Music Lit.]*	
			(607)	*1
2991	_____.			
	1984	25	*General Catalogue. Piano. Organ. Vocal Scores*	
			(618)	*15
2992	_____.			
	1984	26	*General Catalogue [including Music Lit.]*	
			(593)	*15

1 Compiler/State University of New York (Buffalo)   **2** The British Library (London)   **3** Gemeentemuseum (Den Haag)   **4** The Grolier Club (N.Y.C.)   **5** Hirsch Collection, British Library (London)   **6** D.W. Krummel (Urbana)   **7** Library of Congress (Washington, D.C.)   **8** Library and Museum of the Performing Arts (N.Y.C.)   **9** William Reeves (London)   **10** Sibley Library, Eastman School of Music (Rochester)   **11** Nigel Simeone (Tunbridge Wells, Kent)   **12** Vereeniging ter Bervordering van de Belangen des Boekhandels (Amsterdam)   **13** University of Virginia (Charlottesville)   **14** University of California at Los Angeles   **15** Generally available

2993 **MARTIN, PHILIP (York, U.K.) (continued)**
      1984   27   *General Catalogue [including Music Lit.]*
                                      (584)   *15
2994 **MASKE, L. F. (Breslau)**
      1856   33   *... Musikalien*
                                      (16pp.)   *8
2995 _____.
      18__   36   *Musikalische Bibliothek*
                                      (21pp.)   *8
2996 _____.
      18__   66   *Musikalische Bibliothek. Musik und Musikalien*
                                      (569)   *8
2997 _____.
      1900?   111   *Musik und Musikalien*
                                      (45pp.)   *8
2998 **MATHEWS (ELKIN) LTD. (Bishop's Stortford, Herts)**
      1934   58   *First Editions in English Literature and Music*
                                      (491-637)   *4
2999 _____.
      1934   64   *First Editions in Literature and Music*
                                      (468-522)   *4
3000 _____.
      1965   162   *Misc. [including Music. First Eds. ALS. Mss.]*
                                      (392-434)   *4
3001 **MATHEWS (ELKIN) LTD. (London)**
      [1949]   Qrto.   4   *Early Editions of Music. Mss.*
                                      (20pp.)   *7
3002 _____.
      s.d.   List   60   *Music*
                                      (69)   *11
3003 **MAY & MAY (London)**
      1964   2   *[Musical Literature]*
                                      (471)   *8,14
3004 _____.
      1965   3   *[Musical Literature]*
                                      (428)   *8
3005 _____.
      1966   4   *[Music and Music Literature]*
                                      (490)   *8
3006 _____.
      1966   5   *[Music and Music Literature]*
                                      (650)   *8
3007 _____.
      1967   6   *[Music and Music Literature]*
                                      (586)   *8
3008 _____.
      1967   7   *[Music and Music Literature]*
                                      (724)   *8,14

---

1 Compiler/State University of New York (Buffalo)   **2** The British Library (London)   **3** Gemeentemuseum (Den Haag)   **4** The Grolier Club (N.Y.C.)   **5** Hirsch Collection, British Library (London)   **6** D.W. Krummel (Urbana)   **7** Library of Congress (Washington, D.C.)   **8** Library and Museum of the Performing Arts (N.Y.C.)   **9** William Reeves (London)   **10** Sibley Library, Eastman School of Music (Rochester)   **11** Nigel Simeone (Tunbridge Wells, Kent)   **12** Vereeniging ter Bevordering van de Belangen des Boekhandels (Amsterdam)   **13** University of Virginia (Charlottesville)   **14** University of California at Los Angeles   **15** Generally available

3009 **MAY & MAY** (London) (continued)
      1968   8   *Books and Music*
                            (961)   *8,13,14

3010 _____.
      1968   9   *Music Literature and Music*
                            (930)   *8,13,14

3011 _____.
      1969   10   *Music Literature and Music*
                            (1136)   *6,8,13,14

3012 _____.
      1969   11   *Music Literature and Music*
                            (1183)   *6,8,13,14

3013 _____.
      1970   12   *Music Literature and Music*
                            (1298)   *8,13,14

3014 _____.
      1970   13   *Music Literature and Music*
                            (1426)   *6,8,13

3015 _____.
      1971   14   *Books on Music*
                            (886)   *1,6,8,13,14

3016 _____.
      1971   15   *Collected Eds. Full Scores. Pianoforte Music*
                            (1103)   *6,8,13,14

3017 _____.
      1971   16   *General Miscellaneous Literature, A-R*
                            (1137)   *6,8,13,14

3018 _____.
      1971   17   *Music Literature. Singer. Opera*
                            (766)   *6,8,13,14

3019 _____.
      1972   18   *Music for Performers, Scholars*
                            (840)   *1,6,8,13,14

3020 _____.
      1972   19   *Books. General Music literure*
                            (1024)   *1,6,8,13,14

3021 _____.
      1972   20   *Scores of Operas*
                            (574)   *1,6,8,13,14

3022 _____.
      1972   21   *834 Books on Music*
                            (834)   *1,6,8,13,14

3023 _____.
      1973   22   *Books on Conducting, Opera, Singing*
                            (227)   *1,8,13,14

3024 -_____.
      1973   23   *Collected Eds. Vocal Scores. Chamber Music*
                            (338)   *1,6,8,13,14

---

1 Compiler/State University of New York (Buffalo) **2** The British Library (London) **3** Gemeentemuseum (Den Haag) **4** The Grolier Club (N.Y.C.) **5** Hirsch Collection, British Library (London) **6** D.W. Krummel (Urbana) **7** Library of Congress (Washington, D.C.) **8** Library and Museum of the Performing Arts (N.Y.C.) **9** William Reeves (London) **10** Sibley Library, Eastman School of Music (Rochester) **11** Nigel Simeone (Tunbridge Wells, Kent) **12** Vereeniging ter Bervordering van de Belangen des Boekhandels (Amsterdam) **13** University of Virginia (Charlottesville) **14** University of California at Los Angeles **15** Generally available

3025	**MAY & MAY (London) (continued)**			
	1973	24	*Full Scores. Piano Music. Instrumental Sonatas* (277)	*1,8,13,14
3026	_____.			
	1973	25	*Books on Music* (1024)	*1,6,8,13,14
3027	_____.			
	1973	26	*Books on Music* (790)	*1,6,8,13,14
3028	_____.			
	1973	27	*?* ?	[not located]
3029	_____.			
	1973	28	*Full and Vocal Scores* (344)	*6,8,13,14
3030	_____.			
	1973	29	*Full and Vocal Scores* (713)	*1,6,8,13,14
3031	_____.			
	1974	30	*Instrumental, Vocal and Choral Music* (386)	*6,8,13,14
3032	_____.			
	1974	31	*893 Books on Music* (894)	*6,8,13,14
3033	_____.			
	1974	32	*Vocal Scores* (323)	*6,8,13,14
3034	_____.			
	1974	33	*A Musical Miscellany* (131)	*6,8,13
3035	_____.			
	1974	34	*Over 900 Books on Music* (918)	*6,8,13,14
3036	_____.			
	1974	35	*Books on music. Special Liszt Collection* (698)	*6,8,13,14
3037	_____.			
	1975	36	*Second Musical Miscellany* (241)	*6,8,13,14
3038	_____.			
	1975	37	*Over 850 Books on Music* (924)	*8,13,14
3039	_____.			
	1975	38	*Full Scores. Orchestral Materials* (421)	*6,13,14
3040	_____.			
	1975	39	*1001 Books on Music* (1001)	*6,8,13,14

1 Compiler/State University of New York (Buffalo)   **2** The British Library (London)   **3** Gemeentemuseum (Den Haag)   **4** The Grolier Club (N.Y.C.)   **5** Hirsch Collection, British Library (London)   **6** D.W. Krummel (Urbana)   **7** Library of Congress (Washington, D.C.)   **8** Library and Museum of the Performing Arts (N.Y.C.)   **9** William Reeves (London)   **10** Sibley Library, Eastman School of Music (Rochester)   **11** Nigel Simeone (Tunbridge Wells, Kent)   **12** Vereeniging ter Bervordering van de Belangen des Boekhandels (Amsterdam)   **13** University of Virginia (Charlottesville)   **14** University of California at Los Angeles   **15** Generally available

3041	**MAY & MAY** (London) (continued)			
	1975	40	*Full Scores. Orch. Materials. Vocals. Scores* (421)	*8,13,14
3042	_____.			
	1975	41	*715 Books on music* (715)	*6,8,13,14
3043	_____.			
	1975	42	*Chamber Music. Piano Music* (246)	*6,8,13,14
3044	_____.			
	1976	43	*554 Books on Music* (554)	*6,8,13,14
3045	_____.			
	1976	44	*Vocal Music* (221)	*6,13,14
3046	_____.			
	1976	45	*General Music Literature. Pop Music and Jazz* (675)	*6,8,13,14
3047	_____.			
	1976	46	*Collected Editions. Full and Vocal Scores* (416)	*8,13,14
3048	_____.			
	1976	47	*566 Books on music* (566)	*6,13,14
3049	_____.			
	1976	48	*Piano Music. Organ* (382)	*6,8,13,14
3050	_____.			
	1976	49	*728 Books on Music* (728)	*8,10,13
3051	_____.			
	1976?	50	*Vocal Scores* (239)	*8,13
3052	_____.			
	1977	51	*559 Books on Music* (559)	*8,10,13
3053	_____.			
	1977	52	*Full Scores and Orchestral Material* (590)	*8,10,13
3054	_____.			
	1977	53	*620 Books on music* (620)	*8,10,13
3055	_____.			
	1977	54	*Chamber Music* (304)	*8,10,13
3056	_____.			
	1977	55	*566 Books on Music (and some Collected Eds.)* (566)	*8,10,13

1 Compiler/State University of New York (Buffalo)   **2** The British Library (London)   **3** Gemeentemuseum (Den Haag)   **4** The Grolier Club (N.Y.C.)   **5** Hirsch Collection, British Library (London)   **6** D.W. Krummel (Urbana)   **7** Library of Congress (Washington, D.C.)   **8** Library and Museum of the Performing Arts (N.Y.C.)   **9** William Reeves (London)   **10** Sibley Library, Eastman School of Music (Rochester)   **11** Nigel Simeone (Tunbridge Wells, Kent)   **12** Vereeniging ter Bervordering van de Belangen des Boekhandels (Amsterdam)   **13** University of Virginia (Charlottesville)   **14** University of California at Los Angeles   **15** Generally available

3057	**MAY & MAY (London) (continued)**			
	1977	56	*Vocal Scores*	
			(358)	*8,10,13
3058	_____.			
	1977	57	*Piano Music (2 Hands and 4 Hands)*	
			(572)	*8,10,13
3059	_____.			
	1977	58	*?*	
			(?)	[not located]
3060	_____.			
	1977	59	*605 Books on Music*	
			(605)	*8,10,13
3061	_____.			
	1978	60	*Full Scores*	
			(286)	*8,10,13
3062	_____.			
	1978	61	*411 Books on Music*	
			(411)	*10,13
3063	_____.			
	1978	62	*Vocal Music*	
			(403)	*1,10,13
3064	_____.			
	1978	63	*Books on music*	
			(634)	*1,10,13
3065	_____.			
	1978	64	*Chamber Music*	
			(201)	*1,8,13
3066	_____.			
	1978	65	*Books on Music*	
			(567)	*1,8,13
3067	_____.			
	1978	66	*Piano Music, 2 and 4 Hands*	
			(846)	*1,8,13
3068	_____.			
	1978	67	*Books on Music*	
			(748)	*1,8,13
3069	_____.			
	1978	68	*Instrumental Music*	
			(246)	*1,8,13
3070	_____.			
	1978	69	*Books on Music*	
			(583)	*1,8,13
3071	_____.			
	1979	70	*Full Scores*	
			(363)	*1,8,13
3072	_____.			
	1979	71	*Books on Music*	
			(660)	*1,8,13

1 Compiler/State University of New York (Buffalo)   **2** The British Library (London)   **3** Gemeentemuseum (Den Haag)   **4** The Grolier Club (N.Y.C.)   **5** Hirsch Collection, British Library (London)   **6** D.W. Krummel (Urbana)   **7** Library of Congress (Washington, D.C.)   **8** Library and Museum of the Performing Arts (N.Y.C.)   **9** William Reeves (London)   **10** Sibley Library, Eastman School of Music (Rochester)   **11** Nigel Simeone (Tunbridge Wells, Kent)   **12** Vereeniging ter Bevordering van de Belangen des Boekhandels (Amsterdam)   **13** University of Virginia (Charlottesville)   **14** University of California at Los Angeles   **15** Generally available

3073	**MAY & MAY (London) (continued)**			
	1979	72	*Stage Works. Vocal Scores* (229)	*1,8
3074	_____.			
	1979	73	*Books on Music* (632)	*1,8,13
3075	_____.			
	1979	74	*Vocal Music. Songs and Vocal Scores* (324)	*1,8,13
3076	_____.			
	1979	75	*Books on music* (461)	*1,8,13
3077	_____.			
	1979	76	*Full Scores and Orchestral Material* (265)	*1,8,13
3078	_____.			
	1979	77	*Books on music* (704)	*1,8,13
3079	_____.			
	1979	78	*idem.* (497)	*1,8,13
3080	_____.			
	1980	79	*Books on music. Mozart* (704)	*1,8,13
3081	_____.			
	1980	80	*Chamber Music. Instrumental Mussic* (430)	*1,8,13
3082	_____.			
	1980	81	*Books on music* (597)	*1,8,13
3083	_____.			
	1980	82	*Salon Music. Small Orchestral and Ensemble* (523)	*1,8,13
3084	_____.			
	1980	83	*Books on Music* (590)	*1,8,13
3085	_____.			
	1980	84	*Stage Works. Scores* (129)	*1,8,13
3086	_____.			
	1980	85	*Books on Music* (760)	*1,8
3087	_____.			
	1980	86	*Piano Music, 1 (A -G)* (984)	*1,8
3088	_____.			
	1980	87	*Books on music* (461)	*1,8,13

3089 **MAY & MAY (London) (continued)**

	1980	88	*Piano Music, 2 (H -Q)*	
			(891)	*1,8,13
3090	_____.			
	1981	89	*Books on Music*	
			(615)	*1,8,13
3091	_____.			
	1981	90	*Full Scores*	
			(305)	*1,8,13
3092	_____.			
	1981	91	*Books on Music*	
			(529)	*1
3093	_____.			
	1981	92	*Piano Music, 3 (R -Z)*	
			(977)	*1
3094	_____.			
	1981	93	*Books on Music*	
			(518)	*1
3095	_____.			
	1981	94	*Vocal Scores*	
			(315)	*1
3096	_____.			
	1981	95	*Books on music*	
			(498)	*1
3097	_____.			
	1981	96	*Piano Music*	
			(701)	*1
3098	_____.			
	1981	97	*Books on Music*	
			(649)	*1
3099	_____.			
	1981	98	*Orchestra Material*	
			(278)	*1
3100	_____.			
	1982	100	*Chamber and Instrumental Music*	
			(447)	*1
3101	_____.			
	1982	101	*Full Scores, part I: A-K*	
			(360)	*1
3102	_____.			
	1982	103	*547 Books on Music*	
			(547)	*1
3103	_____.			
	1982	104	*Full Scores, part II: L-Z*	
			(475)	*1
3104	_____.			
	1982	105	*Books on music*	
			(646)	*1

1 Compiler/State University of New York (Buffalo)   **2** The British Library (London)   **3** Gemeentemuseum (Den Haag)   **4** The Grolier Club (N.Y.C.)   **5** Hirsch Collection, British Library (London)   **6** D.W. Krummel (Urbana)   **7** Library of Congress (Washington, D.C.)   **8** Library and Museum of the Performing Arts (N.Y.C.)   **9** William Reeves (London)   **10** Sibley Library, Eastman School of Music (Rochester)   **11** Nigel Simeone (Tunbridge Wells, Kent)   **12** Vereeniging ter Bervordering van de Belangen des Boekhandels (Amsterdam)   **13** University of Virginia (Charlottesville)   **14** University of California at Los Angeles   **15** Generally available

3105	**MAY & MAY** (London) (continued)			
	1982	106	*Vocal Miscellany, part I: A-L* (402)	*1
3106	_____.			
	1982	107	*Music Literature* (561)	*1
3107	_____.			
	1982	108	*Full Scores* (285)	*1
3108	_____.			
	1983	109	*Music Literature* (695)	*1
3109	_____.			
	1983	110	*Piano Music, 2- and 4-Hand* (450)	*1
3110	_____.			
	1983	111	*Music Literature* (508)	*1
3111	_____.			
	1983	112	*Vocal Miscellany, part II : M-Z* (445)	*1
3112	_____.			
	1983	113	*Music Literature* (645)	*1
3113	_____.			
	1983	114	*Piano Music, 2-, 4- and 8 -Hand* (554)	*1
3114	_____.			
	1983	115	*Music Literature* (665)	*1
3115	_____.			
	1983	116	*Full Scores* (168)	*1
3116	_____.			
	1983	117	*Music Literature* (792)	*1
3117	_____.			
	1983	118	*Operatic Vocal Scores* (171)	*1
3118	_____.			
	1984	119	*Music Literature* (563)	*15
3119	_____.			
	1984	120	*Chamber and Instrumental Music* (359)	*15
3120	_____.			
	1984	121	*Music Literature* (857)	*15

1 Compiler/State University of New York (Buffalo)   2 The British Library (London)   3 Gemeentemuseum (Den Haag)   4 The Grolier Club (N.Y.C.)   5 Hirsch Collection, British Library (London)   6 D.W. Krummel (Urbana)   7 Library of Congress (Washington, D.C.)   8 Library and Museum of the Performing Arts (N.Y.C.)   9 William Reeves (London)   10 Sibley Library, Eastman School of Music (Rochester)   11 Nigel Simeone (Tunbridge Wells, Kent)   12 Vereeniging ter Bervordering van de Belangen des Boekhandels (Amsterdam)   13 University of Virginia (Charlottesville)   14 University of California at Los Angeles   15 Generally available

3121 **MAY & MAY (London) (continued)**
      1984   122   *Piano Music, 2- and 4-Hand, part I: A-G*
                                 (255)   *15
3122 _____.
      1984   123   *Music Literature*
                                 (852)   *15
3123 _____.
      1984   124   *A Musical Miscellany*
                                 (180)   *15
3124 _____.
      1984   125   *Music Literature*
                                 (740)   *15
3125 _____.
      1984   126   *Piano Music, 2-, 4- and 8-Hand part II: H-R*
                                 (241)   *15
3126 _____.
      1984   127   *Music Lit. Popular Music. Opera. Singing*
                                 (773)   *15
3127 _____.
      1984   128   *Music by British Composers*
                                 (523)   *15
3128 **MECKLENBURG, E. (Berlin)**
      1859   —   *Antiquar. Musikalien, Bücher*
                                 (508)   *5
3129 _____.
      1860   10   *Musik-Katalog, hrsg.*
                                 (30pp.)   [Petzholdt]
3130 _____.
      1861   12   *Musik-Katalog*
                                 (30pp.)   [Petzholdt]
3131 _____.
      1861   13   *Theoretisch und praktische Musik. Autographen*
                                 ?   [Petzholdt]
3132 **LA MEDICEA (Florence)**
      s.d.   —   *Libri rari ... Musica*
                                 (129-55)   *6
3133 _____.
      [1958]   —   *Musica - Teatro. Musica sacra*
                                 (199-419)   *8
3134 **MEDINACELI, LIBRERIA CIENTIFICA (Madrid)**
      s.d.   —   *Musicologia*
                                 (24pp.)   *13
3135 **MEHRING-HAUS, FRANZ (Leipzig)**
      1960   660   *Musik. Theater. Tanz*
                                 (303)   *12
3136 **MEININGEN, BEZIRKANTIQUARIAT (Meiningen)**
      [1975]   27 M   *usik. Theater*
                                 (325)   *1,13

1 Compiler/State University of New York (Buffalo)   **2** The British Library (London)   **3** Gemeentemuseum (Den Haag)   **4** The Grolier Club (N.Y.C.)   **5** Hirsch Collection, British Library (London)   **6** D.W. Krummel (Urbana)   **7** Library of Congress (Washington, D.C.)   **8** Library and Museum of the Performing Arts (N.Y.C.)   **9** William Reeves (London)   **10** Sibley Library, Eastman School of Music (Rochester)   **11** Nigel Simeone (Tunbridge Wells, Kent)   **12** Vereeniging ter Bervordering van de Belangen des Boekhandels (Amsterdam)   **13** University of Virginia (Charlottesville)   **14** University of California at Los Angeles   **15** Generally available

3137   **MEJSTRIK, A. (Vienna)**
     1903   43   *Literatur. Drama .*
                             (3116-872)   *4

3138   **MELLOR & BALLEY (Bryn Teg, Anglesey)**
     1938   2   *Selection from Stock [Music and Music Lit.]*
                             (1248)   *8

3139   _____.
     1939   4   *Selection from Stock [Music and Music Lit.]*
                             (1691)   *8

3140   _____.
     1939   5   *Additional Items to Catalogue 4*
                             (163)   *8

3141   _____.
     1939   6   *Selection from Stock [Music and Music Lit.]*
                             (1480)   *8

3142   _____.
     s.d.   12   *Short Catalogue of Music*
                             (619)   *8

3143   _____.
     s.d.   19   *Music, Musical Books and Autographs*
                             (207)   *4

3144   _____.
     1946   23   *Printed and Manuscript Music*
                             (777)   *4

3145   _____.
     s.d.   38   *Music and Books*
                             (416)   *4,8

3146   _____.
     [1951]   47   *Music and Books*
                             (504)   *4,8,11

3147   _____.
     [1952]   50   *Music, including First Editions. Vocal Scores*
                             (632)   *4,8

3148   _____.
     [195_]   51   *Music and Books*
                             (869)   *4,8

3149   _____.
     [1954]   53   *Music [and Music Literature]*
                             (1050)   *4,8,9

3150   _____.
     1938   List   —   *Short List of Scarce Music*
                             (226)   *4

3151   **MERGENTHALER, WALTER & KARL GEISENDÖRFER (Würzburg)**
     1960   36   *Musik. Musikgeschichte*
                             (52)   [IBAK]

3152   **MERKEL, R. (Erlangen)**
     1890   120   *Sprachen und Literatur. Musik und Kunst*
                             (2773-972)   *12

3153 **MERKEL, R. (Erlangen) (continued)**
         1894   130   *Sprachen und Literatur. Musik und Kunst*
                                    (2553-700)   *12
3154   ____.
         1897   136   *Sprachen und Literatur. Musik und Kunst*
                                    (2597-733)   *12
3155 **MERLANDER, KURT (Burbank, CA.)**
         [1950]   86   *Books on Music (mostly French and German)*
                                    (448)   *8
3156   ____.
         [1952]   111   *Books on Music*
                                    (113)   *8
3157   ____.
         [1952]   121   *Books on music*
                                    (503)   *8
3158   ____.
         [1953]   134   *Books on Music*
                                    (487)   *8
3159   ____.
         [195_]   155   *Books on Music*
                                    (417)   *8
3160   ____.
         [195_]   161   *Music and Musical Literature*
                                    (709)   *8,13
3161   ____.
         [1959]   174   *Books on Music (mostly French and German)*
                                    (291)   *8,13
3162   ____.
         [195_]   179   *Books on music*
                                    (447)   *8
3163   ____.
         [196_]   194   *Books on music*
                                    (613)   *8
3164   ____.
         [196_]   199   *Books on music*
                                    (630)   *8
3165   ____.
         [1965]   204   *Music and Music Literature*
                                    (507)   *6,8,13
3166   ____.
         1969   208   *Music and Music Literature*
                                    (338)   *1,6,8,10,13
3167   ____.
         1970   217   *Music and Music Literature*
                                    (500)   *1,8,10,13
3168   ____.
         [197_]   221   *Music and Music Literature*
                                    (549)   *1,10,13

---

1 Compiler/State University of New York (Buffalo) 2 The British Library (London) 3 Gemeentemuseum (Den Haag) 4 The Grolier Club (N.Y.C.) 5 Hirsch Collection, British Library (London) 6 D.W. Krummel (Urbana) 7 Library of Congress (Washington, D.C.) 8 Library and Museum of the Performing Arts (N.Y.C.) 9 William Reeves (London) 10 Sibley Library, Eastman School of Music (Rochester) 11 Nigel Simeone (Tunbridge Wells, Kent) 12 Vereeniging ter Bervordering van de Belangen des Boekhandels (Amsterdam) 13 University of Virginia (Charlottesville) 14 University of California at Los Angeles 15 Generally available

3169 **MERLANDER, KURT (Burbank, CA.) (continued)**
    [1955]   List   C3   *Musical Literature*
                    (191)   *8

3170 **MEYER, HELLMUT, & ERNST (Berlin)**
    1931   —   *Coll: B... Paganini: Originalporträts /et c.]*
                    (56pp.)   [not located]

3171 _____.
    s.d.   13   *Autogr. v. Musikern, Schauspielern u. Säng ern*
                    (931)   *13

3172 _____.
    [1953]   95   *Autographen I. Musikern und Schauspielern*
                    (348)   *8

3173 **MICALI, GIACINTO E FIGLIO (Livorno)**
    1793   —   *Catalogo dei generi vendibili*
                    (pp.145-66)   *8

3174 **MICHELMORE, G. & CO. (London)**
    s.d.   5   *... Authors' and Composers' Mss.*
                    (417, i.a.)   *4

3175 **MIDDLETON, MAURICE A. (Birmingham, U. K.)**
    1916   6   *[Catalogue, including Music Lit.]*
                    (?)   *7

3176 _____.
    1916   7   *[Catalogue, including Music Lit.]*
                    (?)   *7

3177 _____.
    1916   8   *[Catalogue, including Music Lit.]*
                    (?)   *7

3178 _____.
    1916   9   *[Catalogue, including Music Lit.]*
                    (?)   *7

3179 _____.
    1907   No.   117   *Music, and Books relating to Music*
                    (1475)   *8

3180 _____.
    1917   do.   210   *Music, and Books relating to Music*
                    (?)   *7

3181 _____.
    1968   23   *Books on Musical Literature*
                    (1302)   *1,6,8,10,11,14

3182 **MLYNARSKI, BRONISLAW (Beverly Hills, CA.)**
    1961   11   *Books about Music*
                    (530)   *8,10,11,14

3183 _____.
    1961   12   *Books about Music*
                    (626)   *1,11

3184 _____.
    1962   15   *Books about Music*
                    (900)   *1,8,11

---

1 Compiler/State University of New York (Buffalo)   **2** The British Library (London)   **3** Gemeentemuseum (Den Haag)   **4** The Grolier Club (N.Y.C.)   **5** Hirsch Collection, British Library (London)   **6** D.W. Krummel (Urbana)   **7** Library of Congress (Washington, D.C.)   **8** Library and Museum of the Performing Arts (N.Y.C.)   **9** William Reeves (London)   **10** Sibley Library, Eastman School of Music (Rochester)   **11** Nigel Simeone (Tunbridge Wells, Kent)   **12** Vereeniging ter Bervordering van de Belangen des Boekhandels (Amsterdam)   **13** University of Virginia (Charlottesville)   **14** University of California at Los Angeles   **15** Generally available

3185   **MLYNARSKI, BRONISLAW (Beverly Hills, CA.) (continued)**
        1963   17   *Books on Musical Literature and Instruments*
                                        (604)   *11,14
3186   _____.
        1963   18   *Books about Music*
                                        (1102)   *1,8,10,11
3187   _____.
        1964   20   *Books on Musical Literature*
                                        (1070)   *6,8,11,14
3188   _____.
        1965   21   *Books on Musical Literature*
                                        (1349)   *6,8,10,11,14
3189   _____.
        1967   22   *Books on Musical Literature*
                                        (1158)   *6,8,10,11,14
3190   _____.
        1968   23   *Books on Musical Literature*
                                        (1302)   *1,6,8,10,11,14
3191   _____.
        1969   24   *Books on Music and Musical Literature*
                                        (1250)   *1,6,11,14
3192   _____.
        1971   25   *Books on music and Musical Literature*
                                        (1041)   *1,6,11,13,14
3193   **MONGENET, J. (Geneva)**
        1928   Spec.   3   *Musique bon livres*
                                        (451)   *13
3194   _____.
        s.d.   Liste   16   *Musique. Théâtre*
                                        (357-535)   *13
3195   **MOOY, H. W. (Amsterdam)**
        1907   —   *Muziek*
                                        (?)   *12
3196   **MORETTI, VINCENZO S., BOTTEGA DI LIBRI (Rome)**
        1930   30   *Musica e teatro*
                                        (517)   *9,12
3197   **MORRILL, EDWARD, & SON (Boston)**
        [1954]   41   *American Scene: Books, Pamphlets, Sheet Music*
                                        (415-92)   *8
3198   _____.
        1964   107   *Miscellaneous Books, [including Music]*
                                        (310-524)   *6
3199   **MORTON-SMITH, I. & M. (Maysleith, Hants)**
        5/1981   N.S.1   *Musical Instruments*
                                        (135-53)   [Morton-Smith]
3200   _____.
        8/1981   N.S.2   *"Mercurius Rusticus": Music*
                                        (71)   *8

---

1 Compiler/State University of New York (Buffalo)   2 The British Library (London)   3 Gemeentemuseum (Den Haag)   4 The Grolier Club (N.Y.C.)   5 Hirsch Collection, British Library (London)   6 D.W. Krummel (Urbana)   7 Library of Congress (Washington, D.C.)   8 Library and Museum of the Performing Arts (N.Y.C.)   9 William Reeves (London)   10 Sibley Library, Eastman School of Music (Rochester)   11 Nigel Simeone (Tunbridge Wells, Kent)   12 Vereeniging ter Bervordering van de Belangen des Boekhandels (Amsterdam)   13 University of Virginia (Charlottesville)   14 University of California at Los Angeles   15 Generally available

3201   **MORTON-SMITH, I. & M.** **(Maysleith, Hants) (continued)**
      4/1982   N.S.5   *"Mercurius Rusticus": Music, Books about Music*
                                    (153)   *1

3202   _____.
      5/1982   N.S.6   *Books on Music and the Dance*
                                    (117)   *1

3203   _____.
      8/1982   N.S.8   *Music*
                                    (161-219)   *1

3204   _____.
      6/1984   N.S.9   *"Mercurius Rusticus": Dance [& Music]*
                                    (70)   *1

3205   **MOSER-BUCHHANDLUNG-ANTIQUARIAT (Munich)**
      1967   14   *Kunst. Musik*
                                    (332)   [IBAK]

3206   _____.
      1970   22   *Kunst. Musik*
                                    (459)   *12

3207   **MOTLEY BOOKS LTD. (Mottisfont Abbey, Romsey)**
      1966   7   *Theatre. Cinema. Music & Opera. Dance & Ballet*
                                    (440-503)   *10

3208   _____.
      1966   8   *Theatre. Cinema. Music & Opera. Dance & Ballet*
                                    (327-69)   *10

3209   _____.
      1966   9   *Theatre.... Music and Opera. Dance and Ballet*
                                    (437-91)   *10

3210   _____.
      1968   15   *Books about Music and Theatre*
                                    (269)   *4,6,8,10

3211   _____.
      1968   15   *Dance and Ballet*
                                    (269-725)   *6

3212   _____.
      197_?]   22   *Theatre. Entertainment. Music. Opera. Ballet*
                                    (580-725)   *4

3213   _____.
      1983   57   *Dramatic Theatre. Dance. Musical Theatre*
                                    (852)   *1

3214   _____.
      1983   58   *Dramatic Theatre. Musical Theatre. Cinema*
                                    (580)   *1

3215   _____.
      1984   59   *Dramatic Theatre. Dance. Musical Theatre*
                                    (1025)   *1

3216   _____.
      1984   60   *Dramatic Theatre. Musical Theatre. Dance*
                                    (782)   *1

1 Compiler/State University of New York (Buffalo)   **2** The British Library (London)   **3** Gemeentemuseum (Den Haag)   **4** The Grolier Club (N.Y.C.)   **5** Hirsch Collection, British Library (London)   **6** D.W. Krummel (Urbana)   **7** Library of Congress (Washington, D.C.)   **8** Library and Museum of the Performing Arts (N.Y.C.)   **9** William Reeves (London)   **10** Sibley Library, Eastman School of Music (Rochester)   **11** Nigel Simeone (Tunbridge Wells, Kent)   **12** Vereeniging ter Bervordering van de Belangen des Boekhandels (Amsterdam)   **13** University of Virginia (Charlottesville)   **14** University of California at Los Angeles   **15** Generally available

3217 **MÜLLER, FRIEDRICH (Munich)**
      1928?   10   *Theater - Musik - Tanz*
                             (1927)   *1,5,12,13

3218 _____.
      1929   11   *Theater - Musik - Tanz*
                             (676)   *1,5,12,13

3219 _____.
      1930   13   *Bildnisse, A - K*
                             (71, i.a.)   *13

3220 _____.
      193_   15   *Bildnisse, L - Z*
                             (86, i.a.)   *13

3221 **MÜLLER, MAX (Karl-Marx-Stadt, DDR)**
      1960   67   *Musik. Theater. Tanz*
                             (175)   [IBAK]

3222 _____.
      1963   101   *Musik. Theater. Tanz*
                             (416)   [IBAK]

3223 _____.
      1965   133   *Musik. Tanz. Theater*
                             (396,1316)   *12

3224 _____.
      1970   164   *Literatur- u. Sprachwissenschaft. Musik*
                             (1797)   *12

3225 **MÜLLER, ROBERT A. (Hannover)**
      1961   117   *Musik. Theater. Film. Literatur*
                             (469)   [IBAK]

3226 _____.
      1961   124   *Musikliteratur. Theater. Film*
                             (390)   [IBAK]

3227 _____.
      1962   136   *Kunst. Musik. Kulturgeschichte*
                             (531)   [IBAK]

3228 _____.
      1963   146   *Kunst. Musik. Noten*
                             (532)   *12

3229 _____.
      1965   158   *Musikliteratur. Noten. Theater. Tanz*
                             (609)   [IBAK]

3230 _____.
      1966   174   *Musikliteratur. Theater. Tanz*
                             (561)   [IBAK]

3231 **MÜLLER & GRÄFF (Stuttgart)**
      1955   123   *Musik. Theater. Tanz*
                             (2159)   *6

3232 _____.
      1961   194   *Kunstwissenschaft. Geschichte. Musik. Theater*
                             (2594)   [IBAK]

---

1 Compiler/State University of New York (Buffalo)   **2** The British Library (London)   **3** Gemeentemuseum (Den Haag)   **4** The Grolier Club (N.Y.C.)   **5** Hirsch Collection, British Library (London)   **6** D.W. Krummel (Urbana)   **7** Library of Congress (Washington, D.C.)   **8** Library and Museum of the Performing Arts (N.Y.C.)   **9** William Reeves (London)   **10** Sibley Library, Eastman School of Music (Rochester)   **11** Nigel Simeone (Tunbridge Wells, Kent)   **12** Vereeniging ter Bevordering van de Belangen des Boekhandels (Amsterdam)   **13** University of Virginia (Charlottesville)   **14** University of California at Los Angeles   **15** Generally available

3233 **MÜLLER & GRÄFF (Stuttgart) (continued)**
       1962   210   *Archeol. Kunstgewerbe. Musik. Theater. Tanz*
                                      (2330)   [IBAK]

3234 _____.
       1963   220   *Kunstwissenschaft. Musik. Theater. Tanz*
                                      (2048)   [IBAK]

3235 _____.
       1965   263   *Kunst ... Musik. Theater*
                                      (1738-2274)   *6

3236 **MÜLLER-BUSCHER, HENNING (Laaber)**
       1975   1   *Musikliteratur. Klaviernoten. Varia*
                                      (1128)   *13

3237 _____.
       1975   2   *Neue u. antiq. Musikbücher. Klaviernoten*
                                      (1107)   *13

3238 _____.
       1976   3   *Antiquarische Musikliteratur. Klavierausz.*
                                      (808)   *13

3239 _____.
       197_   4   *Musikalische Erst- u. Frühdrucke*
                                      (1735)   *13

3240 _____.
       1977   5   *Musikliteratur*
                                      (1436)   *13

3241 _____.
       1977   6   *Musica practica*
                                      (3369)   *13

3242 _____.
       1977   7   *Musica theorica*
                                      (1134)   *1,13

3243 _____.
       1977   8   *Musikliteratur*
                                      (1006)   *1,13

3244 _____.
       1978   9   *Reichhaltiges musikalisches Angebot*
                                      (3667)   *1,13

3245 _____.
       197_   10   *Antiquarische Musikliteratur*
                                      (912)   *13

3246 _____.
       197_   14   *Partituren. Klavierauszuege. Musikbücher*
                                      (856)   *13

3247 _____.
       198_?   17   *100 musikalische Seltenheiten. Originaldrucke*
                                      (100)   *10

3248 **MÜNSTER, H. F. (Verona and Leipzig)**
       1878   —   *Coll: Beretta, M. G. B. Libreria musicale*
                                      (?)   [MfM]

---

1 Compiler/State University of New York (Buffalo)   **2** The British Library (London)   **3** Gemeentemuseum (Den Haag)   **4** The Grolier Club (N.Y.C.)   **5** Hirsch Collection, British Library (London)   **6** D.W. Krummel (Urbana)   **7** Library of Congress (Washington, D.C.)   **8** Library and Museum of the Performing Arts (N.Y.C.)   **9** William Reeves (London)   **10** Sibley Library, Eastman School of Music (Rochester)   **11** Nigel Simeone (Tunbridge Wells, Kent)   **12** Vereeniging ter Bervordering van de Belangen des Boekhandels (Amsterdam)   **13** University of Virginia (Charlottesville)   **14** University of California at Los Angeles   **15** Generally available

3249	**MUMMERY, KENNETH** (Bournemouth) [Successor to **HAROLD REEVES, q.v.**]

3249   1949   1   *Autograph Musical Mss. Old and Rare Music* (1001)   *1,8,10,11,13

3250 ____.   1949   2   *Full & Vocal Scores. Violin Music. Opera* (3671)   *1,8,10,11,13

3251 ____.   1951   3   *Biography. Bibliography. Periodicals. Scores* (4221)   *1,8,10,11,13

3252 ____.   1952   4   *Folk Song. Old English Music, 1550-1850* (2133)   *1,8,10,11,13

3253 ____.   1953?   5   *Hymnology. Organ Music* (2157)   *1,8,10,11,13

3254 ____.   1953?   6   *History. Essays. Theory. Full Scores* (4199)   *1,8,10,11

3255 ____.   1952   7   *17th & 18th Century Eds. Libretti. Song Books* (1132)   *1,8,10,11,13

3256 ____.   1954   8   *Opera. Singing. Ballet. Instruments. Music* (3418)   *1,8,10,11

3257 ____.   1955   9   *Biography. Full Scores. Orchestra Sets. Music* (3501)   *1,8,10,11,13,14

3258 ____.   1956   10   *Ancient & Medieval Music. Bibliography. Scores* (2175)   *1,8,10,11,13,14

3259 ____.   1957   11   *Early Beethoven Editions. Autograph Mss.* (687)   *1,8,10,11,13

3260 ____.   1957   12   *Folk Songs. Collected Eds. Theory. Scores* (1868)   *1,6,8,10,11,13

3261 ____.   1957   13   *Treatises. Vocal & Instrumental Music. Mss.* (610)   *1,6,8,10,11,14

3262 ____.   1958   14   *Opera. Biogr. Bibliogr. Violin Music. Scores* (1496)   *1,6,8,10,11,13

3263 ____.   1959   15   *Autograph Mss. Treatises. Scores* (373)   *1,6,8,10,11,13

3264 ____.   1959   16   *Engl.Music. Collected Eds. Hymnology. Scores* (1758)   *1,6,8,10,11,13

1 Compiler/State University of New York (Buffalo)   **2** The British Library (London)   **3** Gemeentemuseum (Den Haag)   **4** The Grolier Club (N.Y.C.)   **5** Hirsch Collection, British Library (London)   **6** D.W. Krummel (Urbana)   **7** Library of Congress (Washington, D.C.)   **8** Library and Museum of the Performing Arts (N.Y.C.)   **9** William Reeves (London)   **10** Sibley Library, Eastman School of Music (Rochester)   **11** Nigel Simeone (Tunbridge Wells, Kent)   **12** Vereeniging ter Bervordering van de Belangen des Boekhandels (Amsterdam)   **13** University of Virginia (Charlottesville)   **14** University of California at Los Angeles   **15** Generally available

3265 **MUMMERY, KENNETH (Bournemouth) (continued)**
     1960   17   *Vocal, Harps. & Chamber Music. Autogr. Mss.*
                    (?)   *6,8,10,11

3266   _____.
     1960   18   *Bibliogr. History. Portraits. Collected Eds.*
                    (1335+)   *1,6,8,10,11,13

3267   _____.
     1961   19   *Treatises. Early Vocal Music*
                    (363+)   *1,6,8,10,11,13

3268   _____.
     1961   20   *[Music and Books on Music]*
                    (1820)   *1,6,8,10,11,13

3269   _____.
     1962   21   *Treatises. Vocal, Harpsichord, Chamber Music*
                    (379)   *1,6,8,10,11,13

3270   _____.
     1962   22   *[Music & Books on Music]*
                    (1252)   *1,6,8,10,11,13

3271   _____.
     1963   23   *Early Vocal, Harps., Chamber Music. Theory*
                    (343)   *1,6,8,10,11,13

3272   _____.
     1963   24   *[Music & Books on Music]*
                    (1845)   *1,6,8,10,11,13

3273   _____.
     1964   25   *Early Vocal, Harps., Chamber Music. Theory*
                    (414)   *1,6,8,10,11,13

3274   _____.
     1964   26   *[Music & Books on Music]. Autograph Mss.*
                    (1484)   *1,6,8,10,11,13

3275   _____.
     1965   27   *Early Vocal, Harps., Chamber Music. Theory*
                    (358)   *1,6,8,10,11,13

3276   _____.
     1966   28   *Bibliography. Coll.Eds. History. Biography*
                    (1626)   *1,6,8,10,11,13

3277   _____.
     1966   29   *Early Vocal, Harps., Chamber Music. Theory*
                    (204)   *1,6,8,10,11,13

3278   _____.
     1966   30   *[Music & Books on Music]*
                    (1368)   *1,6,8,10,11,13

3279   _____.
     1967   31   *Early Treatises. Vocal and Harpsichord Music*
                    (279)   *1,6,8,10,11,13

3280   _____.
     1967   32   *Bibliogr. Coll.Eds. History. Oriental Music*
                    (1936)   *1,6,8,10,11,13

---

1 Compiler/State University of New York (Buffalo)   **2** The British Library (London)   **3** Gemeentemuseum (Den Haag)   **4** The Grolier Club (N.Y.C.)   **5** Hirsch Collection, British Library (London)   **6** D.W. Krummel (Urbana)   **7** Library of Congress (Washington, D.C.)   **8** Library and Museum of the Performing Arts (N.Y.C.)   **9** William Reeves (London)   **10** Sibley Library, Eastman School of Music (Rochester) **11** Nigel Simeone (Tunbridge Wells, Kent)   **12** Vereeniging ter Bervordering van de Belangen des Boekhandels (Amsterdam)   **13** University of Virginia (Charlottesville)   **14** University of California at Los Angeles   **15** Generally available

3281 **MUMMERY, KENNETH (Bournemouth) (continued)**
    1968   33   *[NB: never issued]*

3282 ____.
    1968   34   *Bibliogr. Coll.Eds. History. Oriental Music.*
              (1536)   *1,6,8,10,11,13

3283 ____.
    1969   35   *Early Treatises. Vocal and Harpsichord Music*
              (322)   *1,6,8,10,11,13

3284 ____.
    1969   36   *Bibliogr. Coll.Eds. History. Oriental Music*
              (1723)   *1,6,8,10,11,13

3285 ____.
    1970   37   *Early Treatises. Vocal and Harpsichord Music*
              (289)   *1,6,8,11,13

3286 ____.
    1970   38   *Bibliogr. Coll.Eds. History. Biography. Opera*
              (1440)   *1,6,8,11,14

3287 ____.
    1971   40   *Bibliogr. Coll.Eds. History. Oriental Music*
              (1817)   *1,6,8,10,11,14

3288 ____.
    1972   41   *Early Treatises. Vocal and Harpsichord Music*
              (245)   *1,6,8,11,14

3289 ____.
    1972   42   *Coll.Eds. Bibliogr. History. Theory. Scores*
              (1843)   *1,6,8,13,14

3290 ____.
    1973   44   *Bibliog. Coll. Eds. History. Biography*
              (2149)   *1,6,8,13,14

3291 ____.
    1974   45   *Early Treatises. Vocal and Harpsichord Music*
              (?)   *6,8,13,14

3292 ____.
    1974   46   *Coll.Eds. Bibliography. History. Instruments*
              (1922)   *1,6,8,13,14

3293 ____.
    1975   47   *Collected Eds. Bibliography. History. Theory*
              (1890)   *1,6,8,14

3294 ____.
    1976   48   *Bibliography. Coll.Eds. History. Biography*
              (1838)   *1,6,8,13,14

3295 ____.
    1977   49   *Bibliography. Coll.Eds. History. Biography*
              (1626)   *1,6,8

3296 ____.
    1978   50   *Coll.Eds. Bibliography. History. Instruments*
              (2080)   *1,6,8,13

1 Compiler/State University of New York (Buffalo)   **2** The British Library (London)   **3** Gemeentemuseum (Den Haag)   **4** The Grolier Club (N.Y.C.)   **5** Hirsch Collection, British Library (London)   **6** D.W. Krummel (Urbana)   **7** Library of Congress (Washington, D.C.)   **8** Library and Museum of the Performing Arts (N.Y.C.)   **9** William Reeves (London)   **10** Sibley Library, Eastman School of Music (Rochester)   **11** Nigel Simeone (Tunbridge Wells, Kent)   **12** Vereeniging ter Bervordering van de Belangen des Boekhandels (Amsterdam)   **13** University of Virginia (Charlottesville)   **14** University of California at Los Angeles   **15** Generally available

3297 **MUMMERY, KENNETH (Bournemouth) (continued)**
      1979   51   *Bibliogr. Coll.Eds. History. Biography. Opera*
                         (1472)   *1,6,8,13

3298 _____.
      1980   52   *Bibliogr. Coll.Eds. Hymnology. Full Scores*
                         (1909)   *1,6,8,13

3299 _____.
      1981   53   *Bibliogr. Coll.Eds. Ancient & Medieval Music*
                         (1525)   *1,6,8,13

3300 **MUNS, J. B. (Los Angeles, CA.)**
      196_   102   *Fine Arts. Architecture. Music*
                         (116-25,250-59)   *14

3301 _____.
      1967   103   *Fine Arts. Architecture. Music*
                         (179-299+)   *14

3302 _____.
      1967   105   *Music*
                         (446)   *6,14

3303 _____.
      1967   107   *Books. Scores. Libretti*
                         (526)   *6,14

3304 _____.
      1967   109   *Books. Scores. Libretti*
                         (536)   *6,10,14

3305 _____.
      1967   110   *Books. Scores. Periodicals*
                         (454)   *1,6

3306 _____.
      1968   112   *Books. Scores. Periodicals*
                         (591)   *10

3307 _____.
      1968   114   *Music Books & some Scores*
                         (497)   *1,6,10

3308 _____.
      1969   116   *Scores. Books. Periodicals*
                         (572)   *10,14

3309 **MUNS, J. B. (San Anselmo, CA.)**
      1970   118   *Music. Catalogue of Books*
                         (571)   *1,10,13

3310 _____.
      1971   120   *Music. Catalogue of Books*
                         (581)   *10,13,14

3311 _____.
      1971   122   *Music. Catalogue of Books*
                         (606)   *13,14

3312 _____.
      1971   123   *Art. Music. Architecture*
                         (983-1588)   *10

1 Compiler/State University of New York (Buffalo)   **2** The British Library (London)   **3** Gemeentemuseum (Den Haag)   **4** The Grolier Club (N.Y.C.)   **5** Hirsch Collection, British Library (London)   **6** D.W. Krummel (Urbana)   **7** Library of Congress (Washington, D.C.)   **8** Library and Museum of the Performing Arts (N.Y.C.)   **9** William Reeves (London)   **10** Sibley Library, Eastman School of Music (Rochester)   **11** Nigel Simeone (Tunbridge Wells, Kent)   **12** Vereeniging ter Bervordering van de Belangen des Boekhandels (Amsterdam)   **13** University of Virginia (Charlottesville)   **14** University of California at Los Angeles   **15** Generally available

3313	**MUNS, J. B. (Eugene, Ore.) (continued)**				
	1971		124	*Art. Music. Architecture* (1091-737)	*1,10,13
3314	_____.				
	1974		125	*Books on Art. Music. Architecture* (1901)	*10,13
3315	_____.				
	1975		126	*Books on Art. Music. Architecture* (1834)	*10,13,14
3316	_____.				
	1976?		127	*Books on Art. Music. Architecture* (502-1205)	*6,10,13,14
3317	_____.				
	1977		128	*Books on Art. Music. Architecture* (335-801)	*10,13,14
3318	_____.				
	1978		129	*Books on Art. Music. Architecture* (363-831)	*10,13,14
3319	**MUNS, J. B. (Berkeley, CA.)**				
	1979?		130	*Books on Art. Music. Architecture* (144-560)	*1,10,13
3320	_____.				
	1980		131	*Books on Art. Music. Architecture* (1-457)	*1
3321	_____.				
	1981		132	*Books on Art. Music. Archeology* (158-658)	*1
3322	_____.				
	1982		133	*Books on Art. Music. Architecture* (1-478)	*1
3323	_____.				
	1983		134	*Books [on various topics]. Music. Dance* (144-440)	*1
3324	_____.				
	1984		135	*Books [on various topics]. Music. Dance* (1-433)	*1
3325	_____.				
	1971	List	71-3	*Books on Music* (239)	*10
3326	_____.				
	1972	do.	72-4	*Theory. Jazz. Folk Music. Music Education* (121)	*1,10
3327	_____.				
	1973	do.	73-3	*Music Books* (212)	*1,10
3328	_____.				
	1974	do.	74-1	*Music Books* (198)	*1

1 Compiler/State University of New York (Buffalo)   **2** The British Library (London)   **3** Gemeentemuseum (Den Haag)   **4** The Grolier Club (N.Y.C.)   **5** Hirsch Collection, British Library (London)   **6** D.W. Krummel (Urbana)   **7** Library of Congress (Washington, D.C.)   **8** Library and Museum of the Performing Arts (N.Y.C.)   **9** William Reeves (London)   **10** Sibley Library, Eastman School of Music (Rochester)   **11** Nigel Simeone (Tunbridge Wells, Kent)   **12** Vereeniging ter Bervordering van de Belangen des Boekhandels (Amsterdam)   **13** University of Virginia (Charlottesville)   **14** University of California at Los Angeles   **15** Generally available

3329	**MUNS, J. B. (Berkeley, CA.) (continued)**				
	1977	do.	77-2	*Music & Dance* (88)	*1,10
3330	_____.				
	1977	do.	77-6	*Books on Music* (76)	*1,13
3331	_____.				
	1977	do.	77-8	*Music Books* (124)	*1,13
3332	_____.				
	1979	do.	79-3	*Music Books* (132)	*1,13
3333	_____.				
	1979	do.	79-6	*Music Books* (119)	*1
3334	_____.				
	1980	do.	80-4	*Music Books* (109)	*1
3335	_____.				
	1981	do.	81-2	*Music Books* (97)	*1
3336	_____.				
	1981	do.	81-6	*Music Books* (90)	*1
3337	_____.				
	1982	do.	82-4	*Books on Music. Autographs* (93)	*1
3338	_____.				
	1985	do.	85-5	*Musical Autographs* (143)	*15
3339	**MUSICA ANTIQUA (Copenhagen)**				
	1973	Liste	7	*Klavierpartitur* (299)	*1,10,14
3340	_____.				
	1974	do.	12	*Klaviermusik. Rara. Musikliteratur* (656)	*1,6,10
3341	_____.				
	1975	do.	14	*Chamber Music* (514)	[H.Baron]
3342	_____.				
	1976	do.	15	*Songs. Vocal Scores. Collections. Music Lit.* (1103)	*1,6,10
3343	_____.				
	1976	do.	16	*Theatre. Ballet. Film. Radio* (493 i,a,)	*1
3344	_____.				
	[197-]	do.	20	*Musik. Theater. Ballet* (817)	*14

1 Compiler/State University of New York (Buffalo)   2 The British Library (London)   3 Gemeentemuseum (Den Haag)   4 The Grolier Club (N.Y.C.)   5 Hirsch Collection, British Library (London)   6 D.W. Krummel (Urbana)   7 Library of Congress (Washington, D.C.)   8 Library and Museum of the Performing Arts (N.Y.C.)   9 William Reeves (London)   10 Sibley Library, Eastman School of Music (Rochester)   11 Nigel Simeone (Tunbridge Wells, Kent)   12 Vereeniging ter Bervordering van de Belangen des Boekhandels (Amsterdam)   13 University of Virginia (Charlottesville)   14 University of California at Los Angeles   15 Generally available

3345 **MUSICA ANTIQUA (Copenhagen) (continued)**
      1978   do.   21   *Organ & Church Music. Folkmusic. Books. Jls.*
                            (345)   *1
3346 _____.
      1978   do.   22   *Piano Music. Guitar. Harp. Musical Literature*
                            (865)   *1
3347 _____.
      1979   do.   79/1 *Books on Music. Ballet. Bournonville*
                            (606)   *1
3348 _____.
      1979   do.   79/2 *Books on Music. Songs. Guitar Music*
                            (328)   *1
3349 _____.
      1980   do.   80/1 *Musik. Ballet. Film. Radio*
                            (1145 i.a.)   *1
3350 **MUSICAL AMERICANA (Harry Dichter) (Atlantic City, N. J.)**
      1947   1   *Handbook of American Sheet Music*
                            (2013+)   *1
3351 _____.
      1953   2   *Handbook of American Sheet Music. 2nd Series*
                            (1451)   *1
3352 _____.
      1966   3   *Handbook of American Sheet Music. [3rd Series]*
                            (32pp.)   *1
3353 _____.
      [197_]   10   *Coll: Shenk, J. Songs and Music*
                            (380+)   *10
3354 _____.
      1973   11   *Coll: Shenk, J. Songs and Music*
                            (768)   *10
3355 **MUSICANA UNLIMITED (Chicago, Illinois)**
      1949   7   *Americana. Composers. History. Instruments*
                            (393)   *1
3356 _____.
      1949   8   *[Music and Musical Literature]*
                            (522)   *1
3357 _____.
      1950?   9   *Musical Material, Rare and Scarce*
                            (175)   *1
3358 _____.
      1950   10   *Instruments. The Orchestra. Conducting*
                            (408)   *1
3359 _____.
      1950   11   *Musical Literature and Music, Pt. I, A-CI*
                            (1-400)   *1
3360 _____.
      1950   11   *Musical Literature and Music, Pt. II, CL-FR*
                            (401-788)   *1

---

1 Compiler/State University of New York (Buffalo)   2 The British Library (London)   3 Gemeentemuseum (Den Haag)   4 The Grolier Club (N.Y.C.)   5 Hirsch Collection, British Library (London)   6 D.W. Krummel (Urbana)   7 Library of Congress (Washington, D.C.)   8 Library and Museum of the Performing Arts (N.Y.C.)   9 William Reeves (London)   10 Sibley Library, Eastman School of Music (Rochester)   11 Nigel Simeone (Tunbridge Wells, Kent)   12 Vereeniging ter Bevordering van de Belangen des Boekhandels (Amsterdam)   13 University of Virginia (Charlottesville)   14 University of California at Los Angeles   15 Generally available

3361 **MUSICANA UNLIMITED (Chicago, Illinois) (continued)**
      1951   11   *Musical Literature and Music, Pt. III, FR-LI*
                                     (789)-1212)   *1

3362 _____.
      1951   11   *Musical Literature and Music, Pt. IV, LI-PO*
                                     (1213-1671)   *1

3363 _____.
      1951   11   *Musical Literature and Music, Pt..V, PO-SO*
                                     (1672-2130)   *1

3364 _____.
      1951   11   *Musical Literature and Music, Pt. VI, SP-Z*
                                     (2131-2628)   *1

3365 _____.
      1951   11   *Musical Literature and Music, Pt. VII, Addenda*
                                     (2629-3016)   *1

3366 _____.
      1951   12   *Theatre. Shakespeare. Plays*
                                     (802)   *1

3367 _____.
      1951   13   *Music and Musical Literature*
                                     (542)   *1

3368 _____.
      1951   14   *Scores. Miniature Scores*
                                     (29pp.)   *1

3369 _____.
      1949?   Lists   1   *Miniature Scores and other Music*
                                     (344)   *1

3370 _____.
      1949?   do.   2   *Available Imports*
                                     (259)   *1

3371 _____.
      1949   do.   3   *Miscellaneous Musical Material*
                                     (240)   *1

3372 _____.
      1949   do.   4   *Bibliography. Theory and History of Music*
                                     (234)   *1

3373 _____.
      1952   Nwslt   2-6   *[Musical Literature]*
                                     (4pp. each)   *1

3374 _____.
      1953   do.   7-21   *[Musical Literature]*
                                     (4pp. each)   *1

3375 _____.
      1954   do.   22-23   *[Musical Literature]*
                                     (4pp. each)   *1

3376 **MUTELET, LIBRAIRIE (Metz)**
      196_   238   *Musique et chansons*
                                     (2pp.)   *12

---

1 Compiler/State University of New York (Buffalo)   **2** The British Library (London)   **3** Gemeentemuseum (Den Haag)   **4** The Grolier Club (N.Y.C.)   **5** Hirsch Collection, British Library (London)   **6** D.W. Krummel (Urbana)   **7** Library of Congress (Washington, D.C.)   **8** Library and Museum of the Performing Arts (N.Y.C.)   **9** William Reeves (London)   **10** Sibley Library, Eastman School of Music (Rochester)   **11** Nigel Simeone (Tunbridge Wells, Kent)   **12** Vereeniging ter Bevordering van de Belangen des Boekhandels (Amsterdam)   **13** University of Virginia (Charlottesville)   **14** University of California at Los Angeles   **15** Generally available

3377 **MUTELET, LIBRAIRIE (Metz) (continued)**
    [1965]   342   *Musique et chansons*
                           (2pp.)   *12

3378 **"MUZIEK EN LETTEREN" (Amsterdam)**
    s.d.   —   *Muziek*
                       ?   *12

3379 **NAHR, ED. (Stuttgart) [J. SCHEIBLE'S ANTIQUARIAT NACHF.,q.v.]**
    1921?   8   *Kunst. Musik. Theater*
                       (1508)   *5,12

3380 **NAHR & FUNK (Munich) (FR. KLÜBER'S NACHF.)**
    1910   170   *Kunst. Architecture. Musik. Theater*
                       (991-1226)   *12

3381 **NARDECCHIA, LIBRERIA (Rome)**
    1905   38   *Teatro e musica*
                       (?)   *7

3382 **NAYLOR, F. (London)**
    18__   Spec.   41   *ALS and Historical Documents [all Music]*
                       (8874-9164)   *8

3383 _____.
    18__   do.   42   *ALS and Historical Documents [all Music]*
                       (9165-9376)   *8

3384 **NEBEHAY, CHRISTIAN (Vienna)**
    1949?   18   *Coll: Kalbeck. Musikbibliothek*
                       (344)   *4

3385 _____.
    195_   29   *Coll: Victor Count Wimpfen. Autographen*
                       (72-85)   *4,9

3386 _____.
    195_   50   *Coll: Unnamed*
                       (?)   *4

3387 _____.
    195_   51   *Coll: Herbeck, J. Ritter von. Musik. Theater*
                       (305)   *4,9

3388 _____.
    [1959]   60   *Coll: Spiegel. Autographen*
                       (435-650)   *4

3389 **NEBEHAY, INGO (Vienna)**
    [1962]   Liste   1   *Autographen: Alban Berg, Altenberg, et al*
                       (160)   *12

3390 _____.
    1964   do.   10   *Musik. Theater. Ballet*
                       (547)   [IBAK]

3391 _____.
    1965   do.   15   *Philos. Kulturgeschichte. Philologie. Musik*
                       (1658)   *12

3392 _____.
    1966   do.   19   *Autographen berühmter Musiker*
                       (904)   *1

3393 **NEBEHAY, INGO (Vienna) (continued)**
  1967 do. 25 *Autographen berühmter Musiker*
            (797)   [IBAK]

3394 _____.
  1969 do. 34 *Autographen berühmter Dichter und Musiker*
            (978)   *1

3395 _____.
  197_ do. 43 *Autographen*
            (1-494)   *4

3396 _____.
  1974 do. 50 *Autographen Musiker und Schauspieler*
            (605)   *14

3397 _____.
  [1977] do. 58 *Autographen berühmter Musiker*
            (566)   *14

3398 _____.
  1980 do. 60 *Autographen berühmter Musiker*
            (625)   *14

3399 **NEDERLANDSCHE BOEKHANDEL (Antwerp)**
  1913   K *Schoone Kunsten. Muziek. Tooneel*
            (23pp.)   *B-Br

3400 **NEUMAYER & CO. (London)**
  1912   24 *Old Music and Musical Literature*
            (?)   *7

3401 **NEUWERK BUCH- UND MUSIKHANDEL (Kassel)**
  s.d. Angeb 5 *Musikbücher. Haus- und Kammermusik*
            (16pp.)   *13

3402 _____.
  1963 Angeb NM4 *Klavierauszüge*
            (401)   *12

3403 **NEW YORK PUBLIC LIBRARY**
  1934   — *Music, Parts I-X (Catalogue of Duplicates)*
            (1050+)   *13

3404 **NIELSEN, AXEL V. (Copenhagen)**
  1959   62 *Musik. Theater. Film*
            (826)   *12

3405 **NIJHOFF, MARTINUS (Den Haag)**
  1892   — *Livres anciens et moderne /including Music/*
            (25pp.)   *5

3406 _____.
  1901   — *Coll: Biejers /including Music and Theatre/*
            (3620-707)   *12

3407 _____.
  s.d.   609 *Histoire ecclesiastique des pays-bas, 2*
            (2172-249)   *10

3408 _____.
  [1939]   636 *Music*
            (440)   *5,10,12,13

---

1 Compiler/State University of New York (Buffalo) **2** The British Library (London) **3** Gemeentemuseum (Den Haag) **4** The Grolier Club (N.Y.C.) **5** Hirsch Collection, British Library (London) **6** D.W. Krummel (Urbana) **7** Library of Congress (Washington, D.C.) **8** Library and Museum of the Performing Arts (N.Y.C.) **9** William Reeves (London) **10** Sibley Library, Eastman School of Music (Rochester) **11** Nigel Simeone (Tunbridge Wells, Kent) **12** Vereeniging ter Bervordering van de Belangen des Boekhandels (Amsterdam) **13** University of Virginia (Charlottesville) **14** University of California at Los Angeles **15** Generally available

3409 **NIJHOFF, MARTINUS (Den Haag) (continued)**
       [1941]   643   *Music. Liedboekjes*
                                    (60)   *12

3410 ———.
       [1948]   684   *Music. Liedboekjes*
                                    (1107)   *6,12

3411 ———.
       1954   716   *Music and Theatre*
                                    (672)   *12

3412 ———.
       1963   755   *Varia*
                                    (332-705)   *6

3413 ———.
       1968   791   *Varia*
                                    (551-722)   *10

3414 ———.
       1971   821   *Varia*
                                    (719-849)   *1,10,13

3415 ———.
       19__   List   231   *Music /typescript/*
                                    (70)   *5

3416 ———.
       1959   do.   369   *Books and Periodicals on Music*
                                    (538)   *1,12

3417 ———.
       [1965]   do.   425   *Books and Periodicals on Music*
                                    (31)   *1,12

3418 ———.
       [1965]   do.   434   *Books and Periodicals on Music*
                                    (91)   *1,12

3419 ———.
       [1965]   do.   463   *Music. Dance. Theatre. Film*
                                    (110)   *1,12

3420 ———.
       [1966]   do.   494   *Musical Instruments. Vocal Music*
                                    (71)   *12

3421 ———.
       [196_]   do.   526   *Livres anciens et modernes /including Music/*
                                    (318-67)   *13

3422 ———.
       [196_]   do.   531   *Livres anciens et modernes /including Music/*
                                    (328-416)   *13

3423 ———.
       [1967]   do.   532   *Music*
                                    (53)   *1,12

3424 ———.
       [1968]   do.   544   *Music*
                                    (32)   *1,12

3425   **NIJHOFF, MARTINUS (Den Haag) (continued)**
     [1971]   do.   611   *Music*
                             (69)   *12,13

3426   _____.
     [1972]   do.   636   *Music*
                             (65)   *1,12,13

3427   _____.
     [1973]   do.   644   *Music. History of Music. Theatre*
                             (58)   *1,13

3428   **NIRONI & PRANDI, LIBRERIA (Reggio Emilia)**
     19__   61   *Musica. Danza. Teatro. Feste*
                             (1-421)   *9

3429   **NIZET, A. G. (Paris)**
     1974   N.S.3   *Theatre. Arts du spectacle. Musique*
                             (730)   *14

3430   **NORDDEUTSCHES ANTIQUARIAT (Rostock)**
     [1960]   144   *Kulturgeschichte. Musik*
                             (818)   [IBAK]

3431   _____.
     [1960]   153   *Kulturgeschichte. Musik*
                             (590)   [IBAK]

3432   _____.
     [1960]   168   *Musik. Schoene Literatur*
                             (627)   *6

3433   _____.
     [1961]   188   *Kulturgeschichte. Musikgeschichte*
                             (596)   *6

3434   _____.
     [1961]   199   *Kulturgeschichte. Musikgeschichte*
                             (583)   [IBAK]

3435   _____.
     [1962]   228   *Kulturgeschichte. Musikgeschichte*
                             (1017)   *6

3436   _____.
     [1963]   252   *Kulturgeschichte. Musikgeschichte*
                             (930)   *1,6

3437   _____.
     1965   338   *Belletristik. Musikgeschichte*
                             (1208)   *1

3438   _____.
     [1970]   428   *Buch- und Bibliothekswesen*
                             (621 i.a.)   *13

3439   _____.
     [1969?]   436   *Belletristik. Musik- und Theatergeschichte*
                             (530-999)   *13

3440   _____.
     [1972]   447   *Belletristik. Musik- und Theatergeschichte*
                             (666-1150)   *13

3441 **NORDDEUTSCHES ANTIQUARIAT (Rostock) (continued)**
    [1978]   576   *Belletristik. Musik- und Theatergeschichte*
                              (955-1377)   *13
3442 **NORDSTRØM, ERIK see MUSICA ANTIQUA**

3443 **NOVALIS-ANTIQUARIAT (Freiburg)**
    1960   24   *Klassiker. Literatur und Musik*
                              (356)   [IBAK]
3444 **OBERDORFER, J. (Munich)**
    1862   14   *Musikalien und Bücher ü. Musik*
                              (41pp.)   [Schneider 82]
3445 _____.
    1863   17   *Musikalien und Bücher ü. Musik*
                              (31pp.)   [Schneider 82]
3446 **OELSNER, M. (Leipzig)**
    s.d.   —   *Bücher ü. Musik*
                              (4pp.)   *13
3447 _____.
    s.d.   49   *Antiquarische Musikalien. Bücher ü. Musik*
                              (130pp.)   *13
3448 _____.
    s.d.   123   */Musik und Bücher ü. Musik/*
                              (39pp.)   *13
3449 _____.
    s.d.   124   *Nachtrag zum Katalog 123*
                              (2pp.)   *13
3450 _____.
    s.d.   —   *Bücher ü. Musik*
                              (4pp.)   *13
3451 **O'KEEFE, BRAD (Baltimore, Maryland)**
    1975   —   *Books on Music and Printed Music*
                              (175)   *1,13
3452 **OLB [i.e., OAK LAWN BOOKS] JAZZ (Providence, R.I.)**
    10/1981   812   *Jazz Books/ Jazz Records*
                              (18pp)   *1
3453 **OLSCHKI, LEO S. (Florence)**
    1908   66   *Musique*
                              (529)   *1,3,5,7,8,10,12
3454 _____.
    1909   72   *Liturgie*
                              (310)   *3,7
3455 _____.
    1930   —   *Choix de livres, 8.ptie.: Musique*
                              (359pp.)   *4,7
3456 _____.
    1930   103   *Musique. Théâtre. Danse*
                              (176pp.)   *4,6,7,8,10

---

1 Compiler/State University of New York (Buffalo)   **2** The British Library (London)   **3** Gemeentemuseum (Den Haag)   **4** The Grolier Club (N.Y.C.)   **5** Hirsch Collection, British Library (London)   **6** D.W. Krummel (Urbana)   **7** Library of Congress (Washington, D.C.)   **8** Library and Museum of the Performing Arts (N.Y.C.)   **9** William Reeves (London)   **10** Sibley Library, Eastman School of Music (Rochester)   **11** Nigel Simeone (Tunbridge Wells, Kent)   **12** Vereeniging ter Bervordering van de Belangen des Boekhandels (Amsterdam)   **13** University of Virginia (Charlottesville)   **14** University of California at Los Angeles   **15** Generally available

3457   OLSCHKI, LEO S. (Florence) (continued)
      1938   —   *Une nouvelle collection de musique*
                        (16pp.)   *7

3458   _____.
      1968   —   *Musicologia*
                        (45pp.)   *1

3459   OPERA BOX (N.Y.C. and Brooklyn, N.Y.)
      195_   —   *Opera Biographies*
                        (12pp.)   *6

3460   _____.
      [195_]   —   *Books on Opera*
                        (20pp.)   *6

3461   _____.
      [195_]   —   *Books on opera*
                        (16pp.)   *6

3462   _____.
      [195_]   —   *Books on Opera*
                        (16pp.)   *6

3463   _____.
      [195_]   —   *Books on Opera*
                        (24pp.)   *6

3464   _____.
      1957   —   *Books on Opera*
                        (15pp.)   *14

3465   _____.
      1957   —   *Books on Opera*
                        (15pp.)   *14

3466   _____.
      [196_?]   11   *Books on Opera*
                        (27pp.)   *14

3467   _____.
      [196_?]   12   *Books on Opera. Autographs*
                        (233)   *14

3468   _____.
      196_   13   ?
                        (?)   [not located]

3469   _____.
      196_   14   ?
                        (?)   [not located]

3470   _____
      1963   15   *Books on Opera*
                        (11pp.)   *6,14

3471   _____.
      1963   16   *Books on Opera*
                        (1172)   *6,14

3472   _____.
      196_   17   *Books on Opera*
                        (?)   [not located]

1 Compiler/State University of New York (Buffalo) **2** The British Library (London) **3** Gemeentemuseum (Den Haag) **4** The Grolier Club (N.Y.C.) **5** Hirsch Collection, British Library (London) **6** D.W. Krummel (Urbana) **7** Library of Congress (Washington, D.C.) **8** Library and Museum of the Performing Arts (N.Y.C.) **9** William Reeves (London) **10** Sibley Library, Eastman School of Music (Rochester) **11** Nigel Simeone (Tunbridge Wells, Kent) **12** Vereeniging ter Bervordering van de Belangen des Boekhandels (Amsterdam) **13** University of Virginia (Charlottesville) **14** University of California at Los Angeles **15** Generally available

3473 **OPERA BOX (N.Y.C. and Brooklyn, N.Y.) (continued)**

	196_	18	*Books on Opera*	
			(?)	[not located]
3474	_____.			
	1967	19	*Books on Opera*	
			(1201)	*6,14
3475	_____.			
	1967	20	*Books on Opera*	
			(663)	*1,6,14
3476	_____.			
	1968?	21	*Books on Opera. Scores. Programs*	
			(16pp.)	*1,14
3477	_____.			
	1969	22	*Books on Opera*	
			(17pp.)	*6
3478	_____.			
	1969	23	*Books on Opera. Scores. Programs*	
			(17pp.)	*1,14
3479	_____.			
	1970	24	*Books on Opera*	
			(16pp.)	*14
3480	_____.			
	1970?	25	*Books on Opera*	
			(?)	[not located]
3481	_____.			
	1970?	26	*Books on Opera*	
			(31pp.)	*13
3482	_____.			
	1971	27	*Books on Opera. Scores. Programs*	
			(16pp.)	*1,14
3483	_____.			
	1972	28	*Books on Opera*	
			(21pp.)	*14
3484	_____.			
	197_	29	*Books on Opera*	
			(16pp.)	*14
3485	_____.			
	1973	30	*Books on Opoera*	
			(20pp.)	*14
3486	_____.			
	1973	31	*Books on Opera*	
			(16pp.)	*1,14
3487	_____.			
	1973	32	*Books on Opera*	
			(16pp.)	*1,14
3488	_____.			
	1974?	33	*Books on Opera. Photos*	
			(19pp.)	*1,14

1 Compiler/State University of New York (Buffalo)　**2** The British Library (London)　**3** Gemeentemuseum (Den Haag)　**4** The Grolier Club (N.Y.C.)　**5** Hirsch Collection, British Library (London)　**6** D.W. Krummel (Urbana)　**7** Library of Congress (Washington, D.C.)　**8** Library and Museum of the Performing Arts (N.Y.C.)　**9** William Reeves (London)　**10** Sibley Library, Eastman School of Music (Rochester)　**11** Nigel Simeone (Tunbridge Wells, Kent)　**12** Vereeniging ter Bervordering van de Belangen des Boekhandels (Amsterdam)　**13** University of Virginia (Charlottesville)　**14** University of California at Los Angeles　**15** Generally available

3489   **OPERA BOX (N.Y.C. and Brooklyn, N.Y.) (continued)**
    1975   34   *Books on Opera*   (20pp.)   *1,14

3490   _____.
    1975   35   *Books on Opera. Libretti. Photos*   (20pp.)   *1,14

3491   _____.
    1975   36   *Books on Opera*   (20pp.)   *1,14

3492   _____.
    1976   37   *Books on Opera. Photos. Programs*   (20pp.)   *1,14

3493   _____.
    1977   38   *Books on Opera. Scores*   (20pp.)   *1,14

3494   _____.
    1977   39   *Books on Opera. Scores*   (27pp.)   *14

3495   _____.
    1977   40   *Books on Opera. Photos*   (12pp.)   *1

3496   _____.
    1978?   41   *Books on Opera*   (12pp.)   *1

3497   _____.
    1979   42   *Books on Opera*   (24pp.)   *1

3498   _____.
    1979   43   *Books on Opera. Scores*   (12pp.)   *1

3499   _____.
    1979   44   *Books on Opera*   (20pp.)   *1

3500   _____.
    1981   45   *Books on Opera*   (16pp.)   *1

3501   _____.
    1981   46   *Books on Opera*   (20pp.)   *1

3502   _____.
    1983?   47   *Books on Opera*   (15pp.)   *1

3503   _____.
    1983?   48   *Books on Opera*   (15pp.)   *1

3504   _____.
    1983?   49   *Books on Opera*   (15pp.)   *1

1 Compiler/State University of New York (Buffalo)   **2** The British Library (London)   **3** Gemeentemuseum (Den Haag)   **4** The Grolier Club (N.Y.C.)   **5** Hirsch Collection, British Library (London)   **6** D.W. Krummel (Urbana)   **7** Library of Congress (Washington, D.C.)   **8** Library and Museum of the Performing Arts (N.Y.C.)   **9** William Reeves (London)   **10** Sibley Library, Eastman School of Music (Rochester)   **11** Nigel Simeone (Tunbridge Wells, Kent)   **12** Vereeniging ter Bervordering van de Belangen des Boekhandels (Amsterdam)   **13** University of Virginia (Charlottesville)   **14** University of California at Los Angeles   **15** Generally available

3505 **OPERA BOX (N.Y.C. and Brooklyn, N.Y.) (continued)**
        1983?   50   *Books on Opera*
                                        (19pp.)   *1

3506 _____.
        1984   51   *Books on Opera*
                                        (19pp.)   *1

3507 **OPPERMANN, HENNING [formerly RUDOLPH GEERING] (Basel)**
        9/1928   Jg.4   *Basler Bücherfreund, H.3: Musik-autographen*
                                        (966-3017)   *4,10,13

3508 _____.
        12/1929   Jg.5   *Basler Bücherfreund, H.3/4: Musik ... Autogr.*
                                        (640-1291)   *4,7,9,10,12,13

3509 _____.
        1929   Kat.   274   *Anzeiger neuester Erwerbungen*
                                        (1-220)   *13

3510 _____.
        s.d.   281   *"Raumungs-Anzeiger"*
                                        (pp.43-52)   *3,10,13

3511 _____.
        s.d.   410   *Bücher. Autographen... Alte Musik. Mss.*
                                        (i.a., 60)   *1,4

3512 _____.
        [1931]   421   *Musik. Oper. Lied. Tanz*
                                        (770)   *1,3,4,5,7,10,13

3513 _____.
        [1931?]   422   *Autographen und Autographen-Literatur*
                                        (1000, i.a.)   *7,10

3514 _____.
        1932   425   *Books on Music*
                                        (?)   *7

3515 _____.
        1933   434   *Wertvöller Bücher u. Graphik. Musik. Theater*
                                        (429-56)   *8,10

3516 _____.
        1934   438   *Biographien ... Musik und Theater*
                                        (353-94)   *13

3517 **OTTO'SCHEN BUCHHANDLUNG [F. W. OTTO] (Erfurt)**
        1865   57   *Kunst. Illus. Werke. Werke ü. Musik*
                                        (14pp., i.a.)   *8

3518 _____.
        1874   172   *... Anhang: Bücher ü. Musik*
                                        (655)   *5

3519 **PABEL UND CO. (Bonn)**
        1967   4   *Kulturgeschichte. Musik*
                                        (1270)   *1,12

3520 **PALAU, A. (Barcelona)**
        1921   18   *Musica*
                                        (36pp.)   *12

---

1 Compiler/State University of New York (Buffalo)   **2** The British Library (London)   **3** Gemeentemuseum (Den Haag)   **4** The Grolier Club (N.Y.C.)   **5** Hirsch Collection, British Library (London)   **6** D.W. Krummel (Urbana)   **7** Library of Congress (Washington, D.C.)   **8** Library and Museum of the Performing Arts (N.Y.C.)   **9** William Reeves (London)   **10** Sibley Library, Eastman School of Music (Rochester)   **11** Nigel Simeone (Tunbridge Wells, Kent)   **12** Vereeniging ter Bevrordering van de Belangen des Boekhandels (Amsterdam)   **13** University of Virginia (Charlottesville)   **14** University of California at Los Angeles   **15** Generally available

3521 **PALUDAN, ERIK (Copenhagen)**
      195_?   27   *Musik. Teater*
                               (1-997)   *9,13

3522 _____.
      1957   35   *Musik. Teater. Ballet. Film*
                               (2502)   *12

3523 **PAN AMERICAN BOOKS (Cazenovia, N. Y.)**
      1969   List   2   *Music*
                               (73)   *1

3524 **PANOCHTHUS ANTIQUARIAT (Holten)**
      1965   3   *Muziek. Tooneel. Dans*
                               (230)   *12

3525 _____.
      1965   26   *Muziek. Tooneel. Dans. Film. Ballet*
                               (297)   *12

3526 **PARAMOR, C. D. (Newmarket)**
      11/1982   —   *"Yvolde": Books on Music, Theatre, Ballet*
                               (156)   *1

3527 _____.
      11/1982   —   *"Lutz": Books on Music, Dance, Miscellaneous*
                               (316)   *1

3528 _____.
      12/1982   —   *"Grossmith": Gilbert & Sullivan. D'Oyly Carte*
                               (404)   *1

3529 _____.
      6/1983   —   *"Zeller": Libretti and Vocal Scores*
                               (217)   *1

3530 _____.
      10/1983   —   *"Finck": Books on Music*
                               (470)   *1

3531 _____.
      10/1983   —   *"Serpette": Theatre. Ephemera*
                               (290)   *1

3532 _____.
      11/1983   —   *"Gilbert": Gilbert & Sullivan. D'Oyly Carte*
                               (458)   *1

3533 _____.
      1/1984   —   *"Rosse": Theatre. Music. Cinema. Dance*
                               (317)   *15

3534 _____.
      3/1984   —   *"Kerker": Light Entertainment*
                               (213)   *15

3535 _____.
      4/1984   —   *"Audran": Cinema. Dance. Theatre. Music*
                               (474)   *15

3536 _____.
      8/1984   —   *"Bantock": Cinema. Dance. Theatre. Music*
                               (271)   *15

---

1 Compiler/State University of New York (Buffalo) **2** The British Library (London) **3** Gemeentemuseum (Den Haag) **4** The Grolier Club (N.Y.C.) **5** Hirsch Collection, British Library (London) **6** D.W. Krummel (Urbana) **7** Library of Congress (Washington, D.C.) **8** Library and Museum of the Performing Arts (N.Y.C.) **9** William Reeves (London) **10** Sibley Library, Eastman School of Music (Rochester) **11** Nigel Simeone (Tunbridge Wells, Kent) **12** Vereeniging ter Bervordering van de Belangen des Boekhandels (Amsterdam) **13** University of Virginia (Charlottesville) **14** University of California at Los Angeles **15** Generally available

3537   **PARAMOR, C. D. (Newmarket) (continued)**
       11/1984   —   *"Buttercup": A Gilbert & Sullivan Checklist*
                    (501)   *15

3538   **PARKER 8 SON, LTD. (Oxford)**
       [1965]   195   *Books on Music*
                    (695)   [IBAK]

3539   **PARKINSON, J. A. (Selsden, South Croydon)**
       6/1982   1   *Vocal Scores*
                    (277)   *1

3540   _____.
       9/1982   2   *Instrumental Music*
                    (255)   *1

3541   _____.
       11/1982   3   *Vocal and Orchestral Scores*
                    (279)   *1

3542   _____.
       5/1983   4   *Piano Music*
                    (274)   *1

3543   _____.
       6/1983   5   *Vocal Music*
                    (420)   *1

3544   _____.
       9/1983   6   *Piano Music*
                    (274)   *1

3545   _____.
       10/1983   7   *Vocal Scores*
                    (264)   *1

3546   _____.
       2/1984   8   *Piano Music*
                    (278)   *1

3547   _____.
       2/1984   9   *Organ. Early Keyboard and Choral Music*
                    (225)   *1

3548   _____.
       4/1984   10   *English Songs. Lieder and Folksongs*
                    (426)   *1

3549   _____.
       6/1984   1   *Antiquarian Music*
                    (256)   *1

3550   _____.
       7/1984   12   *Piano Music*
                    (288)   *1

3551   _____.
       8/1984   13   *Scottish Music*
                    (106)   *1

3552   _____.
       9/1984   14   *Vocal Scores*
                    (387)   *1

1 Compiler/State University of New York (Buffalo)   **2** The British Library (London)   **3** Gemeentemuseum (Den Haag)   **4** The Grolier Club (N.Y.C.)   **5** Hirsch Collection, British Library (London)   **6** D.W. Krummel (Urbana)   **7** Library of Congress (Washington, D.C.)   **8** Library and Museum of the Performing Arts (N.Y.C.)   **9** William Reeves (London)   **10** Sibley Library, Eastman School of Music (Rochester)   **11** Nigel Simeone (Tunbridge Wells, Kent)   **12** Vereeniging ter Bevordering van de Belangen des Boekhandels (Amsterdam)   **13** University of Virginia (Charlottesville)   **14** University of California at Los Angeles   **15** Generally available

3553 PARKINSON, J. A. (Selsden, South Croydon) (continued)
      11/1984   15   *Piano Music*
                             (427)   *1

3554 _____.
      12/1984   16   *Organ Music. Hymn Books*
                             (263)   *1

3555 PARNELL, L. & J. (London)
      1894   —   *Rare Original Folio Editions of Old Music*
                             (16pp.)   *8

3556 PARTHENON, LIVRARIA, LTDA. (Sao Paulo)
      1967   —   *Livros sobre musica*
                             (8pp.)   *1

3557 PAS-PERDUS, LES LIBRAIRIE (Paris)
      1964   —   *Musique et musiciens*
                             (296)   *12

3558 PATZER, RUDOLF (Mannheim, Weidenthal)
      [1969]   22   *Musikwissenschaftliche Zeitschriften*
                             (37)   *12

3559 _____.
      s.d.   38   *Musikwissenschaftliche Zeitschriften*
                             (12pp.)   *1

3560 _____.
      1971   Kat.   84   *Musik-Bibliographien*
                             (351)   *1,13

3561 PEARSON, J. (London)
      1905   —   *ALS. Historical Documents. Authors' Mss.*
                             (722, i.a.)   *4

3562 _____.
      1911   —   *Autograph Letters and Mss. of Composers*
                             (75)   *7

3563 PEDERSEN, GROENHOLT (Copenhagen)
      [1962]   87   *Musik. Filologi*
                             (1549)   [IBAK]

3564 _____.
      1968   106   *Antikvaria*
                             (1497-1563)   *13

3565 _____.
      1969   108   *Antikvaria*
                             (1434-508)   *13

3566 _____.
      [1970?]   111   *Antikvaria*
                             (1336-87)   *13

3567 _____.
      [197_?]   114   */Antikvaria/*
                             (1641-78)   *13

3568 PEET, C. J. VAN DER (Amsterdam)
      1971   230   *Music*
                             (133)   *12

3569 **PEET, C. P. J. VAN DER (Haarlem)**
      1966   13   *Small Collection of Books on Music*
                               (80)   [IBAK]
3570 _____.
      1973   --   *... Old Books and Albums. Music and Scores*
                               (11)   *1
3571 **PEET, JAN (Amsterdam-Bussum)**
      1963   492   *Musical Science*
                               (329)   [IBAK]
3572 _____.
      [1966]   757   *Music - Dance - Theatre*
                               (507)   *12
3573 _____.
      [1967]   776   *Music - Dance - Theatre*
                               (488)   *12
3574 _____.
      [1967]   812   *Music - Dance - Theatre*
                               (507)   *12
3575 _____.
      [1968]   831   *Music - Dance - Theatre*
                               (496)   *1,12
3576 _____.
      [1968]   852   *Music - Dance - Theatre*
                               (508)   *1,12
3577 _____.
      [1969]   875   *Music - Dance - Theatre*
                               (502)   *1,12
3578 _____.
      [1969]   894   *Music - Dance - Theatre*
                               (497)   *12
3579 _____.
      [1970]   912   *Music - Dance - Theatre*
                               (526)   *1,12
3580 _____.
      [1970]   932   *Music - Dance - Theatre*
                               (508)   *1,10,12
3581 _____.
      [1970]   953   *Music. Theatre. Ballet*
                               (505)   *10,13
3582 _____.
      [1971]   973   *Music. Dance. Theatre*
                               (499)   *10,12
3583 _____.
      [1971]   993   *Music - Dance - Theatre*
                               (513)   *1,10,12
3584 _____.
      [1972]   1011   *Music - Dance - Theatre*
                               (499)   *1,10,12

1 Compiler/State University of New York (Buffalo)   **2** The British Library (London)   **3** Gemeentemuseum (Den Haag)   **4** The Grolier Club (N.Y.C.)   **5** Hirsch Collection, British Library (London)   **6** D.W. Krummel (Urbana)   **7** Library of Congress (Washington, D.C.)   **8** Library and Museum of the Performing Arts (N.Y.C.)   **9** William Reeves (London)   **10** Sibley Library, Eastman School of Music (Rochester)   **11** Nigel Simeone (Tunbridge Wells, Kent)   **12** Vereeniging ter Bervordering van de Belangen des Boekhandels (Amsterdam)   **13** University of Virginia (Charlottesville)   **14** University of California at Los Angeles   **15** Generally available

3585   **PEET, JAN (Amsterdam-Bussum) (continued)**
       [1972]   1029   *Music - Dance - Theatre*
                          (493)   *1,10,12

3586   _____.
       [1963]   Per.   492   *Periodicals: Musical Science. History of Music*
                          (329)   *12

3587   **PEREBOM, RUDOLF (Amsterdam)**
       1963   23   *Muziek en Theater*
                          (309)   *12

3588   **PERL, MAX (Berlin)**
       [1904?]   64   *Theater und Musik*
                          (604)   *12

3589   _____.
       1906   69   *Coll: Unnamed*
                          (551)   *5

3590   _____.
       1907   77   *Theater und Musik*
                          (676)   *1,5,12

3591   **PERRE, PAUL VAN DER (Brussels)**
       [1938?]   —   *Musique, théâtre & danse. Livres & autogrs.*
                        (1-564)   *10,13

3592   **PETERS, C. F. [Nachf. KOPP & CO.] (Munich)**
       [1937]   60   *Praktische Musik. Musikbücher*
                        (16pp.)   *5

3593   _____.
       s.d.   63   *Musikalische Seltenheiten. Musikbücher*
                        (24pp.)   *5

3594   _____.
       s.d.   List   109   *Musik der Klassik und Vorklassik*
                        (380)   *1,11

3595   **PETIT, A. (Paris)**
       1821   —   *Catalogue de la musique*
                        (?)   *7

3596   **PICARD, ALPHONSE & FILS (Paris)**
       1912   186   *Coll: Amateur. Ouvrages sur la musique*
                        (1072)   *12

3597   **PICARD, AUGUSTE (Paris)**
       1922   214   *Folklore et musique*
                        (87pp.)   *12

3598   **PICKERING & CHATTO (London)**
       1983   651   *Miscellany of Rare & Interesting Books & Mss.*
                        (439-576)   *13

3599   **PINETTE, MAX (Brussels)**
       [1937?]   1   *Musique ancienne et moderne*
                        (400)   *1,5,8,10,13

3600   **PLATTNER, L. (Rotterdam)**
       18__   —   *Musique vocale et instrumentale*
                        (50pp.)   *8

---

1 Compiler/State University of New York (Buffalo)   2 The British Library (London)   3 Gemeentemuseum (Den Haag)   4 The Grolier Club (N.Y.C.)   5 Hirsch Collection, British Library (London)   6 D.W. Krummel (Urbana)   7 Library of Congress (Washington, D.C.)   8 Library and Museum of the Performing Arts (N.Y.C.)   9 William Reeves (London)   10 Sibley Library, Eastman School of Music (Rochester)   11 Nigel Simeone (Tunbridge Wells, Kent)   12 Vereeniging ter Bervordering van de Belangen des Boekhandels (Amsterdam)   13 University of Virginia (Charlottesville)   14 University of California at Los Angeles   15 Generally available

3601	POPPE, KARL MAX (Leipzig)			
	1911	1	*Coll: Weckerlin, J. B. T.* (588)	*3,5
3602	____.			
	1912	2	*Coll: Smolian, A.Musik* (1738)	*3,5
3603	____.			
	1912	3	*Coll: Mottl. Musikgeschichte* (650)	*5
3604	____.			
	1912	4	*Coll: Mottl. Praktische Musik* (1600)	*3,5
3605	____.			
	1913	5	*Coll: Mottl. Musikliteratur* (1798)	*5,7
3606	____.			
	1913	6	*Coll: Koester, K. Praktische Musik* (2806)	*4,5
3607	____.			
	s.d.	7	*Varia /including Music/* (747)	*5
3608	——.			
	1920	16	*Musik* (547)	*5,10
3609	____.			
	1921	18	*Historisch, theoretische und praktische Musik* (808)	*5
3610	____.			
	1924	23	*Musikwissenschaft* (1043)	*5,12
3611	____.			
	1927	34	*Musikwissenschaft* (?)	*5,10
3612	____.			
	1929	40	*Musik. Theater* (?)	*5,10
3613	____.			
	1933	46	*Beethoven und Wagner-Sammlung* (2783)	*1,5,10,13
3614	____.			
	1935	50	*Coll: Heuss, A. Musik. Theater* (3619)	*1,5,10,13
3615	____.			
	1937	51	*Musik, I.Tl. A-F* (3046)	*1,5,9,12,13
3616	____.			
	1937?	52	*Musik, II.Tl. Fétis/Mac* (3047-5993)	*1,9,10,13

1 Compiler/State University of New York (Buffalo)   2 The British Library (London)   3 Gemeentemuseum (Den Haag)   4 The Grolier Club (N.Y.C.)   5 Hirsch Collection, British Library (London)   6 D.W. Krummel (Urbana)   7 Library of Congress (Washington, D.C.)   8 Library and Museum of the Performing Arts (N.Y.C.)   9 William Reeves (London)   10 Sibley Library, Eastman School of Music (Rochester)   11 Nigel Simeone (Tunbridge Wells, Kent)   12 Vereeniging ter Bervordering van de Belangen des Boekhandels (Amsterdam)   13 University of Virginia (Charlottesville)   14 University of California at Los Angeles   15 Generally available

3617 **POPPE, KARL MAX (Leipzig) (continued)**
1938   53   *Musik, III.Tl. McD-Rou*
                           (5994-8674)   *1,5,9,10,13

3618 _____.
1938?   54   *Musik, IV.Tl. Royer-Z*
                           (8675-11544)   *1,9,10,13

3619 _____.
1939   55   *Musik, V.Tl. Wagner. Theater*
                           (11545-13602)   *1,9,10,12

3620 **PORTICO LIBRERIAS (Zaragoza)**
1981   110   *Musica*
                           (93)   *1

3621 _____.
1982   122   *Musica*
                           (335)   *1

3622 _____.
1984   135   *Musica*
                           (480+28)   *1

3623 _____.
12/1984   153   *Musica*
                           (418+20+26)   *1

3624 **PREUSS & JÜNGER (Breslau)**
[1926]   4   *Coll: Mittmann, P.*
                           (2230)   *12.

3625 **PRIEWE, G. (Berlin)**
1910?   73   *Coll: Unnamed. Musik*
                           (358)   *4

3626 **PROUTE, VICTOR & ROBERT (Paris)**
s.d.   46   *Estampes musicales, anciens et modernes*
                           (1042)   [H.Baron]

3627 **PROZENIUM see HACKE, ERNST MAX**

3628 **QUARITCH, BERNARD (London)**
7/1874   20   *Coll: Sandys, Wm. Rare old Music ... [etc.]*
                           (1-50)   *5

3629 _____.
8/1882   343   *Coll: [Engel,C.]: Music. Songs. Games*
                           (8394-977)   *4,12

3630 _____.
188_   —   *General Cat. of Books, Pt.5: Music, Songs, etc.*
                           (?)   *8

3631 _____.
188_   —   *General Cat. of Books, v.2: Music, Games, etc.*
                           (?)   *8

3632 _____.
7/1886   List   77   *Various Libraries. Music. Songs. Dancing*
                           (1047-286)   *4

---

1 Compiler/State University of New York (Buffalo)   2 The British Library (London)   3 Gemeentemuseum (Den Haag)   4 The Grolier Club (N.Y.C.)   5 Hirsch Collection, British Library (London)   6 D.W. Krummel (Urbana)   7 Library of Congress (Washington, D.C.)   8 Library and Museum of the Performing Arts (N.Y.C.)   9 William Reeves (London)   10 Sibley Library, Eastman School of Music (Rochester) 11 Nigel Simeone (Tunbridge Wells, Kent)   12 Vereeniging ter Bervordering van de Belangen des Boekhandels (Amsterdam)   13 University of Virginia (Charlottesville)   14 University of California at Los Angeles   15 Generally available

3633 QUARITCH, BERNARD (London) (continued)

	6/1895	do.	151	*Old Libraries ... Musical Lit. Songs & Ballads* (117-470)	*4
3634	____, 189_	do	154	*Bibliotheca liturgica...Hymnals, Psalters, etc.* (i.a.)	*4,8
3635	____. 1/1899	do.	185	*Games. Sports. Music. Mss. Musical Instruments* (508-808)	*4
3636	____. 2/1903	do.	220	*Music and Songs* (512-632)	*4
3637	____. 6/1903	do.	222	*Music and Music Literature. Treatises* (776-797)	*4
3638	____. 7/1904	do.	232	*[Music and Music Literature. Treatises]* (786-838)	*4
3639	____. 2/1905	do.	237	*Rare and valuable Works ... Eliz. Madrigals* (1-33)	*4,9
3640	____. 1908	do.	270	*Music* (264)	*1,12
3641	____. 3/1911	do.	304	*Rare and Valuable [incl. Music & Music Lit.]* (768-917)	*4
3642	____. 1919	do.	355	*Music* (1314)	*12
3643	____. 1/1925	do.	389	*Africa ... Music. Madrigals. Mss. Autogrs.* (886-1059)	*4
3644	____. 1/1926	do.	397	*Americana [etc.]. Music and Music Literature* (405-549)	*4
3645	____. 2/1927	do.	406	*... Music, incl. Mss., Part-Books, Treatises* (622-801)	*4
3646	____. 1931	do.	447	*Americana [etc.]. Music and Music Literature* (787-931)	*4
3647	____. 1933	do.	471	*... Liturgies. Music [LaBorde Chansonnier]* (776-848)	*4
3648	____. 1935	do.	510	*... Music Mss. [incl. LaBorde Chansonnier]* (987-1176)	*4

1 Compiler/State University of New York (Buffalo) **2** The British Library (London) **3** Gemeentemuseum (Den Haag) **4** The Grolier Club (N.Y.C.) **5** Hirsch Collection, British Library (London) **6** D.W. Krummel (Urbana) **7** Library of Congress (Washington, D.C.) **8** Library and Museum of the Performing Arts (N.Y.C.) **9** William Reeves (London) **10** Sibley Library, Eastman School of Music (Rochester) **11** Nigel Simeone (Tunbridge Wells, Kent) **12** Vereeniging ter Bervordering van de Belangen des Boekhandels (Amsterdam) **13** University of Virginia (Charlottesville) **14** University of California at Los Angeles **15** Generally available

3649 **QUARITCH, BERNARD (London) (continued)**

	1937	do.	530	... *Appendix: Music and Music Literature* (1153-268) *4

3650 _____.

	1937	do.	541	*Books and Mss., Autogrs.... Music. Dancing* (645-706) *4

3651 _____.

	1938	do.	549	*Mss. & printed Books. Music. Books on Music* (902-1046) *4

3652 _____.

	1938	do.	554	... *Music and Music Literature. Dancing* (418-591) *4

3653 _____.

	1939	do.	561	*Fine Arts. Music. Dance* (1314) *12

3654 _____.

	1949	do.	667	*ALS & Documents. Music. Dancing. Mss. Autogrs.* (688-727) *4,12

3655 _____.

	1951	do.	693	*English Literature & History. Music & Dancing* (547-611) *4

3656 _____.

	1953	do.	714	*English Literature & History. Music & Dancing* (733-841) *4

3657 _____.

	1955	do.	743	*English Literature & History. Music & Dancing* (936) *12

3658 _____.

	1957	do.	770	*English Literature & History. Music. Sports* (968) *4,12

3659 _____.

	1958	do.	783	*English Literature & History. Music & Dancing* (570-741) *4

3660 _____.

	1959	do.	795	*English Literature & History. Music & Dancing* (578-739) *1,4

3661 _____.

	1960	do.	807	*English Literature & History. Music & Dancing* (419-694) *4

3662 _____.

	1962	do.	832	*English Literature & History. Music & Dancing* (483-656) *4

3663 _____.

	1964	do.	854	*English Literature & History. Music & Dancing* (584-683) *1,6,10,12

3664 _____.

	1967	do.	878	*English Literature & History. Music & Dancing* (459-602) *4,6,10

1 Compiler/State University of New York (Buffalo)   **2** The British Library (London)   **3** Gemeentemuseum (Den Haag)   **4** The Grolier Club (N.Y.C.)   **5** Hirsch Collection, British Library (London)   **6** D.W. Krummel (Urbana)   **7** Library of Congress (Washington, D.C.)   **8** Library and Museum of the Performing Arts (N.Y.C.)   **9** William Reeves (London)   **10** Sibley Library, Eastman School of Music (Rochester) **11** Nigel Simeone (Tunbridge Wells, Kent)   **12** Vereeniging ter Bervordering van de Belangen des Boekhandels (Amsterdam)   **13** University of Virginia (Charlottesville)   **14** University of California at Los Angeles   **15** Generally available

3665 **QUARITCH, BERNARD** (London) (continued)
    1968   do.   891   *English Literature & History. Music & Dancing*
                     (896-1099)   *1,4,10,12

3666 **RANSCHBURG, OTTO H.** (N.Y.C.)
    s.d.   6   *Old Music*
                     (147)   *1,6,10,13

3667 _____.
    s.d.   8   *Fine Arts. Music. Illustrated Books*
                     (90-173, i.a.)   *1,10

3668 **RAPPAPORT, C. E.** (Rome)
    s.d.   32   *Théâtre. Musique. Danse*
                     (1459)   *5

3669 _____.
    [1961]   137   *Musique. Théâtre*
                     (610)   *1,10,12

3670 **RAU, ARTHUR** (Paris)
    s.d.   —   *Musique française*
                     (176)   *5,10

3671 _____.
    1934   —   *Brief List ... Mss. and Autographs*
                     (?)   *7

3672 _____.
    10/1935   5   *Musique ancienne*
                     (671)   *1,5,10,13

3673 **RAVEN BOOK SHOP** (N.Y.C.)
    s.d.   38   *Theatre. Music Plays*
                     (244-381)   *13

3674 **REEVES, HAROLD** (London) [Succeeded by **KENNETH MUMMERY**, q.v.]
    19__   1   *?*
                     (?)   *8

3675 _____.
    1915   2   *Music & Musical Literature*
                     (24pp.)   *US-CA,8

3676 _____.
    19__   3   *?*
                     (?)   *8

3677 _____.
    1915   4   *Music & Musical Literature*
                     (24pp.)   *US-CA,8

3678 _____.
    1916   5   *350 Full Orchestral Scores*
                     (4pp.)   *8

3679 _____.
    191_   6   *?*
                     (?)   *8

3680 _____.
    1916/17   7   *Music & Musical Literature*
                     (24pp.)   *8

1 Compiler/State University of New York (Buffalo)   **2** The British Library (London)   **3** Gemeentemuseum (Den Haag)   **4** The Grolier Club (N.Y.C.)   **5** Hirsch Collection, British Library (London)   **6** D.W. Krummel (Urbana)   **7** Library of Congress (Washington, D.C.)   **8** Library and Museum of the Performing Arts (N.Y.C.)   **9** William Reeves (London)   **10** Sibley Library, Eastman School of Music (Rochester)   **11** Nigel Simeone (Tunbridge Wells, Kent)   **12** Vereeniging ter Bervordering van de Belangen des Boekhandels (Amsterdam)   **13** University of Virginia (Charlottesville)   **14** University of California at Los Angeles   **15** Generally available

3681	**REEVES, HAROLD (London) (continued)**			
	1917	8	*Colls: Cummings and Southgate* (839)	*US-CA,3
3682	_____.			
	1918	9	*Music & Musical Literature* (36pp.)	*US-CA,8
3683	_____.			
	1918	10	*Books on Music & Musicians* (32pp.)	*US-CA,8
3684	_____.			
	1918/19	11	*Music & Musical Literature* (28pp.)	*US-CA,8
3685	_____.			
	1919	12	*Music and Musical Literature* (32pp.)	*1,8,12
3686	_____.			
	1919	13	*Music & Musical Literature* (32pp.)	*8
3687	_____.			
	1919	14	*Books on Music and Musicians* (32pp.)	*8,9
3688	_____.			
	1919	15	*Music* (16pp.)	*8,12
3689	_____.			
	1919	16	*Old and Rare Music and Musical Books* (336)	*8,9,12
3690	_____.			
	1919	17	*Music and Musical Literature* (32pp.)	*8,12
3691	_____.			
	[1919]	18	*Books on Music & Musicians* (16pp.)	*8
3692	_____.			
	1920	19	*Classical & Modern Music* (16pp.)	*8
3693	_____.			
	1920	20	*Music and Musical Books* ?	*8,12
3694	_____.			
	1920	21	*Music and Musical Books* ?	*8,12
3695	_____.			
	1920	22	*Miscellaneous Music* (16pp.)	*8
3696	_____.			
	1920	23	*Music and Musical Books* ?	*8,12

1 Compiler/State University of New York (Buffalo)   **2** The British Library (London)   **3** Gemeentemuseum (Den Haag)   **4** The Grolier Club (N.Y.C.)   **5** Hirsch Collection, British Library (London)   **6** D.W. Krummel (Urbana)   **7** Library of Congress (Washington, D.C.)   **8** Library and Museum of the Performing Arts (N.Y.C.)   **9** William Reeves (London)   **10** Sibley Library, Eastman School of Music (Rochester) **11** Nigel Simeone (Tunbridge Wells, Kent)   **12** Vereeniging ter Bervordering van de Belangen des Boekhandels (Amsterdam)   **13** University of Virginia (Charlottesville)   **14** University of California at Los Angeles   **15** Generally available

3697   **REEVES, HAROLD (London) (continued)**
       1921   24   *Books on music, Musicians and Instruments*
                                       (32pp.)   *1,8,9,12

3698   _____.
       1920   25   *Music and Musical Literature*
                                       (24pp.)   *8,9

3699   _____.
      [1921]   26   *Miniature Scores*
                                       (8pp.)   *8

3700   _____.
       1920   27   *Music & Musical Literature*
                                       (16pp.)   *8

3701   _____.
       1921   28   *Music and Musical Literature*
                                       (24pp.)   *9

3702   _____.
       1921   29   *Miscellaneous Music*
                                       (20pp.)   *8,9,12

3703   _____.
      [1921]   30   *Miniature Scores*
                                       (8pp.)   *8

3704   _____.
       1921   31   *Music and Books on Music and Musicians*
                                     (8pp.)   *1,8

3705   _____.
       1921   32   *Catalogue of Miscellaneous Music*
                                     (16pp.)   *8,9

3706   _____.
       1921   33   *Rare and Interesting Musical Works*
                                     (844)   *1,8,9

3707   _____.
       1922   34   *Music & Musical Literature. Russian Composers*
                                     (24pp.)   *7,8,9

3708   _____.
       1921!   35   *Music and Musical Literature*
                                     (28pp.)   *8,9,12

3709   _____.
       1922   36   *Music of All Kinds*
                                     (32pp.)   *8,9,12

3710   _____.
       1922   37   *Music and Musical Literature*
                                     (32pp.)   *8,9

3711   _____.
       1922   38   *Old and Rare Musical Works*
                                     (24pp.)   *8,9

3712   _____.
       1922   39   *Music and Musical Literature*
                                     (32pp.)   *8,9

3713   **REEVES, HAROLD (London) (continued)**

	1922/23	40	*Music and Musical Literature* (32pp.)	*8,9
3714	_____. 1923	41	*Music and Musical Literature* (24pp.)	*8,9,12
3715	_____. 1923	42	*Music and Musical Literature* (32pp.)	*8,9
3716	[1923] 1923	43	*Miniature Scores* (6pp.)	
3717	_____. 1923	44	*Musical Literature and all Kinds of Music* (32pp.)	*8,9,12,13
3718	_____. 1923	45	*Old, Rare & Interesting Musical Works* (32pp.)	*US-CA,8
3719	_____. 1923	46	*Music and Musical Literature* (32pp.)	*8,9,12
3720	_____. 1923/24	47	*Music by Classical and Modern Composers* (40pp.)	*8,9
3721	_____. 1924	48	*Nearly One Thousand Miniature Scores* (16pp.)	*8,9
3722	_____. 1924	49	*Music and Musical Literature* (36pp.)	*8,9,12
3723	_____. 1924	50	*Musical Works, Old and Rare* (32pp.)	*8,9,12
3724	_____. 1924	51	*Music. Books on Music. Wagner* (32pp.)	*1,8,9,12
3725	_____. 1924	52	*Books on Musicians* (24pp.)	*1,8,9,12
3726	_____. 1924	53	*All Kinds of Music* (24pp.)	*8,9,12
3727	_____. 1924	54	*Coll: Payne, A. H. American Psalmody* (4210)	*1,3,7,9,12
3728	_____. 1924	55	*One Thousand Miniature Scores* (24pp.)	*5,8,9,10

3729 **REEVES, HAROLD (London) (continued)**

	1924	56	*Music. Books on Music and Musicians* (36pp.)	*1,5,8,9,10
3730	____.			
	1925	57	*Music and Musical Literature* (32pp.)	*1,5,8,9,10
3731	____.			
	1925	58	*Musical Works, Old, Rare and Interesting* (4211-5078)	*1,5,8,9,13
3732	____.			
	1925	59	*Bargain Catalogue of All Kinds of Music* (32pp.)	*5,8,9
3733	____.			
	1925	60	*Coll: Marshall,J. [portion]. Music, Music Lit.* (40pp.)	*1,5,8,9,10
3734	____.			
	1925	61	*Music. Books on Music and Musicians* (44pp.)	*1,8,9,12
3735	____.			
	1926	62	*Musical Works, Old, Rare and Interesting* (5716-6070)	*1,8,9,12,13
3736	____.			
	1926	63	*Coll: Payne, A. H. All Kinds of Music* (32pp.)	*1,8,9,12,13
3737	____.			
	1926	64	*Books Relating to Musical Instruments* (16pp.)	*1,8,9,12
3738	____.			
	1926	65	*Music and Musical Literature* (40pp.)	*1,8,9,10,13
3739	____.			
	1926	66	*Musical Works, Old, Rare and Interesting* (6162-7038)	*1,8,9,13
3740	____.			
	1926	67	*Music and Musical Literature* (36pp.)	*1,8,9,12,13
3741	____.			
	1926	68	*Miniature Scores. Fine Bindings* (28pp.)	*1,8,9,10,12,13
3742	____.			
	1927	69	*Music and Musical Literature* (36pp.)	*8,9,10,12,13
3743	____.			
	1927	70	*Musical Works* (24pp.)	*1,8,9,10,12,13
3744	____.			
	1927	71	*All Kinds of Music* (24pp.)	*1,8,9,10,12,13

1 Compiler/State University of New York (Buffalo)   **2** The British Library (London)   **3** Gemeentemuseum (Den Haag)   **4** The Grolier Club (N.Y.C.)   **5** Hirsch Collection, British Library (London)   **6** D.W. Krummel (Urbana)   **7** Library of Congress (Washington, D.C.)   **8** Library and Museum of the Performing Arts (N.Y.C.)   **9** William Reeves (London)   **10** Sibley Library, Eastman School of Music (Rochester)   **11** Nigel Simeone (Tunbridge Wells, Kent)   **12** Vereeniging ter Bervordering van de Belangen des Boekhandels (Amsterdam)   **13** University of Virginia (Charlottesville)   **14** University of California at Los Angeles   **15** Generally available

3745   **REEVES, HAROLD (London) (continued)**
       1927   72   *Music. Orchestra Sets. Full Scores*
                             (36pp.)   *1,5,8,9,12,13

3746   _____.
       1927   73   *Books on Musical Instruments*
                             (24pp.)   *1,8,9,10,12,13

3747   _____.
       1928   74   *Old and Rare Musical Works*
                             (40pp.)   *1,8,9,10,12,13

3748   _____.
       1928   75   *Music by Classical & Modern Composers*
                             (24pp.)   *5,8

3749   _____.
       1927/28   76   *Books on Music & Musicians*
                             (4pp.)   *5,8

3750   _____.
       1928   77   *Biographies of Musicians, 1: A - L*
                             (20pp.)   *1,8,9,13

3751   _____.
       1928   78   *Music and Books on Music and Musicians*
                             (40pp.)   *1,5,8,9,10,13

3752   _____.
       1928   79   *Music and Books on Music and Musicians*
                             (36pp.)   *8,9,10,13

3753   _____.
       1928   80   *Music. Books on music & Musicians. Schubert*
                             (32pp.)   *5,8,9,10,13

3754   _____.
       1928/29   81   *Selected Miniature Scores*
                             (24pp.)   *1,5,8,9,13

3755   _____.
       1928/29   82   *Old, Rare and Interesting Musical Works*
                             (8891-9615)   *1,8,9,13

3756   _____.
       1929   83   *Music and Musical Literature*
                             (20pp.)   *1,5,8,9,13

3757   _____.
       1929   84   *Music and Musical Literature*
                             (32pp.)   *5,8,9,10,13

3758   _____.
       1929   85   *Biographies of Musicians, 2: M - Z*
                             (24pp.)   *1,8,9,13

3759   _____.
       1929   86   *Old, Rare and Interesting Musical Works.*
                             (36pp.)   *1,8,9,13

3760   _____.
       1929   87   *Music and Musical Lit. Songs. Ballads. Carols*
                             (32pp.)   *5,8,9,10,13

1 Compiler/State University of New York (Buffalo)   **2** The British Library (London)   **3** Gemeentemuseum (Den Haag)   **4** The Grolier Club (N.Y.C.)   **5** Hirsch Collection, British Library (London)   **6** D.W. Krummel (Urbana)   **7** Library of Congress (Washington, D.C.)   **8** Library and Museum of the Performing Arts (N.Y.C.)   **9** William Reeves (London)   **10** Sibley Library, Eastman School of Music (Rochester)   **11** Nigel Simeone (Tunbridge Wells, Kent)   **12** Vereeniging ter Bervordering van de Belangen des Boekhandels (Amsterdam)   **13** University of Virginia (Charlottesville)   **14** University of California at Los Angeles   **15** Generally available

3761	REEVES, HAROLD (London) (continued)			
	1929	88	Music and Musical Literature (35pp.)	*1,5,8,9,10,13
3762	_____.			
	1930	89	Old, Rare and Interesting Musical Works (10579-11515)	*1,5,8,9,10,13
3763	_____.			
	1930	90	Music and Books on Music (32pp.)	*1,7,8,9,10,13
3764	_____.			
	1930	91	Books on Music and Musicians (16pp.)	*1,7,8,9,10,13
3765	_____.			
	1930	92	Music and Musical Literature (32pp.)	*7,8,9,10,13
3766	_____.			
	1930/31	93	Catalogue for Music Lovers (52pp.)	*7,8,9,10,13
3767	_____.			
	1931	94	Music and Musical Literature (44pp.)	*7,8,9,10,13
3768	_____.			
	1931	95	Old, Rare and Interesting Musical Works (52pp.)	*1,7,8,9,13
3769	_____.			
	1931(2?	96	Music, Second-hand and new (36pp.)	*1,7,8,9,13
3770	_____.			
	1931	97	Music and Musical Literature. Spanish Music (36pp.)	*7,8,9,13
3771	_____.			
	1931	98	Books on Musical Instruments *1,7,8,9,13 (32pp.)	
3772	_____.			
	1932	99	All Kinds of Music and Books (48pp.)	*7,8,9,13
3773	_____.			
	1932	100	Enlarged List of Miniature Score (32pp.)	*1,7,8,9,13
3774	_____.			
	1932	101	Music, Second-hand and New (36pp.)	*1,7,8,9,13
3775	_____.			
	1932	102	Coll: Finch, H. Old, Rare & Intresting Music (36pp.)	*1,7,8,9,13
3776	_____.			
	1932	103	Music & Musical Literature (36pp.)	*8,13

3777 **REEVES, HAROLD (London) (continued)**

	1932	104	*Music and Musical Literature* (36pp.) *1,8,9,10,13
3778	____.		
	1932	105	*Catalogue for Music Lovers. Fac. Music Lit.* (36pp.) *8,9,13
3779	____.		
	1932	106	*Chamber Music. Full Orchestra Sores. Books* (40pp.) *1,8,9,13
3780	____.		
	1933	107	*Old, Rare and Interesting Musica Works* (13607-14199) *1,8,9,10,13
3781	____.		
	1933	108	*Music and Musical Literature* (32pp.) *1,8,9,13
3782	____.		
	1933	109	*Music and Books on Music and Muscians* (40pp.) *1,8,9,10,13
3783	____.		
	1933	110	*Second-hand and New Music. Book on Music* (24pp.) *1,8,9,10,13
3784	____.		
	1934	111	*Old, Rare and Interesting Musica Works* (14200-15166+) *1,8,9,10,13
3785	____.		
	1934	112	*All Kinds of Music* (20pp.) *1,8,9,10,13
3786	____.		
	1934	113	*Music Books* (32pp.) *1,8,9,10,13
3787	____.		
	1934	114	*Standard Textbooks. Musical Appeciation* (7pp.) *1,8,9,10,13
3788	____.		
	1934	115	*Music and Musical Literature* (48pp.) *8,9,13
3789	____.		
	1935	116	*Music and Musical Literature* (48pp.) *8,9,10,13
3790	____.		
	1935	117	*Miniature Orchestral Scores* (32pp.) *8,9,13
3791	____.		
	1936	118	*Old, Rare and Interesting Musica Works* (36pp.) *8,9,10,13
3792	____.		
	1935!	119	*Music and Musical Literature* (48pp.) *1,8,9,10,13

1 Compiler/State University of New York (Buffalo)   **2** The British Library (London)   **3** Gemeentemuseum (Den Haag)   **4** The Grolier Club (N.Y.C.)   **5** Hirsch Collection, British Library (London)   **6** D.W. Krummel (Urbana)   **7** Library of Congress (Washington, D.C.)   **8** Library and Museum of the Performing Arts (N.Y.C.)   **9** William Reeves (London)   **10** Sibley Library, Eastman School of Music (Rochester)   **11** Nigel Simeone (Tunbridge Wells, Kent)   **12** Vereeniging ter Bervordering van de Belangen des Boekhandels (Amsterdam)   **13** University of Virginia (Charlottesville)   **14** University of California at Los Angeles   **15** Generally available

3793   **REEVES, HAROLD (London) (continued)**
      1936   120   *Music and Musical Literature*
                                     (44pp.)   *1,8,9,10,13

3794   _____.
      1936/37   121   *Music and Musical Literature*
                                     (64pp.)   *8,9,10,13

3795   _____.
      1937   122   *Old, Rare and Interesting Musica Works*
                                   (15052-17021)   *1,8,9,10,13

3796   _____.
      11938   123   *New Book Publications*
                                   (4pp.)   *9

3797   _____.
      1937/38   124   *All Kinds of Music. Books on muic*
                                   (64pp.)   *1,8,9,10,13

3798   _____.
      1938-39   125   *All Kinds of Music. Books on Muic*
                                   (72pp.)   *1,8,9,13

3799   _____.
      1940   126   *Old, Rare and Interesting Musica Works*
                                   (48pp.)   *1,8,9,10,13

3800   _____.
      1942   127   *Old, Rare and Interesting Musica Works*
                                   (54pp.)   *8,9,13

3801   **REEVES, WILLIAM (London)**
      1875   1   *Interesting Works on Musical Bioraphy & Hist.*
                                   (476)   *1

3802   _____.
      1876   2   _____. *Supplement*
                                   (16+4pp.)   *1

3803   _____.
      1877/78   3   *Musical Biography. History. Tratises*
                                   (21pp.)   *1

3804   _____.
      1878/79   4   *Music and Musical Literature*
                                   (35pp.)   *1

3805   _____.
      1879/80   5   *Music and Musical Literature*
                                   (45pp.)   *1

3806   _____.
      1880   6   *Music and Musical Literature. Ms. Treatises*
                                   (55pp.)   *1

3807   _____.
      1881   7   *Music and Musical Literature. Ms. Treatises*
                                   (55pp.)   *1

3808   _____.
      1881   8   *Music and Musical Literature. Ms. Treatises*
                                   (63pp.)   *1,8

3809   **REEVES, WILLIAM (London) (continued)**
　　　　　1882/83　　　　　9　　_____. *Music from Several Libraies*
　　　　　　　　　　　　　　　　　　(86pp.)　　　　　　　　　　　　　　　　　　　　*1

3810   _____.
　　　　　1883　　　　　　10　*Colls: Engle, Carl, John Hullah,et al*
　　　　　　　　　　　　　　　　　　(pp.87-142)　　　　　　　　　　　　　　　　*1

3811   _____.
　　　　　1883　　　　　　11　*Ancient & Modern Music & Musical Literature*
　　　　　　　　　　　　　　　　　　(pp.143-56)　　　　　　　　　　　　　　　　*1,9

3812   _____.
　　　　　1884　　　　　　12　*Ancient & Modern Music & Musical Literature*
　　　　　　　　　　　　　　　　　　(pp.156-74)　　　　　　　　　　　　　　　　*1

3813   _____.
　　　　　1884　　　　　　13　*Ancient & Modern Music & Musical Literature*
　　　　　　　　　　　　　　　　　　(pp.175-96)　　　　　　　　　　　　　　　　*1,9

3814   _____.
　　　　　1884　　　　　　14　*Ancient & Modern Music. Treatiss. Fine Mss.*
　　　　　　　　　　　　　　　　　　(24pp.)　　　　　　　　　　　　　　　　　　*9

3815   _____.
　　　　　1885　　　　　　15　*Ancient & Modern Music. Treatiss. Fine Mss.*
　　　　　　　　　　　　　　　　　　(24pp.)　　　　　　　　　　　　　　　　　　*9

3816   _____.
　　　　　1886　　　　　　16　*Ancient & Modern Music. Treatise. Full Scores*
　　　　　　　　　　　　　　　　　　(16pp.)　　　　　　　　　　　　　　　　　　*9

3817   _____.
　　　　　1886　　　　　　17　*Colls: Marshall, J. and J. Hulla [portions]*
　　　　　　　　　　　　　　　　　　(15pp.)　　　　　　　　　　　　　　　　　　*9

3818   _____.
　　　　　1887?　　　　　18　*Music & Musical Literature, Ancient & Modern*
　　　　　　　　　　　　　　　　　　(24pp.)　　　　　　　　　　　　　　　　　　*9

3819   _____.
　　　　　1887　　　　　　19　*idem.*
　　　　　　　　　　　　　　　　　　(24pp.)　　　　　　　　　　　　　　　　　　*9

3820   _____.
　　　　　[1887]　　　　　20　*idem.*
　　　　　　　　　　　　　　　　　　(32pp.)　　　　　　　　　　　　　　　　　　*9

3821   _____.
　　　　　1887　　　　　　21　*idem.*
　　　　　　　　　　　　　　　　　　(32pp.)　　　　　　　　　　　　　　　　　　*9

3822   _____.
　　　　　1888　　　　　　22　*idem.*
　　　　　　　　　　　　　　　　　　(36pp.)　　　　　　　　　　　　　　　　　　*9

3823   _____.
　　　　　1888　　　　　　23　*idem.*
　　　　　　　　　　　　　　　　　　(8pp.)　　　　　　　　　　　　　　　　　　*9

3824   _____.
　　　　　1888　　　　　23[!]　*idem.*
　　　　　　　　　　　　　　　　　　(8pp.)　　　　　　　　　　　　　　　　　　*9

1 Compiler/State University of New York (Buffalo)　　**2** The British Library (London)　　**3** Gemeentemuseum (Den Haag)　　**4** The Grolier Club (N.Y.C.)　　**5** Hirsch Collection, British Library (London)　　**6** D.W. Krummel (Urbana)　　**7** Library of Congress (Washington, D.C.)　　**8** Library and Museum of the Performing Arts (N.Y.C.)　　**9** William Reeves (London)　　**10** Sibley Library, Eastman School of Music (Rochester) **11** Nigel Simeone (Tunbridge Wells, Kent)　　**12** Vereeniging ter Bervordering van de Belangen des Boekhandels (Amsterdam)　　**13** University of Virginia (Charlottesville)　　**14** University of California at Los Angeles　　**15** Generally available

3825   **REEVES, WILLIAM (London) (continued)**

	1888	24	*Music & Musical Literature, Ancient & Modern* (36pp.)	*9
3826	_____.			
	1888	25	*idem.* (36pp.)	*9
3827	_____.			
	1888	26	*idem.* (36pp.)	*9
3828	_____.			
	1888	27	*Musical Catalogue* (10pp.)	*9
3829	_____.			
	1889	28	*Music & Musical Literature, Ancient & Modern* (52pp.)	*9
3830	_____.			
	1889	29	*Music & Musical Literature... AS* (32pp.)	*9
3831	_____.			
	1889	30	*Music & Musical Literature ... LS* (48pp.)	*9
3832	_____.			
	1889	31	*Music and Musical Literature* (32pp.)	*9
3833	_____.			
	1889	32	*Music and Musical Literature. AS* (48pp.)	*9
3834	_____.			
	1890	33	*Music and Musical Literature. AS* (56pp.)	*9
3835	_____.			
	1890	34	*Ancient, Modern 2d-hand Music. Teatises. Mss.* (34pp.)	*9
3836	_____.			
	1890	35	*Ancient, Modern 2d-hand Music. Teatises. Mss.* (48pp.)	*9
3837	_____.			
	1890	36	*2nd-hand Music. Treatises. Mss* (40pp.)	*9
3838	_____.			
	1890	37	*Ancient and Modern Music. Musical Literature* (32pp.)	*9
3839	_____.			
	1890	28	*Ancient and Modern Music. Musical Literature* (48pp.)	*9
3840	_____.			
	1890	39	*Ancient and Modern Music. Musical Literature* (48pp.)	*9

1 Compiler/State University of New York (Buffalo)   **2** The British Library (London)   **3** Gemeentemuseum (Den Haag)   **4** The Grolier Club (N.Y.C.)   **5** Hirsch Collection, British Library (London)   **6** D.W. Krummel (Urbana)   **7** Library of Congress (Washington, D.C.)   **8** Library and Museum of the Performing Arts (N.Y.C.)   **9** William Reeves (London)   **10** Sibley Library, Eastman School of Music (Rochester) **11** Nigel Simeone (Tunbridge Wells, Kent)   **12** Vereeniging ter Bervordering van de Belangen des Boekhandels (Amsterdam)   **13** University of Virginia (Charlottesville)   **14** University of California at Los Angeles   **15** Generally available

3841 **REEVES, WILLIAM (London) (continued)**

	1891	40	*Ancient and Modern Music. Musical Literature* (32pp.)	*9
3842 ___.	1891	41	*Ancient and Modern Music. Musical Literature* (40pp.)	*9
3843 ___.	1891	42	*Ancient and Modern Music. Musical Literature* (32pp.)	*9
3844 ___.	1891	43	*Singularly Fine Coll.; Ancient & Modern Music* (32pp.)	*9
3845 ___.	1891	44	*Coll: Costa, Sir M. Musical Lit. Unpubl. Works* (36pp.)	*9
3846 ___.	1891/92	45	*Large Collection of Music* (36pp.)	*9
3847 ___.	1892	46	*Ancient and Modern Music and Muscal Works* (40pp.)	*9
3848 ___.	1892	47	*Music, &c., Ancient and Modern. Programs* (40pp.)	*9
3849 ___.	1892	48	*Music, &c., Ancient and Modern. Programs* (40pp.)	*9
3850 ___.	1892	49	*Music, &c., Ancient and Modern* (40pp.)	*9
3851 ___.	1892-94	50-66	*[These catalogues not located]*	
3852 ___.	[1894]	67	*Old Music and Musical Books* (48pp.)	*9
3853 ___.	n.d.	68	*idem.* (48pp.)	*9
3854 ___.	n.d.	69	*idem.* (48pp.)	*9
3855 ___.	[1895]	70	*idem.* (48pp.)	*9
3856 ___.	4/1895	71	*idem.* (48pp.)	*9

3857 **REEVES, WILLIAM (London) (continued)**
       7/1895   72   *Old Music and Musical Books*
                                      (52+pp.)   *9

3858 _____.
       n.d.   73   *idem.*
                                        (52pp.)   *9

3859 _____.
       1896   74   *idem.*
                                        (56pp.)   *9

3860 _____.
       1896   75   *idem.*
                                        (56pp.)   *9

3861 _____.
       1896   76   *idem.*
                                        (56pp.)   *9

3862 _____.
       1896   77   *idem.*
                                        (56pp.)   *9

3863 _____.
       1896   78   *idem.*
                                        (56pp.)   *9

3864 _____.
       1897   79   *idem.*
                                        (56pp.)   *9

3865 _____.
       1897   80   *idem.*
                                        (56pp.)   *9

3866 _____.
       1897   81   *idem.*
                                        (48pp.)   *9

3867 _____.
       1897   82   *idem.*
                                        (50pp.)   *9

3868 _____.
       1898   83   *Music & Musical Bks. Old & New. 300 Ms. Songs*
                                      (44pp.)   *9

3869 _____.
       1898   84   *Music and Musical Books*
                                      (40pp.)   *9

3870 _____.
       1898   85   *idem.*
                                        (44pp.)   *9

3871 _____.
       1898   86   *idem.*
                                        (44pp.)   *9

3872 _____.
       1898   87   *idem.*
                                        (20pp.)   *9

---

1 Compiler/State University of New York (Buffalo) **2** The British Library (London) **3** Gemeentemuseum (Den Haag) **4** The Grolier Club (N.Y.C.) **5** Hirsch Collection, British Library (London) **6** D.W. Krummel (Urbana) **7** Library of Congress (Washington, D.C.) **8** Library and Museum of the Performing Arts (N.Y.C.) **9** William Reeves (London) **10** Sibley Library, Eastman School of Music (Rochester) **11** Nigel Simeone (Tunbridge Wells, Kent) **12** Vereeniging ter Bervordering van de Belangen des Boekhandels (Amsterdam) **13** University of Virginia (Charlottesville) **14** University of California at Los Angeles **15** Generally available

3873	**REEVES, WILLIAM (London) (continued)**			
	1898	88	*Music and Musical Books* (24pp.)	*9
3874	_____. 1898	89	*idem.* (28pp.)	*9
3875	_____. 1898	90	*idem.* (20pp.)	*9
3876	_____. 1899	91	*idem.* (20pp.)	*9
3877	_____. 1899	92	*idem.* (20pp.)	*9
3878	_____. 1899	93	*idem.* (20pp.)	*9
3879	_____. 1899	94	*idem.* (20pp.)	*9
3880	_____. 1899	95	*Music (Ancient & Modern). Music Bks. Old & New* (24pp.)	*9
3881	_____. 1899	96	*idem.* (28pp.)	*9
3882	_____. 1899	97	*idem.* (24pp.)	*9
3883	_____. 1899	98	*idem.* (24pp.)	*9
3884	_____. 1900	99	*idem.* (2opp.)	*9
3885	_____. 1900	100	*Old & New Music. Musical Bks. Ancient & Modern* (24pp.)	*9
3886	_____. 1900	101	*idem.* (24pp.)	*9
3887	_____. 1900	102	*idem.* (28pp.)	*9
3888	_____. 1900	103	*idem.* (24pp.)	*9

1 Compiler/State University of New York (Buffalo)   2 The British Library (London)   3 Gemeentemuseum (Den Haag)   4 The Grolier Club (N.Y.C.)   5 Hirsch Collection, British Library (London)   6 D.W. Krummel (Urbana)   7 Library of Congress (Washington, D.C.)   8 Library and Museum of the Performing Arts (N.Y.C.)   9 William Reeves (London)   10 Sibley Library, Eastman School of Music (Rochester) 11 Nigel Simeone (Tunbridge Wells, Kent)   12 Vereeniging ter Bervordering van de Belangen des Boekhandels (Amsterdam)   13 University of Virginia (Charlottesville)   14 University of California at Los Angeles   15 Generally available

3889 **REEVES, WILLIAM (London) (continued)**

	1900	104	*Old and New Music, Musical Bks.* (24pp.)	*9
3890	_____.			
	1901	105	*idem.* (24pp.)	*9
3891	_____.			
	1901	106	*Music and Musical Books, Old & Modern* (24pp.)	*9
3892	_____.			
	1901	107	*Old and New Music and Musical Books* (28pp.)	*9
3893	_____.			
	1901	108	*idem.* (24pp.)	*9
3894	_____.			
	1901	109	*idem.* (28pp.)	*9
3895	_____.			
	1902	110	*idem.* (24pp.)	*9
3896	_____.			
	1902	111	*idem.* (24pp.)	*9
3897	_____.			
	1902	112	*idem.* (24pp.)	*9
3898	_____.			
	1902	113	*idem.* (24pp.)	*9
3899	_____.			
	1902	114	*idem.* (24pp.)	*9
3900	_____.			
	1903	115	*idem.* (24pp.)	*9
3901	_____.			
	1903	116	*idem.* (24pp.)	*9
3902	_____.			
	1903	117	*idem.* (24pp.)	*9
3903	_____.			
	1903	118	*Old and New Music and Musical Books* (24pp.)	*9
3904	_____.			
	1904	119	*idem.* (24pp.)	*9

1 Compiler/State University of New York (Buffalo)   **2** The British Library (London)   **3** Gemeentemuseum (Den Haag)   **4** The Grolier Club (N.Y.C.)   **5** Hirsch Collection, British Library (London)   **6** D.W. Krummel (Urbana)   **7** Library of Congress (Washington, D.C.)   **8** Library and Museum of the Performing Arts (N.Y.C.)   **9** William Reeves (London)   **10** Sibley Library, Eastman School of Music (Rochester)   **11** Nigel Simeone (Tunbridge Wells, Kent)   **12** Vereeniging ter Bervordering van de Belangen des Boekhandels (Amsterdam)   **13** University of Virginia (Charlottesville)   **14** University of California at Los Angeles   **15** Generally available

3905	**REEVES, WILLIAM (London) (continued)**				
	1904		120	*Old and New Music and Musical Books* (24pp.)	*9
3906	_____.				
	1904		121	*idem.* (24pp.)	*9
3907	_____.				
	1905		122	*idem.* (24pp.)	*9
3908	_____.				
	1905		123	*idem.* (26pp.)	*9
3909	_____.				
	1905		124	*Colls: Taphouse (Mss.), A Conductor (Scores)* (28pp.)	*9
3910	_____.				
	1905		125	*Music, Musical Lit., Ancient & Modern, 2nd-hand* (32pp.)	*9
3911	_____.				
	1906		126	*idem.* (32pp.)	*9
3912	_____.				
	1906		127	*idem.* (28pp.)	*9
3913	**REEVES, WILLIAM (New Series)**				
	1907	N.S.	1	*Music, Musical Lit., Ancient & Modern, 2nd-hand* (24pp.)	*9
3914	_____.				
	1907	N.S.	2	*idem.* (32pp.)	*9
3915	_____.				
	1907	N.S.	3	*idem.* (32pp.)	*9
3916	_____.				
	1907	N.S.	4	*idem.* (32pp.)	*9,11
3917	_____.				
	1907	N.S.	5	*idem.* (32pp.)	*9
3918	_____.				
	1907	N.S.	6	*idem.* (32pp.)	*9,11
3919	_____.				
	1907	N.S.	7	*idem.* (32pp.)	*9
3920	_____.				
	1907	N.S.	8	*idem.* (32pp.)	*9

1 Compiler/State University of New York (Buffalo)   **2** The British Library (London)   **3** Gemeentemuseum (Den Haag)   **4** The Grolier Club (N.Y.C.)   **5** Hirsch Collection, British Library (London)   **6** D.W. Krummel (Urbana)   **7** Library of Congress (Washington, D.C.)   **8** Library and Museum of the Performing Arts (N.Y.C.)   **9** William Reeves (London)   **10** Sibley Library, Eastman School of Music (Rochester) **11** Nigel Simeone (Tunbridge Wells, Kent)   **12** Vereeniging ter Bervordering van de Belangen des Boekhandels (Amsterdam)   **13** University of Virginia (Charlottesville)   **14** University of California at Los Angeles   **15** Generally available

3921 **REEVES, WILLIAM (New Series) (continued)**
      1908   N.S.   9   *Music, Musical Lit., Ancient & Modern*
                  (32pp.)   *9

3922 _____.
      1908   N.S.   10   *idem.*
                  (32pp.)   *9

3923 _____.
      1908   N.S.   11   *idem.*
                  (32pp.)   *9

3924 _____.
      1908   N.S.   12   *idem.*
                  (32pp.)   *9

3925 _____.
      1908   N.S.   13   *idem.*
                  (36pp.)   *9

3926 _____.
      1908   N.S.   14   *Music & Musical Literature*
                  (36pp.)   *9,11

3927 _____.
      1908   N.S.   15   *idem.*
                  (40pp.)   *9

3928 _____.
      1909   N.S.   16   *Music, Musical Lit., Ancient & Modern, 2nd-hand*
                  (39pp.)   *9,11

3929 _____.
      1909   N.S.   17   *idem.*
                  (40pp.)   *9,11

3930 _____.
      1909   N.S.   18   *idem.*
                  (40pp.)   *9,11

3931 _____.
      1909   N.S.   19   *idem.*
                  (40pp.)   *9

3932 _____.
      1909   N.S.   20   *idem.*
                  (40pp.)   *9

3933 _____.
      1909   N.S.   21   *idem.*
                  (36pp.)   *9

3934 _____.
      1909   N.S.   22   *idem.*
                  (40pp.)   *9,10

3935 _____.
      1910   N.S.   23   *Coll: Alexander, L. Chamber Music*
                  (40pp.)   *7,8,9

3936 _____.
      1910   N.S.   24   *Music & Musical Lit., Ancient & Modern*
                  (40pp.)   *9,11

---

1 Compiler/State University of New York (Buffalo)   **2** The British Library (London)   **3** Gemeentemuseum (Den Haag)   **4** The Grolier Club (N.Y.C.)   **5** Hirsch Collection, British Library (London)   **6** D.W. Krummel (Urbana)   **7** Library of Congress (Washington, D.C.)   **8** Library and Museum of the Performing Arts (N.Y.C.)   **9** William Reeves (London)   **10** Sibley Library, Eastman School of Music (Rochester)   **11** Nigel Simeone (Tunbridge Wells, Kent)   **12** Vereeniging ter Bervordering van de Belangen des Boekhandels (Amsterdam)   **13** University of Virginia (Charlottesville)   **14** University of California at Los Angeles   **15** Generally available

3937 **REEVES, WILLIAM (New Series) (continued)**

	1910	N.S.	25	*Music & Musical Lit., Ancient & Modern*	
				(40pp.)	*9

3938 _____.

	1910	N.S.	26	*idem.*	
				(48pp.)	*9

3939 _____.

	1910	N.S.	27	*Colls: Sawyer (Organ M.), Carrods (Chamber M.)*	
				(48pp.)	*7,8,9,11

3940 _____.

	1910	N.S.	28	*Music & Musical Lit., Ancient & odern*	
				(48pp.)	*9

3941 _____.

	1910	N.S.	29	*idem.*	
				(48pp.)	*9

3942 _____.

	1911?	N.S.	30	*idem.*	
				(48pp.)	*9

3943 _____.

	1911	N.S.	31	*Music & Musical Lit. Rare & Interesting Items*	
				(48pp.)	*9,10

3944 _____.

	1911	N.S.	32	*idem.*	
				(48pp.)	*9,10,11

3945 _____.

	1911	N.S.	33	*idem.*	
				(48pp.)	*9,11

3946 _____.

	1911	N.S.	34	*idem.*	
				(48pp.)	*9,10

3947 _____.

	1911	N.S.	35	*idem.*	
				(48pp.)	*9

3948 _____.

	1912	N.S.	36	*idem.*	
				(48pp.)	*9,11

3949 _____.

	1912	N.S.	37	*idem.*	
				(48pp.)	*9,10

3950 _____.

	1912	N.S.	38	*idem.*	
				(48pp.)	*9

3951 _____.

	1912	N.S.	39	*idem.*	
				(48pp.)	*9

3952 _____.

	1912	N.S.	40	*idem.*	
				(48pp.)	*9

1 Compiler/State University of New York (Buffalo) **2** The British Library (London) **3** Gemeentemuseum (Den Haag) **4** The Grolier Club (N.Y.C.) **5** Hirsch Collection, British Library (London) **6** D.W. Krummel (Urbana) **7** Library of Congress (Washington, D.C.) **8** Library and Museum of the Performing Arts (N.Y.C.) **9** William Reeves (London) **10** Sibley Library, Eastman School of Music (Rochester) **11** Nigel Simeone (Tunbridge Wells, Kent) **12** Vereeniging ter Bervordering van de Belangen des Boekhandels (Amsterdam) **13** University of Virginia (Charlottesville) **14** University of California at Los Angeles **15** Generally available

3953 **REEVES, WILLIAM (New Series) (continued)**
1912 N.S. 41 *Music & Musical Lit. Rare & Interesting Items*
(48pp.)   *9

3954 _____.
1912 N.S. 42 *idem.*
(48pp.)   *9

3955 _____.
1913 N.S. 43 *idem.*
(48pp.)   *9

3956 _____.
1913 N.S. 44 *idem.*
(48pp.)   *9

3957 _____.
1913 N.S. 45 *idem.*
(48pp.)   *9

3958 _____.
1913 N.S. 46 *idem.*
(48pp.)   *9

3959 _____.
1913 N.S. 47 *idem.*
(48pp.)   *9

3960 _____.
1914 N.S. 48 *idem.*
(48pp.)   *9

3961 _____.
1914 N.S. 49 *idem.*
(48pp.)   *9

3962 _____.
1914 N.S. 50 *idem.*
(48pp.)   *9

3963 _____.
1915 N.S. 51 *idem.*
(48pp.)   *9

3964 _____.
1915 N.S. 52 *idem.*
(52pp.)   *9

3965 _____.
1915 N.S. 53 *idem.*
(52pp.)   *9

3966 _____.
1915 N.S. 54 *idem.*
(48pp.)   *9

3967 _____.
1916 N.S. 55 *idem.*
(48pp.)   *9

3968 _____.
1916 N.S. 56 *idem.*
(48pp.)   *9

1 Compiler/State University of New York (Buffalo)   **2** The British Library (London)   **3** Gemeentemuseum (Den Haag)   **4** The Grolier Club (N.Y.C.)   **5** Hirsch Collection, British Library (London)   **6** D.W. Krummel (Urbana)   **7** Library of Congress (Washington, D.C.)   **8** Library and Museum of the Performing Arts (N.Y.C.)   **9** William Reeves (London)   **10** Sibley Library, Eastman School of Music (Rochester)   **11** Nigel Simeone (Tunbridge Wells, Kent)   **12** Vereeniging ter Bervordering van de Belangen des Boekhandels (Amsterdam)   **13** University of Virginia (Charlottesville)   **14** University of California at Los Angeles   **15** Generally available

3969 **REEVES, WILLIAM (New Series) (continued)**

	1917	N.S.	57	*Music & Musical Lit. Rare & Interesting Items* (40pp.)

                                    *9

3970 _____.
  1919 N.S. 58 *idem.*
           (24pp.)   **9,10*

3971 _____.
  1920 N.S. 59 *idem.*
           (24pp.)   **9,10*

3972 _____.
  1921 N.S. 60 *idem.*
           (24pp.)   **9*

3973 _____.
  1923 N.S. 61 *idem.*
           (32pp.)   **9*

3974 _____.
  1923 N.S. 62 *idem.*
           (32pp.)   **9*

3975 _____.
  1925 N.S. 63 *idem.*
           (36pp.)   **9,10*

3976 _____.
  1926 N.S. 64 *idem.*
           (36pp.)   **9,10*

3977 _____.
  1926 N.S. 65 *idem.*
           (36pp.)   **9*

3978 _____.
  1927 N.S. 66 *idem.*
           (40pp.)   **9*

3979 _____.
  1929 N.S. 67 *idem.*
           (44pp.)   **9*

3980 _____.
  1929 N.S. 68 *Music & Musical Literature*
           (44pp.)   **1,9,10,13*

3981 _____.
  1930 N.S. 69 *idem.*
           (48pp.)   **9,13*

3982 _____.
  1931 N.S. 70 *idem.*
           (48pp.)   **9,13*

3983 _____.
  1931 N.S. 71 *idem.*
           (48pp.)   **1,9,10,13*

3984 _____.
  1931 N.S. 72 *idem.*
           (40pp.)   **1,9,13*

1 Compiler/State University of New York (Buffalo) **2** The British Library (London) **3** Gemeentemuseum (Den Haag) **4** The Grolier Club (N.Y.C.) **5** Hirsch Collection, British Library (London) **6** D.W. Krummel (Urbana) **7** Library of Congress (Washington, D.C.) **8** Library and Museum of the Performing Arts (N.Y.C.) **9** William Reeves (London) **10** Sibley Library, Eastman School of Music (Rochester) **11** Nigel Simeone (Tunbridge Wells, Kent) **12** Vereeniging ter Bervordering van de Belangen des Boekhandels (Amsterdam) **13** University of Virginia (Charlottesville) **14** University of California at Los Angeles **15** Generally available

3985	**REEVES, WILLIAM (New Series) (continued)**				
	1932	N.S.	73	*Music and Musical Literature* (36pp.)	*1,9,10,13
3986	_____.				
	1933	N.S.	74	*idem.* (48pp.)	*9,13
3987	_____.				
	1933	N.S.	75	*idem.* (40pp.)	*9
3988	_____.				
	1933	N.S.	76	*idem.* (48pp.)	*9,10,13
3989	_____.				
	1934	N.S.	77	*idem.* (32pp.)	*1,9,10,13
3990	_____.				
	1934	N.S.	78	*idem. (Handel Anniversary)* (40pp.)	*9,10,13
3991	_____.				
	1935	N.S.	79	*Music & Musical Literature* (36pp.)	*9,10,13
3992	_____.				
	1936	N.S.	80	*idem.* (44pp.)	*9,13
3993	_____.				
	n.d.	N.S.	81	*idem.* (36pp.)	*9,13
3994	_____.				
	1937	N.S.	82	*idem.* (52pp.)	*1,9,13
3995	_____.				
	1937	N.S.	83	*idem.* (39pp.)	*1,9,10,13
3996	_____.				
	1938	N.S.	84	*idem.* (51pp.)	*1,9,13
3997	_____.				
	1938	N.S.	85	*idem.* (40pp.)	*1,9
3998	_____.				
	1939	N.S.	86	*idem.* (60pp.)	*1,9
3999	_____.				
	1939/40	N.S.	87	*idem.* (48pp.)	*9,10,13
4000	_____.				
	1940	N.S.	88	*idem.* (56pp.)	*1,9,13

1 Compiler/State University of New York (Buffalo)   2 The British Library (London)   3 Gemeentemuseum (Den Haag)   4 The Grolier Club (N.Y.C.)   5 Hirsch Collection, British Library (London)   6 D.W. Krummel (Urbana)   7 Library of Congress (Washington, D.C.)   8 Library and Museum of the Performing Arts (N.Y.C.)   9 William Reeves (London)   10 Sibley Library, Eastman School of Music (Rochester)   11 Nigel Simeone (Tunbridge Wells, Kent)   12 Vereeniging ter Bervordering van de Belangen des Boekhandels (Amsterdam)   13 University of Virginia (Charlottesville)   14 University of California at Los Angeles   15 Generally available

4001   **REEVES, WILLIAM (New Series) (continued)**

	1941	N.S.	89	*Music and Musical Literature*
				(52pp.) *1,9,10,13

4002   _____.

        1948   N.S¿   90   *idem.*
                                 (28pp.)   *1,9

4003   _____.

        194_   N.S.   91?   *[issued?]*
                                 (?)   [not located]

4004   _____.

        1949   N.S.   92   *Music & Musical Literature*
                                 (28pp.)   *1,9,13

4005   _____.

        194_   N.S.   93?   *[issued?]*
                                 (?)   [not located]

4006   _____.

        194_?   N.S.   94   *Old and Rare Music. Mss. Early Books*
                                 (244)   *1,9,13

4007   _____.

        194_?   N.S.   95   *Opera Scores. Books*
                                 (12pp.)   *1,9

4008   _____.

        195_?   N.S.   96   *[issued?]*
                                 (?)   [not located]

4009   _____.

        195_?   N.S.   97   *Books on Music*
                                 (20pp.)   *1,9

4010   _____.

        195_?   N.S.   98   *Music & Musical Literature. Miniature Scores*
                                 (16pp.)   *1,9,13

4011   _____.

        195_?   N.S.   99   *Music. Musical Lit. Opera. Nat'l Music. Scores*
                                 (20pp.)   *9,13

4012   _____.

        195_   N.S.   100   *Music & Musical Literature. Chamber Music*
                                 (20pp.)   *9,13

4013   _____.

        195_   N.S.   101   *Rare Old Books on Music and First Editions*
                                 (396)   *1,9,13

4014   _____.

        195_   N.S.   102   *Music & Musical Literature*
                                 (16pp.)   *1,6,9,13

4015   _____.

        1958   N.S.   103   *Books on Music*
                                 (1980 lvs.)   *1,9

4016   _____.

        1958   N.S.   103!   *Books on music Second[!] Edition*
                                 (1982 lvs.)   *1,9

---

1 Compiler/State University of New York (Buffalo)   **2** The British Library (London)   **3** Gemeentemuseum (Den Haag)   **4** The Grolier Club (N.Y.C.)   **5** Hirsch Collection, British Library (London)   **6** D.W. Krummel (Urbana)   **7** Library of Congress (Washington, D.C.)   **8** Library and Museum of the Performing Arts (N.Y.C.)   **9** William Reeves (London)   **10** Sibley Library, Eastman School of Music (Rochester)   **11** Nigel Simeone (Tunbridge Wells, Kent)   **12** Vereeniging ter Bervordering van de Belangen des Boekhandels (Amsterdam)   **13** University of Virginia (Charlottesville)   **14** University of California at Los Angeles   **15** Generally available

4017	**REEVES, WILLIAM (New Series) (continued)**				
	195_	N.S.	104	*Books on the Violin* (702)	*1,9,10
4018	____.				
	195_?	N.S.	105	*Books on the Organ. [N.S., Part 03 on cover]* (152)	*1,9,10
4019	____.				
	196_?	N.S,	106	*Musical Literature* (1963-4257)	*1,9,13
4020	____.				
	196_?	N.S.	107	*Musical Periodicals* (7142-301)	*1,9
4021	____.				
	196_?	N.S.	108	*Books about Music* (7405-937)	*1,9
4022	____.				
	196_?	N.S.	109	*idem.* (1021-340)	*1,9
4023	____.				
	196_?	N.S.	110	*idem.* (1341-607)	*1,9
4024	____.				
	196_?	N.S.	111	*idem.* (1608-2062)	*1,9
4025	**REEVES, WILLIAM - Lists**				
	s.d.	Lists	10	*Scholarly Books on Music* (16pp.)	*13
4026	____.				
	s.d.	do.	13	*Books on the Violin and Violoncelo* (24pp.)	[H.Baron]
4027	____.				
	s.d.	do.	15	*Piano Solo* (4pp.)	*9
4028	____.				
	s.d.	do.	19	*Books on the Violin* (35pp.)	[H.Baron]
4029	____.				
	s.d.	do.	21	*Books on the Violin* (34pp.)	[H.Baron]
4030	____.				
	s.d.	do.	22	*Books on the Organ* (337)	*9
4031	____.				
	s.d.	do.	23	*Chamber Music Parts. Textbooks. Operas* (1-680)	*9
4032	____.				
	s.d.	do.	25	*Operas. New Books* (681-1276)	*9

1 Compiler/State University of New York (Buffalo)   2 The British Library (London)   3 Gemeentemuseum (Den Haag)   4 The Grolier Club (N.Y.C.)   5 Hirsch Collection, British Library (London)   6 D.W. Krummel (Urbana)   7 Library of Congress (Washington, D.C.)   8 Library and Museum of the Performing Arts (N.Y.C.)   9 William Reeves (London)   10 Sibley Library, Eastman School of Music (Rochester)   11 Nigel Simeone (Tunbridge Wells, Kent)   12 Vereeniging ter Bervordering van de Belangen des Boekhandels (Amsterdam)   13 University of Virginia (Charlottesville)   14 University of California at Los Angeles   15 Generally available

4033	**REEVES, WILLIAM - Lists (continued)**				
	s.d.	do.	26	*Books on the Organ* (256)	*9
4034	_____.				
	s.d.	do.	28	*Second-hand Music and Books on Msic* (1277-881)	*9
4035	_____.				
	s.d.	do.	30	*Second-hand Music and Books on Msic* (1882-2486)	*9
4036	_____.				
	s.d.	do.	31	*Books on the Organ* (327)	*9
4037	_____.				
	[1952]	do.	32	*Second-hand Music and Books on Msic* (2487-3114)	*6,9
4038	_____.				
	[195_]	do.	33	*Books on the Organ* (317)	*9
4039	_____.				
	[195_]	do.	35	*Second-hand Music and Books on Msic* (3115-542)	*6,9,13
4040	_____.				
	[195_]	do.	36	*Second-hand Music and Books on Msic* (3543-4170)	*9,13,14
4041	_____.				
	[195_]	do.	37	*Items Omitted from Catalogue [N.S.] 104* (1 leaf)	*9
4042	_____.				
	[1959?]	do.	38	*Items Omitted from Catalogue [N.S.] 104* (1 leaf)	*9
4043	_____.				
	[196_?]	do.	39	*Items Omitted from Catalogue [N.S.] 104* (94)	*9
4044	_____.				
	[196_]	do.	40	*New Books* (55)	*9
4045	_____.				
	[196_]	do.	41	*Back Numbers of "The Strad"* (1p.)	*9
4046	_____.				
	[196_]	do.	42	*"Strad" Volumes* (1 leaf)	*9
4047	_____.				
	[196_]	do.	43	*New Books* (52)	*9
4048	_____.				
	[196_]	do.	45	*New Books* (51)	*9

4049	**REEVES, WILLIAM** - Lists (continued)				
	[196_]	do.	46	*Violin Books* (63)	*9,14
4050	____.				
	[196_]	do.	47	*Back Numbers of "The Strad"* (2pp.)	*9
4051	____.				
	[196_]	do.	48	*Books on the Organ* (165)	*9,14
4052	____.				
	[196_?]	do.	49	*Oratorios and Cantatas* (4175-884)	*9,14
4053	____.				
	196_?]	do.	50	*Used Textbooks* (4885-5377)	*9,14
4054	____.				
	[196_?]	do.	53	*Used Textbooks* (5378-490)	*9
4055	____.				
	[196_?]	do.	54	*Miniature Scores* (5491-6664)	*9
4056	____.				
	[196_?]	do.	55	*Violin Music* (6665-902)	*9
4057	____.				
	[196_?]	do.	57	*Chamber Music* (6903-7002)	*9
4058	____.				
	[196_?]	do.	58	*Piano Music* (7003-111)	*9
4059	____.				
	[196_?]	do.	59	*Viola and Cello Music* (7112-222)	*9
4060	____.				
	[196_?]	do.	60	*Organ Music* (7223-355)	*9
4061	____.				
	[196_?]	do.	61	*Bassoon, Oboe, Horn, Harp, Guitar Music* (7356-427)	*9
4062	____.				
	[197_?]	do.	62	*New Music* (7428-655)	*9
4063	____.				
	[197_?]	do.	63	*Books on the Violin* (7656-773)	*9
4064	____.				
	[197_?]	do.	64	*Useful Textbooks* (7774-879)	*9

4065   **REEVES, WILLIAM - Lists (continued)**

	[197_?]	do.	65	*Strad Magazine* (7174-790)	*9
4066	_____.				
	[197_?]	do.	66	*Violin Music* (7791-911)	*9
4067	_____.				
	[197_?]	do.	67	*Opera Vocal Scores* (7912-8151)	*9
4068	_____.				
	[197_]	do.	68	*Books on the Organ* (8152-288)	*9
4069	_____.				
	[197_]	do.	69	*Music* (8289-468)	*9,13
4070	_____.				
	[197_]	do.	70	*Chamber Music* (8469-562)	*9
4071	_____.				
	[197_]	do.	71	*Useful Textbooks* (8563-675)	*9
4072	_____.				
	[197_]	do.	72	*Strad Magazine* (8676-683)	*9
4073	_____.				
	[197_]	do.	73	*Organ Music* (8684-808)	*9
4074	_____.				
	[1974]	do.	74	*Useful Textbooks* (8809-921)	*9,13,14
4075	_____.				
	[1974]	do.	75	*Piano Music* (8922-9029)	*9
4076	_____.				
	[1974]	do.	76	*Music* (9030-214)	*9,13,14
4077	_____.				
	[1974]	do.	77	*Useful Textbooks* (9215-306)	*9
4078	_____.				
	[1974]	do.	78	*National Music* (9307-371)	*9
4079	_____.				
	[1974]	do.	79	*Violin Music* (9371-494)	*9
4080	_____.				
	[1974]	do.	80	*Full Scores and Orchestra Material* (9495-554)	*9

1 Compiler/State University of New York (Buffalo)   **2** The British Library (London)   **3** Gemeentemuseum (Den Haag)   **4** The Grolier Club (N.Y.C.)   **5** Hirsch Collection, British Library (London)   **6** D.W. Krummel (Urbana)   **7** Library of Congress (Washington, D.C.)   **8** Library and Museum of the Performing Arts (N.Y.C.)   **9** William Reeves (London)   **10** Sibley Library, Eastman School of Music (Rochester)   **11** Nigel Simeone (Tunbridge Wells, Kent)   **12** Vereeniging ter Bevordering van de Belangen des Boekhandels (Amsterdam)   **13** University of Virginia (Charlottesville)   **14** University of California at Los Angeles   **15** Generally available

4081   **REEVES, WILLIAM - Lists (continued)**
     [1974]   do.   81   *Books on Violin Making, Repairing*
                                       (9555-566)   *9

4082   _____.
     [1974]   do.   82   *Chamber Music*
                                       (9567-654)   *9

4083   _____.
     [1974]   do.   83   *Oratorios and Cantatas. Useful Textbooks*
                                     (9655-999, 1-20   9) *9

4084   _____.
     [1974]   do.   84   *Opera Vocal Scores*
                                       (210-421)   *9

4085   _____.
     [1974-]   do.   85   *Useful Textbooks*
                                       (422-518)   *9

4086   _____.
     [1974]   do.   86   *Books on Violin Making, Repairing*
                                       (519-29)   *9

4087   _____.
     [1974]   do.   87   *Viola Music. Cello Music*
                                     (530-630)   *9

4088   _____.
     [1974]   do.   88   *Books about Music*
                                     (631-741)   *9

4089   _____.
     [1974]   do.   89   *Books on Subjects apart from Music*
                                     (742-56)   *9

4090   _____.
     [1975]   do.   90   *Useful Textbooks*
                                     (757-855)   *9,13,14

4091   _____.
     [1975]   do.   91   *Piano Music*
                                     (856-965)   *9

4092   _____.
     [1975]   do.   92   *Church Music*
                                     (966-1022)   *9

4093   _____.
     [1975]   do.   93   *Piano Duet and 2 Piano Music*
                                     (1023-140)   *9

4094   _____.
     [1975]   do.   94   *Violin Music*
                                     (1141-254)   *9

4095   _____.
     [1975]   do.   95   *Organ Music*
                                     (1255-383)   *9

4096   _____.
     [1975]   do.   96   *Violin Books*
                                     (1384-443)   *9

1 Compiler/State University of New York (Buffalo)   **2** The British Library (London)   **3** Gemeentemuseum (Den Haag)   **4** The Grolier Club (N.Y.C.)   **5** Hirsch Collection, British Library (London)   **6** D.W. Krummel (Urbana)   **7** Library of Congress (Washington, D.C.)   **8** Library and Museum of the Performing Arts (N.Y.C.)   **9** William Reeves (London)   **10** Sibley Library, Eastman School of Music (Rochester)   **11** Nigel Simeone (Tunbridge Wells, Kent)   **12** Vereeniging ter Bervordering van de Belangen des Boekhandels (Amsterdam)   **13** University of Virginia (Charlottesville)   **14** University of California at Los Angeles   **15** Generally available

4097　**REEVES, WILLIAM - Lists (continued)**
　　　[1975]　　do.　　97　　*Chamber Music*
　　　　　　　　　　　　　　(1444-542)　　　　　　　　　　　　　　*9

4098　_____.
　　　[1975]　　do.　　98　　*Books about Music*
　　　　　　　　　　　　　　(1543-654)　　　　　　　　　*9,13,14

4099　_____.
　　　[1975]　　do.　　99　　*Useful Textbooks*
　　　　　　　　　　　　　　(1655-751)　　　　　　　　　　　　　　*9

4100　_____.
　　　[1975]　　do.　　100　　*Full Scores and Orchestra Material*
　　　　　　　　　　　　　　(1752-899)　　　　　　　　　　　　　　*9

4101　_____.
　　　[1975?]　　do.　　101　　*Piano Music*
　　　　　　　　　　　　　　(1900-2160)　　　　　　　　　　　　　*9

4102　_____.
　　　[1975?]　　do.　　102　　*New Music*
　　　　　　　　　　　　　　(2161-346)　　　　　　　　　　　　　　*9

4103　_____.
　　　[1975?]　　do.　　103　　*Books about Freemasonry*
　　　　　　　　　　　　　　(2347-417)　　　　　　　　　　　　　　*9

4104　_____.
　　　[1975?]　　do.　　104　　*Violin Books*
　　　　　　　　　　　　　　(2418-504)　　　　　　　　　　　　　　*9

4105　_____.
　　　[197_]　　do.　　105　　*Musical Comedies and Comic Opera*
　　　　　　　　　　　　　　(2505-71)　　　　　　　　　　　　　　*9

4106　_____.
　　　[197_]　　do.　　106　　*Books on Violin Making, Repairing*
　　　　　　　　　　　　　　(2719-732)　　　　　　　　　　　　　　*9

4107　_____.
　　　[197_]　　do.　　107　　*Useful Textbooks*
　　　　　　　　　　　　　　(2733-820)　　　　　　　　　　　　　　*9

4108　_____.
　　　[197_]　　do.　　108　　*Opera Vocal Scores*
　　　　　　　　　　　　　　(2821-3041)　　　　　　　　　　　　　*9

4109　_____.
　　　[197_]　　do.　　109　　*Music*
　　　　　　　　　　　　　　(3042-256)　　　　　　　　　　　　　*1,9

4110　_____.
　　　[197_]　　do.　　110　　*Violin Music*
　　　　　　　　　　　　　　(3257-471)　　　　　　　　　　　　　　*9

4111　_____.
　　　[197_]　　do.　　111　　*Piano Duet and 2-hand Music*
　　　　　　　　　　　　　　(3472-588)　　　　　　　　　　　　　　*9

4112　_____.
　　　[197_]　　do　　112　　*Full Scores and Orchestra Material*
　　　　　　　　　　　　　　(3589-789)　　　　　　　　　　　　　　*9

---

1 Compiler/State University of New York (Buffalo)　**2** The British Library (London)　**3** Gemeentemuseum (Den Haag)　**4** The Grolier Club (N.Y.C.)　**5** Hirsch Collection, British Library (London)　**6** D.W. Krummel (Urbana)　**7** Library of Congress (Washington, D.C.)　**8** Library and Museum of the Performing Arts (N.Y.C.)　**9** William Reeves (London)　**10** Sibley Library, Eastman School of Music (Rochester)　**11** Nigel Simeone (Tunbridge Wells, Kent)　**12** Vereeniging ter Bervordering van de Belangen des Boekhandels (Amsterdam)　**13** University of Virginia (Charlottesville)　**14** University of California at Los Angeles　**15** Generally available

4113   **REEVES, WILLIAM - Lists (continued)**
     [197_]   do.   113   *Books on Subjects Apart from Musc*
                           (3790-839)   *9

4114   _____.
     . [197_]   do.   114   *Violin Books*
                           (3840-922)   *9

4115   _____.
     [197_]   do.   115   *Books about Music*
                           (3923-4035)   *9

4116   _____.
     [197_]   do.   116   *Chamber Music*
                           (4036-140)   *9

4117   _____.
     [197_]   do.   117   *Organ Music*
                           (4141-217)   *9

4118   _____.
     [197_]   do.   118   *Bassoon,. Oboe, Horn ... Music*
                           (4218-273)   *1,9

4119   _____.
     [197_]   do.   119   *Oratorios, Cantatas*
                           (4274-589)   *9

4120   _____.
     [197_]   do.   120   ?
                           (4590-624)   [not located]

4121   _____.
     [197_]   do.   121   *Viola Music. Cello Music*
                           (4625-732)   *9

4122   _____.
     [197_]   do.   122   *Books on Organ*
                           (4733-819)   *9

4123   _____.
     [197_]   do.   123   *Violin Books*
                           (4820-885)   *9

4124   _____.
     [197_]   do.   124   *Useful Textbooks*
                           (4886-5006)   *9

4125   _____.
     [197_]   do.   125   *Books about Music*
                           (5007-131)   *9

4126   _____.
     [197_]   do.   126   *Books (not on Music) [reissued as #140]*
                           (5132-176)   *9

4127   _____.
     [197_]   do.   127   *Useful Textbooks*
                           (5177-293)   *9

4128   _____.
     [197_]   do.   128   *Books on Violin Making, Repairing*
                           (5294-308a)   *9

1 Compiler/State University of New York (Buffalo)   **2** The British Library (London)   **3** Gemeentemuseum (Den Haag)   **4** The Grolier Club (N.Y.C.)   **5** Hirsch Collection, British Library (London)   **6** D.W. Krummel (Urbana)   **7** Library of Congress (Washington, D.C.)   **8** Library and Museum of the Performing Arts (N.Y.C.)   **9** William Reeves (London)   **10** Sibley Library, Eastman School of Music (Rochester)   **11** Nigel Simeone (Tunbridge Wells, Kent)   **12** Vereeniging ter Bervordering van de Belangen des Boekhandels (Amsterdam)   **13** University of Virginia (Charlottesville)   **14** University of California at Los Angeles   **15** Generally available

4129	REEVES, WILLIAM - Lists (continued)				
	[197-]	do.	129	Important Violin Books (5309-348c)	*9
4130	_____.				
	[197-]	do.	130	Violin Music (5349-464)	*9
4131	_____.				
	[197-]	do.	131	Violin Books (5465-529)	*9
4132	_____.				
	[197-]	do.	132	Piano Music (5530-655)	*1,9
4133	_____.				
	[197-]	do.	133	Church Music (5656-727)	*1,9
4134	_____.				
	[1978]	do.	134	Min. Scores /often reissued with new prices/ (5728-6240)	*1,9,11
4135	_____.				
	[1978]	do.	135	Chamber Music (6241-355)	*9
4136	_____.				
	[1978]	do.	136	Books about Freemasonry (6356-383)	*9
4137	_____.				
	[1978]	do.	137	Full Scores and Orchestra Material (6384-478)	*9
4138	_____.				
	[1978]	do.	138	Books about Music (6479-578)	*9
4139	_____.				
	[1978]	do.	139	Useful Textbooks (6579-701)	*9
4140	_____.				
	[1978]	do.	140	Books (not Music) (6702-744)	*9
4141	_____.				
	[1978]	do.	141	Clarinet and Flute Music (6745-833)	*1,9
4142	_____.				
	[1978]	do.	142	Violin Books (6834-902)	*9
4143	_____.				
	[1978]	do.	143	Books about Music (6903-7012)	*9
4144	_____.				
	[1978]	do.	144	Useful Textbooks /reissued as Cat. N.S. 180/ (7013-141)	*9

1 Compiler/State University of New York (Buffalo)   2 The British Library (London)   3 Gemeentemuseum (Den Haag)   4 The Grolier Club (N.Y.C.)   5 Hirsch Collection, British Library (London)   6 D.W. Krummel (Urbana)   7 Library of Congress (Washington, D.C.)   8 Library and Museum of the Performing Arts (N.Y.C.)   9 William Reeves (London)   10 Sibley Library, Eastman School of Music (Rochester) 11 Nigel Simeone (Tunbridge Wells, Kent)   12 Vereeniging ter Bervordering van de Belangen des Boekhandels (Amsterdam)   13 University of Virginia (Charlottesville)   14 University of California at Los Angeles   15 Generally available

4145 **REEVES, WILLIAM - Lists (continued)**
     [1978]   do.   145   *National Music*
                                  (7302-404)   *1,9

4146 _____.
     1978   do.   146   *Books on Violin Making, Repairing*
                                  (7405-420)   *9

4147 _____.
     1978   do.   147   *Books about Freemasonry*
                                  (7421-439) '   *9

4148 _____.
     [1978]   do.   148   *New Music*
                                  (7440-602)   *1,9

4149 _____.
     [1978?]   do.   149   *Important Violin Books*
                                  (7604-644)   *1,9

4150 _____.
     [1978?]   do.   150   ?
                                  (?)   [not located]

4151 _____.
     [1979?]   do.   151   ?
                                  (? -8016)   [not located]

4152 _____.
     [1979?]   do.   152   *Books on the Organ*
                                  (8017-071)   *1

4153 _____.
     1979   do.   153   *Musical Comedies and Comic Opera*
                                  (8072-212)   *1,9

4154 _____.
     1979   do.   154   *Violin Auction Sale Catalogues*
                                  (8212-270)   *9

4155 _____.
     1979   do.   155   *Opera Vocal Scores*
                                  (8272-408)   *1,9

4156 _____.
     1979   do.   156   *Oratorios and Cantatas*
                                  (8409-645)   *1,9

4157 _____.
     1979   do.   157   *Books about Music*
                                  (8646-756)   *9

4158 _____.
     1979   do.   158   *Books about Freemasonry*
                                  (8757-770)   *9

4159 _____.
     1979   do.   159   *Violin Music*
                                  (8771-889)   *1,9

4160 _____.
     1979   do.   160   *Chamber Music*
                                  (8890-997)   *1,9

1 Compiler/State University of New York (Buffalo)   **2** The British Library (London)   **3** Gemeentemuseum (Den Haag)   **4** The Grolier Club (N.Y.C.)   **5** Hirsch Collection, British Library (London)   **6** D.W. Krummel (Urbana)   **7** Library of Congress (Washington, D.C.)   **8** Library and Museum of the Performing Arts (N.Y.C.)   **9** William Reeves (London)   **10** Sibley Library, Eastman School of Music (Rochester)   **11** Nigel Simeone (Tunbridge Wells, Kent)   **12** Vereeniging ter Bervordering van de Belangen des Boekhandels (Amsterdam)   **13** University of Virginia (Charlottesville)   **14** University of California at Los Angeles   **15** Generally available

4161	**REEVES, WILLIAM** - Lists (continued)				
	1979	do.	161	*Piano Music* (8998-9111)	*1,9
4162	____.				
	1979	do.	162	*Piano Duet and 2-Piano Music* (9112-231	*1,9
4163	____.				
	1979	do.	163	*Full Scores and Orchestra Material* (9232-309)	*1,9
4164	____.				
	1979	do.	164	*Viola Music, Cello Music* (9310-353)	*1,9
4165	____.				
	1979	do.	165	*Organ Music* (9354-397)	*9
4166	____.				
	1979	do.	166	*Violin Books* (9398-430)	*9
4167	____.				
	1979	do.	167	*Violin Auction Sale Catalogues* (9431-471)	*1,9
4168	____.				
	1979	do.	168	*Music* (9472-523)	*1,9
4169	____.				
	1979	do.	169	*Organ Music* (9254-279)	*1,9
4170	____.				
	1979	do.	170	*Full Scores and Orchestral Material* (9580-665)	*1,9
4171	____.				
	1979	do.	171	*Church Music* (9666-729)	*1,9
4172	____.				
	1979	do.	172	*Piano Music* (9730-831)	*1,9
4173	____.				
	1979	do.	173	*Books about Music* (9832-942)	*1,9
4174	____.				
	1980	do.	174	*Chamber Music* (9942-0041)	*1,9
4175	____.				
	1980	do.	175	*Full Scores and Orchestral Material* (42-157)	*1,9
4176	____.				
	1980	do.	176	*Antiquarian Music* (158-233)	*1,9

1 Compiler/State University of New York (Buffalo)   **2** The British Library (London)   **3** Gemeentemuseum (Den Haag)   **4** The Grolier Club (N.Y.C.)   **5** Hirsch Collection, British Library (London)   **6** D.W. Krummel (Urbana)   **7** Library of Congress (Washington, D.C.)   **8** Library and Museum of the Performing Arts (N.Y.C.)   **9** William Reeves (London)   **10** Sibley Library, Eastman School of Music (Rochester)   **11** Nigel Simeone (Tunbridge Wells, Kent)   **12** Vereeniging ter Bervordering van de Belangen des Boekhandels (Amsterdam)   **13** University of Virginia (Charlottesville)   **14** University of California at Los Angeles   **15** Generally available

4177	**REEVES, WILLIAM** - Lists (continued)				
	1980	do.	177	*Violin Books* (234-290)	*1,9
4178	_____.				
	1980	do.	178	*Books on the Violin* (18pp.)	*1,9
4179	_____.				
	1980	do.	179	*Antiquarian Music* (418-484)	*1,9
4180	_____.				
	1980	do.	180	*Useful Textbooks* (485-559)	*1,9
4181	-_____.				
	1980	do.	181	*National Music* (560-680)	*1,9
4182	_____.				
	1980	do.	182	*Clarinet and Flute Music* (681-843)	*1,9
4183	_____.				
	1980	do.	183	*Opera Vocal Scores* (843-871)	*1,9
4184	_____.				
	1980	do.	184	*Violin, Viola, Cello and Chamber Music* (872-965)	*1,9
4185	_____.				
	1980	do.	185	*Piano Concertos* (966-1020)	*1,9
4186	_____.				
	1980	do.	186	*Strad Magazines* (2pp.)	*1,9
4187	_____.				
	1980	do.	187	*Antiquarian Music* (1021-1101)	*1,9
4188	_____.				
	1980	do.	188	*Music Periodicals* (1102-185)	*1,9
4189	_____.				
	1981?	do.	189	*Violin Books* (1186-235)	*1,9
4190	_____.				
	1981?	do.	190	*Books on the Organ* (1236-407)	*1,9
4191	_____.				
	3/1981	do.	191	*Antiquarian Music* (1408-88)	*1,9,10
4192	_____.				
	1981	do.	192	*Antiquarian Music* (1489-555)	*1,9

1 Compiler/State University of New York (Buffalo)   **2** The British Library (London)   **3** Gemeentemuseum (Den Haag)   **4** The Grolier Club (N.Y.C.)   **5** Hirsch Collection, British Library (London)   **6** D.W. Krummel (Urbana)   **7** Library of Congress (Washington, D.C.)   **8** Library and Museum of the Performing Arts (N.Y.C.)   **9** William Reeves (London)   **10** Sibley Library, Eastman School of Music (Rochester)   **11** Nigel Simeone (Tunbridge Wells, Kent)   **12** Vereeniging ter Bervordering van de Belangen des Boekhandels (Amsterdam)   **13** University of Virginia (Charlottesville)   **14** University of California at Los Angeles   **15** Generally available

4193 **REEVES, WILLIAM - Lists (continued)**

	1981	do.	193	*Antiquarian Music* (1556-631)	*1,9,10
4194 ____.	1982	do.	194	*Antiquarian Music* (2031-110)	*1,9
4195 ____.	1982	do.	195	*Books on the Organ* (2111-163)	*9
4196 ____.	[1982?]	do.	196	*Antiquarian Music* (2164-305)	*1,9,13
4197 ____.	[1982?]	do.	197	*Antiquarian Music. Orchestral Scores* (2306-468)	*1,9
4198 ____.	1982	do.	198	*Opera Vocal Scores* (2469-568)	*1,9
4199 ____.	1982	do.	199	*Antiquarian Music* (2569-706)	*1,9
4200 ____.	1982	do.	200	*Books about Freemasonry* (2707-762)	*1,9
4201 ____.	1982	do.	201	*Antiquarian Music* (2763-904)	*1,9
4202 ____.	1983	do.	202	*Antiquarian Music. Journals* (2905-3027)	*1,9
4203 ____.	1983	do.	203	*Antiquarian Music* (3376-497)	*1,9
4204 ____.	1983	do.	204	*Antiquarian Music* (3498-626)	*1,9
4205 ____.	1983	do.	205	*Antiquarian Music* (3627-798)	*1,9
4206 ____.	1983	do.	206	*Antiquarian Music. National Music* (3799-919)	*1,9
4207 ____.	1983	do.	207	*Miniature Scores* (3920-4157)	*1,9
4208 ____.	1983	do.	208	*Antiquarian Music. National Music* (4156-280)	*1,9

1 Compiler/State University of New York (Buffalo)   2 The British Library (London)   3 Gemeentemuseum (Den Haag)   4 The Grolier Club (N.Y.C.)   5 Hirsch Collection, British Library (London)   6 D.W. Krummel (Urbana)   7 Library of Congress (Washington, D.C.)   8 Library and Museum of the Performing Arts (N.Y.C.)   9 William Reeves (London)   10 Sibley Library, Eastman School of Music (Rochester)   11 Nigel Simeone (Tunbridge Wells, Kent)   12 Vereeniging ter Bervordering van de Belangen des Boekhandels (Amsterdam)   13 University of Virginia (Charlottesville)   14 University of California at Los Angeles   15 Generally available

4209 **REEVES, WILLIAM - Lists (continued)**
　　　　1983　　do.　　209　　*Antiquarian Music*
　　　　　　　　　　　　　　　　(4281-501)　　　　　　　　　　　　　　　　*1,9

4210 _____.
　　　　1984　　do.　　210　　*Antiquarian Music. Oratorios and Cantatas*
　　　　　　　　　　　　　　　　(4402-548)　　　　　　　　　　　　　　　　*1,9

4211 _____.
　　　　1984　　do.　　211　　*Antiquarran Music. Oratorios and Cantatas*
　　　　　　　　　　　　　　　　(4549-752)　　　　　　　　　　　　　　　　*1,9

4212 _____.
　　　　1984　　do.　　212　　*Antiquarian Music*
　　　　　　　　　　　　　　　　(5055-179)　　　　　　　　　　　　　　　　*1,9

4213 _____.
　　　　1984　　do.　　213　　*Antiquarian Music. Oratorios. Journals*
　　　　　　　　　　　　　　　　(5180-287)　　　　　　　　　　　　　　　　*1,9

4214 _____.
　　　　1984　　do.　　214　　*Antiquarian Music. Miniature Scores*
　　　　　　　　　　　　　　　　(5288-444)　　　　　　　　　　　　　　　　*1,9

4215 _____.
　　　　1984　　do.　　215　　*Church Music*
　　　　　　　　　　　　　　　　(5445-627)　　　　　　　　　　　　　　　　*1,9

4216 _____.
　　　　1984　　do.　　216　　*Organ Books*
　　　　　　　　　　　　　　　　(5628-687)　　　　　　　　　　　　　　　　*1,9

4217 _____.
　　　　1984　　do.　　217　　*Opera Scores*
　　　　　　　　　　　　　　　　(5687-856)　　　　　　　　　　　　　　　　*1,9

4218 _____.
　　　　1984　　do.　　218　　*Books on music*
　　　　　　　　　　　　　　　　(5857-992)　　　　　　　　　　　　　　　　*1,9

4219 _____.
　　　　1984　　do.　　219　　*Music and Books about Music*
　　　　　　　　　　　　　　　　(5993-6459)　　　　　　　　　　　　　　　　*1,9

4220 **REICHMAN, ALOIS (Vienna)**
　　　　1966　　　　　117　　*Literatur. Musik - Theater*
　　　　　　　　　　　　　　　　(631)　　　　　　　　　　　　　　　　　　*1

4221 **REICHNER, HERBERT (Stockbridge, Mass.)**
　　　　s.d.　　　　　28　　*Renaissance, part 3: Music and Opera*
　　　　　　　　　　　　　　　　(1375-440)　　　　　　　　　　　　　　　　*10

4222 _____.
　　　　s.d.　　　　　33　　*Medievalia, part : ... Music*
　　　　　　　　　　　　　　　　(3466a-553)　　　　　　　　　　　　　　　　*10

4223 _____.
　　　　s.d.　　　　　35　　*Ref.Books, Bibliographies: Music. Opera. Dance*
　　　　　　　　　　　　　　　　(2013-280)　　　　　　　　　　　　　　　　*10

4224 **RENKA, JACKIE (Munich)**
　　　　1961　　　　　19　　*Theater. Musik. Film*
　　　　　　　　　　　　　　　　(310)　　　　　　　　　　　　　　　　　[IBAK]

---

1 Compiler/State University of New York (Buffalo)　2 The British Library (London)　3 Gemeentemuseum (Den Haag)　4 The Grolier Club (N.Y.C.)　5 Hirsch Collection, British Library (London)　6 D.W. Krummel (Urbana)　7 Library of Congress (Washington, D.C.)　8 Library and Museum of the Performing Arts (N.Y.C.)　9 William Reeves (London)　10 Sibley Library, Eastman School of Music (Rochester) 11 Nigel Simeone (Tunbridge Wells, Kent)　12 Vereeniging ter Bervordering van de Belangen des Boekhandels (Amsterdam)　13 University of Virginia (Charlottesville)　14 University of California at Los Angeles　15 Generally available

4225 **RENKA, JACKIE (Munich) (continued)**
1964 48 *Kunst. Musik. Theater*
(525) [IBAK]

4226 **RENNER, KLAUS (Haar bei München)**
1960 52 *Musikethnologie - Bücher und Schallplatten*
(510) [IBAK]

4227 _____.
1968 84 *Musikethnologie*
(528) *1

4228 _____.
[1971] 184 *Musikethnologie*
(304) *13

4229 **RHEIN, HERMANN (Wismar, DDR)**
[1964] — *Musik*
(1022) [IBAK]

4230 _____.
[1967] 46 *Musik*
(548) [IBAK]

4231 **RICKE, WALTER (Munich & Kottgeisering b. Grafrath)**
s.d. 1 *?*
? ?

4232 _____.
s.d. 2 *?*
? ?

4233 _____.
s.d. 3 *Klavierauszüge*
(1185) [Ricke]

4234 _____.
s.d. 4 *?*
? ?

4235 _____.
s.d. 5 *?*
? ?

4236 _____.
s.d. 6 *Musikliteratur*
(1065) [IBAK]

4237 _____.
s.d. 7 *?*
? ?

4238 _____.
s.d. 8 *?*
? ?

4239 _____.
s.d. 9 *Partituren*
(445) [Ricke]

4240 _____.
s.d. 10 *?*
? ?

4241 **RICKE, WALTER** (Munich & Kottgeisering b. Grafrath) (continued)

	s.d.	11	*Antiquarische Bücher (Musik-Theorie)* (923)	[Ricke]
4242 _____.	s.d.	12	*?* ?	?
4243 _____.	s.d.	13	*?* ?	?
4244 _____.	s.d.	14	*Musiker-Biographien* (1058)	[Ricke]
4245 _____.	1960?	[15]	*Richard Wagner* (383)	[IBAK]
4246 _____.	1960?	16	*Antiquarische Kammermusik* (843)	*1
4247 _____.	1960?	17	*Vokalmusik* ?	[IBAK]
4248 _____.	[1960]	18	*Partituren und Orchestermaterial* (1112)	[IBAK]
4249 _____.	[1960]	19	*Klavierauszüge* (1028)	[IBAK]
4250 _____.	1961?	20	*Klavierauszüge* (422,85)	[IBAK]
4251 _____.	196_	21	*Musikliteratur* (758)	[Ricke]
4252 _____.	196_	22	*?* ?	?
4253 _____.	196_	23	*?* ?	?
4254 _____.	1961?	24	*Aufführungsmaterial. Partituren* (1409)	*6
4255 _____.	1961?	25	*Klavierauszüge* (1224)	*6
4256 _____.	1962?	26	*Musikliteratur* (1856)	[IBAK]

4257 **RICKE, WALTER (Munich & Kottgeisering b. Grafrath) (continued)**

	1962?	27	*Kammer- und Instrumentalmusik*	
			?	[IBAK]
4258	_____.			
	1962?	28	*Vokalmusik*	
			(1001)	[IBAK]
4259	_____.			
	1962?	29	*Theaterliteratur*	
			(169)	[IBAK]
4260	_____.			
	1962?	30	*?*	
			?	?
4261	_____.			
	1962?	31	*Partituren*	
			?	?
4262	_____.			
	1962?	32	*Antiquarische Musikliteratur*	
			(748)	*1,6
4263	_____.			
	1962?	33	*Partituren*	
			?	[Ricke]
4264	_____.			
	1962?	34	*Oper im Erst- und Frühausgaben Operetten*	
			(564)	*1,6,13
4265	_____.			
	1962?	35	*Antiquarische Musikliteratur*	
			(521)	*1,6
4266	_____.			
	1962?	36	*Antiq. /und neu/ Partituren*	
			(875)	*1,6,13
4267	_____.			
	1962?	37	*Coll: Kroyers. Musikliteratur*	
			?	?
4268	_____.			
	1962?	38	*Musikliteratur*	
			(789)	*6,13
4269	_____.			
	1962?	39	*Vokalmusik. Chor- und Kirchenmusik*	
			(1252)	*1,6,13
4270	_____.			
	1962?	40	*Klavierauszüge und Partituren*	
			(916)	*1,13
4271	_____.			
	[1963]	41	*Antiquarische Musikliteratur*	
			(847)	*1,6,12,13
4272	_____.			
	[1963]	42	*Musik f. Tasten- und Saiteninstrumente*	
			(3035)	*1,6,13

4273 **RICKE, WALTER (Munich & Kottgeisering b. Grafrath) (continued)**
     [1963?]   43   *Antiquarische Musikliteratur*
                               (869)   *1,6,13

4274 _____.
     1963?   44   *Antiquarische Musikliteratur*
                               (757)   *1,13

4275 _____.
     1963?   45   *Klavierauszüge und Partituren Mit Nachtrag*
                               (1598)   *1,6,13

4276 _____.
     1963?   46   *Antiquarische Musikliteratur*
                               (471)   *1,6,13

4277 _____.
     1964   47   *Antiquarische Musikliteratur*
                               (9977)   *1,6,13

4278 _____.
     1964   48   *Kammermusik*
                               (1271)   *1,6,13

4279 _____.
     1964   49   *Antiquarische Musikliteratur*
                               (638)   *1,6,13

4280 _____.
     1964   50   *Antiquarische Musikliteratur*
                               (886)   *1,6,13

4281 _____.
     1964   51   *Klavierauszüge. Partituren. Vokalmusik*
                               (1351)   *1,6,13

4282 _____.
     1964   52   *Wagner Literatur. Theater. Literatur*
                               (663)   *1,6,13

4283 _____.
     1964   53   *Antiquarische Musikliteratur*
                               (727)   *1,6,13

4284 _____.
     1965?   54   *Antiquarische Musikliteratur*
                               (704)   *1,6,13

4285 _____.
     1965?   55   *Antiquarische Musikliteratur*
                               (1000)   *1,6,13

4286 _____.
     1965?   56   *Partituren und Klavierauszüge*
                               (1185)   *1,6,13

4287 _____.
     1965?   57   *Antiquarische Musik und Bücher*
                               (1536)   *1,13

4288 _____.
     1966   58   *Antiquarische Musikliteratur*
                               (981)   *6,13

4289   **RICKE, WALTER (Munich & Kottgeisering b. Grafrath) (continued)**

	1966	59	*Antiquarische Musikliteratur*	
			(847)	*1,6,13
4290	____.			
	1966	60	*Partituren. Klavierauszüge. Vokalmusik*	
			(1002)	*6
4291	____.			
	1966	61	*Mozart - Beethoven - Schubert*	
			(749)	*6,13
4292	____.			
	1966	62	*Antiquarische Musikliteratur, mit Beilage*	
			(1101)	*6,13
4293	____.			
	1966	63	*Instrumentalmusik*	
			(1669))	*US-BE,6,13
4294	____.			
	1966	64	*Klavierauszüge. Partituren*	
			(1378))	*US-BE,1,13
4295	____.			
	1966	65	*Antiquarische Musikliteratur*	
			(690)	*1,6,13
4296	____.			
	1966	66	*Musikliteratur*	
			(631)	*1,6,13
4297	____.			
	1966	67	*Antiquarische Partituren und Klavierauszüge*	
			(246)	[IBAK]
4298	____.			
	1967?	68	*Musikliteratur*	
			(1091)	*1,4
4299	____.			
	]1967?	69	*Musik - Theater - Literatur. Bilder*	
			(800)	*1,6
4300	____.			
	1967?	70	*Literatur aus allen Gebieten*	
			(464)	*1,6
4301	____.			
	1967?	71	*Antiquar. Klavierauszüge. Instrumental Musik*	
			(2068)	*1,6,13
4302	____.			
	1967?	72	*Musikliteratur*	
			(1087)	*6,13
4303	____.			
	1967?	73	*Literatur aus allen Gebieten*	
			(441)	*6,13
4304	____.			
	196-?	74	*Österreich. Musik. Geschichte etc.*	
			(1579)	*1,6,13

1 Compiler/State University of New York (Buffalo)   **2** The British Library (London)   **3** Gemeentemuseum (Den Haag)   **4** The Grolier Club (N.Y.C.)   **5** Hirsch Collection, British Library (London)   **6** D.W. Krummel (Urbana)   **7** Library of Congress (Washington, D.C.)   **8** Library and Museum of the Performing Arts (N.Y.C.)   **9** William Reeves (London)   **10** Sibley Library, Eastman School of Music (Rochester)   **11** Nigel Simeone (Tunbridge Wells, Kent)   **12** Vereeniging ter Bervordering van de Belangen des Boekhandels (Amsterdam)   **13** University of Virginia (Charlottesville)   **14** University of California at Los Angeles   **15** Generally available

4305	**RICKE, WALTER (Munich & Kottgeisering b. Grafrath) (continued)**			
	196_	75	*Musiktheorie. Zeitschriften*	
			(1179)	*6,13
4306	____.			
	196_	76	*Geigen*	
			(428)	*1,13
4307	____.			
	1968?	77	*Antiquarische Musikliteratur*	
			(1306)	*1,6,13
4308	____.			
	1969	78	*Musikliteratur*	
			(1051)	*6,12,13
4309	____.			
	[1970]	80	*Klavierauszüge. Partituren*	
			(2590)	*1,6,12,13
4310	____.			
	[1970]	81	*Beethoven - Musikliteratur - Schallplatten*	
			(1272)	*1
4311	____.			
	[1970]	82	*Musikbücher und Musikportraits*	
			(1659)	*1,6
4312	____.			
	[1970?]	83	*Lit. Kulturgeschichte. Theater. Schallplatten*	
			(557-651,665-83	8) *4
4313	____.			
	[1971]	84	*Musikbücher und Musikportraits*	
			(1219)	*1
4314	____.			
	[1971]	85	*Musikbücher*	
			(1171)	*4,12
4315	____.			
	[1971]	86	*Musikbücher*	
			(1670)	*1,4,6
4316	____.			
	[1972]	87	*Musikdrucke in Erst- u. Frühaugaben. Brahms*	
			(1982)	*4,6,13
4317	____.			
	[1972]	88	*Literatur aus allen Gebieten. Schallplatten*	
			(863).)	*US-BE
4318	____.			
	[1972]	89	*Klavierauszüge. Partituren*	
			(1567)	*4,6,12,13
4319	____.			
	[1972]	90	*Musikbücher, antiq. und neu*	
			(1220)	*1,4,6,12,13
4320	____.			
	[1972]	91	*Antiquarische Theater-literatur*	
			(359)	*1,4,12

4321 **RICKE, WALTER** (Munich & Kottgeisering b. Grafrath) (continued)
   [1972]   92 *Musikbücher. Noten. Bilder. Autographen*
             (1779)   *1,4,6,12

4322   ___.
   [1972]   93 *Klavierauszüge. Kammermusik. Bücher*
             (1374+)   *1,4,13

4323   ___.
   [1973]   94 *Musikbücher. Noten. Bilder*
             (1370)   *6,12

4324   ___.
   [1973]   95 *Max Reger*
             (353)   [Ricke]

4325   ___.
   [1973]   96 *Musikbücher. Vocal- und Chormusik*
             (1759)   *1,4,12

4326   ___.
   [1973]   97 *Klavierauszüge. Kammermusik. Bücher*
             (1786)   *1,6

4327   ___.
   [1974]   98 *Musikbücher, antiq. u. neu. Musikerportraits*
             (1551)   *1

4328   ___.
   [1974?]   99 *Musikbücher, antiq. u. neu. Musikerportraits*
             (823+)   *4,6

4329   ___.
   [1974?]   99b *Aus allen Gebieten*
             (1267+)   *6

4330   ___.
   [1974?]   100 *Alte Drucke. Musikbücher*
             (1035)   *6

4331   ___.
   1974-75   101 *Neue Bücher. Klavierauszüge*
             (1397)   *US-BE

4332   ___.
   [197_]   102 *Musikbücher, neu und antiquarisch*
             (962)   *6

4333   ___.
   [197_]   103 *Kammermusik*
             (1385)   *US-BE

4334   ___.
   [197_]   104 *Musikbücher, neu und antiquarisch*
             (1025)   *6

4335   ___.
   [1976]   106 *Musikbücher. Alte Drucke*
             (1303)   *1

4336   ___.
   [1976]   107 *Klavierauszüge. Partituren. Musikbücher*
             (1836)   *1

---

1 Compiler/State University of New York (Buffalo) **2** The British Library (London) **3** Gemeentemuseum (Den Haag) **4** The Grolier Club (N.Y.C.) **5** Hirsch Collection, British Library (London) **6** D.W. Krummel (Urbana) **7** Library of Congress (Washington, D.C.) **8** Library and Museum of the Performing Arts (N.Y.C.) **9** William Reeves (London) **10** Sibley Library, Eastman School of Music (Rochester) **11** Nigel Simeone (Tunbridge Wells, Kent) **12** Vereeniging ter Bervordering van de Belangen des Boekhandels (Amsterdam) **13** University of Virginia (Charlottesville) **14** University of California at Los Angeles **15** Generally available

4337 **RICKE, WALTER (Munich & Kottgeisering b. Grafrath) (continued)**
    [1977]   108   ... *Antiq. Musikbücher. Vocalmusikk*
                  (1309)   *1

4338 _____.
    [1977]   109   *Musikbücher, neu und antiquarisch. Portraits*
                  (797)   *1

4339 _____.
    [1976]   110   *Musikbücher, neu und antiquarisch. Portraits*
                  (970)   *1

4340 _____.
    [1977?]   111   *Musikbücher*
                  (1710)   [Ricke]

4341 _____.
    [1978]   112   *Musikbücher. Klavierauszüge*
                  (1282)   *13

4342 _____.
    [1978]   113   *Musikbücher, neu und antiquarisch*
                  (1248)   *1

4343 _____.
    [1978]   114   *Musikbücher, neu und antiquarisch*
                  (1357)   *1,13

4344 _____.
    [1978]   115   *Musikbücher. Antiq. Musikbücher. Denkmäler*
                  (506)   *1

4345 _____.
    [1978]   116   *[New Books]*
                  (1259+K1-95)   *1,13

4346 _____.
    [1978]   117   *[not Music]*
                  ?   ?

4347 _____.
    [1979]   118   *Musikbücher*
                  (763)   [Ricke]

4348 _____.
    [1980]   119   *Antiquarische Musikbücher. Schallplatten*
                  (918)   *1,13

4349 _____.
    [1981]   121   *Antiquar. Musikbücher. Früh und Erstausgaben*
                  (1031)   *1,13

4350 _____.
    [1981]   122   *Antiq. Musikbücher und Musikalen. Orgelnoten*
                  (1012)   *1

4351 _____.
    1981   123   *Antiquarische Musikliteratur. Schallplatten*
                  (810)   *1

4352 _____.
    1982   124   *Neuerscheinungen. Antiquarische Musikbücher*
                  (1222)   *1

---

1 Compiler/State University of New York (Buffalo) **2** The British Library (London) **3** Gemeentemuseum (Den Haag) **4** The Grolier Club (N.Y.C.) **5** Hirsch Collection, British Library (London) **6** D.W. Krummel (Urbana) **7** Library of Congress (Washington, D.C.) **8** Library and Museum of the Performing Arts (N.Y.C.) **9** William Reeves (London) **10** Sibley Library, Eastman School of Music (Rochester) **11** Nigel Simeone (Tunbridge Wells, Kent) **12** Vereeniging ter Bervordering van de Belangen des Boekhandels (Amsterdam) **13** University of Virginia (Charlottesville) **14** University of California at Los Angeles **15** Generally available

4353 **RICKE, WALTER (Munich & Kottgeisering b. Grefrath) (continued)**
       1982   125   *Neuersch. Antiq. Musikbücher. Kammermusik*
                               (1190)   *1
4354 _____.
       1983   126   *Neuersch. Antiq. Musikbücher. Partituren*
                               (1360)   *1
4355 _____.
       1983   127   *Neuersch. Antiq. Musikbücher. Partituren*
                               (947)   *1
4356 _____.
       1984   128   *Neuersch. Antiq. Musiklit. Taschenpartituren*
                               (1421)   *1
4357 _____.
       1984   129   *Neuersch. Antiq.Musikkbücher. Schallplatten*
                               (1170)   *1
4358 **RICORDI e C., G. (Milan)**
       1957   1   *Libreria musicale*
                               (72pp.)   *6,11
4359 _____.
       1957   —   *Suppl. al Catalogo n.1: Libreria musicale*
                               (17pp.)   *6,11
4360 _____.
       1959   2   *Libreria musicale*
                               (105pp.)   *6,11
4361 _____.
       1960   3   *Libreria musicale*
                               (130pp.)   *6,11,12
4362 **RIEDEL, HANS (Berlin)**
       1952   3   *Musikliteratur*
                               (2000)   *1
4363 _____.
       1953/54   4   *Klavierauszüge*
                               (24pp.)   *1
4364 _____.
       1954/55   5   *Moderne Klaviermusik*
                               (27pp.)   *1,9
4365 _____.
       1955   6   *Alte Drucke. Gesamtausg. Denkmäler. Faks.*
                               (2304)   *1,9
4366 _____.
       195_   7   *Orchestermusik-Partituren*
                               (56pp.)   *9
4367 _____.
       1957   8   *Musik und Musikbücher*
                               (1056)   *9,12
4368 _____.
       1960   11   *Musik und Musikbücher*
                               (1698)   *6,12

1 Compiler/State University of New York (Buffalo)   **2** The British Library (London)   **3** Gemeentemuseum
(Den Haag)   **4** The Grolier Club (N.Y.C.)   **5** Hirsch Collection, British Library (London)   **6** D.W.
Krummel (Urbana)   **7** Library of Congress (Washington, D.C.)   **8** Library and Museum of the Performing
Arts (N.Y.C.)   **9** William Reeves (London)   **10** Sibley Library, Eastman School of Music (Rochester)
11 Nigel Simeone (Tunbridge Wells, Kent)   **12** Vereeniging ter Bevordering van de Belangen des
Boekhandels (Amsterdam)   **13** University of Virginia (Charlottesville)   **14** University of California at Los
Angeles   **15** Generally available

4369   **RIEDEL, HANS (Berlin) (continued)**
  1962   13   *Musik und Musikbücher*
                                       (323)   *6,12
4370   _____.
  1964   15   *Dirigier-Partituren*
                                       (96pp.)   *6
4371   _____.
  1967   18   *Wichtige Nachdrucke*
                                       ([24pp.])   *6
4372   _____.
  1973   20   *Musikbücher. Faksimiles. Gesamtausgaben*
                                       (1684)   *1
4373   _____.
  1974   21   *Vocal Scores. Scores. Orchestral Works*
                                       (1974)   *1
4374   _____.
  1975   23   *New and Second-hand Piano-vocal Scores*
                                       (2578)   *13
4375   _____.
  1976   25   *Musikbücher. Periodica. Faksimiles*
                                       (3331)   *13
4376   _____
  1976/77   27   *Dirigierpartituren und Orchestermateriale*
                                       (4464)   *1
4377   _____
  Au/1979   29   *Second-hand Piano-vocal Scores*
                                       (777)   *1
4378   _____.
  1984   33   *Alte Drucke, Faks., Gesamtausg., Zeitschriften*
                                       (1902)   *1
4379   **RIMELL & SON, J. (London)**
  1921?   259   *Music & Drama*
                                       (?)   *12
4380   **RÖHRSCHEID, LUDWIG (Bonn)**
  [1970]   459   *Musikwissenschaft*
                                       (101pp.)   *4,12,13
4381   **ROMER, G. P. (Hertford)**
  1952   86   *Music in Print and Mss.*
                                       (78)   *1,12
4382   **ROOTHAN & CIE., TH. J. (Amsterdam)**
  s.d.   —   *Muziek*
                                       (?)   *12
4383   **ROOY, JAN DE (Leiden)**
  197_   643   *Musique. Histoire. Théorie. Biographie*
                                       (369)   *1,13
4384   _____.
  197_   672   *Musicologie*
                                       (564)   *1,13

---

1 Compiler/State University of New York (Buffalo)   **2** The British Library (London)   **3** Gemeentemuseum (Den Haag)   **4** The Grolier Club (N.Y.C.)   **5** Hirsch Collection, British Library (London)   **6** D.W. Krummel (Urbana)   **7** Library of Congress (Washington, D.C.)   **8** Library and Museum of the Performing Arts (N.Y.C.)   **9** William Reeves (London)   **10** Sibley Library, Eastman School of Music (Rochester)   **11** Nigel Simeone (Tunbridge Wells, Kent)   **12** Vereeniging ter Bervordering van de Belangen des Boekhandels (Amsterdam)   **13** University of Virginia (Charlottesville)   **14** University of California at Los Angeles   **15** Generally available

4385 **ROOY, JAN DE (Leiden) (continued)**
 1974 691 *Musique et chanson*
 (820) *1

4386 _____.
 197_ 756 *Musique. Histoire. Théorie. Biographie*
 (250) *1

4387 **ROSENKILDE OG BAGGER (Copenhagen)**
 [1959] 114 *Ballet. Musik. Theater*
 (1223) *12

4388 _____.
 [1971] 153 *Old and Rare Books on Music*
 (46) *1,12,13

4389 _____.
 1976 178 *Schauplatz der Künste ... Musik. Tanz*
 (170-203+) [H. Baron]

4390 **ROSENTHAL, ALBI (London) [Successor to OTTO HAAS, q.v.]**
 1946 6 *Rare Books*
 (2411-551+) *4,10

4391 _____.
 1948 10 *Rare Books*
 (1503-850) *1,4,6,10,13

4392 _____.
 1950 20 *500 Rare Books and Mss.*
 (i.a.) *1,4,10

4393 _____.
 195_ 22 *Musicology. Rare Original Editions*
 (273) *1,4,6,10,12

4394 _____.
 195_ 29 *Instrumental Music. Books on Instruments*
 (880) *1,4,6,10,12,13

4395 _____.
 195_ 32 *Musicology*
 (273) *1,4,6,10,12

4396 _____.
 s.d. Lists 1 *Music Reference Works*
 (73) *9

4397 _____.
 s.d. do. 5 *Musik Books and Editions*
 (200) [not located]

4398 _____.
 s.d. do.? — *Books & Studies on Greek & Byzantine Music*
 (31) *13

4399 **ROSENTHAL, HEINRICH (Lucerne)**
 s.d. — *Musik [typewritten]*
 (?) *5

4400 **ROSENTHAL, JACQUES (Munich)**
 s.d. N.S.1 *Musique*
 (758) *5,12

---

1 Compiler/State University of New York (Buffalo) **2** The British Library (London) **3** Gemeentemuseum (Den Haag) **4** The Grolier Club (N.Y.C.) **5** Hirsch Collection, British Library (London) **6** D.W. Krummel (Urbana) **7** Library of Congress (Washington, D.C.) **8** Library and Museum of the Performing Arts (N.Y.C.) **9** William Reeves (London) **10** Sibley Library, Eastman School of Music (Rochester) **11** Nigel Simeone (Tunbridge Wells, Kent) **12** Vereeniging ter Bervordering van de Belangen des Boekhandels (Amsterdam) **13** University of Virginia (Charlottesville) **14** University of California at Los Angeles **15** Generally available

4401 **ROSENTHAL, JACQUES (Munich) (continued)**
    s.d.   N.S.   86   *Alte Musik, 1500-1850*
                      (640)   *3,5,6,7,12

4402 _____.
    1934?   N.S.   95   *Humanisme*
                      (?)   *7,10

4403 **ROSENTHAL, LUDWIG (Hilversum)**
    1972   List   7373   *[Plainchant]*
                      (3pp.)   *13

4404 _____.
    1973   do.   7428   *Music*
                      (11pp.)   *13

4405 _____.
    1974   do.   7638   *Music*
                      (5pp.)   *13

4406 **ROSENTHAL, LUDWIG (Munich)**
    s.d.   26   *Musica I*
                      (248pp.)   *4,5,7

4407 _____.
    1880   30   *Musica II*
                      (4257)   *4

4408 _____.
    [1908]   121   *... Musik. Kirchengesang*
                      (1782)   *4,5,6,12

4409 _____.
    1909   130   *Musik*
                      (?)   *4

4410 _____.
    s.d.   150   *Bibliotheca liturgica.*
                      (2v.)   *4,5

4411 _____.
    1913   153   *Alte und neue Musik*
                      (?)   *4,5,7,10,12,13

4412 **ROSENTHAL, R. B. (Lisbon)**
    1969   Bol.   114   *Suplemento (Musica)*
                      (5827-865)   *1

4413 _____.
    1971   do.   125   *Suplemento (Musica. Canto popular)*
                      (9191-261)   *1

4414 **ROSSBERG'SCHEN BUCHHANDLUNG (Leipzig)**
    s.d.   4   *Coll: Küschner, Jos. Theater und Musik*
                      (3024)   *10

4415 **ROSSI, DARIO GIUSEPPE (Rome)**
    1914   —   *Jolie collection de portraits de musiciens*
                      (650)   *3

4416 **ROUNDELAY BOOK AND MUSIC SHOP (Chicago)**
    [196_?]   List   5   *Rare and Early Editions ... Violin Makers*
                      (53)   *6

1 Compiler/State University of New York (Buffalo)   2 The British Library (London)   3 Gemeentemuseum (Den Haag)   4 The Grolier Club (N.Y.C.)   5 Hirsch Collection, British Library (London)   6 D.W. Krummel (Urbana)   7 Library of Congress (Washington, D.C.)   8 Library and Museum of the Performing Arts (N.Y.C.)   9 William Reeves (London)   10 Sibley Library, Eastman School of Music (Rochester)   11 Nigel Simeone (Tunbridge Wells, Kent)   12 Vereeniging ter Bevordering van de Belangen des Boekhandels (Amsterdam)   13 University of Virginia (Charlottesville)   14 University of California at Los Angeles   15 Generally available

4417   **ROUNDELAY BOOK AND MUSIC SHOP (Chicago) (continued)**
       [196.?]   do.   6   *Books on music: The Writings of R. Wagner*
                                      (73)   *6
4418   _____.
       [196.?]   do.   7   *Books on Music: Richard Wagner's Life*
                                      (116)   *6
4419   _____.
       [1964]   do.   8   *The Wagner Collection*
                                      (1016)   *6
4420   **RYMSHA, VITALI (Maywood, CA.)**
       1956   List   3   *Books about Violins and Violin Makers*
                                      (9 lvs.)   *9
4421   **SABA, UMBERTO (Paris)**
       1957   150   *Musica. Danza*
                                      (776))   *12
4422   _____.
       1965   181   *Libro antico. Musica e teatro*
                                      (950)   [IBAK]
4423   _____.
       1966   182   *Libri antichi, Sicilia. Arte. Musica*
                                      (899)   [IBAK]
4424   **SAGGIORI, R. (Meylan, France)**
       8/1974   —   *L'Autographe*
                                      (143, i.a.)   *8
4425   _____.
       12/1974   —   *L'Autographe*
                                      (125, i.a.)   *8
4426   _____.
       4/1975   —   *L'Autographe*
                                      (112, i.a.)   *8
4427   _____.
       n.d.   —   *L'Autographe: Feuilles musicales*
                                      (180)   *8
4428   **SAGOT, EDMOND (Paris)**
       1887   —   *Coll: Vervoitte. Livres. Partitions*
                                      (1027)   *8
4429   _____.
       1892   34   *Musique. Dessins*
                                      (38pp.)   *12
4430   **ST. GOAR, ISAAC (Frankfurt a.M.)**
       1883   57   *[... Musik]*
                                      (780-991)   *5
4431   _____.
       1886   —   *Coll: Oppel. [Musiktheorie]*
                                      (582)   [MfM]
4432   _____.
       1909   103   *Theater und Musik*
                                      (614)   *5

1 Compiler/State University of New York (Buffalo)   **2** The British Library (London)   **3** Gemeentemuseum (Den Haag)   **4** The Grolier Club (N.Y.C.)   **5** Hirsch Collection, British Library (London)   **6** D.W. Krummel (Urbana)   **7** Library of Congress (Washington, D.C.)   **8** Library and Museum of the Performing Arts (N.Y.C.)   **9** William Reeves (London)   **10** Sibley Library, Eastman School of Music (Rochester) **11** Nigel Simeone (Tunbridge Wells, Kent)   **12** Vereeniging ter Bervordering van de Belangen des Boekhandels (Amsterdam)   **13** University of Virginia (Charlottesville)   **14** University of California at Los Angeles   **15** Generally available

4433 **ST. GEORGE'S GALLERY (London)**
    1946   3   *Books on Art and Music*
                    (425-521)   *1

4434 **SALISBURY, JESSE (London)**
    1885   5   *Musical Literature. Topography. Misc.*
                    (134-48 & i.a.)   *4

4435 _____.
    1887   13   *Musical Literature*
                    (136-96 & i.a.)   *4

4436 _____.
    1888   16   *Americana. Drama. Music. Topography*
                    (258-323)   *4

4437 _____.
    1888   17   *Americana. Drama. Music. Topography*
                    (225-321)   *4

4438 _____.
    1888   18   *Americana. Drama. Music. Topography*
                    (323-67)   *4

4439 _____.
    1889   19   *Americana. Drama. Music. Topography*
                    (282-404)   *4

4440 **SALLOCH, WILLIAM (Ossining, N. Y.)**
    1939-40 Lists unn.   *[6 small Lists: Books on Musical History]*
                    (?)   [Salloch]

4441 _____.
    1939-40 Lists unn.   *[3 small Lists: Ballads and Folksongs]*
                    (?)   [Salloch]

4442 _____.
    1941   Cat.   34   *Music and Books on Music*
                    (28pp.)   *10,13

4443 _____.
    1941   35   *Old Ballads, Folksongs, Songsters*
                    (?)   *13

4444 _____.
    1943   41   *Music and Books on Music*
                    (449)   *6,10

4445 _____.
    1944   45   *Early American Music. Songsters. Folksongs*
                    (1-466)   *10

4446 _____.
    1945   47   *Music and Books on Music*
                    (809)   *1,10

4447 _____.
    1945   50   *Renaissance - Humanism - Music & Art*
                    (810-41)   *1

4448 _____.
    1945   51   *Middles Ages - Art - Music - Literature*
                    (208-53)   *1,10

4449	**SALLOCH, WILLIAM (Ossining, N. Y.) (continued)**				
	1946		58	*Music, First & Early Editions. Schumann* (236)	*1,10
4450	———.				
	1947		61	*Music and Books on Music* (809)	*1,10
4451	———.				
	1948		79	*History of Music* (457)	*6,13
4452	———.				
	1949		96	*History of Music* (378)	*1,10
4453	———.				
	1951		104	*History of Music* (402)	*1
4454	———.				
	1952		113	*History of Music* (473)	*1
4455	———.				
	1953.		120	*The Seventeenth Century* (235-79)	*1
4456	———.				
	1953		125	*History of Music* (571)	*1,6
4457	———.				
	1955	Misc.	143	*Summer Miscellany* (502-633)	*6
4458	———.				
	1958	Cat.	164	*History of Music* (352)	*1
4459	———.				
	1958		171	*History of Music* (750)	*1,6,11
4460	———.				
	1959		182	*History of Music* (479)	*6,12
4461	———.				
	1961		198	*World of Music* (523)	*1,12
4462	———.				
	1963		217	*World of Music* (538)	*1,6,13,14
4463	———.				
	1966		237	*World of Music* (444)	*1,6,10,13,14
4464	———.				
	1968		257	*The Seventeenth Century, Pt. 2: Music* (169-213)	*1,14

1 Compiler/State University of New York (Buffalo)   **2** The British Library (London)   **3** Gemeentemuseum (Den Haag)   **4** The Grolier Club (N.Y.C.)   **5** Hirsch Collection, British Library (London)   **6** D.W. Krummel (Urbana)   **7** Library of Congress (Washington, D.C.)   **8** Library and Museum of the Performing Arts (N.Y.C.)   **9** William Reeves (London)   **10** Sibley Library, Eastman School of Music (Rochester) **11** Nigel Simeone (Tunbridge Wells, Kent)   **12** Vereeniging ter Bervordering van de Belangen des Boekhandels (Amsterdam)   **13** University of Virginia (Charlottesville)   **14** University of California at Los Angeles   **15** Generally available

4465   **SALLOCH, WILLIAM (Ossining, N. Y.) (continued)**
   1969   268 *World of Music*
              (279)   *1,6,12,14

4466   _____.
   1972   293 *Drama (including Opera, Ballet)*
              (225)   *1,13,14

4467   _____.
   1973   301 *World of Music, Pt. 1: Early American Music*
              (106)   *1,10,13,14

4468   _____.
   1973   302 *World of Music, Pt. 2: Musical Miscellany*
              (314)   *1,6,10,12,13,14

4469   _____.
   1974   316 *Music. Middle Ages. Renaissance. Baroque*
              (284)   *1,6,10,12,13,14

4470   _____.
   1975   319 *Ancient and Oriental Music*
              (421)   *1,13

4471   _____.
   1975   321 *Music and Musical History, Pt. 3*
              (666)   *1,6,10,13,14

4472   _____.
   1975   323 *Music & Musical History, Pt.4: Opera, etc.*
              (913)   *1,10,13,14

4473   _____.
   1975   324 *From Bach to Bartok*
              (913)   *1,10,13

4474   _____.
   1976   331 *Eighteenth Century, including Music. Ma-Z*
              (450)   *1

4475   _____.
   1976   334 *Music in America*
              (230)   *1,13,14

4476   _____.
   1977   338 *Medieval, Renaissance and Baroque Music*
              (307)   *1,14

4477   _____.
   1977   341 *Bach. American Music*
              (272)   *1,13,14

4478   _____.
   1978   349 *Music of the Twentieth Century*
              (400)   *1,10,13,14

4479   _____.
   1980   361 *World of Music: Rare Music, Books, Mss.*
              (361)   *1,6,14

4480   _____.
   1983   387 *World of Music*
              (410)   *1

1 Compiler/State University of New York (Buffalo)   **2** The British Library (London)   **3** Gemeentemuseum (Den Haag)   **4** The Grolier Club (N.Y.C.)   **5** Hirsch Collection, British Library (London)   **6** D.W. Krummel (Urbana)   **7** Library of Congress (Washington, D.C.)   **8** Library and Museum of the Performing Arts (N.Y.C.)   **9** William Reeves (London)   **10** Sibley Library, Eastman School of Music (Rochester)   **11** Nigel Simeone (Tunbridge Wells, Kent)   **12** Vereeniging ter Bervordering van de Belangen des Boekhandels (Amsterdam)   **13** University of Virginia (Charlottesville)   **14** University of California at Los Angeles   **15** Generally available

4481 **SALOMON, GUSTAV (Dresden)**
      18__   —   *Music*
                                      (140)   *8

4482 _____.
      18__   47   *Geschichte und Theorie der Musik. Portraits*
                                      (483)   *8

4483 _____.
      1883   —   *Coll: Rietz. Autogr. Tonkünstler, etc.*
                                      (?)   *8

4484 **SANDERS & CO. (Oxford)**
      195_   NS 1   *Music and Musical Literature*
                                      (948)   *2,11

4485 _____.
      10/1954   NS 4   *Antiquarian Books, Music and Musical Lit.*
                                      (754-918)   *11

4486 **SANSONI (Florence)**
      1952?   —   *Scaffaleto 3: Teatro e musica*
                                      (566)   *8

4487 **LA SCALA AUTOGRAPHS (Hopewell, N.J.)**
      1976?   7   *Opera [autographs]*
                                      (88)   *8

4488 _____.
      1976   10   *Historic American Performers [autographs]*
                                      (108)   *8

4489 _____.
      1976   11   *Opera [autographs]*
                                      (98)   *8

4490 _____.
      1977?   17   *Wagnerian Singers & Conductors [autographs]*
                                      (86)   *8

4491 _____.
      1/1978   —   *Unsigned Photographs of Opera Singers*
                                      (223)   *8

4492 _____.
      7/1978   —   *Autograph Programmes*
                                      (18)   *8

4493 _____.
      8?/1978   22   *Opera - Theatre - Ballet [autographs]*
                                      (103)   *8

4494 _____.
      11/1978   —   *Christmas Cards, Posters, Photos [autographs]*
                                      (123)   *8

4495 _____.
      4?/1979   24   *Music and Theatre Autographs*
                                      (81)   *8

4496 _____.
      9?/1979   26   *Autograph Musical Quotations*
                                      (69)   *8

---

1 Compiler/State University of New York (Buffalo)   **2** The British Library (London)   **3** Gemeentemuseum (Den Haag)   **4** The Grolier Club (N.Y.C.)   **5** Hirsch Collection, British Library (London)   **6** D.W. Krummel (Urbana)   **7** Library of Congress (Washington, D.C.)   **8** Library and Museum of the Performing Arts (N.Y.C.)   **9** William Reeves (London)   **10** Sibley Library, Eastman School of Music (Rochester)   **11** Nigel Simeone (Tunbridge Wells, Kent)   **12** Vereeniging ter Bevrordering van de Belangen des Boekhandels (Amsterdam)   **13** University of Virginia (Charlottesville)   **14** University of California at Los Angeles   **15** Generally available

4497 **LA SCALA AUTOGRAPHS (Hopewell, N.J.) (continued)**
       3?/1980   28   *Opera, Theatre, Dance, Music [autographs]*
                                (77)   *8
4498 _____.
       11/1981   —   *Opera, Music, Theatre Autographs*
                                (77)   *8
4499 _____.
       3?/1980   32   *Around Wagner, v.2 [autographs]*
                                (71+)   *8
4500 _____.
       5?/1981   33   *Opera and Ballet Autographs*
                                (100)   *8
4501 _____.
       11/1981   —   *Holiday Book Supplement and Autographs*
                                (21+67)   *8
4502 _____.
       6/1982   Hdlst   3   *Composers [autographs]*
                                (26)   *8
4503 _____.
       11/1982   Cat.   —   *Holiday Catalogue [autographs]*
                                (114)   *8
4504 _____.
       3/1983   40   *Opera Composers and Creators [autographs]*
                                (78)   *8
4505 **SCANDINAVIAN MUSIC-CENTRE (Hellerup, Denmark)**
       4/1952   —   *Old and Rare: Instruments. History. Scores*
                                (332)   *8
4506 **SCHAB, WILLIAM H. (N.Y.)**
       s.d.   4   *Original musical Mss. Autographs*
                                (1-42)   *8,10
4507 _____.
       s.d.   6   *Fine, rare old Books, Autographs, Manuscripts*
                                (81-93)   *10
4508 _____.
       s.d.   11   *Rare Books and Mss.*
                                (113-21)   *8,10
4509 _____.
       s.d.   13   *Rare Books and Medieval Manuscripts*
                                (96-113)   *8
4510 _____.
       s.d.   14   *Important fine Books*
                                (136-52)   *8,10
4511 _____.
       s.d.   15   *A Renowned Library from a European Castle*
                                (155-70)   *8
4512 _____.
       s.d.   24   *First and Early Editions. Early Music*
                                (158-75)   *10

---

1 Compiler/State University of New York (Buffalo) **2** The British Library (London) **3** Gemeentemuseum (Den Haag) **4** The Grolier Club (N.Y.C.) **5** Hirsch Collection, British Library (London) **6** D.W. Krummel (Urbana) **7** Library of Congress (Washington, D.C.) **8** Library and Museum of the Performing Arts (N.Y.C.) **9** William Reeves (London) **10** Sibley Library, Eastman School of Music (Rochester) **11** Nigel Simeone (Tunbridge Wells, Kent) **12** Vereeniging ter Bervordering van de Belangen des Boekhandels (Amsterdam) **13** University of Virginia (Charlottesville) **14** University of California at Los Angeles **15** Generally available

4513	**SCHAB, WILLIAM H. (N.Y.) (continued)**			
	s.d.	30	*Early Printed & Illustrated Books. Music* (206-51)	*10
4514	_____.			
	s.d.	41	*Great Books of Art, Science and Music* (153-64)	*10
4515	_____.			
	s.d.	46	*Art, Science, Lit., Theatre, Ballet, Music* (119-58)	*8,10
4516	_____.			
	s.d.	47	*Monuments of Book Illus. Music & Ballet* (158-77)	*10
4517	**SCHEER, LEO (Louisville, Ky.)**			
	s.d.	—	*[Music]* (88)	*8,13
4518	**SCHEIBLE, J. [later ED. NAHR, q.v.] (STUTTGART)**			
	s.d.	96	*Musik. Theater. Tanzkunst* (693)	*12
4519	_____.			
	s.d.	205	*Musik. Dramaturgie. Theater. Tanz* (1029)	*12
4520	_____.			
	s.d.	240	*Literatur Seltenheiten. Musikwissenschaft* (1922)	*5
4521	**SCHLOSS, OSKAR (Munich)**			
	1928	2	*Musik. Literatur. Kunst* (1111)	*12
4522	**SCHLÖHLEIN, MUSIKAMT (Basel)**			
	6/1977	1	*Musikliteratur des 18.-20. Jahrhunderts* (659)	[Baron]
4523	_____.			
	1978?	2	*Vokalmusik, 1: Partituren und Klavierausz.* (452) 1:	*1
4524	_____.			
	1979?	3	*Vokalmusik, 2: Gesanglehren. Vocalisen* (?)	?
4525	_____.			
	1980?	4	*Vokalmusik, 3: Lieder, A-Z* (1213)	*1
4526	_____.			
	3/1983	5	*100 musikalische Sammelstücke* (100)	*1
4527	_____.			
	4/1984	6	*Kinderlieder* (254)	*1
4528	_____.			
	4/1984	7	*Musikalisches Mancherlei* (75)	*1

(SCHMIDT)
4529 - 4544

4529 **SCHMIDT, C. F. (Heilbron. [At *8 as CLASS, J. D. (C. F. SCHMIDT)]**
    s.d.   55   *Verzeichnis antiquarischen Musikalien*
                      (28pp.)   *8

4530 _____.
    s.d.   101   *Verzeichnis einer ... Musikalien-Lagers*
                      (58pp.)   *8

4531 _____.
    1871   126   *Theoretisch und praktische Musikwerke*
                      (?)   ?

4532 _____.
    187_   175   *Bücher ü. Musik*
                      (?)   *5

4533 _____.
    187_   176   *Gesang. Lieder*
                      (?)   *5

4534 _____.
    187_   177   *Claviermusik. Orgel*
                      (?)   *5

4535 _____.
    187_   178   *Orchester- und Instrumentalmusik*
                      (?)   *5

4536 _____.
    1880   180   *Gesangmusik. Kirchenmusik*
                      (?)   *5

4537 _____.
    188_   181   *Musikliteratur*
                      (?)   *5

4538 _____.
    188_   182   *Ein- und zweistimmige Lieder*
                      (?)   *5

4539 _____.
    188_   183   *Claviermusik. Orgel*
                      (?)   *5

4540 _____.
    188_   184   *Orchester-Musik*
                      (?)   *5

4541 _____.
    188_   185   *Instrumental-Musik mit Pianoforte*
                      (?)   *5

4542 _____.
    188_   186   *Instrumental-Musik ohne Pianoforte*
                      (?)   *5

4543 _____.
    188_   187   *Musik-literatur*
                      (?)   *5

4544 _____.
    1883   188   *Vokalmusik*
                      (?)   *5

---

1 Compiler/State University of New York (Buffalo) **2** The British Library (London) **3** Gemeentemuseum (Den Haag) **4** The Grolier Club (N.Y.C.) **5** Hirsch Collection, British Library (London) **6** D.W. Krummel (Urbana) **7** Library of Congress (Washington, D.C.) **8** Library and Museum of the Performing Arts (N.Y.C.) **9** William Reeves (London) **10** Sibley Library, Eastman School of Music (Rochester) **11** Nigel Simeone (Tunbridge Wells, Kent) **12** Vereeniging ter Bervordering van de Belangen des Boekhandels (Amsterdam) **13** University of Virginia (Charlottesville) **14** University of California at Los Angeles **15** Generally available

284

4545 **SCHMIDT, C. F.(Heilbron.) (continued)**
      1899   282   *Musikliteratur. Opern-partituren*
                                    (46pp.)   *8

4546 _____.
      1900   288   *Vocalmusik. Chor-Musik. Lieder*
                                    (98pp.)   *8

4547 _____.
      1901   292   *Kirchenmusik. Theoretische Werke*
                                    (?)   *5

4548 _____.
      1901   294   *Militärmusik. Nachtrag: Orchestermusik*
                                    (?)   *5

4549 _____.
      1901/02   297   *Musikliteratur. Partituren. Opern-partituren*
                                    (54pp.)   *8

4550 _____.
      1903/04   311   *Musikliteratur. Partituren. Opern. Chorwerke*
                                    (62pp.)   *8

4551 _____.
      190_   316   *Kirchenmusik aller Art*
                                    (40pp.)   *5

4552 _____.
      190_   324   *Musikliteratur. Facsimile ältere Werke*
                                    (40pp.)   *5,8

4553 _____.
      1907/08   337   *Musikliteratur. Portraits*
                                    (32pp.)   *3

4554 _____.
      1909-10   350   *Musikliteratur. Portraits.*
                                    (40pp.)   *3

4555 _____.
      1910/11   356   *Musikliteratur. Portraits*
                                    (40pp.)   *3

4556 _____.
      12/1910   —   —   *Mitteilungen aus ...*
                                    (32pp.)   *8

4557 **SCHMORL UND VON SEEFELD NACHFOLGER (Hannover)**
      [1966]   66   *Geschichte. Literatur. Musikwissenschaft*
                                    (1212)   [IBAK]

4558 _____.
      1968   77   *Literatur. Musik. Theater*
                                    (950)   *12

4559 **SCHNASE, ANNEMARIE (Scarsdale, N.Y.)**
      [1960]   3   *Periodicals in ... Music*
                                    (124)   *10,13

4560 _____.
      [1960]   4   *idem.*
                                    (248)   *10,13

4561 SCHNASE, ANNEMARIE (Scarsdale, N.Y.) (continued)

	[196_]	5	*Periodicals in Art - Music - Theatre* (300)	*10
4562	[1961?]	7	*Periodicals* (235)	*6
4563	[196_]	9	*Periodicals* (289)	*6
4564	[1963]	10	*Periodicals in the Field of Music* (355)	*6,13
4565	[196_]	11	*Rare Books* (i.a.)	*6,10
4566	[196_]	12	*Periodicals in the Field of Music* (385)	*6,13
4567	[1965]	14	*Periodicals in the Field of Music* (334)	*6,13
4568	[1967]	20	*Selection of Music Periodicals* (245)	*6,13
4569	[1968]	21	*Selection of Music Periodicals* (514)	*6,13
4570	1969	22	*Selection of Music Periodicals* (551)	*6,13
4571	1969-70	23	*Selection of Music Periodicals* (170)	*13
4572	1970	24	*Music Periodicals* (542)	*10,13
4573	1971	25	*Music Periodicals* (464)	*6,8,13
4574	1972-73	26	*Music Journals* (635)	*13
4575	1973-74	27	*Music Journals* (741)	*10,13
4576	1975-76	28	*Music Periodicals* (744)	*10,13

1 Compiler/State University of New York (Buffalo)   **2** The British Library (London)   **3** Gemeentemuseum (Den Haag)   **4** The Grolier Club (N.Y.C.)   **5** Hirsch Collection, British Library (London)   **6** D.W. Krummel (Urbana)   **7** Library of Congress (Washington, D.C.)   **8** Library and Museum of the Performing Arts (N.Y.C.)   **9** William Reeves (London)   **10** Sibley Library, Eastman School of Music (Rochester) **11** Nigel Simeone (Tunbridge Wells, Kent)   **12** Vereeniging ter Bervordering van de Belangen des Boekhandels (Amsterdam)   **13** University of Virginia (Charlottesville)   **14** University of California at Los Angeles   **15** Generally available

4577 **SCHNEIDER, HANS (Tutzing ü. München)**

| | 1949 | 1 | *Varia* | |
| | | | (588) | [Schneider] |

4578 _____.
| | 1949 | 2 | *Musikliteratur* | |
| | | | (100) | [Schneider] |

4579 _____.
| | 1949 | 3 | *Varia* | |
| | | | (575) | [Schneider] |

4580 _____.
| | 1949 | 4 | *Varia* | |
| | | | (735) | [Schneider] |

4581 _____.
| | 1950 | 5 | *Varia* | |
| | | | (384) | [Schneider] |

4582 _____.
| | 1950 | 6 | *Varia* | |
| | | | (1100) | [Schneider] |

4583 _____.
| | 1950? | 8a[7] | *Varia* | |
| | | | (305) | [Schneider] |

4584 _____.
| | 195_ | 8 | *Musikalische Frühdrucke. Autographen. Faks.* | |
| | | | (433) | *1,10 |

4585 _____.
| | 195_ | 9 | *Musikwissenschaft. Bibliographie* | |
| | | | (490) | *1,10 |

4586 _____.
| | 195_ | 10 | *Musiker Biographien* | |
| | | | (490) | *1,10 |

4587 _____.
| | 1953 | 11 | *Gesamtausgaben.Partituren* | |
| | | | (908) | *1,10 |

4588 _____.
| | 1953 | 12 | *Klavierauszüge. Taschenpartituren* | |
| | | | (447) | *1,10 |

4589 _____.
| | 1953 | 13 | *Musikliteratur* | |
| | | | (908) | *1,10 |

4590 _____.
| | 1953 | 17 | *Musikliteratur* | |
| | | | (1540) | *1,10 |

4591 _____.
| | 1953 | 18 | *Musikliteratur* | |
| | | | (208) | *1,10 |

4592 _____.
| | 1953 | 19 | *Dirigierpartituren* | |
| | | | (158) | *1,10 |

1 Compiler/State University of New York (Buffalo)   2 The British Library (London)   3 Gemeentemuseum (Den Haag)   4 The Grolier Club (N.Y.C.)   5 Hirsch Collection, British Library (London)   6 D.W. Krummel (Urbana)   7 Library of Congress (Washington, D.C.)   8 Library and Museum of the Performing Arts (N.Y.C.)   9 William Reeves (London)   10 Sibley Library, Eastman School of Music (Rochester) 11 Nigel Simeone (Tunbridge Wells, Kent)   12 Vereeniging ter Bevordering van de Belangen des Boekhandels (Amsterdam)   13 University of Virginia (Charlottesville)   14 University of California at Los Angeles   15 Generally available

4593   **SCHNEIDER, HANS (Tutzing ü. München) (continued)**

	1953	22	*Musik des l6.-l9. Jahrhunderts*	
			(149)	*1,10
4594 _____.				
	1953	23	*Musikgeschichte. Musikwissenschaft*	
			(492)	*1,10
4595 _____.				
	1953	24	*Musiker-Autographen*	
			(272)	*1,10
4596 _____.				
	1953	25	*Musikalische Seltenheiten*	
			(100)	*1,10
4597 _____.				
	1954?	26	*Musiker-Biographien, 1: A-Haydn*	
			(412)	*1,10
4598 _____.				
	1954?	27	*Musiker-biographien, 2: Hein-Z*	
			(415)	*1,10
4599 _____.				
	1954	28	*Denkmäler & Gesamtausgaben*	
			(47)	*1,10
4600 _____.				
	1954	29	*Musikwissenschaft. Musikgeschichte*	
			(101)	*1,10
4601 _____.				
	1954	30	*Kammermusik, l7.-l9. Jahrhunderts. Erstausg.*	
			(193)	*1,10,13
4602 _____.				
	1954	31	*Vokalmusik*	
			(256)	*1,10
4603 _____.				
	1954	32	*Mss.-Ungedruckte Kammermusik d. l8.Jahrhdts.*	
			(160)	*1,10
4604 _____.				
	1954	33	*Musik-geschichte, -wissenschaft. Biograph.*	
			(464)	*1,10
4605 _____.				
	1954	34	*Musikliteratur. Denkmäler. Gesamtausgaben*	
			(180)	*1,10,13
4606 _____.				
	1954	35	*Musiktheorie*	
			(788)	*1,10,13
4607 _____.				
	1954	36	*Vokalmusik [with 2 Supplements]*	
			(1102)	*1,6,10,13
4608 _____.				
	1954	37	*Biographien, Schriften und Briefe*	
			(600)	*1,6,10,13

4609	SCHNEIDER, HANS (Tutzing ü. München) (continued)			
	1954	38	*Kammermusik [with Supplement]* (558)	*1,10,13
4610	_____. 1954	39	*Musikalische Faksimiles und Bildwerke* (83)	*6
4611	_____. 1954	40	*Partituren* (491)	*1,6,10
4612	_____. 1954	41	*Musikliteratur und Musikhandschriften* (338)	*1,6,10,13
4613	_____. 1954	42	*Alte Musik* (280)	*1,6,10,13
4614	_____. 1954	43	*Musiktheorie* (732)	*1,6,10,13
4615	_____. 1955	44	*Biographien, Schriften und Briefe* (313)	*1,6,10,13
4616	_____. 1955	45	*Musikalische Seltenheiten* (144)	*1,6,10,13
4617	_____. 1955	46	*Musik der letzte 80 Jahre* (618)	*1,6,10,13
4618	_____. 1955	47	*Musikliteratur* (312)	*1,6,10,13
4619	_____. 1956	48	*Zeitschriften, Almanache, etc.* (371)	*1,6,10,13
4620	_____. 1956	49	*Musikdrucke und Mss., l6.-l8. Jahrhunderts* (140)	*1,6,10,13
4621	_____. 1956	50	*Musikliteratur* (278)	*1,6,10,13
4622	_____. 1956	51	*Mozart* (600)	*1,6,10,13
4623	_____. 1956	52	*Coll: Krauss, C. Dirigierpartituren* (725)	*1,6,10,13
4624	_____. 1956	53	*Musikdrucke und Mss. des l9. Jahrhunderts* (290)	*1,6,10,13

1 Compiler/State University of New York (Buffalo)   2 The British Library (London)   3 Gemeentemuseum (Den Haag)   4 The Grolier Club (N.Y.C.)   5 Hirsch Collection, British Library (London)   6 D.W. Krummel (Urbana)   7 Library of Congress (Washington, D.C.)   8 Library and Museum of the Performing Arts (N.Y.C.)   9 William Reeves (London)   10 Sibley Library, Eastman School of Music (Rochester)   11 Nigel Simeone (Tunbridge Wells, Kent)   12 Vereeniging ter Bervordering van de Belangen des Boekhandels (Amsterdam)   13 University of Virginia (Charlottesville)   14 University of California at Los Angeles   15 Generally available

4625	**SCHNEIDER, HANS (Tutzing ü. München) (continued)**			
	1956	54	*Musikalische Seltenheiten* (100)	*1,6,10,13
4626	_____.			
	1956	55	*Musik-geschichte, -theorie, -wissenschaft* (535)	*1,6,10,13
4627	_____.			
	1957?	56	*Mss. u. Autographe. Musikdrucke. Musiklit.* (363)	*1,6,10,13
4628	_____.			
	1957?	57	*Biographien* (477)	*1,6,10,13
4629	_____.			
	1957	58	*Klavierauszuege* (551)	*1,6,10,13
4630	_____.			
	1957	59	*Musikliteratur* (260)	*1,6,10,13
4631	_____.			
	1957	60	*Instrumentalmusik* (226)	*1,6,10,13
4632	_____.			
	1957	61	*Vokalmusik* (262)	*1,6,10,13
4633	_____.			
	1957	62	*Musikliteratur* (1152)	*1,6,10,13
4634	_____.			
	1957	63	*Opern. Klavierausz. Partituren. Libretti* (691)	*1,6,10,13
4635	_____.			
	1958	64	*Klavierauszüge* (950)	*1,6,10,13
4636	_____.			
	1958	65	*Kammermusik* (708)	*1,6,10,13
4637	_____.			
	1958	66	*Klaviermusik* (405)	*1,6,10,13
4638	_____.			
	1958	67	*Musikliteratur. Denkmäler. Gesamtausgaben* (466)	*1,6,10,13
4639	_____.			
	1958	68	*Musikliteratur* (321)	*1.6,10,13
4640	_____.			
	1958	69	*Musik aus fünf Jahrhunderten* (441)	*1,6,10,13

1 Compiler/State University of New York (Buffalo) **2** The British Library (London) **3** Gemeentemuseum (Den Haag) **4** The Grolier Club (N.Y.C.) **5** Hirsch Collection, British Library (London) **6** D.W. Krummel (Urbana) **7** Library of Congress (Washington, D.C.) **8** Library and Museum of the Performing Arts (N.Y.C.) **9** William Reeves (London) **10** Sibley Library, Eastman School of Music (Rochester) **11** Nigel Simeone (Tunbridge Wells, Kent) **12** Vereeniging ter Bervordering van de Belangen des Boekhandels (Amsterdam) **13** University of Virginia (Charlottesville) **14** University of California at Los Angeles **15** Generally available

4641 **SCHNEIDER, HANS (Tutzing ü. München) (continued)**

	1958	70	*Musikdrucke. Mss. Musikliteratur*	
			(500)	*1,6,10,13
4642	_____.			
	1958	71	*Musikerautographen*	
			(135)	*1,10,13
4643	_____.			
	1959	72	*Musikerautographen. Mss. Partituren*	
			(5000)	*1,6,10,13
4644	_____.			
	1959	73	*Musikliteratur*	
			(585)	*1,6,13
4645	_____.			
	1959	74	*[Not Published]*	
4646	_____.			
	[1960]	75	*Coll.: Erdmann, E.*	
			(1000)	*10
4647	_____.			
	1961	76	*Musikerautographen. Musikdrucke. Musiklit.*	
			(1140)	*1,6,10,13
4648	_____.			
	1961	77	*Vokalmusik*	
			(1017)	*1,6,10,13
4649	_____.			
	1962	78	*Musikliteratur*	
			(814)	*1,6,10,13
4650	_____.			
	1962	79	*Instrumentalmusik*	
			(500)	*1,6,10,13
4651	_____.			
	1962	80	*M.-autographen. Dirigierpartituren. M.-lit.*	
			(684)	*1,6,10,13
4652	_____.			
	1962	81	*Musikerautographen. Musiklit. Musikdrucke*	
			(1054)	*1,6,10,13
4653	_____.			
	1962	82	*Musikalische Bibliographie*	
			(357)	*1,6,10,13
4654	_____.			
	1962	83	*Coll.: Haas, R. Musikliteratur*	
			(634)	*1,6,10,13
4655	_____.			
	1962	84	*Musikalische Seltenheiten*	
			(100)	*1,6,10,13
4656	_____.			
	1962	85	*Musikliteratur*	
			(462)	*1,6,10,13

1 Compiler/State University of New York (Buffalo)   2 The British Library (London)   3 Gemeentemuseum (Den Haag)   4 The Grolier Club (N.Y.C.)   5 Hirsch Collection, British Library (London)   6 D.W. Krummel (Urbana)   7 Library of Congress (Washington, D.C.)   8 Library and Museum of the Performing Arts (N.Y.C.)   9 William Reeves (London)   10 Sibley Library, Eastman School of Music (Rochester)   11 Nigel Simeone (Tunbridge Wells, Kent)   12 Vereeniging ter Bevordering van de Belangen des Boekhandels (Amsterdam)   13 University of Virginia (Charlottesville)   14 University of California at Los Angeles   15 Generally available

4657   **SCHNEIDER, HANS (Tutzing ü. München) (continued)**
       1962   86   *Dirigierpartituren*
                               (461)   *1,6,10,13

4658   _____.
       1962   87   *Musikliteratur*
                               (705)   *1,6,13

4659   _____.
       1962   88   *Musikliteratur*
                               (367)   *1,6,13

4660   _____.
       1962   89   *Oper und Oratorium*
                               (1123)   *1,6,13

4661   _____.
       1962   90   *Klaviermusik*
                               (210)   *1,6,13

4662   _____.
       1963?   91   *Musikliteratur*
                               (687)   *1,6,13

4663   _____.
       1963?   92   *Kammermusik*
                               (465)   *1,13

4664   _____.
       1963?   93   *Partituren*
                               (216)   *1,6,13

4665   _____.
       1963   94   *Vokalmusik*
                               (530)   *1,6,13

4666   _____.
       1963   95   *Klaviermusik*
                               (292)   *1,6,13

4667   _____.
       1963   96   *Coll.: Hamel, F. Musikliteratur*
                               (890)   *1,6,13

4668   _____.
       1963   97   *Musikliteratur*
                               (303)   *1,6,13

4669   _____.
       1963   98   *Musikalische Seltenheiten*
                               (64pp.)   *1,6,13

4670   _____.
       1964   99   *Erstausgaben und Frühdrucke Chopin et al*
                               (824)   *1,6

4671   _____.
       1964   1   00   *Johannes Brahms*
                               (1750)   *1,6

4672   _____.
       1964   1   01   *Coll.: Anderson, E. Bücher. Musikdrucke*
                               (815)   *1, 6

4673 **SCHNEIDER, HANS (Tutzing ü. München) (continued)**
       1964   1   02   *Musikliteratur*
                                 (545)   *1,6

4674 _____.
       1964   1   03   *Musikliteratur*
                                 (354)   *1,6

4675 _____.
       1964   1   04   *Musikdrucke*
                                 (320)   *1,6

4676 _____.
       1964   1   05   *Coll.: Haraszti, Emil. Neuerwerbungen*
                                 (92)   *1,6

4677 _____.
       1965   1   06   *Musikerautographen*
                                 (333)   *1,6

4678 _____.
       1965   1   07   *Musikliteratur*
                                 (562)   *1,6

4679 _____.
       1965   1   08   *Schöner und seltener Musikdrucke*
                                 (156)   *1,6

4680 _____.
       1965   1   09   *Musik der letzten hundert Jahre*
                                 (816)   *1,6

4681 _____.
       1965   1   10   *Musikalisches Quodlibet*
                                 (594)   *1,6

4682 _____.
       1965   1   11   *Musikgeschichte. Musikwissenschaft*
                                 (1000)   *1,6

4683 _____.
       1965   1   12   *Biographien. Faksimiles. Portraits*
                                 (1600)   *1,6

4684 _____.
       1965   1   13   *Musikalisches Tafel-Confect*
                                 (1283)   *1,6

4685 _____.
       1965   1   14   *Musikliteratur*
                                 (640)   *1,6,13

4686 _____.
       1965   1   15   *Musikalisches Seltenheiten*
                                 (100)   *1,6,13

4687 _____.
       1965   1   16   *Oper und Oratorium*
                                 (721)   *1

4688 _____.
       1966?   1   17   *Musikliteratur. Musikzeitschriften*
                                 (861)   *1,6,13

1 Compiler/State University of New York (Buffalo)   **2** The British Library (London)   **3** Gemeentemuseum (Den Haag)   **4** The Grolier Club (N.Y.C.)   **5** Hirsch Collection, British Library (London)   **6** D.W. Krummel (Urbana)   **7** Library of Congress (Washington, D.C.)   **8** Library and Museum of the Performing Arts (N.Y.C.)   **9** William Reeves (London)   **10** Sibley Library, Eastman School of Music (Rochester)   **11** Nigel Simeone (Tunbridge Wells, Kent)   **12** Vereeniging ter Bervordering van de Belangen des Boekhandels (Amsterdam)   **13** University of Virginia (Charlottesville)   **14** University of California at Los Angeles   **15** Generally available

4689 **SCHNEIDER, HANS (Tutzing ü. München) (continued)**

	1966?	1	18	*Klaviermusik. Kammermusik*
				(684)	*1,6

4690 _____.

	1966	1	19	*Coll.: Mozart Sohn. Erst- und Frühdrucke*
				(384)	[IBAK]

4691 _____.

	1966	1	20	*Musikdrucke seit 1850*
				(700)	*1,6,13

4692 _____.

	1966	1	21	*Musikerautographen aus vier Jahrhunderts*
				(200)	*1,6,13

4693 _____.

	1966	1	22	*Musikalisches Lustwäldchen*
				(537)	*1,6,13

4694 _____.

	1966	1	23	*Partituren*
				(1000)	*1,6,13

4695 _____.

	1966	1	24	*Musikliteratur. Seltene Klavierauszüge*
				(660)	*1,6,13

4696 _____.

	1966	1	25	*Autographen aus verschiedenen Gebieten*
				(400)	*1,6,13

4697 _____.

	1966	1	26	*Coll.: Jolles, Henri*
				(1950)	*1,6

4698 _____.

	1966	1	27	*Coll.: Schreinzer, K. Kammermusik, 1.Tl.*
				(888)	*1

4699 _____.

	1967	1	28	*Musikalische Selenheiten. Autographen*
				(55)	*1,6

4700 _____.

	1967	1	29	*Musikalische Mancherley*
				(1600)	*1,6

4701 _____.

	1967	1	30	*Musikalisches Quodlibet. Erstausg. Autogr.*
				(535)	*1,6

4702 _____.

	1967	1	31	*Musikliteratur. Violinliteratur. Faksimiles*
				(512)	*1,6

4703 _____.

	1967	1	32	*Musikalisches Seltenheiten*
				(132)	*1,6

4704 _____.

	1967	1	33	*Wertvolle Kammermusik, 2ter Tl.*
				(1321)	*6,14

---

1 Compiler/State University of New York (Buffalo)   2 The British Library (London)   3 Gemeentemuseum (Den Haag)   4 The Grolier Club (N.Y.C.)   5 Hirsch Collection, British Library (London)   6 D.W. Krummel (Urbana)   7 Library of Congress (Washington, D.C.)   8 Library and Museum of the Performing Arts (N.Y.C.)   9 William Reeves (London)   10 Sibley Library, Eastman School of Music (Rochester)   11 Nigel Simeone (Tunbridge Wells, Kent)   12 Vereeniging ter Bervordering van de Belangen des Boekhandels (Amsterdam)   13 University of Virginia (Charlottesville)   14 University of California at Los Angeles   15 Generally available

4705 **SCHNEIDER, HANS (Tutzing ü. München) (continued)**

	1967	1	34	*[In Japanese]*

4706 _____.

	1967		135	*Musikliteratur. Musikalisches Frühdrucke*
				(714) *1,6

4707 _____.

	1967		136	*Musiker-autographen. Mss. und Briefe*
				(644) *1,6

4708 _____.

	1968		137	*Coll.: Ney, Elly*
				(2216) *1,6

4709 _____.

	1968	1	38	*Musikliteratur. Frühdrucke*
				(381) *1,6

4710 _____.

	1969	1	39	*Musikliteratur. Frühdrucke*
				(280) *1,6

4711 _____.

	1969	1	40	*Coll.: Markgrafen zu Limpurg.*
				(550) *1,6,10

4712 _____.

	1969	1	41	*250 Jahre Breitkopf & Härtel*
				(250) *1,6,10

4713 _____.

	1969	1	42	*Autographen aus verschiedenen Gebieten*
				(341) *1,10

4714 _____.

	1969	1	43	*Erstausgabe. Frühdrucke und Ms.*
				(353) *1,10

4715 _____.

	1969	1	44	*Musikliteratur, A-E*
				(977) *1,10,13

4716 _____.

	1969	1	45	*Musikliteratur, F-K*
				(950) *1,10,13

4717 _____.

	1969	1	46	*Musikliteratur, L-R*
				(1003) *1,10,13

4718 _____.

	1969	1	47	*Musikliteratur, S-Z*
				(1355) *1,10,13

4719 _____.

	1970	1	48	*Faks. Denkmäler. Gesamtausg. Zetschriften*
				(837) *1,10,13

4720 _____.

	1970	1	49	*Erst- und Frühdrucke*
				(263) *1,10,13

1 Compiler/State University of New York (Buffalo)   2 The British Library (London)   3 Gemeentemuseum (Den Haag)   4 The Grolier Club (N.Y.C.)   5 Hirsch Collection, British Library (London)   6 D.W. Krummel (Urbana)   7 Library of Congress (Washington, D.C.)   8 Library and Museum of the Performing Arts (N.Y.C.)   9 William Reeves (London)   10 Sibley Library, Eastman School of Music (Rochester) 11 Nigel Simeone (Tunbridge Wells, Kent)   12 Vereeniging ter Bevordering van de Belangen des Boekhandels (Amsterdam)   13 University of Virginia (Charlottesville)   14 University of California at Los Angeles   15 Generally available

4721   **SCHNEIDER, HANS (Tutzing ü. München) (continued)**
      1970   1   50   *Musica noster amor*
                         (95)   *1,10,13

4722   _____ .
      1970   1   51   *Musikalisches Quodlibet*
                         (3471)   *1,10,13

4723   _____ .
      1970   1   52   *Musikalische Blumenlese*
                         (97)   *1

4724   _____ .
      1970   1   53   *200 Jahre B. Schott's Söhne*
                         (1910)   *1

4725   _____ .
      1970   1   54   *Musikliteratur*
                         (989)   *1

4726   _____ .
      1970   1   55   *Klavierauszüge. Klavier- und Orgelmusik*
                         (1530)   *1

4727   _____ .
      1970   1   56   *Musikerautographen. Manuskripte*
                         (750)   *1

4728   _____ .
      1970   1   57   *Kammermusik*
                         (2060)   *1,10

4729   _____ .
      1970   1   58   *Dirigierpartituren*
                         (1756)   *1,10

4730   _____ .
      1971   1   59   *Erst- und Frühdrucke*
                         (300)   *1,10

4731   _____ .
      1971   1   60   *Coll.: Georg V, Koenig. Musikliteratur*
                         (321)   *1

4732   _____ .
      1971   1   61   *Coll.: George V, Koenig. Musikliteratur*
                         (948)   *1

4733   _____ .
      1971   1   62   *Musikerautographen. Mss. Briefe*
                         (400)   *1

4734   _____ .
      1971   1   63   *Sumer is icumen in*
                         (366)   *1

4735   _____ .
      1971   1   64   *Coll.: Ivoguen & Raucheisen. Deutsche Lied*
                         (888)   *1

4736   _____ .
      1971   1   65   *Historische Musikinstrumente. Sammelstücke*
                         (307)   *1

1 Compiler/State University of New York (Buffalo)   **2** The British Library (London)   **3** Gemeentemuseum (Den Haag)   **4** The Grolier Club (N.Y.C.)   **5** Hirsch Collection, British Library (London)   **6** D.W. Krummel (Urbana)   **7** Library of Congress (Washington, D.C.)   **8** Library and Museum of the Performing Arts (N.Y.C.)   **9** William Reeves (London)   **10** Sibley Library, Eastman School of Music (Rochester)   **11** Nigel Simeone (Tunbridge Wells, Kent)   **12** Vereeniging ter Bervordering van de Belangen des Boekhandels (Amsterdam)   **13** University of Virginia (Charlottesville)   **14** University of California at Los Angeles   **15** Generally available

4737 SCHNEIDER, HANS (Tutzing ü. München) (continued)

4737	1971	1	66	*Tutzinger Tafelconfekt* (128)	*1
4738	1971	1	67	*Musik-autographen* (250)	*1
4739	1972	1	68	*Musikliteratur. Partituren* (1526)	*1,13
4740	1972	1	69	*Klaviermusik des 19. Jahrhunderts* (563)	*1
4741	1972	1	70	*Musiker-autographen* (400)	*1
4742	1972	1	71	*Kammermusik* (447)	*1
4743	1972	1	72	*Olimpia und andere schöne Musiksachen* (164)	*1
4744	1972	1	73	*Musikliteratur* (849)	*1
4745	1972	1	74	*Oper und Oratorium* (286)	[Schneider]
4746	1972	1	75	*Musikerautographen* (206)	*1
4747	1973	1	76	*Klaviermusik in Erst- und Frühdrucken* (450)	*1
4748	1973	1	77	*Max Reger zu seinen 100 Geburtstag* (333)	*1
4749	1973	1	78	*Kammermusik* (337)	*1
4750	1973	1	79	*Musikliteratur.Klavier-ausz.* (763)	*1
4751	1973	1	80	*Musikerautographen* (289)	*1
4752	1973	1	81	*Vokalmusik* (336)	*1

1 Compiler/State University of New York (Buffalo)   2 The British Library (London)   3 Gemeentemuseum (Den Haag)   4 The Grolier Club (N.Y.C.)   5 Hirsch Collection, British Library (London)   6 D.W. Krummel (Urbana)   7 Library of Congress (Washington, D.C.)   8 Library and Museum of the Performing Arts (N.Y.C.)   9 William Reeves (London)   10 Sibley Library, Eastman School of Music (Rochester)   11 Nigel Simeone (Tunbridge Wells, Kent)   12 Vereeniging ter Bervordering van de Belangen des Boekhandels (Amsterdam)   13 University of Virginia (Charlottesville)   14 University of California at Los Angeles   15 Generally available

4753 **SCHNEIDER, HANS (Tutzing ü. München) (continued)**
       1973   1   82   *Coll: Danckert, Werner. Musikbilbiothek*   *1
                                 (915)
4754 _____.
       1973   1   83   *Musikalische Erst- und Frühdrucke*   *1,14
                                 (179)
4755 _____.
       1974   1   84   *Klaviermusik des 19. Jahrhunderts*   *1
                                 (384)
4756 _____.
       1974   1   85   *Kammermusik*   *1
                                 (388)
4757 _____.
       1974   1   86   *Musikliteratur. Partituren. Klaviermusik*   *1
                                 (920)
4758 _____.
       [1975]   1   87   *Sumer is (abermals) icumen in*   *1,13
                                 (360)
4759 _____.
       1975   1   88   *Robert Schumann*   *1
                                 (256)
4760 _____.
       1975   1   89   *Musikdrucke*   *1,13
                                 (500)
4761 _____.
       1975   1   90   *Coll: Pringsheim, H. Musikliteratur*   *1
                                 (695)
4762 _____.
       1975   1   91   *Musikverlag N. Simrock*   *1
                                 (745)
4763 _____.
       1975   1   92   *Musikerautographen*   *1
                                 (300)
4764 _____.
       1975   1   93   *Frühausgabe. Musikliteratur. Klavierausz.*   *1,13
                                 (1035)
4765 _____.
       1975   1   94   *Richard Strauss, 1. Tl: Mss. und Briefe*   *1
                                 (131)
4766 _____.
       1975   1   95   *Kammermusik*   *1
                                 (379)
4767 _____.
       1975   1   96   *Musik zum Jahre der Frau*   *1
                                 (218)
4768 _____.
       1976   1   97   *Klaviermusik*   *1
                                 (440)

1 Compiler/State University of New York (Buffalo)   2 The British Library (London)   3 Gemeentemuseum
(Den Haag)   4 The Grolier Club (N.Y.C.)   5 Hirsch Collection, British Library (London)   6 D.W.
Krummel (Urbana)   7 Library of Congress (Washington, D.C.)   8 Library and Museum of the Performing
Arts (N.Y.C.)   9 William Reeves (London)   10 Sibley Library, Eastman School of Music (Rochester)
11 Nigel Simeone (Tunbridge Wells, Kent)   12 Vereeniging ter Bervordering van de Belangen des
Boekhandels (Amsterdam)   13 University of Virginia (Charlottesville)   14 University of California at Los
Angeles   15 Generally available

4769 **SCHNEIDER, HANS (Tutzing ü. München) (continued)**
       1976   1   98   *Musikliteratur*
                                (1386)   *1

4770 _____.
       1976   1   99   *Musiker-autographen*
                                (400)   *1

4771 _____.
       1976   2   00   *Musikalisch Sammelstücke*
                                (200)   *1

4772 _____.
       1976   2   01   *Musikalisches Quodlibet. Bücher. Autographen*
                                (2376)   *1

4773 _____.
       1976   2   02   *Instrumentalmusik*
                                (611)   *1

4774 _____.
       1976   203   *Musikalische Mancherley*
                                (111)   *1

4775 _____.
       1976   204   *Musiker-autographen*
                                (279)   [Schneider]

4776 _____.
       1977   205   *75 Jahre Universal Edition*
                                (1840)   *1

4777 _____.
       1977   206   *Einige schöne Musiksachen*
                                (64)   *1

4778 _____.
       1977   207   *Coll: Mies, Prof. Dr. Paul. Musikbibliothek*
                                (2294)   *1

4779 _____.
       1977   208   *Partituren. Kammermusik. Bücher. Autographen*
                                (989)   *1

4780 _____.
       1977   209   *Coll: Diaghilev, et al. Opernpartituren*
                                (600)   *1

4781 _____.
       1977   210   *Richard Wagner, 1.Tl.: Dokumente 1829-1849*
                                (31)   *1

4782 _____.
       1977   211   *Seltene Musikdrucke*
                                (172)   *1

4783 _____.
       1977   212   *Musikerautographen*
                                (185)   *1

4784 _____.
       1978   213   *Klaviermusik*
                                (966)   *1

4785 **SCHNEIDER, HANS (Tutzing ü. München) (continued)**
       1978   214   *Kammermusik*
                                (288)   *1
4786 _____.
       1978   215   *Richard Wagner, 2.Tl.: Dokumente 1850-1864*
                                (76)   *1
4787 _____.
       1978   216   *Klavierauszüge*
                                (1875)   *1
4788 _____.
       1978   217   *Partituren. Vokalmusik*
                                (306)   *1
4789 _____.
       1978   218   *Coll: Aign, W. Wagner-Sammlung. Musiklit.*
                                (1130)   *1
4790 _____.
       1978   219   *Kleinere Musikerautographen*
                                (610)   *1
4791 _____.
       1978   220   *Abermals kleinere Musikerautographen*
                                (777)   *1
4792 _____.
       1978   221   *Partituren*
                                (692)   *1
4793 _____.
       1978   222   *Gruss an die Schweiz*
                                (233)   *1
4794 _____.
       1978   223   *Richard Wagner, 3.Tl.: Dokumente 1865-1883*
                                (150)   *1
4795 _____.
       1978   224   *Franz Schubert*
                                (457)   *1
4796 _____.
       1978   225   *Musikerautographen*
                                (229)   *1
4797 _____.
       1978   226   *Oper und Oratorium*
                                (1126)   *1
4798 _____.
       1978   227   *Musikalisches Quodlibet*
                                (1983)   *1
4799 _____.
       1979   228   *Schöne und seltene Musikdrucke*
                                (139)   *1
4800 _____.
       1979   229   *Coll: Engel, Hans. Musikbibliothek*
                                (1208)   *1

1 Compiler/State University of New York (Buffalo)   2 The British Library (London)   3 Gemeentemuseum (Den Haag)   4 The Grolier Club (N.Y.C.)   5 Hirsch Collection, British Library (London)   6 D.W. Krummel (Urbana)   7 Library of Congress (Washington, D.C.)   8 Library and Museum of the Performing Arts (N.Y.C.)   9 William Reeves (London)   10 Sibley Library, Eastman School of Music (Rochester)   11 Nigel Simeone (Tunbridge Wells, Kent)   12 Vereeniging ter Bervordering van de Belangen des Boekhandels (Amsterdam)   13 University of Virginia (Charlottesville)   14 University of California at Los Angeles   15 Generally available

4801   **SCHNEIDER, HANS (Tutzing ü. München) (continued)**
      1979   230   *Vokalmusik*
                                  (393)   **1*

4802   _____.
      1979   231   *Klaviermusik*
                                  (600)   **1*

4803   _____.
      1979   232   *Musikerautographen*
                                  (179)   **1*

4804   _____.
      1979   233   *Musikalischer Schrebergarten*
                                  (710)   **1*

4805   _____.
      1979   234   *Bücher, älter als 100 Jahre*
                                  (666)   **1*

4806   _____.
      1979   235   *Musikverlag André*
                                  (437)   **1*

4807   _____.
      1979   236   *Musikerautographen*
                                  (303)   **1*

4808   _____.
      1979   237   *Musikdrucke. Musikliteratur*
                                  (187)   **1*

4809   _____.
      1980   238   *Erst- und Frühdrucke*
                                  (192)   **1*

4810   _____.
      1980   239   *Bücher. Musikalien. Autographen*
                                  (2161)   **1*

4811   _____.
      1980   240   *Musikalisch Albumblätter*
                                  (363)   **1*

4812   _____.
      1980   241   *Bedeutende Musikerautographen*
                                  (86)   **1*

4813   _____.
      1980   242   *Kammermusik, 1.Tl.: A-L*
                                  (409)   **1*

4814   _____.
      1980   243   *Musik f. Kenner und Liebhaber*
                                  (100)   **1*

4815   _____.
      1980   244   *Kammermusik, 2.Tl.: M-Z*
                                  (906)   **1*

4816   _____.
      1980   245   *Musikliteratur. Klavierauszüge*
                                  (1465)   **1*

---

1 Compiler/State University of New York (Buffalo)   **2** The British Library (London)   **3** Gemeentemuseum (Den Haag)   **4** The Grolier Club (N.Y.C.)   **5** Hirsch Collection, British Library (London)   **6** D.W. Krummel (Urbana)   **7** Library of Congress (Washington, D.C.)   **8** Library and Museum of the Performing Arts (N.Y.C.)   **9** William Reeves (London)   **10** Sibley Library, Eastman School of Music (Rochester) **11** Nigel Simeone (Tunbridge Wells, Kent)   **12** Vereeniging ter Bervordering van de Belangen des Boekhandels (Amsterdam)   **13** University of Virginia (Charlottesville)   **14** University of California at Los Angeles   **15** Generally available

4817	**SCHNEIDER, HANS (Tutzing ü. München) (continued)**			
	1980	246	*Musikerautographen, A-L* (200)	*1
4818	_____. 1980	247	*Aufführungs-Materialen* (756)	*1
4819	_____. 1981	248	*Musikalische Lehr- und Studienwerke* (565)	*1
4820	_____. 1981	249	*Musiker-Autographen, M-Z* (250)	*1
4821	_____. 1981	250	*Musiker-Autographen* (25)	*1
4822	_____. 1981	251	*Klaviermusik ... auch Werke für Orgel* (786)	*1
4823	_____. 1981	252	*Oper und Operette ... Handschriften* (355)	*1
4824	_____. 1981	253	*Partituren. Klavierausz. Klavier- u. Orgelm.* (1465)	*1
4825	_____. 1981	254	*Musikliteratur* (960)	*1
4826	_____. 1981	255	*Vokalmusik. Erst- u. Frühdrucke. Prakt. Werke* (757)	*1
4827	_____. 1981	156	*Klaviermusik [2-8 Hdn.]* (703)	*1
4828	_____. 1981	257	*Musikerautographen (verschiedenen Gebieten)* (1-351)	*1
4829	_____. 198_	258	*?* (?)	*15
4830	_____. 1982	259	*?* (?)	*15
4831	_____. 1982	260	*300 Musikerautographen [mostly ALS]* (300)	*15
4832	_____. 1982	261	*Kammermusik* (523)	*15

4833 **SCHNEIDER, HANS (Tutzing ü. München) (continued)**
 1982   262   *Coll: Heger, R., H. Kaminsky, R. Kraus.*
                         (1173)   *15

4834 _____.
 1982   263   *Dirigierpartituren und Orchestermaterialen*
                         (622)   *15

4835 _____.
 1982   264   *Joseph Haydn, 250 Geburtstag*
                         (524)   *15

4836 _____.
 1982   265   *Seltene Musikbücher und Musikdrucke*
                         (129)   *15

4837 _____.
 1982   266   *Musikdrucke und Musikhandschriften*
                         (943)   *15

4838 _____.
 1982   267   *Libretti aus vier Jahrhunderten*
                         (823)   *15

4839 _____.
 1982   268   *Partituren. Kammermusik. Klaviermusik*
                         (803)   *15

4840 _____.
 1982   269   *Musikliteratur*
                         (1025)   *15

4841 _____.
 1983   270   *Zweihundertsiebzig Musikerautographen*
                         (270)   *15

4842 _____.
 1983   271   *Musikliteratur. Klavierauszüge*
                         (1125)   *15

4843 _____.
 1983   272   *"Einige schöne Musiksachen"*
                         (117)   *15

4844 _____.
 1983   273   *"Sammelsurium musicale"*
                         (1600)   *15

4845 _____.
 1983   274   *Musikautographen*
                         (272)   *15

4846 _____.
 1984   275   *R. Wagner zum 101 Todestag, 1.Tl.: Dokumente*
                         (188)   *15

4847 _____.
 1984   276   *R. Wagner ... 2. Tl.*
                         (1535)   *15

4848 _____.
 1984   276A   *R. Wagner ... 3. Tl.*
                         (4pp.)   *15

1 Compiler/State University of New York (Buffalo)   2 The British Library (London)   3 Gemeentemuseum (Den Haag)   4 The Grolier Club (N.Y.C.)   5 Hirsch Collection, British Library (London)   6 D.W. Krummel (Urbana)   7 Library of Congress (Washington, D.C.)   8 Library and Museum of the Performing Arts (N.Y.C.)   9 William Reeves (London)   10 Sibley Library, Eastman School of Music (Rochester)   11 Nigel Simeone (Tunbridge Wells, Kent)   12 Vereeniging ter Bervordering van de Belangen des Boekhandels (Amsterdam)   13 University of Virginia (Charlottesville)   14 University of California at Los Angeles   15 Generally available

4849 **SCHNEIDER, HANS (Tutzing ü. München) (continued)**

	1984	277	*Musikalisches Divertissement*	
			(145)	*15
4850	_____.			
	1984	278	*Vokalmusik A-G*	
			(382)	*15
4851	_____.			
	1984	279	*Musikliteratur*	
			(1173)	*15
4852	_____.			
	1984	280	*VokalMusik H-P*	
			(627)	*15
4853	_____.			
	1984	281	*Musikalisches Mancherlei*	
			(106)	*15
4854	_____.			
	3/1958	Angeb	—	*Alte Klavierauszüge*
			(103)	*8,9
4855	_____.			
	4/1958	do.	---	*Partituren*
			(189)	*9
4856	_____.			
	10/1958	do.	18	*Musikliteratur*
			(294)	*9
4857	_____.			
	12/1958	do.	22	*Kammermusik*
			(139)	*9
4858	_____.			
	12/1958	do.	23	*Musikliteratur/Musikdrucke*
			(171)	*9
4859	_____.			
	3/1959	do.	25	*Erstausgaben und Frühdrucke*
			(95)	*9
4860	_____.			
	3/1959	do.	26	*Vokalmusik*
			(116)	*9
4861	_____.			
	4/1959	do.	28	*Vokalmusik*
			(145)	*9
4862	_____.			
	6/1959	do.	31	*Musikliteratur/Musikdrucke*
			(372)	*9

4863 **SCHNEIDER, PIERRE (Paris)**

	12/1928	—	*Catalogue des éditions du Magasin musical*
			(18pp.)	*8
4864	_____.		
	2/1932	—	*Livres d'occasion sur la musique*
			(1563)	*8,13

4865	**SCHOENINGH, FERD.** (Osnabrück)			
	1930?	280	*Theater und Musik*	
			(2364)	*5
4866	**SCHUMANN, HELLMUT** (Nachf. A RAUSTEINS) (Zürich)			
	194_	418	*Literatur. Musik. Theater*	
			(?)	*4
4867	_____.			
	1952	434	*Musik. Theater*	
			(?)	*4
4868	_____.			
	195_?	451	*Musik. Theater. Wagner-Sammlung*	
			(1344 -1880)	*1
4869	_____.			
	[1964]	461	*Coll: Wälterlein*	
			(?)	*4
4870	_____.			
	197_	List	5	*Occasional List: Old Music*
			(33)	*1
4871	**SCHWAB, EUGENE L.** (Brooklyn, N. Y.)			
	1964?	M-64	*Early American Sheet Music*	
			(76)	*8
4872	**SCHWEIZERISCHES ANTIQUARIAT** (Zürich)			
	1868	22T	*heoretische und praktische Musik*	
			(335- 637)	*8
4873	_____.			
	19_	418	*Philosophie. Psychologie ... Musik und Theater*	
			(813- 904)	*4
4874	_____.			
	1951	430	*Literatur. Theater. Musik*	
			(1236)	*12
4875	_____.			
	195_	434	*Musik und Theater*	
			(537)	*12
4876	_____.			
	[1959]	451	*Deutsche Literatur. Musik und Theater*	
			(1880)	*12
4877	_____.			
	[1963]	461	*Deutsche Literatur. Musik und Theater*	
			(1632)	*12
4878	**SCIENTIFIC LIBRARY SERVICE** (N.Y.C.)			
	1952	10	*Musicology. Full Scores*	
			(317)	*1
4879	_____.			
	1952	13	*Music Books and Scores*	
			(495)	*1,6,8
4880	_____.			
	1953	17	*Music Books and Scores*	
			(904)	*1,6,8,10,13

1 Compiler/State University of New York (Buffalo)   2 The British Library (London)   3 Gemeentemuseum (Den Haag)   4 The Grolier Club (N.Y.C.)   5 Hirsch Collection, British Library (London)   6 D.W. Krummel (Urbana)   7 Library of Congress (Washington, D.C.)   8 Library and Museum of the Performing Arts (N.Y.C.)   9 William Reeves (London)   10 Sibley Library, Eastman School of Music (Rochester)   11 Nigel Simeone (Tunbridge Wells, Kent)   12 Vereeniging ter Bervordering van de Belangen des Boekhandels (Amsterdam)   13 University of Virginia (Charlottesville)   14 University of California at Los Angeles   15 Generally available

4881 **SCIENTIFIC LIBRARY SERVICE (N.Y.C.) (continued)**
      1954   21   *Music, 1500-1954. Books. Scores*
                                (1421)   *1,6,8,10,13

4882 ____.
      195_   22   *Music, Instrumental and Vocal*
                                (508)   *1,6,8,13

4883 ____.
      1955   24   *Music, Books and Scores*
                                (1954)   *6,8,10

4884 ____.
      1956   28   *Music, Books and Scores, Rare, Early*
                                (2720)   *1,6,8,10

4885 ____.
      1957   31   *Music, Books and Scores, Rare, Early*
                                (2576)   *1,6,10,8,12,13

4886 ____.
      1958   34   *Music, Books and Scores, Rare, Early*
                                (2643)   *1,6,8,12,13

4887 ____.
      1959   37   *Music, Books and Scores, Rare, Early*
                                (2861)   *1,6,8,10,11,13

4888 ____.
      1960   40   *Music Books, Rare, Early. Mozart Ms.*
                                (2344)   *1,6,8,10,11,13

4889 ____.
      1960   41   *Music Scores, Rare, Early*
                                (1121)   *1,6,8,10,11,13

4890 ____.
      1960   45   *Music Books, Prints, Autographs*
                                (2756)   *1,6,8,10,11,13

4891 ____.
      1960   46   *Music - Scores*
                                (1117)   *1,6,8,12,13,14

4892 ____.
      1962   48   *Music, Books, Prints, Periodicals*
                                (2710)   *6,8,10,11,13

4893 ____.
      1963   49   *Music Scores, Rare, Early, Modern*
                                (1202)   *6,8,11,13,14

4894 ____.
      1963   51   *Music*
                                (3367)   *6,8,10,12,13,14

4895 ____.
      1964   52   *Music Scores, Rare, Early, Modern*
                                (1287)   *6,8,13,14

4896 ____.
      1964   53   *Music Scores - Vocal*
                                (578+53)   *6,8,10,13,14

---

1 Compiler/State University of New York (Buffalo)   **2** The British Library (London)   **3** Gemeentemuseum (Den Haag)   **4** The Grolier Club (N.Y.C.)   **5** Hirsch Collection, British Library (London)   **6** D.W. Krummel (Urbana)   **7** Library of Congress (Washington, D.C.)   **8** Library and Museum of the Performing Arts (N.Y.C.)   **9** William Reeves (London)   **10** Sibley Library, Eastman School of Music (Rochester)   **11** Nigel Simeone (Tunbridge Wells, Kent)   **12** Vereeniging ter Bervordering van de Belangen des Boekhandels (Amsterdam)   **13** University of Virginia (Charlottesville)   **14** University of California at Los Angeles   **15** Generally available

4897   **SCIENTIFIC LIBRARY SERVICE (N.Y.C.) (continued)**
     1965   55   *Music Books, 1830-1965*
                               (2473)   *6,8,10,13,14

4898   _____.
     1965   56   *Autographs: Scientists, Musicians, etc.*
                               (762)   *6,8,11,13,14

4899   _____.
     1966   59   *Music Books, 1830-1966*
                               (2407)   *6,8,11,13,14

4900   _____.
     1966   60   *Rare and Early Music Books and Scores*
                               (469)   *1,6,8,13,14

4901   _____.
     1966   61   *Music Scores*
                               (1466)   *6,8,12,13

4902   _____.
     1967   64   *Music Books, 1820-1967*
                               (1981)   *1,6,8,12,13,14

4903   _____.
     1968   65   *Rare and Early Music Books and Scores*
                               (849)   *1,6,8,13,14

4904   _____.
     1968   66   *Masic Scores, Vocal and Instrumental*
                               (925)   *1,6,8,13,14

4905   _____.
     1969   68   *Autographs: Musicians, Actors*
                               (664)   *1,6,8,10,13,14

4906   _____.
     1969   69   *Music Books, 1820-1969*
                               (1931)   *1,6,8,13,14

4907   _____.
     1969   70   *Music Scores, Vocal and Instrumental*
                               (662)   *1,6,8,10,13,14

4908   _____.
     1971   72   *Music Books, 1820-1970*
                               (2106)   *1,8,13,14

4909   _____.
     1972   75   *Music Scores, Vocal and Instrumental*
                               (1915)   *1,8,13,14

4910   _____.
     1973   76   *Music Books, 1820-1973*
                               (3049)   *1,6,8,13,14

4911   _____.
     1975   77   *Rare and Early Music Books and Scores*
                               (816)   *1,6,8,13

4912   _____.
     1977   80   *Music Books, 1820-1977*
                               (2881)   *1,6,8,13

1 Compiler/State University of New York (Buffalo)   **2** The British Library (London)   **3** Gemeentemuseum (Den Haag)   **4** The Grolier Club (N.Y.C.)   **5** Hirsch Collection, British Library (London)   **6** D.W. Krummel (Urbana)   **7** Library of Congress (Washington, D.C.)   **8** Library and Museum of the Performing Arts (N.Y.C.)   **9** William Reeves (London)   **10** Sibley Library, Eastman School of Music (Rochester)   **11** Nigel Simeone (Tunbridge Wells, Kent)   **12** Vereeniging ter Bervordering van de Belangen des Boekhandels (Amsterdam)   **13** University of Virginia (Charlottesville)   **14** University of California at Los Angeles   **15** Generally available

4913	**SCLARANDIS, PAOLO, LIBRAIO** (Turin)			
	1972	---	*Letteratura musicale*	
			(691)	*1
4914	____.			
	12/1972	—	*Letteratura musicale. Spartiti d'opera*	
			(627)	*1,8
4915	**SCOTT, B. J.** (**Winthrop Harbor, Illinois**)			
	196_	77	*Literature of Music*	
			(206)	*1
4916	____.			
	1968	89	*Literature of Music and Ballet*	
			(126)	*1
4917	**SCRIBNER & WELFORD** (**N.Y.C.**)			
	1886?	unn.	*Select List: Music and Musical Literature*	
			(30pp.)	*8
4918	**SCRIBNER BOOK STORE** (**N.Y.C.**)			
	s.d.	5	*First Editions of Music by Famous Composers*	
			(72)	*9
4919	____.			
	s.d.	95	*First Editions of Music*	
			(78)	*1,6,8,10
4920	____.			
	1935	100	*First Editions of Music*	
			(184)	*1,8,10,13,14
4921	____.			
	1936?	105	*First Editions of Music. Famous American Songs*	
			(437)	*8
4922	____.			
	[1937]	111	*Books. Manuscripts. Music*	
			(50pls.)	*1,8
4923	____.			
	1940	112	*Bach to Stravinsky. First Editions*	
			(188)	*1,6,8,9,10,13
4924	____.			
	1940	119	*First Editions. Bach, Beethoven, Brahms*	
			(74)	*8,9,10,11,13
4925	____.			
	194_?	120	*Famous Operas, from Lully to Strauss*	
			(127A)	*8,9,10,13
4926	____.			
	194_?	121	*First Editions of Music*	
			(157)	*8,9,10,13
4927	____.			
	s.d.	127	*First Editions of Music*	
			(181)	*8,10,13
4928	____.			
	s.d.	133	*Music. First Editions*	
			(196)	*8,10

1 Compiler/State University of New York (Buffalo)   2 The British Library (London)   3 Gemeentemuseum (Den Haag)   4 The Grolier Club (N.Y.C.)   5 Hirsch Collection, British Library (London)   6 D.W. Krummel (Urbana)   7 Library of Congress (Washington, D.C.)   8 Library and Museum of the Performing Arts (N.Y.C.)   9 William Reeves (London)   10 Sibley Library, Eastman School of Music (Rochester)   11 Nigel Simeone (Tunbridge Wells, Kent)   12 Vereeniging ter Bevordering van de Belangen des Boekhandels (Amsterdam)   13 University of Virginia (Charlottesville)   14 University of California at Los Angeles   15 Generally available

4929 **SCRIBNER'S, CHARLES, SONS (N.Y.C.)**
      1899?   —   *Musical Literature List. New, rev. & enl. ed.*
                             (96pp.)   *8

4930 **SCRIPTORIUM (Beverly Hills, CA.)**
      197_?   3   *Manuscripts and Documents of Famous People*
                             (6, i.a.)   *8

4931   _____.
      197_?   4   *Manuscripts and Documents of Famous People*
                             (8, i.a.)   *8

4932   _____.
      1976   5   *Manuscripts and·Documents of Famous People*
                             (9, i.a.)   *8

4933 **SELE, ERNEST (Antwerp)**
      [1923?]   2   *Musique. Peintre. Sculpture*
                             (610-1158)   B-Br

4934 **SELIGSBERG, B. (Bayreuth)**
      s.d.   274   *Literatur. Musik. Theater. Portraits*
                             (329-1077)   *12

4935   _____.
      1912   305   *Musik und Theater. Wagner*
                             (2472)   *8,12

4936   _____.
      [1925]   335   *Wagner*
                             (925)   *5,12

4937 **SEXL UND CO. (Vienna)**
      1960   74   *Sprach- u. Lit.wissenschaft. Musik. Theater*
                             (328)   *12

4938 **SEYFFARDT, N. V. (Amsterdam)**
      1874   —   *Buecher und Schriften von Musik*
                             (?)   *12

4939   _____.
      1891   —   *Goedkoope Muziek*
                             (?)   *12

4940   _____.
      s.d.   —   *Afd. III: Piano-muziek*
                             (130pp.)   *12

4941   _____.
      s.d.   —   *Afd. IV*
                             (39pp.)   *12

4942   _____.
      s.d.   —   *Harmonium-muziek*
                             (?)   *12

4943   _____.
      s.d.   —   *Muziek*
                             (?)   *12

4944   _____.
      s.d.   —   *Afd. VIII: Musikalien*
                             (2678)   *3

---

1 Compiler/State University of New York (Buffalo) **2** The British Library (London) **3** Gemeentemuseum (Den Haag) **4** The Grolier Club (N.Y.C.) **5** Hirsch Collection, British Library (London) **6** D.W. Krummel (Urbana) **7** Library of Congress (Washington, D.C.) **8** Library and Museum of the Performing Arts (N.Y.C.) **9** William Reeves (London) **10** Sibley Library, Eastman School of Music (Rochester) **11** Nigel Simeone (Tunbridge Wells, Kent) **12** Vereeniging ter Bervordering van de Belangen des Boekhandels (Amsterdam) **13** University of Virginia (Charlottesville) **14** University of California at Los Angeles **15** Generally available

4945 SEYFFARDT, N. V. (Amsterdam) (continued)
　　　　1916　　　　　　　—　　*Muziek-portefeuille*
　　　　　　　　　　　　　　　　(7pp.)　　　　　　　　　　　　　　　　*12

4946　＿＿．
　　　　1926　　　　　　　—　　*Koorwerken*
　　　　　　　　　　　　　　　　(24pp.)　　　　　　　　　　　　　　*3

4947 SHAPIRO, OSCAR (Washington, D. C.)
　　　　1966　　　　　　　5　　*Rare Music and Music Treatises*
　　　　　　　　　　　　　　　　(111)　　　　　　　　　　　　　　　*8,12

4948　＿＿．
　　　　1967　　　　　　　6　　*Rare Music and Music Treatises. Autographs*
　　　　　　　　　　　　　　　　(395)　　　　　　　　　　　　　　*1,10,13

4949　＿＿．
　　　　1968　　　　　　　7　　*Rare Music and Music Treatises. Autographs*
　　　　　　　　　　　　　　　　(381)　　　　　　　　　　　　　　　*1,8

4950　＿＿．
　　　　1970　　　　　　　8　　*Beethoven. Opera Scores*
　　　　　　　　　　　　　　　　(407)　　　　　　　　　　　　　　*6,8,13

4951　＿＿．
　　　　1971　　　　　　　9　　*Opera Scores. Rare Music and the Violin*
　　　　　　　　　　　　　　　　(494)　　　　　　　　　　　　　　*1,8,13

4952　＿＿．
　　　　1971　　　　　　　10　　*Music and Musical Autographs*
　　　　　　　　　　　　　　　　(331)　　　　　　　　　　　　　　*1,8,10

4953　＿＿．
　　　　1972　　　　　　　11　　*The Violin Family*
　　　　　　　　　　　　　　　　(372)　　　　　　　　　　　　　　　*10

4954　＿＿．
　　　　1974　　　　　　　12　　*The Violin Family. Autographs*
　　　　　　　　　　　　　　　　(296)　　　　　　　　　　　　　　*1,8,10

4955　＿＿．
　　　　1976　　　　　　　13　　*Rare Music*
　　　　　　　　　　　　　　　　(227)　　　　　　　　　　　　　　　*1,8

4956　＿＿．
　　　　1978/79　　　　　14　　*The Violin Family*
　　　　　　　　　　　　　　　　(374)　　　　　　　　　　　　　　　*10

4957　＿＿．
　　　　1980　　　　　　　15　　*Musical Miscellany and Violin Books*
　　　　　　　　　　　　　　　　(397)　　　　　　　　　　　　　　　*10

4958　＿＿．
　　　　1981　　　　　　　16　　*The Violin Family*
　　　　　　　　　　　　　　　　(189)　　　　　　　　　　　　　　　*10

4959　＿＿．
　　　　1982　　　　　　　17　　*Niccolo Paganini: Music, Music Lit. Documents*
　　　　　　　　　　　　　　　　(238)　　　　　　　　　　　　　　　*8

4960　＿＿．
　　　　1983　　　　　　　18　　*The Violin Family*
　　　　　　　　　　　　　　　　(220)　　　　　　　　　　　　　　　*1

---

1 Compiler/State University of New York (Buffalo)　2 The British Library (London)　3 Gemeentemuseum (Den Haag)　4 The Grolier Club (N.Y.C.)　5 Hirsch Collection, British Library (London)　6 D.W. Krummel (Urbana)　7 Library of Congress (Washington, D.C.)　8 Library and Museum of the Performing Arts (N.Y.C.)　9 William Reeves (London)　10 Sibley Library, Eastman School of Music (Rochester)　11 Nigel Simeone (Tunbridge Wells, Kent)　12 Vereeniging ter Bervordering van de Belangen des Boekhandels (Amsterdam)　13 University of Virginia (Charlottesville)　14 University of California at Los Angeles　15 Generally available

4961 **SHAPIRO, OSCAR (Washington, D. C.) (continued)**
  1984   19   *The Violin Family*
             (186)   *8

4962 _____.
  1984/85   20   *The Violin Family*
             (284)   *8

4963 **SHEP, R. L. (Seattle, Washington)**
  [1976]   66   *Performing Arts*
            (688-831)   *8,10,13

4964 _____.
  1977   69   *Performing Arts·*
           (1375)   *13,14

4965 _____.
  1977   70   *Music and Dance*
           (601)   *13

4966 _____.
  1979   75   *Music and Dance*
           (1374)   *1

4967 _____.
  1980   77   *Performing Arts and Costume*
           (1396)   *8

4968 **SHOTTON, J. (Durham, U. K.)**
  s.d.   —   *List of Music*
           (274)   *13

4969 **SILVER, MARTIN A. (Santa Barbara, CA.)**
  1970   4   *Musical Literature*
           (400-505)   *1

4970 _____.
  1972   1   *Antiquarian, New and Reprint Titles*
           (297+)   *1,13

4971 _____.
  1973   1   *Antiquarian Books and Music. Duckles Titles*
           (224)   *1,6,10

4972 _____.
  1974   1   *Duckles Titles*
           (19pp.)   *1,6,8

4973 _____.
  1975   1   *[Music and Musical Literature]*
           (330)   *1,6,14

4974 _____.
  1975   2-3   *[Music and Musical Literature]*
           (608)   *1,6,8,10,14

4975 _____.
  1976   1   *[Music and Musical Literature]*
           (326)   *1,6,8,10,13,14

4976 _____.
  1977   1   *[Music and Musical Literature]*
           (271)   *1,8,10,14

1 Compiler/State University of New York (Buffalo)   2 The British Library (London)   3 Gemeentemuseum (Den Haag)   4 The Grolier Club (N.Y.C.)   5 Hirsch Collection, British Library (London)   6 D.W. Krummel (Urbana)   7 Library of Congress (Washington, D.C.)   8 Library and Museum of the Performing Arts (N.Y.C.)   9 William Reeves (London)   10 Sibley Library, Eastman School of Music (Rochester)   11 Nigel Simeone (Tunbridge Wells, Kent)   12 Vereeniging ter Bervordering van de Belangen des Boekhandels (Amsterdam)   13 University of Virginia (Charlottesville)   14 University of California at Los Angeles   15 Generally available

4977 **SILVER, MARTIN A. (Santa Barbara, CA.) (continued)**
       1977   2   *[Music and Musical Literature]*
                              (265)   *1,6,8,10,14
4978 _____.
       1977   3   *[Music and Musical Literarture]*
                              (286)   *1,8,10,14
4979 _____.
       1978   15   *[Music and Musical Literature]*
                              (295)   *1,13
4980 _____.
       1978   16   *[Music and Musical Literature]*
                              (280)   *1,8,14
4981 _____.
       2/1982   —   *l00 Books of importance to the Music Librarian*
                              (100)   *1
4982 **SLATKINE, M., & FILS (Geneva)**
       10/1950   187   *Livres anciens et d'occasion*
                              (661-718)   *8
4983 _____.
       1973   30   *Musicology*
                              (777)   *1,8
4984 **SMETRYNS, J. (PARIS)**
       S.D.   5   *Livres anciens et modernes*
                              (?)   *12
4985 **SMIT, B. H. (Amsterdam/Haarlem)**
       s.d.   —   *Muziek*
                              (?)   *12
4986 **SMIT, C. B. (Amsterdam/Arnhem)**
       s.d.   —   *Muziek*
                              (?)   *12
4987 **SMITH, GEORGE see ELLIS (Marlborough, U.K.)**

4988 **SMITH, JOHN RUSSELL (London)**
       1856   —   *English Broadside Ballads*
                              (141pp.)   *12
4989 **SNELL, K. R. and J. E. (Malvern 3144, Victoria)**
       11/1984   1   *American Popular Music, c.1900-1940*
                              (2pp.)   *1
4990 **SOTHERAN, HENRY, LTD. (London)**
       1936   Notes   19   *... including a Mendelssohn Collection [Mss.]*
                              (lot 3545, 16 i   tems) *10
4991 **SOTHMANN, MAGDALENE (Amsterdam)**
       [1950]   9   *Muziek*
                              (577)   *12
4992 **SPIRGATIS, M. (Leipzig)**
       1895   34   *Lieder in Originaldrucken*
                              (269)   *12

4993 **STAP, J. M. (Haarlem)**
    1896?   —   *Muziek van Voorhanden*
                        (32pp.)   *12

4994 **STACEY (GILBERT) (London and Stoneleigh, Epsom)**
    s.d.   List   51   *Full Orchestra Scores. Rare Musical Items*
                        (5pp.+60 lots)   *11

4995 _____.
    1/1951   do.   —   *Second-hand full Scores. Orch. and Vocal Works*
                        (8pp.)   *8

4996 _____.
    1951?   do.   —   *Books on or by Composers*
                        (11pp.)   *8

4997 _____.
    7/1956   do.   —   *Second-hand Cello Music*
                        (421)   *8

4998 _____.
    9/1956   do.   —   *Supplementary List of Cello Music*
                        (120)   *8

4999 _____.
    10/1956   do.   —   *Organ Music*
                        (146)   *8

5000 _____.
    ?/1956   do.   —   *Organ List No. 2*
                        (424)   *8

5001 _____.
    11/1956   do.   —   *November List of Second-hand Music*
                        (889+38)   *8

5002 _____.
    1960?   do.   —   *Addenda to List 50*
                        (pp.31-36)   *8

5003 _____.
    1961   do.   60   *A List of Second-hand Chamber Music*
                        (499)   *8

5004 _____.
    [1962]   do.   64   *"Spring Miscellany"*
                        (425)   *6

5005 _____.
    [1964]   do.   68   *Revised: A List of Full Scores*
                        (500)   *6

5006 **STAGE HOUSE II (REITSMA & SCHWARZ) (Lyons, CO.)**
    9/1971   List   VII   *Early American Sheet Music*
                        (192)   *8

5007 **STARGARDT, J. A. (Berlin)**
    s.d.   252   *Autographen [including musicians]*
                        (1-88)   *4

5008 _____.
    1929   292   *Autographen [including musicians]*
                        ?   *4,9

---

1 Compiler/State University of New York (Buffalo)　**2** The British Library (London)　**3** Gemeentemuseum (Den Haag)　**4** The Grolier Club (N.Y.C.)　**5** Hirsch Collection, British Library (London)　**6** D.W. Krummel (Urbana)　**7** Library of Congress (Washington, D.C.)　**8** Library and Museum of the Performing Arts (N.Y.C.)　**9** William Reeves (London)　**10** Sibley Library, Eastman School of Music (Rochester)　**11** Nigel Simeone (Tunbridge Wells, Kent)　**12** Vereeniging ter Bervordering van de Belangen des Boekhandels (Amsterdam)　**13** University of Virginia (Charlottesville)　**14** University of California at Los Angeles　**15** Generally available

5009 **STARGARDT, J. A. (Berlin) (continued)**
    s.d.   296   *Selbschriften berühmter Künstler*
                                    (1-188)   *3

5010 _____.
    s.d.   309   *Porträts, A - C*
                                      (i.a.)   *3

5011 _____.
    s.d.   330   *Autographen [including musicians]*
                                      (i.a.)   *4,10

5012 _____.
    s.d.   345   *Autographen [including musicians]*
                                      (i.a.)   *4

5013 _____.
    s.d.   357   *Autographen [including musicians]*
                                      (130-58)   *3

5014 _____.
    s.d.   481   *Musiker-Autographen*
                                      (200)   *8

5015 _____.
    1983   623   *Autographen und Urkunden*
                                      (47, i.a.)   *8

5016 _____.
    1937   A.-S.   *Autographen-Sammler, 2.Jg., Nr.2: [music Mss.]*
                                      (100)   *9

5017 **STARR BOOKS SHOP (Cambridge, Massachusetts)**
    1977   401   *Music List*
                                      (236)   *1

5018 **STECHERT, G. E., & CO¿ (N.Y.C.)**
    10/1941   List   238   *Musical List*
                                      [18pp.]   *10

5019 **STECHERT-HAFNER, INC. (N.Y.C.)**
    1952   202   *Music [Literature]*
                                      (1680)   *8,10

5020 _____.
    1953   219   *Musicology. Scores. Librettos. Journals*
                                      (971)   *8,10,13

5021 _____.
    1955   233   *Musicology. Scores. Librettos*
                                      (1266)   *8,10,13

5022 _____.
    1957   248   *Musicology. Scores. Librettos. Journals*
                                      (1245)   *8

5023 _____.
    1961   List   543   *Music*
                                      (166)   *8

5024 _____.
    1965   do.   611   *Music [Literature]*
                                      (50)   *10

---

1 Compiler/State University of New York (Buffalo)   **2** The British Library (London)   **3** Gemeentemuseum (Den Haag)   **4** The Grolier Club (N.Y.C.)   **5** Hirsch Collection, British Library (London)   **6** D.W. Krummel (Urbana)   **7** Library of Congress (Washington, D.C.)   **8** Library and Museum of the Performing Arts (N.Y.C.)   **9** William Reeves (London)   **10** Sibley Library, Eastman School of Music (Rochester)   **11** Nigel Simeone (Tunbridge Wells, Kent)   **12** Vereeniging ter Bervordering van de Belangen des Boekhandels (Amsterdam)   **13** University of Virginia (Charlottesville)   **14** University of California at Los Angeles   **15** Generally available

5025	**STEIN, KURT (Springfield, PA.)**				
	9/1982		982	*Early American Sheet Music* (112)	*1
5026	_____.				
	1/1983		--	*American Sheet Music, 1800-1825* (134)	*1
5027	_____.				
	2/1983		283	*Early American Sheet Music* (108)	*1
5028	_____.				
	5/1983		583	*Early American Sheet Music* (108)	*1
5029	_____.				
	9/1983		983	*Early American Sheet Music* (111)	*1
5030	_____.				
	2/1984		284	*Early American Sheet music* (115)	*1
5031	_____.				
	5/1984		584	*Early American Sheet Music* (112)	*1
5032	_____.				
	9/1984		984	*Early American Sheet Music* (109)	*1
5033	**STEINKOPF, FERDINAND (Stuttgart)**				
	1874		131	*Theoretische und praktische Musikwerke* (?)	[MfM]
5034	_____.				
	1879		215	*Hymnologie* (16pp.)	*8
5035	_____.				
	1881		267	*Hymnologie* (18pp.)	*12
5036	**STENDERHOFF ANTIQUARIAT (Münster)**				
	[1972]		263	*Natur- und Musikwissenschaft* (2193-2500)	*4,12
5037	**STERN-VERLAG OPHOFF & CO. (Düsseldorf)**				
	1963	Liste	106	*Kunst und Musik* (679)	[IBAK]
5038	_____.				
	1964	do.	118	*Musik. Theater und Kunst* (538)	[IBAK]
5039	_____.				
	1965	do.	132-3	*Kunst. Musik (2 vols.)* (635,705)	[IBAK]
5040	_____.				
	1966	do.	146	*Bildende Kunst. Musik. Theater* (601)	[IBAK]

1 Compiler/State University of New York (Buffalo) **2** The British Library (London) **3** Gemeentemuseum (Den Haag) **4** The Grolier Club (N.Y.C.) **5** Hirsch Collection, British Library (London) **6** D.W. Krummel (Urbana) **7** Library of Congress (Washington, D.C.) **8** Library and Museum of the Performing Arts (N.Y.C.) **9** William Reeves (London) **10** Sibley Library, Eastman School of Music (Rochester) **11** Nigel Simeone (Tunbridge Wells, Kent) **12** Vereeniging ter Bervordering van de Belangen des Boekhandels (Amsterdam) **13** University of Virginia (Charlottesville) **14** University of California at Los Angeles **15** Generally available

5041 **STERN-VERLAG OPHOFF & CO. (Düsseldorf) (continued)**
  1967 do. 156 ... *Kunst. Musik. Theater. Tanz*
              (865)   [IBAK]

5042 **STEVENS & BROWN (London)**
  1943/44   4 *Rare and Interesting Books*
              (422a-530)   *8,10

5043 _____.
  1950   11 *Rare old Music Books and Mss.*
             (611)   *8

5044 **STEVENS, ERIC AND JOAN (London)**
  1976   73 *Drama and Music*
             (263)   *8

5045 **STILLER'SCHEN HOFBUCHHANDLUNG (Rostock i. Mecklenberg)**
  1861   — *Antiquarische Musik*
             (34pp.)   [Petzholdt]

5046 **STOCKUM, W. P. VAN, EN ZOON (Den Haag)**
  1891   2 *Beaux livres*
             (484-558)   *3

5047 _____.
  1893   3 *Beaux livres*
             (817-33)   *3

5048 _____.
  1894   4 *Beaux livres*
             (i.a.)   *3

5049 _____.
  1895   5 *Théâtre. Musique*
             (92)   *12

5050 **STOCKUM'S ANTIQUARIAAT, VAN (Den Haag)**
  s.d.   30 *Portraits ... musiciens*
             (779)   *12

5051 _____.
  s.d.   33 *Portraits ... musiciens*
             (2076)   *12

5052 _____.
  s.d.   48 *Musique*
             (1852)   *5,7,8,12

5053 **STODDARD, RICHARD (N.Y.C.)**
  3/1977 List 2 *Theatre and Opera. Mss.*
             (69)   *1,8

5054 _____.
  1/1978 do. 6 *Theatre ... Drama. Dance. Opera. Music*
             (121)   *8

5055 _____.
  5/1978 do. 8 *Theatre. Stage Design. Opera*
             (114)   *1,8,13

5056 _____.
  ?/1979 do. 12 *Theatre and Music*
             (142)   *1,8

5057   **STODDARD, RICHARD (N.Y.C.) (continued)**
       ?/1980   do.   16   *[Theatre and Music]*
                               (250)   *1

5058   _____.
       3/1981   do.   19   *[Theatre and Music]*
                               (103)   *1,8

5059   _____.
       ?/1981   do.   20   *[Theatre and Music]*
                               (120)   *1

5060   _____.
       9/1981   do.   21   *[Theatre and Music]*
                               (245)   *1

5061   _____.
       11/1981   do.   22   *[Theatre and Music]*
                               (103)   *1,8

5062   _____.
       5/1982   do.   25   *[Theatre and Music]*
                               (94)   *1

5063   _____.
       11/1982   do.   27   *Theatre and Drama. Musical Comedies*
                               (113)   *8

5064   _____.
       3/1983   do.   29   *[Theatre. Music Literature]*
                               (94)   *1

5065   _____.
       9/1984   do.   33   *[Theatre. Drama. Music Literature]*
                               (94)   *1

5066   _____.
       9/1984   do.   36   *Music. Dance*
                               (129-70)   *1

5067   **STOLL & BADER (Freiburg)**
       1882   40   *Theater. Kunst. Musik*
                               (536)   *5

5068   **STONEHILL, C. A., LTD. (N.Y.C.)**
       1942   148   *Clearance! Books ... and Music*
                               (216-461)   *8

5069   **"STRAD" OFFICE (London)**
       s.d.   List   —   *Selection of Rare and Out of Print Works*
                               (4pp.)   *8,13

5070   **STREISAND, HUGO (Berlin)**
       [1965]   296   *Theater. Musik*
                               (536)   *12

5071   **STRUCK, HARTWIG (Goslar)**
       1961   19   *Musik*
                               (275)   [IBAK]

5072   **SÜDDEUTSCHES ANTIQUARIAT (Munich)**
       1900   V   *Seltene Werke*
                               (958-1104)   *8

5073 **SÜDDEUTSCHES ANTIQUARIAT (Munich) (continued)**

	1902	27	*Musik. Theater* (546)	*5
5074	_____. 1903	28	*Musik. Theater.* ?	*5,8
5075	_____. 1903	47	*Musik und Theater* (637)	*8
5076	_____. s.d.	57	*Musik und Theater* (637)	*5
5077	_____. 1906	83	*Drama. Theater. Musik. Libretti* (800-1131)	*5,12
5078	_____. 1909	105	*Coll: Scherer* (?)	*4
5079	_____. 1909	112	*Coll: Scherer. 4.Tl: Musik. Lied. Theater* (1644)	*12

5080 **SURASKY, RUBIN (Baltimore)**

	1942	List	2A	*Secondhand and o. p. Books on Music* (4pp.)	*8
5081	_____. 194_	do.	4A	*Supplement to #4 (Violins). Misc. Books* (61)	*8
5082	_____. 194_	do.	5	*Musical Literature. Opera Scores. Periodicals* (283)	*8,10
5083	_____. 1949	do.	—	*Musical Lit. Periodicals. Theory. Songsters* (319)	*8

5084 **SWETS EN ZEITLINGER (Amsterdam)**

	[1940]	List	164	*Muziek. Liederen. Tooneel* (176)	*12
5085	_____. 1947	do.	323	*Bibliography. Biography and Ref. Bks. on Music* (280)	*8
5086	_____. 2/1948	do.	339	*Music* (244)	*8
5087	_____. 11/1948	do.	352	*Music* (502)	*8
5088	_____. ?/1948	do.	353	*Music* (519)	*12

---

1 Compiler/State University of New York (Buffalo) **2** The British Library (London) **3** Gemeentemuseum (Den Haag) **4** The Grolier Club (N.Y.C.) **5** Hirsch Collection, British Library (London) **6** D.W. Krummel (Urbana) **7** Library of Congress (Washington, D.C.) **8** Library and Museum of the Performing Arts (N.Y.C.) **9** William Reeves (London) **10** Sibley Library, Eastman School of Music (Rochester) **11** Nigel Simeone (Tunbridge Wells, Kent) **12** Vereeniging ter Bervordering van de Belangen des Boekhandels (Amsterdam) **13** University of Virginia (Charlottesville) **14** University of California at Los Angeles **15** Generally available

5089 **SWETS EN ZEITLINGER (Amsterdam) (continued)**

| | 1950 | do. | 373 | *Music* (554) | *8 |

5090 _____.

| | 8/1966 | do. | 552 | *Music* (145) | *8 |

5091 _____.

| | 12/1967 | do. | 5098! | *Music* (127) | *8 |

5092 _____.

| | 1968 | do. | 595 | *Music (Periodicals)* (86) | *6 |

5093 _____.

| | 1970 | do. | — | *Catalogue on Music* (73pp.) | *1 |

5094 _____.

| | 1971 | do. | 765 | *Music and Theatre* (94) | *13 |

5095 _____.

| | 1978 | do. | 853 | *Backsets on Music* (177) | *14 |

5096 _____.

| | 11/1981 | do. | 887 | *Backsets of Music. Theatre. Film* (356) | *1,8 |

5097 _____.

| | 1950 | Cat. | 71 | *... Fine Arts. XXIV. Music* (2297-2400) | *8 |

5098 **TAUSSIG, I. (Prague) [NB: #92-125 are cited in #133]**

| | s.d. | Verz. | 32 | *Coll: Skraup, J. N. Werke ü. Musik* (982) | *8 |

5099 _____.

| | s.d | Kat. | 92 | *Harmonium-Musik* (?) | [not located] |

5100 _____.

| | s.d. | | 102 | *Piano- und Violin-Musik* (?) | [not located] |

5101 _____.

| | s.d. | | 106 | *Music für das Piano* (?) | [not located] |

5102 _____.

| | s.d. | | 107 | *Musik für Viola und Cello* (?) | [not located] |

5103 _____.

| | s.d. | | 108 | *Musik für Clarinette und Fagott* (?) | [not located] |

5104 _____.

| | s.d. | | 109 | *Musik für Fluegelhorn* (?) | [not located] |

1 Compiler/State University of New York (Buffalo)   **2** The British Library (London)   **3** Gemeentemuseum (Den Haag)   **4** The Grolier Club (N.Y.C.)   **5** Hirsch Collection, British Library (London)   **6** D.W. Krummel (Urbana)   **7** Library of Congress (Washington, D.C.)   **8** Library and Museum of the Performing Arts (N.Y.C.)   **9** William Reeves (London)   **10** Sibley Library, Eastman School of Music (Rochester) **11** Nigel Simeone (Tunbridge Wells, Kent)   **12** Vereeniging ter Bervordering van de Belangen des Boekhandels (Amsterdam)   **13** University of Virginia (Charlottesville)   **14** University of California at Los Angeles   **15** Generally available

5105   **TAUSSIG, I. (Prague) (continued)**
        s.d.   110   *Musik für Flöte*
                                      (?)   [not located]

5106   _____ .
        s.d.   111   *Musik für Klavier*
                                        (?)   [not located]

5107   _____ .
        s.d.   112   *Musik für Klavier-quartette*
                                        (?)   [not located]

5108   _____ .
        s.d.   118   *Musik für Violine*
                                        (?)   [not located]

5109   _____ .
        s.d.   119   *Musik für Orgel*
                                        (?)   [not located]

5110   _____ .
        s.d.   120   *Musik für 2-4 Violinen*
                                        (?)   [not located]

5111   _____ .
        s.d.   122   *Musik für Blasinstrument*
                                        (?)   [not located]

5112   _____ .
        s.d.   123   *Musik für Streichquartette*
                                        (?)   [not located]

5113   _____ .
        s.d.   125   *Musik für Mandoline*
                                        (?)   [not located]

5114   _____ .
        s.d.   133   *Musikbücher und Portraits*
                                        (1417)   *5,8

5115   _____ .
        s.d.   141   *Mozart: Sein Leben und Werke*
                                        (362)   *3,12

5116   _____ .
        s.d.   148   *Die Musik in Böhmen*
                                        (1468)   *3,5

5117   **TERL, MARGARETE (Berlin)**
        [1959]   60   *Musik. Theater. Tanz. Volkslied*
                                        (445)   *12

5118   _____ .
        [1959]   67   *Musik. Theater. Tanz. Volkslied*
                                        (457)   *12

5119   _____ .
        1961   102   *Musik. Theater. Tanz*
                                        (270)   [IBAK]

5120   _____ .
        [1962]   108   *Musik*
                                        (370)   [IBAK]

5121   **TERL, MARGARETE (Berlin) (continued)**
       [1962]   114   *Musik. Tanz. Theater. Film*
                              (301)   *12

5122   ———.
       [1963]   118   *Musik*
                              (370)   *12

5123   ———.
       [1963]   120   *Geschichte. Orientalia. Musik*
                              (429)   *12

5124   ———.
       [1963]   124   *Musik. Theater*
                              (344)   *12

5125   ———.
       [1965]   136   *Musik. Theater. Tanz*
                              (495)   *1,12

5126   ———.
       [1965]   140   *Musik. Literatur. Kunst*
                              (1337)   [IBAK]

5127   ———.
       [1967]   150   *Musik. Tanz. Theater. Folklore*
                              (619)   *1,12

5128   ———.
       [1969   165   *Musik. Theater. Tanz*
                              (625)   *1,6,12

5129   ———.
       [196_]   212   *Sprache. Literatur. Musik. Theater. Volkslied*
                              (684-1019)   *10

5130   ———.
       [196_]   219   *Musikwissenschaft. Theater. Tanz. Film*
                              (1-856)   *13

5131   **TEUBNER, F. (Bonn/Düsseldorf)**
       s.d.   155   *Volkslieder*
                              (341)   *12

5132   **THEATRE BOOKSHOP (Brighton)**
       1968   List   —   *Theatre. Drama. Film. Music. Ballet*
                              (304)   *12

5133   **THIN, JAMES (Edinburgh)**
       1960   —   *Books on Music*
                              (674)   *1,12

5134   ———.
       [1969]   —   *Books on Music*
                              (697)   *6

5135   **THOL, VAN (Den Haag)**
       1741   —   *... Muzyk-boeken en Muzyk-instrumente*
                              (?)   [BoB]

5136   **THOMAS, LIBRAIRE (Paris)**
       1934   —   *Catalogue*
                              (?)   *7

---

1 Compiler/State University of New York (Buffalo) **2** The British Library (London) **3** Gemeentemuseum (Den Haag) **4** The Grolier Club (N.Y.C.) **5** Hirsch Collection, British Library (London) **6** D.W. Krummel (Urbana) **7** Library of Congress (Washington, D.C.) **8** Library and Museum of the Performing Arts (N.Y.C.) **9** William Reeves (London) **10** Sibley Library, Eastman School of Music (Rochester) **11** Nigel Simeone (Tunbridge Wells, Kent) **12** Vereeniging ter Bervordering van de Belangen des Boekhandels (Amsterdam) **13** University of Virginia (Charlottesville) **14** University of California at Los Angeles **15** Generally available

5137 **THOMPSON, GEORGE** (Middleton-on-Sea, U.K.)
    1965   593   *Books on Music and Lives of Composers*
                                (101)   *1

5138 _____.
    1965   594   *Miniature Scores and Piano Music*
                                (136)   *1

5139 _____.
    1965   619   *Books on Music and Lives of Composers*
                                (149)   *1

5140 **THORP, THOMAS** (Guildford, U.K.)
    4/1954   List   36   *Ballet. Drama. Music. Films*
                                (40-222)   *8

5141 **THORPE, THOMAS** (London)
    1847   —   *Pt. 2 for 1847, Coll: J. Williams. Ms. Music*
                                (i.a.)   [H. Horblit]

5142 _____.
    1848   —   *Pt. 2 for 1848, Coll. of Music, Printed and Ms.*
                                (1931-57)   [H. Horblit]

5143 **TIEDEMANN, H.** (Berlin)
    2/1955   —   *Musikliteratur*
                                (959)   *9

5144 _____.
    1951   —   *Musik-Literatur*
                                (365)   *8

5145 _____.
    1951   —   *Literatur betr.: Musik*
                                (253)   *8

5146 _____.
    1951   —   *Literatur betr.: Musik*
                                (80)   *8

5147 _____.
    1952   —   *Musikliteratur*
                                (251)   *8

5148 _____.
    1957   —   *Musikliteratur*
                                (1203)   *6,13

5149 _____.
    1958   —   *Musikliteratur*
                                (1310)   *1,6,12,13

5150 _____.
    1959   —   *Musikliteratur*
                                (1544)   *12

5151 **TIVOLI BOOK CO.** (San Francisco)
    1975   1   *Music. Dance. A-L*
                                (485)   *10,14

5152 **TOSCANINI, WALTER, ANTIQUARIATO** (Milan)
    12/1927   —   *Raccolta d'autografi: Musicisti, Cantanti, ecc.*
                                (1-458)   *8

---

1 Compiler/State University of New York (Buffalo)   **2** The British Library (London)   **3** Gemeentemuseum (Den Haag)   **4** The Grolier Club (N.Y.C.)   **5** Hirsch Collection, British Library (London)   **6** D.W. Krummel (Urbana)   **7** Library of Congress (Washington, D.C.)   **8** Library and Museum of the Performing Arts (N.Y.C.)   **9** William Reeves (London)   **10** Sibley Library, Eastman School of Music (Rochester) **11** Nigel Simeone (Tunbridge Wells, Kent)   **12** Vereeniging ter Bervordering van de Belangen des Boekhandels (Amsterdam)   **13** University of Virginia (Charlottesville)   **14** University of California at Los Angeles   **15** Generally available

5153	**TOSCANINI, WALTER, ANTIQUARIATO** (Milan) (continued)				
	1928	Cat.	1	*[Musica]*	
				(1357)	*8
5154	____.				
	5/1929		2	*[Musica]*	
				(1190)	*8
5155	____.				
	1929		3	*[Musica]*	
				(3361)	*US-Bp,10
5156	____.				
	1931		—	*Reprints: Early Books on Music, Theatre, Dance*	
				(?)	*7,13
5157	____.				
	1931		—	*Libri, manoscritti, incunabuli*	
				(?)	*7,13
5158	____.				
	s.d.		—	*Teatro - Musica - Danza*	
				(150)	*10

5159 **TRAVIS & EMERY** (London and Salisbury)
"LONDON CATALOGUES"

5160	____.				
	1960		1	*Vocal Music. Folksong. Oratorio*	
				(240)	*1,11
5161	____.				
	1960		2	*Books on Music*	
				(282)	*1,14
5162	____.				
	1960		3	*Instrumental Music*	
				(244)	*1,11
5163	____.				
	1961		4	*Opera*	
				(361)	*1,8
5164	____.				
	1961		5	*Books on Music*	
				(353)	*1,11
5165	____.				
	1961		6	*Vocal Music*	
				(239)	*1,11
5166	____.				
	1962		7	*Books on Music*	
				(354)	*1,11
5167	____.				
	1962		8	*Instrumental Music*	
				(340)	*1,11
5168	____.				
	1963		9	*Vocal Music*	
				(267)	*1

1 Compiler/State University of New York (Buffalo)   2 The British Library (London)   3 Gemeentemuseum (Den Haag)   4 The Grolier Club (N.Y.C.)   5 Hirsch Collection, British Library (London)   6 D.W. Krummel (Urbana)   7 Library of Congress (Washington, D.C.)   8 Library and Museum of the Performing Arts (N.Y.C.)   9 William Reeves (London)   10 Sibley Library, Eastman School of Music (Rochester)   11 Nigel Simeone (Tunbridge Wells, Kent)   12 Vereeniging ter Bervordering van de Belangen des Boekhandels (Amsterdam)   13 University of Virginia (Charlottesville)   14 University of California at Los Angeles   15 Generally available

5169   **TRAVIS & EMERY (London and Salisbury) (continued)**

	1963	10	*Books on Music* (378)	*1
5170	_____.			
	1963	11	*Opera* (400)	*1
5171	_____.			
	11/1964	S/64	*Vocal Music* (158)	*11
5172	_____.			
	3/1965	B/65	*Piano Music* (205)	*11
5173	_____.			
	1965	12	*Musical Biography* (388)	*1,10,11
5174	_____.			
	1966	13	*Opera* (289)	*1,10,11
5175	_____.			
	1967	14	*Sacred Music* (334)	*10,11
5176	_____.			
	1967	15	*Books on Music* (642)	*1,6,8,10
5177	_____.			
	1967	16	*Chamber Music* (364)	*1,6,8
5178	_____.			
	1968	17	*Opera* (714)	*1,8
5179	_____.			
	1968	18	*Music [and Musical Literature]* (626)	*1,6,8,10
5180	_____.			
	1969	19	*Chamber Music* (672)	*1,6,8
5181	_____.			
	1969	20	*Vocal Music* (496)	*1,6,8,10,13,14
5182	_____.			
	1970	21	*Piano Music* (938)	*1,6,8,10,13,14
5183	_____.			
	1970	22	*Orchestral Music* (558)	*1,10,13
5184	_____.			
	1970	23	*Opera* (508)	*1,6,10

1 Compiler/State University of New York (Buffalo)   **2** The British Library (London)   **3** Gemeentemuseum (Den Haag)   **4** The Grolier Club (N.Y.C.)   **5** Hirsch Collection, British Library (London)   **6** D.W. Krummel (Urbana)   **7** Library of Congress (Washington, D.C.)   **8** Library and Museum of the Performing Arts (N.Y.C.)   **9** William Reeves (London)   **10** Sibley Library, Eastman School of Music (Rochester)   **11** Nigel Simeone (Tunbridge Wells, Kent)   **12** Vereeniging ter Bervordering van de Belangen des Boekhandels (Amsterdam)   **13** University of Virginia (Charlottesville)   **14** University of California at Los Angeles   **15** Generally available

5185 **TRAVIS & EMERY (London and Salisbury) (continued)**
| | 1971 | 24 | *Instrumental Music* | |
| | | | (822) | *1,8,10 |

5186 _____.
| | 1971 | 25 | *Books on Music* | |
| | | | (869) | *1,8,10,13 |

5187 _____.
| | 1971 | 26 | *Music* | |
| | | | (803) | *1,8,10,13 |

5188 _____.
| | 1972 | 27 | *Musical Literature* | |
| | | | (782) | *1,8,10 |

5189 _____.
| | 1973 | 28 | *Opera* | |
| | | | (346) | *1,8,10 |

5190 _____.
| | 1974 | 29 | *Musical Literature* | |
| | | | (1008) | *1,8,13 |

5191 _____.
| | 1975 | 30 | *Books on Music & Musicians* | |
| | | | (850) | *1,8 |

5192 _____.
| | 1976 | 31 | *Chamber Music* | |
| | | | (499) | *1,8 |

5193 _____.
| | 1977 | 32 | *Opera* | |
| | | | (496) | *1,8,10 |

5194 _____.
| | 1977 | 33 | *Music for Performance* | |
| | | | (928) | *1,10,14 |

5195 _____.
| | 1977 | 34 | *Books on Music & Musicians* | |
| | | | (1271) | *1,10,14 |

5196 _____.
| | 1978 | 35 | *Vocal Music* | |
| | | | (466) | *1,10,14 |

5197 _____.
| | 1979 | 36 | *Books on Music & Musicians* | |
| | | | (922) | *1,8,10,14 |

5198 _____.
| | 1979 | 37 | *Vocal Music* | |
| | | | (564) | *1,8,10,14 |

5199 _____.
| | 1980 | 38 | *Music* | |
| | | | (1197) | *1,8,10,14 |

5200 _____.
| | 1980 | 39 | *Books on Music & Musicians* | |
| | | | (1392) | *8,14 |

1 Compiler/State University of New York (Buffalo)   **2** The British Library (London)   **3** Gemeentemuseum (Den Haag)   **4** The Grolier Club (N.Y.C.)   **5** Hirsch Collection, British Library (London)   **6** D.W. Krummel (Urbana)   **7** Library of Congress (Washington, D.C.)   **8** Library and Museum of the Performing Arts (N.Y.C.)   **9** William Reeves (London)   **10** Sibley Library, Eastman School of Music (Rochester)   **11** Nigel Simeone (Tunbridge Wells, Kent)   **12** Vereeniging ter Bervordering van de Belangen des Boekhandels (Amsterdam)   **13** University of Virginia (Charlottesville)   **14** University of California at Los Angeles   **15** Generally available

5201   **TRAVIS & EMERY (London and Salisbury) (continued)**

	1980	40	*Vocal Music* (633)	*1,10
5202	_____. 1981	41	*Music. Miniature and Study Scores* (1116)	*1,8,10
5203	_____. 1981	42	*Books on Music & Musicians* (1006)	*1,10
5204	_____. 1982	43	*Opera. Songs. Choral Works. Hymn Books* (590)	*1,8
5205	_____. 1983	44	*Books on Music & Musicians* (1038)	*1,8
5206	_____. 1983	45	*Stage Works. Songs. Choral Works* (600)	*1,8
5207	_____. 1984	46	*Books on Music & Musicians* (1120)	*1,8
5208			*"SARUM CATALOGUES"* (Salisbury)	
5209	_____. 1972?	1	*300 Years of London Music* (204)	*1,8,10
5210	_____. 1073?	2	*Full Scores and Orchestral Material* (211)	*1,8,10,11
5211	_____. 1975	3	*Music from Europe* (358)	*1,10,11
5212	_____. 1976	4	*Music Publishing in England* (403)	*1,8,10
5213	_____. 1978	5	*Music, Old and New* (490)	*1,8,10,14
5214	_____. 1979	6	*Music* (535)	*1,8,10,14
5215	_____. 1980	7	*Music* (635)	*1,8,10
5216	_____. 1981	8	*Music* (707)	*10

1 Compiler/State University of New York (Buffalo)   **2** The British Library (London)   **3** Gemeentemuseum (Den Haag)   **4** The Grolier Club (N.Y.C.)   **5** Hirsch Collection, British Library (London)   **6** D.W. Krummel (Urbana)   **7** Library of Congress (Washington, D.C.)   **8** Library and Museum of the Performing Arts (N.Y.C.)   **9** William Reeves (London)   **10** Sibley Library, Eastman School of Music (Rochester)   **11** Nigel Simeone (Tunbridge Wells, Kent)   **12** Vereeniging ter Bervordering van de Belangen des Boekhandels (Amsterdam)   **13** University of Virginia (Charlottesville)   **14** University of California at Los Angeles   **15** Generally available

5217 **TRAVIS & EMERY (London and Salisbury) (continued)**
      1982   9   *Music*
                          (581)   *1,8

5218 _____.
      1983   10   *Music*
                          (581)   *1,8

5219 _____.
      1984   11   *Music*
                          (750)   *1,8

5220 _____.
      1984   12   *Books on Music and Drama. Programmes*
                          (266)   *1,8

5221
                                "NEWSLETTERS"

5222 _____.
      12/1971   —   *[Instrumental Music, ca. 1760]*
                          (1p.)   *8

5223 _____.
      2/1972   —   *Periodicals. Prokofiev Works*
                          (67)   *10

5224 _____.
      3/1972   —   *Opera*
                          (222)   *1,8,10

5225 _____.
      4/1972   —   *Orchestral Materials*
                          (99)   *1,8,10

5226 _____.
      5/1972   —   *English Musical Drama. Italian Opera in London*
                          (66)   *10

5227 _____.
      9/1972   —   *Mendelssohn*
                          (131)   *1,8,10

5228 _____.
      11/1972   —   *Opera and Ballet*
                          (89)   *1,10

5229 _____.
      1/1973   —   *Orchestral Scores*
                          (139)   *1,8,10

5230 _____.
      4/1973   —   *Instrumental and Chamber Music*
                          (225)   *1,10

5231 _____.
      12/1973   —   *Piano Music*
                          (198)   *1,8,10

5232 _____.
      1/1974   —   *Gustav Holst, R. V. Williams, Havergal Brian*
                          (432)   *13

---

1 Compiler/State University of New York (Buffalo)   **2** The British Library (London)   **3** Gemeentemuseum (Den Haag)   **4** The Grolier Club (N.Y.C.)   **5** Hirsch Collection, British Library (London)   **6** D.W. Krummel (Urbana)   **7** Library of Congress (Washington, D.C.)   **8** Library and Museum of the Performing Arts (N.Y.C.)   **9** William Reeves (London)   **10** Sibley Library, Eastman School of Music (Rochester)   **11** Nigel Simeone (Tunbridge Wells, Kent)   **12** Vereeniging ter Bervordering van de Belangen des Boekhandels (Amsterdam)   **13** University of Virginia (Charlottesville)   **14** University of California at Los Angeles   **15** Generally available

5233 **TRAVIS & EMERY (London and Salisbury) (continued)**
      2/1974   —   *Orchestral Music*
                                        (401)   *1,6,8

5234 _____.
      3/1975   —   *Vocal Scores and Songs*
                                        (156)   *10,13

5235 _____.
      9/1975   —   *Opera*
                                        (161)   *1

5236 _____.
      2/1965   List   A-65   *Orchestral Scores*
                                          (54)   *6

5237 **TREGASKIS, JAMES (London)**
      s.d.   1022   *Caxton Head Catalogue. Manuscripts ... Music*
                                        (67-79)   *10

5238 **TULKENS, FL. (Brussels)**
      1950   70   *Musique, ancien et moderne. Theatre. Danse*
                                        (1235)   *1,11,13

5239 **TURRI, LIBRERIA (Milan)**
      1939   6   *Medicina. Musica e varia*
                                        (1184)   *12

5240 **TYROLIA ANTIQUARIAT (Vienna)**
      [1928]   17   *Kunstgeschichte. Kunstblätter. Theater. Musik*
                                        (778)   *12

5241 **UNGER, C. W. (Pottsville, PA.)**
      1922   List   371   *Early American Songs and Hymns in Sheet Music*
                                        (142)   *8

5242 _____.
      192_   do.   460   *Sheet Music with Songs or Poetry by Americans*
                                        (147)   *8

5243 _____.
      1924   do.   478   *American Minstrel & Ethiopian Songs.*
                                        (201)   *8

5244 _____.
      1924   do.   501   *Early Amer. Sheet Music with Pictorial Covers*
                                        (181)   *8

5245 _____.
      1931   do.   822   *Early American Sheet Music, Part III*
                                        (89)   *8

5246 _____.
      1931   do.   887   *Early Amer. Minstrel, Negro & Ethiopian Songs*
                                        (192)   *8

5247 _____.
      1933   do.   25   *Americana, including Music and Autographs*
                                        (?)   *7

5248 **UNIVERSAL BOOKS (Hollywood, CA.)**
      1969   137   *Music & Dance*
                                        (442)   *14

5249 **UNIVERSITÄTSBUCHHANDLUNG (Rostock)**
    1959   118   *Film. Tanz. Theater. Musik*
                          (778)   *12

5250 **UPDIKE, JOHN (Edinburgh)**
    [1966]   2   *First Editions. Books. Music. Drawings*
                          (250)   *12

5251 **VALLERI, GIOVANNI (FIRENZE)**
    4/1965   50   *Teatro. Musica. Cinema*
                          (363-498,1861-1   938)*6

5252 _____.
    5/1965   51   *Teatro. Musica. Cinema*
                          296-413)   *6

5253 _____.
    6/1965   52   *Teatro. Musica. Cinema*
                          (583-707)   *6

5254 _____.
    9/1965   53   *Teatro. Musica. Cinema*
                          (437-550)   *6

5255 _____.
    1/1966   56   *Teatro. Musica. Cinema*
                          (1012-1105)   *6

5256 _____.
    3/1966   60   *Teatro. Musica. Cinema*
                          (1170-1327)   *6

5257 _____.
    5/1966   60   *Teatro. Musica. Cinema*
                          (875-950)   *6

5258 _____.
    6/1967   69   *Musica. Teatro. Cinema*
                          (301-86)   *6

5259 _____.
    10/1967   72   *Musica. Teatro. Cinema*
                          (514-723)   *6

5260 _____.
    6/1958   80   *Music. Teatro. Cinema*
                          (958-1059)   *6

5261 _____.
    5/1978   Cat.   25   *Teatro - Musica - Cinema*
                          (131-87)   *8

5262 _____.
    10/1981   58   *Teatro - Musica - Cinema*
                          (145-215)   *8

5263 _____.
    12/1981   60   *Teatro - Musica - Cinema*
                          (302-402)   *8

5264 _____.
    9/1983   76   *Teatro - Musica - Cinema*
                          (161-217)   *8

1 Compiler/State University of New York (Buffalo)   **2** The British Library (London)   **3** Gemeentemuseum (Den Haag)   **4** The Grolier Club (N.Y.C.)   **5** Hirsch Collection, British Library (London)   **6** D.W. Krummel (Urbana)   **7** Library of Congress (Washington, D.C.)   **8** Library and Museum of the Performing Arts (N.Y.C.)   **9** William Reeves (London)   **10** Sibley Library, Eastman School of Music (Rochester)   **11** Nigel Simeone (Tunbridge Wells, Kent)   **12** Vereeniging ter Bervordering van de Belangen des Boekhandels (Amsterdam)   **13** University of Virginia (Charlottesville)   **14** University of California at Los Angeles   **15** Generally available

5265 **VALLERI, GIOVANNI (FIRENZE)** (continued)
6/1984   79   *Teatro - Musica - Cinema*
(225-73)   *8

5266 **VANDERSTOEL, GRAEME (El Cerrito, CA.)**
[1977]   List   28   *Ethnomusicology and Dance*
(57)   *13

5267 _____.
s.d.   do.   33   *Jazz*
(59)   *13

5268 _____.
[1978]   do.   36   *Ethnomusicology*
(56)   *13

5269 _____.
1980   do.   47   *Ethnomusicology*
(56)   *8

5270 **VERBANDES DER ANTIQUARE ÖSTERREICHS**
1966   [3]   *Musik und Theater in Österreich*
(251)   [IBAK]

5271 **VITALI IMPORT CO. (Maywood, CA.)**
[1966]   —   *Books [on Music]*
(4pp.)   *1

5272 _____.
1970/71   —   *Books [on Music]*
(98)   *1

5273 _____.
1973   —   *Books [on Music]*
(124)   *1

5274 **VITTORIO, LIBRERIA (Firenze) [each cat. more than 35 lots of music]**
1969   65   *Libri antichi e moderni*
(593-670)   *13

5275 _____.
1969   68   *Libri antichi e moderni*
(1448-1495)   *13

5276 _____.
1969   70   *Libri antichi e moderni*
(893-956)   *13

5277 _____.
1969   72   *Libri antichi e moderni*
(408-480)   *13

5278 _____.
1970   75   *Libri antichi e moderni*
(311-46)   *13

5279 _____.
1970   76   *Libri antichi e moderni*
(547-613)   *13

5280 _____.
1970   80   *Libri antichi e moderni*
(390-427)   *13

5281   **VITTORIO, LIBRERIA (Firenze) (continued)**
         1971   83   *Libri antichi e moderni*
                                     (508-49)   *13
5282   _____.
         1971   84   *Libri antichi e moderni*
                                     (731-73)   *13
5283   _____.
         1971   85   *Libri antichi e moderni*
                                     (331-89)   *13
5284   _____.
         1971   88   *Libri antichi e moderni*
                                     (634-74)   *13
5285   _____.
         1971   91   *Libri antichi e moderni*
                                     (357-96)   *13
5286   _____.
         1971   92   *Libri antichi e moderni*
                                     (1411-463)   *13
5287   _____.
         1972   95   *Libri antichi e moderni*
                                     (400-43)   *13
5288   _____.
         1972   96   *Libri antichi e moderni*
                                     (618-76)   *13
5289   _____.
         1972   100   *Libri antichi e moderni*
                                     (646-78)   *13
5290   _____.
         1972   1   *Libri antichi e moderni*
                                     (1195-231)   *13
5291   _____.
         1972   2   *Libri antichi e moderni*
                                     (1460-498)   *13
5292   _____.
         1973   3   *Libri antichi e moderni*
                                     (436-80)   *13
5293   **VLETTER, W. C. de (Rotterdam)**
         s.d.   Bull.   20   *Muziek*
                                     (?)   *7,12
5294   _____.
         s.d.   Cat.   1-10   *Muziek*
                                     (?)   *7
5295   **VLOEMANS, H. A. (Den Haag)**
         1961   13   *Musik. Kunst*
                                     (250)   [IBAK]
5296   **VOERSTER, J. (Stuttgart)**
         1967   1   *Musik in Erst- u. Frühdrucken. Musikliteratur*
                                     (131)   *4,8,12,13,14

1 Compiler/State University of New York (Buffalo)   **2** The British Library (London)   **3** Gemeentemuseum (Den Haag)   **4** The Grolier Club (N.Y.C.)   **5** Hirsch Collection, British Library (London)   **6** D.W. Krummel (Urbana)   **7** Library of Congress (Washington, D.C.)   **8** Library and Museum of the Performing Arts (N.Y.C.)   **9** William Reeves (London)   **10** Sibley Library, Eastman School of Music (Rochester)   **11** Nigel Simeone (Tunbridge Wells, Kent)   **12** Vereeniging ter Bervordering van de Belangen des Boekhandels (Amsterdam)   **13** University of Virginia (Charlottesville)   **14** University of California at Los Angeles   **15** Generally available

5297 **VOERSTER, J. (Stuttgart) (continued)**
  1968   2   *Musik und Theater. Seltene Musikdrucke*
                                   (410)   *4,6,8,12,13,14

5298 _____.
  1969   3   *Musiker- und Dichter-Autographen*
                                   (266)   *1,4,8,12,13

5299 _____.
  1970   4   *Musikliteratur*
                                   (944)   *1,6,8,12,13,14

5300 **VRIN, J. (Paris)**
  1933   NS188   *... 1re partie: Musicologie*
                                   (2317-552)   *8

5301 **VYT, CAMILLE (Gand)**
  1895   374   *Musik. Theater*
                                   (744)   [MfM]

5302 **WAGNER, PAUL (Houston)**
  s.d.   —   *Sheet Music of the Period 1842-1865*
                                   [15pp.]   *8

5303 **WALFORD, G. W. (London)**
  s.d.   TM/2   *Theatre and Music*
                                   (212)   *14

5304 _____.
  s.d.   TM/3   *Theatre and Music. Scores*
                                   (241)   *14

5305 _____.
  s.d.   TM/9   *[Books on Instruments. Scores. Dance. Theatre]*
                                   (259)   *14

5306 _____.
  s.d.   TM/10   *Theatre and Music*
                                   (253)   *14

5307 _____.
  s.d.   TM/11   *[Organ. Instruments. Opera. History]*
                                   (311)   *14

5308 _____.
  [1964]   TM/12   *[Theatre. Music]*
                                   (194)   [IBAK]

5309 _____.
  1964   TM/13   *Theatre and Music*
                                   (276)   *14

5310 _____.
  1965   TM/15   *Theatre and Music*
                                   (201)   *14

5311 _____.
  s.d.   TM/19   *Theatre and Music*
                                   (169)   *14

5312 _____.
  [1970]   TM/23   *Theatre and Music*
                                   (183)   *12

5313 **WALKER, JOHN W. (London)**
    1923   5   *Coll: Hervey, Arthur. Scores. Music Criticism*
                          (530-813)   *8

5314 **WALLISHAUSSER BUCHHANDLUNG (Vienna)**
    1957?   2   *Theater - Musik - Kostümkunde*
                          (1-338-,830-53)   *8

5315 **WASTIAU, LIBRAIRE (Brussels)**
    1963   —   *Costumes. Musique et théâtre*
                          (100)   [IBAK]

5316 **WEIGEL, ADOLF (Leipzig)**
    s.d.   83   *Theater. Musik. Lied*
                          (828-1380)   *8,12

5317 **WEIGEL, OSWALD (Leipzig)**
    1896   NF74   *M.-Geschichte, Theorie. Prakt.-Musik. Theater*
                          (856)   *8

5318 _____.
    1901   NF98   *... Hymnologie. Liturgik. Geistliche Musik*
                          (1859-2293)   *8

5319 _____.
    1904   NF111   *Musik Festlichkeiten - Opern - Ballete - Tanz*
                          (843)   *8

5320 **WEINGART, E. (Erfurt)**
    s.d.   139   *Musikalien und Werke ü. Musik*
                          (40pp.)   *5

5321 _____.
    1860   157   *Musikalien und Werke ü. Musik*
                          (56pp)   [Petzholdt]

5322 _____.
    [1862]   209   *Musikalien und Werke ü. Musik*
                          (?)   [Petzholdt]

5323 _____.
    s.d.   273   *Dissertationen ... Musikalien*
                          (92pp.)   *12

5324 _____.
    s.d.   278   *Musikalien und Schriften ü. Musik*
                          (4pp.)   *8

5325 _____.
    s.d.   281   *Kirchenmusik. Compositionen für die Orgel*
                          (16pp.)   *8

5326 **WEINSTEIN BOOK (Cerritos, CA.)**
    1970   2   *Music and Dance*
                          (192)   *,14

5327 _____.
    [1971]   6   *Music, Theatre and Dance*
                          (842)   *10,13

5328 **WEISS, SIGMUND (N.Y.C.)**
    [1949?]   1   *Music Sale List [books]*
                          (289)   *8

5329　**WEISS, SIGMUND (N.Y.C.) (continued)**
　　　　[1953]　　　　　3　　*Third Music Sale List [books]*
　　　　　　　　　　　　　　(407)　　　　　　　　　　　　　　　　　*8

5330　_____.
　　　　s.d.　　　　　　4　　*4th Music Sale List*
　　　　　　　　　　　　　　(307)　　　　　　　　　　　　　　　　　*14

5331　**WELTER, HUBERT (Paris)**
　　　　[1900]　　　　110　　*Musique et theatre*
　　　　　　　　　　　　　　(23pp.)　　　　　　　　　　　　　　　*12

5332　**WESTERMAN, B., CO., INC. (N.Y.C.)**
　　　　s.d.　　　　　　3　　*Autographs. Scores. Mss. Original Eds. Facs.*
　　　　　　　　　　　　　　(344)　　　　　　　　　　　　　　　*8,10,13

5333　**WHELDON & WESLEY (London)**
　　　　1924　　　　　NS11　　*Elizabethan Madrigals. Early English Music*
　　　　　　　　　　　　　　(184)　　　　　　　　　　　　　　　*7,8,12

5334　_____.
　　　　1929　　　　　NS21　　*Elizabethan Madrigals. Early English Music*
　　　　　　　　　　　　　　(21)　　　　　　　　　　　　　　　　*8

5335　**WHITE, HENRY, AND SONS (London)**
　　　　1861　　　　　Pt.3!　　*Music and Musical Literature*
　　　　　　　　　　　　　　(1401-2059)　　　　　　　　　　　　*8

5336　_____.
　　　　1878　　　　　Pt.1　　*Music and Musical Literature*
　　　　　　　　　　　　　　(774)　　　　　　　　　　　　　　　　*8

5337　_____.
　　　　1878　　　　　Pt.2　　*Music and Musical Literature*
　　　　　　　　　　　　　　(775-1555)　　　　　　　　　　　　*8

5338　**WHITELOCKE, HERBERT (London)**
　　　　1950　　　　　1　　*Music and Musicians*
　　　　　　　　　　　　　　(218)　　　　　　　　　　　　　　　　*6

5339　_____.
　　　　s.d.　　　　　—　　*The World of Entertainment*
　　　　　　　　　　　　　　(235)　　　　　　　　　　　　　　　　*6

5340　**WHITTINGHAM, ALFRED (London)**
　　　　1860?　　　　3　　*Scarce and Curious Music*
　　　　　　　　　　　　　　(1038)　　　　　　　　　　　　　　　*3

5341　_____.
　　　　1860?　　　　4　　*Valuable Ancient and Modern Music*
　　　　　　　　　　　　　　(700)　　　　　　　　　　　　　　　　*3

5342　**WIELENGA, W. (Harderwijk)**
　　　　s.d.　　　　　—　　*Muziek*
　　　　　　　　　　　　　　(?)　　　　　　　　　　　　　　　　　*12

5343　**WIJNEKUS, G. H. (Amsterdam)**
　　　　s.d.　　　　　—　　*Muziek-Voordrachten*
　　　　　　　　　　　　　　(?)　　　　　　　　　　　　　　　　　*12

5344　**WILLIAMS BOOK STORE (Boston)**
　　　　[1941]　　Bull.　　1　　*Original Amer. Music and Early Amer. Reprints*
　　　　　　　　　　　　　　(4pp.)　　　　　　　　　　　　　　　*8

5345	**WILSON, B. & L. (London)**			
	[1949]	4	*General Music List*	
			(648)	*8
5346	_____.			
	1949	5	*idem.*	
			(1105)	*6
5347	_____.			
	1949-50	6	*idem.*	
			(1842)	*1,6
5348	_____.			
	1950	7	*idem.*	
			(1072)	*1,6
5349	_____.			
	1950	8	*idem.*	
			(1093)	*6
5350	_____.			
	1951	9	*idem.*	
			(6774)	*1,6,8
5351	_____.			
	S/1951	—	*idem.*	
			(934)	*6,9
5352	_____.			
	1951	10	*idem.*	
			(1311)	*6
5353	_____.			
	1951-52	—	*idem.*	
			(475)	*6
5354	_____.			
	1952	11	*idem.*	
			(1104)	*1,6
5355	_____.			
	1952	—	*idem.*	
			(595)	*6
5356	_____.			
	1952-53	12	*idem.*	
			(1940)	*1,6,8,9
5357	_____.			
	1952	12A	*Music in 18th Century Editions*	
			(1089)	*6
5358	_____.			
	1952-53	—/	*General Music Catalogue*	
			(1234)	*6,9
5359	_____.			
	1953	14	*idem.*	
			(3504)	*6,8,9
5360	_____.			
	S/1953	—	*idem.*	
			(1050)	*6,9

1 Compiler/State University of New York (Buffalo)   **2** The British Library (London)   **3** Gemeentemuseum (Den Haag)   **4** The Grolier Club (N.Y.C.)   **5** Hirsch Collection, British Library (London)   **6** D.W. Krummel (Urbana)   **7** Library of Congress (Washington, D.C.)   **8** Library and Museum of the Performing Arts (N.Y.C.)   **9** William Reeves (London)   **10** Sibley Library, Eastman School of Music (Rochester)   **11** Nigel Simeone (Tunbridge Wells, Kent)   **12** Vereeniging ter Bevordering van de Belangen des Boekhandels (Amsterdam)   **13** University of Virginia (Charlottesville)   **14** University of California at Los Angeles   **15** Generally available

5361	**WILSON, B. & L. (London) (continued)**			
	1953-54	15	*idem.*	
			(3177)	*1,6,8,9
5362	_____.			
	1953-54	—	*idem.*	
			(986)	*6,8,9
5363	_____.			
	1954	16	*idem.*	
			(1704)	*1,6,9
5364	_____.			
	S/1954	—	*idem.*	
			(1199)	*6,8,9
5365	_____.			
	1955	17	*idem.)*	
			(2563)	*1,6,8
5366	_____.			
	1955	—	*idem.*	
			(1453)	*6,9
5367	_____.			
	1955	18	*idem.*	
			(3946)	*1,6,9
5368	_____.			
	1956	19	*idem.*	
			(941)	*1,6,9
5369	_____.			
	1956	20	*Vocal Music. Instr. Music. Miscellaneous*	
			(30pp.)	*9
5370	_____.			
	1956	21	*General Music Catalogue*	
			(2225)	*9
5371	_____.			
	1958	24	*idem.*	
			(1147)	*1,6,9
5372	_____.			
	10/1958	25	*idem.*	
			(1844)	*1,6,9
5373	_____.			
	1959	26	*idem.*	
			(1496)	*9
5374	_____.			
	1960	27	*idem.*	
			(1626)	*1,9
5375	_____.			
	196_	29	*idem.*	
			(1010)	*1
5376	_____.			
	196_	30	*Full Scores and Orchestral Material*	
			(110)	*8

1 Compiler/State University of New York (Buffalo)   **2** The British Library (London)   **3** Gemeentemuseum (Den Haag)   **4** The Grolier Club (N.Y.C.)   **5** Hirsch Collection, British Library (London)   **6** D.W. Krummel (Urbana)   **7** Library of Congress (Washington, D.C.)   **8** Library and Museum of the Performing Arts (N.Y.C.)   **9** William Reeves (London)   **10** Sibley Library, Eastman School of Music (Rochester)   **11** Nigel Simeone (Tunbridge Wells, Kent)   **12** Vereeniging ter Bervordering van de Belangen des Boekhandels (Amsterdam)   **13** University of Virginia (Charlottesville)   **14** University of California at Los Angeles   **15** Generally available

5377 **WILSON, B. & L. (London) (continued)**
          n.d.   31   *General Music Catalogue*
                                             (1731)   *6

5378 _____.
          1961   33   *idem.*
                                             (1731)   *6

5379 **WILSON, BERNARD (London)**
          1964   —   *Orch. Materials. Min. Scores. Instr. Music*
                                             (5623)   *1,13

5380 _____.
          1965   —   *Books on Music. Vocal Scores. Songs*
                                             (1338)   *1

5381 _____.
          1966   —   *Spring: Books. Organ Music*
                                             (419)   *1

5382 _____.
          1966/67   —   *Winter: Keyboard Music. Plectral Music*
                                             (492)   *1,8

5383 _____.
          1968   —   *Spring: Songs. Vocal Scores. Wind Music*
                                             (471)   *1,8

5384 _____. **(moved to Hythe, Kent)**
          1968   —   *Interim Summer: Full Scores. Pfte. & Vocal M.*
                                             (388)   *1,6,8

5385 _____.
          1968   —   *Orchestral Music*
                                             (17pp.)   *1,6,8

5386 _____.
          1970   —   *Spring: Scores. Books. Orchestral Music*
                                             (10pp.)   *1,6

5387 _____.
          1971   —   *Spring: Scores and Books. Orchestral Sets*
                                             (10pp.)   *1,13

5388 _____.
          1972   —   *Scores. Orchestral Sets.*
                                             (10pp.)   *9

5389 _____.
          1975   —   *Summer: Ballet. Chamber Music*
                                             (5pp.)   *1,8,13

5390 _____. **(now WILSON'S, Caenarvon, N. Wales)**
          1975   —   *Summer: Chamber Music. Scores. Books*
                                             (14pp.)   *1,8

5391 **WILSON, GAIL (Toronto)**
          1984   List   —   *[Books on] Jazz*
                                             (40)   *1

5392 **WILSTON BUREAU (N.Y.C.)**
          s.d.   List   22   *Music [books about]*
                                             (107)   *8

---

1 Compiler/State University of New York (Buffalo)   **2** The British Library (London)   **3** Gemeentemuseum (Den Haag)   **4** The Grolier Club (N.Y.C.)   **5** Hirsch Collection, British Library (London)   **6** D.W. Krummel (Urbana)   **7** Library of Congress (Washington, D.C.)   **8** Library and Museum of the Performing Arts (N.Y.C.)   **9** William Reeves (London)   **10** Sibley Library, Eastman School of Music (Rochester)   **11** Nigel Simeone (Tunbridge Wells, Kent)   **12** Vereeniging ter Bervordering van de Belangen des Boekhandels (Amsterdam)   **13** University of Virginia (Charlottesville)   **14** University of California at Los Angeles   **15** Generally available

5393 **WILSTON BUREAU (N.Y.C.) (continued)**
       s.d.   do.   54   *Music [books about]*
                                       (243)   *8
5394 _____.
       s.d.   do.   —   *Music [books about]*
                                       (8pp.)   *8
5395 **WITSEN, A., VAN (Rotterdam)**
       [1937]   16   *Muziek. Partituren*
                                       (592)   *12
5396 _____.
       [1942]   N.S.4 *Muziek. Partituren*
                                       (664)   *12
5397 **WITT, RICHARD (London)**
       [1980]   —   *Music and Books about Music*
                                       (454)   *8
5398 **WITTMANN'SCHE BUCHHANDLUNG (Berlin)**
       [1953]   3   *Musik. Bücher und Zeitschriften*
                                       (375)   *8,9
5399 _____.
       s.d.   15   *Music. Books and Periodicals. Alte Musikalien*
                                       (557)   *9
5400 _____.
       s.d.   23   *Musik. Theater. Tanz. Film*
                                       (622)   *9
5401 _____.
       s.d.   34   *Musik*
                                       (752)   *12
5402 _____.
       s.d.   S.-A.   24   *Sonderangebot. Musik*
                                       (605)   *12
5403 _____.
       [1963]   do.   27   *idem.*
                                       (845)   *6,12
5404 **WOOD, PETER (Cambridge, U.K.)**
       1973   1   *Theatre. Music*
                                       (763)   *12
5405 _____.
       1973   2   *... Music. Theatre*
                                       (730-68)   *10
5406 _____.
       1973   2A   *Suppl. Performing Arts*
                                       (216)   *10
5407 _____.
       1974   3   *Theatre. Musical Literature. Dance. Cinema*
                                       (1099-2118)   *8,10
5408 _____.
       197_   7   *Musical Literature. Jazz. Opera*
                                       (980   *8,10

1 Compiler/State University of New York (Buffalo)   **2** The British Library (London)   **3** Gemeentemuseum
(Den Haag)   **4** The Grolier Club (N.Y.C.)   **5** Hirsch Collection, British Library (London)   **6** D.W.
Krummel (Urbana)   **7** Library of Congress (Washington, D.C.)   **8** Library and Museum of the Performing
Arts (N.Y.C.)   **9** William Reeves (London)   **10** Sibley Library, Eastman School of Music (Rochester)
11 Nigel Simeone (Tunbridge Wells, Kent)   **12** Vereeniging ter Bevordering van de Belangen des
Boekhandels (Amsterdam)   **13** University of Virginia (Charlottesville)   **14** University of California at Los
Angeles   **15** Generally available

5409 **WOOD, PETER** (Cambridge, U.K.) (continued)

| | 197_ | 10 | *Fine and Rare Books ... on Performing Arts* (189-290) | *10 |

5410 _____.

| | 197_ | 12 | *Performing Arts. Ballet. Music. Theatre* (1-312) | *10 |

5411 _____.

| | 197_ | 15 | *Performing Arts. Ballet. Opera. Music* (51-381) | *10 |

5412 _____.

| | 197_ | 18 | *Musical Lit. Jazz. Programs. Min. Scores* (1160) | *10 |

5413 _____.

| | 197_ | 19 | *Performing Arts. Ballet. Opera. Music* (1041-1467) | *10 |

5414 _____.

| | 1979 | 21 | *Music and Opera* (1271) | *1,8 |

5415 _____.

| | 1980 | 24 | *Art. Ballet. Bibliography. Music. Opera* (872) | *1 |

5416 _____.

| | 1981 | 29 | *Performing Arts* (409-702, 1083- | 1195) *1 |

5417 _____.

| | 1982 | 33 | *idem.* (895) | *1 |

5418 _____.

| | 1983 | 35 | *Performing Arts. Music Literature. Theatre* (758) | *1 |

5419 _____.

| | 1983 | 36 | *Entertainment Ephemera. Song Sheets. Posters* (2403) | *1 |

5420 _____.

| | 1983 | 36-1 | *Supplement [to 36]. Programmes* (2404-4177) | *1 |

5421 _____.

| | 1983 | 36-2 | *Supplement 2: Ephemera of Entertainment* (4187-4708) | *1 |

5422 _____.

| | 1983 | 37 | *Performing Arts. Ballet. Opera. Jazz/Pop* (824) | *1 |

5423 _____.

| | 1984 | 40 | *Music and Music Literature. Opera. Jazz/Pop* (441) | *1 |

5424 _____.

| | 1984 | NS10 | *Ballet. Music. Opera. Theatre. Jazz* (337) | *1 |

---

1 Compiler/State University of New York (Buffalo) **2** The British Library (London) **3** Gemeentemuseum (Den Haag) **4** The Grolier Club (N.Y.C.) **5** Hirsch Collection, British Library (London) **6** D.W. Krummel (Urbana) **7** Library of Congress (Washington, D.C.) **8** Library and Museum of the Performing Arts (N.Y.C.) **9** William Reeves (London) **10** Sibley Library, Eastman School of Music (Rochester) **11** Nigel Simeone (Tunbridge Wells, Kent) **12** Vereeniging ter Bervordering van de Belangen des Boekhandels (Amsterdam) **13** University of Virginia (Charlottesville) **14** University of California at Los Angeles **15** Generally available

5425 **WOOD, PETER (Cambridge, U.K.) (continued)**
      1984   NS11   *Ballet. Music. Jazz. Opera...Libretti*
                              (648)   *1

5426 **WRIGHT'S MUSIC SHOP (Madison, Wisconsin)**
      [1962]   2   *Music*
                              (546)   *6

5427 ____.
      [1962]   3   *Used Music*
                              (1231)   *6

5428 ____.
      [1963]   3-2   *Full Scores. Orchestral Parts*
                            (293)   *6,8,11

5429 ____.
      [1963]   4   *Music History*
                            (715+)   *6,11

5430 ____.
      [1964]   5   *Music Literature*
                            (1402)   *6,8,11,13

5431 ____.
      [196_]   6   *Music of Max Reger*
                            (16pp.)   *1,6,8,10,11

5432 ____.
      [196_]   7   *Music Lit. Facsimiles. Reference Books*
                            (1702)   *1,6,8,10,11,13

5433 ____.
      [196_]   8   *Full Scores. Oratorio Full Scores*
                            (552)   *1,6,8,10,11

5434 ____.
      [196_]   9   *Music Literature*
                            (1705)   *1,6,8,10,11

5435 ____.
      [196_]   10   *Piano-Music - Used*
                            (412)   *1,6,8,10,11

5436 ____.
      1964   List   —   *Study Scores, Recent and Modern*
                            (57)   *1

5437 ____.
      1965   do.   1   *Books and Music*
                            (216)   *6,14

5438 ____.
      1965   do.   [2]   *New and Used Opera Scores*
                            (316)   *6,14

5439 ____.
      1965   do.   3   *Music for Voice*
                            (517)   *8,14

5440 ____.
      [1966]   do.   4   *Chamber Music*
                            (557)   *1,8,10,14

---

1 Compiler/State University of New York (Buffalo)   **2** The British Library (London)   **3** Gemeentemuseum (Den Haag)   **4** The Grolier Club (N.Y.C.)   **5** Hirsch Collection, British Library (London)   **6** D.W. Krummel (Urbana)   **7** Library of Congress (Washington, D.C.)   **8** Library and Museum of the Performing Arts (N.Y.C.)   **9** William Reeves (London)   **10** Sibley Library, Eastman School of Music (Rochester)   **11** Nigel Simeone (Tunbridge Wells, Kent)   **12** Vereeniging ter Bervordering van de Belangen des Boekhandels (Amsterdam)   **13** University of Virginia (Charlottesville)   **14** University of California at Los Angeles   **15** Generally available

5441   WÜNSCHMANN, HEINZ (Berlin)
        1966   45   *Musik. Theater. Tanz. Film. Rundfunk*
                                    (362)   [IBAK]
5442   _____.
        1966   56   *Musik. Theater. Film*
                                    (374)   [IBAK]
5443   WULKOW, O. (Magdeburg)
        1875   14   *Architectur. Kunst. Musik*
                                    (?)   *12
5444   WYLER, MICHAEL (West Moors, Wimborne, Dorset)
        197_   MB102   *Books on Music and Musicians*
                                    (230)   *8
5445   _____.
        [1973]   Ma103   *Musical Autographs. Cartes-de-visite*
                                    (365)   *8,13
5446   _____.
        [1973]   MB103   *Books on Music and Musicians*
                                    (372)   *8,13
5447   _____.
        s.d.   MA104   *Catalogue of Musical Autographs*
                                    (277)   *8
5448   _____.
        s.d.   MB104   *Books on Music and Musicians*
                                    (306)   *8
5449   _____.
        3/1977   —   *Antiquarian Music*
                                    (321)   *11
5450   XERXES RARE BOOKS (N.Y.C.)
        198_   List   359   *Music. Autographs. Mss. Music Lit. Scores*
                                    (132)   *1
5451   YOUNG, ISRAEL (N.Y.C.)
        1957   2   *Folk Song, Folk Lore, Folk Dance. Jazz*
                                    (597+27)   *8
5452   VON ZAHN, R. & JÄNSCH (Dresden)
        s.d.   111   *Musik und Theater*
                                    (1168)   *12
5453   _____.
        1906   191   *Coll: Stockhausen & Schwender. Musik*
                                    (2333)   *3,5
5454   _____.
        1915   270   *Musikgeschichte und Theorie*
                                    (2312)   *5
5455   _____.
        1925   313   *Musik. Theater. Musiktheorie*
                                    (1528)   *5
5456   _____.
        [1938]   343   *Kunstgeschichte. Literatur. Musik . Reisen*
                                    (834)   *12

1 Compiler/State University of New York (Buffalo)   2 The British Library (London)   3 Gemeentemuseum (Den Haag)   4 The Grolier Club (N.Y.C.)   5 Hirsch Collection, British Library (London)   6 D.W. Krummel (Urbana)   7 Library of Congress (Washington, D.C.)   8 Library and Museum of the Performing Arts (N.Y.C.)   9 William Reeves (London)   10 Sibley Library, Eastman School of Music (Rochester) 11 Nigel Simeone (Tunbridge Wells, Kent)   12 Vereeniging ter Bervordering van de Belangen des Boekhandels (Amsterdam)   13 University of Virginia (Charlottesville)   14 University of California at Los Angeles   15 Generally available

5457 **ZENTRAL-ANTIQUARIAT DER DDR (Berlin)**

	1960?]	A.-A.	304	*Antiq.-Angebot: Musik* (486)	[IBAK]
5458	[1961]	do.	354	*Musik. Theater. Tanz* (387)	[IBAK]
5459	1964	do.	664	*Musik. Theater. Tanz* (550)	*12
5460	[1966]	do.	794	*Theaterwissenschaft und Musik* (426)	[IBAK]
5461	1966	do.	828	*Theaterwissenschaft und Musik* (492)	*12
5462	1967	do.	871	*Musik. Theater* (329)	*12
5463	1967	do.	891	*Musik* (218)	*6,8,12
5464	1967	do.	911	*Musik. Theater. Tanz* (515)	*1,8,12
5465	1968	do.	919	*Musik* (257)	*12
5466	1968	do.	935	*Musik. Theater. Tanz* (459)	*8,12
5467	1968	do.	947	*Musik. Theater. Tanz* (367)	*12
5468	1968	do.	961	*Musik* (270)	*1,8,12
5469	1968	do.	977	*Musik. Theater* (300)	*1,6,8,12
5470	1968	do.	985	*Musik. Theater* (302)	*1,6,12
5471	1969	do.	999	*Musik* (257)	*12
5472	1969	do.	1017	*Musik* (217)	*1,8,12

1 Compiler/State University of New York (Buffalo)   **2** The British Library (London)   **3** Gemeentemuseum (Den Haag)   **4** The Grolier Club (N.Y.C.)   **5** Hirsch Collection, British Library (London)   **6** D.W. Krummel (Urbana)   **7** Library of Congress (Washington, D.C.)   **8** Library and Museum of the Performing Arts (N.Y.C.)   **9** William Reeves (London)   **10** Sibley Library, Eastman School of Music (Rochester)   **11** Nigel Simeone (Tunbridge Wells, Kent)   **12** Vereeniging ter Bervordering van de Belangen des Boekhandels (Amsterdam)   **13** University of Virginia (Charlottesville)   **14** University of California at Los Angeles   **15** Generally available

5473 **ZENTRAL-ANTIQUARIAT DER DDR** (Berlin) (continued)

	1969	do.	1044	*Musik* (254)	*1,12
5474	_____.				
	1969	do.	1054	*Musik. Theater. Tanz* (330)	*1,8,12
5475	_____.				
	1969	do.	1076	*Musik. Literatur* (212)	*1,8,12
5476	_____.				
	1969	do.	1085	*Musik. Literatur* (301)	*12
5477	_____.				
	1970	do.	1099	*Musik. Theater. Tanz* (220)	*12
5478	_____.				
	1970	do.	1115	*Musik. Literatur* (1353)	*1,12,13
5479	_____.				
	1970	do.	1152	*Musikalien* (484)	*1,10,12,13
5480	_____.				
	1971	do.	1216	*Musik, A-L* (293)	*12
5481	_____.				
	1972	do.	1241	*Musikliteratur* (431)	*1,8,10,12,13
5482	_____.				
	1972	do.	1247	*Theater. Tanz* (232)	*1,10,13
5483	_____.				
	1973	do.	1338	*Musik, A-M* (414)	*1,8,10,13
5484	_____.				
	1973	do.	1351	*Musikliteratur* (335)	*1,10,13
5485	_____.				
	1974	do.	1387	*Musikliteratur* (491)	*1
5486	_____.				
	1975	do.	1427	*Theater. Film. Tanz* (269)	*1
5487	_____.				
	1975	do.	1445	*Theater. Film. Tanz* (547)	*1
5488	_____.				
	1976	do.	1490	*Musikliteratur* (522)	*1,8,13

1 Compiler/State University of New York (Buffalo)   **2** The British Library (London)   **3** Gemeentemuseum (Den Haag)   **4** The Grolier Club (N.Y.C.)   **5** Hirsch Collection, British Library (London)   **6** D.W. Krummel (Urbana)   **7** Library of Congress (Washington, D.C.)   **8** Library and Museum of the Performing Arts (N.Y.C.)   **9** William Reeves (London)   **10** Sibley Library, Eastman School of Music (Rochester) **11** Nigel Simeone (Tunbridge Wells, Kent)   **12** Vereeniging ter Bervordering van de Belangen des Boekhandels (Amsterdam)   **13** University of Virginia (Charlottesville)   **14** University of California at Los Angeles   **15** Generally available

5489 **ZENTRAL-ANTIQUARIAT DER DDR (Berlin) (continued)**

	1976	do.	1502	*Theater. Tanz. Film* (449)	*1
5490	_____.				
	1977	do.	1504	*Musikliteratur* (641)	*1,10
5491	_____.				
	1978	do.	1544	*Musikliteratur* (479)	*1,10
5492	_____.				
	[1978]	do.	1551	*[Includes Musikliteratur]* (pp.31-35)	*13
5493	_____.				
	1979	do.	1585	*Musik- und Theaterliteratur* (480)	*1,10,13
5494	_____.				
	1980	do.	1624	*Musik- und Theaterliteratur* (672)	*1,8
5495	_____.				
	1981	do.	1665	*Musikliteratur* (487)	*1,8,10
5496	_____.				
	1981	do.	1696	*Theater. Film. Tanz* (361)	*1
5497	_____.				
	1981	do.	1705	*Musikliteratur* (673)	*1
5498	_____.				
	1982	do.	1753	*Kunst - Theater - Musik* (286)	*1,13
5499	_____.				
	1983	do.	1799	*Theater. Film. Tanz* (471)	*1
5500	_____.				
	[1967]	S.-A.	89	*Sonder-Angebot: Kunst - Musik - Theater* (184)	[IBAK]
5501	_____.				
	s.d.	do.	200	*Musik - Theater - Tanz* (160)	*13
5502	_____.				
	[1972]	do.	237	*Musik - Theater* (150)	*13
5503	_____.				
	1982	do.	329	*Kunst - Theater - Musik* (286)	*1
5504	_____.				
	1983	do.	335	*Kunst - Musik - Theater* (326)	*1

1 Compiler/State University of New York (Buffalo)   **2** The British Library (London)   **3** Gemeentemuseum (Den Haag)   **4** The Grolier Club (N.Y.C.)   **5** Hirsch Collection, British Library (London)   **6** D.W. Krummel (Urbana)   **7** Library of Congress (Washington, D.C.)   **8** Library and Museum of the Performing Arts (N.Y.C.)   **9** William Reeves (London)   **10** Sibley Library, Eastman School of Music (Rochester) **11** Nigel Simeone (Tunbridge Wells, Kent)   **12** Vereeniging ter Bervordering van de Belangen des Boekhandels (Amsterdam)   **13** University of Virginia (Charlottesville)   **14** University of California at Los Angeles   **15** Generally available

5505 **ZENTRAL-ANTIQUARIAT DER DDR** (Berlin) (continued)
    1968   Kat.   43   *Musik*
                       (1076)   *12

5506 .
    1971   do.   163   *Musik*
                       (585)   *12

5507 .
    1973   do.   172   *Musik. Theater*
                       (714)   *4,12

5508 .
    1983   do.   152!   *Musikliteratur*
                       (1482)   *13

5509 .
    [1983]   Liste   212   *Antiquariatsliste: Musik*
                       (761)   *13

5510 **ZEUNE, R.** (Berlin/Dresden/Weimar)
    1862   [17]   *Theoretisch und praktische Musik. Portraits*
                       (22pp.)   [Petzholdt]

5511 - .
    [1864]   —   *Bücher. Portraits*
                       (19pp.)   [Petzholdt]

5512 .
    1864?   19   *Coll: [unnamed]*
                       (16pp.)   [Petzholdt]

5513 .
    1905?   20   *Autographen ... Musiker, Sänger...*
                       (309)   *1,4

5514 **ZIMMERMAN** (Straubenhardt)
    [1984]   Liste   4   *Fotos. Porträts. Musik. Albumblätter*
                       (293)   *8

5515 .
    [1984]   Kat.   13   *[Musik und Musikliteratur]*
                       (500)   *8

5516 .
    [1985]   16   *Erst- u. Frühdrucke Musikliteratur. Portraits*
                       (316)   *8

5517 **ZLATIN, Madame S.** (Paris)
    1967   40   *Théâtre - Marionettes - Musique - Danse*
                       (299-319)   *1

5518 .
    1968   41   *Théâtre - Marionettes - Musique - Danse*
                       (367-416)   *1

5519 .
    1971   45   *Théâtre - Danse - Cirque - Musique*
                       (598-727)   *1,8

5520 .
    1972   46   *Théâtre - Danse - Cirque - Musique*
                       (671-740)   *1

1 Compiler/State University of New York (Buffalo)   **2** The British Library (London)   **3** Gemeentemuseum (Den Haag)   **4** The Grolier Club (N.Y.C.)   **5** Hirsch Collection, British Library (London)   **6** D.W. Krummel (Urbana)   **7** Library of Congress (Washington, D.C.)   **8** Library and Museum of the Performing Arts (N.Y.C.)   **9** William Reeves (London)   **10** Sibley Library, Eastman School of Music (Rochester)   **11** Nigel Simeone (Tunbridge Wells, Kent)   **12** Vereeniging ter Bervordering van de Belangen des Boekhandels (Amsterdam)   **13** University of Virginia (Charlottesville)   **14** University of California at Los Angeles   **15** Generally available

5521 **ZLATIN, Madame S. (Paris) (continued)**
      1972   47   *Théâtre - Danse - Cirque - Musique*
                              (749-857)   *1

5522 _____.
      1973   48   *Théâtre - Danse - Cirque - Musique*
                              (961-1066)   *1

5523 _____.
      1976   51   *Théâtre - Danse - Cirque - Musique*
                              (906-42)   *1

5524 _____.
      1977   52   *Théâtre - Danse - Cirque - Musique*
                              (318-500)   *1

5525 _____.
      1978   53   *Théâtre - Cirque - Danse*
                              (i.a., 872)   *1

5526 _____.
      1979   54   *Cirques. Music hall. Danse. Théâtre*
                              (372)   *1

5527 _____.
      1981   56   *Cirques. Music hall. Danse. Théâtre*
                              (i.a., 819)   *1

5528 _____.
      1982   57   *Cirques. Music hall. Théâtre. Musique. Danse*
                              (761)   *1

5529 _____.
      1983   58   *Cirques. Music hall. Théâtre. Musique*
                              (756)   *1

5530 _____.
      1984/85   59   *Cirques. Music hall. Théâtre. Musique. Danse*
                              (869)   *1

5531 **ZOBEL BOOK SERVICE (Clintondale, N. Y.)**
      196_   1-MU *Music - Theatre - Dance*
                              (24pp.)   *1,13

1 Compiler/State University of New York (Buffalo)   2 The British Library (London)   3 Gemeentemuseum (Den Haag)   4 The Grolier Club (N.Y.C.)   5 Hirsch Collection, British Library (London)   6 D.W. Krummel (Urbana)   7 Library of Congress (Washington, D.C.)   8 Library and Museum of the Performing Arts (N.Y.C.)   9 William Reeves (London)   10 Sibley Library, Eastman School of Music (Rochester)   11 Nigel Simeone (Tunbridge Wells, Kent)   12 Vereeniging ter Bervordering van de Belangen des Boekhandels (Amsterdam)   13 University of Virginia (Charlottesville)   14 University of California at Los Angeles   15 Generally available

Indexes

There are two indexes:
I   Subject and Type of Material Index
II   Place and Dealer Index

References are to item numbers

ACOUSTICS   2736

AESTHETICS   321, 1570, 1777, 2753

AFRICAN MUSIC 3643

ALS   see   AUTOGRAPH LETTERS, SIGNED

AMERICAN MUSIC   21, 577-78, 791, 2054, 2422,
    2425, 2429, 2436, 2446, 3197, 3355, 3644,
    3727, 4445, 4467, 4475, 4871, 4921, 2989,
    5006, 5025-32, 5241-47, 5344

ANDRE, publisher   4806

ARIAS   204

AUSTRIA   4304, 5270

AUTOGRAPH LETTERS, SIGNED   175, 194, 199,
    210, 318, 585, 623-25, 854, 876, 879, 950,
    989, 1007, 1009, 1046, 1050, 1415, 1550,
    1583, 1648, 1651, 1665, 1669, 1671, 1674,
    1728-29, 1968, 2027, 2045-46, 2831, 2869,
    2871-73, 2877, 2879-2900, 2902, 3000,
    3382-83, 3561-62, 3654, 3830-31, 3833-
    3834, 4831

AUTOGRAPH MANUSCRIPTS   see   HOLOGRAPHS

AUTOGRAPHS (handwritten signatures)   76-77,
    80, 82, 271, 279, 311, 326, 330, 333, 336,
    338, 344, 348, 371-72, 419, 456, 551, 559,
    567, 569, 573, 649, 775, 798-99, 801-03,
    804, 821, 824, 832, 872 (Mozart), 1029,
    1031-32, 1036, 1038, 1043, 1299, 1422,
    1424, 1519-20, 1526-28, 1540-41, 1558,
    1572, 1577-78, 1580-81, 1716, 1798, 1800-
    1801, 1805, 1809-10, 1813, 1816, 1820,

1822-25, 1830, 1836, 1846, 1872, 1884-87,
1937, 1946, 1992, 2039, 2041, 2244, 2376-
2377, 2555, 2561, 2567, 2616, 2627, 2631,
2639, 2643-44, 2646, 2649, 2656-57, 2661,
2668, 2672, 2679, 2687, 2690, 2684, 2703,
2714, 2717, 2721, 2744, 2748, 2754, 2764,
2774, 2778, 2781, 2812-13, 2818, 2835,
2843-45, 2848-49, 2874, 2877, 2879-82,
2909, 2915, 2931, 2963, 3131, 3143, 3171-
3172, 3174, 3249, 3337-38, 3385, 3388-
3389, 3392-98, 3467, 3507-08, 3511, 3513,
3591, 3643, 3650, 3654, 3671, 4321, 4424-
4427, 4483, 4487-4504, 4506-07, 4584,
4595, 4627, 4642-43, 4647, 4651-52, 4677,
4692, 4696, 4699, 4701, 4707, 4713, 4727,
4733, 4738, 4741, 4746, 4751, 4763, 4770,
4772, 4775, 4779, 4783, 4790-91, 4796,
4803, 4807, 4810, 4812, 4817, 4820-21,
4828, 4831, 4841, 4845, 4890, 4898, 4905,
4948-49, 4952, 4954, 5007-16, 5157, 5247,
5298, 5332, 5445, 5447, 5450, 5513

BALLET   (see also DANCE)   638, 923, 952,
    955, 968-69, 982, 986, 997, 1009-10,
    1021-22, 1024, 1063-64, 1092, 1101, 1171,
    1191, 1217, 1267, 1974, 2043, 2217, 2220,
    2222, 2227, 2268, 2388, 2865, 2876, 2884,
    2886, 2895, 2901, 2905, 3207-09, 3211-12,
    3256, 3343-44, 3347, 3349, 3390, 3522,
    3535-36, 4466, 4493, 4500, 4516, 4916,
    5132, 5140, 5228, 5319, 5389, 5411-12,
    5413, 5415, 5422

BARTOLUCCI, DOMENICO   541

BASSOON   (see also WIND MUSIC)   4061, 4118,
    5103

BAYREUTH   (see also WAGNER)   923

CHAMBER MUSIC (cont'd.)   3275, 3277, 3341,
   3401, 3779, 3935, 3939, 4012, 4031, 4057,
   4070, 4082, 4097, 4116, 4135, 4174, 4184,
   4246, 4257, 4278, 4322, 4326, 4333, 4353,
   4601, 4603, 4609, 4636, 4663, 4689, 4704,
   4728, 4742, 4749, 4756, 4766, 4779, 4785,
   4813, 4815, 4832, 4839, 4857, 5003, 5107,
   5112, 5177, 5180, 5192, 5230, 5389-90,
   5440

CHANT   2467-68, 4398, 4403

CHILDRENS' MUSIC   2195, 2316, 2321, 4527

CHORAL MUSIC   146, 204, 1088, 1213, 1222,
   1287, 1355, 1389, 1704, 2307, 2397, 2416,
   2511, 2521, 2773, 3547, 4269, 4325, 4546,
   4550, 4946, 5204, 5206

CHURCH MUSIC   2, 5, 171, 188, 201, 230,
   320, 331, 1094, 1102, 1117, 1184, 1224,
   1524, 1536, 1559, 1569, 2111, 2311, 2337,
   2340, 2842, 2807, 2986, 3133, 3345, 3407,
   4133, 4171, 4215, 4269, 4408, 4428, 4536,
   4547, 4551, 5175, 5318, 5325

CLARINET (see also WIND MUSIC)   4141, 4182,
   5103

COLLECTED EDITIONS   65, 91, 254-55, 259-60,
   652, 658, 660, 943, 948, 957, 961, 1144,
   1160, 1199, 1516, 1649, 1652, 2771, 2780,
   2950, 2955, 2958, 2961, 2971, 3016, 3024,
   3047, 3056, 3260, 3264, 3266, 3276, 3280,
   3282, 3284, 3286-87, 3289-90, 3292-99,
   4365, 4372, 4378, 4587, 4599, 4605, 4638,
   4719

COLLECTIONS (Collectors unnamed)   6, 538,
   580-84, 1266, 3386, 3589, 3625

COLLECTIONS (by Collector)   Aign, Walter,
   4789; d'Albert, Eugen, 1934; Alexander,
   Lesley, 3935; Almeria, Countess of Ester-
   hazy, 457; An Amateur, 3896; Anderson,
   Emily, 4672; Apunn, Anton, 2815; Auberlen,
   Ad., 834; B..., 2476, 3170; Bach, August
   Wilhelm, 2792; Barb, H. A., 471; Baumgart,
   Expedit Felix, 2794; Becker, Hans, 2826;
   Beijers, ?, 3406; Beretta, Giovanni Bat-
   tista, 3248; Berri, Pietro, 239; Bieber,
   Albert A., 23; Birch-Reynardson, H., 1008;
   Black, Frank, 314; Böhme, Franz Magnus,
   2813; Boers, Jan Conradus, 2814; Bois-
   siere, P. de la, 778; Bovet, Alfred,
   2717; Brahms, Johannes, 1815; Broedelet,
   H. W., 826; Calvocoressi, Michel Dimitri,
   975-76; Carrodus, John Tiplady, 3939;
   Cartier, J. B., 2472, 2614, 2713, 2725,
   2727; Choron, Alexandre Étienne, 2613;
   Clarence, O. B., 1025; Cohn, Albert, 563;
   A Conductor, 3609; Costa, Sir Michael,
   3845; Commer, Franz, 2647-48; Cronheim,
   Paul, 2197-98; Cummings, William Hayman,
   893, 3681; Danckert, Werner, 4573; Dann-
   reuther, Edward, 239; David, Ferdinand,
   1796; Dent, Edward J., 162-63; Diaghilev,
   Serge, 4780; Eitner, Robert, 2715, 2720,
   2723; Engel, C., 2131; Engle, Carl, 3810,
   [Engel, Charles], 3629; Engel, Hans, 4800;
   Erdmann, Eduard, 4646; Finch, Heneage,
   3775; Fischer, Dr. (of Grossottersleben),
   2811; Fleischer, Oskar, 828; Fürster,
   Friedrich, 2717; Fokker, A. D., 781;
   Friedländer, Max, 2551, 2782-83; Fuchs,
   Albert, 2738; Galluzzi, Giuseppe, 2818;
   Georg V, King, 4731-32; Grabau, Johann
   Andr., 2802; Grell, Eduard August, 571,
   2640, 2642; Grüters, August, 2738; Haas,
   Robert, 4654; Haeberlin, Carl, 804; Hahn,
   Albert, 2798; Hamel, Fred., 4667; (contd.)

COLLECTIONS (contd.)

EAST EUROPEAN MUSIC   1450

EPHEMERA   5419, 5421

"ETHIOPIAN" SONGS   5243, 5246

ETHNOMUSICOLOGY   32, 1441, 2455, 4226-28,
   5266, 5268-69

EXOTIC MUSIC   2771

FACSIMILES   91, 202, 222, 643, 792, 1149,
   1321, 3778, 4365, 4372, 4375, 4378, 4552,
   4584, 4610, 4683, 4702, 4719, 5332, 5432

FESTSCHRIFTEN   2328

FILM AND FILM MUSIC   548, 594-95, 597, 622,
   972, 1579, 1636, 1699, 1708, 1710-11,
   1724-26, 2082, 2138, 2140-41, 2146, 2217,
   2275, 2278, 2280, 2285, 2327, 2332, 2851,
   2860, 2936-37, 3207-08, 3214, 3225-26,
   3343, 3349, 3404, 3419, 3525, 3533, 3535-
   3536, 4224, 5096, 5121, 5130, 5132, 5140,
   5249, 5251-64, 5400, 5407, 5441, 5486-87,
   5489, 5496, 5499

FIRST EDITIONS   371, 373, 626, 653, 668-70,
   735, 792, 915, 928-29, 931-34, 1097-99,
   1139-40, 1167, 1172, 1195, 1207, 1210,
   1234, 1281, 1283, 1321, 1555, 2021, 2122,
   2262, 2517, 2527, 2533, 2538, 2543, 2875,
   2959, 2998-3000, 3147, 3239, 3247, 4012,
   4264, 4316, 4349, 4449, 4512, 4601, 4670,
   4690, 4701, 4714, 4720, 4730, 4747, 4754,
   4809, 4826, 4859, 4918-24, 4926-28, 5296

FLUEGELHORN   (see also WIND MUSIC)   5104

FLUTE MUSIC   (see also WIND MUSIC)   1278,

1337, 1354, 2378, 2384, 2412, 4141, 4182,
5105

FOLKMUSIC AND DANCE   74, 91, 179, 193, 227,
   269, 520-29, 592, 1080, 1117, 1149, 1156,
   1184, 1200, 1213, 1220, 1226, 1236, 1250,
   1340, 1366-67, 1374-77, 1559, 1567, 1623,
   1627, 1632, 1804, 1903, 1931-32, 2192,
   2224, 2267, 2325, 2334, 2399, 2414, 2454-
   2461, 2565, 3252, 3260, 3326, 3345, 3548,
   3897, 4443, 4445, 5117-18, 5127, 5129,
   5131, 5160, 5451

FREDERIK, D.   2418

FRENCH MUSIC   249. 829, 930

FRÜHDRUCKE   see   EARLY EDITIONS

FULL SCORES   121, 208, 212, 217, 240, 252,
   262-63, 501, 663, 684, 711, 761, 768-69,
   949, 962, 964, 973, 1100, 1106, 1108,
   1115, 1133, 1162, 1164, 1180, 1218, 1255,
   1260, 1280, 1294, 1350, 1650, 2393, 2397,
   2402, 2464, 2766, 2951, 2955, 2957-58,
   2961, 2966, 2969, 2971-72, 3016, 3025,
   3029-30, 3039, 3041, 3047, 3053, 3061,
   3071, 3077, 3091, 3101, 3103, 3107, 3115,
   3250, 3254, 3257, 3678, 3745, 3816, 4100,
   4112, 2137, 4163, 4170, 4175, 4197, 4248,
   4254, 4261, 4270, 4275, 4281, 4286, 4290,
   4294, 4296, 4309, 4318, 4354-55, 4366,
   4370, 4373, 4376, 4523, 4549-50, 4587,
   4592, 4611, 4623, 4634, 4651, 4657, 4664,
   4694, 4729, 2739, 4779, 4783, 4788, 4792,
   4824, 2834, 4839, 4855, 4878, 4994-95,
   5005, 5210, 5376, 5384, 5395-96, 5428,
   5433

GADE, NIELS   1141, 1143

(continued)

BERLIN (continued)
  Riedel, Hans   4362-78
  Stargardt, J. A.   5007-16
  Streisand, Hugo   5070
  Terl, Margarete   5117-30
  Tiedemann, H.   5143-50
  Wittman'sche Buchhandlung   5398-403
  Wunschmann, Heinz   5441-42
  Zentralantiquariat der DDR   5457-509
  Zeune, R.   5510-13

BERN
  Alder, Robert   16

BETHANY, CONN.
  Antiquarium   39

BEVERLY HILLS, CA.
  Front, Theodore
  Mlynarski, Bronislaw   3182-92
  Scriptorium   4930-32

BILTHOVEN
  Creyghton   626-748

BIRMINGHAM, U. K.
  Middleton, Maurice A.   3175-81

BISHOP'S STORTFORD, HERTS
  Mathews, Elkin, Ltd.   2998-3000

BOLOGNA
  Antiquariato   38
  Forni, Arnaldo, Libreria   1385-87

BONN
  Bouvier, H., & Co.   453
  Carthaus, J. F.   537
  Cohen, Friedrich   559
  Lempertz   2548
  Pabel und Co.   3519
  Rohrscheid, Ludwig   4380
  Teubner, F.   5131

BORDEAUX
  Lefevbre, Charles   2453

BOSTON
  Morrill, Edward, & Son   3197-98
  Williams Book Store   5344

BOURNEMOUTH, U. K.
  Mummery, Kenneth   3249-99

BRESLAU
  Friedrich, Georg   1410
  Lesser, H.   2564
  Maske, L. F.   2994-97
  Preuss & Jünger   3624

BRIGHTON, U. K.
  Holleyman & Treacher   1900-01
  Theatre Bookshop   5132

BRISTOL, U. K.
  George's, William, & Sons, Ltd.   1523-25

BRNO
  Brecher, L. & A.   457
  Karafiat   2086

BROOKLYN
  Dance Mart   775
  Schwab, Eugene L.   4871

BRUSSELS
  Les Amis de la musique   25
  Le Grenier du collectionneur   1598
  Librairie des académies   257
  Librairie encyclopédique
  Librairie musicale   2578-86
  Perre, Paul van der   3591
  Pinette, Max   3599
  Tulken, Fl.   5238
  Wastiau, Libraire   5315

BRYN TEG, ANGLESEY
  Mellor & Balley   3138-50

BUDAPEST
  Kultura   2287

BURBANK, CA.
  Merlander, Kurt   4155-69

CAMARILLO, CA.
  Edwards, H. E.   837-38

CAMBRIDGE, MASS.
  Cantabrigia   520-29
  Starr Books Shop   5017

CAMBRIDGE, U. K.
  Bowes & Bowes   454-55
  Heffer, W., & Sons   1858-70
  Wood, Peter   5404-40

CAZENOVIA, N. Y.
  Pan American Books   3523

CERRITOS, CA.
  Weinstein Books   5326-27

CHAMPAIGN, ILL.
  Foster, Mark   1389

CHESTNUT HILL, MASS.
  Book and Tackle Shop   439

CHICAGO
La Cerra, Patrick   2288
Musicana Unlimited   3355-75
Roundelay Book & Music Shop   4416-19

CHUMLEIGH, U. K.
Cox, Lisa   623-25

CLINTONDALE, N. Y.
Zobel Book Service   5531

COLOGNE
Lengfeld, M.   2549-63

COPENHAGEN
Fog, Dan   1079-1371
Gad, G. E. C.   1455
Gronholt, Pedersens Boghus   1602
Haase, P., & Sons   1683-84
Larsen, Knud   2378-2418
Levin, Richard   2569
Levin & Munksgaard   2570
Lynge og Sohn   2863-66
Musica Antiqua   3339-49
Nielsen, Axel V.   3404
Paludan, Erik   3521-22
Rosenkilde of Bagger   4387-89

CORAL GABLES, FLA.
La Scala Autographs   4487-4504

DARMSTADT
Dörffel, Felix   798-806

DERBY
Drewry, John   1790
Murray, F.   1886

DODRECHT
de Hart   1828

DOETINCHAM
Jong, E. D. De   2080

DRESDEN
Alicke, Paul   17
Bertling, Richard   323-48
Dannapel, E.   776
Dresdner Antiquariat   810-18
Salomon, Gustav   4481-83
Von Zahn, R. & Jänsch   5452-56

DÜSSELDORF
Bayrhoffer Nachfolger J. Jaeger   274

DUN LAOGHAIRE, EIRE
Fenning, J. O'D.   925

DURHAM, U.K.
Shotton, J.   4968

EAST ROCHESTER, N. Y.
Gatsby's Music   1515

EDINBURGH
Grant, John   1586-95
Thin, James   5133-34
Updike, John   5250

ELBERFELD
Arnold, F. W.   44

EL CERRITO, CA.
Vanderstoel, Graeme   5266-69

ERFURT
Otto'schen Buchhandlung   3517-18
Weingart, E.   5320-25

ERLANGEN
Krische, Theodor   2273
Merkel, R.   4152-54

EUGENE, ORE.
Muns, J. B.   3313-18

EXMOUTH, U. K.
Holmes, T., & Co. (by A. N. May)   1913-18

FALMOUTH, U. K.
Browser's Books   473-83

FLORENCE
Lapiccirella, Leonardo   2376-77
Libreria Dante   2588
Licosa Sansoni   2599
Marini & Co., T., de   2933
La Medicea   3132-33
Olschki, Leo S.   3453-58
Sansoni   4486
Valleri, Giovanni   5251-65
Vittorio, Libreria   5274-92

FOREST HILLS, N. Y.
Ganley, Eric H.   1456-95

FORT WORTH, TEXAS
Cultura   749-69

FRANKFURT A. M.
Baer, Joseph   71-86
Kauffman, J.   2124-29
St. Goar, Isaac   4430-32

FREDERICKSBURG, VA.
Leamington Book Shop   2442-50

FREIBURG I. BR.
Albert, Eberhard   15
Novalis-Antiquariat   3443
Stoll & Bader   5067

(continued)

PARIS (continued)
  Loliée, Marc 2831
  Pas-Perdus, Les Librairie 3557
  Petit, A. 3595
  Picard, Alphonse & fils 3596
  Picard, Auguste 3597
  Proute, Victor & Robert 3626
  Rau, Arthur 3670-72
  Saba, Umberto 4421-23
  Sagot, Edmond 4428-29
  Schneider, Pierre 4863-64
  Smetryns, J. 4984
  Thomas, Libraire 5136
  Vrin, J. 5300
  Welter, Hubert 5331
  Zlatin, Madame S. 5517-30

PLAINFIELD, VT.
  Keonig's, Benjamin, Country Bookshop 2214

PLAINSBORO, N. J.
  La Scala Autographs 4487-504

PORT WASHINGTON, N. Y.
  College Book Service 574

PORTSMOUTH, N. H.
  Hanrahan, J. & J. 1733

POTTSVILLE, PA.
  Unger, C. W. 5241-47

PRAGUE
  Taussig, I. 5098-116

PROVIDENCE, R. I.
  OLB (Oak Lawn Books) 3452

REGGIO EMILIA
  Nironi & Prandi, Libreria 3428-29

READING, U. K.
  Hyman, Leonard 1937-77

RICHMOND, U. K.
  Kew Books 2147-49

ROME
  Belmore, H. W. 310
  Casamiri-Capra 540-42
  Chiappini, Libreria 549-50
  Corbellini, Mario 586-99
  Gerra, Ferdinando 1526-28
  Hortus Musicus 1920-22
  Lang, C. 2370-72
  Libreria Romana 2598
  Loescher, Ermanno 2830
  Moretti, Vincenzo S., Bottega 3196
  Nardecchia, Libreria 3381
  Rappaport, C. E. 3668
  Rossi, Dario Giuseppe 4415

ROSTOCK
  Norddeutsches Antiquariat 3330-41
  Stiller'schen Hofbuchhandlung 5045
  Universitätsbuchhandlung 5249

ROTTERDAM
  Dunk, J. H. 826-27
  Plattner, L. 3560
  Vletter, W. C. de 5293-94
  Witsen, A., van 5395-96

SALISBURY, U. K.
  Travis & Emery 5209-20

SALZBURG
  Huber, Alois Hilmer 1933

SAN ANSELMO, CA.
  Muns, J. B. 3309-12

SAN FRANCISCO, CA.
  Harpagon Associates 1762-63
  Tivoli Book Co. 5151

SANTA BARBARA, CA.
  Silver, Martin 4969-81

SANTA MONICA, CA
  Karno, Howard 2088-91

SAO PAULO
  Parthenon, Livraria 3556

SAUSALITO, CA.
  Glaser, Edwin V. 1544

SCARSDALE, N. Y.
  Schnase, Annemarie 4559-76

SCHAFFHAUSEN
  Lamlin, H. 2290

SCHENECTADY, N. Y.
  Hammer Mountain Book Halls 1730

SCHLOSS KAIBITZ B. KEMNATH-STADT
  Hacke, Ernst Max 1686-1711

SEATTLE, WASH.
  Shep, R. L. 4963-67

SELSDEN, U. K.
  Parkinson, J. A. 3539-54

SMITHTOWN, N. Y.
  Cadenza Bookseller 509-15

SONDERSHAUSEN
  Bertram, Gustav 359

SOUTH LEE, MASS.
  Lubrano, J. & J. 2843-56

WEILBURG
   Lanz, L. G.   2375

WELLINGSBOROUGH, U. K.
   Collett's Holdings, Ltd.   575

WEST KIRBY, U. K.
   Donald, W.   808

WEST MOORS, WIMBORNE, U. K.
   Wyler, Michael   5444-49

WEST PALM BEACH, FLA.
   Hazlett, Dick   1802-03

WEST STOCKBRIDGE, MASS.
   Elsberg, Dorothy   895-912

WIESBADEN
   Harrassowitz, Otto   1766-73

WILMINGTON, DEL.
   Grobe, Charles   1600

WINDSOR, U. K.
   Goldscheider, Gaby   1549

WINDSOR, VT.
   Kolvoord, R.   2228

WINTHROP HARBOR, ILL.
   Leakley Book Search   2451
   Scott, B. J.   4915-16

WISMAR, DDR
   Rhein, Hermann   4229-30

WÜRZBURG
   Frank, J., Antiquariat   1405-06
   Liebing, Arnulf   2600-01
   Mergenthaler, Walter & Karl Giesen-
      dörfer   4151

YORK, U. K.
   Gard Book   1513-14
   Martin, Philip   2974-93

ZARAGOZA
   Portico Librerias   3620-23

ZÜRICH
   Hug & Co.   1934-35
   Lang, C.   2370-72
   Schumann, Hellmut   4866-70
   Schweizerisches Antiquariat   4872-77